The Business of Sport Management

The Business of Sport Management

Second edition

Edited by
John Beech and Simon Chadwick

PEARSON

Harlow, England • London • New York • Boston • San Francisco • Toronto • Sydney • Auckland • Singapore • Hong Kong
Tokyo • Seoul • Taipei • New Delhi • Cape Town • São Paulo • Mexico City • Madrid • Amsterdam • Munich • Paris • Milan

Pearson Education Limited
Edinburgh Gate
Harlow
Essex CM20 2JE
England

and Associated Companies throughout the world

Visit us on the World Wide Web at:
www.pearson.com/uk

First published 2004 (print)
Second edition published 2013 (print and electronic)

ISBN: 978-0-273-72133-8 (print)
978-0-273-72137-6 (PDF)
978-0-273-77963-6 (eText)

British Library Cataloguing-in-Publication Data
A catalogue record for this book is available from the British Library

Library of Congress Cataloging-in-Publication Data
A catalog record for this book is available from the Library of Congress

ARP impression 98

Typeset in 10/13pt Minion by 35
Printed and bound by Ashford Colour Press Ltd., Gosport

Brief contents

Contents

22 Sports media and PR   488

Stephen W. Dittmore

23 The internationalisation of sport   510

Simon Chadwick

24 Sports agents and intermediaries   527

Anna Semens and Adam Pendlebury

About the authors

Andy Adcroft

Andy is the Director of Academic Development for the Faculty of Business, Economics and Law at the University of Surrey. His main research interest is in expertise studies where he has published widely on issues such as performance and competitiveness in sport and the relationship between training and performance.

Dave Arthur

Dave is a widely published academic, an accomplished practitioner, and a sought-after consultant as well as an inveterate user of Twitter in all aspects of sport business. English by birth but living and working in Australia, his abiding love is his wife and three children closely followed by rugby union.

Michael Barker

Michael is a Senior Lecturer at Coventry University specialising in Management Accounting. As a keen sports fan, Michael has developed his research interest in sports finance, predominately in football, cricket and the financial legacies of major tournaments. Outside sport Michael also has interests in internationalisation, especially improving the experience of Chinese students studying at Coventry.

Karen Bill

Karen is Associate Dean in the School of Sport, Performing Arts and Leisure at the University of Wolverhampton responsible for research and income generation. She is editor of *Sport Management* (Exeter: Learning Matters, 2009) and has completed the Post Graduate Diploma in Legal Studies (CPE) having published in the areas of sports entrepreneurship and sports law.

John Beech (co-editor)

John is a Senior Research Fellow at Coventry University, where he is the Head of Sport and Tourism at the Applied Research Centre for Sustainable Regeneration. He is a Visiting Professor at the University of the Applied Sciences, Kufstein, Austria, and the IE Business School, Madrid, Spain. His research interests include internet marketing by soccer clubs, football finance and governance, mega sports events and sports tourism. In 2010 he won the Football Supporters' Federation Writer of the Year Award for his Football Management blog (http://footballmanagement.wordpress.com).

Terry Brathwaite

Terry is Senior Lecturer in International Human Resource Management and Founding Programme Manager for the flagship MSc Degree in Global Development & International Law at Coventry University. A former Lecturer on Human Relations in Sport at the University of the West Indies, he has also served as Sports Marketing Manager for the

Ontario Amateur Football Association in Canada. Terry has held visiting lectureships at Harvard University, the CENTRUM Católica Business School (Lima, Peru), the National Normal University of Taiwan, and the American University in London. He is also a member of various professional bodies including the American Society of International Human Resource Management.

Terri Byers

Terri is Principal Lecturer in Sport Management at Coventry University. She teaches on undergraduate and postgraduate courses, supervises Masters by Research and PhD students and is an active researcher in organisation studies generally and the management of sport specifically. Her current research interests are focused on recruiting and training volunteers in sport, understanding the control of voluntary sport organisations and new methodological approaches (particularly Critical Realism) to enhance research into sport management. Her new book, co-authored with Trevor Slack and Milena Parent, *Key Concepts in Sport Management* by Sage Publications is due out in 2012.

Simon Chadwick (co-editor)

Simon is Professor of Sport Business Strategy and Marketing, and Director of the Centre for the International Business of Sport, at Coventry University. He has published and commented extensively and internationally on the subject of sport. Among the outlets in which Chadwick's work has appeared or been quoted are the *Journal of Advertising Research*, *The Wall Street Journal*, Elsevier Publishing and CNN. He has also worked with many of the world's leading sport organisations including UEFA, Mastercard, the International Tennis Federation, FC Barcelona and Octagon.

Leon Culbertson

Leon is Assistant Director of the Graduate School at Edge Hill University and teaches the philosophy of psychology in the Department of Social and Psychological Sciences. Most of his work in the philosophy of sport is concerned with the ethics of sports medicine. He has published a number of articles on various aspects of the ethics of performance-enhancement. He also still occasionally writes on the work of Jean-Paul Sartre, which was the topic of his doctoral thesis. His other philosophical interests include the philosophy of mind and psychology, aspects of the philosophy of language, metaethics and the work of Ludwig Wittgenstein.

Stephen W. Dittmore

Stephen is Assistant Professor of Recreation and Sport Management Health, Human Performance and Recreation at the University of Arkansas. He worked as a sport management faculty member at East Stroudsburg University from 2006–08, University of Louisville, 2004–06, and Wichita State University, 2002–04. Prior to that, he spent 12 years working in sport public relations. He was a staff member for the 2002 Olympic Winter Games and 1996 Olympic Games, and he has worked at sports events in ten different countries.

Dominic Elliott

Dominic is Professor of Business Continuity and Strategic Management at the University of Liverpool and has published widely in the fields of crisis and strategic management and has particular interests in organisational learning from crisis and business continuity management, with some interest in the sports sector.

Simon Gardiner

Simon is a Reader in Sports Law at Leeds Metropolitan University and Senior Research Fellow at the Asser International Sports Law Centre. His particular research interests include sports governance, racism and the construction of national identity in sport. He is lead author of Gardiner et al., *Sports Law*, 4th edn (Oxford: Routledge, 2011).

Ted Graham

Ted is a senior executive and management consultant with a focus on brand management and strategy. Currently with PriceWaterhouseCoopers, he previously held senior positions with Interbrand, McKinsey, Hill & Knowlton, and National Public Relations. He specialises in working with leading global institutions in the areas of brand value measurement; product and service innovation; social networks and brand building. He holds an MBA from Queen's University in Kingston, Ontario.

Jon Guest

Jon is a National Teaching Fellow of the Higher Education Academy and a Principal Lecturer in Economics at Coventry University. He also became the first Government Economic Service approved tutor in 2005 and won the student-nominated award from the Economics Network in the same year. He supports Portsmouth Football Club.

Boris Helleu

Boris is a Senior Lecturer in Sports Management at Université de Caen Basse-Normandie, France. His thesis was devoted to the geographic aspects of the regulation of professional sport. His work looks at professional sport, combining contributions from economics (models of sports regulation), geography (the globalisation and metropolisation of professional sport), and marketing (fans and the digital matchday experience). He has headed the Sports Management diploma at the University of Caen since 2010.

Sebastian Kaiser

Sebastian is Professor for Sport Management at SRH University Heidelberg, Germany, a post he previously held at the University of Applied Sciences in Kufstein, Austria, where he was also Vice Director of Studies for Sports, Culture and Event Management. Sebastian holds university teaching positions at several German universities. His fields of research are sport economics, the culture of sport organisations and services management.

Maxence Karoutchi

Maxence is a Rugby Agent and Consultant with a focus on sports social media and sponsorship. He develops sports social media strategy for professional athletes and sports teams. Founder of Sportbizinside, a Sports business blog, Maxence was previously business developer at IBM and a semi-professional Soccer Team (Sporting Toulon Var, France). He has also held visiting lectureships at Cafam (Bogota, Colombia), and Escuela Superior de Periodismo Deportivo (Buenos Aires, Argentina).

Robert Kaspar

Robert is the Director of Studies of the Department of Sports, Culture and Event Management as well as Marketing and Communication Management, based in Kufstein in the Tyrol, Austria. Kaspar obtained his Doctorate in International Business Administration at the Vienna University of Economics after having researched and studied in New Zealand, Spain and Sweden. Since 1994, he has served in a number of mega-event companies, ranging from Expos to World Championships including the position of managing director for the Salzburg 2010 Olympic Winter Games bid.

Mike McNamee

Mike is Professor of Applied Ethics at Swansea University. He is a former President of the International Association for the Philosophy of Sport, and the founding Editor of *Sport, Ethics and Philosophy*. Recent books include *Sports, Virtues and Vices: Morality Play* (Routledge, 2008), *Sports Ethics: A Reader* (Routledge, 2010) and *Doping and Anti-Doping Policy* (Routledge, 2011).

Yue Meng-Lewis

Yue is a Lecturer in Marketing Communications at the Media School, Bournemouth University, and completed her doctoral studies at Leeds University Business School. Her research interests focus on sport marketing and sponsorship, celebrity endorsement and international communication strategy.

David Morris

David is Professor of Business Development at Coventry University. Over 20 years ago he was instrumental in setting up the first ever undergraduate degree programme with a focus on developing equine industry professionals. As part of this he developed a long-term interest in the relationship between the betting industry, gambling and sports. He does not bet himself.

Cameron O'Beirne

Cam is Lecturer in Wine Marketing and Business at Curtin University, and specialist in eCommerce, new media and sports management, with a focus in aquatics. He consults internationally on beach safety to governments, volunteer organisations and Hollywood films.

Norm O'Reilly

Norm is an Associate Professor of Sport Business at the University of Ottawa. He has previously taught at Syracuse, Stanford, Laurentian and Ryerson universities in sport marketing, marketing, sport finance and sport management. A holder of BSc, MA, MBA and PhD degrees and the CGA accounting designation, he has published three books, over 50 articles in refereed management journals and more than 75 conference proceedings and case studies. The North American Editor of the *Journal of Sponsorship* and a winner of eight Best Paper awards, he is the lead researcher on the Canadian Sponsorship Landscape Study, a highlight of the annual Canadian Sponsorship Forum since 2007, and a three-time member (2004, 2008 and 2010) of the Mission Staff for the Canadian Olympic Committee at the Olympic Games.

John Old

John is an Associate Teaching Fellow of Warwick Business School, and formerly a Principal Lecturer at Coventry University, as well as working for, among others, Aston and Durham Universities. He is also a freelance business consultant and writer on a range of subjects, from business and management to sport and politics.

Chris Parker

Chris is Principal Lecturer in Sport and Leisure Management at Nottingham Trent University. He is an experienced management consultant and trainer. He is the author of *If I Take The Lead Will You Walk By My Side? 101 Communication Tips for Managers* and the co-author of *Campaign It!* and *Five Essential Ingredients for Business Success*.

Adam Pendlebury

Adam is a Senior Lecturer in Law and coordinator of the Centre for Sports Law Research at Edge Hill University. He has published in peer reviewed journals and given papers at a number of international conferences. His research interests are in the regulation of sportsfield violence, the governance of sport and the regulation of doping.

Lindsay Rennie

Lindsay is an experienced marketing professional who has a vast array of experiences with properties, agencies and entrepreneurial organisations. Prior to his current position as Account Director at MacLaren Momentum, Rennie was Senior Account Director at Bensimon Byrne, Marketing Director at Discover Boating and the Founder of Highland Sports Management. He also spent three years as Retail Marketing Group Supervisor at Nike Canada. He holds an MBA from Queen's University in Kingston, Ontario.

Emily Ryall

Emily is a Senior Lecturer in Philosophy in the Faculty of Applied Sciences at the University of Gloucestershire. She is on the executive committee of the International Association for the Philosophy of Sport and the British Philosophy of Sport Association, and is the author of *Critical Thinking for Sports Students*.

Anna Semens

Anna is Director of Development in Football Industries at the University of Liverpool. She has published on various aspects of the commercial sports industry in both academic and practitioner publications. Anna has consulted for various sport stakeholders in the UK and abroad providing event and economic impact analysis, and her current research interests include agents and intermediaries, football transfer markets, league structure, media rights values, sponsorship and events.

Harry Arne Solberg

Harry is a Professor of Economics at Trondheim Business School, Sør-Trøndelag University College. He also holds a 20 per cent position as Professor at Molde University College. Harry holds a PhD from Sheffield Hallam University, UK, 2003. He has research interests in the economic analysis of various sporting activities, with special attention on sporting events and media related issues. Together with Professor Chris Gratton, he has published the book: *The Economics of Sport Broadcasting*. He has published a number of articles in scientific journals including *European Sport Management Quarterly*, *International Journal of Sport Marketing and Sponsorship* and *Journal of Media Economics*. He has also published several book chapters.

Leigh Sparks

Leigh is Professor of Retail Studies at the Institute for Retail Studies, University of Stirling, Scotland. At Stirling he teaches Sport Marketing at undergraduate and postgraduate levels, to students in both Sports Studies and Marketing. His sports marketing research interest is on sports goods distribution and retailing. Leigh has a life-long interest in sport generally, but particularly in the joys and disappointments of Welsh rugby.

Des Thwaites

Des is Senior Lecturer in Marketing at Leeds University Business School. His research interests focus on marketing strategy and his publications have appeared in leading journals such as *Product Innovation Management*, *European Journal of Marketing*, *Journal of Advertising*, *Industrial Marketing Management*, *Psychology and Marketing* and *Journal of Advertising Research*.

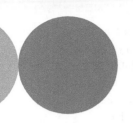

Preface

When the first edition of *The Business of Sport Management* was published more than eight years ago, it was in many ways a portent of things to come. While back in 2004 there was clearly a need for a book of this nature, as a business or industry sport outside the United States was essentially still in its formative years. Now in the twenty-first century, things have changed dramatically: it is estimated that sport may account for as much as 3 per cent of global economic activity; sport is increasingly being used as a pillar of government policy (such as in the case of Qatar's 2030 Vision); sporting events are generating economic and commercial impacts worth billions of pounds (the Olympic Games often being seen as the most prominent example of this); sports brands such as Manchester United and Real Madrid are appearing in league tables of the world's best brands; and so the list goes on.

In part, we hope that the first edition of our book played even just a small role in the dynamic and rapidly changing sport industry. The book was adopted by numerous universities across the world and so has been read by students who then graduated and moved on to become professionals in the world of sport business and management. Yet as is clear from this introductory statement, the sport industry has changed rapidly and dramatically over the last decade.

As such, this second edition has been produced both to reflect the changes that are taking (and have taken) place in sport, and to predict some of the changes that will take place in sport over the coming years. While many of the chapters from the first edition of the book have been retained, each of these has been extensively updated to incorporate latest developments in theory as well as current case studies in sport. In addition, several new chapters have been introduced into the second edition, including chapters on the international and global development of sport, sports agents and social media. It is hoped that these chapters will not only give *The Business of Sport Management* greater scope and depth, but will also ensure that the book remains at the cutting edge of thinking in the field of sport business and management.

In general terms, therefore, the main objective of this book is to provide an introduction to key aspects of sport management for both undergraduate and postgraduate students. The book will also serve as a useful resource for staff involved in teaching on sport-related modules and programmes, and for practitioners working as managers of sport businesses.

The book now consists of 25 chapters, which are split into three sections: Context, Business Functions, and Management Issues in Sport. A concluding chapter looks at the future of sport and its management. The rationale for this structure is a reflection of the underlying aim outlined above.

The first section, Context, explains how sport management exists within the worlds of both business and sport. It shows how professional sport has evolved, and how sport businesses operate within a broader context of governing bodies and state involvement. It is essential when approaching the subject to be familiar with this context; otherwise the more advanced areas of study are not realistically accessible.

Once an understanding of the context of sport management has been achieved, the student can begin to assimilate the basics of business management theory, the subject of Section B. This section is divided into chapters whose titles would not be unfamiliar to the general business studies student. The content of each chapter is, however, presented with particular reference to sport businesses. It thus concentrates on functions of business which are generic but which are presented from a sport business perspective.

While it is generally accepted that any business needs to be customer-focused, a number of sectors have faced the difficulty of equating its 'customers' with the generic view of 'customers'. Examples are the health sector, the education sector and even the transport sector, where 'patients', 'students' and 'passengers' are more complex notions than simply 'customers'. In the sport business sector, many organisations face difficulties with matching the notions of 'customers' and 'fans'. As a result, a number of management issues have to be addressed that are unique to sport businesses. These issues are covered in the ten chapters of Section C of the book, which concludes with a consideration of the future prospects for sport businesses.

Each of the chapters in this book contains the following:

- a statement of learning outcomes;
- a chapter overview;
- subject content appropriate to one of the sections mentioned above;
- case studies, including one extended case;
- a conclusion;
- keywords;
- guided reading;
- recommended websites;
- a bibliography.

At the time of writing, all recommended websites were live. However, it may be the case that sites become inaccessible. In the event of this happening, readers are asked to contact the publisher with details of any problems.

Acknowledgements

The editors would like to thank each of the chapter authors for their hard work and commitment in getting the book written. Special thanks are extended to those chapter authors who worked under especially tight time constraints.

We would also like to thank the ever-patient staff of Pearson Education who have been involved with the production of 'BOSM2'.

John dedicates his work on the book to Sue, who continues to tolerate a considerable amount of displacement activity.

Simon dedicates his work on the book to his family.

Publisher's acknowledgements

We are grateful to the following for permission to reproduce copyright material:

Figures

Figure 6.1 from *The Economics of Staging the Olympics*, Edward Elgar Publishers (H. Preuss and H.-J. Weiss 2003) 24; Figure 8.1 from *Motivation and Personality,* 3, Pearson Education Inc. (Maslow, Abraham H.; Frager, Robert D. (Editor); Faidman, James (Editor), 1987), MASLOW, ABRAHAM H.; FRAGER, ROBERT D.; FAIDIMAN, JAMES, MOTIVATION AND PERSONALITY, 3rd edn, copyright 1987. Reprinted and electronically reproduced by permission of Pearson Education, Inc., Upper Saddle River, New Jersey; Figure 12.2 from Theories, Concepts and the Rugby World Cup: Using management to understand sport, *Management Decision*, 46, 4 (A. Adcroft and J. Teckman 2008), Emerald Publishing; Figure 12.3 from *Competitive Strategy: Techniques for Analyzing Industries and Competitors*, The Free Press, Simon and Schuster (Michael E. Porter 1998), Reprinted with the permission of Free Press, a Division of Simon & Schuster, Inc., from COMPETITIVE STRATEGY: TECHNIQUES FOR ANALYZING INDUSTRIES AND COMPETITORS by Michael E. Porter. Copyright © 1980, 1998 by The Free Press. All rights reserved; Figure 13.1 from *Structure of the BEF*, British Equestrian Foundation (R.H.G. Suggett 2010), British Equestrian Federation www.bef.co.uk; Figure 13.4 from *Operations Management: Focusing on Quality and Competitiveness* (R.S. Russell and B.W. Taylor III 1998); Figure 13.5 from A conceptual model of service quality, *International Journal of Operations and Production Management*, 8 (6), 36–44 (J. Haywood-Farmer 1988); Figure 18.1 from *The Economics of Sports Broadcasting* 1st edn, Routledge (Gratton C., Solbergm, H.A.) p. 69 (July 18, 2007); Figure 19.1 from Beyond Contingency Planning: Towards a model of crisis management, *Industrial Crisis Quarterly*, 4 (4), 263–75 (D. Smith 1990), © 1990, Sage publications. Reprinted by Permission of SAGE Publications; Figure 19.2 from *Business Continuity Management: A Crisis Management Approach*, 2nd edn, Routledge (Elliott, D., Swartz, E. and Herbane, B. 2010), Copyright 2010 From Business Continuity Managemet: A Crisis Management Approach, by Elliott, D., Swartz, E. and Herbane, B. Reproduced by permission of Taylor and Francis Group, LLC, a division of Informa plc.

Tables

Table 6.1 from *The New Sports Organisation*, TSE Consulting (Lars Haue-Pedersen); Tables 10.5 and 10.6 from Arsenal Holdings plc; Table 14.1 from Meeting relationship-marketing goals through social media: A conceptual model for sport marketers, *International Journal of Sport Communication*, 10 (3), 422–37 (J. Williams and S.J. Chin 2010), Reprinted, with permission, from J. Williams and S.J. Chin, 2010, 'Meeting relationship-marketing goals through social media: A conceptual model for sport marketers,' International Journal of Sport Communication 3 (4): 422–27; Table 17.1 from Corporate sponsorship by the Financial Services Industry, *Journal of Marketing Management*, 10, 743–63 (D. Thwaites 1994), copyright © Westburn Publishers Limited, reprinted by permission of Taylor & Francis Ltd, www.tandfonline.com on behalf of The Westburn Publishers Limited; Table 18.1 from multimedia.olympic.org/pdf/en_report_344.pdf, Table 18.1 http://www.olympic.org/Documents/marketing_fact_file_en.pdf; Table 18.2 from TV Sports Markets, *TV Sports Markets Journal*, 11, 13 (2010); Table 18.3 from Safety in numbers Annual review of football finance, tvsportsmarkets.com, Sport Business Group June 2009; Table 18.4 from The international trade of players in European Club football – The consequences for national teams, *Journal of Sport Marketing and Sponsorship*, 10, 1 (H. Solberg and K. Haugen 2008); Table 19.2 from Strategic Management of Corporate Crises, *Columbia Journal of World Business*, Spring (1), 5–11 (Shrivastava, P. and Mitroff II 1987). Copyright Elsevier 1987; Table 22.1 from *The New Rules of Marketing and PR*, John Wiley & Sons (Scott, D.M. 2009); Table 25.1 adapted from 10 ways to shake up sport, *Observer Sport Monthly*, 03/10/2004, observer-guardian.co.uk, Copyright Guardian News & Media Ltd 2004.

Text

Case Study on pages 36–7 from Supporters Direct, enquiries@supporters-direct.coop; Extract 13.3 from www.goodform.info; Case Study 14.3 from Teams on Facebook and Twitter, www.sportsfangraph.com, www.coylemedia.com; Case Study 14.5 from London 2012 Olympics: Twitter action at Games could be every bit as competitive as the sport by Simon Hart 30 March 2012, blogs@telegraph.co.uk, The Telegraph Group, copyright © Telegraph Media Group Limited; Case Study 17.2 from www.sportbusiness.com/news/160182/nationwide-secures-new-sponsorship-of-english-fa; Case Study 18.2 from Central sale paves the way for Serie A's cultural revolution, *TV Sports Markets*, 13, 3 Sport Business Group; Case Study 18.3 from SABC listed-events lobbying 'unlikely' to change much, *TV Sports Markets Journal*, 12, 1 (Catherine Davies 2008); Case Study 22.1 from The use of an organizational weblog in relationship building: The case of a Major League Baseball team, *International Journal of Sport Communication*, 1 (3), 384–97 (Dittmore, S.W., Stoldt, G.C. and Greenwell, T.C. 2008), Adapted, with permission; Case Study 23.2 from Li Na serves an ace by flying solo, *The Financial Times*, 28/01/2011 (Dyer, G.), © The Financial Times Limited. All Rights Reserved; Case Study 25.1 from Race Industry takes the Lead, *The Financial Times*, 11/09/2007 (Griffiths, J.); Case Study 25.2 from UEFA warning over Ronaldo £80 million signing, *The Financial Times*, 12/06/2009 (Blitz, R. and Mulligan, M.)

Picture credits

Top row: images left to right:

© *John Foxx Collection. Imagestate. POD_P77092*
© *Photolink. Photodisc. POD_P9726*

Bottom row, images left to right:

© *Image Source. POD_P59769*
© *John Foxx Collection. Imagestate. POD_P77048*
© *John Foxx Collection. Imagestate. POD_P77017*

In some instances we have been unable to trace the owners of copyright material, and we would appreciate any information that would enable us to do so.

Abbreviations

AMA	American Marketing Association
AML	Anthropomaximological
ASA	Advertising Standards Authority
ASP	Association of Surfing Professionals
ATP	Association of Tennis Professionals
AWP	Amusement with prizes
B2B	Business-to-business
B2C	Business-to-customer
B2F	Business-to-fans
BBC	British Broadcasting Corporation
BCP	Business continuity plan
BEF	British Equestrian Federation
BEP	Break-even point
BISL	Business in Sport and Leisure
BOA	British Olympic Association
BRI	Basket related income
CAAWS	Canadian Association for the Advancement for Women in Sports and Physical Activity
CAD	Computer-aided design
CAE	Computer-aided engineering
CAF	Confederation of African Football
CAM	Computer-aided manufacturing
CAS	Court for Arbitration in Sport
CBA	i) Cost-Benefit Analysis
	ii) Collective Bargaining Agreement
CCC	County Cricket Club
CCTV	Closed-circuit television
CEO	Chief Executive Officer
CEP	Culture and Education Programme
CFU	Caribbean Football Union
CHV	Conversational human voice
CIC	Community Interest Company
CIMA	Chartered Institute of Management Accountants
CM	Crisis management
CNS	Cybercast News Service
CONCACAF	Confederation of North, Central American and Caribbean Association Football
COPS	Culture, Organisation, and People/HR Systems
CRC	Communicated relational commitment
CSR	Corporate social responsibility

CVA	Company Voluntary Arrangement
CVP	Cost–volume–profit
DGR	Defined gross revenue
DRO	Digital return optimisation
EBU	European Broadcasting Union
EC	European Community
ECJ	European Court of Justice
EEMS	Energy efficient motor sports
EEO	Equal employment opportunity
EFL	English Football League
EFQM	European Foundation for Quality Management
EPIC	Ethanol Promotion and Information Council
EPL	English Premier League
EQ	Emotional intelligence
EQSM	Extensible System Quality Management
ESPN	Entertainment and Sports Programming Network
EU	European Union
F1	Formula One
FA	(English) Football Association
FC	Football Club
FEI	Federation Equestrian Internationale
FIA	Fédération Internationale de l'Automobile
FIBA	Fédération Internationale de Basketball (known in English as the International Basketball Association)
FIFA	Fédération Internationale de Football Association
FINA	Fédération Internationale de Natation
FIS	International Ski Federation/Fédération Internationale de Ski
FMA	Facility Management Association of Australia
FOA	Formula One Administration
FSA	Full service agency
GDP	Gross domestic product
HBR	Harvard Business Review
HR	Human resource
HRM	Human resource management
HSE	Health and Safety Executive
HSWA	Health and Safety at Work Act 1974
IAAF	International Association of Athletics Federations
IBF	International Boxing Federation
ICASA	Independent Communications Authority of South Africa
ICC	International Cricket Council
ICT	Information and communication technologies
iDTV	Integrated digital television
IMC	Integrated marketing communications
IOC	International Olympic Committee
IPL	Indian Premier (cricket) League
IPR	Intellectual property right

ISO	International Organization for Standardization
ITV	Channel 3 (formerly, Independent Television)
KRA	Key results area
LOCOG	London Organising Committee of the Olympic Games
LPGA	Ladies Professional Golf Association (USA)
MBA	Masters in Business Administration
MCC	Marylebone Cricket Club
MLB	Major League Baseball
MLS	Major League Soccer
MMC	Membership Management Company
NAL	North American (Baseball) League
NAPBBP	National (US) Association of Professional Base Ball Players
NASCAR	National Association for Stock Car Auto Racing
NBA	i) National (US) Basketball Association
	ii) National (USA) Boxing Association (now, WBA *qv*)
NBC	National (US) Broadcasting Company
NCAA	National (US) Collegiate Athletic Association
NFL	National (US) Football League
NHL	National (Canada & US) Hockey League
NPSO	Not-for-profit sport organisation
NSGB	National sport governing body
OAPA	Offences against the Person Act
ODA	Olympic Delivery Authority
OFT	Office of Fair Trading
OHS	Occupational Health and Safety
OLA	Occupiers' Liability Act
PE	Physical Education
PEST	Political, Economic, Social and Technological
PESTLE	Political, Economics, Social, Technological, Legal and Environmental
PFA	Professional Footballers Association
PGA	Professional Golfers' Association
plc	Public limited company
PM	Personnel management
PR	Public relations
QC	Queen's Counsel
R&D	Research and development
RFU	Rugby Football Union
RIDDOR	Reporting of Injuries, Diseases and Dangerous Occurrences Regulations 1995
ROCE	Return on capital employed
ROI	Return on investment
RoSPA	The Royal Society for the Prevention of Accidents
RPC	Restrictive Practices Court
RYA	Royal Yachting Association
SABC	South African Broadcasting Corporation
SARS	Severe acute respiratory syndrome

SE	Sport England
SEO	Search engine-optimised
SHRM	American Society of Human Resource Management
SLSWA	Surf Life Saving Western Australia
SME	Small to medium size enterprise
SMR	Social media release
SP	Starting Price
STP	Segmentation, targeting and positioning
SUP	Stand up paddle surfing
SWOT	Strengths, weaknesses, opportunities and threats
TAB	Totaliser Agency Board (Australia and New Zealand)
TOP	The Olympic Partner programme
TSIF	The Sports Industries Federation
UEFA	Union of European Football Associations/Union des Associations Européennes de Football
UFC	Ultimate Fighting Championship
UNICEF	United Nations Children's Fund (formerly, United Nations International Children's Emergency Fund)
USBA	United States Boxing Association
WADA	World Anti-Doping Agency
WBA	World Boxing Association
WBC	World Boxing Council
WBO	World Boxing Organization
WCT	World (Surfing) Championship Tour
WRU	Welsh Rugby Union
WTA	Women's Tennis Association
WTCC	World Touring Car Championship
WWE	World Wrestling Entertainment (formerly, World Wrestling Federation)
WWF	World Wildlife Fund
WYOG	Winter Youth Olympic Games
YOG	Youth Olympic Games

Section A

The context of sport

This section sets the context for the book. Given the main focus of the book – that of private sport businesses – the section charts a path to the start of sport in the twenty-first century. The section nevertheless acknowledges that sports businesses must still adhere to certain morally acceptable practices, and that the State still has a big role to play in influencing sport.

The purpose of the section is to examine the development of sport from amateurism to professionalism to commercialism. As a counterpoint to the model of private, profit-oriented sport businesses which this book implies, the section also considers the role of the State in sport and details the importance of ethics and governance for sport businesses. As such, the section establishes an agenda within which the rest of the book is written.

This section contains the following chapters:

The commercialisation of sport

Governance in sport

Ethics in sport

The role of the State in sport

The economics of competitive balance in sport

The impacts of sport

Introduction: the commercialisation of sport

John Beech, Coventry Business School
Simon Chadwick, Coventry Business School

I can remember the day when, as a goalkeeper playing for Reading against Millwall in a reserve match at the Den in 1951, I collected nine pence in old pennies which had bounced off my skull. We needed the money in those days.

(Edward Bird in a letter to the *Daily Telegraph*, 31 January 2002)

Learning outcomes

Upon completion of this chapter the reader will be able to:

- outline the various processes which take place as a sport moves from a pure sport activity to a sport business;
- identify the scope of the business of sport and of sport businesses;
- identify the main business factors which are relevant to the management of sports organisations;
- explain the facets of sport which make it different from conventional businesses;
- identify the main contents of this book.

Overview

This introductory chapter sets out the three basic elements of the book:

The main focus of this book

This is a perspective driven by management theory but recognising the uniqueness of the sport industry. This perspective is implicit in the various chapters, written by a variety of authors from a variety of educational institutions in the UK, continental Europe and Australia.

The development of professional sports and their subsequent commercialisation

A two-part case study which looks at the split between Rugby Union and Rugby League is used as an example of this, and explores the continuing paradox of these two sports which split over the issue of payments to players but are now both amateur and professional. This leads to an exploration of basic themes – professional and amateur sport, professional and amateur players, the processes of professionalisation and commercialisation in sport, sport as competitive event-based activity and the limits of the book in terms of what is within and what is outside the limits of 'sport business'.

Its content on a chapter-by-chapter basis

The contents of the book are introduced in terms of business functions applied to sport and management issues specific to sports businesses.

The two-part case study is presented with discussion questions, as are more general discussion questions offered at the end of the chapter, a method used throughout the book.

The main focus of the book

The concept of sport and the ideals it encompasses are often seen as emerging from amateur and altruistic principles in a historical perspective. This approach to sport as one of activity exemplifying 'muscular Christianity' – a nineteenth century public school approach to sport – has been a popular one, and a rich source of research by sports sociologists. Similarly, sports scientists have brought their academic expertise to bear on the analysis of sport activity, considerably expanding our understanding of sport in general and of particular sports.

It is only in recent years that sport management has begun to emerge as a study with its own particular characteristics. This is perhaps surprising as the notion of sport as inherently amateur and altruistic is misguided even in its origins, athletes at the original Olympic Games being known to have received payment. A moment's reflection makes clear that it is difficult to generalise in this respect, some sports more clearly being identifiable with an Olympian ideal, while others have no historical connection with that ethos, or indeed with the Games themselves.

Although professional sport has been with us in the United Kingdom for over a century, it has generally attracted little academic interest other than from social historians. This has changed very noticeably as professional sport has moved from a long-standing and fairly steady state of 'professional' to a rapidly evolving process of large-scale 'commercialisation', a distinction which is discussed below. In general, commercialisation has happened to sports that had already reached the 'professional' stage in their development. Some sports, however, have progressed directly from 'amateur' to 'commercial' and, in this respect, this book generally restricts itself to sports which have moved beyond 'amateur'.[1]

The development of a sport as a business

Sports vary considerably in the extent to which they have become 'big business'. Those that have have generally followed a similar sequence (summarised in Figure 1.1). This sequence is best understood by distinguishing between *evolutionary* phases, where change is slow and incremental, and *revolutionary* phases, where change is rapid and the phase is characterised by high levels of uncertainty.

The three revolutionary phases (codification, professionalisation and commercialisation) are necessarily relatively short. In the case of codification and professionalisation a specific date for the 'revolution' can be identified, although, of course, the implications of the revolutionary changes will rarely be instantaneous. The commercialisation revolution can also often be associated with a particular event, but generally it will be a series of events, making the commercialisation peak of high uncertainty and high rate of change take place over a longer time period than the two preceding revolutions.

The evolutionary phases between the revolutionary peaks can be of quite differing lengths of time. For example, in the cases of English and Scottish football there was an

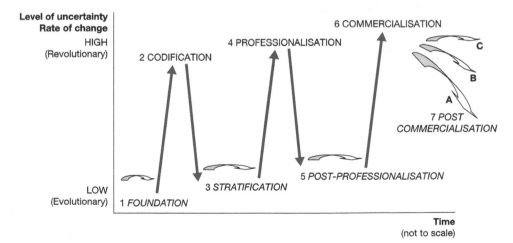

Figure 1.1 Framework: the development of a sport as business

Note: Curved arrows indicate periods of time the length of which will vary from sport to sport. In some cases the period may be very short, in others as long as a century.

---

[1] 'Amateur' sports are not excluded from consideration as amateur clubs still need to be managed, to promote themselves in a marketing sense, to control their finances etc.

evolutionary phase between professionalisation and commercialisation of roughly a century, whereas in the case of rugby union commercialisation rapidly followed professionalisation.

It should be noted that the model is a model of the mainstream activity in the particular sport. When applying it to athletics, for example, it takes no account of the pocket of sprinting for prize money which has been taking place in Scotland for well over a century, but which cannot be considered as part of the mainstream development of athletics. The model also makes no attempt to accommodate anomalous occurrences such as the one-off awarding of prize money in sports that were otherwise essentially amateur.

The phases are:

Foundation (Evolutionary) The sport emerges through ancient folk tradition (e.g. soccer).

Codification (Revolutionary) Codification may take place as a formalisation of practice (e.g. cricket), as the outcome of an organisational breakaway (e.g. rugby league) or through the need to define the game at the time of invention (e.g. snooker). In cases like rugby league, the sport may in fact see its foundation as coincident with codification; in cases like snooker, they are coincident.

Stratification (Evolutionary) As a sport grows, the body responsible for codification sets up or administers through merger a variety of leagues, typically with an element of promotion and relegation, and normally characterised by a regional dimension, especially at lower levels. In this phase, the sport remains amateur. The changes in the governance of the game may be considered revolutionary, but the effects of these changes have relatively little impact on the overall stability of the game, and growth is slow but steady.

Professionalisation (Revolutionary) As a sport gains popular appeal, the willingness of spectators to pay to watch, and the willingness of investors to support clubs, for altruistic reasons as well as commercial ones, allows the payment of players. Initially payment is in terms of expenses. This may extend to payment for loss of earnings. At this point the distinction between amateur and professional status may become blurred. Where full-blown professionalisation occurs, the elite players are able to play sport as a full-time job.

Post-professionalisation (Evolutionary) During this phase, a senior game which is professionalised typically sits alongside an amateur junior game.

Commercialisation (Revolutionary) As the sport develops an overtly business context, external organisations see the opportunity of using the sport for their own purposes, typically marketing in the forms of sponsorship – involving governing bodies, leagues and clubs – and endorsement – involving players. If the sport organisations, leagues and clubs are inept in their management of the greatly increased financial revenues which become available, they will come under pressure to the extent that some professional clubs in particular may be forced out of existence.

Post-commercialisation (Evolutionary/Revolutionary) Outside the 'Big Four' North American sports, few major sports can claim to have reached this phase. European soccer is entering this phase, and certainly F1 motor racing and cycling have been in this phase for a number of years. The phase may often appear to be evolutionary – a period of stability and growth following the commercialisation phase – but, because major revenues derive from outside the sport, sudden dramatic change (i.e. revolutionary change) may be thrust upon the sport since it has a reduced level of control over the steadiness and predictability of its income.

A review of sports that have reached post-commercialisation suggest that, unlike other phases in the model, there is a lack of consistency in that, in particular, some have reverted to a relatively stable state of low uncertainty and slow rate of further change, wrestling for example (indicated by path A in Figure 1.1), whereas others such as soccer have maintained high levels of uncertainty and rates of change (indicated by path C). Yet others, such as Rugby Union, have shown a slow return towards a fairly stable evolutionary phase (path B). In the bigger historical picture, our experience of post-commercialised sport is relatively short, and it will take many more years before the post-commercialised phase can be definitively analysed.

Table 1.1 is an application of the framework to English soccer which shows the timescale of the phases. It should be noted that the evolutionary stratification phase in fact lasted for a shorter time than the revolutionary commercialisation phase. The table also includes examples of the iterative nature of the process – the creation of the Premiership and the ongoing review of the structure of leagues at lower levels in the pyramid. This highlights a further important dimension to the model – the level within the sport. In sports which are large enough to support a 'tall' structure of leagues, development through the various phases is more rapid at higher (professionalised) levels, with lower levels remaining at the earlier stratification (amateur) level.

The progression from each phase to the next is not necessarily a process which has been completed by every sport. Sports which have not progressed beyond phase 2 are generally outside the scope of this book. The significance of phase 2 is that it defines the governing body of the sport, and the role of the governing body in the management of the sport becomes clear as the sport progresses to higher phases.

Those at phase 3 are certainly within its scope, as the sport as 'organisation' has emerged, and there will be financial, marketing and human resource dimensions to the operation of the business. Although the sport will have no professional players, it may well have employed administrators on a full-time or part-time basis. Section 2 of this book will be relevant, although section 3 will probably not.

When a sport reaches phase 4 the business dimension covered in Section 2 of the book is of great significance. This is because people are employed in the sport at the level of clubs in particular. The club now has revenues and expenditures – it must at least balance its books, it needs to promote its activities, and as an employer it has to consider the needs of its staff.

The business dimension is to the fore in sports which have reached phase 6. Now the clubs and the leagues have strong business relations with sponsors and with broadcasters. These organisations need to consider how they will manage risk, what legal liabilities they may incur, and how they might maximise the revenues generated by their main physical asset – their stadium or ground.

The further the organisation progresses through the phases, the greater the tendency for iteration – the revisiting of previous steps. The best examples of this lie in English and Scottish soccer. Clubs at the phase of Commercialisation revisited Stratification in the sense that their developing relationship with sports broadcasters influenced the way in which the games were structured – the English Premiership and the Scottish Premier League emerged in the process of strengthening the sports links with broadcasters.

Table 1.1 An example of the application of the framework: English soccer

Phase	Commentary
Foundation	The game emerged from various forms of two teams kicking a ball around with a view to scoring by reaching a goal.
Codification	Codification by the [English] Football Association (FA) in 1863 – the first codification of 'football', and the basis of the English claim to have 'invented' the game – standardised the game as one between two teams of 11 players and defined the characteristics of the 'goals'.
Stratification	The game grew rapidly and a range of leagues, national and local, became affiliated to the Football Association.
Professionalisation	By the mid-1870s, some clubs had begun to employ semi-professional and even professional players, and in 1885 such practices were authorised by the FA.
Post-professionalisation	The game entered a steady state, with a structure of leagues surmounted by three national leagues, ultimately developed into four national leagues. The players in these top leagues were professionals.
Commercialisation	A commercial dimension began to enter the game in the late 1960s. Early examples are the sponsorship of cups by Texaco (an oil company) and Watneys (a brewery), and the emergence of shirt sponsorship, a practice initially banned by the FA but which Jimmy Hill's Coventry FC attempted to circumvent.
	The major event in this phase was the formation of a new Premiership (league), driven by the clubs in the existing 'top flight' who sought to gain a larger share of the new available funding from broadcasting rights.
	By the end of the 1990s commercialisation had become firmly embedded across the whole of the top four leagues as well as the FA, with sponsorship of a range of events and facilities, including individual stadia, common practice. Club websites had become integrated with betting companies, mobile phone companies and other external organisations, typically offering directly soccer-related services. Weaker (in terms of financial success) clubs have faced major pressures such as being forced into administration.
Post-commercialisation	As we move beyond the first decade of the twentieth century, a clear case can be made that English soccer has reached this phase. The involvement with external bodies seems to have reached a natural limit, with further expansion by sponsors generally being limited to becoming involved with the lower levels of the game. However, it is still perhaps too early to judge, and further restructuring may yet happen – in particular, the relationship between soccer and sports broadcasters can be seen as still potentially 'revolutionary'. With the move towards the UEFA-imposed Financial Fair Play protocol, still in outline at the time of writing, a high level of uncertainty remains.

Clearly there are implications for players and stakeholders which derive from the steady-state phase that the sport has reached. These are set out in Table 1.2.

Great attention has been paid by academics to the business of soccer in the past ten years, no doubt because it is in this sport that the largest sums of money have been invested. This coverage has frequently shown a censorial tone, implicitly protesting at the loss of control of the game to the external paymasters – sponsors and broadcasters – (but less often protesting at the loss of control to the particular sport's highly paid elite participants) and frequently has lacked analysis using management theory. This book has been written to provide a source which:

Table 1.2 Stakeholder phases in the commercialisation of sport

The amateur game (phases 1 to 3)	The professional game (phases 4 and 5)	The commercial game (phases 6 and 7)
Players are unpaid. Stakeholders consist progressively of players, fans, clubs and governing bodies.	Players are paid, although a strong supporting amateur structure persists. Stakeholders now include investors.	Players at the highest level are very highly paid. Other players are paid, and still an amateur structure persists. Stakeholders now go well beyond players, fans, clubs, governing bodies and investors; they include external sponsors with only contractual loyalty, and broadcasters.

- sets the management of sport businesses in theoretical frameworks from a range of management disciplines;
- reflects the growing range of sports that have clear commercial dimensions.

The book focuses on sports which are familiar in the UK and Europe, and hence there is relatively little coverage of North American sports, although they are not ignored.

How significant is the scale to which many sports have become commercialised? Exhibit 1.1 gives some indications for a range of stakeholders.

Exhibit 1.1 How significant is the commercialisation of sport?

When it comes to who is involved in the commercialisation of sport, what is spent and who benefits, there are too many examples to mention. However, here is a brief selection of recent events that help to illustrate just how commercial the world of sport has become:

The performer

'Musicians, sports stars and actors are rapidly overhauling established business tycoons as some of America's wealthiest young people.'

The gambler

'Merrill Lynch has revealed that the online gambling industry in total will be worth an estimated £123bn by 2015, while online sports betting will be valued at £100bn.'

The spectator

'Since it began 14 years ago, the sport [World Super Bikes] has become ever more popular with over 1m spectators in 2001, double that of 1996.'

The club

'A report published by Deloitte & Touche and Sport-Business Group has revealed that Manchester United heads football's rich list with turnover of £117m. It is based upon turnover for the season 1999–2000. In 2nd place is Real Madrid with turnover of £103.7m.'

(continued)

The consumer

'The Sport Industry Research Centre at Sheffield Hallam University, in a report entitled "Sport Market Forecasts 2001–2005", revealed that UK spending on sport in 2000 was £15.2 billion. This ensures that sport accounts for approximately 3% of consumer spending. In the 1990s this market has grown by more than 70%, an estimated 64% of which is spent on sports services, while 20% goes on clothing and footware.'

The corporation

'Over the past 4 years the corporate hospitality industry has experienced huge growth. The sector is now worth more than £100m a year. A major investment and service-driven approach adopted by many sporting venues has not only served the hospitality industry, it has also opened the floodgates for conference opportunities.'

The sponsor

'Kellogg has signed its biggest ever UK sports sponsorship deal. It is linking its Nutri-Grain brand with the Rugby League's Challenge Cup. Kellogg will invest more than £1 million into the sponsorship.'

The governing body

'World Snooker, the governing body of professional snooker, is to invest £100m to promote the sport. World Snooker is expected to unveil details of a five-year plan to spark greater interest in the game next month.'

The merchandiser

'Hays and Robertson is planning a two-way split, by floating International Brands Licensing, the Admiral and Mountain Equipment brand business on Aim in June 2002, in an attempt to raise its market value to £11.5m. Hays and Robertson will then join with Sky in a deal to sell England kits and other football kits later on in the year and focus on purchasing licenses for other brands for UK distribution.'

The venue

'According to Wembley, the events company, a good performance from its 6 grey-hound tracks in the UK helped to boost interim profits 12.5% to £16.2m.'

The rights owner

'Formula One Administration (FOA), the company which owns the rights to Formula One motor racing, posted an 8% increase in profits in 2001. FOA's pre-tax profits rose to $180m, up from $165m in the previous year. Turnover jumped to $594m, up from $538m in 2000.'

Sources: 'Wealthiest men and women under 40', *Evening Standard*, 5 September 2001, p.3; 'Online sports gambling', *Sport Business*, 1 October 2001, p.2; 'The World Superbike Championships', *Sports Business*, 1 March 2002, p.8; 'Richest football clubs report', *Financial Times*, 1 December 2001, p.2; 'Consumer spending on sports increases', *Leisure Management*, 10 August 2001, p.10; 'Corporate hospitality industry has experienced massive growth over the past 4 years', *Marketing*, 20 September, 2001, p.47; 'Kellogg signs its biggest ever UK sports sponsorship deal', *Marketing*, 6 December 2001, p.4; 'World Snooker to invest £100m to promote the sport', *Sunday Business*, 7 October 2001, p.7; 'Hays and Robertson to float IBL', *Daily Express*, 20 May 2002, p.54; 'Income from greyhound tracks boosts Wembley', BBC News Online, 16 August 2001, www.bbc.co.uk; 'FOA posts 8% rise in profits', *The Business*, 21 April 2002, p.5.

The development of professional sport and professional players

There are sports in which it is clear when an individual 'turns professional'. This act may have two distinct aspects, although the two aspects may be irrevocably entwined:

- the decision to seek to make a living by earning money from participating in the sport;
- the changing of status with respect to membership of sport governing bodies.

These two aspects lie at the core of the Development of Rugby Case Study (A). The sport of rugby has been chosen because of its interesting extra dimension – the emergence of two varieties of the sport, arising out of the differing views held at the time on whether professionalisation was an appropriate way forward for the then single sport, and the similar ways the two varieties faced up to commercialisation at a much later date, albeit from different starting points.

Case 1.1a The development of rugby (a)

The Rugby Football Union was founded in 1871 on a strictly amateur basis. In 1893 the Union received reports that a Yorkshire Club had made a financial offer to induce a player to leave another club and join them. Payment to cover 'broken time' – pay that was lost through being absent from work in order to play rugby – was not unknown.

The Union was warned that the chief clubs in Lancashire and Yorkshire would react by breaking away, no insignificant threat as many of the national team came from these clubs. The particular club was suspended. In August 1895, 22 clubs made the threatened break and formed the splinter Northern Union. Within two years a total of 80 clubs were members of the Northern Union. In 1922 the Northern Union changed its name to the Rugby Football League.

As an entity quite separate from the Rugby Football Union, the Northern Union was responsible for the laws of the game its members played. In the early days a number of changes were made, including the reduction in the number of players in a team from 15 to 13.

Thus began a clear divide between the amateur Union and the professional League.

As the League game quickly became distinct from Union, it required an amateur base from which to draw its professional players. However, control of Rugby League remained completely in the hands of the professional clubs. In 1973 the amateur League clubs, fed up with lack of democracy, formed the British Amateur Rugby League Association, a move that initially was contested vigorously but unsuccessfully by the League. Within a few years the League relented, giving the amateur League Association its blessing.

Discussion questions

1 Why do you think the Northern clubs were willing to force their case through?

2 Why do you think the League introduced new rules of play?

In the case of rugby, differences over payment led to the emergence of two distinct sports – Rugby Union and Rugby League. In other sports, such as boxing, two sports, one amateur and one professional, coexist with essentially the same rules, any differences being relatively minor and insufficient for the two sports to be seen as 'different sports'.

Some sports have sought to allow the two statuses, 'amateur' and 'professional', to co-exist. Cricket maintained the two categories of 'Gentleman' and 'Player' (amateur and professional respectively) until 1963. This distinction had by the end of its life become both blurred and absurd. It was not uncommon for County Cricket clubs to find patrons who would offer token jobs to a cricketer to ensure that he could retain his amateur status, or even to employ them as club officials. This allowed the club to continue with the myth that the team captain was a 'Gentleman' and not a 'Player'. The absurdity of the distinction is best illustrated by the story Fred Titmus tells of the announcement over the PA system at Lords which sought to clarify that he was a professional rather than an amateur: 'We apologise for the error on your scorecards – "F.J. Titmus" should read "Titmus, F.J."' Clearly the earning status of the sportsman was of vital importance, and had to be reflected in the way his name was on the scorecards!

Whatever the attitude that the governing body of a particular sport had taken to the issue of 'professionalism', by the end of the twentieth century it might well, depending on the sport, have found itself under pressure to accept money from broadcasters and sponsors. The former sought a ready-made and familiar product to sell to its customers; the latter sought to align their particular brands with the lifestyle surrounding the sport, and hence to gain an enhanced public perception of their products. While normally working well in terms of synergy, the matching of team and sponsor can seem incongruous – the sponsorship of the England soccer team by a Danish lager manufacturer, for example, arguably working rather better for the sponsor than for the sponsee. Not infrequently some sponsors have sought marketing outlets that were needed to replace ones that were blocked through restrictive legislation, cigarette and spirits manufacturers being good examples of this.

Rugby is, of course, untypical in that the early conflict between 'amateurism' and 'professionalism' led to the divergence of a splinter group to found a new and distinct sport. This schism was not however to remain as clear-cut as the steady state of the first half of the century was to suggest.

Case 1.1b The development of rugby (b)

Throughout the twentieth century, there had continued to be a total schism between the Union and the League, the Union debarring for life anyone who dared to cross to League. The climate within Union began to change in the late 1980s amid isolated reports of Union players compromising their totally amateur status by accepting unreasonably high expenses which amounted to appearance money. In 1987 two-way movement of players between Union and amateur League was allowed by both parties. In the early 1990s, for the first time since the original rift, a significant number of senior players 'defected' from Union to League.

(continued)

The Union game, as far as the vast majority of its participants was concerned, remained thoroughly amateur. The world of sport was changing fast nevertheless, and in 1987 the Union negotiated a £1.6m sponsorship deal with the brewers Courage. 1995 saw the International Board announce that the Union game would be opened up to the payment of players. In a move prompting comparisons with the formation of soccer's Premiership in 1992 as well as with the events of almost 100 years previously, in 1997 the top two Union leagues in England (a total of 24 clubs) received a £7.5m sponsorship package over three years from Allied Dunbar, the financial services organisation. The attraction to Allied Dunbar was the televising of these clubs by Sky Sports, a deal worth £87.5m, negotiated jointly through the auspices of English Professional Rugby Union Clubs, subsequently replaced by the English First Division Rugby body.

Discussion questions

3 Given the context of history, is it an absurdity that there is a British Amateur Rugby League Association and, recently, there has been a body called English Professional Rugby Union Clubs?

4 As a Rugby Union club manager in the early 1990s (i.e. before the permitting of payment to players), how might you have addressed the problem of stopping players moving to the paid world of Rugby League?

5 Compare the distribution of wealth between particular clubs and players in the two games, noting where the balance has changed over time.

6 Why do you think there was a rapprochement between the two amateur 'wings' but not between the two games as a whole?

This two-part case study together with some significant dates, from a business perspective, in the development of sport, as given in Table 1.3, provides a basis from which we can identify the features of this book:

● key themes that underpin the book's contents and which are implicit throughout the chapters;

● key topics that consist of business functions which are applied to the particular context of sport businesses;

● key issues that are specific to 'sport' as 'business' and which determine the uniqueness of applying management theory to sport businesses.

Table 1.3 Some significant dates in the development of sport as business

1806	First 'Gentleman' v. 'Players' match organised by the MCC.
1863	Foundation of the (English) Football Association (FA) (and the myth that the English invented soccer) on an amateur basis.
1880s	Widespread rumours of illegal cash payments to soccer players, succeeded by clubs openly admitting it. Leads to . . .
1885	FA approval of professionalism.
1888	Foundation of (English) Football League and league match system.

(continued)

Table 1.3 (*continued*)

1890	(English) Football League imposes transfer restraints on players changing clubs.
1900	Introduction of Maximum Wage Rule for soccer players (£4 per week).
1901	Professional Golfers Association founded; first sponsored tournament follows in 1903.
1906	Alf Common becomes the first footballer to be valued at £1,000 when he transfers from Sunderland to Middlesbrough.
1907	Foundation of soccer Players' Union.
1909	Soccer players' strike. Advances prove more psychological than tangible.
1922	Syd Puddefoot is sold by West Ham to Falkirk for a record fee of £5,000.
1928	David Jack becomes the first £10,000 footballer when transferring from Bolton Wanderers to Arsenal.
1936	First television broadcasts of an Olympic Games, restricted to a small number of viewers in Berlin.
1937	First sports broadcast by BBC – 25 minutes of tennis from Wimbledon.
1948	Foundation of Pegasus Football Club to champion the ideal of amateur soccer and sport in general.
1955	Kent Walton first introduced wrestling to a wider British public on ITV's 'World of Sport'.
1961	Professional Footballers Association achieves the abolition of the maximum wage.
1963	Abolition of distinction between 'Gentlemen' and 'Players' in Cricket.
	Transfer restrictions in amateur soccer introduced to curtail the unauthorised transfer market.
1968	Lawn Tennis Association accepts professionals and prize money at Wimbledon.
1969	'Pot Black' begins a 17-year run of snooker programmes on BBC television.
1975	Giuseppe Salvoldi becomes the first £1,000,000 football player when transferring from Bologna to Naples.
1976	The Oxford v. Cambridge Boat Race becomes sponsored.
1977	Kerry Packer establishes the short-lived breakaway World Series Cricket, introducing night matches and one-day games.
1979	First PGA National Pro-Am Championship, sponsored by State Express, a brand of cigarettes.
1981	International Amateur Athletics Federation relaxation of rules on amateur status.
1992	Senior English soccer clubs form breakaway Premier League, BSkyB acquires the broadcasting rights.
	Aldershot and Maidstone United, both then in the fourth tier, fold.
1995	The International Rugby Board removes the ban on payments to players.
	Rupert Murdoch's News Corporation begins multinational negotiations for the rights to broadcast Rugby Union.
1996	The Atlanta Olympic Games hit a new high in commercialisation. IOC President Juan Antonio Samaranch broke with precedent by describing them as 'most exceptional' rather than the traditional 'best Games ever'.
	Rugby League introduces 'video referees'.
1998	First women's boxing bout sanctioned in the UK.
	BSkyB introduces UK's first digital broadcasting allowing interactive programming.
2001	EU Directive bans sponsorship by tobacco companies.
2002	Collapse of ITV Digital.
	British Horseracing Board sells major bookmakers rights for use of data in betting shops and internet betting operations.
2007	Wimbledon adopt equal prize money for men and women for the first time.
2009	Roman Abramovic converts an interest-free loan to Chelsea of £340m into equity to make the club 'virtually debt free'.
	Cristiano Ronaldo transfers from Manchester United to Real Madrid for £80,000,000.
2010	Tiger Woods continues to lose endorsement contracts following his car crashing incident.

Key themes

'Professional sport' and 'amateur sport'

This book is not about the difference between 'professional sport' and 'amateur sport'. It *is* about 'professional sport' and 'sport businesses'. This distinction has clear implications for which sports are covered and what aspects of sport are covered.

'Professional sport' is taken broadly to mean sport which derives income from non-participants and which is dependent on that income to survive in the form that it currently has. Such income may come from one or more of a variety of sources which the sport organisations – governing bodies, clubs, events organisers – have control over. These might include gate revenue, broadcasting rights, branding and merchandising.

It will be helpful if you start to see any particular sport as part professional and part amateur. It is not difficult, for example, to see that the world of Sunday morning soccer in the local park is a very different world from that of Manchester United. The causes of the emergence of the former from the latter is the domain of sport sociologists and sport historians, and is an important area of academia. It is not the domain of this book, although it provides an interesting background to it. This book is about the management of the Celtics, the Ferrari Teams and the Wigan Warriors of sport.

'Professional players' and 'amateur players'

The distinction between amateurs and professionals has been the subject of more soul-searching and debate by the governing bodies of all the major sports than any other issue. The distinction received particular attention in two eras. In the last 20 years of the nineteenth century, the governing bodies of many sports, dominated as they were by Oxbridge 'gentlemen', resisted the realities of payment to players by clubs that were run by local businessmen seeking to make a profit as well as to promote local sporting pride. How they handled this perceived issue varied from sport to sport. We have seen how rugby was split into two sports; soccer accommodated professionals, and within 20 years only clubs that employed professionals made any significant contribution at the highest level of the sport; athletics ignored the problem in reality, although maintaining a total opposition to commercial athletic activity as practised, for example, in parts of Scotland.

Whatever the matters of 'ideal' were, it became clear in every sport that the only chance of achieving excellence was by a total time commitment to sport. The 'amateur' road could not lead to such excellence as the norm. The distinction matters less and less, and in this book we will be looking at the David Beckhams, the Tim Henmans, the Colin Montgomeries and the Lennox Lewises of sport, and their less well known professional colleagues.

Professionalisation and commercialisation

The professionalisation of a sport – the appearance of money-earning players – became, as noted above, an issue in many sports in the late Victorian era. The existence of professional players became, in many but not all sports, an acceptable modus operandi, a means to a healthy and vibrant set of sporting competitors who offered a clear focus to Saturday afternoon leisure activity. 'Professionalisation' was thus a practical measure, and a sacrifice most sports were prepared to make.

In the last decade of the twentieth century, however, a different process took place in the major sports: the emergence of satellite broadcasting and the opportunities for sports, and hence the top players, to earn previously unimagined sums. With the potential to earn much larger sums, players began to make use of professional agents. When, in 1961, the Professional Footballers Association (PFA) managed to get the maximum wage for professional soccer players abolished, that maximum wage stood at £20 per week.[2] In 2002, David Beckham was rumoured to be seeking a wage of £100,000 per week from Manchester United, on the grounds that he would be paid that by other clubs eager to sign him up. In 2009, Cristiano Ronaldo, then aged 24, negotiated a contract with Real Madrid which would, over a six-year period, offer him, as salary and image rights, a staggering £106,000,000. His salary increases year by year, but, if he sees the contract out, he will have earned an average £340,000 per week.

The previous 20 or so years have seen the injection of vast sums of money into the game through television rights and sponsorship deals. Typically these sums have gone straight through 'the game' and to the players and, to a much lesser extent, their agents. This process is the 'commercialisation' of sport and has attracted much academic interest, especially with respect to soccer. It should be noted that for some sports – Rugby Union, for example – 'professionalisation' has been driven through alongside 'commercialisation', the latter not making the former irresistible any more.

Written in the current era, it follows that this book is interested in both professionalisation and commercialisation.

Sport as competitive event-based activity

In applying management principles to sport businesses it is inevitable that the unique nature of sport makes for interesting problems. Unlike other businesses, sport businesses have the following particular characteristics:

- Each organisation has no meaningful existence without direct competitors with which it must literally compete. On the other hand, competition cannot take place without co-ordination, and collaboration with those competitors.
- The organisation of competition is controlled by governing bodies which operate like a cartel, in a way that would that might be considered illegal in other more conventional businesses where their trade associations wield far less power.
- The focus of this activity is an event, sometimes held on the organisation's own premises, sometimes on its immediate competitor's premises, or, rarely, on neutral ground. An event carries with it the factors of fixed place, fixed time and fixed duration.
- The set of competitors is defined in terms of 'leagues', and changes annually as a result of performance in the sport during the year. These changes impact on income but not on costs. (It's costly being relegated, in other words!)

---

[2] In very broad terms, this wage equated roughly to the earnings achievable by someone newly graduated from university, or to a manual worker. In today's world, allowing for the inflation which has taken place since 1961, a comparable figure would be a salary of roughly £30,000 per year. The fact that a comparison is made between a footballer's *wages* in the 1960s and a footballer's *salary* today reflects a change in the way that society sees their job, as, of course, does the marked difference in level between payment over 40-plus years.

- Direct income from such competition is usually seasonal.

- The essence of sport is thus competitive, seasonal, event-based activity, and, as a direct result, organisations seek indirect and more regular income streams through activities such as merchandising. With more and more commercialisation, direct revenue forms less and less as a percentage of total revenue.

- The uncertainty of outcome in matches forms the basis of a sport's attractiveness.

Rogan Taylor, the sports sociologist, has famously remarked about the passion and commitment of soccer fans, in comparison with brand loyalty to supermarkets, that 'nobody ever wanted to get married in their local supermarket', unlike the albeit limited, but nonetheless real appeal of home football grounds for this purpose, and this contrast helps when looking at the business aspect of sport. Supermarkets can seek sites where they have local monopolies, they do not operate other than in their own premises, they compete in a relatively free market, uncontrolled in any formal sense by their fellow supermarket chains, they are never 'promoted' or 'relegated', and they don't get serious income from television sponsorship. Their customers don't buy branded shirts to wear provocatively when visiting their competitors. The business of sport *is* different from most business, but in practical operational aspects, not just in emotive, sociological ways. In this book, having explored the context of sport business, we explore first the similarities with which business functions can be applied to sport businesses, in Chapters 7 to 14, and then the distinctive characteristics, the management issues that are specific to sport businesses, in Chapters 15 to 24.

The broader sport industry

Sport businesses are not confined to professionalised sports clubs and players. The following are all participants in the sport industry:

Players	Players' agents
Clubs and their teams	Stadia owners and operators
Leagues	Tournament and event organisers
Governing bodies	Sports equipment manufacturers
Players' associations	Sponsors of players, clubs, leagues, events etc.

Beyond these organisations, it becomes less clear where the boundary lies. Certainly organisations such as MUTV, the television subsidiary of Manchester United, are within the industry, but few would include the manufacturers of the branded merchandise that all major organisations sell to maintain revenue streams. This indicates the general boundaries adopted by this book. The main criterion for inclusion is that the organisation is essentially based in or around sport – Sky Sports therefore qualifies, but the parent Sky Television does not.

Sponsors generally fall into one of two categories:

- those that qualify by virtue of their core business – Nike qualifies as a manufacturer of sports footwear, for example, irrespective of its sponsorship activity;

- those that qualify with respect to their sponsorship role – the sponsorship activities of Benson & Hedges, for example, are within the sport industry, whereas their core business clearly is not.

See Case Study 1.2 on The changing Olympics for an idea of the role of sponsorship in a sports tournament.

Case 1.2 The changing Olympics

The summer Olympics take place every four years and last 16 days. The right to host the event is always fiercely contested. In the past this was an issue of city and/or national pride rather than any commercial aspect. Until the 1984 Games in Los Angeles, the outcome was a considerable financial deficit – the citizens of Montreal were paying for the 1976 Games until November 2006, when the last payment to clear the debt was finally paid.

The trend for a more commercialised Olympics is epitomised by the centennial Games, held in Atlanta in 1996. Only 26 per cent of the income for these games came from direct sales of tickets. The largest income stream was from television rights (34 per cent), followed closely by corporate sponsorship (32 per cent). A further 8 per cent derived from retailing and product licensing. NBC, the Games' host broadcaster, supplied 3,000 hours of broadcasting, which compares with the 100 hours provided by the previous soccer World Cup. They guaranteed to earn the International Olympic Committee $500m through selling the broadcasts, and still expected to make $70m from the deal.

Since 1986 the International Olympic Committee has offered sponsors the opportunity to be a member of the Olympic Programme (TOP), restricted to ten members and costing the member $40–$50m. For the Atlanta Games the TOP sponsors were Bausch & Lomb (manufacturers of Ray-Ban sunglasses), Coca-Cola, John Hancock (US insurance group), Kodak, IBM, Panasonic, Rank Xerox, *Sports Illustrated* (US magazine), UPS (parcel delivery service) and Visa. As well as exposing their logos in an Olympic context, sponsors expose the Olympic logo in their own advertisements. Sponsors also sponsor individual athletes, and their success offers another opportunity to advertise.

During the Atlanta Games Nike ran a series of advertisements which included the Games-oriented strap lines 'You don't win silver. You lose gold' and 'If you are not here to win, you're a tourist'.

Success in the Olympics leads to individual sponsorship deals, and those successful in high-profile sports can negotiate very favourable deals. The self-sustaining nature of personal promotion by sports individuals is well illustrated by the Xerox presence at the Atlanta Games. They recruited a team of 100 ex-sports stars to promote Xerox, led by Mark Spitz, the winner of a record-breaking seven gold medals at the 1972 Munich Olympics.

Sources include *The Independent*, *Independent on Sunday* and *The Sunday Business*.

Discussion questions

7 To what extent is it possible to view the Atlanta Games as representing an Olympian ideal?

8 How do individuals in team sports rise above their team-mates in securing sponsorship deals?

9 Review the ways in which Olympic sponsorship enhances the brands of each of the ten TOP sponsors.

Key topics and issues

At the heart of any understanding of sport management is a common core of management theory. It is in the application of this theory that there is a need for a book such as this one. We have already seen that the various sectors of sport have distinctivenesses which prompt characteristic behaviour. This phenomenon is by no means confined to sport – it is certainly not being argued that sport is unique in being different, only that sport is uniquely different. John Spender (1989) argued:

> Having worked in several different industries before I began my research work, I already suspected that managers often deal with the problems that uncertainty creates in ways that are characteristic of that industry. (p. 6)

> [T]he industry recipe is the business-specific world-view of a definable 'tribe' of industry experts, and is often visibly articulated into its rituals, rites of professional passage, local jargon and dress. (pp. 7–8)

> [Practising managers and industry analysts] could use [the industry recipe], for instance, to diagnose corporate performance, measure the fitness of the firm for its industry, guide strategic thinking and evaluate the appropriateness of mergers. (p. 8)

> I see the industry recipe as part of a particular firm's response to the varying competitive conditions, work practices, technologies, public policies, legislation, and so forth prevailing at the time. (p. 8)

The Treaty of Lisbon, finally enacted on 1 December 2009, will lead to a more formalised approach within the European Union to this notion that sport is uniquely different. Over two years previously, the European Commission had published its White Paper on Sport (Commission of the European Union, 2007). A far-ranging report, it includes sections on the economic dimension of sport and the organisation of sport. The latter includes the following statement:

> [S]port has certain specific characteristics, which are often referred to as the 'specificity of sport'. The specificity of European sport can be approached through two prisms:
> - The specificity of sporting activities and of sporting rules, such as separate competitions for men and women, limitations on the number of participants in competitions, or the need to ensure uncertainty concerning outcomes and to preserve a competitive balance between clubs taking part in the same competitions;
> - The specificity of the sport structure, including notably the autonomy and diversity of sport organisations, a pyramid structure of competitions from grassroots to elite level and organised solidarity mechanisms between the different levels and operators, the organisation of sport on a national basis, and the principle of a single federation per sport.

Just how this will impact on sports business is as yet unclear, but it may well have direct impacts on areas such as employment law and contract law, and the assignment and negotiation of broadcasting rights.

It is with these notions of 'industry recipe' and 'specificity of sport' that we are concerned, and on which the following chapters focus.

The remaining chapters in this first section continue to develop an understanding of the context of sport business. Chapter 2 considers the *Governance* of sports, and how the playing of a sport is organised. Issues raised include who controls sport, who should control sport and whether there is any place for 'fan power'. Chapter 3 explores the *Ethics* of sport, covering topics such as doping and the dominant values of elite competitive sport. Next, Chapter 4, the *role of the State* is considered, with particular reference to the United Kingdom. A new Chapter 5 explores *leagues and competitions*, looking at how their structure influences uncertainty of outcome and competitive balance, and it is followed by another new chapter on the *Impacts of sport*.

The second section, on business functions, opens with Chapter 7, which is on *organisational behaviour*, the study of how people behave individually and collectively within organisations, how they communicate, how they are motivated and how they exercise and react to different forms of leadership. The issues which concern us are the 'off the pitch' commercial and professional dimensions, rather than those on the pitch, which would be appropriate in a textbook on sports coaching rather than sport management.

A closely related field is that of *human resource management*, the subject of Chapter 8. This explores further the notions of motivation and looks at the problematic area of reward systems, systems which in professional sport have shot off at a tangent from the reward systems of conventional businesses. The disparity between the top players and the lowest professional players has become extreme in the last ten years. The employment of professional sportsmen and sportswomen has been contentious and confrontational in many areas – soccer, rugby, tennis and golf, for example – and has attracted more than its fair share of case law, such as soccer's Bosman Ruling. *Law* and its particular application to sport are the subject of Chapter 15.

After its players, a club's greatest tangible asset is usually its stadium, and by the nature of sport it is often a greatly under-utilised asset. *Events and facility management* form the subject of Chapter 16, which includes a look at the phenomenon of fans travelling to away matches – sport tourism and its impact.

As the product of a sport business is essentially different from conventional businesses (see above: Sport as competitive event-based activity), it follows that their *marketing* will have essentially different characteristics. Chapter 9 outlines basic marketing principles as applied to the world of sport. It looks at the segmentation of fans in particular – who are sports fans in business rather than sociological terms. The specialist areas so important to the marketing of sport businesses – *sponsorship and endorsement* are covered in Chapter 17, while Chapter 21 looks at *retailing and merchandising*.

Since money is the fundamental issue that separates professional from amateur sport, it comes as no surprise that *finance* merits a chapter of its own, Chapter 10. Here, the distinctive characteristics of sport accounting are considered. For example, the greatest assets of any team are its players, yet they do not appear in the financial accounts. In terms of managerial accounting, the most obvious aspects of most professional sports organisations are that (a) they are not financially viable in terms of direct revenue and (b) they are vulnerable to changing fortunes arising from poor team performance or players' injury. *Risk management* is investigated in Chapter 19, and a significant industry in its own right, the *sports betting industry*, is explained in Chapter 20.

Such problems are obviously not unique to the big names of sport, and even the smallest amateur club has to worry about risk, about finance, about marketing and so on. The particular issues of *managing small and not-for-profit sports organisations* are analysed in Chapter 11. Similarly, all clubs have to worry about the business environment they operate in, at the mercy of political, economic, social and technological changes and developments. Chapter 12 explains *strategy and environmental analysis*. The smaller clubs are the ones that most often need the support of the public sector. Both quangoes which promote sport and the National Lottery play significant roles in sports development.

Managing operations, quality and performance is also an area that managers must be familiar with if their businesses are to be successful, and it is considered in Chapter 13. Today's businesses have been quick to take advantage of the possibilities which new technology has presented. Chapter 14 covers *information technology and management information systems.*

Broadcasting has had the most amazing impact on the top levels of sport. The technological innovation of colour television made snooker a national sport for the first time. The advent of satellite television and the escalating rates being paid for the rights to broadcast sports events are investigated in Chapter 18.

There are entirely new chapters in this third section to reflect the emerging significance of *media and PR* (Chapter 22), *international and global sport* (Chapter 23), and *sports agents and intermediaries* (Chapter 24).

The book concludes with a look at *the future of sport businesses* (Chapter 25).

 ## Conclusion

Studying the business of sport management can be challenging. If you come to this book with a background of sports studies, it will be hard to take on board that management is at the core of sport business – the sociology of sport will help to explain the social environment which influences the development of sport business, but will in itself prove totally inadequate to explain sport business strategy, for example. If you come from a sports sciences background, this book will offer an entirely different set of analytical tools to apply in a fundamentally different dimension.

If, on the other hand, you approach this book with a basic understanding of business principles, you may feel that you come with a flying start. Be careful! While the idea that sport management is the application of general management to sport underpins this book (Section B: Chapters 7 to 14), it is also clear that the *distinctiveness* of sport business – the 'industry recipe' – is also at the core (Section C: Chapters 15 to 24).

Although the majority of research into sport management, at least from the European perspective, has concerned soccer, the examples and case studies have been chosen from a wide variety of sports, including, albeit on a small scale, from North American sports. By developing a set of business skills which you will have built in a range of applications, this book should help you not only with sport management studies, but with your personal development regarding a career in sport management. Such careers should span a working lifetime and are more realistic in terms of opportunity for most students.

Discussion questions

10 'As businesses go, the sport industry is like the music industry.' Explore this statement by comparing and contrasting the two industries.

11 'Sport management and the sociology of sport are irrevocably interconnected'. Discuss.

12 In the 1880s, Preston North End regularly fielded teams with up to nine 'imported' Scottish players. How, if at all, is this different from today's Chelsea fielding a team of 11 overseas non-home nationals?

Keywords

Business; commercialisation; management; organisation; professional; specificity.

Guided reading

For further information on professionalism in the original Olympic Games, see Slack (1998).

The early professionalisation of soccer in England is well covered by Tischler (1981). Hill (1998) provides some interesting personal insight into the final fight for the abolition of the maximum wage for soccer players, and also into the commercial development of a soccer club. See also Douglas (1973) for an insight into English soccer as it began to progress from the post-professionalisation phase to the commercialisation phase.

Smith and Porter (2000) gives excellent coverage of the recent amateur/professional issue in soccer, cricket, golf, athletics, horse racing and rugby union, and is highly recommended.

Quirk and Fort (1992) provides a good example of the commercialisation of sport in North America. For the commercialisation of English soccer, see, for example, Conn (1997) or Hamil, Michie and Oughton (1999). There are many texts on the commercialisation of soccer but very little on the professionalisation or commercialisation of other sports in the UK.

The impact of broadcasting on professional soccer is comprehensively covered by Hamil et al. (2000), but the contributions to this collection need to be read selectively. Lee (1999) is particularly relevant, giving a clear picture of how modern professional sport is developing from a management perspective.

As a basis for Chapters 7 to 14, students will find it useful to have access to standard texts in organisational behaviour, human resource management, finance, marketing and corporate strategy. Suitable texts are recommended in the appropriate sections of these chapters. For someone with no prior knowledge of business studies, Lynch (1997) is recommended.

Recommended websites

Websites which are relevant to the case studies include the following:

Rugby Union   www.irfb.com/index.html
Rugby League   www.rfl.uk.com/default.asp
Forbes Magazine   www.forbes.com
Olympic Games   www.olympic.org

References

Commission of the European Communities (2007) *White Paper on Sport*, Brussels, European Commission.

Conn, D. (1997) *The Football Business*, Edinburgh: Mainstream.

Douglas, P. (1973) *The Football Industry*, London: George Allen and Unwin.

Hamil, S., Michie, J. and Oughton, C. (eds) (1999) *The Business of Football – A Game of Two Halves?*, Edinburgh: Mainstream.

Hamil, S., Michie, J., Oughton, C. and Warby, S. (eds) (2000) *Football in the Digital Age: Whose Game Is it Anyway?*, Edinburgh: Mainstream.

Hill, J. (1998) *The Jimmy Hill Story*, London: Hodder & Stoughton.

Lee, S. (1999) 'The BSkyB bid for Manchester United Plc', in S. Hamil, J. Michie and C. Oughton (eds). *The Business of Football – A Game of Two Halves?*, Edinburgh: Mainstream Publishing, pp. 82–111.

Lynch, R. (1997) *Corporate Strategy*, London: Pitman.

Quirk, J. and Fort, R.D. (1992) *Pay Dirt*, Princeton: Princeton University Press.

Slack, T. (1998) 'Studying the commercialisation of sport: the need for critical analysis', *Sociology of Sport On-Line*, 1 (1).

Smith, A. and Porter, D. (2000) *Amateurs and Professionals in Post-War British Sport*, London: Frank Cass.

Spender, J.-C. (1989) *Industry Recipes: The Nature and Sources of Managerial Judgement*, Oxford: Basil Blackwell.

Tischler, S. (1981) *Footballers and Businessmen*, London: Holmes & Meier.

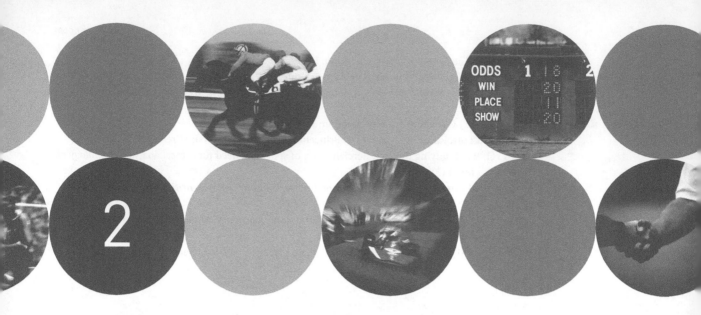

Governance in sport

John Beech, Coventry Business School

Learning outcomes

Upon completion of this chapter the reader will be able to:

- differentiate three concepts of governance – systemic governance, corporate, organisational or good governance, and political governance – and explain the relevance of these concepts to management in the sports industries;

- clarify changes in the nature of systemic governance in terms of the environment, and skills demanded, of managers in sports systems;

- identify and apply criteria for the evaluation of good governance and related ethical practices in sports management contexts;

- clarify the nature of the relationship between normative governance concerns and ethical business practices in the context of the commercialisation and professionalisation of sport;

- highlight the nature of political governance of sport and the implications for managers in the delivery of services and the implementation of policies.

Overview

The term 'governance' is one which is used in a variety of subtly different ways. It can generally be taken to mean 'the act of governing' or 'the process of governing'. In the case of sports it is inevitably related to those who govern – the governing bodies. In an ideal world we might wish for a single governing body for each sport, but this is unlikely to happen if only because sports governing bodies find themselves in hierarchies determined geographically. In English football, for example, County Football associations do not act autonomously; they fall within the remit of the national Football Association, which is itself one of 53 members of the Union des Associations Européennes de Football, much more widely known by its abbreviation, UEFA. Above UEFA in the geographical hierarchy is the Fédération Internationale de Football Association (FIFA), although, to add complexity to an already complex subject, it is national associations rather than regional associations that comprise the 208 members of FIFA.

An extended view of this hierarchical context to governance, together with examples of how governance may affect those involved at different levels of the hierarchy is given in Table 2.1.

It is important to note at this point that the word 'club' is used in three different ways, as set out in Table 2.2, and that, depending on which meaning we are using, the governance implications vary considerably.

Table 2.1 Hierarchical dimensions of governance

Tier	Example of organisation	Example of governance implications
International	FIFA	Determines eligibility of national associations to enter international competitions
Continental	UEFA	Introduction of Financial Fair Play protocol, which imposes restraints on the financial policies of clubs wanting to play in European competitions
National	FA	Investing money in grass-roots football
National organisational	Premier League	Selling broadcasting rights and disbursing the revenues from them
Club	Portsmouth FC	Imposed: operational restrictions in both the sporting and business areas
Player		Imposed: regulation of disciplinary codes, and possible punishments as a result

Table 2.2 A 3Cs model of 'club' – as 'construct', 'company' and 'crew'

	'Club' as construct	*'Club' as company*	*'Club' as crew*
Example	'Pompey'	Portsmouth City Football Club Limited	The team which played Tottenham Hotspur in the semi-final of the FA Cup in April 2010
Characteristics	The 'till I die' element of fans' loyalty The heritage, culture, mentality and mythology; fans' tattoos The fans' construct It survives discontinuities in the 'club as company' It doesn't physically exist yet it's the most permanent dimension	The owner(s), the board of directors, the Chief Executive Officer The business element Finance and accounts Making a profit – or at least not making a loss Subject to complete discontinuity when the company is sold or goes into administration; can result in 'phoenixing' or 'resurrection'	'Ship of Theseus' or 'Trigger's broom' Constantly changing Transfer to opposing clubs Days of local identity and 'one club' players long gone, with very few exceptions Still the fans' 'heroes' or 'zeroes' Highly transient in definition
Governance implications	Governance cannot directly influence the 'club as construct' *because* it is a construct	The 'club as company' is ever aware that it must comply with the rules and regulations imposed upon it by governing bodies	In essence, governance implications impose limited restrictions, typically with respect to discipline and employer changes (i.e. transfers)

Context

Governing is itself not conducted in isolation, and governance is therefore shaped by the external environment, especially the legal and political environments. Where once a sporting body just drew up the rules by which a sport was played, sporting bodies increasingly find themselves having to take note of not only national laws but also international laws. This is particularly the case within the European Union (EU), where membership of the EU by a particular nation brings with it specific obligations to comply with European law. Within a professionalised sport this means compliance with EU laws in areas such as contract law, employment law and competition law.

The nature of sport as business is a problematic one. Sport is a sector in which there is a requirement for competitive balance, and thus a requirement for a degree of collaboration between business competitors. Put more simply, leagues cannot allow one team to totally dominate the league, and the clubs that constitute the membership of the league need to act collectively on occasions. In ways such as this the nature of sport business is in marked contrast with other business sectors – there is, for example, no implicit need for, say, the top 20 supermarket chains in a country to remain roughly equal in terms of market share. Indeed, it can be argued that it is in the public interest for market forces to determine that the efficient and customer-oriented chains survive at the cost of the weaker and inefficient ones. The European Union recognises the principle that sport as business is different from other business sectors, and this principle is explicitly stated in the Treaty of

Lisbon as the 'specificity of sport'. The precise definition of the specificity, or uniqueness, of sport as business has yet to be agreed however.

Any study of governance needs to focus on the practice of good governance, and, as we shall see, the issues of, on the one hand, corruption, and on the other, fair and ethical practice, have become increasingly matters for debate. With the commercialisation of sports, governing bodies increasingly have to deal with external stakeholders, and situations can arise when there is a tension between acting fairly and ethically for the greater good of the sport and its participants, and meeting the needs of external stakeholders.

These themes are explored in the following sections.

Governance as part of the evolutionary process

In Chapter 1 we have seen how professional sports have evolved through a process featuring three key periods – codification, professionalisation and commercialisation.

With respect to codification, two distinct cases should be distinguished. In the first, codification predates the founding of a governing body. A good example of this case is the sport of boxing. As the sport moved on from the bare-knuckle form, there was a need for a code which made clear that a new variety of the sport was to be defined, one in which the glove was an essential feature. This was embodied in the formulation of the Marquis of Queensbury rules by John Graham Chambers in 1867. They represent a new definition of the sport of boxing, incorporating not only the requirement to wear boxing gloves but also such then novel features as three-minute rounds and the count-of-ten. They should not be thought of as a formulation in isolation however; in particular they explicitly incorporate elements of a previous code, the London Prize Ring Rules.

The definition of the sport by a code which lacks the hand of a pre-existing governing body leaves open the possibility of more than one governing body 'claiming' the sport and seeking to govern it. Case 2.1 shows the problems this has created for the governance of boxing.

Case 2.1 Boxing's international governing bodies

Boxing provides an example of a sport where there is not one universally accepted governing body – at least three bodies see themselves as the 'official' world governing bodies.

The World Boxing Association (WBA) is the oldest of these. It began life as the (USA) National Boxing Association (NBA) in 1921, and it was in 1962 that it adopted its present name, with its implicit claim to be the global governing body. The following year, however, representatives of 11 national boxing federations (including one from the United States) met to form a body which, in the organisation's own words, 'would achieve the unity of all commissions of the world to control the expansion of a sport which desperately needed it'. This body was the World Boxing Council (WBC). Two of its founding members had sanctioned world title fights – the European Boxing Union (and its forerunner, the International Boxing Union) since 1913, and the New York State Athletic Commission since 1920 – as had the NBA. (Claims to be 'world champion' predate these various formal titles however, going as far back as John L. Sullivan in 1885.)

(continued)

In 1976 the United States Boxing Association (USBA) was formed, when 24 US boxing Commissions 'decided it was time to form a new organization based in the United States and comprised of legitimate boxing commissioners from the United States and its territories'. In some respects this filled a gap in US boxing governance following the internationalisation of the National Boxing Association, and in its early days the USBA 'served as a springboard for its boxers to the rankings of the World Boxing Association'.

In 1980 Robert W. Lee, Sr., then a vice-president of the WBA, stood unsuccessfully for the presidency of that organisation. He then sought to extend the influence of the USBA internationally, and in 1983 the USBA-I was formed, adopting the name International Boxing Federation (IBF) the following year. Lee remained heavily involved with the IBF until he was indicted on federal charges of racketeering, money laundering and tax fraud in 1999.

In 1988 a group splintered off from the WBA to form the World Boxing Organization (WBO).

In the public's eye the multiplicity of governing bodies is most noticeable in terms of the champions it recognises and the rankings they publish. A current list of champions at the various weights is maintained at http://en.wikipedia.org/wiki/Boxing_champions. At most weights there are four different 'world champions', one from each of the four above organisations. At the time of writing, the current heavyweight champions were David Haye of the UK (WBA), Vitali Klitschko of the Ukraine (WBC), and his brother, Wladimir Klitschko (IBF and WBO).

To add to this complexity, it should be noted that amateur boxing has an entirely separate international body, the Association Internationale de Boxe Amateur.

Sources: Websites of the four bodies.

Discussion questions

1 To what extent does boxing suffer as a sport through the proliferation of governing bodies? Are there any advantages to this atypical state of affairs?

2 Is the objective of unified titles an effective step in producing a unified body?

The more common case is that where the codification either coincides with or follows the foundation of a governing body. In many sports the growth of the sport then followed in a relatively simple 'straight-line' process. The uniquely complex case of those sports which include the word 'football' in their name yet today must be considered as quite distinct sports must be noted. Table 2.3 shows the foundation dates of the earliest national governing bodies of such sports.

Hughes (2009) sets out how these various sports, distinct though we see them as today, have, with the exception of Gaelic football, evolved through adaptation and schism in a single 'family tree'. Even within this family tree there are complicated histories, as in the cases of the emergence of Australian football, and of American football, which has no single governing body that bears direct comparison with other sports.

Before moving on from the codification phase of evolution, it is worth noting that having a single governing body in a sport and a single set of rules does not guarantee the smooth conduct of a sport, as Case 2.2 shows – rules may prove problematic when tested in practice!

Table 2.3 The foundation of early governing bodies in the 'football family'

Code	Governing body	Year
Association	(English) Football Association	1863
Rugby Union	Rugby Football Union	1871
Gaelic Football	Gaelic Athletic Association	1884
Canadian Football	Canadian Rugby Football Union	1884
Australian Football	Australasian Football Council	1890
Rugby League	Northern Rugby Football Union	1895
American Football	Intercollegiate Athletic Association of the United States	1906

Case 2.2 Problems at the Caribbean Cup

The (English) Football Association first organised its famous cup competition as long ago as 1871, and FIFA organised its first World Cup in 1930. Whatever problems might have arisen in association football's early days, one might have expected that by 1994 sufficient experience in running cup competitions had been accumulated for major disruption caused by the inadequacy of the rules under which they operate to have been long avoided.

In the latter year, the Confederation of North, Central American and Caribbean Association Football (CONCACAF) organised its fifth Caribbean Cup. In the qualifying tournament the 21 national teams were arranged into six groups of either two, three or four nations and played one another once. The winner of each group, plus the second placed team in the two larger groups (with four nations) then proceeded to further group rounds, which produced four teams for a conventional knockout cup format.

Things in Group 1 of the qualifying round took a turn that might have been predicted in a perfect world, but in fact was not. The fact that there had to be a clear winner of the group had resulted in the organisers laying down two specific rules:

1 Since the clubs only played each other once, every game must produce a winner. If the game was tied after 90 minutes, there would be sudden death extra time.

2 For reasons that are not clear, it was decided by CONCACAF that, for this competition, any goal which was scored in that extra time would count double. In other words, the team which scored a single goal win in extra time would be deemed to have achieved a two-goal victory.

On the face of it perhaps, nothing appears amiss with these rules. The first two games played led to the following results:

Barbados	0:1	Puerto Rico
Grenada	2:0	Puerto Rico

Grenada thus went into the game with a superior goal difference, but Barbados had home advantage. The latter could move to the top of the table, and hence on to the next round, if they could beat Grenada by at least two goals.

(continued)

Barbados in fact led 2:0 until the 83rd minute, when Grenada pulled a goal back as a result of an own goal by a Barbadian defender. This meant that Barbados could only proceed to the next round if they scored again. Grenada not surprisingly started to play very defensively as, with the score at 2:1, they would top the group.

Somebody on the Barbadian side realised that a better option than trying to score a further goal in the last seven minutes of play was to force the game into extra time by scoring an own goal, which they proceeded to do, anticipating a score of 2:2 after 90 minutes, and then 30 minutes of extra time in which to score a single goal (a goal that would give them victory of 4:2 because of the second rule noted above, and progress to the next round).

The Grenadians however quickly realised that there were two possible strategies: they could score a third goal, or, if they scored an own goal in the dying minutes, the Barbadians would win by three goals to two, which would mean that Grenada progressed.

The Grenadians then attacked *both* goals, as a goal at either end would see them through, and the Barbadians were forced to defend at both ends. This may be football, but not as we would expect it to be played!

The outcome was no further goals in normal time, Barbados scored a golden goal, which counted double (giving them a nominal 4:2 victory), and thus progressed to the next stage.

Sources: Gardiner (2005); Snopes (2008).

Discussion questions

3 Might this bizarre and dysfunctional situation have reasonably been anticipated?

4 Are there any circumstances where games should be replayed because the original result might be considered unsound?

Three approaches to governance

Henry and Lee (2004) argue that are three interrelated approaches to governance, as outlined in Table 2.4.

The three approaches are not mutually exclusive. All approaches are ultimately systemic, and it can be argued that organisational and political approaches are in fact subsets of systemic governance. In attempting to map their interrelationships it is important to recognise that the relationships are not static, but change over time. Two key factors which drive these changes are the evolutionary nature of sport as business, as discussed in Chapter 1, and the increasing internationalisation of sport as business and globalisation of sports (see Chapter 23). These two factors have brought increasing complexity to the way in which sports are conducted, and this has required changes in how the sports are governed.

A good example of how governance has changed is provided by the Olympic Games. In the early Olympic Games, that is, prior to the First World War, the Games were organised and conducted by the ultimate governing body, the International Olympic Committee, but

Table 2.4 Approaches to governance

Approach	Concern	Example of where the approach has been practised
Systemic	Concerned with competition, co-operation and mutual adjustment between organisations	Leagues consisting of clubs which play against one another, such as the Premier League, the Football League and the Football Conference
Organisational	Concerned with normative, ethically-informed standards of managerial behaviour	The European Club Association The League Managers Association The Professional Footballers Association
Political	Concerned with how governments or governing bodies in sport 'steer', rather than directly control, the behaviour of organisations	The Football Task Force The House of Commons Select Committee Inquiry on Football Governance

Source: Developed from Henry and Lee (2004)

operated by a host city. Choice of the host city was not decided in the context of a fiercely competitive bidding process as it is today, and cities which were chosen often added the Olympic Games onto a larger pre-existing event. For example, in 1904 the St Louis Olympic games were 'bolted on to' the Louisiana Purchase exposition, and, as a result, took place over a period lasting almost five months, in stark comparison to today's three-week calendar of events.

National Olympic associations as we know them today were not the basis for entering individual athletes or teams. Entry to the competition was a much more open process, and this resulted in what we today consider to be anomalies. For example, at the St Louis Games, the two most represented nations were the United States of America (523 athletes) and Canada (52 athletes), with only ten other nations sending athletes. In the latter group were two athletes who chose to represent Austria. Austria was then part of the dual monarchy of the Austro-Hungarian Empire, yet, in the pre-1914 Games, athletes from the Dual Monarchy chose to represent their self-defined countries of Austria, Hungary and Bohemia (today's Czech Republic, but then part of a considerably larger Austria). Because competitors were not selected as they are today, there were many examples of 'national teams' that were not in any way representative of the country they came from. In the 1900 Paris Games, cricket was an Olympic sport, although only two nations competed – Great Britain and France. Great Britain's team was in fact the Devon and Somerset Wanderers, a club on a continental tour, and the French team consisted of British expatriates working in France. In a similar vein, the tug-of-war was contested from 1900 to 1920, but the entrants were individual clubs, and in 1904 and 1908 the same country won all three medals (the United States in 1904 and Great Britain in 1908, with the City of London Police team winning the gold medal).

As the production of an Olympic Games became more formalised in the inter-war years, a more sophisticated form of governance was needed, and a model emerged which contained, in addition to the International Olympic Committee, a series of National Olympic Associations, a local Organising Committee for each Games, and International

Federations representing each sport, each of them at the top of a hierarchy of national federations. The IOC's role in systemic governance began to take on an additional organisational governance perspective.

In more recent years, in a post-commercialised era, external stakeholders have become increasingly important stakeholders in the Olympic Games, and IOC governance has had to extend to the governance of partners such as sponsors and broadcasters. Sponsors, for example, were still the responsibility of the Local Organising Committee up until the 1976 Montreal Games, where there were 628 sponsors. In an attempt to regulate this seemingly anarchic market, and, it must be said, in order to profit-maximise, the IOC introduced The Olympic Partner (TOP) programme, where a handful of sponsors pay very large sums to the IOC for the right to exploit the Olympic logo in their own advertising. This in turn has seen a growth in activity by the IOC to protect the Olympic brand legally.

The involvement of external stakeholders and the increasing levels of money moving around in sports, and out to external profit-takers, an inevitable outcome in the post-commercialised era, have brought into question a need for governance which retains an emphasis on 'the sporting ethic'. Similarly commercialisation and increased cashflows have resulted, in some sports, in an increased incidence of financial doping – the attempt to buy success by distorting the balance of competition.

Effectiveness, transparency and accountability

At the time of writing, the UK Government, in the form of a House of Commons Select Committee, had just issued a report on the state of football governance. In the lead-up to the Committee's hearings, Hugh Robertson, the UK Sports Minister had described football as 'the worst governed sport in this country' (Winter, 2011). Attempts to improve football's governance have been manifold over the years, with arguably only the Taylor report, which followed stadium disasters at Bradford City and Hillsborough, producing any significant outcomes (see Table 2.5).

In a broader context, and in terms of different sports and internationally, the biennial *Play the Game Conference* has in its last three occurrences carried papers on governance shortcomings in athletics, cricket, cycling, F1, field hockey, football, handball, horse racing, the Olympics, tennis, weight-lifting and wrestling, covering such diverse issues as ambush marketing, broadcasting rights, child abuse, disability, doping, fan violence, financial doping, financial fair play, money laundering, gender identity, homophobia, match-fixing, sexism and sport mega-events and their impacts.

Allegations about corruption in FIFA, especially with respect to the process of selecting the hosts for specific World Cups, have dominated sports media reporting throughout 2011. The suspension of members has gradually increased, the most high profile being the lifetime ban on Mohammed Bin Hammam, Qatar, and Jack Warner, Trinidad and Tobago and head of CONCACAF and CFU. Investigations by FIFA into the Warner allegations have ceased, because he pre-emptively resigned, but Bin Hammam continues to fight his suspension.

The general state of sports governance cannot be described as healthy overall, and inevitably much discussion centres on how good practice can be achieved. A key question is '*quis custodiet custodiens?*', or 'who will guard the guardians?'

Table 2.5 Parliamentary-inspired reviews of and inquiries into British football

Year	Report	Author	Any specific prompt
1923	Report of the Departmental Committee on Crowds	Shortt	Disturbances at 1923 FA Cup Final
1946	Moelwyn Hughes	Hughes, Home Office	Burnden Park disaster
1968	Report of the Committee on Football	Chester	
1968	Soccer Hooliganism	Commissioned by Ministry of Sport	
1969	Crowd Behaviour at Football Matches	Lang	
1972	Report of the Inquiry into Safety at Sports Grounds	Wheatley, Home Office	Ibrox disaster
1977	Report of the Working Group on Football Crowd Behaviour	McElhone, Scottish Education Department	
1984	Football Spectator Violence	Department of the Environment	
1985	Interim Report of the Committee of Inquiry into Crowd Safety and Control at Sports Grounds	Popplewell, Home Office	Bradford City fire disaster
1986	Final Report of the Committee of Inquiry into Crowd Safety and Control at Sports Grounds	Popplewell, Home Office	Bradford City fire disaster
1988	Football National Membership Scheme	Ministry for Sport	
1989	The Hillsborough Stadium Disaster Interim Report	Taylor	Hillsborough disaster
1990	The Hillsborough Stadium Disaster Final Report	Taylor	Hillsborough disaster
1993	Kick It!	Commission for Racial Equality	
1994	Let's Kick Racism Out of Football	Commission for Racial Equality	
1995	Kick It Again	Commission for Racial Equality	
1996	The Director General's Review of BSkyB's Position in the Wholesale Pay TV Market	Office of Fair Trading	
1998	Eliminating Racism from Football	Football Task Force	
1998	Improving Facilities for Disabled Supporters	Football Task Force	
1998	Review of Football Related Legislation	Home Office	
1999	Investing in the Community	Football Task Force	
1999	Football: Commercial Issues	Football Task Force	
1999	British Sky Broadcasting Group plc and Manchester United	Monopolies and Mergers Commission	Proposed merger
2004	English Football and Its Finances	All Party Football Group	
2009	Football and Its Governance	All Party Parliamentary Group	
2011	Report of House of Commons Select Committee on Football Governance	House of Commons Select Committee	

One approach is to separate out specific issues from the remit of individual governing bodies, and two higher-level bodies have been established in specific areas:

- **The World Anti-Doping Agency** (WADA) was established in 1999, its mission being 'to lead a collaborative worldwide campaign for doping-free sport'. It is an independent agency, and is funded equally by the sport movement and governments of the world. It has a Foundation Board, the supreme decision-making body, consisting of 38 members drawn equally from the Olympic Movement and governments. Additionally it has a 12-member Executive Committee, again with members drawn equally from the Olympic Movement and governments, and a President, who comes alternately from the Olympic Movement and governments.

  It has been active in establishing anti-doping codes, in scientific research, in testing and in educating against doping among sportsmen and sportswomen.

- **The Court for Arbitration in Sport** (CAS) was established in 1984. In its own words, 'At the beginning of the 1980s, the regular increase in the number of international sports-related disputes and the absence of any independent authority specialising in sports-related problems and authorised to pronounce binding decisions led the top sports organisations to reflect on the question of sports dispute resolution.'

  As well as making judgments in specific court-related cases, it offers both arbitration and mediation services.

It is not of course possible to devolve all governance issues to such meta-bodies, and sports governing bodies need to establish models of best practice internally.

In reviewing the state of sports governance, Bruyninckx (2011) notes the fact that the world of sports and the world of government have largely been separate 'or, more precisely, perceived as separate'. He sees three main approaches emerging from the literature on governance as useful:

- **Governance as steering** He suggests that governance is being steered towards efficiency and effectiveness, and hence performance.

- **Networked or participatory governance** Here there is more emphasis on the process of rule and norm setting.

- **Good governance** Here the emphasis is on qualities such as legitimacy, transparency, clear legal and ethical frameworks, etc., and thus on setting out 'a sort of normative benchmark to judge governmental practices'.

The last of these three approaches remains the most contentious. As Bruyninckx puts it:

> Transparency, accountability and legitimacy at times seem to be as rare in the functioning of the largest sport federations as a snowball in the desert. This precondition for the creation of functional governance arrangements remains therefore highly problematic.
>
> Bruyninckx (2011)

Pielke (2011) has suggested that the literature on general governance provides a good indication of the way sports governance needs to turn. In particular he draws attention to the work of Grant and Koehne (2005) on evaluating accountability mechanisms in international politics. Their framework is summarised in Table 2.6.

Table 2.6 Accountability mechanisms

Mechanism of accountability	Characteristics
Hierarchical	The power that superiors have over subordinates within an organisation
Supervisory	Relationships between organisations
Fiscal	Mechanisms of control over funding
Legal	The requirement that international bodies and their employees must abide by the laws of relevant jurisdictions in which those laws are applicable
Market	Influence that is exercised by investors or consumers through market mechanisms
Peer	The evaluation of organisations by their peer institutions
Public reputational	The reputation of an organisation among 'superiors, supervisory boards, courts, fiscal watchdogs, markets and peers' and this is related to each of the other six forms of accountability listed above

Conclusion

The current state of sport governance is undoubtedly sub-optimal, although its quality varies considerably from sport to sport. We turn finally to the issue of the 'governance of governance', and a broader discussion of the key question of '*quis custodiet custodiens?*', or 'who will guard the guardians?' Although the highest level of the governance of specific issues such as doping and legal issues has been addressed with differing measures of success through the establishment of WADA and CAS respectively, there is as yet no ultimate authority for the governance of sport.

The *Play the Game Conference 2011* saw the issuing of the 'Cologne Consensus' (Play the Game, 2011) in order to move the debate forward and ensure that action is taken. It invited international sports federations and the IOC to take the lead in making the necessary changes by organising a conference for all relevant stakeholders that should look at a number of issues:

1 Governance documents and practices, and democratic procedures.

2 Representation principles, including age, gender, ethnicity, tenure and stakeholder issues.

3 Principles of autonomy and co-operation with governments.

4 Transparency and accountability, both operational and financial.

5 Monitoring, compliance and enforcement, including the feasibility of an independent agency to this end.

6 Development of grass-root sport.

7 Education, sharing of information and best practices.

8 Equity, inclusiveness, non-discrimination and minority protection.

Such a step is just the beginning, and it remains to be seen how the IOC will respond. Among the issues that will have to be resolved if this path is to be pursued is how the IOC will accommodate the 'barely Olympic sports' such as cycling, football and tennis, and the 'non-Olympic sports' such as the North American 'Big 4' sports, Formula One, golf and the various codes of rugby.

Other possible bodies which might undertake such a task include Transparency International, a global organisation of more than 90 locally established national chapters and chapters-in-formation, which is dedicated to fighting corruption. It already has shown in interest in sport governance – for example, recently calling on 'world football's governing body, FIFA, to carry out comprehensive governance reforms overseen by a group composed of representatives from outside FIFA (elder statesmen, sponsors, media and civil society) and inside football (federations, clubs, professional leagues, players, women's football, referees, supporters) in a way that ensures its independence'. The inclusion of both players and spectators is significant – it recognises two very important stakeholder groups often excluded from the governance process.

While there is an impetus to reform sport governance 'from the top down', there are also signs of improving micro-governance at the club level, i.e. new ownership models designed to improve internal governance in a club. Supporters' Trusts are appearing in a widening range of sports, and in a widening range of countries. Case 2.3 shows the increasing role of Supporters Direct in this movement.

Case 2.3 Supporters Direct and the Supporters Trust movement

Supporters Direct arose from the third report of the Football Task Force, *Investing in the Community*, and began its work in October 2000. Its earliest remit was to help in establishing Supporters' Trusts at English football clubs, but over the years it has expanded, to Scotland and then Europe, and to other sports, particularly Rugby League.

Its mission statement is 'Our goal is to promote sustainable spectator sports clubs based on supporters' involvement and community ownership', and it describes itself on its website (www.supporters-direct.org/page.asp?p=3977) thus:

- Supporters Direct campaigns for the wider recognition of the social, cultural and economic value of sports clubs
- Sports clubs and competitions are increasingly being put at risk by short-term vested interests, poor financial management and inadequate standards of governance; we are the UK's leading body working to ensure that clubs are run responsibly and are financially sustainable
- Supporters Direct aims to create the conditions in which supporters can secure influence and ownership of sports clubs
- Supporters Direct provides guidance and support to groups in more than 16 countries throughout Europe
- Supporters Direct promotes the value of supporter ownership to sports fans, empowering them to set up supporters' trusts or become members of existing trusts
- Supporters Direct is a community benefit society, owned by its members

It headlines the following achievements:

Since October 2000, Supporters Direct and the trust movement has ensured the survival of approximately 50 clubs – mostly in English professional football, and brought at least £30m of investment alone into football and Rugby League in Britain.

(continued)

Supporters Direct estimate that because of their direct intervention and supporters' trusts, 50 clubs have been saved or reformed.

Across Europe Supporters Direct work in over 20 countries, including Spain, Belgium, the Republic of Ireland, France and Sweden.

The highest placed clubs with supporter involvement in their ownership are [at the end of November 2012] Dundee FC (100% fan owned), Swansea City (20 per cent and an elected director), and Doncaster Rovers (director on the club board).

Across the UK, 32 clubs are owned and controlled by their supporter's trust.

The highest placed clubs in England, Wales and Scotland owned by their supporters are Dundee FC, AFC Wimbledon, Exeter City and Wycombe Wanderers.[1] Wrexham FC was bought by its supporters' trust in 2011, and AFC Telford United were reborn in 2004, and owned by the Telford United Supporter's Trust, whilst Chester FC were reformed by their fans in 2010. In Scotland, Clyde and Stirling Albion were bought out by their supporters.

> *Source*: http://www.supporters-direct.org/
> homepage.aboutsupportersdirect/facts-figures/

The Trusts it assists tend to be formed as mutuals, a loose term which can embrace industrial and provident societies, co-operatives, social enterprises and employee-owned businesses. A few Supporters' Trusts which have taken over clubs, and, for legal and organisational reasons, have needed to constitute the legal entity which owns the club distinct from the legal entity which is the football club itself, have done so as Community Interest Companies (CICs). This is a legal form of business which is appropriate to a sports club. This is described on their regulator's website thus:

> Community interest companies (CIC) are a new type of limited company designed specifically for those wishing to operate for the benefit of the community rather than for the benefit of the owners of the company. This means that a CIC cannot be formed or used solely for the personal gain of a particular person, or group of people.
>
> CICs can be limited by shares, or by guarantee, and will have a statutory 'Asset Lock' to prevent the assets and profits being distributed, except as permitted by legislation. This ensures the assets and profits are retained within the CIC for community purposes, or transferred to another asset-locked organisation, such as another CIC or charity.

Supporters' Trusts have met with mixed fortunes in achieving fan ownership. Currently the following English, Scottish and Welsh football clubs are owned 100 per cent by Supporters' Trusts: AFC Telford, Enfield Town, FC United of Manchester, Fisher, Gretna, Hendon, Merthyr Town, Runcorn Linnets and Scarborough Athletic, with Supporters' Trusts holding the majority of shares in AFC Wimbledon, Brentford, Clydebank and Exeter City. This is in stark contrast with fan ownership in the German Bundesliga, where the norm is for clubs to have a majority of shares owned by fans, the so-called '50 [per cent] +1' rule, although there are two exceptions, Bayern 04 Leverkusen and Wolfsburg, which remain owned by the companies, Bayer and Volkswagen, of which they were originally the 'works team'.

---

[1] At the time of writing, Pompey Supporters Trust was in an advanced stage of negotiating the purchase of Portsmouth Football Club from its Administrator.

> ## Discussion questions
>
> **5** How might being owned by a Supporters Trust, as opposed to being owned by a millionaire 'benefactor' for example, impact on the ways in which a club is run?
>
> **6** Fan ownership is clearly viable in large clubs, as the German Bundesliga evidences. How might a Supporters Trust at a Premier League club, as for example in the cases of Manchester United and Newcastle United, raise enough capital to make a credible bid for buying the club while still keeping to the principle of supporter ownership?
>
> **7** The track record of success for Supporters Trusts which have taken over clubs in England is patchy. Suggest reasons why this is the case.

Discussion questions

8 Investigate the ways that the IOC and/or FIFA are structured, and the ways in which they operate. Using the Grant and Koehne (2005) model of accountability mechanisms (see Table 2.6), evaluate their accountability.

9 What are the advantages and disadvantages of the idea of establishing a single global body as the ultimate authority for sport governance?

Keywords

Accountability; corruption; governance; specificity; transparency.

Guided reading

A useful textbook is *Governance and Policy in Sport Organizations* (2009) by Mary A. Hums and Joanne C. MacLean, although it has a strong North American perspective, while *Sport Governance* (2007) by Russell Hoye and Graham Cuskelly is similarly useful, although skewed towards an Australian perspective. A broader perspective is offered by James E. Thoma and Laurence Chalip's *Sport Governance in the Global Community* (2007).

Readers especially interested in football governance are recommended *Regulating Football* by Steve Greenfield and Guy Osborn (2001), and *What is the Feasibility of a Supporters Direct Europe?* (2009) produced by Antonia Hagemann.

Other recommendations include *Professional Sport in the EU: Regulation and Re-regulation* (2000), edited by Andrew Caiger and Simon Gardiner, and the more contemporary *Social Capital and Sport Governance in Europe* (2011), edited by Barrie Houlihan and Fabien Ohl. The latter includes a number of chapters focusing on individual EU countries.

The select Committee's Report on Football Governance is downloadable from www.publications. parliament.uk/pa/cm201012/cmselect/cmcumeds/792/79202.htm; the individual written submissions are downloadable from www.publications.parliament.uk/pa/cm201012/cmselect/cmcumeds/792/792we01.htm. John Beech's Football Management blog (http://footballmanagement.wordpress.com/) frequently covers aspects of football governance.

Recommended websites

All Sports International has a website with links to many sports governing bodies, albeit a rather UK-centric selection: www.allsportsinternational.co.uk/governingbodies.html

Wikipedia offers a set of links to International Sports Federations: http://en.wikipedia.org/wiki/List_of_international_sport_federations

The *Play the Game* website (www.playthegame.org/) is very useful as a resource of news on various sports governance issues. It is also provides a database of presentations at its conferences.

Transparency International has its website at www.transparency.org/

The *Supporters Direct* website can be found at www.supporters-direct.org

Investigative journalist Andrew Jennings maintains a website at www.transparencyinsport.org/, and Jens Weinreich writes a blog (in German) at www.jensweinreich.de/

References

Bruyninckx, H. (2011) 'Sports governance: between the obsession with rules and regulations, and the aversion of being ruled and governed', Play the Game Conference 2011, Cologne, 3–6 October.

Caiger, A. and Gardiner, S. (eds) (2000) *Professional Sport in the EU: Regulation and Re-regulation*, The Hague: TMC Asser Press.

Gardiner, S. (2005) *Sports Law*, London: Routledge Cavendish.

Grant, R.W. and Koehne, R.O. (2005) 'Accountability and abuses of power in world politics', *American Political Science Review*, 99 (1), 29–43.

Greenfield, S. and Osborn, G. (2001) *Regulating Football*, London: Pluto Press.

Hagemann, A. (2009) *What is the Feasibility of a Supporters Direct Europe?*, London: Supporters Direct, http://clients.squareeye.net/uploads/sd/documents/SDEurope-Full-Report.pdf

Henry, I. and Lee, P.C. (2004) 'Governance and ethics in sport', in J. Beech and S. Chadwick (eds), *The Business of Sport Management*, 1st edn, Harlow: Pearson Education.

Houlihan, B. and Ohl, F. (eds) (2011) *Social Capital and Sport Governance in Europe*, London: Routledge.

Hoye, R. and Cuskelly, G. (2007) *Sport Governance*, Oxford: Elsevier.

Hughes, G. (2009) *A Develyshe Pastime*, Cheltenham: SportsBooks Limited.

Hums, M.A. and MacLean, J.C. (2009) *Governance and Policy in Sport Organizations*, 2nd edn, Scottsdale, AZ: Holcomb Hathaway Publishers.

Pielke, R. Jr. (2011) 'How can FIFA be held accountable?', Play the Game Conference 2011, Cologne, 3–6 October.

Play the Game (2011) *Cologne Consensus: Towards a Global Code for Governance in Sport*, www.playthegame.org/fileadmin/documents/Cologne_Consensus.pdf

Snopes (2008) *Football Follies*, www.snopes.com/sports/soccer/barbados.asp

Thoma, J.E. and Chalip, L. (2007) *Sport Governance in the Global Community*, Morgantown, WV: Fitness Information Technology.

Winter, H. (2011) 'Hugh Robertson: football is the worst governed sport in Britain', *Daily Telegraph*, 20 January.

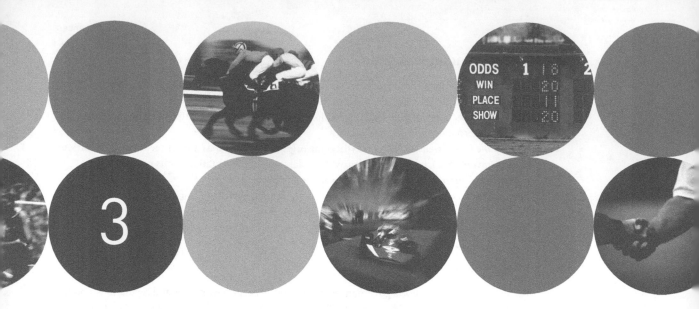

Ethics in sport

Leon Culbertson, Edge Hill University
Mike McNamee, Swansea University
Emily Ryall, University of Gloucestershire

Learning outcomes

Upon completion of this chapter the reader should be able to:

- describe the distinction between 'ethics' and 'morality';
- explain the distinction between descriptive ethics and normative ethics;
- morally evaluate examples of sporting conduct;
- evaluate the central arguments in the debate on doping in sport;
- compare and contrast criticisms of the dominant values of elite competitive sport;
- discuss the interrelationships between conduct in sport, performance enhancement and the commodification of sport.

Overview

This chapter begins with a discussion of ethics as an academic subject. A distinction is drawn between 'ethics' and 'morality' and an outline of the role of ethical theories in consideration of ethical issues in sport is given. In addition, a further distinction is made between descriptive ethics and normative ethics. The chapter then has three sections, each dealing with a topic in the ethics of sport. Sporting conduct is considered first, before moving to consideration of some of the various arguments in relation to the use of performance-enhancing drugs in sport. Finally, there is a discussion of the values of professional sport. The chapter concludes with a brief account of the interrelationships between these three topics.

Introduction

Competitive sport is a deeply moral business. It is a rule-bound activity, so issues of duties, fairness and cheating frequently emerge in discussion of sport. There appears to be a form of implicit contract entered into by contestants who play sport. If you and I are going to play some sport or other, we implicitly agree to play by the rules and in a particular spirit. Such agreements, whether implicit or explicit, suggest a sense of duty to abide by the agreement. Sport values performance, and, as a result, the means of performance enhancement (what permissible and what is not) are covered by the rules of the various sports. This raises moral questions of at least two basic kinds – those relating to the morality of rule keeping and breaking, and those relating to the moral concern athletes ought to have in relation to specific performance-enhancement practices adopted by athletes and the values and purposes of the adoption of such practices. Elite competitive sport raises further issues. At this level of participation, athletes are part of commercial enterprises. As such they raise many moral questions. For example, are athletes mere commodities; is their activity to be viewed as alienated labour; are the sums of money paid to some elite athletes offensive and morally reprehensible given the global prevalence of extreme poverty?

While there are many different areas of sport that philosophers and social scientists have found to be of moral interest (and concern) – such as issues of gender equity, the treatment of children in sport, whether physical education can be morally educative etc. – this chapter will focus on the three issues briefly outlined above: fair play, performance enhancement and the ethics of sport as a business. The three issues may, of course, be related. Sports that are publicly seen to be plagued by cheating suffer in financial terms. Equally, someone might argue that the pursuit of profit is a major incentive to cheat. There are two reasons why this chapter focuses on these three areas. First, it simply is not possible to give any kind of comprehensive discussion of all the major topics commonly dealt with in the ethics of sport, and the three considered here provide a good representative sample to enable the reader to grasp not only some of the debates in the ethics of sport but the way philosophers approach thinking about ethical issues in sport. Second, the connections between the three issues and between those issues and the concerns of this book suggest that they are an appropriate selection from the range of possibilities. Before considering the three issues, however, it is necessary to provide a more detailed discussion of ethics as an academic field, including some discussion of the role of ethical theories in consideration of ethical issues in sport. The chapter, therefore, comprises five sections – 'Morality, ethics and sport', 'Ethical theories in the ethics of sport', 'Sporting conduct: between rules and ethos', 'The ethics of performance enhancement in sport: doping' and 'Sport, business and money'.

Morality, ethics and sport

Some confusion surrounds the precise nature and scope of the concept 'sports ethics' itself. While it is both difficult and undesirable to police language and to prescribe usage that dissipates conceptual confusion effectively, it may be helpful to observe some important distinctions before describing the work of philosophers in the area of 'ethics of sport'.

The words 'ethics' and 'morality' are used interchangeably in everyday language. Many philosophers have come to question the concept 'morality' as a peculiarly modern Western convention whose desire to universalise guides to right conduct is often thought to be overly ambitious in scope in the face of anthropological knowledge regarding the variety of values and lifestyles in the world.

Along with the project of modernity, philosophers were looking to universalise ethics along the lines that scientists had so powerfully done in discovering natural laws and thereby 'mastering' the world. A number of traditions of moral thinking emerged which shared certain features in their development of systems of thought that ought to guide the conduct of people across the world regardless of where they live. In this modern philosophical vein, 'ethics' was used to refer to the systematic study of morals – i.e. universal codes or principles of right conduct. The distinction between rules, guidelines, mores or principles of living ('morality') that exist in time and space and systematic reflection upon them ('ethics') is still worth observing. The idea that morality refers to that which all reasonable persons ought to conform requires much more careful attention.

Having suggested, then, a distinction between 'morality' and 'ethics', it is worth noting that the very concept of 'ethics' itself is a hotly contested one. There are a host of theoretical accounts of morality too numerous to list here (but including contractarianism, emotivism, intuitionism, and rights theory in the West, and a host of religio-ethical systems such as Confucianism in the East). One common way of capturing the contested nature of the terrain has been caught up in the terms 'descriptive ethics' and 'normative ethics'. Ultimately, the distinction cannot survive close logical scrutiny, but it can be useful in detecting what are at least prima facie differences in the aims of certain philosophical and social scientific scholars interested in a range of concepts and practices such as admiration, cheating, deceiving, lying, promising, respecting, virtues and vices and so on.

In the sports-related literature, much of what is called 'ethics' is simply social science by another name. It is better, perhaps, to give it the label social scientific descriptions of ethically problematic practices, persons or policies. The older label 'descriptive ethics' was designed to capture precisely such research. Here researchers seek to describe that portion of the world that is ethically problematic by the received methods of social science – observation, ethnography, interview, questionnaire and the like.

The most common examples of 'ethics' in sport that emerge in casual conversations, as well as the academic literature, are matters of equity (i.e. social justice in terms of unequal pay for male and female sports stars) and/or of access and respect (e.g. in relation to disabled sportspersons or racism), deviant sub-cultures and practices (e.g. so-called football 'hooliganism' and cheating, sexual abuse/harassment or doping), the prevalence of sport as a site of child abuse and exploitation, homophobia and so forth.

There is another conception of 'ethics' that, as noted above, is quite simply moral philosophy. Under this conception of ethics, academics are engaged in systematic conceptual enquiry in relation to reflective questions regarding how we ought to live our lives. This entails the analysis of central concepts such as duty, right, harm, pain, pleasure and promise within (often ignored) theoretical perspectives such as deontology, utilitarianism, virtue ethics and so forth. Each of these moral philosophical traditions aims to systematise thinking about human nature in the contexts of good and right living and conduct.

Nevertheless, their form and scope differs widely. At some points they are coherent and comparable, at other times, and when pushed to answer particular questions, they throw up radically divergent norms for conduct.

The distinction between descriptive ethics – which was originally supposed to be a value-free endeavour, and normative ethics – which was supposed to be issued in authoritative guidance – is, unsurprisingly enough, a contentious one. It is conceived of differently according to how one understands the nature of 'ethics' itself. Questions such as whether there are moral facts; whether there is a clear distinction between facts and values; how the fact/value relationship is characterised; whether moral obligations override considerations of virtue and so on, are not answerable from outside a given theoretical perspective. But there are difficulties with any attempt to distinguish one programme that sets out to describe the world from another that prescribes a programme for action; the two are intertwined in complex ways. Most philosophers working in mainstream ethics and in the ethics of sport have given up the idea of a neutral, descriptive ethics (of sports) and pursue normative programmes for which they attempt to give reasonable support in terms of the clarity and coherence of their developed position. Nonetheless, the distinction need not be sharp to be important.

Ethical theories in the ethics of sport

In most writings in the ethics of sport, one or more of three families of theories have been adopted, two modern and one ancient. Modern moral philosophy was dominated by the universalistic ethics of either consequentialism or deontology (McNamee, 2010). Over the last 30 years or so – a relatively recent time period in philosophical thought – there has been a revival of virtue theory in mainstream ethics and in the ethics of sport. Some introductory remarks and references to indicative sources in the literature must suffice here.

Deontology (from the Greek word 'deon'; roughly, duty) is the classical theory of right action. Before we act, deontologists (the German philosopher Immanuel Kant is the key figure here) argue that we must consider those duties (usually in the form of principles or rights), which we owe others in our transactions with them. The system of principles is usually thought to have its foundation in a super-rule (often called the Golden rule – enshrined in Christian thought among others) that one ought always to treat others with respect. To lie, cheat, deceive or harm people is to disrespect them. Warren Fraleigh's classic *Right Actions in Sport* is a beautiful statement of the deontological ethic in sport. It attempts to cash out a system of guides to right conduct for participants and coaches engaged in sports. In other cases (see Lumpkin et al., 1999) philosophers have simply assumed a deontological framework and applied it to good effect without necessarily interrogating the theoretical basis upon which their ethics of sport is based.

Of course, philosophically troubling questions such as 'what is meant by respect?', 'does respect always trump other moral values?', 'does respect entail not harming others even when they consent to it?' and so on still trouble deontological ethicists. Fraleigh (1984), for example, argues that boxing is immoral since it involves disrespecting the opponent by intentionally harming them – even though both boxers consent to that harm. While deontology (whether as rights or duties) remains a common-sense ethic for many people, there are others who think it simply starts from the wrong place.

In apparent contrast, consequentialism is a teleological theory (from the Greek word 'telos', which means roughly 'nature/purpose'). It is a family of theories of the good, which justify actions according to their yielding the most favourable and least unfavourable consequences. The dominant strand of thinking here is 'utilitarianism' which comes in a variety of shapes and sizes but is based upon the maximising of 'utility' or good. In distinguishing good from bad we merely need to add up the potential consequences of different courses of action and act upon that which maximises good outcomes.

There are very few sustained efforts at utilitarian thinking in sports but see Claudio Tamburrini's (2000a) defence of Maradona's infamous 'Hand of God' incident. He also attempts to argue, from a utilitarian perspective, for controversial conclusions to the doping issue (he is in favour of abolishing bans) and gender equity (he is often in favour of non-sex-segregated sports).

Consequentialism and deontology, while taking opposing foundations for the justification of moral action (in sports, as in life) share certain important conceptual features. In the first instance they are universal in scope: moral rules apply in all places and times – it's just that they have different moral principles (respect and utility). Equally important is the idea (often ignored in naïve discussion of utilitarianism as an ideology) that they enshrine impartiality.

In both theoretical traditions, no one person or group must be favoured over another. Everyone is equally deserving of respect, just as everyone should be counted in the decisions as to which course of action should be taken – not just whether to commit a strategic foul in terms of good consequences for my team, but the opposition and the good of the game.

Finally, they share the idea that the moral rules have force: once you understand them you must act in a manner that brings the conclusion to life in your actions, for to fail to do so would be irrational, not just immoral. But it is difficult to imagine any ethical theories (or religious theories for that matter) that did not make such a claim.

The recent revival of virtue theory has usually taken the form of a resuscitation of Aristotle's work. Here ethics is based upon good character, and the good life will be lived by those whose character embodies a range of virtues such as courage, co-operativeness, sympathy, honesty, justice, reliability, and the absence of vices such as cowardice, egoism and dishonesty.

Russell Gough's (1997) admirable book is an accessible application of virtue ethics in sports. This language has an immediate application in the contexts of sports in theory, but in practice spitefulness, violence and greed often characterise elite sports. Moreover, we often question the integrity of certain coaches or officials just as we chastise players who deceive the officials. One final aspect of virtue ethics pertinent to sport is a consideration that the virtuous player should also feel the right way according to the choices they make and the actions they perform. This is one reason why we criticise those who feel *Schadenfreude* – the pleasure at the suffering of, for example, their opponents, or those who fail to feel certain emotions such as compassion or sympathy (McNamee, 2008).

This sketch of underlying ethical theory and its application to sports is not merely suggestive; it is also a rather traditional one. Scholars have more recently been questioning an exciting array of issues; the use of genetic engineering in sports, the ethics of sports medicine, the place of adventurous activities in a risk-avoiding culture, the role of sports in sustaining and subverting communities, identities and sexualities; environmental ethics for sports in a global world; ethical audits of sports organisations and cultures; and much more.

Abstract discussions of ethics, ethical theories and the ethics of sport only go so far in providing an understanding of ethics and sport; the best approach is to consider some particular cases. The chapter will first address the issue of sporting conduct before moving to a particular form of morally problematic conduct in sport – performance enhancement. The chapter will then address ethical issues raised by the status of sport as a business.

Sporting conduct: between rules and ethos

Irrespective of win, draw (tie) or loss, sports participants attempt to demonstrate superiority of some range of athletic action. While we may acknowledge qualitative differences in the ways in which people perform skills, it is only through a certain agreed structure that the demonstration of superiority can be displayed. In colloquial terms this structure is often called 'fair play'. The rules define the nature of every sport but they also regulate how players may (and more commonly may not) act. These sets of rules are typically referred to in the literature as constitutive rules and regulative rules (see Loland, 2002).

It is often said that when an athlete or player breaks the rules they are not 'playing the game'. Now while this phrase is often used in a metaphorical sense, in sports it has a strict logical application too. If the rules of the activity define the activity, then the athlete or player who breaks them is engaging in behaviours that exist outside of the activity itself. This logical thesis is called formalism. Nevertheless, it is also said that the rules do not fully determine what goes in games playing. Often it is the ethos or spirit of the activity that guides conduct therein. Adherents to this view argue that the rules – though necessary – are insufficient to describe games playing and to regulate conduct therein (see McFee, 2004).

A very practical difficulty arises when space opens up between widely shared behaviours that are at odds with the rules of the activity. In such cases adherents to the ethos view will say that the practice is 'all part of the game' while formalists will deny that it is part of the game constituted by the rules. Take, for example, the voluntary suspension of play as it arises in football (soccer). When a player is seriously injured it is widely held that whichever team is in possession of the ball should kick the ball out of play in order that the injured player can receive medical treatment. This norm is an attempt to recognise the importance of players' safety and that the game is not more important than the health of a player who is seriously injured. When the resultant throw-in occurs the team which has the ball should throw the ball back to the opposition in order to give the opposing team possession of the ball, which they had before they voluntarily stopped play. It is a norm of restorative justice; an act of fairness to recognise the merit of the team who deliberately eschewed the advantage they had in favour of allowing treatment to the opposing team player. Clearly it is an ethically admirable norm.

In a famous case, while Arsenal FC played Sheffield United FC in the Football Association Cup (the oldest knockout sports competition) in the UK, instead of returning the ball to the opposition, an Arsenal player threw the ball to a team-mate who (instinctively he said) shot and scored. The resultant outrage that the team had exploited a convention of fairness that, though not obligatory or part of the constitutive rules of the activity, ended when the Arsenal manager offered to re-play the game. His response was seen as a laudatory one: upholding the spirit of the game. Other commentators, philosophers

45

included, think that the voluntary suspension of play opens up too much latitude for teams to feign injury in order to gain a competitive advantage or to forestall a potentially important attacking move by their opponents. The idea that the spirit of sport can be used as normative leverage over athletes and players has gained significant momentum in practice recently in the World Anti-Doping Agency's policy of banning certain performance-enhancing products and processes. They argue that if a product or process allows two of three criteria – that it is performance enhancing, (potentially) harmful or is against the spirit of sport – it may be considered to be banned. The contravention of the rules against banned doping products or processes is among the most controversial in sports ethics. We turn to a general consideration of the ethical problems concerning performance enhancement next.

Case 3.1 FIFA World Cup qualification, 2009: Ireland v France

In the play-offs to determine the final participants at the 2012 FIFA (soccer) World Cup France were drawn against Ireland. The game comprised a home and away fixture. In the Irish home fixture France won 1:0 and were strong favourites to go through, as they only required a draw (tie) in their home fixture. However, Ireland scored, forcing the game into extra time (overtime). During this period French player Thierry Henry was involved in an incident that sparked considerable controversy. He received the ball near the edge of the line of play near the Irish goal, and handled the ball twice in one movement (to prevent the ball going out of play, and then to caress the ball in the direction of his feet) before crossing it to his teammate (William Gallas) who scored what was the winning goal. Neither the referee nor the assistant saw the rule-breaking handball and the goal was awarded. France went through to the World Cup finals while Ireland exited the competition. The act was condemned and Henry himself, one of the finest players in the modern era, clouded his reputation and felt highly embarrassed.

Discussion questions

1 Was it Henry's responsibility to tell the referee of his rule-breaking or is it the job of officials to enforce the rules of the game as they see it?

2 How does Henry's intention (or lack of) to deliberately break the rules have a bearing on this as an ethical problem? Is it appropriate to label Henry a 'cheat'?

3 Ought FIFA to have replayed the game? Or, should the French Football Association to have requested a re-match?

The ethics of performance enhancement in sport: doping

In sport the rules force competitors to use inefficient means in the pursuit of their ends (victory). In boxing one cannot use a machine gun or a machete to render one's opponent defenceless for at least ten seconds. Nor may one punch them in restricted areas such as the genitals or the back of the head. Equally, if all sprinting was about was breasting the finishing line first, then one would clearly win every time by using a jet pack or motorbike. But the rules prevent athletes from employing the most efficient means towards the end; and that is the heart of their attraction. The contest challenges athletes because they must develop skills, strategies and embodied powers in order to overcome these gratuitous difficulties.

In keeping with this general feature of sports we can see that the use of performance-enhancing products (typically steroids, or human growth hormone) or processes (like the removal and re-introduction of blood after heavy training to increase oxygen-carrying capacity) may be problematic. While it is widely accepted that there is (at least) something morally problematic about the use of performance-enhancing drugs in sport, it has proved remarkably difficult to develop a broadly uncontested argument for the contention that doping is morally wrong. Schneider and Butcher (2000) offer a clear introduction to the general ethical framework for deciding the im/permissibility of doping. They categorise the types of arguments on doping under four headings: cheating and unfairness; harm; perversion of sport; and unnaturalness and dehumanisation. The category of harm is further divided into harm to athletes who dope (the users); harm to other (clean) athletes; harm to society; harm to the sports community; and harm caused by bans. Each of these categories and sub-categories of arguments will be outlined here, but while certain ways out of the impasse will be suggested, no particular position will be advanced.

The claim that the use of performance-enhancing drugs in sport should be banned because they cause harm to those who use them seems, on the face of it, to be plausible. Some problems emerge from the application of this criterion. First, there is a problem of consistency or, to be more accurate, inconsistency. Tamburrini (2000b) points out that even if we accept that the use of performance-enhancing drugs *does* harm those who use them, it is rather difficult to justify the claim that we should act to prevent such harm given some of the other dangers that are standardly tolerated in sport. For example, boxing, Formula One motor racing, mountaineering, downhill skiing and many other sports are demonstrably dangerous activities. Considerable harm and even death result from such activities, if not frequently, then at least on a fairly regular basis. If sport tolerates such risks and harm, the argument that performance-enhancing drugs harm those who use them would seem to be insufficient on its own as a justification for banning the use of such drugs. Others have argued that from the fact that we allow some harms in sports it does not follow that we should allow any or all (McNamee, 2009; Murray, 2009).

It is also necessary to ask whether all banned substances necessarily harm those who take them. The medical evidence is mixed, and much will depend on dosages and cycles of usage and so on. Some banned substances certainly *do not* harm those who take them, such as ingredients in some cold remedies. The prohibition of some substances is justified, irrespective of harmful consequences, on the grounds that they are known to mask other doping products.

An additional problem is the fact that to ban performance-enhancing drugs on the grounds that they harm those who use them is designed to protect athletes from their own choices and actions. This form of paternalism is often criticised. For example, Tamburrini (2000b) claims that no other area has laws to protect people from their own choices and actions. He rejects the view that laws requiring the use of safety helmets or seatbelts and the law prohibiting narcotics are equivalent cases. He claims that the real aim in the case of seatbelts and narcotics is to protect society as a whole, and that in the case of safety helmets the aim is to protect employees from their employers. Regardless of what one might make of Tamburrini's specific arguments, it certainly seems that there is something quite different between the nature of the risk in cases involving safety helmets, seatbelts and narcotics, and the risk in cases of the use of most performance-enhancing drugs.

An alternative form of the harm argument is that which claims that the use of performance-enhancing drugs harms other people. For example, it is sometimes argued that athletes who take such drugs coerce others to take drugs in order to be able to achieve the higher standard set by those who take performance-enhancing drugs. It is worth noting that this argument seems to rely on an implicit assumption that there is something necessarily harmful about taking performance-enhancing drugs, an assumption that may be disputed. Others worry that it may lead to a problem of slippery slopes where the use of certain potentially harmful but advantageous products may become normalised, where-upon athletes may endeavour to gain the competitive advantage by taking products that promise greater benefits at the risk of greater harms.

This problem may be avoided when 'the harm to others argument' is stated slightly differently: 'Young athletes may copy their role models, so lifting the ban on performance-enhancing drugs may result in doping on the part of junior athletes.' This argument does not suffer from the same difficulty as the first version of the harm to others argument – that of not actually being able to say what the harm is. The harm, in the revised version, is based on a fairly general concern that most people have for the welfare of the young. We tend to regard certain activities as either perfectly acceptable or at least tolerable in adults, but unacceptable in children and young people – such as drinking alcohol, smoking and sex. So the similarity here between the concern to protect the young from doping and concerns in other cases suggests a reasonable basis for a claim to harm (McNamee, 2009).

Two rejoinders might be made by sceptical critics at this point. First, they might contest the empirical claim that young athletes emulate their role models who take performance-enhancing drugs. Second, they might point out that it is uncertain that doping is necessarily harmful. While the concern for the welfare of young people present in this formulation of the harm to others argument is consistent with other paternalistic positions that are generally accepted (such as those on alcohol, smoking and sex), that does not tell us what the harm is.

It is important to recognise that coercion cannot, on its own, be taken to be the problem because sport is already (in certain instances) coercive; heavier training regimes, use of sports scientists, technological advances in the design of equipment, altitude training, warm weather training and use of dietary supplements all exert a coercive pressure (Simon, 1991). Moreover, alcohol is not banned in sport, yet it is far more likely that young athletes will copy their sporting role models in alcohol consumption than in use of performance-enhancing drugs. There are no regulations relating to the amount of training that athletes can undertake, yet, again, this can be both harmful and something that young athletes are likely to emulate.

An alternative to arguments that claim doping causes harm to people is the claim that it harms sport. However, this argument has difficulty avoiding the charge of simply being an assertion of a particular conception of sport. The problem rests in the fact that it is not possible to give an account of the essence of sport (although many have tried – see Suits, 2005 for the classic attempt, and McFee, 2004 for an account of why this cannot work in principle). As a result, it is difficult to counter the claim that sport involving legal doping is just different from modern sport as we have known it thus far, but not necessarily any better or worse; and certainly not morally so.

Arguments based on the claim that doping is unnatural encounter objections because there is so much that is artificial (for example, technological products) that is essential to many sports. Equally, the claim that doping is dehumanising ultimately requires the articulation of other objections to support it because the term 'dehumanise' does not refer to the loss of a thing called 'human-ness' (Culbertson, 2007). Effectively, to say that doping is 'dehumanising' is to identify it as morally troubling in any one of a range of different ways, but that means it is still necessary to offer a further account to explain in which of those ways it is morally troubling. Many of those morally troubling features (such as the fact that doping often appears to treat human beings as if they were machines) are not necessarily sufficient on their own to carry the conclusion that doping should be banned.

Fairness may seem an obvious basis for an argument against doping in sport, but even that is not as straightforward as it might at first appear. If someone is to claim that doping is unfair, the basis for that claim cannot be that it is cheating because that would form a circular argument in which doping is taken to be unfair because it is cheating and cheating because it is unfair. Yet attempts to explain why doping is unfair without referring to the fact that it is cheating can easily run into problems. There are a number of things that give some athletes an unfair advantage over others. Some of these are thought of as unavoidable, such as the genetic constitution of the athlete, money, place of birth, attitude of parents etc. Others are clearly avoidable, such as sponsorship and access to technology. The existence of such factors means that sport never has been and never will be *fair*. Exposure of fairness in sport (in any complete sense) as a myth clears the way for a debate about a whole range of ways that sport might be made fairer. A final counter-intuitive argument in this debate is Tamburrini's (2000b) claim that the existence of a doping ban places those who do not take performance-enhancing drugs at a distinct disadvantage, a disadvantage that could be eliminated by the lifting of the ban.

Case 3.2 2002 Men's Olympic Slalom: Alain Baxter

Scottish skier Alain Baxter lost his bronze medal from the 2002 Olympic slalom because he was found to have ingested the banned substance methamphetamine from a nasal decongestant. The product had been previously used by Baxter in the United Kingdom (where it does not contain anything on the IOC list of banned substances), but in the United States the product contains levomethamphetamine.

The IOC did not allow the isomer separation test necessary to show that Baxter's sample contained levomethamphetamine rather than dextromethamphetamine (commonly known as 'speed'). The IOC does not distinguish between the two, yet Baxter's lawyers argued that only the latter is performance-enhancing. This is important because such a test would have provided corroboration of Baxter's claim to have ingested the banned substance by using the inhaler. The Court of Arbitration for Sport cleared Baxter of suspicion of intentionally taking the banned substance (and therefore intent to enhance performance), but did not overturn the decision of the IOC to withdraw Baxter's medal. The president of the IOC, Jacques Rogge,

(continued)

claimed that Baxter had broken the rules and therefore deserved to be punished. He claimed that to do otherwise would be to open a Pandora's box. Despite this, Baxter generally found support for his case. The Snowsport Industries of Great Britain (the trade body for snowsports in the United Kingdom) confirmed its support for Baxter. Similar support came from other skiers, including Benjamin Raich, who finished fourth, the British Olympic Association, Baxter's sponsors (Peugeot UK and Drambuie) and members of the Scottish Parliament. In addition, the International Ski Federation acknowledged that the contravention of the rules by Baxter was an innocent mistake.

Since Baxter's case WADA doping rules have been formalised into a new World Anti-Doping Code. The code operates a condition known in legal terms as 'strict liability'. This means that there is no need for authorities to show that the athlete intended to ingest a banned substance. If it is found in their body they have committed a doping offence irrespective of how it got there. Effectively it is the athlete's duty not to have a doping product in his or her body.

Discussion questions

4 Should Baxter have been held responsible for what appears to have been an innocent mistake?

5 Should the IOC have ordered an isomer separation test to determine whether the type of methamphetamine in Baxter's sample was performance enhancing?

6 Is the 'strict liability code' fair to athletes?

Sport, business and money

Morgan (2006) claims that, in the West generally and in the USA specifically, we have abysmally low moral expectations of professional sports. He writes that this is because:

> they are mainly businesses and, therefore, are usually content to let the market do their bidding for them unless they run up against something (say, trust-busting legislation) that threatens to compromise their market share; only then do they drag out their big guns and try to pass themselves off as respectable moral enterprises.
>
> (Morgan, 2006: 25)

There is, however, much more to the moral critique of professional sport than the simple claim that the influence of market forces has had a morally degrading impact on such sport. While regarding the role of the market as central to the problem, Morgan expands on the impact of market forces by claiming that they have led to professional sport and (as a result of the fact that professional sport generally sets the tone for other sport) sport more widely, becoming overly individualistic. He also claims that the influence of the market has resulted in the dominance of instrumental reason in sport. This, he argues, has led to a decline in the quality of play, and standards of athletic excellence, in sport.

Morgan is not the only person to have pursued these lines of criticism. John Hoberman (1995: 203) argues that 'high-performance sport has become an exercise in human engineering that aims at producing not simply an athletic type, but a human type as well'. For Hoberman, the concern is not simply that technology has come to dominate sport, with a resulting modification of the goals and values of sport, but that such changes are symptomatic of, and instrumental in perpetuating, shifts in wider societal values. Torbjörn Tännsjö (2000: 10) has similar concerns. He claims that:

> Our admiration for the achievements of the great sports heroes, such as the athletes who triumph at the Olympics, reflects a fascistoid [Tännsjö's neologism] ideology. While nationalism may be dangerous, and has often been associated with fascism, what is going on in our enthusiasm for individual athletic heroes is even worse. Our enthusiasm springs from the very core of fascist ideology: admiration for strength and contempt for weakness.

So it is the values associated with professional elite competitive sport, and, by their influence on other levels of sport, sport in general, that concern Hoberman and Tännsjö. Morgan, like many other philosophers and social scientists, is concerned about those values. He also argues that a proper concern for sport raises issues about the negative impact of individualism, the emphasis on winning at all costs and the role the market has on people involved in sport, whether competitors or spectators.

This suggests two positions that could be adopted among critics concerned about the values of elite competitive sport: first, one might adopt a view similar to Morgan's and argue that sport can be repaired if only the right action is taken as soon as possible. Second, one might adopt a position that seems to follow from Tännsjö's view – that elite competitive sport is unsalvageable because of the centrality of certain values and their close association with certain morally reprehensible ideological positions. One might hold this view solely in relation to professional sport, or in relation to all elite competitive sport, depending on which values one regards as problematic.

Loland (2000), like Morgan, is concerned with putting sport right. He draws a distinction between the logic of quantifiable progress and the logic of qualitative progress. Loland favours the latter and suggest ways of altering sport to enable it to more consistently reflect the logic of qualitative progress. A central problem here seems to be the fact that the logic of quantifiable progress (emphasis on records over quality of performance and competition) produces the most marketable spectacle in those sports where it dominates. So while it might be the case that soccer is an extremely marketable commodity (in most parts of the world), yet is not dominated by the logic of quantifiable progress, soccer has other features (such as the central role of allegiance to teams) that is lacking in the record-based sports. As a consequence, it is not possible to claim that the case of soccer shows that individual sports involving racing need not rely on the logic of quantifiable progress to improve their marketability; soccer is simply too different to be a relevant comparison.

What these critiques of sport appear to show is a contradiction between some of the values dominant in sport (such as those alluded to in the Olympic motto, *Citius, Altius, Fortius* – Faster, Higher, Stronger), sporting nationalism and emphasis on the market in professional sport on the one hand, and other values prevalent in sport (such as fair play) and the desire to prevent radical change to the nature of specific sports and the methods of performance enhancement employed by athletes on the other. Technological developments can make it easier to market sport, but frequently at a cost – sports are often gradually modified to sustain interest within a competitive market, or simply to gain an advantage and a greater market share (for example, Twenty20 Cricket). Technological developments also alter the means available to athletes to pursue the logic of quantifiable progress. With all these changes moral concerns arise. So the contradiction outlined above is not simply a practical one, it is a practical/moral contradiction because the pursuit of the goals of the market, or the logic of quantifiable progress, often leads to moral concerns. This, in turn, has practical implications because the moral concerns can result in reduced public interest in specific sports and a negative impact on their marketability (this was a problem, for example, in cycling in the late 1990s).

The professionalisation, internationalisation and marketing of sports are not things that leave sport unchanged. They are processes that alter sport at all levels (not just professional, international and heavily marketed sport). This creates concern over the nature of sport, but more importantly it creates moral concern over the changing role of the athlete or sportsperson. The commodification of sporting talent renders athletes commodities. Not only do athletes sell their labour in a market; sportsmen and women involved in team sports are themselves bought and sold in a market. In addition, sportsmen and women who compete in international sport often become representatives of nationalist sentiment (not necessarily intentionally), and the pursuit of records heightens the role of technology in performance enhancement, prompting analogies between athletes and laboratory specimens (see Hoberman, 1995).

Case 3.3 The scheduling of Olympic distance running events

In recent years the scheduling of Olympic events has often been planned in accordance with peak viewing times in the United States (the most lucrative market for sports sponsors). For example, at the Beijing Olympics in 2008 both the men's and women's marathons began at 7.30am local time, which meant that they could be shown live on television in the United States at 7.30pm Eastern Standard Time. The scheduling of distance running events in this manner can have serious implications for the performance of the athletes, and, in some cases, their health. At the very least, it changes the nature of the test the athletes face. Acclimatisation to weather conditions, atmospheric conditions (altitude, pollution) and different time zones is difficult enough for athletes without the added test of running the marathon at 7.30 in the morning, or worse, during the hottest part of the day.

However, this is not as simple a matter as it might at first appear. The choice of the venue for the Olympic Games is partly influenced by commercial considerations, yet the venue can have an impact on the performance and the health of individual athletes (consider the problems of pollution in Los Angeles in 1984 and Beijing in 2008, and the issue of altitude in Mexico City in 1968). So someone might argue that scheduling, like the choice of host city, is simply another example of decision-making that must necessarily consider a range of factors, including commercial considerations and the impact on athletes. Nonetheless, someone else might counter this by pointing out that the decisions frequently accord with commercial considerations to the detriment of the participating athletes.

Discussion questions

7 Do the IOC or other international sports federations have a moral duty to prioritise the health of athletes over commercial considerations when making scheduling decisions?

(continued)

8 Are the specific conditions under which, for example, an Olympic event takes place, simply part of the sporting challenge faced by the athletes, like the lane draw in the 200m, or the barriers in the steeplechase?

9 Does professional sport have a duty to focus more on fulfilling the desires of the (paying) spectator (i.e. ensuring that it is an entertaining and aesthetic performance) over the aims and values of the participating athlete (i.e. winning, enjoyment, solidarity and co-operation with others).

Conclusion

While the three topics from the ethics of sport outlined in this chapter were chosen to provide an introduction to ethics and sport in general, they are not discrete topics. They were chosen partly for their ability to illustrate the relationship between ethics and sport, but also because of the interrelationships between the three topics. Conduct in sport, performance enhancement and the commodification of sport can be, and often are, considered individually, but treated in this way they can appear to be issues that are really only problematic for those expressly concerned with ethics. However, when the interrelationships between these topics are considered it is possible to achieve a clearer view of the problems that they raise for those involved in sports management who may otherwise have regarded conduct in sport and performance enhancement as of little relevance to their concerns and the commodification of sport as something simply to be unquestioningly accepted and not worthy of comment. This chapter has attempted to show that quite the opposite is true. Sport as a business is dependent on its product, and a product that is morally troubling will not maximise market appeal, and may lose that appeal altogether.

Discussion questions

10 In what specific ways might there be interconnections between the issues of conduct in sport, performance enhancement and the dominant values of professional sport? List as many interconnections as you can think of.

11 What impact might these interconnections have on sports as businesses? Construct a diagram to illustrate the influence of conduct, performance enhancement and values on sports as businesses, and the impact that they might have.

12 Can the future of sport be profitably left to market forces? Write a 1,000-word assessment of this issue considering the results of your responses to the two questions above.

Keywords

Deontology; doping; ethos; formalism/formalist; paternalism; rules (constitutive and regulative); utilitarianism; virtue theory.

Guided reading

For edited collections on ethical issues in sport see Boxill (2003); McNamee (2010); McNamee and Parry (1998); Morgan (2007); Tännsjö and Tamburrini (2000); and Morgan and Meier (1995).

Readers wishing to see a fuller picture of the scope of sports ethics may see the Ethics and Sports book series co-edited by Mike McNamee, Jim Parry and Heather Reid at http://www.routledge.com/books/series/Ethics_and_Sport (accessed January 2010). It includes Walsh and Giulianotti's (2006) book that considers the relationship between ethics, sport and money.

Single authored books that are worth reading to develop a more detailed understanding of particular ethical issues and normative perspectives are Feezell (2004); Fraleigh (1984); McNamee (2008); Morgan (2006); and Suits (2005).

For students wishing to develop their skills in evaluating and formulating (ethical) arguments, Ryall's (2010) text is specifically dedicated to helping students studying sports-related subjects improve their critical thinking abilities.

The two main journals in the philosophy and ethics of sport are *The Journal of the Philosophy of Sport* (http://hk.humankinetics.com/JPS/journalAbout.cfm) and *Sport, Ethics and Philosophy* (www.tandf.co.uk/journals/titles/17511321.asp).

Recommended websites

British Philosophy of Sport Association: www.philosophyofsport.org.uk
Ethics Updates: http://ethics.sandiego.edu/
Higher Education Academy: Philosophy of Sport Resource www.heacademy.ac.uk/assets/hlst/documents/resources/philosophy_ethics_sport.pdf
International Philosophy of Sport Association: http://iaps.net
Philosophy of Sport Blog: http://philosophyandsports.blogspot.com/2009/12/intellectual-muscle.html
WADA: www.wada-ama.org/

References

Blair, T. (2000) *A Sporting Future for All*, London: DCMS.

Boxill, J. (ed.) (2003) *Sports Ethics: An Anthology*, Oxford: Blackwell.

Coakley, J. (1997) *Sport in Society: Issues and Controversies*, London: Mosley.

Culbertson, L. (2007) '"Human-ness", "dehumanisation" and performance-enhancement', *Sport, Ethics and Philosophy*, 1 (2), 195–208.

DNH (1995) *Sport – Raising the Game*, London: Department of National Heritage.

Feezell, R. (2004) *Sport, Play and Ethical Reflection*, Urbana: University of Illinois Press.

Fraleigh, W. (1984) *Right Actions in Sport: Ethics for Contestants*, Champaign, IL: Human Kinetics.

Gough, R. (1997) *Character is Everything*, Fort Worth, TX: Harcourt Brace.

Hardman, A. and Jones, C. (eds) (2010) *The Ethics of Sports Coaching*, London: Routledge.

Hoberman, J. (1995) 'Sport and the technological image of man', in W.J. Morgan and K.V. Meier (eds) *Philosophic Inquiry in Sport*, 2nd edn, Champaign, IL: Human Kinetics, 321–27.

Loland, S. (2000) 'The logic of progress and the art of moderation in competitive sports', in T. Tännsjö and C.M. Tamburrini (eds), *Values in Sport: Elitism, Nationalism, Gender Equality and the Scientific Manufacture of Winners*, London: Routledge, 39–56.

Loland, S. (2002) *Fair Play in Sport: A Moral Norm System*, London: Routledge.

Loland, S. and McNamee, M.J. (2000) 'Fair play and the ethos of sports: an eclectic philosophical framework', *Journal of the Philosophy of Sport*, XXVII, 63–80.

Lumpkin, A., Stoll, S.K. and Beller, J.M. (1999) *Sport Ethics: Applications for Fair Play*, New York: McGraw-Hill.

McFee, G. (2004) *Sport, Rules and Values: Philosophical Investigations into the Nature of Sport*, London: Routledge.

McNamee, M.J. (2008) *Sports, Virtues and Vices*, London: Routledge.

McNamee, M.J. (2009) 'Beyond consent: the ethics of paediatric doping', *Journal of the Philosophy of Sport*, XXXVI (2), 111–26.

McNamee, M.J. (2010) *The Ethics of Sport: A Reader*, London: Routledge.

McNamee, M.J. and Moller, V. (2011) *Doping and Anti-Doping Policy: Ethical, Legal and Social Perspectives*, Abingdon: Routledge.

McNamee, M.J. and Parry, S.J. (eds) (1998) *Ethics and Sport*, London: Routledge.

Morgan, W.J. (2006) *Why Sports Morally Matter*, London: Routledge.

Morgan, W.J. (ed.) (2007) *Ethics in Sport*, 2nd edn, Champaign, IL: Human Kinetics.

Morgan, W.J. and Meier, K.V. (eds) (1995) *Philosophic Inquiry in Sport*, 2nd edn, Champaign, IL: Human Kinetics.

Murray, T. (2009) *Performance Enhancing Technologies in Sports*, ed. T.H. Murray, K.J. Maschke and A.A. Wasunna, Baltimore: Johns Hopkins University Press.

Ofsted (2001) *Specialist Schools: An Evaluation of Progress*, London: HMSO.

Ryall, E. (2010) *Critical Thinking for Sports Students*, Exeter: Learning Matters.

Schneider, A.J. and Butcher, R.B. (2000) 'A philosophical overview of the arguments on banning doping in sport', in T. Tännsjö and C.M. Tamburrini (eds), *Values in Sport: Elitism, Nationalism, Gender Equality and the Scientific Manufacture of Winners*, London: E & FN Spon, 185–99.

Simon, R.L. (1991) *Fair Play: Sports, Values, and Society*, Colorado: Westview Press.

Suits, B. (2005) *The Grasshopper: Games, Life and Utopia*, Toronto: Broadview Press.

Suits, B. (2006) 'Games and their institutions in *The Grasshopper*', *Journal of the Philosophy of Sport*, XXXIII (1), 1–9.

Szymanski, S. (2002) 'The economic impact of the World Cup', *World Economics*, 3 (1), 169–78.

Tamburrini, C.M. (2000a) 'Sports, fascism and the market', in T. Tännsjö and C.M. Tamburrini (eds), *Values in Sport: Elitism, Nationalism, Gender Equality and the Scientific Manufacture of Winners,* London: E & FN Spon.

Tamburrini, C.M. (2000b) 'What's wrong with doping?', in T. Tännsjö and C.M. Tamburrini (eds), *Values in Sport: Elitism, Nationalism, Gender Equality and the Scientific Manufacture of Winners*, London: E & FN Spon, 200–16.

Tännsjö, T. (2000) 'Is it fascistoid to admire sports heroes?', in T. Tännsjö and C.M. Tamburrini (eds), *Values in Sport: Elitism, Nationalism, Gender Equality and the Scientific Manufacture of Winners*, London: Routledge, 24–48.

Tännsjö, T. and Tamburrini, C.M. (eds) (2000) *Values in Sport: Elitism, Nationalism, Gender Equality and the Scientific Manufacture of Winners*, London: E & FN Spon.

Walsh, A. and Giulianotti, R. (2006) *Ethics, Money and Sport: This Sporting Mammon*, London: Routledge.

Whannel, G. (1983) *Blowing the Whistle*, London: Pluto Press.

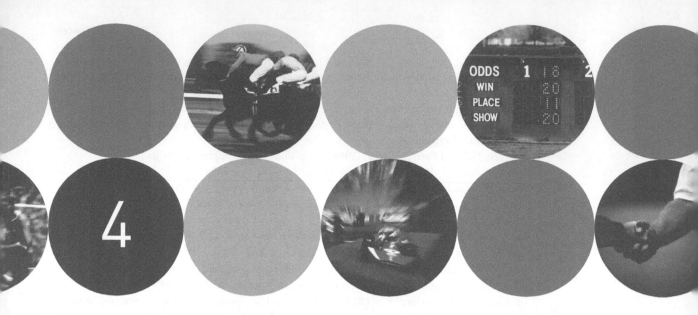

4

The role of the State in sport

Chris Parker, Nottingham Trent University

Learning outcomes

Upon completion of this chapter the reader should be able to:

- identify pathways highlighting the State's influence and role in sport;
- understand how government funding and attitudes determines the profile and perceived value of specific sports;
- recognise how and why sport bodies and businesses respond to government initiatives;
- understand the relationship between State and sport from a number of perspectives;
- place this relationship in a historical context.

 ## Overview

This chapter focuses on the role of the State on the development of sport at all levels within the UK. It asks the question 'What role should the State play – and why?' and considers several different answers. It explores recent and current government initiatives and attitudes and the implications of these for all concerned. Throughout the chapter the reader is encouraged to examine the relationship between State and sport from a number of perspectives, including those of the government, sports administrators and elite athletes.

Specific case studies are provided although, in one sense, the discussion of the current situation can be seen as an extended case in its own right: by placing it in a historical context and exploring the pathways of influence that derive from the government's stated vision and aims, the reader will be encouraged to consider possible – or likely – future roles of the State and associated changes in the performing, supporting, selling, sharing and teaching of sport at all levels. There is a perhaps inevitable focus on the 2012 London Olympics.

The chapter progresses from a historical overview of the role of the State to a consideration of the government, the Olympic Games and the value and nature of legacy.

Essentially, this chapter argues that in order to understand fully the role of the State on the business of sport management it is necessary to identify the degree and expressions of the State's influence at all levels of sport, including those beyond the pure context of business, to recognise the relationships that exist between these levels and to understand what drives the State to adopt the role that it does.

A historical overview

I went skiing and broke a leg. Fortunately it wasn't mine.   (Anon)

Sport influences us as individuals and as a society in myriad ways, irrespective of whether or not we are sportsmen or women. It is impossible to be on the mountain and not be influenced by the skiers. (Although the influence need not be a negative one as in the case referred to above.) In the same way, it is impossible to be involved in the business of sport management and not be influenced explicitly or implicitly by the role the State plays in shaping the industry.

Sport fulfils a number of important functions in society; it provides employment, entertainment and escapism; it improves physical and mental well-being and creates a sense of belonging and sharing on a local and national level. Sport itself is transient, subjective and immediate. For some, their sporting involvement defines their personal identity. For others, it is simply the way they make their living. The sport industry in the UK is growing rapidly and, whilst the industry has not always been so large, sport has always played an important role in society on a variety of levels; which is why, to some extent, the argument can be made that those who control the nature, practices and development of sport wield considerable national power. Whannel, writing in 1983, argued that: 'Only in the last 20 years has the State played much of a role' (cited in Critcher et al., 2001: 222).

In the eighteenth century, for example, sport was influenced significantly – if not controlled – by aristocratic patronage. However, in the nineteenth century concern for the physical condition of the working class led to legislation that included the Public Baths and Washroom Act of 1846 (which was actually intended to encourage the working class to bathe in disinfected water rather than take up swimming), and the Education Act of 1870 which introduced physical education into the curriculum. These concerns, however, were not to go away and were not simply the result of governments moving philosophically towards the creation of a welfare state. As Haywood et al. (1995: 173) report:

The impetus for the introduction of school meals came from the Report of the Inter-departmental Committee on Physical Deterioration in 1904, which expressed concern about fitness for military service. The Boer War and a recognition of the need for readiness to defend the Empire did much to stimulate support for this apparently altruistic concern.

By the end of the nineteenth century aristocratic patronage had been replaced by the rise of sport institutions controlled predominantly by sections of what Whannel described as 'the upper-middle class . . . These predominantly amateur-paternal sport organisations dominated English sport until the post-war era' (cited in Critcher et al., 2001: 222).

By the 1930s an increased sense of the value of physical culture expressed by members of the medical and physical education professions helped spur the many voluntary bodies that felt the need for a co-ordinating body to organise their activities into action. In 1935 the Central Council for Recreation and Training was formed. The Council enjoyed royal patronage as well as support from the Board of Education. Its stated aim was:

> to help improve the physical and mental health of the community through physical recreation by developing existing facilities for recreative physical activities of all kinds and also by making provision for the thousands not yet associated with any organisation.

The government demonstrated its concern with the nation's fitness by creating a National Fitness Council. It did not last long. The outbreak of the Second World War turned concerns away from physical fitness towards matters of far more immediate importance. With the war over, the Council focused on the provision of facilities, an initiative that led to the development of seven National Recreation Centres, serving as residential centres for elite performers in a variety of sports. The aim now was to increase Britain's chances of success in international competition.

In the 1950s, the increasing internationalisation of sport and the growth of media coverage – particularly the effects of television – and associated sponsorship led to an increasingly marked difference between the worlds of amateur and professional sport, and the need for governments to recognise and manage the social, national and international values of a growing industry. In 1957, the Council established the Wolfenden Committee. Its task was to suggest how statutory bodies could assist in promoting the general welfare of the community in sport and leisure. The twin needs of developing a sporting elite and encouraging and enabling sporting participation amongst the general public were now clearly visible.

In 1960, the Wolfenden Committee produced the 'Sport and the Community' report, in which it argued for statutory funding of sport and the development of a sports council made up of six to ten people to control expenditure of approximately £5 million per year. When a Labour government was formed in 1964, it expressed its commitment to the creation of a sports council and, as an initial step, set up an advisory council. By 1969 sport funding was removed from the education budget and consequently gained greater status. One year later, the Conservative government determined to establish a statutory sports council with the power to disburse funding and, in 1971, the Sports Council, with a Royal Charter giving it control over its own budget, finally came into being.

The Sports Council's brief reflected the twin needs identified previously. It had to work with sports governing bodies to help develop the highest possible levels of performance and skill, whilst simultaneously developing knowledge of, and participation in, all forms of physical recreation in the interests of social welfare. Haywood et al. (1995: 191) write:

> These extrinsic rationales (supporting provision because of its side effects) and intrinsic rationale (supporting provision as worthwhile in its own right) were echoed in both the House of Lords Select Committee Report Sport and Leisure and the subsequent White Paper Sport and Recreation. Indeed, the latter document argues that leisure provision is a need and, therefore, constitutes a necessary welfare service.

This latter argument was not and – as will be demonstrated shortly – has not been accepted, even though the political perception at the time was that leisure time would increase and, commensurate with it, levels of participation would grow. It was also acknowledged that provisions to meet this expected increase in sport and recreational pursuits were seriously lacking. Whannel reported: 'In 1964 there was just one purpose-built sport centre in the whole of England and Wales. By 1972 there were still only 30. By 1978 there were 350' (cited in Critcher et al., 2001: 225).

In the 1970s the rationale for leisure provision – and particularly sport – changed from one emphasising the State's role in ensuring social equality by providing access for all (an example being 'Sport for All'), to one of economic benefit. From the mid-1970s the Sports Council provided funding for 'Football in the Community' and 'Action Sport' amongst other initiatives intended, in part at least, to alleviate the costs of policing inner cities and repairing vandalised properties by targeting the energy and relieving the boredom and frustration of the young and unemployed. However, user surveys of sports facilities carried out throughout the 1970s indicated that usage was dominated by groups other than dis-advantaged inner city dwellers. (These groups were predominantly middle class users, the young, those with cars and white males.) The Sports Council, with encouragement from the government, came to the conclusion that the provision of facilities alone was not sufficient; there was a need also to invest in personnel who could stimulate awareness, interest and participation within target groups.

As the State's rationale for involvement in sport and other forms of recreation changed during the decade, so too did the Sport Council's clearly defined independence from central government. The provision of a Royal Charter had been intended to ensure no direct government involvement in the Council's policy-making; the principle had been that the government would allocate a sum of money, but would not attempt to influence how it was spent. In 1978, though, the Labour government gave over £800,000 to the Sports Council to be spent specifically on alleviating urban deprivation, and a further £1.7 million for schemes linking football clubs more fully with their local communities. Haywood et al. (1995: 193) argue that:

> The Council, in accepting these funds and agreeing to implement policies decided by the government, assisted the breaching of their own independent status. Since the election of the Conservative government in 1979, this erosion of independence has continued.

Certainly this rationale and relationship continued in the early years of the Thatcher government until, according to Bull et al. (2003: 173):

> [T]he government began to squeeze the funding given to the leisure quangos as it attempted to take more direct control over many areas of policy . . . During this period both the Arts Council and the Sports Council were being encouraged to raise more private sponsorship (Treasury 1988, 1990), and were increasingly having to justify their claims for grant aid in terms of the externalities that might accrue, rather than intrinsic value.

After John Major's election win in 1992, another shift occurred. A new department was created – the Department of National Heritage (to be renamed the Department for Culture, Media and Sport five years later) – with responsibility for sport, tourism, broadcasting, heritage and the arts. David Mellor was its first Minister and the main emphasis was, once again, on the intrinsic value of these activities. Indeed, in his introduction to *Sport: Raising the Game*, the Conservative government's sports policy statement (DNH, 1995), John Major wrote:

> I have never believed that the quality of life in Britain should revolve simply around material success. Of equal importance, for most people, is the availability of those things that can enrich and elevate daily life in the worlds of arts, leisure and sport.

The Sports Council was subsequently restructured. It became less independent of the government, but its role and capabilities increased.

In 1997, Tony Blair's Labour government swept to victory and, according to Bull et al. (2003: 174), their:

> more recent initiatives . . . appear to indicate that the brief flirtation with intrinsic rationales for provision is at an end . . . both sport and the arts have played a significant part in the Blair government's social policy agenda. This has been made possible as a result of the revised directions regarding the National Lottery in 1998. These directions allowed agencies such as Sport England and the Arts Council to be strategic in their distribution of funds within guidelines laid down by the Department for Culture, Media and Sport. Such guidelines directed Lottery funding, particularly in the sports sector where programmes are now almost exclusively based on the Lottery Sports Fund Strategy (Sport England, 1998) towards initiatives such as social inclusion and the delivery of Best Value.

In the Thatcher era leisure policy was viewed as relatively insignificant; in subsequent years its profile has raised markedly helped, in part at least, by the work of high-profile politicians such as Chris Smith and the late Tony Banks.

The decision to bid for the 2012 Olympic Games, a commitment driven by the then Labour Minister for Sport, Tessa Jowell, brought the issue of the value, benefits and costs of sport into the public consciousness more than ever before. (Which is why it warrants more detailed consideration later in this chapter.)

Only three influences?

The prediction of increased participation and diversity has proven true. Some (see Whannel 1983) argue that despite this growth and diversification, the State influences sport in three essential ways. Firstly, it works to ban certain activities. Examples cited could include attempts to ban football in the seventeenth century, anti-cruel-sport legislation in the nineteenth century and current debates regarding the futures of fox hunting and boxing. Secondly, the State regulates and licenses activities. One obvious example of this is the 1960 Betting and Gaming Act, which led to the creation of the off-course betting shop. In London in 1953 police made 4,000 arrests because of street betting. The fact that they made only three arrests for the same offence in 1967 indicates clearly that a new industry had been developed. Thirdly, as discussed, the State provides required facilities. At local authority level, the degree of funding available for this is determined by the ways in which services are categorised. Wilson and Game (1994: 86, with Leach and Stoker) provide the following categorisation:

- *Need services*, provided for all, regardless of means . . . Education and Social Services are the main examples.
- *Protective services*, provided for the security of the people, to national guidelines . . . Police and fire services are examples.
- *Amenity services*, provided largely to locally-determined standards to meet the needs of each local community. Cleaning and lighting of streets . . . are examples.
- *Facility services*, for people to draw upon if they wish.

Sport facilities fit into this last category and, as need services receive the greatest percentage expenditure, facility services invariably receive the least. According to Haywood et al. (1995: 192): 'Sports provision might seem to represent the "luxury" end of welfare and therefore to be most likely to suffer cuts when central government is looking to reduce public expenditure.'

Wilson and Game (1994: 27) also note that: 'In many cases the local authority is the regulator and monitor of the activities of other agencies and organisations.' This includes 'the certification of sports ground safety, as the public became acutely aware following the Bradford and Hillsborough football disasters'.

Whilst the above is undoubtedly true, the State's pathways of influence are more complex and far-reaching than is suggested by the three broad influences outlined.

Discussion question 1

Before reading any further, identify ways in which the State influences sport by considering the following sectors:

- education;
- health;
- business;
- amateur sport;
- professional sport.

Explore the relationships that exist between these sectors; identify ways in which influences on one sector impact upon the others.

Whatever the precise nature and reach of the State's pathways of influence on sport, one fact that is beyond discussion is that in England the State does now play a significant role.

Why is the State involved? A modern perspective: from 1997 to the 2012 London Olympic Games

Sport matters. From 73,000 spectators packed into Wembley Stadium and roaring their support for England to a girl hitting a tennis ball for hour after hour against a wall, sport inspires a passion and a dedication which plays a central part in many people's lives. Whether it is watching some of our great sportsmen and women strive at the very edge of their ability or the rest of us working hard in a Sunday morning local league team, whether it is supporting our children in sport at school or swimming lengths in the local pool to get fit, sport matters to us all – to individuals, to families and in bringing people together for a common aim, to communities at every level.   (Blair, 2000)

The former Labour Prime Minister's foreword to the Labour government's paper 'A Sporting Future For All' provides one answer to the question posed. The State has a role to play because 'sport matters' in a variety of ways. But what is that role? According to Blair, it is not to control sport. In the same foreword he states:

The Government does not and should not run sport. Sport is for individuals, striving to succeed – either on their own or in teams. However those individuals, together or alone, need the help of others – to provide the facilities, the equipment, the opportunities. So there is a key role to play for those who organise and manage sport – local authorities, sports clubs, governing bodies, the Sports Councils and the Government . . . We need to see new thinking and new action about ways to improve sport in our country.

A study of the ways the State currently impacts upon sport reveals three areas of focus different in many regards to the three influences suggested earlier. These are:

- the provision of funding;
- sporting bodies: Sport England, UK Sport, SportScotland, Sports Council for Wales and Sports Council of Northern Ireland;
- sport in education.

All three of these are brought together, along with a number of other significant factors, in Case 4.1 relating to the 2012 London Olympics. Part One of the case outlines the process and campaign that led to London winning the 2012 Olympics. Before reading that, though, consider the following discussion question:

Discussion question 2

'The Government does not and should not run sport.'

Do you agree with Tony Blair's statement? What should the government's role be?

Case 4.1 The 2012 London Olympic Games
Part 1: The vision

'The London 2012 bid was a vision.'
Tessa Jowell, Secretary of State for Culture, Media and Sport (in conversation with the author)

The vision for the London Olympic Games was built upon two key legacy objectives. Tessa Jowell described it as: 'a vision that was tied to legacy objectives. The first was

(continued)

to transform a generation of young people through sport and the second was to transform East London through the accelerated regeneration of the Lower Lea Valley' (all quotes taken from an interview by the author). These two objectives were to be achieved through five key themes presented in the form of the following five promises:

Promise 1: Making the UK a world-leading sporting nation

This was to be achieved in three ways. Firstly, by inspiring young people through sport. (This focus on the role and importance of the Games for young people was to become a powerfully evocative part of the bid process.) This particular commitment would, it was pledged, result in:

1 offering all 5–16-year-olds in England five hours of high-quality sport a week and all 16–19-year-olds three hours a week by 2012;
2 more coaches in schools and the community;
3 further education sports co-ordinators;
4 four hundred and fifty disability multi-sports clubs.

Secondly, by helping at least 2 million people in England to be more active by 2102. This would be achieved, in part, by:

1 the offer of free funding swimming initiatives focusing on the under 16s and the over 60s, beginning in April 2009;
2 cycling and walking schemes;
3 healthy living campaigns;
4 Sport England's 'Grow, Sustain and Excel Strategy' which had aims that included ensuring that 1 million people were taking part in sport, fewer 16–18-year-olds were dropping out of sport, and improving talent development in at least 25 sports.

Thirdly, through a focus on elite achievement with the aim of being fourth in the Olympic medal table and at least second in the Paralympic medal table in 2012. This was to be supported in a variety of ways, not least of which was an investment of £600 million.

Promise 2: To transform the heart of East London

Transformation would be demonstrated in three ways. By:

1 transforming places;
2 transforming communities;
3 transforming prospects.

Aims included:

1 creating a well-planned and well-managed environment in and around the Olympic Park that would attract business and investment and promote long-term cultural and recreational use;
2 building over 9,000 new homes and accompanying, sport, health, leisure and education facilities;
3 creating 12,000 new job opportunities in the area of the Park after the Games had ended and 20,000 unemployed Londoners into permanent employment by 2012.

(continued)

Promise 3: To inspire a generation of young people

This was arguably the most emotive and far-reaching part of the vision, with a global focus reaching out to 3 million young people overseas. To inspire a generation of youngsters both in the UK and abroad, the campaign team promised there would be:

1 tens of thousands more young people giving their time to their local communities and engaging in cultural activities as a consequence of the Games;

2 thousands of schools, colleges and universities inspiring learners through the adoption of the Olympic values;

3 over 3 million youngsters overseas accessing quality physical education and sport, with at least 1 million of these participating regularly by 2012.

The emphasis throughout would be on:

● education – physical education and school links;

● sport – development and sporting excellence;

● development – of children in schools and communities through sport.

Promise 4: To make the Olympic Park a blueprint for sustainable living

Here again, the proposed legacy was based on sustainability and inspiration. The promise specified:

1 a 50 per cent reduction in carbon emissions for the built environment of the Olympic Park within a year of the Games;

2 encouragement for people to live more sustainably, with a focus on local sustainability initiatives and a Capital Clean Up campaign, enabling people to reduce their carbon footprint, be more energy efficient and/or recycle on a greater scale, because of the Games.

Promise 5: To demonstrate that the UK is a creative, inclusive and welcoming place to live in, to visit, and for business

The three key elements were:

1 increasing and sustaining growth in UK business, including small-to-medium sized enterprises;

2 helping the workforce to get and stay in work and develop their skills;

3 making the UK a welcoming place that offers world-class customer service.

Related initiatives and projects included the London 2012 Business Network, an emphasis on promoting the UK overseas, the development of the London Employment and Skills Taskforce for 2012 Action Plan, pre-Games training camps, the 2012 Tourism Strategy alongside a Nation Skills Strategy for hospitality, and a commitment to improving access for disabled visitors.

When asked about the selection of the two legacy objectives upon which the vision for the Olympic bid was based, Tessa Jowell, said:

East London had always been a priority for regeneration as and when investment became available and so there was never any serious question that if we ever going to stage the Olympics we would stage them in East London. What the effect has been is to accelerate that

(continued)

regeneration by about 25 years . . . So, linked to that is the importance of that legacy promise being not only focused on the physical infrastructure of the Park . . . but also the change in the demography and aspirations of the five Olympic Boroughs.

On the second legacy objective, the transformation of a generation of young people through sport, that is what has driven, or drove, our Labour government's School Sport partnership and we started back in 2002 – maybe even earlier – to promise that every child in primary or secondary school would have at least two hours per week of high-quality sport or physical education. That increased to three hours and was set to increase to five hours for about 70 per cent of children by the time we got to 2012, and that was linked with a growth in facilities, a growth in the number of coaches and, critically, a growth in the number of sports that children could choose from.

Discussion questions

3 Do you agree with the selection of the two legacy objectives?

4 Are there any other objectives you would have prioritised? (If so, which and why?)

5 Consider the tactics used to achieve each objective. Analyse their appropriateness, their relative strengths and weaknesses. Would you do anything differently?

6 'The decision to focus on the regeneration of East London was made because the government is London-based. If the government was situated in Newcastle, the East End of London would not have been chosen.' Do you agree?

Major sporting events: benefits and funding

Governments that choose to bid for and then host major sporting events are in one sense obliged to highlight the benefits of doing so. The five benefits that are most frequently cited are:

- tourism and image benefits;
- wider economic benefits;
- urban regeneration benefits;
- sporting legacy benefits;
- social and cultural benefits.

Hosting a major event may well increase revenues from tourism and international recognition for the host city – particularly if it was not already well known globally. However, as tourism is influenced by so many other factors, the long-term benefits are not so clear. Tourist visits to Sydney, for example, have decreased since the 2000 Olympics, but this could be due primarily to the effects of 9/11. The potential downsides of bidding for and/ or hosting a major event are:

- increasing costs of bidding for an event;
- the negative 'fall-out' following an unsuccessful bid (e.g. England's bid to hold the 2006 Football World Cup);
- the negative image created if the event is not a great success;
- the potential financial loss if the event is mismanaged or unsuccessful.

Wider economic benefits are also difficult to quantify. Although economic growth is often put forward as a justification for hosting an event, Jeanrenaud (2000) warns:

> Not only are the results of many economic impact studies misinterpreted . . . in order to support . . . policy beliefs, but the results themselves are often miscalculated by economists, sometimes deliberately to please the sponsors of the research project, sometimes unintentionally, the number of pitfalls in estimating the net benefits of a public investment being numerous.

Similarly, some economists are sceptical of the claimed urban regeneration benefits of hosting major events. Clearly, some regeneration takes place but, to date, there is minimal statistical or economic evidence of significant impacts in this regard. Barcelona, host city of the 1992 Olympics, experienced significant regeneration in its downtown area as a result of the Games. However, this has to be set against the estimated $12 billion it cost to host the event; leaving one to wonder if the same benefits could have been achieved at less cost? In the UK, Manchester City Council – host of the 2002 Commonwealth Games – began work after the Games developing a framework for the long-term evaluation of benefits. For Manchester, the Games were one significant aspect of a wider vision for regeneration, with the City highlighting sustainable after-use of venues as a clear priority. Given the above, it would seem that economic justifications for bids to host major sporting events need to be assessed rigorously. Perhaps the best argument that can be made is that these events act primarily as a catalyst for leveraging funding for regeneration.

The case is often put that the sporting legacy benefits of hosting a major event are new facilities, increased mass participation and sustained levels of international success. Again, the case is not as simple as it might first appear. Compare Olympic hosts Sydney and Barcelona, both left with a legacy of under-used facilities and stadia, with Manchester, which built new facilities for the Commonwealth Games that were designed to have long-term viability. (Examples would be the swimming facilities, which were criticised for inadequate seating during the Games but have met all subsequent needs, and – by way of comparison with Stade de France – the athletics stadium which was conceived and built on the agreement that it would become the home of Manchester City Football Club.) The message would seem to be to plan facilities for the long term, not just the event.

There is also limited data available to support the increased participation and international success claims. Certainly, many sports claim increased participation and interest following significant international success – especially if it was televised – but how long such increases last and their impact on future international achievement is not clear. For example, the number of people playing curling does not appear to have increased greatly despite Britain's success in the recent Winter Olympics.

Social and cultural benefits – the so-called 'feel-good' factor discussed earlier – are also difficult to measure and impossible to ignore. Szymanski (2002) moves away from the economic debate by arguing that the primary reason for hosting an event is celebration and reward. This argument alone might be sufficient reason for governments to encourage such events: 'Rather than thinking of an event as investment in generating an economic return, it should be considered a form of public consumption – a reward for past efforts.'

The perceived benefits of international sporting success are worthy of mention, providing another insight into why 'sport matters' and, by extension, why many governments feel they have a role to play. These benefits are identified as:

- the 'feelgood factor';
- a heightened sense of national pride and identity;
- an increased positive image of the country.

The 'feel-good factor', a euphoria in society, is usually created by victory or a performance that exceeds expectation. Such a benefit is difficult to measure and has attracted very little academic research. This sense of 'feel-good' has been linked, though, to the concept of 'social capital' which, in turn, has been defined as: 'the relationships and norms that shape the quality and quantity of a society's social interactions' (SU discussion paper Social Capital 2002).

The suggestion has been made that social capital increases with the 'feel-good factor', resulting in a decrease in crime and an increase in social bonding and, possibly, GDP. While it is possible, therefore, that the 'feel-good factor' might have positive long-term benefits beyond the immediate euphoria of success, the case has not been proven. A study undertaken by the London School of Economics, for example, on the effect of international sporting success and failure in consumer confidence and productivity failed to show any significant link between sporting accomplishment and economic performance.

National pride is also associated with the 'feel-good factor'. Bairner (1996) suggests that an increased sense of national pride, spawned by great sporting achievement, may enhance social inclusion and help unite a nation.

Clearly, though, the extent to which the nation feels good is linked directly to the amount of media coverage a particular sporting event receives. In June 2002, for example, the British men's athletics team won the European Cup and yet received only limited media attention. Consequently, there was little evidence of increased public euphoria.

Sport can create a positive image of a country on the international stage. In research carried out by the British Council, people in a variety of countries aged 25–34 were asked which images best summed up the home countries: 11 per cent of respondents associated football with England and 6 per cent associated rugby with Wales. When the same people were presented with a list of famous Britons and asked to identify them, 33 per cent recognised Linford Christie and 13 per cent Tim Henman. (It should be noted, though, that musicians, models and actors were more widely recognised than sports stars.)

The argument can also be made, however, that these benefits can be reversed. If a national team is perceived to under-perform, there is a likelihood of a 'feel-bad' factor and a diminishing of national pride. If such a performance also leads to outbreaks of hooliganism, a negative image is created.

What needs to be borne in mind is that, whatever the eventual outcomes of hosting a major event, there is inevitably a significant financial implication. Given that these outcomes cannot be guaranteed, the question always has to be asked: 'Is it (whatever the particular event is) worth the risk?'

Let's return to the 2012 Olympic Games. On 15 March 2007 Tessa Jowell announced that the predicted cost of hosting the event would be £9.35 billion. The money was to come essentially from three sources as follows:

1 £2,175 million was to be provided by the National Lottery;

2 £1,175 million was to come from London funding;

3 £6,000 million would be provided by central government.

However, some fear that the final cost might be significantly greater – the costs are reported as having exceeded £9.35 billion (*The Guardian* gives a figure of £11 billion – excluding security). (*The Guardian*, 4 April 2012.) citing the experiences of previous Olympic hosts as worrying examples. If we consider the 2004 Athens Olympics, the initial budget was a mere £840 million and yet the final cost rose to over £4.4 billion – approximately five times over budget.

If the London Games overrun to the same degree the final cost will be £12.6 billion. And this at a time when the country is experiencing financial difficulties that are arguably unknown and unparalleled.

Case 4.2 The role of the State in sport and the 2012 Olympics: one man's perspective

Jerome Goudie is Head Coach at Loughborough University for Women's Hockey and a centrally contracted coach for England Hockey. He began his international hockey career in Hong Kong before playing for Great Britain and England. He has 127 caps and previously played in the 2006 and 2002 World Cups, the European Cup of 2005 and 2003 and the 2003 Commonwealth Games.

What follows is a summary of an interview with Jerome. His answers to the questions that are at the heart of this chapter provide an insight into the attitudes, needs and desires of one elite sportsman and coach.

Q What is, or should be the role of the government in terms of sport?

A The government should assist, both financially and politically, with international sporting events, for example the Olympics. They should be in charge of the policy for participation, including participation from young people. They should be responsible for:

- developing a healthy lifestyle through sport for children;
- implementing a sport syllabus within schools;
- developing public sporting facilities for certain sports and activities and in certain areas;
- developing sport through clubs. Assisting clubs financially and strategically to achieve this.

They should take a more active role in ethical issues, for example introducing independent bodies to deal with drug taking, bribery, match fixing, any illegal aspects of sport.

Q What should the priority be: elite sport, education, national health?

A Education and participation. The government should provide opportunities for youngsters to play sport. Additional assistance should be given to the amateur sports.

Q What effects of government decision-making have you noticed?

A The introduction of National Lottery funding has had a large impact on elite sport and facility provision for non-elite sport. Also, the introduction of projects to increase youth participation, for example 'Kids Active'.

(continued)

Q The Olympics will cost over £9 billion. What would your advice be to the Minister for Sport?

A Ensure the Games are a legacy not just a short-term success. Make sure they are available to the general public and that interest is maintained, or harnessed, afterwards. Ensure that facilities are available and used. Help the National Governing Bodies to build on the success of their athletes.

Q Any other comments?

A The government is responsible for children benefiting from PE. It is too easy for children not to participate in PE and just sit at the side. PE should be compulsory and fun.

Independent commissioners need to be introduced to improve the morals and role models in sport.

Government policy should make sure children play several sports each week. Focus on sport for fun!

Discussion question

7 To what extent, if any, is it the government's responsibility to ensure that professional sportsmen and women are appropriate role models for children?

Sport in education

Whilst there are few, if any, who would debate the fact that schools, and indeed educational establishments in general, are important and obvious places in which people can learn sport and engage in physical activity, the actual relationship between sporting achievement and academic standards is worthy of more consideration.

Current sociological research into the links between sport participation and educational achievement focuses on three specific mechanisms:

1 Pre-existing conditions: Athletic performance does not influence academic performance and those sportsmen and women who do well academically do so only because of pre-existing conditions such as personality traits.

2 Zero-sum theory: As students have a finite amount of time and energy, those who participate in sport have fewer reserves to apply to their academic studies.

3 Developmental theory: Through involvement in sport, students can develop a variety of skills and attitudes, like time management, self-discipline and interpersonal skills, which can improve academic performance.

The results of research carried out in the USA appear to support the developmental theory, and there is case study evidence from the UK which suggests that:

1 Playing sport may impact positively on emotional and cognitive development and thus lead to improved academic performance.

2 Sports can encourage students who under-achieve academically to pursue educational programmes.

In support of the above, an Ofsted evaluation report (*Specialist Schools: An Evaluation of Progress* 2001) talked positively about the broad impact of Sports Colleges on youngsters' development. However, the following observations need to be borne in mind.

Much of the early American research has been criticised, as the samples chosen made it difficult to determine causality (that is, whether participation in sport led to improved educational performance or whether those who do well academically are more likely to play sport). Whilst Coakley (1997) argues that academic improvements are the result of a variety of adults paying particular attention to sporting youngsters, rather than the actual playing of sport itself.

It would appear, therefore, that whilst it is reasonable to claim that 'sporting achievement and academic standards go hand in hand', the actual nature of the relationship and the key influences operating within it are still open to debate.

There is also an increased focus on sport-related programmes in higher education, with many universities offering sports science and/or sports management courses and some making the quality of their sports facilities an integral part of their 'sales pitch' to prospective students. It should be noted, too, that the Football Association has established a women's centre of excellence at Loughborough.

Governments and governing bodies

Case 4.3 The complexity of the relationship

Jason Hughes has worked extensively in global football, having been a member of two FIFA Committees, Deputy General Secretary of CONCACAF, Director of International Development for Celtic FC as well as having worked in international relations at the FA. What follows are his thoughts about the relationship between government and football's governing bodies.

In the case of football it is a well-established principle, upheld by FIFA, that the National Association governing football within its member nations be 'free from political interference'.

FIFA defends this principle vigorously, even suspending member associations in cases where government interference is found to be occurring. In recent history, the National Associations of countries such as Brunei, Iraq, Kuwait, Peru have found themselves suspended and unable to enter or compete in FIFA-sanctioned events and suspension has even been threatened of Portugal and briefly applied to Greece while European champions (though these cases were not necessarily down to government interference).

It's not difficult to see why governments might seek involvement in football. Football brings with it attention, public interest and the prospect of glory. Even in countries where the on-field performance cannot be expected to be fillip to national pride on a regular basis, football's governors enjoy significant annual investment in football administration: the FIFA Financial Assistance Programme (through which each national association in good standing receives US$250,000 per annum towards running costs) and funding is readily available for FIFA Goal! Capital Projects, through the Goal 1 and Goal 2 programmes. Add to this invitations to an annual FIFA Congress held in various host cities in the world, and attendance at the opening game of the World Cup itself, and you can see that the ability to control these assets and interests would appeal to many politicians.

(continued)

So, that's it then – football is independent and any threat to that independence from governments will be vigorously defended.

Simple, right? Well, in reality, there is much more to it.

Firstly the differences between how governments and countries are run are so wide and varied that actually relationships between National Associations and governments have to be much more nuanced. In countries where dictators are in government, is it really possible for a National Association to operate without the support and sanction, be it implicit or explicit, of the government? Is, for example, North Korea as fully separate and independent of government influence as, say the US Soccer Federation?

What about in the UK? Does the on-going Select Committee investigation into the governance of football (in England) amount to 'political interference?'. Or does the fact that football's governing bodies are willing participants mean that it amounts to something different?

Then there's the simple fact that, in many ways, football relies on the State and government in order to function. Attend any professional game in any major league around the world and you will see police in attendance to uphold public order. Police are generally public employees and, in many countries, without police sanction games cannot go ahead.

Even FIFA itself, despite urging political separation, requires government involvement in hosting of its major events. Bids to host tournaments are only valid with a government guarantee to support it in various ways. This might include, in the case of the World Cup at least, alterations to various tax regulations in order to ensure participants are free from incremental tax liabilities and guaranteeing security. It would be unthinkable, of course, to host an event of the scale of the World Cup without the co-operation of the host government. How can a major football event, even such as the Champions League Final or FA Cup Final, go ahead without the co-operation of public authorities such as transport and the police?

Then again, just as FIFA takes very seriously its independence from government interference, so, too, do governments take their responsibilities seriously. We need look no further than the UK where, following the tragedy at Hillsborough in 1989, Lord Justice Taylor's report made a number of recommendations, including the 'all-seater stadium model' affecting when standing terraces would be permitted in stadia, and also concerning the sale of alcohol, use of crush barriers and other matters affecting stadium safety. In this case, government legislation, based on Taylor's recommendations, directly impacted on what football stadiums would look like in the modern game. Along with the investment of TV money in English football, few acts did as much as the Taylor report to bring about a modernising of football's infrastructure and this played a pivotal role in the subsequent growth in the appeal of football across England.

Finally, what about labour laws? At the European level, legislation protecting a right to transfer your skills as a worker led directly to the 'Bosman ruling', which had a massive impact on the way that football transfers operated. More recently, it seems likely that European courts could rule that media rights bought in one member state of the EU can be offered to consumers in another. A landlady in an English pub may be able to choose, if she wishes, to buy her coverage of the FA Premier League from the Greek satellite provider rather than from ESPN or Sky. Yet Sky and ESPN have paid handsomely for the exclusive right to show the FA Premier League in the territory of the UK.

And so the question is, does a paradox exist? No interference on the one hand, but a reliance on government support to operate on the other. Is 'political interference' in one country just the way things are done in another?

Certainly the relationship between governments and football is much more complicated than simply one of separation. The reality is that government and politics influences football in many ways. These include: stadium health and safety; media rights; labour laws and company law. Football also needs governments to function. Governments provide policing, transport and stadium infrastructure, for example. Major projects, such as hosting a World Cup

(continued)

or building a new Wembley, could not happen without government support. With all this public money comes a need for accountability and a desire to influence. Relations between sport and governments are therefore bound to be complex.

Discussion question

8 'There is no such thing as unhealthy "political interference" in sport. It is all just a matter of culture, of the way "things are done around here".' Discuss.

Times change, governments change, the Games go ahead

In 2010 a coalition government came into office at a time that most have described as one of 'financial crisis'. Changes, both philosophical and pragmatic, were inevitable and yet the focus on sport continues.

For example, the Culture Secretary Jeremy Hunt and Education Secretary Michael Gove announced that 'competitive sport' will be revived in England's schools with the launch of a national competition based around the Olympic Games. Since 2011, schools have been able to compete against each other in district leagues. The successful athletes and teams will qualify for county finals, with the winners going on to compete in national finals. The first championship will take place in the run-up to the 2012 Games, with paralympic-style events taking place also for young people with disabilities. This new competition will be funded by the National Lottery, with up to £10 million being provided to create the necessary league structure.

Whatever the future holds and however dire the state of the nation's finances, the Games will go ahead.

Case 4.4 The 2012 London Olympic Games

Part 2: The bid

> To make an Olympic champion it takes eight Olympic finalists. To make Olympic finalists, it takes 80 Olympians. To make 80 Olympians it takes 202 national champions, to make national champions it takes thousands of athletes. To make athletes it takes millions of children around the world to be inspired to choose sport.
>
> Sebastian Coe, the Chief Executive of the London 2012 bid team

Sebastian Coe began his opening statement to the IOC Commission in Singapore on 6 July 2005 with a direct reference to one of the legacy objectives upon which the London bid was based: the need to inspire and develop children through sport.

Before that, in November 2004, the official London bid book had been delivered to the IOC by Amber Charles, a gifted 14-year-old basketball player from East London. With this one act both legacy objectives were represented symbolically. It was an approach that was to run throughout the campaign, culminating on the final day when

(continued)

Amber and dozens of other children from the East End of London took to the stage in Singapore. They were one, crucial part of a bid team that had to persuade the decision-makers to ignore the relatively recent project difficulties that had affected both the building of the new Wembley stadium and the Millennium Dome.

The team included Olympians Steve Redgrave, Kelly Holmes, Daley Thompson, Denise Lewis, Matthew Pinsent and paralympian Tanni Grey-Thompson, supported by leaders from industry, Tony Blair and the Queen – who, on the last night of the IOC's visit to London in 2004, hosted a gala dinner at Buckingham Palace.

Interestingly, Coe had not been the original leader of the bid team. That had been Barbara Cassani, the American executive responsible for the creation of the British Airways low-budget airline, 'Go!' She led the bid through the first round of voting before making way for Coe. From that point on, a Conservative MP led the Labour government's bid to secure the Olympic Games.

Although Paris was the original favourite to win the Games, London had achieved the highest international press coverage by the time the final vote was cast. By the time 30 East End children took to the stage in Singapore, the Princess Royal had shared a press conference with Ade Adepitan, a black wheelchair basketball player, and David Beckham, an international sporting superstar and East End boy, demonstrating their support for the London vision and associated legacy. The bid was emotive, powerfully campaigned and successful.

Conclusion

Sport matters because it fulfils a variety of important functions at a variety of levels. It can have both positive and negative effects, raise ethical and moral questions and influence public feeling and perception. For that reason, those who play roles in managing, shaping and delivering sport have significant power and responsibility. In the last 50 years the internationalisation of sport has combined with increased media coverage and sponsorship to raise the profile – and therefore significance – of elite sport and mark a difference between amateur and professional sport. Subsequent English governments have brought their own philosophies and approaches to address the twin needs of developing a sporting elite and encouraging sporting participation amongst the general public.

The many claims and assertions made by governments about the positive benefits of sport don't always have the validity of extensive academic research to support them, but they are compelling for all that. As fans and/or participants many people have experienced – *do* experience – the emotional, social and physical benefits of sporting involvement. On the economic level, sport is providing those benefits associated with rapidly growing industries.

The State can influence sport in a variety of explicit ways. These include:

- banning certain activities;
- regulating and licensing;
- providing facilities (or supporting facility provision);
- interacting with sporting bodies;
- encouraging and supporting major sporting events;

- providing funding;
- through education (including health education);
- encouraging and supporting major sporting events.

The extent to which the above provide 'opportunities' and 'encouragement' – and to whom – is determined by myriad factors and is inevitably open to interpretation and debate. As has been discussed previously, the State's involvement through these activities creates, at the very least, ripples of influence throughout all aspects of sport: from sport development and amateur sport to professional sport and international competition; from sport in schools to the many businesses dependent on sport; from improving the nation's health (and all associated savings) to improving infrastructure, national pride and even global recognition. It is the complexity of these interactions that make the role of the State – whatever role it chooses – of such importance. It is because of this importance that one vital aspect of the business of sport management is understanding and influencing that role.

> The futility of arguing whether sport is good or bad has been observed by several authors. Sport, like most activities, is not a priori good or bad, but has the potential of producing both positive and negative outcomes . . . Questions like 'What conditions are necessary for sport to have beneficial outcomes?' must be asked more often.
>
> (Patriksson, 1995)

Discussion questions

9 What are the conditions necessary for sport to have beneficial outcomes?

10 Are the Olympic legacy objectives worth at least £9 billion?

Keywords

Amenity services; Central Council for Recreation and Training; facility services; National Recreation Centres; need services; protective services; scenario planning; Sports Council; Wolfenden Committee

Guided reading

In *An Introduction to Leisure Studies*, Bull, Hoose and Weed (2003) provide a number of chapters that explore the role of the State from different perspectives. The most obvious of these discuss: the historical development of leisure (and the influences of a variety of political, economic and social factors); the economic and political significance of leisure; the political framework for leisure provision and leisure and local government.

Wolsey and Abrams (2001) include two chapters of particular interest in *Understanding the Leisure and Sport Industry*. These are: 'The UK and International Sports Organisations', which considers the different perspectives of the various sectors, the range of organisations involved and the impact of the marketplace; and 'Globalisation', which identifies six dimensions of globalisation, and discusses global firms and responses to globalisation.

Scase's work *Britain in 2010* (2000) is a useful read not only for this chapter but also for Chapter 12, Strategy and environmental analysis in sport; sport managers need to be managing not only (for) today but (for) the future, and Scase provides insights and raises questions in an entertaining and, in some ways, challenging book.

Recommended websites

Department of Culture, Media and Sport: www.culture.gov.uk
Sport England: www.sportengland.org
Sports Council for Wales: www.sports-council-wales.co.uk
Sports Council of Northern Ireland: www.sportni.net
SportScotland: www.sportsscotland.org.uk
The Game Plan: www.strategy.gov.uk/2002/sport/report.shtml
UK Sport: www.uksport.gov.uk

References

Bairner, A. (1996) 'A sportive nationalism and nationalist politics: a comparative analysis of Scotland, The Republic of Ireland, and Sweden', *Journal of Sport and Social Issues*, 23, 314–34.

Blair, T. (2000) *A Sporting Future for All*, London: DCMS.

Bull, C., Hoose, J. and Weed, M. (2003) *An Introduction to Leisure Studies*, Harlow: FT/Prentice Hall.

Coakley, J. (1997) *Sport in Society: Issues and Controversies*, London: Mosley.

Critcher, C., Bramham, P. and Tomlinson, A. (2001) *Sociology of Leisure. A Reader*, London: Spon.

DNH (1995) *Sport – Raising the Game*, London: Department of National Heritage.

Haywood, L., Kew, F., Bramham, P., Spink, J., Caperhurst, J. and Henry, I. (2002) *Understanding Leisure*, Cheltenham: Nelson Thomas.

Jeanrenaud, C. (ed.) (2000) *The Economic Impact of Sports Events*, Neuchâtel: Centre International d'Etude du Sport.

Ofsted (2001) *Specialist Schools: An Evaluation of Progress*, London: HMSO.

Patriksson, G. (1995) *The Significance of Sport for Society – Health, Socialisation, Economy: A Scientific Review*, Scientific Review Part 2, Council of Europe Press.

Scase, R. (2000) *Britain in 2010*, Oxford: Capstone Publishing.

Szymanski, S. (2002) 'The economic impact of the World Cup', *World Economics*, 3 (1), 169–78.

Whannel, G. (1983) *Blowing the Whistle*, London: Pluto Press.

Wilson, D., Game, C. with Leach, S. and Stoker, G. (1994) *Local Government in the United Kingdom*, Basingstoke: Macmillan.

Wolsey, C. and Abrams, J. (eds) (2001) *Understanding the Leisure and Sport Industry*, Harlow: Pearson Education.

The economics of competitive balance in sport

Jon Guest, Coventry University Business School

Learning outcomes

Upon completion of this chapter the reader should be able to:

- outline the peculiar economics of professional team sports;
- appreciate different aspects of uncertainty of outcome/competitive balance;
- understand and apply some different measures of competitive balance;
- assess the extent to which leagues will tend towards competitive imbalance;
- outline a number of different restrictive policies that have been introduced by the governing bodies of various team sports;
- critically assess the rationale and impact of these policies.

Overview

The chapter will initially discuss the factors that influence the willingness of people to pay to watch sporting contests and then go on to consider how sport might differ from other industries. The concepts of uncertainty of outcome and competitive balance will be discussed in some detail including a case study on how seasonal uncertainty in the English Premier League can be measured. The natural tendency of leagues towards competitive imbalance will be analysed before considering the policies that have been employed by sports governing bodies in order to influence the level of competitive balance. This will include detailed descriptions of the reserve clause, the retain and transfer system, salary caps, luxury taxes and the sharing of gate/broadcasting revenue. The theoretical effect of these schemes will be analysed using economic theory. A case study is included which considers the impact of 'soft' and 'hard' salary caps in American sports. The chapter will conclude by briefly considering how the predictions of the economic analysis are altered by changing the assumptions on which it is based.

Introduction

Fans are willing to pay to watch sporting contests for a number of reasons and these are not mutually exclusive. For some fans, watching their team win will be the most heavily valued factor. Some may simply enjoy watching exceptionally talented athletes demonstrating their skills on the field of play. For example, a particular football match may attract more spectators because of the participation of players such as Kaka, Messi, Ronaldo or Rooney. Attendance at a rugby match may be boosted by the involvement of Dan Carter or a basketball game may generate a larger television audience if Kobi Bryant is playing. This is often referred to as the absolute quality of the players. Another factor that might attract people is the perceived closeness of the contest. Fans may gain greater pleasure from winning games where their own team and the opposition are evenly matched. Some great rivalries include Liverpool and Manchester United in football and the Los Angeles Lakers and the Boston Celtics in basketball. The idea that fans enjoy watching matches between equally matched teams is known as uncertainty of outcome. It has been argued that the greater the uncertainty of outcome the greater will be the interest in the sport. The argument is clearly summarised by Quirk and Fort (1992: 242).

> For every fan who is a purist who simply enjoys watching athletes with outstanding ability perform regardless of the outcome, there are many more who go to watch their team win, and in particular watch their team win a close game over a challenging opponent.

The perceived importance of uncertainty of outcome to fans has played a key role in the development of the economics of professional team sports.

The peculiar economics of sport and uncertainty of outcome

In most industries the profit motive will provide firms with strong incentives to outperform their rivals. Profits will be maximised if the firm can drive all of its rivals out of business and become the sole supplier – a monopoly. The same may not be true in the sports sector. If all of a team's competitors were relatively weak then the sport would become very predictable. The team would win almost all of its games. The championship would become a procession instead of a contest. The fans of all the weaker teams would gradually lose interest and attendances would decline. Revenues would eventually fall to a level where it would be impossible for the teams to stay in business. The dominant team would be left on its own. It would have a monopoly but no other teams to play! Unlike other industries, in sport a single firm (i.e. a team) cannot supply the entire market. In the words of Neale (1964: 2), 'Pure monopoly is a disaster'.

In sports, teams need to both compete and co-operate with each other in order to produce the product, i.e. a game. Neale argued that this was a 'peculiar' characteristic of sport.

In the retail sector, Tesco does not require the co-operation of Asda or Sainsbury's in order to sell a loaf of bread or a pint of milk. On the other hand, the Chicago Bulls need the co-operation of other teams in the National Basketball Association (NBA) such as the LA Lakers or Orlando Magic in order to produce a game of basketball. Unlike other industries, a monopoly in any sport would be less profitable than having some competition. Clubs need competition to produce matches and generate revenue.

Although any sport requires strong rivalry in order to be successful, the strength of that competition may vary from one sport to another. There may not be a dominant team, but some teams usually win more often than others. In order to assess the degree of competition analysts often refer to two key concepts: competitive balance and uncertainty of outcome.

Competitive balance

Competitive balance refers to the equality in the playing strengths of the teams in any league or cup competition. To what extent are the most talented players concentrated amongst just a few of the teams? To what extent are they equally distributed amongst all the teams in the league? The greater the distribution across all the teams the more competitively balanced is the league. If the best players are employed by just a few teams then those teams would be expected to win most of their games. The league would become competitively imbalanced.

Uncertainty of outcome

There is no single definition of the uncertainty of outcome. Instead there are a number of different facets to the concept, each of which is interconnected. For example, Szymanski (2003) argues that there are three kinds of uncertainty – uncertainty of match outcome, seasonal uncertainty and championship uncertainty.

Uncertainty of match outcome or short-run uncertainty

How predictable is the outcome of an individual match or game? What are the chances of the home team winning, or the away team winning? A fan would take into account factors such as the talent of the players on both teams, the current form of the two teams and any injuries to key players. If the game cannot be drawn then the uncertainty of match outcome is at its greatest when the probability of the home team winning is 0.5. (Hence the probability of the away team winning must also be 0.5.) If fans value uncertainty of match outcome then they should prefer games like this to ones where they judge it very likely that either the home or away team will win. An interesting way to infer the predictability of a match is to use the odds quoted by bookmakers. For soccer matches in England, bookmakers use fixed odds. This means that the odds are initially set by the bookmaker and remain unaffected by the weight of bets placed by the public. These odds should reflect the objective view of the book-makers about the chances of either side winning a game. The bookmaker will need to make a profit so the odds will be set so that the payout is less than the true chance of the event occurring. This is referred to as over-round on the book. However, they should provide a reasonable guide to the level of unpredictability of any individual game. Bookmakers quote odds in the form a/b. For example if the bookmaker offers odds of evens or 1/1 that a particular team will win, then a = 1 and b = 1 in the previous expression. The corresponding probability odds figure is b/(a + b). Therefore, with odds of 1/1 the probability odds figure would equal 1/(1 + 1) = 0.5. In other words, if a bookmaker offers odds of 1/1 this means that they believe that there is approximately a 50 per cent or 1 in 2 chance of the team winning that particular match. The outcome of the game is very uncertain. If the bookmaker offers odds of 4/1 on to win a game (odds of 1/4) then this means the bookmakers believe that there is approximately an 80 per cent or 4 in 5 chance that the team will win that particular match. In other words, the outcome of the game is very predictable. Data from bookmakers has been used to estimate the importance of uncertainty of match outcome in determining the attendance at games in the English Football League (EFL).

Seasonal uncertainty

As well as the level of uncertainty about individual matches, sports fans may also care about the predictability of outcomes over one season. These factors will obviously be interconnected. If a large number of matches are highly predictable then so too are the seasonal outcomes. There are a number of different aspects to seasonal uncertainty. Firstly, there is the level of uncertainty at the beginning of the season. For example, in the major American closed leagues such as the National Basketball Association (NBA), Major League Baseball (MLB), National Football League (NFL) or National Hockey League (NHL) how much uncertainty is there at the beginning of the season as to which team will eventually triumph and become champions? How predictable is the eventual winner of the NFL Super Bowl in August or the MLB World Series in March? Secondly, how quickly will the level of uncertainty change as the season progresses? For example, for how long are a large number of teams in contention for the championship? Are only a few teams in contention at a relatively early point in the season or are a large number of teams in contention right up until the end of the season? In open leagues such the English Premier League (EPL) and Serie A, as well as the degree of unpredictability over the identity of the eventual champions, there is also the degree of unpredictability over which clubs will get relegated. How certain are fans in August over the identity of the three clubs that will be relegated from the EPL and Serie A the following May?

Seasonal uncertainty may generate interest in different ways amongst different types of fans. Some fans' interest may be greater if the team they support is involved. For example, a fan of one of the stronger teams in the league will be more interested, all other things being equal, the greater chance that team has of winning the championship at the beginning of the season and as the season progresses. If the team drops out of contention as the season develops then interest and attendance might decline. This may be a particular issue at the end of the season when games appear to have little championship significance. Soccer fans sometimes refer to the concept of 'mid-table obscurity'. A fan of a weaker team will have similar interests in the relegation battle. Greater uncertainty over the identity of the eventual champions and relegated clubs may not just generate greater interest and attendance from the fans of the clubs involved. It may also generate more interest from (a) fans of other clubs not involved in the championship race or relegation battle or (b) people who do not support a particular club but enjoy watching the sport. For example, fans of clubs knocked out of a cup competition may be more likely to watch the games in later rounds if they believe there is more uncertainty over the eventual winner of the competition. The 'purist' fan of the sport may be more interested in a league where there are lots of clubs in contention for the championship even though the fan does not identify with a particular club.

Case 5.1 Measuring seasonal uncertainty of outcome

There are a number of different ways that seasonal uncertainty of outcome can be measured. In American sports the most common method is to calculate the percentage of games that each club wins in a season – its winning percentage. The variation or spread in the winning percentages of all the teams is then analysed. If the teams in the league are equally matched then they should approximately win the same number of games. This means the variation in the win percentage of the different clubs would be small. However, if the variation in the winning percentage of the clubs is high then this would indicate that the league is not competitively balanced. Some teams would have won a lot more games than others. This variation in winning percentage can be tracked over time to see if a league is becoming more or less unbalanced. In European soccer the analysis is complicated by the fact that teams can draw matches. To overcome this problem researchers have tended to analyse the variation in the number of points won by teams in a league. A particular issue of concern in the EPL has been the dominance of the top four teams. This can be examined by using the concept of a concentration ratio. A four-team concentration ratio (C4) measures the degree of inequality between the top four clubs and all the other clubs in the league. It is calculated in the following way

For example, in the 2008/09 EPL season the total number of points won in the league was 1043. The top four clubs won 331 of these points, giving a C4 figure of 0.317. The larger the C4 figure the greater the dominance of the top four teams and the more competitively imbalanced the league. Data for the years 1996–2009 is shown in Figure 5.1 with a trend line.

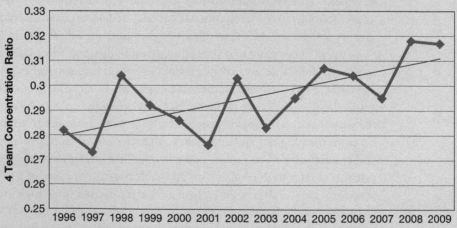

Figure 5.1 Dominance of the top four teams in the EPL 1996/7–2008/09

Discussion questions

1 Comment on the data in Figure 5.1.

2 Consider some of the limitations of using the C4 ratio as a measure of competitive balance.

Championship/inter-seasonal uncertainty of outcome

Rather than focusing on the unpredictability of outcomes in any given season, championship uncertainty focuses on the unpredictability of outcomes over a number of seasons. How often does one club win the league championship or cup competition? How many different clubs are in contention for the league championship over a number of years? If the same team dominates a sport and wins the league championship for a number of years is there a danger that the fans of that club and other clubs will begin to lose interest?

Competitive balance v. uncertainty of outcome

Many authors use the terms competitive balance and uncertainty of outcome interchangeably. The equality of the playing strengths of the teams in the league will have an obvious impact on the uncertainty of match, seasonal and championship outcomes. The more concentrated star players are amongst a few clubs the more likely those clubs are to win matches and championships. However, other authors have argued that although the concepts are similar they do in fact refer to different things. For example, Forrest and Simmons (2000, p. 229) state that 'Competitive balance and uncertainty of outcome are two important, but easily conflated concepts'.

If competitive balance simply refers to the equality of the playing strengths of the teams in the league this is not the only factor that determines the uncertainty of outcome. For example, research has found that home advantage has a strong impact on the chances of a team winning. Data from the English Football League (EFL) shows that the home team won twice as many matches as the visiting team. This might mean that if teams were equally balanced then some home games would become more predictable than others. In order to illustrate this argument, assume that there are two unequal teams – i.e. the skill of the players in one team is on average much higher than the skill of the players in the other team. The team with the better players is team S and the team with the weaker players is team W. Initially if team W is the home team then the game may be unpredictable. The negative impact on the chances of team W winning caused by the fact that it has less able players is offset by the positive impact on its chances of winning because of home advantage. If the playing strengths of the teams were equalised then the outcome of the game would become much more predictable. It would now be far more likely that team W would win because of the impact of home advantage. The predictability of seasonal outcomes in any sport is also influenced by the design of the tournament. Two key factors that will determine the success of any team are the talent of its players and luck or random factors. Whenever a competition contains a 'knock-out' phase, random factors will have relatively greater impact on determining the success of the team. One bad day, being drawn away or an exceptional one-off performance by the opposition could knock the team out of the competition. In a league format with repeated fixtures it is more likely that the good and bad pieces of luck will cancel each other out. The effort and talent of the players will have a much greater impact determining the team's success. In other words, the team with the most talented players is likely to win.

Summary

Sport is different from other industries because strong competition makes teams more profitable. In order to analyse the strength of the competition in any sport the concepts of competitive balance and uncertainty of outcome are used. Sometimes the concepts are used interchangeably although some authors have stressed differences in their exact meaning. The uncertainty of outcome is a multi-dimensional term with no single definition. Some have argued that the concept has often been used in a rather general and vague manner. Competitive balance and uncertainty of outcome are often used when referring to uncertainty over seasonal outcomes.

Market restrictions and competitive balance

Although becoming a monopoly may not be in the interests of the owners of any team, they will still want to win games. This raises some important questions.

- Will unregulated competition in a league produce the 'right' level of competitive balance?
- Do leagues have a natural tendency to become competitively imbalanced?
- Can governing bodies in sport introduce policies that will have an impact on competitive balance?

Background

Concerns have recently been expressed about the increasing predictability of seasonal outcomes in English soccer. Research by Lee and Fort (2009) suggests that seasonal uncertainty of outcome in English soccer has deteriorated significantly since 1995. The chairman of the English Football League, Lord Mawhinney, stated in May 2009 that competitive balance is 'perhaps the biggest threat facing the modern game' (*Daily Telegraph*, 21 May, 2009). The 'Blue Ribbon' panel was created because of concerns over competitive balance in Major League Baseball (MLB) in the late 1990s (Levin et al. 2000). From 1995 to 2000 the New York Yankees won four out of the six World Series. The panel concluded that 'large and growing revenue disparities exist and are causing problems of chronic competitive imbalance'. These concerns are not new and date back over 100 years to the formation of professional leagues in sport. For example, the English Football League was established in 1888 with 12 teams playing each other home and away. The champions in the first season were Preston, which did not lose a single game. The team was nicknamed the 'Invincibles', also winning the FA Cup that year without conceding a goal. Out of the nine league championships between 1892 and 1900, Aston Villa claimed the title on five occasions, while Sunderland won the championship on three occasions. The first national league in baseball was established in 1871 (National Association of Professional Base Ball Players – NAPBBP). In 1872 the Boston Red Sox led the league, winning 83 per cent of their games. In 1875 they won 71 games and lost only eight – a winning percentage of 89 per cent. The Chicago White Sox went on to to dominate the newly formed National League under the leadership of William Hulbert.

A natural tendency towards competitive imbalance

The attendance at any team's games will be influenced by a number of specific demographic factors. In particular:

- the size and wealth of the local population;
- the traditional interest amongst the local population in the sport;
- the level of 'loyalty' amongst the potential fans.

This means that teams of a given quality can generate different match day attendances depending on where the team is based. For example, imagine the impact of a winning team in soccer for (a) a team based in a large city such as Manchester or Liverpool and (b) a team based in a relatively small city or town such as Cheltenham or Crewe. An improvement in the winning record of a large market team may produce an extra 10,000 fans whereas for a small market team it may only generate an extra 500 fans. Assuming no differences in the quality of managers and coaches, a team will improve its winning record on the pitch by recruiting more talented players. In other words, the participation of very talented players in a big city/market team such as Manchester United will generate greater extra revenue through higher match day attendances than they would if they played for a small city/market team such as Crewe. If there is free competition in the labour market the most talented players will tend to play for big market teams which can generate larger revenues and therefore pay much higher salaries.

If a league contains some teams with much larger local populations with a greater traditional interest in the sport than others then the previous line of reasoning suggests that competitive imbalance will exist. Given the structure of the competition, this will lead to increasingly predictable seasonal outcomes as the most talented players move to the big market teams.

Even if all the teams came from approximately equal sized cities/towns competitive imbalance may still exist. Another important factor is the responsiveness of potential fans to a winning team. Economists refer to this as the win elasticity of demand. The responsiveness of fans in cities of a given size might vary. Some cities/towns may have a large proportion of 'fickle' fans. These fans will only pay to watch a winning team and their interest quickly wanes if the team starts losing a large percentage of the games. They can be described as win responsive or win elastic. Other cities may have a high proportion of 'loyal' fans. These fans are prepared to pay whether the team wins or loses. These fans are relatively unresponsive or win inelastic. The more responsive or elastic attendance is to a winning team, the greater the salary a team would be willing to pay for a star player in order to improve its on-pitch performance. As the team start to win more games, match day attendance rises significantly as the 'fickle' fans are willing to pay to watch the team. A team with a high proportion of 'loyal' fans would have attendances that are less win responsive. Signing star players would have a smaller impact on attendances and generate less extra revenue. Therefore talented players that have a large incremental impact on the team's performance could command higher salaries from clubs with win-elastic or 'fickle' fans.

If the win elasticity of demand varies between teams then even a league composed of teams from equal sized markets could still have a natural tendency towards competitive imbalance.

Profit incentives and externalities

Early economic analysis of professional team sports was based on a number of key assumptions:

- team owners run their clubs in order to make as much money as possible;
- players will move to clubs that offer them the most money;
- potential fans value uncertainty of outcome very highly and it is an important factor that determines the attendance at games;
- the number of talented players is fixed.

The assumption of profit maximisation has been used widely in economic theory and its application to sports economics is a very controversial topic area. If clubs are run in order to maximise profits then they should buy/employ players until the point where the extra revenue generated from the last player employed is just equal to the extra cost of employing that player. A star player will generate extra revenue by boosting attendance at the team's games and increasing the number of televised matches which, depending on the broadcast deal, could also increase the team's revenue. The signing of the player may also boost the revenue from merchandise sales. The extra cost of signing another star player will include his/her wages, any transfer fees that had to be paid and any potential impact on the wages of players already at the club. This last point could be an important factor. If existing players were already earning £50,000/week and a new star player was signed for £100,000/week then the existing players may start asking for the wage terms of their contract to be renegotiated. In other words, they will ask for their wages to be increased so that they are equal to the salary of the new star player. Therefore, whenever a club signs a new player it needs to be aware of the potential impact on its total wage bill.

Previously it has been argued that people are willing to pay to watch a sporting contest for three key reasons: they like to see their team win, they like to watch players who are very skilful and they also like close contests that are unpredictable. Different fans will value these reasons differently. However, most of the early research in sports economics focused on the importance of the last of these factors – the uncertainty of outcome. This is clearly illustrated by the following statement by El-Hodiri and Quirk (1971: 1306): 'The essential economic fact concerning professional team sports is that gate receipts depend crucially on the uncertainty of outcome of the games played within the league.'

The combination of these two assumptions has important implications for the predicted behaviour of teams in a league and in particular the revenue implications of signing new players. Initially the theory predicts that as a club signs star players its revenue should increase. These players improve the playing performance of the club and so its attendances increase. However, if it continues to buy all the best players then its games will become increasingly predictable. Given the importance attached to uncertainty of outcome in this analysis, the prediction is that a point will be reached where fans get bored, and both match day attendance and revenue fall. When it becomes highly likely that a team will win all of its games El-Hodiri and Quirk (1971: 1306) argue that its 'gate receipts fall substantially. Consequently, every team has an economic motive for not becoming too superior in playing talent compared with other teams in the league'.

This last point is very important. The argument is that the profit motive will provide incentives for large market teams not to buy all the star players. The teams are aware that if they keep signing star players, then the games in which they play will become very predictable and attendances/revenues will begin to fall. The profit motive alone may limit the otherwise natural tendency of the league towards competitive imbalance. Whether it will deliver the 'right' or optimal level of competitive balance for the league is less clear. As

Zimbalist (2002: 11) notes, 'Competitive balance is like wealth. Everyone agrees it is a good thing to have, but no one knows how much one needs'.

Although the profit incentive may to some extent limit competitive imbalance, its impact may be muted if there are significant externalities. Externalities exist if one club's actions have an impact on the costs and revenues of other clubs, but the club taking the action does not take this into account. In other words, its actions have a 'spillover' effect on the prosperity of the other teams in the league. For example, imagine a situation where a large market club, Manchester United, is considering whether or not to buy a star player like Rooney or Berbatov. The player will help the team to win more games but this could lead to the matches becoming very predictable. The improvement in playing performance will have a positive impact on attendance and revenue while the increased predictability of matches could have a negative impact. Let's assume in this particular example that the positive impact on attendance outweighs the negative impact. The owner must then decide if the increase in revenue is greater than the cost (salary plus transfer fee) of buying the player. If the extra revenue is greater than the extra cost then the profit-maximising owner of Manchester United should buy the star player. The important point is that the owner only takes into account the impact on the costs and revenues of his own team. The problem for the league is that if Manchester United purchases the star player it could make the league more predictable and boring. The increased seasonal certainty that Manchester United will win the league could reduce attendance at other games in which Manchester United are not involved. The impact of Manchester United buying the star player has a negative impact on the revenue of other clubs and Manchester United does not take this account when buying the player.

In this situation, if the net benefit to the club of buying the player is less than the negative impact on the revenues of the other clubs in the league, then it would be best for the league if the player transfer did not take place. However, if the club is only responding to its own benefits and costs then it will buy the player. This reduces the positive impact of profit incentives on competitive imbalance.

An interesting example of this took place in baseball in the 1920s. The Yankees won the championship in 1926 and then completely dominated the 1927 season, winning 110 games and losing just 44. The attendance at Yankee games increased from 1,027,000 in 1926 to 1,164,000 in 1927. However, attendances in the American league as a whole fell from 4,913,000 to 4,613,000 as the fans of other teams lost interest.

Restrictions

Concerns surrounding this natural tendency of leagues towards competitive imbalance were used by governing bodies in a number of sports in order to justify the introduction of a number of regulations and restrictions. These policies fall broadly into three key areas:

- Restrictions on the freedom of players to move from one team to another. In theory one method of making sure that the most talented players do not all end up at the large market teams is to (a) allocate the most talented younger players to the smaller market teams and then (b) prevent the large market clubs from buying all the best players by limiting the ability of players to move between clubs. Real world examples of this type of policy include the reverse-order-of-finish draft, the reserve clause and the retain and transfer system.

- Restrictions on the amount that teams can spend on players' salaries. In theory if the league could equalise the amount teams spend on players' wages then this should result in competitive balance. Real world examples of this type of policy include the salary cap schemes introduced in the NBA, NFL, NHL, Guinness Premiership in rugby union and the Super League in rugby league. A luxury or payroll tax has been introduced into MLB and the NBA.

- Redistributing revenue from the large market teams to the small market teams. Real world examples of this type of policy include the sharing of gate and broadcasting revenues.

The reserve clause and reverse-order-of-finish draft

For many years the contracts of professional Baseball players typically started in March and lasted for 12 months. If the club and player had not agreed a new contract by the 1 March of the following year then the reserve clause came into operation. This gave the club the unilateral right to renew the player's contract for another year. As long as the contract was offered to the player before 11 March and it offered the same terms as the previous contract then it could not be rejected! Whether he signed the deal or not the player was tied to the club for another year, when the reserve clause would come into operation and the club could unilaterally extend the player's contract by yet another year! The reserve clause effectively bound a player to a club for his entire career with the club having a perpetual option to renew the player's contract. Not surprisingly, the legality of the system was challenged on a number of occasions. For example there were famous Supreme Court cases in 1922 and 1972. On each occasion it was challenged the system was defended on the grounds that it helped to maintain competitive balance. For example in 1972, team owners argued that 'without the balance provided by the reserve system, the clubs with greater financial resources would attract the most outstanding players and as a result successful and reasonably balanced league play would be impossible to maintain' (Ross, 1999: 4). The scheme remained in place until 1976 when an agreement was reached that players could be free agents after they had played for six years or more in MLB.

Whatever its impact on competitive balance the reserve clause did limit competition between teams for the services of a player. Without it, players would have been free to bargain with as many clubs as they wished. This competition would have put upward pressure on their wages. By suppressing this competition the reserve clause helped to hold players' wages below what they would have been in a free and competitive labour market. Players may not have been poor but without the scheme their wages would have been much higher. This can be clearly illustrated by looking at what happened to players' salaries once free agency was introduced. Between 1973 and 1975 the average annual real (adjusting for inflation) increase in players' salaries was between 0 and 2 per cent (i.e. the last two years of the reserve clause). This annual figure jumped to 10 per cent in 1976 and 38 per cent in 1977!

Teams in American sport recruit young players from amateur college football. They could compete for this new talent but instead they use the reverse-order-of-finish draft. In this system the teams take it in turns to choose which young player they want to sign. The order in which the choices are made is determined by the playing record of the team in the previous season. The team with the worst playing record gets to choose first and so on. By giving the weakest teams first pick of the most talented young players it is hoped that the scheme will have a positive impact on competitive balance.

The retain and transfer system

In 1885 the FA introduced a requirement on all clubs to register their players annually with the Football Association and this helped the Football League to establish a retain and transfer system. The scheme proved to be very similar to the reserve clause in the US. Players initially signed one-year contracts with a club and at the end of the season the club would decide whether they wanted to retain that player's services or not. A player that the club decided it did want to retain was simply placed on a 'retained list' and had to be offered terms equal to a minimum retaining wage. If the player refused the offer they were not entitled to (a) any pay and (b) to seek employment with another club. The club could do this as it was able to hold on to a player's registration even if a new contract was not agreed. The scheme gave all the bargaining power to the clubs. Rather like the reserve clause, it meant that players were bound to a club once they had signed an initial contract. If they wanted to play for another club they were not free to do so. It was completely at the discretion of the club with which they had originally signed. Players who were no longer required were placed on a 'transfer list' with a fee that the club was willing to sell them at. If a deal was agreed, the buying club effectively took ownership of the player's registration off the selling club which that club could then retain. The rationale given for this scheme by the EFL was the same as the one provided by the owners of teams in MLB. As Dabscheck (1986: 353) states: 'It is argued that in the absence of such controls the rich clubs would secure the most skilled players, and, through their continual domination of the various competitions, interest in the game would decline and spectators would find other forms of entertainment'.

The system was challenged on a number of occasions and major changes were made in 1963 (George Eastham case), 1977 and 1995 (Bosman case). Following the Bosman case, players over the age of 24 were free to leave their clubs at the end of their contracts and no transfer fee had to be paid.

Salary caps and luxury taxes

There are a number of different salary cap schemes. They could set limits on:

- The maximum amount that could be paid to an individual player. For example, the Football Association introduced a maximum wage of £4/week in 1901. The system lasted until 1961 by which time the maximum wage was £20/week.

- The maximum amount that could be spent on the wages of the entire team. This could be an absolute amount. For example, the NFL had a salary cap of $102 million/team in 2006. In this system, large revenue clubs and small revenue clubs face the same limit. An alternative to this would be to set the cap as a percentage of each team's revenue. For example, in 2003/04 each club in League Two of the EFL agreed to limit their spending on wages to 60 per cent of their turnover. In absolute terms this would allow clubs with bigger turnovers to spend more on wages than clubs with small turnovers.

These policies are not mutually exclusive. If limits were placed on the wages paid to an individual player this would to some extent limit the wage bill for the whole team. If every player was paid the maximum amount, team wage bills could still vary if there were no limits on the number of players a team could employ. A limit on the wage bill of the entire team does not place a direct limit on the amount that can be paid to an individual player. However, the pay of any individual player is constrained because the salaries of all the players added together must not be greater than the cap on the team's payroll. The NHL salary cap contains both elements. In 2005/06 teams could spend a maximum of $39 million on the team and $7.8 million (20 per cent of the team cap) on an individual player. As well as limiting the maximum amount, salary cap schemes often place restrictions on the minimum amount teams must spend on players' wages. For example, the NFL salary cap in 2006 specified that teams had to spend a minimum of 84 per cent of the salary cap, or $85.7 million, on players' wages.

A luxury tax fines teams that spend over a certain amount on the salaries of the players. The luxury tax in MLB is actually called the 'competitive balance tax'. For 2009 it specified that any team that spent over $162 million on players' salaries would have to pay tax at a rate of 22.5 per cent. If the team repeatedly exceeded the payroll limit then the rate of tax would increase to 30 per cent and then 40 per cent. Any money raised by the tax is redistributed to the small market teams.

Case 5.2 Hard v. soft salary caps

One of the first caps on team pay was introduced into the NBA in the 1984/85 season. The size of the cap was determined by the revenue of the league. Revenue streams from sources such as gate receipts and national TV money were aggregated and referred to as Basket Related Income (BRI). A collective bargaining agreement between the team owners' and players' union specified that 53 per cent of BRI should be spent on players' salaries. The system worked as an absolute cap on all teams. Once 53 per cent of BRI was calculated, this figure was split equally between all 30 teams in the NBA and this represented each team's salary cap. For example in 1984/85:

$$BRI = \$203.8 \text{ million}$$
$$53\% \ (BRI) = \$108 \text{ million}$$
$$108/30 = \$3.6 \text{ million}$$

In theory, whether it was a large market team (e.g. LA Lakers or New York Knicks) or a small market team (e.g. Seattle Supersonics or Milwaukee Bucks) the maximum amount that could be spent on players' wages that year was $3.6 million. The collective bargaining agreement also specified that teams had to spend a minimum of 90 per cent of the cap on players' wages or $3.24 million.

The scheme became known as a 'soft' cap because it had various exceptions built into it. The most famous of these is known as the Larry Bird Exception. This worked in the following way. A player who had completed his contract and became a free agent was free to negotiate with any team. If the original club re-signed the player, his salary did not count towards that club's salary cap. Larry Bird re-signed for the Boston Celtics in 1985, hence the name of the exception. The exceptions meant that by 1997/98 more than half the clubs in the NBA broke the agreed salary cap ($26.9 million) that year. The Chicago Bulls re-signed Michael Jordan for a salary of $33 million – i.e. more than the salary cap for the whole team!

(continued)

The NFL introduced a salary cap in 1994 that was very similar to the one used by the NBA. Revenues generated by the league were called Defined Gross Revenue (DGR) and it was agreed that 64 per cent of this figure could be spent on players' salaries. The salary cap for each club in the 1994/95 season was $34.6 million. However, unlike the NBA there were no exceptions to this scheme so the NFL cap became known as a 'hard' cap. In 2009, the cap was $128 million per team, while the floor was set at 87.6 per cent of the cap, which meant that each team had to spend a minimum of $112.1 million on players' salaries.

We might anticipate that the large market clubs would want to find ways of signing more star players and avoiding the constraints of the salary cap. While teams in the NBA had an easy way of circumventing the soft cap – the Larry Bird Exception – teams in the NFL had to be more innovative.

One approach was to 'backload' players' contracts. A team could agree a four-year contract with a player worth $10 million. Instead of allocating the salary equally over the contract (i.e. $2.5 million/year) it could be allocated in the following way:

Year 1 – $500,000
Year 2 – $1 million
Year 3 – $2 million
Year 4 – $6.5 million

This would free up space in the early years so that more could be spent on other players' salaries. The team could then release the player at the end of the third year of his contract to avoid having to pay the large 'backloaded' part of the salary.

The team could also pay players by using 'signing on' bonuses. These bonuses would not count towards the cap in a given year. Instead, they were spread evenly (i.e. prorated) over the length of the contract. Hence if a player signed a four-year contract with a signing on bonus of $2 million, they would receive the cash immediately. However, only $500,000 would count towards the team's salary cap for that year with the remainder prorated over the following three years.

Discussion question

3 Recently proposed schemes in European soccer have tried to set salary caps as a percentage of each team's revenue rather than an absolute salary cap. Why would an absolute salary cap be more difficult to introduce into European soccer than the leading American team sports?

Revenue sharing

There are a number of different revenue sharing schemes. These include:

- **Gate revenue sharing between the home and away team.** For example, when the English Football League was established, William McGregor argued that the gate money should be shared equally between the home and away team. His proposal was rejected by 10 out of the original 12 clubs in the league and instead it was agreed that the away team would be given a fixed sum of £12. In 1919 the league agreed that the home team would keep 80 per cent of its gate revenue and give 20 per cent to the away team. This system remained in place until it was abolished in 1983. In the NFL, home teams keep 60 per cent of their gate revenue while away teams receive the other 40 per cent.

- **Central pool revenue sharing.** In these schemes each club pays money into a central pool which is then distributed between all the clubs. Clubs' contribution into the pool is often based on a given percentage of their revenues. This means that in absolute terms the larger market clubs pay greater amounts into the pool than smaller market clubs. In many of these schemes the money is then distributed evenly between the teams. These are 'straight pool' schemes. For example, the English Football League agreed in 1917 that each club would pay 1 per cent of its gate receipts into a pooled account. This money was then equally distributed between the clubs. After gate revenue sharing between home and away clubs was abolished in 1983 the amount was increased to 4 per cent. The 2006 Collective Bargaining Agreement (CBA) in MLB specified that each team must pay 31 per cent of its net local revenue into a central pool. Net local revenues are local revenues less stadium expenses. Local revenue in MLB includes the income teams generate from match day attendance and local television deals. (NB Teams in the MLB sell most of their games through local rather than national broadcasting contracts.) This was also a 'straight pool' scheme as the money from the pool is then distributed equally between the teams. In some pool sharing schemes the money is not distributed equally. These are 'split pool' schemes. In the 1996 MLB CBA, teams had to pay 20 per cent of their net local revenue into a central pool. Twenty-five per cent of this pooled money went only to the teams whose local revenues were below the average for the league as a whole. The further the team was below the average the more money it received.

- **Sharing of revenue generated from the collective sale of broadcasting rights.** This could be from television, radio and the internet. For many years broadcasting revenue from English football was divided equally between the clubs in all four divisions. For example, in 1980 all 92 clubs in the EFL received £23,900 from the television deal. However, when the top division broke away from the EFL and formed the EPL they negotiated a separate broadcasting deal. Under this deal, 50 per cent of the money is split equally amongst all the premier clubs. Twenty-five per cent is split on the basis of final league position – i.e. the higher up the league a club finishes the greater the share of TV money – it receives. The final 25 per cent is divided on the basis of the number of times a given club's games are televised. In both the NBA and NFL revenue from national broadcasting deals is divided equally between the teams.

The impact of restrictions on player mobility in the labour market

Economic theory built on the previous assumptions concluded that restrictions on player mobility in the labour market would have no impact on competitive balance – a result completely at odds with the claims made by the sport's governing bodies. What later became known as the invariance principle predicted that players would end up at the same clubs under a system of restricted mobility as they would under a system where they were free to move to the highest bidder. Another important assumption in reaching this conclusion is that there are no limits on the sale of players for money. In this case players would move from small market clubs to large market clubs where there impact on club revenues would be greater. The large market club could agree to pay a price for the player which was greater than his value to the small club but less than his value to the large club. In this case if the teams aim to maximise profits it would be in both their interests if the trade took place. The argument can be clearly illustrated with a simple example. Imagine a situation where a player is initially employed by a small market club. Assume that by playing for this club for his entire career the player will generate an extra £3 million of revenue for the club but is only paid £1 million. (NB Given the restrictions on his mobility the player can be paid considerably less than his value to the team as there is no competitive bidding for his services.) Assume the same player would generate an extra £5 million of revenue if he played for a large market team. A transfer fee of between £2 million and £4 million could be agreed and both teams would be better off following the trade. For example, if a fee of £2.1 million was agreed the small market team would be better off from selling the player (receiving a fee of £2.1 million) than it would be if it kept the player (£3 million – £1 million = £2 million). The large market team would also be better off signing the player as the value to it of having the player (£5 million – £1 million = £4 million) is greater than the transfer fee it has paid (£2.1 million). If the transfer fee was £3.9 million the net gain for the small club of selling the player would be greater than before (£3.9 million v. £2 million) while the net gain for the large market club from buying the player would be smaller than before (£4 million v. £3.9 million). The final transfer fee would depend on the relative bargaining power of the two clubs but there is a range of prices where trade would increase the profits of both clubs. The previous example clearly illustrates how restrictions on player mobility have no impact on competitive balance. If there were no restrictions the player would still end up playing for the large market team. However, free competition for his services would lead to his wages being bid up to a level much closer to £5 million. Economic theory predicts that the major impact of the scheme is to hold players' wages below the levels that would exist in a competitive players' labour market. Income is effectively redistributed away from the players to smaller market teams via the transfer fees paid by the larger market teams. Although it is difficult to isolate the impact of one change, evidence from the major American sports suggests that the removal of the reserve clause and the introduction of the reserve draft had no significant impact on different measures of competitive balance (Fort and Quirk, 1995).

The impact of a salary cap

If a salary cap places an absolute upper and lower limit on the amount that teams can spend on players' wages then economic theory predicts that this could improve the level of competitive balance in a league. The cap should have the impact of equalising expenditure on players' so preventing the large market teams from employing all of the most talented athletes. The NFL example from 2006 illustrates how each team had to spend a minimum of $85.7 million/year and a maximum of $102 million/year on players' wages. However, the league would have to enforce the cap because profit-maximising team owners of both small and large market clubs will have an incentive to cheat. In effect the salary cap is forcing the large market clubs to spend less on players than the profit-maximising level for those teams. If the cap includes a minimum limit it also forces the small market clubs to spend more on players' wages than the profit-maximising level for those teams. If the most talented players are equally distributed across all the teams in the league this is not a profit-maximising position for the clubs. Some talented players would generate more revenue if they moved from a small market club to a large market club. Both profit-maximising teams would benefit if the player was traded. In summary, unlike the reserve clause, economic theory predicts that a salary cap could have an impact on competitive balance. However, governing bodies should anticipate that teams will try to cheat the system (see Case 5.2). Evidence on the impact of salary caps is mixed. Using data from the NFL, Larsen, Fenn and Spenner (2006) found that the introduction of the salary cap had a positive impact on competitive balance. However, research from Barriger et al. (2004) contradicted these results and found no impact. Endo et al. (2003) also found no significant impact of the soft cap in the NBA.

The impact of revenue sharing

Early economic analysis predicted that the sharing of gate revenue would have no impact on competitive balance. Teams would take into account the impact of winning more games on the share of revenue they receive from both home and away games. In particular it is assumed that if teams win more games it will have a negative impact on the revenue generated from its away fixtures. This causes each team's marginal return from winning more games to fall by the same amount. Hence the policy has no impact on the distribution of playing talent and hence competitive balance. The scheme does reduce the revenue for both teams from improved performance, so profit-maximising owners will respond by paying players lower wages. Central pool sharing could have an impact on competitive balance but depending on the precise details of the scheme it might actually lead to more imbalance. For example, split pool schemes might actually give the small market clubs a disincentive to employ better players and improve their performance. As their performance improves they would receive lower payments from the split pool scheme! If this outweighs any revenue gains from improved performance then a rational profit-maximising owner would simply bank the redistributed revenue and not spend any of it on players' wages! In summary, sharing gate revenue between the home and away team is predicted to have no impact on competitive balance and lead to lower wages for the players. Pool sharing could have an impact but it may be perverse given the precise details of the scheme. Evidence on the impact of gate sharing is very limited. Recent work by Robinson and Simmons (2009) found that the abolition of gate sharing in the EFL increased the probability that players would move from the second division in the league to the first division. This suggests that gate sharing does have an impact on competitive balance.

Summary

The previous theoretical analysis suggests that competitive balance will be relatively unchanged by policies that restrict player mobility in the labour market – i.e. the invariance principle. This is supported by evidence from the abolition of the reserve clause in major American sports. The theoretical analysis also suggests that gate sharing will have no impact. However, recent empirical research throws some doubt on this prediction. A salary cap was the one policy that economic theory predicts can have an impact on competitive balance as long as it can be enforced. The evidence from the NFL and NBA is mixed.

Extending the analysis

Recent research has extended the initial economic analysis in order to examine situations where:

- Team owners are trying to maximise success on the pitch subject to breaking even. If owners are win maximisers instead of profit maximisers then they may be willing to hold on to talented players who could otherwise be more profitably traded to other clubs.
- Fans care as much about the absolute quality of the players as they do about the perceived closeness of the game – i.e. uncertainty of outcome.

If teams are win maximisers then:

- Unregulated leagues will have a tendency to become more competitively imbalanced.
- Sharing gate revenue will increase competitive balance (see Késenne, 1997).

If fans care strongly enough about the absolute quality of the players:

- Sharing gate revenue will increase competitive balance even when team owners are trying to maximise profits.

Conclusion

If leagues contain teams with very different local markets then there will be a tendency towards competitive balance. If uncertainty of outcome is very important for fans then the profit incentive for teams may ensure that the league does not become too imbalanced. However, negative externalities could limit the impact of profit incentives and lead to competitive imbalance. Sports governing bodies have used three different methods in order to improve competitive balance:

1. restricting the mobility of players in the labour market;
2. restricting the amount that clubs can spend on players' salaries; and
3. redistributing revenue from the large to the small market teams.

Early economic theory predicted that two of these measures – restricting mobility and revenue sharing – would have little impact on competitive balance. However, they would reduce players' wages. A salary cap could have an impact on competitive balance if it could be enforced, but teams would have incentives to circumvent the cap. The evidence does support some of the predictions of the theory. The movement from the reserve clause to free agency did not have an impact on competitive balance.

Discussion questions

4. Compare and contrast at least three different methods of measuring seasonal uncertainty of outcome in a professional sports league.
5. Using one of these measures, calculate what has happened to the uncertainty of outcome over the last 20 years in a league of your choice.
6. Outline some non-financial measures that have been used by governing bodies to make sporting outcomes less predictable.

7 Explain why a league with teams from equal sized markets might still become competitively imbalanced.

8 Analyse how the profit motive may provide incentives so that a reasonable level of competitive balance is maintained in a league. Clearly state any assumptions that you have made in the analysis.

Keywords

Competitive balance; externalities; invariance principle; luxury tax; pooled revenue sharing; reserve clause; reverse-order-of-finish draft; salary cap; transfer system; uncertainty of outcome; win elasticity of demand.

Guided reading

Interesting discussions of how the retain and transfer system evolved in football and the reserve clause in baseball are provided in chapters 5, 6 and 7 in Szymanski and Zimbalist (2005), Dabscheck (1986), chapter 5 in Quirk and Fort (1992) and chapter 8 in Fort (2011).

A good summary of current league policies and recent changes in the NFL, MLB, NBA and NHL can be found in Vrooman (2009). Dietl et al. (2009) focus on the implications of introducing salary caps into professional sports leagues.

Different ways of measuring the uncertainty of outcome are outlined in chapter 6 in Fort (2011) and chapter 8 in Downward et al. (2009). For recent trends in the uncertainty of outcome in football see Lee and Fort (2012). For recent trends in the NFL, MLB, NBA and NHL see chapter 6 in Fort (2011) and Vrooman (2009).

The theoretical analysis on the impact of the reserve clause, salary cap and revenue sharing outlined in this chapter is developed in more detail in chapter 6 of Fort (2011), chapter 9 in Downward et al. (2009) and Fort and Quirk (1995).

Finally, a collection of interesting articles on many different aspects of competitive balance were published in the *Journal of Sports Economics* in 2002.

Recommended websites

PremierSoccerStats: www.premiersoccerstats.com/epl.html
Rod's Sports Economics: www.rodneyfort.com/Rods_Sports_Economics/Welcome.html
The Sports Economist: http://thesportseconomist.com/
Vrooman Sports Economics: www.vanderbilt.edu/Econ/faculty/Vrooman/sports.htm

References

Barriger, A., Sharpe, J., Sullivan, B. and Sommers, P. (2004) 'Has a salary cap in the NFL improved competitive balance?' Middleburg College Discussion paper No. 04-02.

Bowdin, G., et al. (2011) *Events Management* (Events management series), 3rd edn, Amsterdam: Elsevier/Butterworth-Heinemann.

Chang, W.-H. (2001) 'Variations in multipliers and related economic ratios for recreation and tourism impact analysis', Thesis of the Department of Park, Recreation and Tourism Resources, Michigan State University.

Dabscheck, B. (1986) 'Beating the off-side trap: the case of the professional footballers' Association', *Industrial Relations Journal* (Winter), 350–61.

Daniels, M.J., Norman, W.C. and Henry, M.S. (2004) 'Estimating income effects of a sport tourism event', *Annals of Tourism Research*, 31 (1), 180–99.

Dietl, H., Franck, E., Lang, M. and Rathke, A. (2009) 'Revenue sharing, reserve clause and salary caps in professional team sports leagues', *International Journal of Global Business and Economics*, 2, 44–50.

Downward, P., Dawson, A. and Djonghe, T. (2009) *Sport Economics: Theory, Evidence and Policy*, Oxford: Butterworth-Heinemann, Chapters 7–9.

Edgell, D.L. (2008) *Managing Sustainable Tourism: A Legacy for the Future*, Philadelphia, PA: Haworth Press.

El-Hodiri and Quirk, J. (1971) 'An economic model of a professional sports league', *Journal of Political Economy*, 79, 1302–19.

Endo, M., Florio K.M., Gerber J.B. and Sommers, P. (2003) 'Does a salary cap improve competitive balance?', *Atlantic Economic Journal*, 31 (4), 388.

Forrest, D., and Simmons, R. (2002) 'Outcome uncertainty and attendance demand in sport: the case of English soccer', *The Statistician*, 91, 229–41.

Fort, R. (2011) *Sports Economics*, 3rd edn, Prentice Hall.

Fort, R. and Quirk, J. (1995) 'Cross-subsidization, incentives, and outcomes in professional team sports leagues', *Journal of Economic Literature*, 33, 1265–99.

Johnson, A. and Sack, A. (1996) 'Assessing the value of sports facilities: the importance of non-economic factors', *Economic Development Quarterly*, 10 (4), 3296–381.

Jones, C. and Munday, M. (2004) 'Evaluating the economic benefits from tourism spending through input-output frameworks: issues and cases', *Local Economy*, 19 (2), 117–33.

Larsen, A., Fenn, A. and Spenner, E. (2006) 'The impact of free agency and the salary cap on competitive balance in the National Football League', *Journal of Sports Economics*, 7, 374–90.

Lee, C.-K. and Taylor, T. (2005) 'Critical reflections on the economic impact assessment of a mega-event: the case of 2002 FIFA World Cup', *Tourism Management*, 26 (4), 595–603.

Lee, Y. and Fort, R. (2012) 'Competitive balance: Time series lessons for the English Premier League', *Scottish Journal of Political Economy*, 59 (3), 266–82.

Levin, R., Mitchell, G., Volcker, P. and Will, G. (2000) The report of the Independent members of the Commissioner's Blue Ribbon Panel on Baseball Economics, July.

Neale, W. (1964) 'The peculiar economics of professional sports', *Quarterly Journal of Economics*, 78, 1–14.

Preuss, H. (ed.) (2007) *The Impact and Evaluation of Major Sporting Events*, Abingdon: Taylor & Francis Ltd.

Preuss, H. (2010) 'The economic impact of visitors at major multi-sport events', in J. Connell and S.J. Page (eds), *Event Tourism: Critical Concepts in Tourism*, London: Routledge, 257–77.

Quirk, J. and Fort, R. (1992) *Pay Dirt: The Business of Professional Team Sports*, Princeton: Princeton University Press.

Raj, R. and Musgrave, J. (2009) *Event Management and Sustainability*, Wallingford: CABI Publishing.

Robinson and Symonds (2009) 'Gate sharing and talent distribution in the English Football League', Manchester Business School Research Paper, No. 570.

Ross, S.F. (1999) 'Restraints on player competition that facilitate competitive balance and player development and their legality in the United States and Europe', in C. Jenrenaud and S. Késenne (eds) *Competition Policy and Professional Sports*, Neuchâtel: International Centre for Sports Studies, p. 4.

Szymanski, S. (2003) 'The economic design of sporting contests', *Journal of Economic Literature*, 41 (4), 1137–87.

Szymanski, S. and Zimbalist, A. (2005) *National Pastime: How Americans Play Baseball and the Rest of the World Plays Soccer*, Washington DC: Brookings Institution Press.

Vrooman, J. (2009) 'Theory of the perfect game: competitive balance in monopoly sports leagues', *Review of Industrial Organization*, 34 (1), 5–44.

Zimbalist, A.S. (2002) 'Competitive balance in sports leagues: an introduction', *Journal of Sports Economics*, 3, 111–21.

The impacts of sport

Robert Kaspar, University of Applied Sciences, Kufstein, Austria
Sebastian Kaiser, SRH University Heidelberg, Germany

Learning outcomes

Upon completion of this chapter the reader should be able to:

- define the impacts of mega sports events;
- describe the benefits of sports for a city/destination/nation;
- describe the foundations of cost–benefit analysis in sports;
- critically reflect on the methods for evaluating the impacts of sports mega events (economic, socio-cultural, environmental, political);
- explore the stages of the event life cycle.

 ## Overview

This chapter addresses the multiple impacts of sports using sports mega events as examples. Within the area of sports mega events an area is singled out which has gained increasing importance in public, media and economic discussion over recent years. The procedures for measuring the various impacts are problematic and are discussed below. This controversy derives from the high political relevance of sports mega events, the large number of impacts to be measured as well as the multiple connections between sports economic activities with general economic development. Furthermore, the number and heterogeneity of the different stakeholders with their specific demands have to be taken into account.

Next to the economic impact there are a number of relevant impacts which need to be considered in the decision-making for or against the holding of a sports mega event, but which are difficult to measure empirically.

The following discussion will cover the fundamental and different aspects of impact measurement of sports mega events as well as central methodological challenges. In the first instance general principles of (economic) impact and cost–benefit analysis are introduced and some central methodological challenges are discussed. Subsequently, as possible impacts affect different target groups (i.e. have differing degrees of relevance for respective stakeholders), a comprehensive heuristic of the socio-economic impact of sports mega events' relevant aspects is presented. Because impacts occur at different times and their importance varies in the long term, the life cycle methodological framework is a useful tool when examining the impacts of major sports events. The event life cycle takes a broader, integrative approach looking at the event from the ideas stage to the long-term sports positioning of a destination; a special view is taken of how the advances in sports and general infrastructure are accelerated by a sports mega event.

 ## The impacts of sport

There are various effects associated with sport and participation in it, both positive and negative. Correspondingly, there are a range of academic disciplines working on the impacts of sport. For example, the disciplines of sports medicine and biomechanics are researching the impact of sport on the muscular-skeletal system of the human body, whilst sports sociologists research the social structures and processes within sport – for example its role in the areas of socialisation and integration processes. There is often a clear and distinctive instrumental understanding behind these research efforts. Of special interest across the differing academic disciplines and research areas are the specific functions which sports are able to offer in order to solve problems within society. This can be grounded on the particular embedding of sport in many areas of society. In the course of dealing with the impact of sports there are, therefore, next to the impartation of sports values, a notable number of economic and social factors to be considered. For example, Pedersen (2009) looks at the direct and indirect economic and social impacts of sports activities, including major events, professional teams, amateur sports and leisure sports (see Table 6.1).

Table 6.1 Impacts of sports activities

	Major events	*Professional teams*	*Amateur sports*	*Leisure sports*
Income – Direct economic impact	Create an increase in volume	Secure consistent revenues	Raise the number of participants	Stimulate spending
Marketing – Indirect economic impact	Foster positive image branding	Develop strong association	Generate promotion of local sport	Raise interest in sporting activities
Health – Direct social impact	Drive sport activation	Motivation for participation	Build awareness of activities	Incorporate sport into lifestyle
Behaviour – Indirect social impact	Inspire community involvement	Cultivate a sense of local pride	Encourage team values	Promote inclusion for all

Source: Pedersen, 2009

The term 'impact' has a number of different meanings. In order to enable broad access, and in order to prevent obstructing the view of relevant factors, a wide terminology is used in this chapter, which also includes non-economic meanings of the term.

Economic impact of sports

Of special interest within the framework of sports-economics research are the economic prospects of sports. As a result of traditional and distinctive distance between the role of economists and sports the academic study of the subject was limited for a long time. The main focus of economists was and remains the analysis of organisation and professional asset production within companies, for markets. The leisure/voluntary nature of production of (sport) services from members of non-profit organisations on which until now the sports system in Europe has been based has been of little interest to economists and has not fit within their economic models (Horch, 1994). From the opposing perspective, the particular distance of sport to the economy should be mentioned (ibid.). Traditionally, sport was perceived as part of leisure time. Therefore, in view of club-based sports' own perception of being a counterpart to the job market and wage-earning, for a long time there was no cause for economic research. Not least, as a result of the unique resource structure whereby clubs are mainly financed by club members, donations as well as high public subsidies minimised the need for economic expertise (ibid.). Amateur as well as restrictive advertising regulations of sports organisations additionally limited/slowed the economic exploitation of sport.

In the course of the process of commercialisation and professionalisation this framework has changed fundamentally over recent years. The economic significance of sports is high and increasing and there is an even greater integration between sport and economy. Against the backdrop of these developments and the high and rising economic importance of sport, the understanding of its impacts as well as the discussion of appropriate acquisition methods are emerging as more relevant. Not least the political dimension of this debate has to be considered. Amongst others, reliable information about the actual effects of sport are of particular interest for decision-making in the process of the awarding of public funds, e.g. in the course of institutional funding or in the discussion regarding the construction of sports facilities.

Within previous years in both European and non-European countries numerous studies have been conducted to analyse the complex relationship between sport and the economy. This research can be classified roughly into three categories (Meyer and Ahlert, 2000): firstly, strongly theoretically orientated studies which try to apply economic approaches especially from general economics to sports. Secondly, partial analytic studies which merely investigate single economic aspects of sports, e.g. sports sponsorship. Thirdly, studies which aim to capture monetary flows and economic activities resulting from sports (and sports events). Those studies can be further differentiated (see Pawlowski, 2009) in macroeconomic (economic impact of the sports sector for an economy, e.g. Rigg and Lewney, 1987; Jones, 1989, 1990; Couder and Késenne, 1990; Andreff et al., 1995; Weber et al., 1995; Meyer and Ahlert, 2000; Nelson, 2001) and microeconomic studies (for example, studies investigating consumption patterns of specific societal groups or with regard to specific types of goods and/or services, e.g. Thrane, 2001; Breuer and Hovemann, 2002; Weagley and Huh, 2004; Lera-López and Rapún-Gárate 2005, 2007). A comprehensive summary of the state of research can be found in Pawlowski (2009).

The impacts of sports mega events

This section addresses the impacts of sports using sports mega events as examples. It is an area that has won increasing importance in public and economic discussion over recent years. This increase in importance results on one hand from the increasingly high social and economic relevance of sports mega events. On the other hand, as already indicated, the measuring of impacts is contentious. This controversy derives from the large number of impacts to be measured as well as multiple connections between sports economic activities and general economic development. Furthermore, the number and heterogeneity of the different stakeholders with their specific demands are an essential anomaly which has to be taken into account. The following will discuss the fundamental aspects concerning the different perspectives of impact measurement of sports mega events as well as central methodological challenges.

Defining mega events

In the academic discussion a multitude of definitions and distinctions between different event types, like mega, hallmark and recurring events, has emerged over recent decades (see Kaspar and Schnitzer, 2011). Roche defines mega events as 'large-scale cultural (including commercial and sporting) events, which have a dramatic character, mass popular appeal and international significance' (Roche, 2000: 1; cf. Getz, 1998). For Roberts, what defines certain sports events as 'mega' is that they are 'discontinuous', out of the ordinary, international and simply big in composition. What Roberts refers to as 'megas' have the ability to transmit promotional messages to billions of people via television and other developments in telecommunications (Roberts, 2004). Hallmark events are major (sporting) events with a limited duration and rotate between different host cities and/or host countries. Host cities are selected after a tendering (bidding) process, are faced with an international audience, usually have high media coverage and have various impacts (economic, social, ecological, sporting, touristic, infrastructural, political) on the host region. Recurring events occur on a regular basis, may also rotate between host cities/ countries, but are definitely staged on a regular basis (for example each year) in the same host cities as they may be part of a circuit. Many characteristics of the recurring events are similar to the hallmark events. Direct impacts might be smaller, but they can have greater cumulative effect in the long run (see Kaspar and Schnitzer, 2011).

Measuring the impact of sports mega events

Scientific discussion about the measurement of the impact of major sports events has formed a focal point for sports economic research over recent years (see, for example, Getz, 1994; Jeanrenaud, 1999; Preuß, 1999; Gratton et al., 2000; Gans et al., 2003; Kurscheidt, 2006). The importance of event-related tourism is emphasised. Tourist-induced consumer spending is an important dimension of autonomous cash inflow into a region; such inflow is independent from the existing redistribution of expenditure that is already taking place in the area (Preuß et al., 2009; Chang, 2001; Preuß and Weiss, 2003). In order to forecast the economic impact of a mega sports event it is necessary first of all to determine the primary impulses of the consumer. Subsequently its impact can be calculated with the help of a macroeconomic model (Preuß et al., 2009; cf. Daniels et al., 2004). One such leading forecasting model internationally recognised within the sports economy (Kurscheidt, 2006) is the macroeconomic model INFORGE (INterindustry FORecasting GErmany), as well as INFORGE/SPORT as a sectorally disaggregated model which as an extension of the INFORGE model refers directly to active and passive sports consumption.

In order to establish the primary economic impulse, the specific consumer behaviour of event tourists has to be considered alongside the question whether the cash inflow consists of regionally generated or autonomous funds. Therefore, in the context of the respective research focus, tourism-related analysis of mega sports events are especially emphasised (Preuß et al., 2009; Lee and Taylor, 2005; Jones and Munday, 2004).

Basically, appropriate studies are discussed not least due to their often high political relevance. Furthermore, from a methodological perspective they are especially full of pre-conditions. The reason for this is largely due to the fact that in addition to the economic impact there are a number of further relevant impacts which need to be considered in the decision for or against the holding of a sports mega event, which are, however, difficult to measure empirically. Therefore, in the first instance general principles of (economic) impact and cost-benefit analysis are introduced and some central methodological challenges are discussed. Subsequently a comprehensive heuristic of the socio-economic impacts of mega sports events' relevant aspects is presented.

If the organisation of sports or cultural events were per se a profitable business, the private sector could organise and manage such events without utilising taxpayer's money. But since large sporting and cultural events can mostly only be realised with substantial public support and subsidies, it is crucial that the funds are allocated selectively. Therefore, a government must be provided with strong arguments for supporting an event, which also means examining the opportunity costs in consideration of alternative uses. The main questions in this respect are under which conditions such investments are justifiable and how the viewpoints of different stakeholders can be properly integrated on the path to successful realisation. However, ex post investigations usually show that the fantastic predictions about the outcomes made prior to the event could not be achieved. This, on the one hand, can be explained by the fact that the interest-related arguments of many stakeholders do not fulfil the necessary requirements of solid appraisals and interpretations from a political-economic point of view (Thöni, 2008). On the other hand, respective studies are often suspected of having been commissioned in order to be used by sports lobbyists to demonstrate the benefit of the respective event for the local or national economy in order to justify public support for subsidies (Késenne, 2005; Johnson and Sack, 1996).

> In some studies benefits are a priori over-estimated resp. costs are underestimated or in surveys only the benefits are emphasised, only microeconomic concepts are used, only short-term aspects are analysed, particular time definitions are used, particular spatial delimitations are conducted, special reference institutions, sectors, groups, people are chosen.
> (Thöni, 2008: 31)

Impact v. cost–benefit studies

When deciding whether or not to bid for and organise a sports and/or cultural event, it is essential – in advance – to thoroughly assess the potential direct and indirect effects.

To this end, cost–benefit and impact studies are carried out. According to Késenne (2005) there are two main types of impact studies: the first type only measures the flow of foreign money into the country and assumes that locals spending their money on tickets would have simply spent money on other goods in the absence of the event. The second type tries to assess the amount of additional income (value added) from the event, for example extra jobs and government tax returns (ibid.). In contrast, cost–benefit analysis seeks to assess the benefits for the population and which of the relevant money flows are to be considered as costs taking into account also crowding-out effects and opportunity costs: 'In many cases, notwithstanding many nice economic impact figures, sports events turn to yield negative net benefits, where some people gain but more people lose' (Késenne, 2005: 3).

Cost–benefit analyses are studies which, in parallel with microeconomic capital budgeting, investigate costs and benefits of alternative measurements from a macroeconomic point of view (allocation problem). In contrast to microeconomic capital budgeting, profit orientation is not of primary importance, but social welfare and indirect as well as intangible (that is not measurable, in terms of quantities and prices on the market) effects are taken into account. The extended cost–benefit analysis additionally considers the distribution effects of time, place and group (distribution problem). Therefore, cost–benefit analyses are considered to be more suitable as they provide better arguments for a government to support an event (Késenne, 1998, 2005; Crompton, 1995; Porter, 1999; Preuss, 2000, 2004; Preuss et al., 2009).

Foundations of cost–benefit analysis (CBA)

The CBA is an established economic procedure to assess public measurements. Its central purpose is to measure the negative (costs/cash outflows) and positive (benefits/cash inflows) impacts connected with the realisation of events on the social welfare of a specifically defined region or country for a limited period of time. All cash outflows are labelled as costs within the considered region. Cash outflow implies the removal of the financial means (i.e. for the population of a region this doesn't lead to more income and jobs). Qualitatively all other negative impacts of the major event are also assessed in terms of social welfare and are considered under the terms of intangible costs (i.e. non-fulfilment of aims related to the welfare function) in the qualitative report. The benefits in a CBA are all cash inflows in a region. Expenditures that originate from financial means of the region and lead to income in the region are called redistributions. Expenditure, depending upon its purpose, can lead to opportunity costs or can create additional benefits, if the means are applied to less productive or more productive applications. This aspect is not often considered, as alternative projects to a major sports event are hard to find (Preuss, 2003). Before assessing the costs and benefits the research field has to be defined. This could be a town, a region or even a country. In this context all financial means flowing within the research field are described as imports whereas all financial means which flow into the region stem from exports and represent autonomous expenditures. The problem of being driven out of the market arises if the demand is greater than the supply and the consumer then abstains from consuming or transacts their business outside of the region. In the situation where unemployment is typical, cash inflow leads to target achievement and therefore is a benefit. But all other positive impacts of major sports event on social welfare are also described as benefits. These are considered in the qualitative part of the CBA (ibid.).

As an essential benefits potential, additional incomes through event-induced increase in tourists, who also use the shopping opportunities of a big city, are emphasised in the argumentats for holding a major event. In contrast to this, possible economic costs which can arise in connection with this problem are often neglected, commonly leading to an overestimation of the mentioned effects for regional value creation. If sport event tourists crowd out the city tourists in a 1:1 ratio then the hotel and restaurant industry merely has an exchange of neutral costs. However, it has to be taken into account that sports tourists show different consumer behaviour than normal city tourists (Preuß et al., 2009). Their time budget is mainly invested in visiting the event and less time is spent in usual tourist activities. Conversely the turnover in the food and restaurant industry, etc., is increasing. Furthermore, Preuß et al. (2009) show that sports event tourists have a higher total expenditure than normal city tourists. Therefore, a crowding out in a 1:1 ratio would result in a macroeconomic gain (concerning the driving-out effects and its methodological relevance, see ibid.).

Direct (Organisation Committee, State) and indirect spending (for example, tourism) induce multiplier effects that also have to be taken into consideration. A multiplier is a factor which indicates to what extent total sales (i.e. income, employment) within the region are changed in the case of consumer or investment expenditure shifting by one monetary unit. Initial spending within the region thus generates further rounds of re-spending. The primary impulse is used, with the help of a regional multiplier for consumer spending through a multiplier for investments, to measure the economic impact of a mega event over a given period of time. Along with that, the size of the multiplier depends on how much of the autonomous spending remains in the specified region and is re-spent (Crompton, 1995; Wang, 1997; for general principles of the multiplier effect see Howard and Crompton, 2004). Secondly, the primary impulse forms the basis for the calculation of the overall economic effect with the help of a macroeconomic model (Preuß, 2003; see also Chapter 2.).

In summary the ideal steps of a CBA are as follows:

1 Definition of a target system and the welfare function.
2 Definition of alternative projects/events within the same target system/welfare function and examination of additional factors.
3 Determination of region and time horizons.
4 Assessments of all costs and benefits (cash inflow/outflow).
5 Chronological homogenisation with the help of discounting using a base year.
6 Identification of the net present value under the consideration of uncertainty and risk.
7 Decision for or against the mega sport event taking into account the qualitative report.

An overview of the process of conducting a CBA of a major sports event is given in Figure 6.1.

Socio-economic impact of sports mega events

All the possible methodological problems arising in connection with analysing the cost effectiveness of major events cannot be dealt with sufficiently in this instance. However, in the following, a few essential aspects which need to be considered in the course of a reliable estimation are described. In order to allow for a blanket appraisal of the socio-economic value it is essential, beyond the aforementioned aspects, to take three basic facets into account.

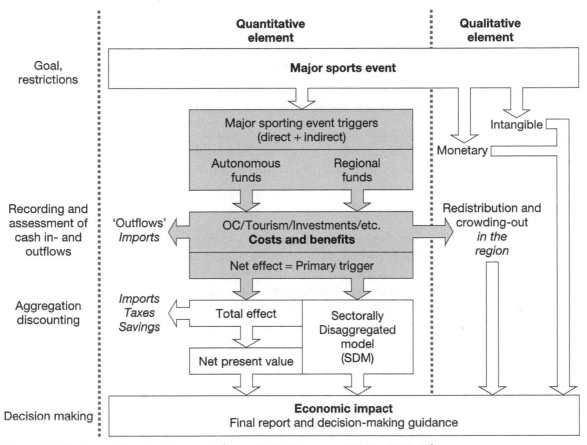

Figure 6.1 Cost-benefit analysis in sports (according to Preuß and Weiss, 2003: 24)

First, it is of vital importance to take all relevant impacts into consideration if possible. It has been demonstrated time and again that temporary, large events are not a rational instrument for stimulating short- or medium-term economic growth (Preuß et al., 2009). What's more, the economic effects that can be seriously considered are too insignificant to influence regional or national economies. But that of course does not necessarily mean that a sports event with a negative net economic benefit for the country should not be organised, or should not be supported by the government (Késenne, 2005). It depends on what is included in the analysis and what is left out (ibid.). Large events bring with them an additional range of effects such as positive external effects which take on the character of public goods, for instance national pride, image or sports participation. As these benefits are hard to estimate or quantify, they cannot be directly captured in the impact or net product studies. Alongside the quantifiable and presentable economic impacts are social and ecological impacts, which also cannot be given a direct monetary value, being impossible to assess in terms of quantities and market prices (concerning the assessment of intangible event effects see e.g. Dwyer et al., 2000; Heyne et al., 2009). Secondly, it should be taken into account that the relevant impacts occur at different times and vary regarding their importance from a long-term perspective. For this reason the event life cycle (Kaspar, 2006) as a methodological framework for the examination of the impact of major sports events is discussed below. Thirdly, it should be considered that possible impacts affect different target groups – i.e. have differing degrees of relevance for respective stakeholders. For this reason, a typology for the classification of possible impacts of major sports events is presented which might serve as a heuristic tool to derive the relevant effects.

Classification of the impact of sports mega events

In the following, referring to Gans, Horn and Zemann (2003), the impact of major sports events will be presented from two perspectives: (1) stakeholders and (2) type of impact. Each of the stakeholders can be assigned a different number of single impacts.

Economic impacts

Expenditures of the hosts, the spectators, competitors/athletes, coaches and journalists cause economic impacts on the hotel, restaurant and retail sectors. In addition to the economic effects concerning the population of the host town/city, there are benefits due to supplementary income-generating activities and jobs as well as the costs originating from price increases on the occasion of the event that have to be taken into account. Entrance fees, catering and transport to and from the venue are among the economic costs for visitors. The economic costs for the host consist of personnel and material costs for planning and realisation of the major sports event (administration, logistics, rentals, assisting participants, insurance etc.), third party expenses (security, waste management etc.), costs for construction and operation of sports facilities and other event-related infrastructure such as funding costs. In opposition to this, on the beneficial side there are revenues from entrance fees, media rights, advertising and sponsorship contracts, merchandising as well as catering and so on. Expenses for public administration in the host town/city can also include costs of personnel and materials. Additionally, where necessary, the host can face costs for construction and maintenance of infrastructure in connection with a major sports event, costs for construction and operation of sports facilities and other event-related infrastructure as well as costs for grant-giving. In public administration, the host town/city gains income from, for example, taxes, fees and leasing. The hotel and restaurant industry and retail sectors can be faced with loss of income as a result of other tourists being crowded out (without compensation through sports event tourists) as well as loss of income through deterioration of the tourist image of the host town/city (e.g. due to event-related violence). Other businesses at the host venue might have to face loss of time due to overcrowding as a possible result of the sports event. Price increases due to the major sports event and loss of time due to congestion are economic costs for the resident population at the venue (Gans et al., 2003).

Ecological impacts

Ecological impacts in the classification according to Gans et al. (2003) have to be assigned to the population at the host town/city as the regional and temporal concentration of big crowds are a burden to the land, the air, the flora and fauna as well as being a burden imposed on the locals. These impacts result particularly from the arrival and departure of visitors and participants, the accumulating waste and the stress on public spaces caused by erosion, unauthorised camping and noise pollution. This includes interference with the aesthetic quality of the rural and urban landscape, with protected countryside through loss of open spaces, energy consumption due to the major event (the event itself and transport), emissions of air pollutants (event itself and transport), noise pollution (both the event and traffic) as well as waste production caused by the event. In some cases, the construction of venues, especially in natural environments as is a requirement at winter events, impacts heavily on the fauna/flora of the location. Likewise, possible positive effects of major sports events on the environment have to be considered; for example, easing of traffic congestion can occur as a result of new road construction or through the improvement of the public transport network.

Case 6.1 The Nordic Ski World Championships in Ramsau/Dachstein (Austria)

The Styrian (Austrian) village of Ramsau/Dachstein hosted the 1999 FIS Nordic Ski World Championships. In an innovative approach, sustainability – being prominent on the global agenda through the 1994 UN Rio Summit on Sustainable Development – became a key issue in the planning and organisational stages of the Nordic event. Seven days after the awarding of the event to the Austrian organisers, Secretary General Wolfgang Mitter had already declared the objective as being the organisation of a 'green event'. Consequently, 21 environmental projects were carried out before and during the Nordic Ski World Championships. The environmental impacts of the event were integrated in all areas before, during and after the event. In the planning stage, the newly built small jumping hill was integrated into the landscape whereas for the large hill an existing venue nearby was used instead of a new venue being constructed on site. Regarding the construction of the cross-country trails, a mere 700 metres were built rather than the originally planned 5 kilometres of new trails. All building issues were developed in close dialogue with citizens and environmental groups. During the event the main focus of the environmental projects was put on transport (with two-thirds of the spectators travelling on public transport), waste management (recycling, multi-use cups), energy issues (biomass energy was utilised for heating the VIP tents) and the integration of local farmers and organic products amongst many other projects. Most importantly, Ramsau utilised the event to position itself as both an international Nordic training centre as well as a Nordic winter tourism destination. Additionally, Ramsau has developed into a winter and summer sports tourism and athlete training destination with the establishment of Nordic running trails and a high-performance indoor training centre. All sports venues are not only very well maintained, but the gold medal winner of the event is overseeing the developments and venue operations as Nordic director. Consequently, the Nordic training centre is used by both athletes and tourists from all over the world.

Discussion questions

1 What are the positive/negative environmental impacts related to sports mega events? What efforts can be undertaken to minimise negative environmental impacts?

2 How does sports tourism benefit from hosting a sports event?

Social/socio-cultural impacts

Social impacts concerning the bearers of the costs and benefits, according to existing taxonomy, occur predominantly for the population. On the side of costs, crime and vandalism have to be taken into account. The social effects that concern the population in the host town/city can also arise independently from a visit to the event, if the holding of a sports mega event brings about a sense of identity, strengthens the sense of togetherness and increases the interest of the citizens in urban and regional concerns. On the side of the costs, it should be noted that there can be a negative perception of the development of social and cultural traditions due to event-related tourism, resulting in the emergence of social dissent about holding such events. On the other hand, successful events or successful athletes may also increase the self-esteem of a nation and contribute to a positive identity. Social costs for visitors to the event have to be distinguished from the aforementioned costs. These include the implications of possible conflict situations between spectators as well as potential health impairments caused by the visit to the event (accidents, loss of hearing etc.). On the side of the benefits, amongst others the recreational and entertainment effects have to be mentioned, in addition to the generation of a collective spirit or the sharing of values. These positive effects are opposed to the possible conflict situations amongst spectators or potential health impairments on the cost side (Gans et al., 2003).

Case 6.2 The 2010 Olympic Winter Games in Vancouver/Canada

A sustainable approach to a sport event through cultural aspects

Including cultural aspects in a sport event is a great challenge, but with the Olympic Games it is far more hazardous. The organising committee of the Olympic Winter Games in Vancouver 2010 took this chance to introduce the Cultural Olympiad. Concentrating not only on the real impact can jeopardise the project through a lack of resources, which may reach from insufficient staff to running out of time. There is a chance to strengthen national pride and also to achieve increased media presence and attention, and not only for sports persons – national and international.

By implementing the Nation Touring Program, the main idea of the organising team was, as Burke Taylor (Vice President of Culture and Celebrations for the Vancouver Organizing Committee for the 2010 Olympic and Paralympic Games) stated, that they 'want all Canadians to feel they can share in the cultural celebrations surrounding the 2010 Winter Games in their own hometowns'. This cultural programme extended from ballet and theatre to up-and-coming musicians and puppetry. Taking this show all over Canada gave a chance to include everyone. In order to reduce conflict and strengthen national pride there was close co-operation with the four First Nations. By working together with this aboriginal organisation, which includes the four main tribes, a better understanding was ensured. The logo was based on the Canadian Inuit inukshuk and became a symbol for leadership, co-operation, friendship and the human spirit, the mascots, showing aboriginal legends, and the Olympic medals were developed in close co-operation with the First Nations and considered the values of the national aboriginal tribes.

(continued)

As a bridge to another discussion concerning land rights and the construction of the venues, this project was awarded to a First Nations construction company. A voice for the Lil'wat Nation and the Squamish Nation could be guaranteed in this way and a broader understanding between the organising committee and the two aboriginal tribes was reached. Aboriginal participation in the Cultural Olympiad was essential to the structure of the event, by including the culture of the country. The last stage in the event's life cycle has been a sustainable sports and tourism development for Canada all due to the Olympic Winter Games 2010.

Discussion questions

3 Why is it critical to involve all local and regional stakeholders in the planning and organising of a sports event?

4 What are the socio-cultural impacts associated with events?

The concept of the event life cycle

Hallmark events such as the Olympic Games, World and Continental Championships (Asian and Pan-American Games, Commonwealth Games, African Soccer Cup) and periodically recurring events (FIS World Cup ski, Formula One Grand Prix) are used to attracting global media and business attention in order to position or rebrand the host city or host country. Sports events attract investments into general and sports infrastructure and contribute to an increased attractiveness of the destination from both a tourism and a business perspective. In a positive scenario, the sports event may accelerate the development of a destination and contribute to its revitalisation for generations to come (e.g. the Barcelona Olympic Summer Games have spurred the city on to become a major business destination with a high quality of life for its citizens).

While most authors and studies discuss the multi-faceted impacts of events, Kaspar (2007: 476) argues that a wider angle has to be opened when interpreting the impact of sports events. Based on the theories of the product life cycle (e.g. Sääksvuori and Immonen, 2008), the destination life cycle (Howie, 2003) following earlier discussions by Getz (1998) and Ritchie (2000) on event legacy, Kaspar assumes that the complete event life cycle has to be considered in order to accurately assess the impacts of a sports event for a host city or a host nation. Kaspar (2007: 476) defines the stages of the event life cycle (applicable to both sports as well as cultural and business events) from the bid to the long-term development of the host city/nation as follows:

1 The idea (why a bid is launched, who drives the bid decision).

2 The feasibility (venues, host destination infrastructure, budget, risks, sports experience).

3 The bidding campaign (or the event decision).

4 The organisational make-up of the organising committee.

5 Developing the sports venue master plan and post-event management plan.

6 Decision on the general infrastructural developments (media, accommodation, transport and city infrastructure).

7 Planning the event.
8 Designing the event branding strategy.
9 Hosting the event.
10 Development of the long-term positioning of the destination and creation of an event strategy.
11 Execution of post-event venue management plans.
12 Sports and tourism product development.

Each stage of the event life cycle can be perceived with a varying level of activity and is visualised in the event life cycle helix in Figure 6.2. In some events certain stages of the event life cycle may be ignored (e.g. the feasibility study) or other stages set at a different time frame (e.g. the event branding strategy is designed at an early stage as part of a strategic destination brand development process). The helix can be seen as a spiral developing from the initial idea, passing the stages with differing levels of activity to the actual hosting and delivering of the event. After the event, the impacts will vary greatly depending on the planning and management of the post-event impacts.

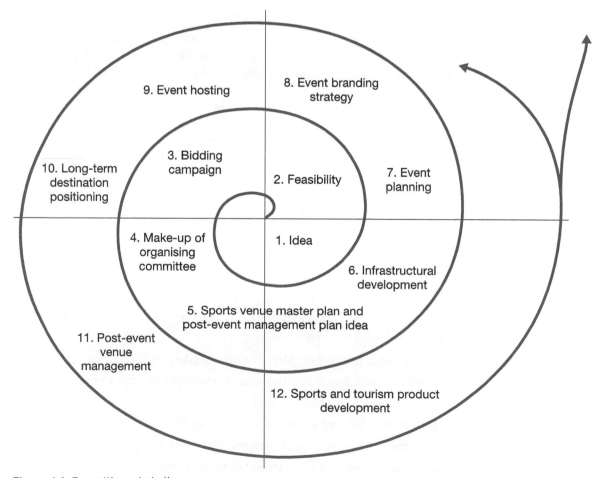

Figure 6.2 Event life cycle helix

The ideas stage may well be the most critical stage for the creation of long-term impacts of a sports event. While the initial idea may be launched by a sports federation, the business sector, politicians or other key stakeholders, it is of paramount importance to reflect on 'why' a bid is proposed. What are the main expectations for all the stakeholders involved? What are the key potential areas of conflict? What is the vision for the destination? In many cases the idea to bid is driven by the obvious impacts of the world's leading sports mega events (Olympic Summer and Winter Games, FIFA Soccer World Cup and UEFA European Football Championship, IAAF Athletics or FINA Swimming World Championships) such as global media coverage, financial and sports issues. Nevertheless, the enduring impact is the sports and general infrastructure created for successful event delivery and its benefits for athletes, clubs and wider sports participants as well as the citizens of and visitors to the destination.

When a destination considers bidding for an international sports event, a proper feasibility study has to be carried out in order to assess both the requirements and the potential benefits of the event. Any sports mega event has to fulfil specific requirements, defined by the sports governing body owning the event rights, in order to become a legitimate candidate city. Firstly, sports venues need to be carefully selected and located and the options for utilising existing venues, upgrading or enlarging existing venues, building brand new venues or using temporary structures need to be considered. Secondly, the event infrastructure such as accommodation (for athletes, stakeholders, spectators and the media) and transport (airports, railways and train stations, roads) needs to be analysed. For any infrastructural requirement, the following issues should be discussed and resolved:

- budgeting and financing the infrastructure;
- infrastructure ownership;
- venue management;
- post-event management concepts.

A strategic review needs to take place in order to assess how the sports event and its potential impacts on the development of the destination's infrastructure are in line with the long-term development strategy and destination master plans. Further important areas for a feasibility study are security, accommodation requirements and the risks involved with hosting the event (especially the clear definition of who will assume responsibility for any potential event deficits).

Given the positive conclusions of the feasibility study (including the financial commitments of the stakeholders concerned) the next step in obtaining the right to host an event is the bidding campaign. Naturally this applies more to hallmark events that are awarded to new destinations each time in contrast to recurring events that take place in the same location periodically. In the Olympic sports business it can be seen that both the 2014 Olympic Winter Games (Sochi, Russia) and the 2016 Olympic Summer Games (Rio de Janeiro, Brazil) were awarded to destinations with development issues and dramatic infrastructural requirements rather than to destinations with existing sports infrastructure (e.g. Salzburg, Austria for 2014 or Chicago, Madrid or Tokyo for 2016). A further important factor to be considered in a feasibility study is continental rotation, as mega events tend to be held in different continents over time and back-to-back events are an exception (e.g. the 1992 Albertville and the 1994 Lillehammer Olympic Winter Games, both in Europe).

In the twenty-first century, bidding for mega sports events has become part of the strategic master plan for many nations and cities around the globe based on both global marketing considerations and key infrastructural developments. To conceptualise a bid, the requirements of the event owner need to be identified and cross-checked with the findings of the feasibility study. In an ideal scenario the destination master plan is in tune with the infrastructural commitments described in the bidding documents. In the bidding documents the bidder formulates the key plans for the successful delivery of the event, such as the sports venue master plan, infrastructural assets and operational issues such as transport management. At this stage, decisions are already being taken that will heavily impact on the success of the event. Most sports federations now carry out assessments of the bidding documents before the candidate is submitted for a final vote on criteria such as:

- government support and public opinion;
- general infrastructure;
- sports venues;
- environmental conditions and impacts;
- accommodation (athletes, media, guests);
- transport;
- security;
- experience from past sports events.

Once the bid is submitted the focus of the bidder is on an international marketing and lobbying campaign in order to secure the event rights based on the decision of the sports' governing body. Their evaluation reports are made available to the sports federation's voting members and nowadays usually to the general public at the final stage of any bidding campaign. Some event owners, such as the International Olympic Committee, have even split the process into two stages in order to limit the costs for a city that is acknowledged not to have the current capacity to host the Olympic Games. Whereas every National Olympic Committee can nominate an applicant city, the executive board of the IOC decides which cities can actually go on to be submitted to the candidate city stage.

The most complex issue is the lobbying process, winning the hearts and minds of the decision makers based on the technical excellence of the bid and unknown success factors.

The host city/country announcement signifies both the end of a sometimes gruelling bidding competition and the launch of the planning stage of the event. If the focus on optimising the event impacts is strongly anchored with the decision makers, the organisational structures are implemented at a very early stage. In Athens (see Case 6.3), it took the organising committee three years from awarding the event before major decisions were taken and the planning process was firmly structured. This had a dramatic impact on event budgets and time constraints. The development of the sports master plan for multi-sports (Olympic Games, Commonwealth Games, Pan-American Games) and multi-venue (FIFA World Cup, European Football Championships) events is unquestionably the area with the highest impact as the costs incurred in the building of sports venues are unlikely ever to be recovered.

Kaspar (2007: 481) argues that in the building of any permanent sports venue, a venue life-cycle process should be initiated to consider the following factors:

- building costs;
- operation (facility management) costs;
- multifunctionality;
- venue ownership;
- venue utilisation (elite sport, sports clubs, leisure, culture, business).

If the venue forecasts an operational profit in the medium to long term or clear benefits for athletes, sports clubs, residents and guests then a permanent venue should be built considering the non-sports potential, such as the venue being utilised for concerts, congresses and exhibitions. If the benefits for the event owner (public, private or public-private) and potential users are not expected to be positive, the installation of a temporary venue or the enlargement of an existing facility should be discussed. As described in Case 6.3, the Greek government wasted hundreds of millions of euros as a result of building all venues as permanent venues and not placing the focus on the development of sensible post-event venue ownership and management plans.

Case 6.3 The Athens Olympic Summer Games 2004

Athens had hoped, and arguably deserved, to host the Centennial Games in 1996, 100 years after the first modern Olympic Games in Athens in 1896. After losing its bid to Atlanta, a second attempt was successful in 1997. Despite warnings from international federations and the IOC it took the Greek organisers until 2000 to start building the enormous number of sports venues required. Whereas the logical approach is to build the necessary general transport infrastructure as a permanent benefit for the population, the decision was taken to build all sports venues as permanent venues as opposed to finding alternatives such as temporary venues for sports not very popular locally. Doubts and media criticism were directed at Athens before the Olympic Summer Games. The Greek government eventually managed to get all the infrastructure (airport, trains, waterfront development, inner city regeneration) and sports venues (11 indoor and 15 outdoor venues) ready just in time for the opening ceremony. The post-Olympic situation is both positive and critical. On the one hand, the Athenians now benefit and heavily use the modernised transport infrastructure and benefit from a refurbished inner city and coastal redevelopment, thereby attracting an increasing number of international city tourists. On the other hand, post-Olympic venue utilisation has left many venues in a very challenging situation. Some venues are fenced off, with no prospect of new ownership, some are used only occasionally (Olympic Stadium) and only a few can be seen as positive examples. Had Athens diligently considered post-Olympic venue ownership and management in the initial stages, hundreds of millions of euros would have been saved in construction costs and in permanent operation expenses.

Discussion questions

5 What are the advantages and disadvantages of building permanent venues v. the utilisation of temporary venues for a multi-sports event?

6 How can a city benefit from an event?

In many cases the hosting of a prestigious hallmark event motivates local, provincial and federal governments and private investors to accelerate investment in the general urban infrastructure. In all of the investments, a clear distinction needs to be made between the needs of the (indeed very short) duration of the event and the long-term impacts on the destination. It is generally agreed that new or improved airports, train stations and railways have benefits for both citizens and guests, however the building of new roads often creates heated discussions. A further key element is the beautification and redevelopment of urban spaces such as inner cities, waterfronts and underprivileged areas (e.g. the developments for the London Olympic Games in East End). If the planned impacts are strategically managed, a city may be able to compete in a new league of cities or nations, the indicators being business or lifestyle driven. Brazilian President Lula even argued that hosting both the Olympic Summer Games 2016 and the FIFA Soccer World Cup 2014 will bring Brazil from a second league nation into the first league of nations ('Brazil stopped being a second-class country and definitively joined the level of first-class nations').

Once the master plans and the organisational structures are implemented and running, the operational planning stage is key to the successful delivery of the event. The responsibilities are split between the event owner and the local organising committee to different degrees. The International Olympic Committee oversees the general event master plan, but leaves full responsibility and risks with the local organising committee. The Union of European Football Associations (UEFA), in contrast, assumes full responsibility for the event, only leaving the areas of sports venues, security and fan zones to the host nation and host cities. For the host city/country, complete ownership indicates that the event can be organised with a view to achieving a long-term impact on the destination whilst also bearing all the associated risks. Sports federations' requirements regarding the size of the sports venues is one important constraint. Generally sports federations require large venues, and have little or no regard for optimal use of the venue after the event. In the case of the EURO 2008 in Austria/Switzerland some of the venues were only enlarged to the required spectator capacity for three matches before being rebuilt again at substantial cost.

Successful organisers of sports events set up a global event master plan and execute professional project management to plan the magnitude of operational issues relevant during the hosting of the event. One key aspect in order to optimise the event's impact is the careful planning of the destination branding process. First of all, the destination should have defined a clear, unique selling position to be communicated to the global television audience during the event. The definition of key televised icons (e.g. the fan zone in the Vienna imperial city centre during EURO 2008, the Sydney Opera House and Harbour Bridge during the 2000 Sydney Olympic Games, the ancient Olympic stadium at the 2004 Athens Olympic Games) and offering the media scenic shots of the country and city as well as offering excellent support and featured press stories about the destination are of key importance. In many cases the hosting of the sports event is planned to brand or rebrand a destination, such is described in Case 6.4 on the first Winter Youth Olympic Games in Innsbruck 2012, reloading the city's DNA (host city of the Olympic Winter Games in 1964 and 1976) with Olympic values and a young, urban sports spirit.

Case 6.4 Winter Youth Olympic Games, Innsbruck 2012

The International Olympic Committee (IOC) awarded the first Winter Youth Olympic Games (WYOG) in 2012 to Innsbruck. The Youth Olympic Games (YOG) have been newly created by the IOC in order to reach a young, global audience, promoting Olympic values and sport. Innsbruck's credibility and expertise in hosting winter sports as well as its modern youth culture should now facilitate the delivery of a truly innovative Olympic event and intercultural exchange.

Innsbruck hosted the Olympic Winter Games in 1964 and 1976, thus being positioned as an Olympic city. Since the 1990s Innsbruck has invested millions of euros in the revitalisation of its snow and ice sports venues (bobsleigh, luge and skeleton track, ski jumping hill by Zaha Hadid, ice hockey venues, Patscherkofel alpine venue). Additionally, Innsbruck has hosted and will host a series of hallmark (including the Ice Hockey World Championships 2005 and 2008, Winter Special Olympics, Winter Universiade 2005) and recurring (FIS four hill ski jumping tournament, Air and Style snowboard contest) winter sports events. Innsbruck's (and the Tyrol's) worldwide reputation is still shaped by hosting the Olympic Winter Games more than 30 years ago. Innsbruck now is positioned as a university and alpine town in the heart of the Alps and the Winter Youth Olympic Games ideally fit with the destination brand.

An event with ideals and innovative elements, such as the Culture and Education Programme (CEP) within the WYOG, and an ideal host city such as Innsbruck, with already existing venues, a lot of event know-how and a high credibility in the youth culture may offer opportunities for both participating athletes and active organisational contributions by local youth and students.

Discussion questions

7 Why is it important that the planned image boost of an event relates to the destination positioning and brand?

8 Will the International Olympic Committee (IOC) be successful in attracting a younger target audience by launching the Youth Olympic Games?

The impact of actually hosting the event can vary greatly. If well managed, the sports, business and tourism sector benefit enormously from the media exposure, revenues generated by media rights, sponsoring, ticketing and operational expenses by the organising committee associated with the delivery of the event. Additionally, the sports spectators and stakeholders during the event may bring major benefits to the destination, as key studies proved during the FIFA World Cup in Germany 2006 and at other events (e.g. Preuss et al., 2009). Nevertheless the negative impacts of the event, such as traffic congestion and crowding-out effects (negative impacts on cultural and conference tourism), have to be taken into consideration. Negative media reports occur quickly if the safety of the event is jeopardised or operational organisation in areas such as traffic management or competition management fail.

Since the EURO 2004 in Portugal the official event is made available to a wider general public, within so-called 'fan zones', creating a positive impact for the citizens of a host city, who enjoy a free event while experiencing a classic venue atmosphere; this leads once more to a positive image being portrayed to the world, such as demonstrated by Germany which hosted the broadly acknowledged 'friendly and welcoming' World Cup in 2006.

Once the last spectator has left the closing ceremony the actual event is history, but the fortune of the destination is at stake. If the planned legacy and its associated impacts are managed positively, the successful event delivery and global media exposure kicks off the destination's development based on an improved sports and general infrastructure and exploiting a better image and awareness within the global tourism community (Chappelet and Kübler-Mabbott, 2008; Ritchie, 2000; Shipway, 2007).

Case 6.5 The 1994 Winter Olympic Games in Lillehammer, Norway

The Lillehammer Olympic Winter Games 1994 were globally perceived as the green games, pioneering efforts to balance the economic, socio-cultural and environmental challenges of hosting the world's largest winter sports mega event. As concluded by the president of the organising committee and now IOC member and head of the marketing commission, Gerhard Heiberg, the 16 days of sports events were followed by Norwegians with enthusiasm and passion and a great pride in the achievements of a small city in a small country. This was also reflected in the excellent results achieved by Norwegian athletes.

In the 1980s the idea to bid for the Olympic Winter Games was developed and local businesses lobbied for the event with a clear view of the economic impact of the event for the region of Oppland. Once Lillehammer was awarded the event, international federations made Lillehammer build five large new ice venues, whereas the snow sports venues were developed with the objective of establishing national winter sports training centres. A clear strategic decision was taken by the Norwegian government, namely to create a 15-year post-Olympic fund in order to maintain the venues and to position the region as a winter sports destination. The environmental impact was optimised by carefully selecting venue locations and by implementing a series of innovative environmental projects resulting in improved transport and water quality for the Lillehammer residents. The socio-cultural impacts were widely seen as positive by the local population as well as by the wider Norwegian spectators and television audience.

Spinning the event life cycle concept from the bid to the current state of Lillehammer, it can be concluded that despite the fact that Lillehammer is a comparatively small city for hosting the Olympic Winter Games, nearly all of the purpose-built infrastructure has been developed and is now used for the benefit of non-sporting activities (e.g. the international broadcasting centre being a university of applied sciences, the Hamar speed skating oval being used as an exhibition and event location, the bobsleigh and luge venue as a tourist attraction) and sport stakeholders (national training centres, ice-hockey league venues).

Discussion questions

9 Should indoor sports venues at a winter sports event be concentrated in the host city or spread out to include other host communities?

10 How can changes in national pride or national identity be considered as an impact of an event?

Naturally, sports spectators and tourists tend to forget the host city/nation if no smaller recurring events follow the key hallmark event. Once a host city has opted to position itself for example as a winter sports destination, a sports event strategy needs to be developed both to utilise the sports venues continuously and to be present in the sports media on a regular basis.

Another option is the establishment of sports athlete training centres that attract the top athletes before, during or after the competition period on a regular basis. Both issues require permanent maintenance and upgrading of the sports tourism infrastructure to cater for the needs of both athletes and sports tourists.

If the destination and the government stakeholders have not overspent on the sports and general infrastructure, both citizens and visitors can see the positive impacts for decades to come and enjoy a regenerated host city. It is clear therefore that the careful co-ordination of all future international bidding, hosting and tourism planning taking place within the context of a cleverly managed transfer of knowledge involving all the retiring and the emerging stakeholders is key to the success of this almost unique sports business sector.

Conclusion

The impacts of sports are varied, ranging from personal (health, attitude to life, fitness) to societal impacts. Sports mega events attract global, national and local media interest and in many circumstances are the highlight of an athlete's career, inspiring the broader general sports participant to actively participate in sports. Large events bring with them an additional range of effects, such as positive external effects which take on the character of public goods – for instance national pride, image or sports participation. As these benefits are hard to estimate or quantify, they cannot be directly captured in the impact or net product studies. Alongside the quantifiable and presentable economic impacts, it also has social and ecological impacts, which cannot be given a direct monetary value, an economic assessment in terms of quantities and market prices being impossible. Secondly, it should be considered that possible impacts affect different target groups – i.e. have differing degrees of relevance for respective stakeholders. Thirdly, it should be taken into account that the relevant impacts occur at different times and vary regarding their importance from a long-term perspective. For this reason the event life cycle (Kaspar, 2006) has been introduced as a methodological/heuristic framework for the detection and examination of the impacts of sports mega events. The event life cycle analyses the event impacts from the idea for an event to the long-term positioning of a destination and includes discussion of the benefits, such as the improvement of the sports and general infrastructure and the development of sports tourism years after the successful hosting of any sports event.

Discussion questions

11 What are the differences between mega, hallmark and special events?

12 What different approaches of assessing the impacts of mega sports events can be distinguished?

13 Describe the ideal steps of a cost–benefit analysis using the example of a mega sports event.

14 Discuss the stages of the event life cycle.

Keywords

Cost–benefit analysis; event life cycle; hallmark events; mega events; multiplier effects; opportunity costs.

Guided reading

The various impacts of sport are discussed and analysed from different perspectives in sport management literature, with a clear focus on the economic impacts so far. Especially the impacts of sport events as well as consumption pattern of sport event tourists have been well researched in the last few years (e.g. Preuss 2007, 2010). Numerous textbooks on the various challenges for events management have been published, for example, Bowdin et al. (2011). The various impacts of sport are discussed and analysed from different perspectives in sport management literature, with a clear focus on the economic impacts so far.

Within practice-related and academic sport event research, the aspect of sustainability is gaining in importance. A book which provides valuable insights into the field is Raj and Musgrave (2009).

As events are directly connected with tourism, there is also literature focusing on tourism and sustainability (for example, Edgell, 2008). Furthermore, sport-specific academic journals such as the *International Journal of the History of Sport*, *Journal of Sport Management* (see e.g. Vol. 22 (4): 'Special Sport Events – Part I' and Vol. 22 (5): 'Special Sport Events – Part II') and *Journal of Sport and Tourism* provide plenty of information. Further valuable sources which give a practical insight are the various reports of event host destinations, while some new approaches are given via the research of the Olympic Studies Centre (www.olympic.org/olympic-studies-centre).

Recommended websites

Games Bids: www.gamesbids.com
Lillehammer: www.lillehammer.com
Olympic Movement: www.olympic.org
Olympic Summer Games London 2012: www.london2012.com
Olympic Summer Games Rio 2016: www.rio2016.com
Olympic Winter Games Sochi 2014: www.sochi2014.ru
Olympic Winter Games Vancouver 2010: www.vancouver2010.com
Ramsau am Dachstein: www.ramsau.com
Winter Youth Olympic Games Innsbruck 2012: www.innsbruck2012.com

References

Andreff, W., Bourg, J.F., Halba, B. and Nys, J.F. (1995) *Les enjeux économiques du sport en Europe: Financement at impact économique*, Paris: Dalloz.

Bowdin, G., et al. (2011) *Events Management* (Events management series), 3rd edn, Amsterdam: Elsevier/Butterworth-Heinemann.

Breuer, C. and Hovemann, G. (2002) 'Individuelle Konsumausgaben als Finanzierungsquelle des Sports', in H.-D. Horch, J. Heydel and A. Sierau (eds), *Finanzierung des Sports*, Aachen: Meyer & Meyer, 61–79.

Chang, W.-H. (2001) 'Variations in multipliers and related economic ratios for recreation and tourism impact analysis', Thesis of the Department of Park, Recreation and Tourism Resources, Michigan State University.

Chappelet, J.-L. and Kübler-Mabbott, B. (2008) *The International Olympic Committee and the Olympic System. The Governance of World Sport*, New York: Routledge.

Couder, J. and Késenne, S. (1990) 'The Economic Impact of Sport in Flanders', *Sport Science Review*, 13, 60–63.

Crompton, J.L. (1995) 'Economic Impact analysis of sports facilities and events: eleven sources of misapplication', *Journal of Sport Management*, 9, 14–35.

Daniels, M.J., Norman, W.C. and Henry, M.S. (2004) 'Estimating income effects of a sport tourism event', *Annals of Tourism Research*, 31 (1), 180–99.

Dwyer, L., Mellor, R., Mistilis, N. and Mules, T. (2000) 'A frameword for assessing "tangible" and "intangible" impacts of events and conventions', *Event Management*, 3 (6), 175–89.

Edgell, D.L. (2008) *Managing Sustainable Tourism: A Legacy for the Future*, Philadelphia, PA: Haworth Press.

Gans, P., Horn, M. and Zemann, C. (2003) *Sportgroßveranstaltungen – ökonomische und ökologische und soziale Wirkungen*, Schorndorf: Hofmann.

Getz, D. (1994) 'Event tourism: evaluating the impacts', in J.R.B. Ritchie and C.R. Goeldner (eds), *Travel, Tourism and Hospitality Research: A Handbook for Managers and Researchers*, New York et al.: Wiley, 437–50.

Getz, D. (1998) 'Trends, strategies, and issues in sport-event tourism', *Sport Marketing Quarterly*, 7 (2), 8–13.

Gratton, C., Dobson, N. and Shibli, S. (2000) 'The economic importance of major sports events: a case study of six events', *Managing Leisure*, 5 (1), 17–28.

Heyne, M., Maennig, W. and Süßmuth, B. (2009) 'Die intangiblen Effekte der Fußball-WM 2006TM in Deutschland – Eine Bewertung mit der Contingent-Valuation-Methode', in S. Bogusch, A. Spellerber, H.H. Topp and C. West (eds), *Organisation und Folgewirkung von Großveranstaltungen: Interdisziplinäre Studien zur FIFA Fussball-WM 2006™*, Wiesbaden: VS Verlag für Sozialwissenschaften.

Horch, H.-D. (1994) 'Besonderheiten einer Sport-Ökonomie', *Freizeitpädagogik*, 16 (3), 243–57.

Howard, D.R. and Crompton, J.L. (2004) *Financing Sport*, Morgantown: Fitness Information Technology Inc.

Howie, F. (2003) *Managing the Tourist Destination*, London: Thomson Learning.

Jeanrenaud, C. (ed.) (1999) *The Economic Impact of Sport Events*, Neuchâtel: Editions CIES.

Johnson, A.T. and Sack, A. (1996) 'Assessing the value of sport facilities: the importance of non-economic factors', *Economic Development Quarterly*, 10 (4), 369–81.

Jones, C. and Munday, M. (2004) 'Evaluating the economic benefits from tourism spending through input-output frameworks: issues and cases', *Local Economy*, 19 (2), 117–33.

Jones, H.G. (1989) *The Economic Impact and Importance of Sport: An European Study*, Strasbourg: Council of Europe.

Jones, H.G. (1990) 'The economic impact and importance of sport: a Council of Europe co-ordinated study', *Sport Science Review*, 13, 26–30.

Kaspar, R. (2006) 'The event life cycle approach – the long marathon from bidding to hosting and finally positioning the host city on the world destination map', *Valencia Summit 2006: Major Sports Events as Opportunity for Development: The International Promotion of the City*. Noos Institute, Spain, 112–119.

Kasper, R. (2007) 'Der Ansatz des Event Cycle Life', in W. Garber, *Tourismus Manager Austria*, Arblinger & Garber, Hall: Austria, 475–82.

Kaspar, R. and Schnitzer, M. (2011) 'Recurring vs. hallmark events', in L. Swayne, *Encyclopedia of Sports Management and Marketing*, Thousand Oaks, CA: Sage Publications.

Késenne, S. (1998) 'Cost–benefit analysis of sport events', *European Journal for Sport Management*, 5 (2), 44–49.

Késenne, S. (2005) 'Do we need an Economic Impact study or a cost–benefit analysis of a sports event?', *Working Papers 2005018*, University of Antwerp, Faculty of Applied Economics.

Lee, C.-K. and Taylor, T. (2005) 'Critical reflections on the economic impact assessment of a mega-event: the case of 2002 FIFA World Cup', *Tourism Management*, 26 (4), 595–603.

Lera-López, F. and Rapún-Gárate, M. (2005) 'Sports participation versus consumer expenditure on sport: different determinants and strategies in sport management', *European Sport Management Quarterly*, 5 (2), 167–86.

Lera-López, F. and Rapún-Gárate, M. (2007) 'The demand for sport: sport consumption and participation models', *Journal of Sport Management*, 21 (1), 103–22.

Meyer, B. and Ahlert, G. (2000) *Die ökonomischen Perspektiven des Sports*, Schorndorf: Verlag Karl Hofmann.

Nelson, J.P. (2001) 'Hard at play! The growth of recreation in consumer budgets, 1959–1998', *Eastern Economic Journal*, 27 (1), 35–53.

Pawlowski, T. (2009) *Die Dienstleistungsnachfrage im Freizeitsektor – Eine Analyse des Ausgabenverhaltens von Privathaushalten in Deutschland*, Saarbrücken: SVH.

Pedersen, L-H. (ed.) (2009) *The New Sports Organisation*, Lausanne: TSE Consulting.

Porter, P. (1999) 'Mega-sports events as municipal investments: a critique of impact analysis', in J. Fizel, E. Gustafson and L. Hadley (eds), *Sports Economics: Current Research*, Ch. 5. Westport: Preager, 61–73.

Preuss, H. (1999) *Ökonomische Implikationen der Ausrichtung Olympischer Spiele on München 1972 bis Atlanta 1996*, Kassel: Agon Sportverlag.

Preuss, H. (2000) *Economics of the Olympic Games*, Sydney: Walla Walla Press.

Preuss, H. (2004) 'Calculating the regional economic impact of the Olympic Games', *European Sports Management Quarterly*, 4 (42), 234–54.

Preuss, H. (ed.) (2007) *The Impact and Evaluation of Major Sporting Events*, Abingdon: Taylor & Francis Ltd.

Preuss, H. (2010) 'The economic impact of visitors at major multi-sport events', in J. Connell and S.J. Page (eds), *Event Tourism: Critical Concepts in Tourism*, London: Routledge, 257–77.

Preuss, H. and Weiss, H.-J. (2003) *Torchholder Value Added. Der ökonomische Nutzen Olympischer Spiele 2012 in Frankfurt RheinMain*, Eschborn: AWV.

Raj, R. and Musgrave, J. (2009) *Event Management and Sustainability*, Wallingford: CABI Publishing.

Rigg, J. and Lewney, R. (1987) 'The economic impact and importance of sport in the U.K.', *International Review for the Sociology of Sport*, 22 (3), 149–70.

Ritchie, J.R.B. (2000) 'Turning 16 days into 16 years through Olympic legacies', *Event Management*, 6 (3), 155–65.

Roberts, K. (2004) *The Leisure Industries*, Houndmills and New York: Palgrave Macmillan.

Roche, M. (2000) *Mega-events and Modernity – Olympics and Expos in the Growth of Global Culture*, London and New York: Routledge.

Sääksvuori, A. and Immonen, A. (2008) *Product Lifecycle Management*, Berlin and Heidelberg: Springer-Verlag.

Shipway, R. (2007) 'Sustainable legacies for the 2012 Olympic Games', *The Journal of the Royal Society for the Promotion of Health*, 127 (3), 119–24.

Thöni, E. (2008) 'UEFA EURO 2008TM: Stadienbauten und Eventumsetzung – Probleme ihrer öffentlichen sozio-ökonomischen Effektediskussion', *WKO Wirtschaftspolitische Blätter* 1/2008, (55), 21–37.

Thrane, C. (2001) 'The differentiation of personal sport expenditures: the Norwegian case', *International Journal of Sport Management*, 2 (3), 237–51.

Wang, P.C. (1997) 'Economic impact assessment of recreation services and the use of multipliers: a comparative examination', *Journal of Park and Recreation Administration*, 15 (2), 32–43.

Weagley, R.O. and Huh, E. (2004) 'Leisure expenditure of retired and near-retired households', *Journal of Leisure Research*, 36 (1), 101–27.

Weber, W., Schnieder, C., Kortlüke, N. and Horak, B. (1995) *Die Wirtschaftliche Bedeutung des Sports*, Schorndorf: Verlag Karl Hofmann.

Business functions applied to sport

This section examines sport businesses from a functional perspective, considering the roles, operations and challenges facing a range of departments typically found in a sport business. You should note that you may not find all of these departments inside a sport business. Even in cases where sport business managers are involved in activities that can be characterised by the chapters in this section, a single designated manager may be involved in a number of activities that overlap what is presented.

The purpose of the section is to help the reader become familiar with business functions, and to ensure that the importance of managing the organisation, human resources, marketing, finance, information, quality and performance are all recognised. The section also embraces a longer-term perspective and considers a range of strategic challenges facing sport businesses.

> **This section contains the following chapters:**
>
> Organisational behaviour in sport organisations
>
> Human resource management in sport
>
> Branding and marketing in sport
>
> Sports finance
>
> Managing small and not-for-profit sports organisations
>
> Strategy and environmental analysis in sport
>
> Managing sport operations: quality, performance and control
>
> The internet, online social networks and the fan digital experience

Organisational behaviour in sport organisations

John Old, Coventry Business School

Learning outcomes

Upon completion of this chapter the reader should be able to:

- identify the internal aspects, functions and processes of organisations;
- examine different group behaviours;
- examine individual behaviours within a group;
- explain different models which classify organisational culture;
- recognise the features of different communications systems.

 ## Overview

It is probably not an exaggeration to say that the ability to organise themselves is one of the key factors that has made the human race so successful as a species. Other creatures may have more spectacular physical attributes, or even larger brains, but none appear to have the ability consciously to co-ordinate the activities of a large number of individuals to achieve collectively what is impossible for them working alone. The word 'consciously' is central to the above statement: 'eusocial' insects such as ants and bees can produce fantastic collective work in their nests and hives, while many other animals appear to have complex organisational structures that help them achieve certain ends, but only human beings appear to have the ability continuously to organise and re-organise themselves towards any number of goals. In this chapter we examine the nature of organisations, how they are structured, key processes that take place inside organisations and how people behave inside organisations.

Organising and organisations

Organising is not the same as organisation

Human activity can be organised in all sorts of ways. For example, what we do, and how we relate to each other, are also governed by laws, traditions, customs and family relations. Managers of organisations need to note that there are other ways to organise the activities that go into producing 'output'. Using the *market* is another way of co-ordinating activity. For example, instead of having our own departments for cleaning or transport, we can simply contract these out to other agencies, and save ourselves the problems of having to run and co-ordinate these activities 'in-house'. Instead of having to recruit, direct, motivate and control the people undertaking these functions directly, the task of management becomes one of agreeing with an outside supplier the service to be provided (a 'service level agreement'), negotiating a contract based upon this and then monitoring the performance of the contract.

The important point here is that simply because something has to be 'organised' does not mean that it has to be done inside the organisation. An alternative is to buy it in from outside suppliers. Many organisations have come to see this in recent years, and sports-based organisations are no exceptions. For example, many professional soccer and rugby clubs have contracted out the advance sales and distribution of tickets to specialist firms such as Ticketmaster. Nike, the sportswear manufacturer, effectively outsources all the manufacture of its athletic shoes to partners, and concentrates on research, design and marketing.

Like the managers of any organisation, the managers of sports organisations have to ask themselves of any activity: is this one we should organise for ourselves or one that we should buy in? Even the committee of a village cricket club must consider whether ground maintenance can be safely entrusted to volunteer members, or whether it should be contracted out. The answer to these questions will be strongly affected by the relative ease with which a function or activity can be organised in-house compared with how easily it can be contracted out.

One other very important practical implication of recognising that organising through organisations and organising through markets are distinctly different alternatives is that organisations and markets require managing in quite different ways. For example, if work is put out to a contractor, the manager's skill will lie in negotiating the contract, and then monitoring its performance. If instead the work is done 'in-house', the relationship between the manager and the employees is very different. It is rare that one can specify precisely in advance exactly what the employee is required to do (and it probably wouldn't be very efficient to do so). Instead, at least up to a point, the employee is a resource at the disposal of the organisation, and it becomes the manager's responsibility to use that resource effectively. As an example, managers sometimes wonder why they can't 'motivate' their employees simply by offering them more money for more or 'better' work – after all this is the way things work in markets. But inside organisations it's much more complex. Do we know in advance what 'better' work will be? Who will say whether it's 'better'? Can the manager monitor precisely what had been done, and will they be judged by the employee to assess it impartially? To what extent is the performance of the employee under their control, and to what extent is it affected by the performance of others – including, crucially, the manager? None of these questions arise when we buy something in, whether it be cleaning services or a ground maintenance contract.

So what is an organisation?

An organisation is a deliberate arrangement of people to achieve a particular end. If we are members of an organisation, then our behaviour is affected by the fact of that membership. Of course, other things also influence our behaviour, such as custom, laws, traditions and our own personality, but membership of that organisation is also crucially important. For example, my behaviour as school governor, academic, business consultant and sports club secretary has been affected by the different organisations concerned.

Crucially, an organisation may be said to comprise three elements:

- members;
- 'rules';
- purpose.

Members

Crucially, organisations are made up of people, and managing organisations is first and foremost about managing people. But an organisation is more than simply a collection of people, even if they share the same purpose. People watching a professional sports event, or in the club's bar or store, share a common purpose, but they are not members of the organisation. Another way of looking at this is to say that an organisation has boundaries, which separate activities undertaken inside the organisation from those conducted outside, and members from non-members. Membership of the organisation implies that to some extent at least your behaviour is governed by its rules.

'Rules'

By rules we mean all the structures and procedures that determine who does what inside the organisation, and the way they interact with each other. These 'rules' may be formally laid down, or emerge informally, but either way they determine:

- **Tasks, roles, and responsibilities** – who is responsible for what. One of the great advantages of organisations is that they get the benefits of the division of labour by creating a number of specialised jobs. Formal *job descriptions* will often specify exactly what the responsibilities of each person are – for example, at a cricket club, who has the final say on the type of grass that is used and the pitch that is produced: the cricket manager, the groundsman or the stadium manager?
- **Patterns of communication** – is important information communicated verbally or in writing? Can people communicate freely with anyone they wish to within the organisation? Or, at the other extreme, must everything go through a formal 'chain of command' – up through one manager, across to another and then back down? This is related to authority relationships.

- **Authority relationships** – in simple terms, who is whose boss? who can give orders to whom? More formally, we talk of 'superior–subordinate' relationships, or 'reporting lines'. Is the organisation one with many layers of management, so that communication tends to be *vertical*, or is it very flat, with few layers of management? If the latter, then clearly each manager becomes responsible for more people, and more activities – the '*span of control*' is larger. It becomes more difficult for the manager to be involved with the detail of work, and there must be more *delegation* and *lateral* communication (directly, between people at the same level of the organisation, rather than through their superiors).

It is possible to distinguish between members and non-members of an organisation in terms of the extent to which they accept these 'rules'. Those who operate within this framework are members. Those who don't – for example customers and suppliers – are not. Managers need to recognise this when they deal with non-members – these latter are not bound by the rules of the organisation. There are few more effective ways of antagonising suppliers, and especially customers, than to insist that they behave in a certain way which suits the internal workings of the organisation, for example by insisting that they can only purchase from the organisation in a certain way, or join excessively long queues at turnstiles because it does not suit the organisation to open more. Organisations should also recognise that, to the outsider, internal distinctions of rank and authority mean nothing. To a customer, the person they deal with at the gate or over the phone represents the organisation just as much – probably much more – than the chief executive.

Purpose

All these rules and structures exist for a purpose, and it is the responsibility of managers to ensure that the efforts of all the members contribute to the achievement of that purpose. This may be particularly problematic for sports organisations. On the face of it, the purpose of a sports club may appear to be straightforward – to be successful in that sport – but in reality it is much more complex. If the objective were simply 'to win' then by the nature of the business only a very few professional sports organisations achieve their purpose, as most rarely if ever win trophies. The founders of the Football League recognised from the outset that their primary purpose was to provide a form of entertainment. At a local level, amateur clubs have as a primary purpose the provision of opportunities for individuals to engage in sport and other recreation. A cricket club such as Warwickshire CCC not only wishes to produce a successful county side, but also supports the development of local cricket. In addition, it has a major asset, in the form of its stadium at Edgbaston, that it can look to use for other, non-cricketing uses. Many professional sports clubs are also subsidiaries of larger commercial organisations, and success on the field may have to take second place to financial requirements to make profits, or at least reduce losses. In 2009 and 2010 a number of English professional soccer clubs faced financial difficulties, which among other things involved the transfer out of leading players, with obviously detrimental effects on playing performance. In contrast, in January 2010 the 'Northern League', representing soccer clubs at the ninth and tenth levels of the English soccer 'pyramid', launched a 'Just Give it a Go' campaign, emphasising the role of 'non-League' soccer as a source of affordable and 'grass-roots' entertainment, and a chance to engage with local community activity.

Reconciling these perhaps conflicting objectives is a major task of management.

Types of organisation

It is beyond the scope of this book to examine the different types of structure that organisations may employ, but a useful distinction can be made between those that are more, and less *bureaucratic*.

Bureaucracy

To most people, the term 'bureaucracy' conjures up pictures of red tape, narrowmindedness, timidity and buck-passing. But it is probably true that *all* organisations are bureaucratic to a greater or lesser extent. 'Bureaucracy' of itself is neither 'good' nor 'bad', but simply a description of an organisation which has the following features:

- **Precise definition of jobs and responsibilities** – which means that everyone knows exactly what is expected of them, and full use can be made of specialised skills.

- **A hierarchy of subordinate–superior relations and communications** – everyone knows whom they report to, and which subordinates they are responsible for. Communication within the organisation tends to be formal, in the sense that important communications are written down, and records kept; and it tends to take place vertically – information flowing upwards to superiors, and information and instructions flowing downwards to subordinates.

- **An impersonal approach to work**, epitomised by the use of set *procedures* to solve problems and *rules* to govern what people do. The use of such rules and procedures can speed up decision making. It also increases the predictability of everyone's behaviour in the organisation, which has major advantages for management. It is a mistake to think of bureaucracies as organisations as ones in which 'bosses' are forever giving instructions to subordinates. On the contrary, in a well-organised bureaucracy, people's job descriptions, along with the use of plans, routines, rules and set procedures, mean that people can work unsupervised for long periods, and yet management can be confident that work is proceeding as planned. It is a form of *control* that does not require constant intervention by managers to tell people what to do.

Defined like this, many familiar work patterns and processes can be described as 'bureaucratic', from the work of the finance office, to a refreshment bar having to dispense large quantities of food and drink in a short period of time at a major stadium. In the latter, speed is essential – every customer unserved may mean the loss of several pounds' worth of revenue. Reducing the production and sale of tea, coffee and a few other basic refreshments to a routine speeds customer throughput and maximises efficiency.

Bureaucratic structures and systems can clearly aid organisational efficiency, which is why they are so widely used. They allow the maximum use of the division of labour. They give management confidence that the work of the organisation is being carried out as intended. Because people have to concentrate only on a fairly narrow range of activities, in which they may develop specialised skills, they may develop greater confidence in their work. If they leave, then the tight job descriptions and the structure of the organisation allow them to be replaced without widespread disruption.

> Fundamentally, good organisational design is about a clear chain of command and identification of specific responsibilities – such structures make organisations very much more effective when compared to agencies in which everybody wanders around wondering what exactly their specific roles and tasks are.
>
> (Watt, 1998: 125)

However, it is true that bureaucracies can be frustrating places to work, and frustrating organisations to deal with. Their procedures may slow down activities, as information is processed 'through channels' and passed between individuals and departments; decisions sometimes appear narrowminded or arbitrary, and people working within them can feel that new ideas are discouraged or ignored. Efforts are sometimes made to cut out or at least reduce bureaucracy, but it is important to recognise that the advantages and disadvantages of bureaucracy are often two sides of the same coin. For example, specialisation allows people to develop and use particular skills, but it also tends to make people lose sight of 'the big picture' and concentrate only on their own work, sometimes to the detriment of the organisation a whole. (Some leading sportsmen have sometimes been accused of being poor 'team players', as they appear to be too concerned with their own performance – for example, Test cricket batsmen who appear to be more concerned with preserving their wicket, and therefore their average, rather than taking a chance and speeding up their scoring for the benefit of the team.) The use of rules can speed up decision making, and ensure that everyone is treated 'fairly' – i.e. the same – but it can also lead to arbitrary and sometimes bizarre decisions. You can't solve this problem by rewriting the rules, or by telling people to ignore the rules when they don't seem to apply – because then they're no longer rules. You have to decide whether to use rules, or instead to rely on people using their own judgement. (This is an insoluble dilemma that underpins the constant calls for soccer referees on the one hand to be consistent, and on the other to 'use their common sense'. The latter implies that the referee will *not* apply the 'letter of the law', and therefore conflicts with the demand that every instance be treated the same way.)

Whether or not a bureaucratic approach is best for an organisation depends on a number of factors, for example:

- Is the work *routine*, or is each job that comes along different, requiring a different approach? For example, processing ticket enquiries, or handling sales at a till, are jobs that are probably best reduced to best-practice routines, whereas planning a new clubhouse, devising a new advertising campaign or negotiating a new sponsorship contract are one-off tasks that may require novel and creative approaches.

- How fast-moving, changeable or unpredictable is the *environment* within which different sections of the organisation operate? The more settled this is, the easier it is to plan and control things centrally. If individual people, or departments, need to be very responsive to changes 'on the ground', or to grasp opportunities, then they need more freedom and flexibility to adapt their working methods to these changes.

- How *large* is the organisation? Bureaucratic procedures, including standardised ways of working, clear responsibilities and clearly laid down rules for communication, can help ensure that all the different parts of the business are working towards the same end, or that the customer receives the same (hopefully high!) standard of service from everyone in the organisation.

● What sort of structure suits the *people* – both managers and subordinates – within the organisation? For example, if we have a large number of part-time employees, employed to do particular jobs at particular times, a more bureaucratic structure which defines and schedules their work may be preferable. Many 'sports organisations' change dramatically in size and structure at certain times of the year – for example staging a major golf or tennis tournament. Many employees are brought in, as marshals, programme sellers or whatever, for a brief period. It is important that their duties and responsibilities are carefully planned and communicated to them before the event begins. Younger or inexperienced workers may also work better in a more 'settled' way than more experienced employees who can make better use of a situation where they are empowered to make their own decisions.

It is a mistake to think that one way of structuring and organising work is always more effective than another – it depends on the type of work to be done.

Alternatives to bureaucracy

It is often said that it is not a question of whether an organisation is to be bureaucratic, but *how* bureaucratic it is to be. In other words, it is difficult to imagine an organisation that did not make at least some use of specialisation, routines and so on, but there are other ways in which management can control the organisation. It is important in this respect to understand the meaning of management 'control'. It does not mean direct physical control of everything and everyone inside the organisation – among other things this would be enormously inefficient, if not impossible. (This is one reason why prisons are so expensive to run, and why it is so exhausting to 'control' young children!)

Instead, it is 'control' in the sense that a thermostat controls a central heating system – it monitors performance, and then makes adjustments accordingly. Bureaucracies emphasise *control of process*. Through specialisation, plans, rules and routines, management determines *how* activities must be conducted. If all is designed, and works as planned, the desired outcome is produced. If it does not, then management reviews and redesigns the procedures, etc. The analogy is with trying to produce a well-designed and efficient machine, or with the design of the many new sorts of stadia built in the 1990s and early twenty-first century. Careful attention to planning how people enter the stadium, find their seat, and leave at the end should ensure that the aims of reduced congestion and increased safety are met.

An alternative is *control of outcome* – management sets targets, against which performance is measured, and intervention is focused on where significant deviations occur. However, rather than try to 'mastermind' or re-engineer all the processes in the problem area, a review will take place of whether the targets are realistic, or whether support (training, resources, etc.) is required – or even whether the personnel should be replaced. Much greater freedom is allowed to people inside the organisation as to how they do their work, how they communicate with each other, and so on.

You might note that whether the emphasis is on control of process or control of outcome, senior management should not be continuously involved in directing day-to-day operations. Not least, this would mean that they had insufficient time to focus on their own jobs – setting and overseeing the overall strategy of the business, reviewing the performance of its various parts, negotiating with major outside investors, customers and suppliers, and so on. This is the major value of *delegation* in any situation – it frees up your time to do what only you can do. It may have other advantages – for example, people may feel more motivated, or trusted, if work is delegated to them, and they don't waste time waiting for the boss to make a decision. But the big gain is the time liberated for the delegator to do their own job more effectively. The manager of a Premiership soccer club will be concerned to discover new talent, but cannot afford to spend all his time with the youth and reserve teams, or 'scouting' at other clubs' games. So these tasks – of coaching the reserves and juniors, and watching other games, are likely to be delegated to others who are both competent and trusted by the manager. The last point – *trust* – is essential. Having set out what needs to be done, the delegator must have the confidence to trust the work and judgement of the subordinate. If they don't, not only are they likely to waste their own time 'checking up', but they are likely to undermine the confidence and motivation, and hence the performance, of the subordinate.

Examples of non-bureaucratic approaches to organising work

- **Project teams**: groups of workers with a variety of skills are drawn together for a particular purpose. Workers may be members of several project teams simultaneously. The project usually has a defined object; when this is achieved the workers move to new projects. In some organisations project teams are combined with specialised departments in *matrix structures*. While workers are 'based' in specialist departments, they join project teams as and when required. We have already referred to the new stadia built in the 1990s: typically the planning of these involved not just architects, but also financial experts, representatives from the sporting side of the organisation, grounds maintenance staff and even representatives of supporters.

- **Self-managing teams**: instead of work being done by a group in which each worker specialises in a particular task, a group has responsibility for a whole activity – they organise the work between themselves, rather than be directed by a manager or supervisor. We have already noted that 'organisations' and 'markets' are two ways of organising human activity: a third is '*self-organisation*'. Thousands of people can be relied upon to make their way to and from a sporting event without colliding with each other: it should be possible for them to organise at least some aspects of their work without having to rely on rules and procedures laid down by someone else. If this can work with thousands of people, there is a good chance it will work with a few.

- **Network communication**: in bureaucracies, communication tends to take place vertically, between manager and subordinate, and be in written form (or at least permanent electronic records). Instead, workers can be encouraged to communicate with whomever they need and want to, whether in writing, verbally or electronically.

- **Autonomous units**: different parts of the business are structured and run in ways that are different, according to their purpose. Typically they are set targets and budgets, and their managers are given a high degree of discretion as to how they are organised – performance is measured not in terms of how well they carry out processes laid down by senior management, but how well they achieve their objects. (Recall that an alternative to carrying out a function 'in-house' is to contract it out to an independent supplier. The use of 'autonomous units' can be seen as a 'halfway house' – the activity is still carried out by the organisation itself, but by a unit which is semi-independent from the rest of the organisation.) Stadium catering is often organised this way.

These alternative methods of working often appeal to both managers and workers. They appear to offer more flexibility and freedom; they can be stimulating and motivating ways in which to work; and they appear to free people from some of the restrictions of bureaucracy. However, we should not lose sight of the advantages of bureaucratic ways of working. There is the danger that these alternative methods of working can give rise to inefficiency in a number of ways, for example:

- If the same activity is being carried out in a number of different project teams, autonomous units, or whatever, there is a danger that the economies of scale associated with *specialisation* will be lost. Put simply, a lot of effort may be wasted in duplicated effort.

- It may be unrealistic to expect people to master the range of skills necessary to make this sort of system work. This can be a source of *stress*, and lead to *demotivation*. People may be happier doing one job, and feel that they are doing it well.

- *Information* flows round a bureaucracy on a 'need to know' basis, and the use of standard ways of reporting means that the meaning of information should be fairly unambiguous. If, in contrast, everyone can communicate with everyone else, and in any way they like, there is a danger that people will be swamped with information, and in the end unable to cope with it all. (It is sometimes said that if you tell everybody everything, you end up telling nobody anything – they simply can't process it all.) Managers who practise an 'open door' policy often find that they end up working very long hours, but achieve disappointingly little, as they are continually taking queries from subordinates. In turn the latter sometimes feel that they have to 'run things past other people' – especially the boss – before acting, and the whole organisation slows down.

The point is, bureaucratic systems suit some situations and non-bureaucratic systems others. Part of a manager's skill lies in identifying which is which.

One can demonstrate the difference between bureaucratic and other ways of working through a rather striking sporting parallel (Suutari, 2001). American football is a game made up of a succession of set plays. On each play someone (usually the coach) determines the tactics. Players each have their specialist roles to perform during the play – in professional American football specialist players come on to the field for different tactics – for example, whether the team is in offensive or defensive mode. Once the play is complete, the coach reappraises the situation, and draws up the plan and designates the roles for the next play.

In rugby (especially Rugby League, but increasingly Rugby Union), while there may be superficial parallels with American football, play is much more continuous. For example, players may have to switch from offensive to defensive mode and back again in the same passage of play. It is impossible to determine in advance the details of the play. Instead the coach can only give broad directions, and then rely upon players with a variety of skills to interpret these as play unfolds.

In terms of the discussion of this chapter so far, American football is more 'bureaucratic' than rugby. Ray Suutari, the author of the article cited here, asks 'Are you playing American football when you should be playing rugby?' with the implication that in business, rugby is a better metaphor for how things should be organised. But this is an oversimplification. The tight control of process, specialisation and planning of American football suit the type of game which is being played – and, as we have seen, bureaucratic systems are appropriate for some business situations, but not for others.

The individual and the organisation

The specific issue of how organisations manage their 'human resources', especially individual employees, is covered in the next chapter. In this chapter we are mainly concentrating on some of the other unique characteristics of organisations, and issues that these raise for managing them.

However, organisations are made up of people, and an examination of organisational behaviour has to take account of how people behave as individuals, as well as how they behave when they interact. For example, a major concern of human resource management, as we shall see, is what 'motivates' people – why do they do what they do? A very influential view of motivation was (and still is) that people are largely 'instrumental' in what they do – that is they do one thing (typically work) in order to obtain another (typically money).

This view – that people's attitude and motivation towards work was largely a matter of how much money they could earn – was one of the planks of what came to be known as 'Scientific Management' (see Case 7.1). This system of organising work involved specialisation, the separation of 'planning' from 'doing' and financial rewards. It undoubtedly raised productivity, and in many ways, with its emphasis on specialisation and top-down control, fitted well with 'bureaucratic' ways of structuring organisations.

However, it rapidly became apparent that, at least in the way it was applied in practice, 'Scientific Management' had severe shortcomings and limitations. Deteriorating industrial relations, among other things, indicated that some workers at least were dissatisfied with the working methods that it involved. From the 1930s, and certainly after the Second World War, there was increasing emphasis on trying to tap into other sources of human motivation – for example, perhaps what people sought from work was not financial reward but the opportunity for social interaction, or simply the satisfaction of using and developing their skills, or of a 'job well done'. Such approaches to managing individuals tend to be incompatible with 'Scientific Management' and this has contributed to the search for other ways to structure work and organisations.

Case 7.1 Taylorism and Scientific Management

'Scientific Management' is often described, with some justification, as being the single most influential idea in the whole of management theory and literature. It is sometimes called 'Taylorism', partly out of deference to its pioneer, Frederick W. Taylor, and partly because many critics have argued that the term 'Scientific Management' is misleading – that it's not particularly 'scientific', and that it takes a very partial view of 'management' (it's not to be confused with 'management science', which is the application of sophisticated mathematical and statistical techniques to decision making).

Taylorism is probably best known for its use of time and motion studies (Taylor called them time studies; the 'motion' part was added by Frank and Lilian Gilbreth) in which jobs are analysed to find the best way of performing them; a way which is then broken down into simple routines (the Gilbreths identified each separate movement, known as 'therbligs'). However, there was more to Taylorism than that: Taylor was concerned with what he termed 'systematic soldiering', or deliberate underperformance by workers. He ascribed this, in part, to workers' experience of

(continued)

management setting incentives for higher performance, then, when these were achieved, removing the bonuses. As well as the adoption of work study, Taylor's system involved large (potentially unlimited) bonuses for workers who adopted the new methods, careful selection of the right people for the job, and 'continuous co-operation' between workers and management. This co-operation wasn't just a slogan or an aspiration but something that would arise:

(a) because workers and managers would share an objective – they'd both be financially better off and

(b) workers would recognise that they could only achieve their ends if managers were able to do their jobs of planning and organising the work.

Taylor ascribed some of the apparent failures of Scientific Management to management refusing to undertake the required 'mental revolution' and apply the other parts of the system (such as the higher pay). Lillian Gilbreth, a trained psychologist, maintained that Scientific Management should be presented as a system which allowed workers to achieve the most out of themselves, and Taylor himself believed that a 'job' should consist of more than doing the work in hand – it was also preparation for the next job. So it is not true to say that Taylorism totally ignored the human aspects of work. However, it certainly emphasised money as the major motivating factor, and, to take a particular factor to which we will return, Taylor believed that influence of groups on human behaviour was almost totally pernicious, as it interfered with wholly individualistic behaviour and motivation, could lead to time being 'wasted' on social interaction, and breed social 'norms' of timewasting, under-performance and so on.

Although all the well-known examples of Taylorism are applications to manual labour, Taylor maintained that it could be applied to all work – but failed to show how it could be applied to management. Note that Taylorism rigorously separated 'planning' from 'doing'. In other words someone – the manager – would plan and organise what was to be done, and someone else – the worker – would do it. It is difficult to see how this could be applied to management itself.

Taylorism and sport

Taylor himself was a great sports fan, and drew many examples and insights from sport, especially American sport. American team sports, such as football and baseball, tend to place a great emphasis on individual expertise in a particular aspect of the game (as noted by Suutari in the article mentioned earlier); and the insight that one does not have to be a great 'doer' to be a good 'planner' – or conversely that great players do not necessarily make great coaches – is clearly borne out in sport. Even the greatest sports practitioners see the value in coaches who can objectively assess their performance and suggest ways to improve.

Taylorism today?

We can still see all around us examples of Taylorite methods. Modern call centres are often quoted as examples, but we can also see examples in quite sophisticated areas. For example, *some* aspects of 'Total Quality Management', such as designing jobs so that they can only be done one way, appear straightforward applications of Taylorite ideas. Furthermore, in an age when many organisations feel that their major assets are their 'intellectual capital', a growing area of interest is 'knowledge management', where firms try to gather and use all the expertise 'locked' in the minds of their employees. This can range from simple cataloguing of the areas in which their employees appear to be 'experts', to more sophisticated techniques – e.g. monitoring email enquiries throughout the organisation to see which experts are resorted to most.

Motivating individuals in organisations

A key theme of this chapter is that people's behaviour is affected by the organisational setting in which they work. If we recognise that their motivation is more complex than simply wishing to maximise their pay, then this implies that different people are likely to behave differently in the same situation, and also that people with similar motivations are likely to react and behave differently in different organisational settings.

Different motivations – similar settings

We often speak of 'older workers' or 'part-time workers' as though all members of these groups will be motivated, and behave, in the same way. But, as an example, a firm's 'part-time workers' may include some who are indeed 'instrumental': for whom the job offers an (often vital) supplement to household income, and who may well be expected to respond positively to structures and incentives that offer well-defined if routine and undemanding work with steady pay (and might therefore be quite happy with 'Taylorite' systems). On the other hand, for others the work may be primarily an opportunity for social interaction, or gaining experience and developing skills, and for these workers such a situation would be very frustrating. (Think of the work that students undertake – some may be working for a much-needed supplement to their income, while others are looking at it as a valuable first step in their career.)

Similar motivations – different settings

It follows from the above that people with the same motivation may perform very differently in different situations. An older worker looking for the opportunity to 'remain active' – mentally and/or physically – is unlikely to be happy with work that provides them with no challenge, and accordingly appear frustrated and unproductive. In a job offering variety and opportunities to use their experience and knowledge they may be an invaluable member of the organisation.

Learned behaviour

One further point we should note is that human behaviour does not necessarily arise from some innate characteristics (attitudes, motivation, etc.) of the individual, but can also be learned responses to particular situations. It is beyond the scope of this chapter to examine this in depth, but note that another consequence of a particular organisational setting is that it may 'teach' people the 'appropriate' responses. Someone working in a group-based organisation will rapidly learn the importance of developing interpersonal skills, or they will be unproductive, or possibly leave. An organisation which emphasises financial rewards should not be surprised if the workers' response to any new initiative is 'What's in it for us?'

To summarise this section, an understanding of individual behaviour, and what drives and motivates it, is important for managers, but it should always be seen in an organisational context. Remember this when you study the material on Human resource management in sport in the next chapter.

Managing groups and teams

'Every manager is a manager of people.' This is heard so often that it has become a cliché (one that is ignored, for example, by every manager who tries to pass off 'people problems' to their human resources specialists). But it encapsulates a profound truth: that managers only achieve what they do through the efforts of other people. So managers of organisations have to be aware of how to produce the best from other people.

We have dealt briefly with issues which arise in managing people as individuals, and this is developed in much greater depth in the next chapter; here we concentrate on looking at their behaviour in groups. Managers need to understand that people may behave differently when working in groups or teams – a group is more than simply a collection of individuals. Knowledge of some of the forces which shape group behaviour is invaluable as a management tool.

For example, we often talk of 'peer group pressure', or *esprit de corps* – influences that may have a profound effect on the behaviour of people when they work collectively, rather than on their own. Sometimes these effects may be positive for the organisation – for example, schoolteachers and army officers use them to help enforce discipline. The success of many leading sports teams has been ascribed to this, rather than the individual skills of their members. Sometimes they can be negative – for example, an individual may feel inhibited from giving as much effort as they could for fear of being thought to be 'sucking up' to management. Or a group may have established its own 'norms' which are below those wanted by the organisation, and group members adhere to these norms for fear of retribution from the group. Some sports clubs have in the past allowed or even encouraged players to socialise in heavy drinking sessions – initially it was thought this would help to build 'team spirit', but later the damaging effects on performance became obvious and were difficult to eradicate. (Group norms are standards of behaviour and performance that develop from the interaction of the group. Although they emerge informally, they can often influence people as much as, or even more than, the formal standards laid down by management.)

When managing people as a group, and even more so when considering whether to establish a group to perform a task, managers need to consider the likely balance of these 'process gains' – the positive effects – and 'process losses' – the negative effects – likely to flow from group working. Both are likely to be greater, the more *interdependent* are the members of the group – in other words, to what extent does the work of one person depend on the work of another?

The simplest form of interdependence is 'pooled' interdependence.[1] Here each individual can work on their own, and at their own pace, but the outcome depends upon them all performing their own work satisfactorily, when it is all brought together. Here, of course, people may not even have to work together as a group at all, but there may be process gains if having them work together – for example, in an open plan office – helps encourage performance, or monitor slacking. However, there may also be losses if their working together encourages wasteful social interaction, or the development of inefficient group norms. On the other hand, if interaction between people is deliberately suppressed, this can reduce efficiency. For example, unbeknown to each other, they may be duplicating the same work; and often 'social interaction' is not wasteful at all, but helps remove feelings of isolation,

---

[1] The original work on which this analysis of interdependence was based was published by Thompson (1967).

can satisfy the very human need for social contact and can build positive *esprit de corps*. Remember that group norms can have positive as well as negative effects – a group may take pride in its performance which leads it to exceed what is expected by management.

All of the preceding also applies to 'sequential' interdependence. Here one person's work depends on another's being done first. This is epitomised in manufacturing industry by the assembly line, but also affects all sorts of other work – for example a sports team's performance when on tour could be affected by the efficiency with which those responsible for travel arrangements, hotel bookings, etc., have done their job. (The underperformance of many British athletes at the 1960 Rome Olympics was ascribed to poor planning and scheduling of their accommodation, allowing insufficient time for acclimatisation. In contrast, 50 years on, many participating teams at the 2010 Football World Cup were researching and booking accommodation, training facilities and so on even before qualifying.) There are many gains to be had from this type of interdependence – for example, the ability of people to specialise – but a potential loss is that everyone can only proceed at the speed of the slowest; and that the whole 'chain' is only as strong as its weakest link. A failure by one part of the organisation impacts on all the rest.

The greatest interdependence is 'reciprocal' interdependence – I cannot do my job unless you do yours, and vice versa. This is where it really makes sense to talk of a 'team', and the best examples are in team sports, where success depends on the performance of everybody, and not least on their willingness to support and cover for colleagues who are underperforming. Here it makes sense to redefine your own job along the following lines: 'My job is to help *us* perform well'. The potential process gains are the greatest, but so are the potential losses. For example, any member of the team may reason that as long as the others are performing, they can take it easy; and if the others aren't performing, why should they try anyway? The opportunities for 'social loafing' of this sort are at their greatest, not least because in a team situation it is very difficult to detect. And other members of the team may rapidly grow frustrated, and *de*motivated, if they feel they are being required to 'carry' other people who aren't pulling their weight.

Table 7.1 summarises these different types of interdependence.

Effective management of groups and teams also requires attention to the type of people in the group – for example their age, skills, background and personality. If group members are very similar, the group is likely to be more *cohesive* – that is, more willing to work together and contribute to group goals. Other factors that are likely to contribute to cohesiveness

Table 7.1 Types of interdependence in a group

Type of interdependence	Examples of process gains	Examples of process losses
'Pooled' (all work separately, pool the results)	Division of labour 'Audience' and 'co-action' effects ('peer group pressure')	Wasteful duplication of effort Co-ordination costs
'Sequential' (my work depends on you doing yours first)	Economies of scale Specialisation, 'assembly line' effects	Governed by the slowest, or 'weakest link'
'Reciprocal' (we're continually dependent on each other)	Motivation Positive support and help from other team members	Opportunities for free riding

include the size of the group (large groups are likely to be less cohesive), past successes and a sense of exclusivity, and outside groups with which one is in rivalry. Managers can build more cohesive groups by manipulating these factors – for example, by 'bringing through' a group of young players from the youth to the first team most of the conditions for high cohesiveness are likely to be met – but beware! Cohesive groups can be a major source of process gains, and increased productivity, as long as the goals of the group are well aligned with those of the organisation. If they are not, they may be a positive hindrance.

Another factor that contributes to the effective functioning of groups is a balance of *role*s that people play within it. A well-balanced group requires a number of roles to be undertaken – for example, not everyone can be a leader, and there is a place both for those who can plan what has to be done, and those who can make sure it is finished on time. The group may need someone who can contribute creative ideas, and someone who can be 'practical', and check that ideas are practical, and can be resourced. There is a role for people who can keep the group working together happily, and also for those who can make sure it does not lose sight of the job to be done.

Recognition of the different roles to be played within a group gives an insight into effective leadership. Being a 'leader' is best viewed as fulfilling a particular *group role*, as it is possible to conceive of a group functioning without a leader, but a leader without followers is meaningless. In this context, effective leaders are likely to be those who identify the greatest need in their followers – whether it be for guidance, training, motivation, or whatever – and provide it. Some followers – for example, young and inexperienced members of the organisation – probably require a rather authoritarian leader who can tell them what to do, and how to do it. More experienced members, who probably have useful ideas to contribute, probably appreciate a leader who takes a more 'participative' approach, and puts more effort into building harmony and motivation.

In recent years there has been a fashion for promoting 'teams' in the workplace, as if these were always the best basis on which to organise. In practice, some work is best organised on an individual basis. The manager must first ask: what is it that needs to be done, and if I form a group to do it, what is the likely balance of process gains and losses? If a group is to be formed, how cohesive should it be, and how can I affect this? What roles have to be carried out within it – do I have the people who are suited to these roles? Last but not least, do people have the necessary skills to work in teams? Not everyone is naturally suited to this – for example, are they prepared to trust other people; do they have the necessary communication skills? – and extensive training may be required. In professional team sports there are such obvious advantages to be gained from effective teamwork in the actual playing of the game that it is tempting to believe that the rest of the organisation must benefit from being run on the same lines, but this is not necessarily the case – for example, a better playing surface may be produced where it is the unambiguous responsibility of a single individual.

 ## Communication

Inside organisations, we have many options as to how we communicate with each other – verbally, in writing, over the phone or by email; face to face, individually or in groups. Yet many organisational failures, large and small, are often put down to a 'failure of communication'. Why is this?

It is important to remember that there are three key elements to communication:

- the sender;
- the message; and
- the recipient.

If you 'send' a 'message' you presumably have some purpose. For example, if you ask someone to 'check if the mail has come', what do you expect them to do? Report back to you? Bring the mail with them? Open the mail and respond to it? If it hasn't come, and you're expecting a confirmation from a customer or supplier, phone them up and find out what's going on? The important point is, does the recipient know what you want them to do?

As the sender, you must always try to imagine the *context* in which the recipient receives your message, because this will govern how they respond to it. The 'bureaucratic' approach to this problem is to write messages in a standard, unambiguous way, and send them to people whose job description and/or expertise will mean they know exactly what they are supposed to do with it. So a secretary may know that it is their job, on collecting the mail, to open it, arrange standard responses to routine enquiries, and take the rest to the manager for action. In Rugby Union, at a line out, the hooker will call out a coded instruction to his forwards so that they know where he intends to throw the ball and therefore what they should do, in a similar way to the signals exchanged between baseball pitchers and catchers.

If it is not possible to standardise communication in this way, then we need other ways to clarify the context. Alternatives include:

- **Include the context in the message**. For example, 'Please check the mail – I'm looking out for that confirmation from the bus company – if it's not there please phone them and ask what is going on'.

- **Allow two-way communication**. Allow the recipient to check back with you what you want them to do, and why – don't be tempted to say 'Just do it!' Quite apart from anything else, they might impart useful information to you, for example that the bus company have just phoned to confirm the booking.

- **Consider face-to-face communication**. We don't only communicate with what we say, but also how we say it, through our body language, etc. For example, the recipient will get a much clearer idea of how important the message is if they see that you are agitated about it.

- **Use group meetings**. Communicating to a group allows them to see the context of the message. ('If Baljit would check the mail, and let Les know if the confirmation is through, we can get the team together, and I'll confirm our arrival time.') It also allows members of the group to share ideas and discuss problems.

 ## Organisational culture

We often talk of an organisation exhibiting or being pervaded by a particular type of 'culture' – e.g. a 'blame culture' 'an innovative culture' or 'a culture of fear'. Management 'guru' Tom Peters has claimed that he can assess an organisation by a few minutes in its reception area, as it exudes and demonstrates the organisation's culture.

What do we mean by 'culture'?

There are a large number of definitions of culture, but it is generally agreed it is *not* simply a question of 'how things are done around here', though this may be the most notable element. The notion of 'culture' goes deeper: it also refers to similar ways of thinking, and, at a deeper level still, our subconscious or unconscious psychological frameworks for ordering our experiences and perceptions. 'How things are done' both *reflects* these and *reinforces* them. For example, in a particular organisation, people may wear business suits to work. Why? Because that's what they believe is the norm. And everybody does it, so that belief is reinforced.

When observing cultures we may notice what Gert Hofstede calls 'practices' – for example, the 'rituals' (how people behave, the language they use, the stories they tell which reinforce the culture, such as what the group has achieved in the past, or what was done to it, even the 'heroes' – the present or past members admired and held up as examples) – but it is the *values* of the culture which give these practices meaning, and are the most deep-rooted parts of the culture.

The significance of this 'psychological' aspect of culture (as opposed to the observable practices) can be seen when considering how an organisation tackles a totally new problem. If there is a 'team culture' there will be an immediate tendency to involve people collectively; if individualistic, then emphasis may be placed upon the efforts of people working on their own to come up with ideas, and to tackle 'their part' of the problem. Again, in either scenario, how much emphasis is placed on building consensus? 'A lot' will mean that a solution will be sought (however arrived at) that commands widespread support; 'not much' means that 'consensus' will not be regarded as an important factor in deciding what is the 'best' course of action.

Importance of culture

Particular cultures are compatible with other aspects of management and organisation. For example, a culture which encourages concern for detail, stability and adherence to process will fit better with a bureaucratic rather than non-bureaucratic system. An organisation which seeks to pursue a strategy of growth through innovation will find it easier to do so if it has a culture which puts a high value on creativity, and a low value on stability. Human resource management policies which emphasise teamwork and/or personal development are more likely to flourish in a supportive culture.

Subcultures

Within a dominant culture there may be a number of subcultures – e.g., the sales and research departments of an organisation may have distinctive cultures. For example, to the designers of a new sports kit and the people whose job it is to sell it, the simple word 'urgent' may have a totally different meaning. The former may have months to develop a new design, but the latter have much sharper deadlines – the majority of sales occur in a few weeks after product launch before the new season. So for some groups 'urgent' may mean 'in the next couple of months', but for others 'by 3.30 this afternoon'. It is worth noting that sometimes this 'clash of cultures' may be so great that a major problem for the organisation – its management – may be to find ways to keep the different sections 'pulling together'. The managers of the different sections may need to be particularly skilled in appreciating the differences in the different cultures, and in negotiating methods of working together that keep the different parts 'pulling in the same direction', rather than trying to impose a culture which is appropriate for one on another.

Impact of culture on behaviour

The effect of a culture, or subculture, on its members depends not just on the *extent* to which it is shared, but the *intensity* with which it is shared. We may all (in a group) be comfortable doing things the way they are, but does that matter that much to us compared with, say, the survival of the firm, or our own job prospects, or a pay rise? An issue for a globalised business can be: what will have the strongest impact on how a particular national branch of the company performs and behaves, the 'organisational' culture or the national culture of the host country? Hofstede's research indicates that while it is possible for an organisational culture to override national ones, this requires a very strong 'corporate culture'. In industry, transnational firms often try to develop this by training, and by moving managers around between different geographical settings. It can be a greater problem where an international organisation is more federal in nature, and where the members are representatives of national organisations, within which they retain significant responsibilities. This of course is true of many international sports organisations.

Some famous 'models' of culture

The Harrison/Handy model

Charles Handy has popularised the idea (originally put forward by Harrison) that organisational cultures can be typified as:

- **Power** (e.g. the small entrepreneurial firm). There is little emphasis on formal procedures and job descriptions; the organisation revolves around one or a few people who control all its resources. Tasks tend to be undertaken on the basis of direct instructions from the power-holders, or, in their absence, on the basis of what subordinates know, or believe, the power-holders would want. Jobs are ill-defined; decisions are made quickly. Speed is often possible as people are often able to decide what to do on their knowledge of 'the boss' and what s/he wants, so formal communication and instructions aren't necessary. This type of culture is typical of small businesses, but also of some political dictatorships. In individual sports, such as golf or tennis, many players surround themselves with professional and technical assistants who operate in this way. In team sports, some long-serving and successful soccer managers have successfully created this type of culture revolving around themselves; but problems can arise if this causes clashes with other types of culture – for example if the soccer club is only part of a larger organisation with a different culture.

- **Role** (e.g. the classic bureaucracy). There is an emphasis on rationality, order and predictability. Emphasis is put on doing your own job, in the correct way, following the laid-down procedures of the organisation. This culture fits well with 'bureaucratic' structures and procedures. The day-to-day commercial operations of many sports organisations (e.g. stadium maintenance) may exhibit a subculture of this type.

- **Task** (e.g. emphasis on new technologies, project teams). The emphasis is on problem solution, and harnessing human and other resources to tackling a succession of new and unpredictable challenges. You don't expect to concentrate on simply your own role, but bring your skills to bear wherever they help solve the problems of the organisation. This culture is often found in organisations where teamwork and project-based operations are common. The actual playing of team sports exhibits this type of culture.

- **Person** (where key individuals have a high degree of autonomy). In the first three cultures the individual is subordinate to the organisation. Here the picture is reversed – the organisation is there to support the work of (typically highly skilled) individuals. Examples include medical general practices and some university departments. Some sports agencies, and, of course, the 'entourage' of individual sports stars mentioned earlier, may also reflect this culture, as their only purpose is to further the interest of their star clients.

Exhibit 7.1 A party game – what does someone do for a living?

Ask someone what they do for a living. Suppose they work for Lord Chadwick on the Beech Estate as a gamekeeper. How do they reply to your question?

'I work for Lord Chadwick' = power culture

'I work for the Beech Estate' = role culture

'I work in gamekeeping' = task culture

'I'm a gamekeeper, and a ****** good one' = person culture

The Deal and Kennedy model – risks and feedback

Deal and Kennedy (1982) identify two key factors that shape culture:

- the *types of risks* assumed – high or low. Are the consequences of actions or decisions potentially very serious for the individual or organisation?

- and the *speed of feedback from decisions* – fast or slow. How long does it take before you know what the consequences of actions or decisions are?

On the basis of this they identify four main organisational cultural types.

- **'Tough guy/macho'** cultures (high risk, fast feedback) tend to be characterised by rapid 'gut instinct' decision making, high individualism, competitiveness, even superstition. Examples include television, advertising, and professional sports organisations.

- **'Bet your company'** cultures (high risk, slow feedback) may exhibit high regard for expertise, meticulous planning, and mentoring of younger by older staff. Examples include investment banking, the armed forces.

- **'Work hard, play hard'** cultures (low risk, rapid feedback) – high volume, low risk activities such as mass retailers and many (particularly amateur) sports teams. There is likely to be an emphasis on hard work, teams and dynamism.

● 'Process' cultures (low risk, slow feedback) – employees find it difficult to measure directly the success of what they do (at least in the short run) but, unlike in a 'bet your company' culture, are unlikely to make decisions that could be catastrophic for the organisation. Hence there is an emphasis on 'doing things right', rather than on the long-term outcome, and the value placed on mastering and maintaining the internal systems. Examples include public administration and national sports administration bodies. (Interestingly, banking often used to be quoted as one such occupation – before the 'Credit Crunch', which has been widely ascribed to banks taking, perhaps unconsciously, inordinate risks. It may be that the Credit Crunch was due at least in part to the predominant culture of organisations getting out of step with the realities of their business.)

Exhibit 7.2 Another party game

Deal and Kennedy (1982) believe that certain types of physical recreation appeal to people in different types of culture. So what type of physical activity do you take part in?

'Tough guy/macho' types like highly competitive individual games – like squash

'Work hard, play hard' types like team sports

'Bet your company' types like games where the outcome remains in doubt as long as possible – like golf

'Process' types like activities where the emphasis is more on the participation than the outcome – like swimming, aerobics or jogging

---

Structure, behaviour, communications and culture – bringing them all together

It should by now be clear that these four aspects of organisations cannot be dealt with in isolation from each other. For example, a bureaucratic structure tends to go with a 'role' or 'process' culture; communication is likely to be hierarchical, and be written, in a standardised form; and there is probably more emphasis on individual specialised work. Team-based organisations, in contrast, may have 'task' or 'work hard/play hard' cultures, be flatter and less hierarchical, and encourage network, verbal communication and meetings. This can extend to other aspects of management and organisations that we have not considered here. For example, in making *decisions*, should managers consult their subordinates, or even delegate decisions to them? In a bureaucratic hierarchy, subordinates may be used to the manager making decisions at one level, but leaving lower level decisions to them to take, as they fall within their area of competence and responsibility. What is seen as 'excessive' communication and consultation about decisions may be viewed as unnecessary, unexpected and disruptive. In contrast, in another organisation, where it is felt that subordinates have vital inputs to make into decisions, or where it is felt that commitment by subordinates to decisions is vital (so they need to feel that their views, ideas and fears have been taken into account), consultative decision making, built around meetings and verbal communication, may be the norm.

Managers need to be aware of how these organisational and work practices link together for organisational efficiency. At any one time there are always fads and fashions in management, whether it be for teamwork, electronic communication, 'culture change' or whatever. It is important to recognise that, while there is no 'magic formula' for success, it is more likely to come if management recognise that organisational structure, communications, culture, people management methods and decision making are part of a single 'system', one part of which affects all the others, and no part of which can be treated or altered in isolation.

Case 7.2 The changing face of Formula One: F1 teams in 2011

by John Old and Martin Smith

A Formula One 'team' typically employs between 140 and 500 people. These range from business specialists such as accountants and secretaries, who could, and often have, worked in quite different types of business, through specialist engineers to race drivers on seven-figure contracts.

As with most sporting organisations, while the team may have aspirations to win its tournament – in this case the F1 World Championship, for either drivers or constructors – this is not a realistic business goal for the medium term, as in the last decade only five teams (Ferrari, Renault, Maclaren, Brawn and Red Bull) have achieved this. Realistically, success is measured in terms of achieving 'points' (top ten) and in particular 'podium' (top three) finishes in races.

In recent years teams have had to cope with a number of major changes, both externally and within the sport. Partly as a result of the economic environment, major auto manufacturers such as Honda, Toyota and BMW have withdrawn from direct involvement in running teams, and teams have had to work hard to maintain sponsorship and marketing income. Rule changes and a threat (so far unimplemented) of a 'budget cap' have also forced teams to rethink and reorganise. One particularly significant change has been in the supply of engines and how they are used. There are now only three engine suppliers – Ferrari, Mercedes and Cosworth – and there are strict FIA rules on how these are used. For example, all teams must now use a standardised electronic controller. (This standardised controller was introduced by the FIA as a means of wresting back the contents and applications within the controller software. For many years the FIA had banned the use of 'driver aids', meaning such things as 'launch control', traction control and stability control, within the controller software, but this was notoriously difficult to police and teams were circumventing the rules by clever manipulation of the engine controllers.) These changes have weakened the previously intimate relations between the teams and engine suppliers, but have placed an even greater premium on skill and ingenuity within these constraints.

Business planning, and activities, work in a series of cycles of decreasing length. There is a long-term objective, achievable only over several seasons, to develop better technology, and better cars, that will increase the likelihood of points or podium finishes.

(continued)

On an annual basis, there is the need to generate sufficient revenues[2] to maintain the team, largely through sponsorship and marketing, and negotiate supplies of competitive key components such as engines and tyres. During the season, there is a two-weekly cycle of competing in the current race and preparing for the following one.

Figure 7.1 is a representation of the organisational structure of the team. This may look unnervingly complex to people familiar with much more straightforward 'organisation charts', but attempts to capture the reality of a number of groups whose

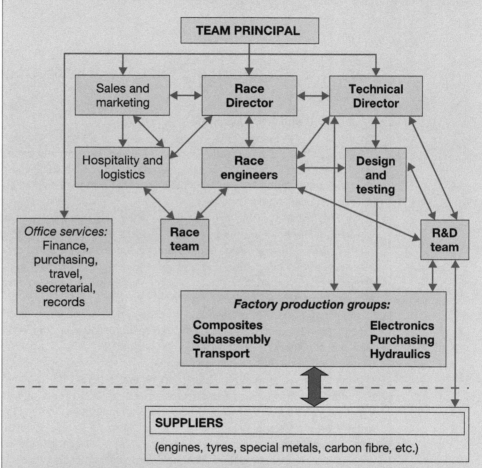

Figure 7.1 Organisation of a Formula One team, c. 2011

Notes:

Production is 'factory based', working what would be considered 'normal' hours unless urgent parts are required due to crashes, parts failure or new designs.

Design is again 'factory based' but may attend test sessions with the test team, and also work closely with the R&D dept.

Office services is the sort of organisation one would expect to find in any place of manufacturing, with the exception of sales and marketing which will attend test sessions and races to provide hospitality support to sponsors and sponsors' guests.

(*continued*)

---

[2] Teams are reticent about publishing their costs or expenditures, but independent estimates range from around $120 million to over $400 million per annum.

work interacts and overlaps. In addition, there are intricate relations with outside firms (the 'boundaries' of the team are shown by broken lines). Tyre suppliers, for example, are keen that their products are seen to perform well, and will work intimately with members of the Formula One team to improve performance (shown on the chart by the interaction between the Chief Engineer of the suppliers and the team Technical Director, and between the team R&D and suppliers). Indeed, at times employees of the supplier may be based with the team – for example with the specialist groups – and working alongside them in a way that would make it difficult for an outsider to distinguish the difference between them. This interaction may link back to the suppliers of the suppliers – for example, from the team's R&D, to the engine supplier's race engineering group, to the latter's R&D section, and then back to their suppliers.

These working practices involving the suppliers, if anything, have been further reinforced by both the recent rule changes and the threat of a 'budget cap' on the teams.

The different business horizons of the firm are reflected in the working patterns of the various groups within the organisation. For example, the race team are involved in intensive bursts of preparation for the races, when all-night working may not be uncommon, while the R&D team are working on a more regular pattern towards longer term objectives – though even they may find themselves diverted to a short-term problem such as a cure for a 'grenading' gearbox or failing crankshaft. FIA rules now ban in-season testing, so considerable responsibility has fallen on engineers running computer-assisted engineering programmes. These serve the race, design and R&D teams, and their work patterns may therefore reflect whatever is the greatest imperative. While the specialist work groups have the most regular work patterns, at any time these may have to be adjusted to meet urgent requirements of the race, design or R&D teams.

In-factory activities are typically organised with managers and section heads reporting back and up. Race team mechanics are organised via the Chief Mechanic, who liaises with (and receives instructions from) the Technical Director, the Senior Chassis Race Engineer, and the Senior Engine Race Engineer. He passes on instructions to the No. 1 Mechanic on each car (No. 1 Mechanic is responsible for the preparation of the car), who in turn is aided by the No. 2 Mechanic, and then the Front End and Rear End Lead Mechanics.

The Engine and Chassis Race Engineers then also liaise with the No. 1s for their relevant car. The Senior Race Engineer (in both chassis and engine areas) give instructions to and receive information from their subordinate engineers. At any time boundaries can be crossed as needs dictate. It is not uncommon for Senior Race Engineers to join in with working on a chassis or to be found preparing a race engine. In these circumstances they will be told what to do by the Engine Dresser (a specialised mechanic whose function is to fit the engine to the chassis).

The intricacies of this structure, and its links with suppliers, places particular demands on the organisation. There is network rather than vertical communication. With sporting success possibly being measured in tenths, or even hundredths of a second, expertise and ideas are invaluable, wherever they are located in the organisation. Post-race Monday meetings of all employees (the 'prayer meetings') help set priorities. Employees must be prepared to work flexibly, and be comfortable with joining ad hoc project teams. Managers must be able to negotiate their requirements, rather than rely upon being able to command what they need. For example, at any

(continued)

one time, the immediate orientation of the business – which tasks take priority – must be negotiated by the Race and Technical (and even Sales and Marketing) Directors. There is obviously a danger that one or other of these could prevail on a consistent basis, which could result in either the short- or medium-term interests of the team being overlooked. The Team Principal can intervene to arbitrate, but if this were to happen on a regular basis it would represent a failure in the organisation. Similarly, at the level of the engineers in the specialist groups, while specialist skills are valued, it is also important that individuals recognise and are prepared to adapt to the needs of other sections.

Discussion questions

1 Why does an Formula One team have such an intricate structure? Would this be appropriate or necessary in other sports organisations, for example a soccer or rugby club?

2 Managers in Formula One teams must often deal with people who work elsewhere in the automobile industry, where organisation structures are often much more 'bureaucratic' in the sense described in the text. What 'culture clashes' might this give rise to?

3 In the case it states that if the Team Principal were to have to intervene on a regular basis to arbitrate disputes, this would represent a failure of organisation. Why, and what sense?

4 Although there is significant international ownership and sponsorship of Formula One teams, most are still based in (Southern) England. What are the implications and advantages of this from an organisational point of view?

Keywords

Bureaucracy; control; culture; group norms; leadership; organisation.

Guided reading

Robbins and Judge (2006) gives a very readable introduction to all of the topics covered in this chapter. Mullins (2007), and Robbins and Coulter (2007) give more depth, explanations of relevant research, and a wealth of examples. For an expanded view of the issues and topics in this chapter, particularly organisational design and culture, set in a sports context, see Slack (1997). Chapter 6 of Pedersen et al. (2011) is a brief but rather intense overview of organisational behaviour in a sports context, and shows how different aspects of organisational design and behaviour work together as a single 'system'.

For a really in-depth view of modern thinking about organisations, see Morgan (1997). This is a deliberately challenging book, but for someone who wants to study organisations it provides a stimulating variety of different perspectives on what organisations are, and how they work.

For further reading on corporate culture, see Deal and Kennedy (1982) and especially Handy (1991). The latter uses a metaphor (which has become quite famous) of four Greek Gods to represent the four cultures, and explores what the 'worship' of these four gods means for an organisation.

Smith and Stewart (1999) includes chapters on organisational structure and culture. Parkhouse (2001) has chapters on organisational design and group decision making.

Recommended websites

The website businessballs.com (www.businessballs.com) contains a wealth of short, punchy definitions, articles, and activities on business topics, many of which are relevant to this chapter.

References

Deal, T.E. and Kennedy, A.A. (1982) *Corporate Cultures: The Rites and Rituals of Corporate Life*, Harmondsworth: Penguin Books.

Handy, C. (1976) *Understanding Organisations*, Harmondsworth: Penguin Books.

Handy, C. (1991) *The Age of Unreason*, Harvard, MA: Harvard Business Press Review.

Harrison, R. (1972) 'Understanding your organisation's character', *Harvard Business Review* (May–June), 119–28.

Hofstede, G. (1994) *Cultures and Organisations: Software of the Mind*, London: Profile Books.

Morgan, G. (1997) *Images of Organization*, London: Sage.

Mullins, L.J. (2007) *Management and Organisational Behaviour*, 8th edn, Harlow: FT/Prentice-Hall.

Parkhouse, B.L. (2001) *The Management of Sport*, 4th edn, New York: McGraw Hill.

Pedersen, P.M., Parks, J.B., J. Quarterman and L. Thibault (2011) *Contemporary Sport Management*, 4th edn, New York: McGraw Hill.

Robbins, S.P. and Judge, T.A. (2012) *Essentials of Organizational Behavior*, 11th edn, Upper Saddle River, NJ: Prentice Hall.

Slack, T. and Parent, M.M. (1997) *Understanding Sports Organizations*, 2nd edn, Champaign, IL: Human Kinetics.

Smith, A. and Stewart, B. (1999) *Sports Management: A Guide to Professional Practice*, St Leonards NSW: Allen & Unwin.

Suutari, R. (2001) 'Organizing for the new economy', *CMA Management*, April.

Thompson, J.D. (1967) *Organizations in action*, New York: McGraw-Hill.

Watt, D.C. (1998) *Sports Management and Administration*, London: E & F Spon.

Human resource management in sport

Terrence Wendell Brathwaite, Coventry Business School

Learning outcomes

Upon completion of this chapter the reader should be able to:

- explain the main theories of motivation;
- apply them to different professional sports scenarios;
- assess the importance of human resources (HR) to the overall strategic position of an organisation;
- explain the key functions of HR within an organisation;
- explain and assess the key HR processes within an organisation;
- explain the factors of human resource management (HRM) which are particular to professional sports.

 ## Overview

In this chapter[1] we explore the essence of managing the human capital in sports organisations. The people factor in sports can essentially be placed into the following categories – technicians (i.e. amateurs, self-employed professionals, employed professionals), technical specialists (including operatives and support staff) and managers (who may be either

---

[1] Dedicated to my two daughters and talented female (blue cord) *capoeiristas*: Tesha-Dawn at Oxford University Medical School and Alyssa at Cambridge University Law School. Respectively, you are my eternal 'pride' and 'joy'. Axé!

volunteer or paid administrators). In its contextual criss-crossing of each category, this chapter's trajectory will be threefold and based on a voyage of discovery not in seeking new landscapes, but in having new eyes for responding quickly to market forces in this generation of uncompromising global competition. First of all, we shall consider the nature and dynamics of psychological motivation in people management and leadership performance within the sports industry, bearing in mind how *power* is performed and manifested by 'playing without fear'. At this juncture, the discussion will centre on the function of people management and leadership as being further determined from a triad of ancillary fundamental aspects:

- a system of *interaction* – that is, the basic nature of any interpersonal relations;
- a system of *influence* – in other words, a system of reciprocal impact between a sports organisation's situational factors, the human resources manager or leader (coach) and the subordinates (employees, athletes or team) upon each other;
- and a system of *empowerment* – within the employer–employee relationship, human resource managers or leaders have a greater potential for exerting influence, due to the intrinsic power of their position.

Savants in management science have suggested that the main underlying dispositional attribute which correlates this threesome to managerial leadership is *intelligence*, which is generally acknowledged as the ability to cope with uncertainties in a discerning fashion via planning, organising, co-ordinating and evaluating various options of action using innate cognitive abilities (or 'common sense'). But while the twentieth century has witnessed a continuous review of intelligence as an oversimplified notion,[2] the advent of the millennium has ushered in a modernistic model of multiple intelligences that is more reflective of the phenomenal matrix of psychosocial diversity and personal excellence in sports management today. Moreover, neuroscientific research (see Cooper et al., 2009 and Knutson et al., 2003) confirms that the presence of a thought in the mesial prefrontal cortex of the brain, whether impulsive or spawned in response to environmental stimuli received through our five senses, has been determined to contain autonomic control, emotional introspection and even reaction control. This is particularly in response to monetary rewards, à la professional basketball, football or the over 200-year-old tales of bribery and match-fixing in cricket, which as a team game was initially organised as a means for wealthy eighteenth-century English landowners to gamble. The chapter thus commences by exploring the reality that there is more than one way of being a discerning motivator and manager of people in the sports industry, where, like all places of work, there can be found any and every emotion – affirmation, rejection, love, anger, envy, jealousy, sense of well-being and a sense of emotional patterns revisited – that together make up part of the human experience.

---

[2] Cross-cultural psychologists (see Segall et al., 1990) have challenged the stereotypical idea of intelligence by advocating that just because a test is identified as an intelligence test does not guarantee that it actually measures intelligence. The line of reasoning has been made, perhaps most convincingly, by earlier empirical studies which establish that benchmark IQ intelligence tests measure only the current aptitude of individuals to partake efficiently in Western (Euro-American and Australian) schools (see LeVine, 1970: 581). Therefore, it is established within a hard-core scientific context that this is all IQ tests do measure and whether they measure anything else is quite dubious.

Within this context, the chapter also asserts that the key to understanding the motivational and multiple intelligence theories of human experience in sports management is the fact that the workplace is not a mechanised apparatus, because those who inhabit it are not mechanical appliances as defined by Frederick Taylor's scientific management ideals and re-manifested throughout our modern-day impersonal corporate leadership culture(s).[3] To help explain the many social and emotional aspects of motivational relationships within the sports industry, consideration will be given to a poignant case study featuring the 'bodymind-kinesomatic' activity in the Brazilian Capoeira Roda,[4] followed by a situational analysis of an anthropomaximological (AML) approach to inspirational leadership in American high school basketball, which deem powerlessness as the root cause of many human relations problems in the workplace today, where physical and mental potential are sometimes squandered or not fully discovered. The AML approach embraces the analysis of the reserve potential of the physical motor system and the psychofunctional system of a healthy employee (or sports competitor), and the broad beliefs controlling their performance under extreme stress conditions, when thought becomes tacit.

Supported by a complementary case study which signifies the advantage of positive feedback loops at work in the Rugby League, the chapter will then move on to explore the key dimensions of a sports organisation and the importance of developing an *Ubuntu* value-based leadership philosophy (humanitarian and communitarian) and a 'Yenza' (proactive and synchronous) strategy for managing employees. Within this context, there are obvious lessons for the industrialised world from the rest of the world, and consideration will thus be given to the historiographical constitution of the HR Manager's influential authority, and the current need to develop a more focused, coherent but flexible 'people-centric' strategy in a rapidly changing and globalised sports milieu. By acknowledging the development of such a holistic stratagem from which mutually caring attitudes and actions of interdependence flow to rekindle the spirit of participatory humanism in the business of sport, the chapter will also address the questions of (a) quality staffing, (b) people programmes and initiatives and (c) the key seven corporate dimensions of sports organisations.

---

[3] Frederick Winslow Taylor was an American engineer who pioneered what is now known as the neo-Cartesian dogma of scientific management, based on the medieval matrix of organisational structure of the monastic military order of the Knights Templar (see Bruno and Thompson, 2000). His functional doctrines provided the 'cornerstone' for work design throughout the early twentieth century. And in many circumstances, those Protestant work ethics and martial virtues of the past have emerged as the vices of the new millennium, whilst the 'survival of the fittest' industrial vices of the past have become the necessities of an existing 'new world order', which involves bullying and overworking staff who are paid to leave their brains outside, bring their bodies into the workplace, and simply be cogs in the organisational wheel (see Swindall, 2010; Tyler, 2010; Head, 2005; Morgan, 1997 and Egan, 1994).

[4] Capoeira or 'Dance of War' is an African-derived martial arts dance game, created in Brazil by slaves from Africa, sometime after the sixteenth century. As a national sport, it is 'played', not fought, and requires the use of intuition and foresight, so the players are not dependent exclusively on the use of physical strength. During the game the *capoeiristas* enter a *Roda* or sacred circle where they skilfully expose the limitations of their opponents while interacting in stylised playful attacks and counter-attacks to percussion-driven music/chants, thus better enabling each competitor to realise their personal inner power. The leading musical instrument is a one-stringed, bow-shaped instrument called a *berimbau* with a gourd attached to one end to give resonance. The *berimbau* is also supported by a drum called an *atabaque* and a *pandeiro* (tambourine).

To conclude, the chapter will address the logistics of managing social and technological change while transforming people performance in professional sports, and volunteer groups through effective communications, 'emotional intelligence' (EQ), an equitable rewards determination process, and the dynamics of current employment legislation with particular emphasis being placed on the importance of dispute procedures, the energies of organisation and innovation in building bridges within the sports company as a learning milieu.

The 'impact of expectancy' and managing people in sport

In a world where the scheme of work, infrastructure and corporate spirit of contemporary sports have been radically influenced and institutionalised by the globalisation of capitalism and its protestant work ethic, HRM in general terms has been charged with becoming too insular as a function and in need of broadening its aspirations transculturally and from an interdisciplinary perspective. Originally instituted in the USA and concerned with the human aspect of enterprise management and employees' relationships with their companies, HRM is underpinned by the findings of industrial psychology and applies consolidated systems and strategies commonly accepted as personnel management (PM) in the UK.

As a significant part of the HRM panorama, PM deals with the more practical, utilitarian and instrumental application of policies and management techniques, including employee resourcing, appraisal, employee training and development, business–employee relations and employment law. However, with businesses across the planet recognising that a competitive advantage and sustained customer contentment are heavily dependent on creating employee satisfaction, corporate strategists are now ensuring that the customer's needs, the company's brands and the commitment of employees are all synchronous. Therefore, as we venture further into this digital age, we see the empowerment of human capital becoming even more of a strategic imperative, while chief executives look for HR functions to move beyond a legalistic 'commitment to the people mantra' and play a greater integral role in getting more out of the minds of employees by really understanding how they learn, create and perform best. In sports, as in other areas, this motivational (rather than aptitudinal) approach to managing human (and intellectual) capital is geared towards delivering value to different parts of the business and making a contribution to improving productivity levels.

To advance their roles and address the monetary and pecuniary rewards synonymous with the 'bottom line', it is important that HR professionals in sports better understand why people behave the way they do and the organisational practices for the optimum utilisation of all human resources. This involves managers, coaches and trainers acknowledging the importance of internal forces and those external to a person that stimulate enthusiasm and devotion to persevere along a particular course of action towards the accomplishment of goals and the accrual of rewards. With reference to sports and other business enterprises, the rewards for an individual's drive to take initiative are both intrinsic and extrinsic. The intrinsic rewards refer to the inner satisfaction one derives from performing and completing a challenging task, while the extrinsic motivating forces are normally the more substantial earnings such as promotion and 'hard currency'. However, while professional sports performers and aspirant professionals are without a doubt animated by money, there are other components which also account for their expectancy of motivation.

Throughout the twentieth century and continuing into the new millennium, sports psychologists have provided a number of different phenomena and various conceptual perspectives to interpret energising, directing and stopping human behaviour. These include:

- **The drive theory.** In terms of sport and physical activity research, drive is the energiser for behaviour while habits (or learned behaviours) account for the direction and pattern of an individual's preferred initiatives during certain stages of the decision-making process (see Hull, 1952 and Spence, 1956).

- **The optimal-level theory.** This model is summarised by the proposal that a congruous relationship exists between the intensity of arousal and the effectiveness of performance during individual decision-making processes (see Landers, 1978).

- **The attribution theory.** This is viewed as a 'common-sense' model individuals use in everyday situations to account for behaviour. Thus they see the result of an action or outcome as being attributed to (a) cultural and socio-environmental contexts, (b) specific properties of the situation, (c) the nature of the activity and (d) the personal traits of the participants/competitors (see Heider, 1958).

When these models of motivation are applied to the sports organisational context, we see them as the inducement factor of an employee's thoughts and actions through appeals to that individual's specific needs and personality to work toward organisational goals. The expectation is that the employee will be able to see that s/he can achieve personal objectives by achieving the company's goals, while the employer can tap the deepest levels of intellectual creativity and the highest levels of productivity of that worker. However, motivation is convoluted by the fact that we are addressing people and their attitudes – both tremendously complex factors in their own right. The employee in the office who has entered into or works under a contract of employment is therefore no different to the employee out of the office, or the athlete on the track, who is working towards a better intuitive understanding of the general AML principles governing normal regulation of the functioning of physiological systems in circumstances of ultra-intense activity. In the same vein, the coach in the gym can be juxtaposed to the employer who seeks to know more about the true potential of the employee as a healthy organism who is socially active and emotionally inspired, while engaged in activities that involve strict occupational selection. On a daily basis s/he transfers to the work environment those attitudes, prejudices, feelings, tensions and emotions developed by the total life pattern of preferred initiatives.

In some way the employer also has to communicate to the employee(s) a sense of mission and organisational vision which focuses on:

- Why is the sports organisation in business?

- What is/should be our purpose?

- What values does it offer to users, the community?

- What are the constituency needs?

- What activities should we undertake/avoid?
- How unique or special is the sports organisation?
- What do we stand for (style, relationship)?

As such, the sports organisation's vision must be systematically checked (see Exhibit 8.1) and objectives recognised at multiple levels, along with the cultivation of a feeling of commitment to these objectives which can only be accomplished via a consistent communication programme based not just on lip-service, but through deeds. Furthermore, for the employees to believe in and be committed to their management, they must be provided with very clear objectives and know that their achievements would finally be given recognition. It is only in a climate such as this that management can expect their staff to be truly motivated, because the integration of human resources and overall company objectives safely establishes the workforce as a supportive or facilitating function, constructing a milieu and a culture within which valuable contributions can be provided by all employees.

This is the crux of the 'HRM' concept and forms a key part of the sports industry's organisational reorientation for 'employee resourcing' in its widest context. It can thus be argued that HRM in sports and other industries today represents a shift in the pragmatics of traditional personnel management, from that of an 'odd job' to being a strategic contribution which focuses not only on obtaining skilled healthy people who are in short supply, but in making the best use of the employees' reserve potential in the mental, psychological and physical spheres of their occupational activity, for the purpose of increasing instruction levels, working capacity and creative longevity. The Sports HR Manager's input to this AML approach can be consolidated through training and development, rewards, organisational culture, strategic planning and checking that the vision is shared (see Senge, 1990: 205–32).

Exhibit 8.1 Motivation and the Sports HR Manager as a visionary

Diagnose the present state of your chosen sport as you perceive it.

Checking the vision of the sports organisation

	Strongly Agree			Strongly Disagree

There is a clear understanding in our sports organisation of the fundamental reasons why we are in business.

1	2	3	4	5

We know what particular values we intend to provide to the users we serve.

1	2	3	4	5

We know what particular values are provided to those who serve in the organisation (volunteers, staff).

1	2	3	4	5

(continued)

We clearly know the needs of the constituencies that we hope to address.

                                                    1   2   3   4   5

We have defined the programmes and services that we will undertake.

       1   2   3   4   5

We have dealt with and stated the activities and temptations that we will avoid.

       1   2   3   4   5

In general, we know what distinguishes us as unique or special in the community we serve.

       1   2   3   4   5

In particular, we know what advantages we have over our competition (other organisations offering programmes in the same sport, other sports, other recreational time pursuits, etc.).

       1   2   3   4   5

We are clear about the values and principles we stand for as an organisation.

       1   2   3   4   5

We are clear about how we intend to operate externally, i.e. with the public and users.

       1   2   3   4   5

Motivation as theory and praxis in HRM

Notably, we have the benefit of recent neurobiological findings that (at least on the atomic level) our human consciousness observes and creates its own 'reality'. This has led to the exciting suggestion from both neuroscientists and management psychologists that human behaviour is motivated by what we observe as our 'reality of needs' (see Pert, 1997; Lucas, 2001). This principle also represents the driving force behind all activities in one or more of our personal unfulfilled needs. The 'reality of needs' here can therefore be easily correlated with the work of Abraham Maslow, the noted behavioural scientist.

Maslow (1943) theorised that human needs are hierarchial in nature and while it is often stated that *Man does not live by bread alone*, the crux of the matter is that this is only 'a reality' for the man who has bread. Maslow's construct on a hierarchy of needs is perhaps the most widely known model which has offered formulae to account for what animates people. He contends that those personal needs which are not satisfied will operate as motivators within the contextual framework of physiological needs, being the most basic, followed by psychological and social needs and ultimately the crowning AML need for self-actualisation (see Figure 8.1).

Within the sports industry we will find individuals (whether technicians, technical specialists or managers) repositioning up and down the hierarchy of needs, with class, age, gender, ethnic origin and other psycho-cultural variables impinging on the definition of needs at the upper levels. At the lower levels, the individual whose tummy is unfilled will tend to be quite obsessed with thoughts about 'bread'. Thus the need to find a meal as soon as possible will be the motivational force behind his behaviour. On the other hand, once

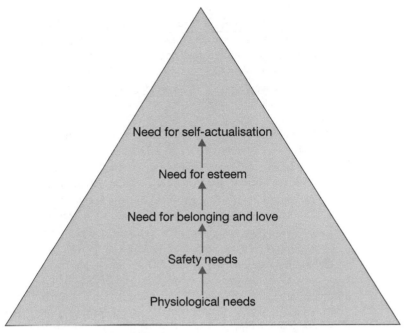

Figure 8.1 Maslow's Hierarchy of Needs

Source: From *Motivation and Personality*, 3rd edn, Pearson Education Inc. (Maslow, A.H., Frager, R.D. and Faidman, J. (1987)).
Reprinted and electronically reproduced by permission of Pearson Education Inc., Upper Saddle River, New Jersey.

that meal has been obtained and the tummy filled, the motivation to find food will no longer be of significance and a higher need will emerge until the individual reaches that AML point of self-actualisation. This is a point where the normal that lies hidden in the pathological becomes manifest (Pavlov, in Kutznetsov, 1982: 282), and s/he simply feels the need to be what s/he must be, in the same way that dolphins have the natural urge to swim and humming birds must fly. This behavioural construct of 'what a wo/man can be s/he would be' is well illustrated in Case 8.1, which features the nature of 'playing without fear' in the Capoeira Roda.

Case 8.1 Motivation and true potentialities within the Capoeira Roda

'Pure love' or 'playing without fear'

> The East has Zen
> Psychoanalysis was developed in the West
> In Brazil we have Capoeira.   (Capoeira, 1992: 106)

According to the laws of aerodynamics as defined by modern physicists, it is asserted that a bumble bee should not be able to fly. However, someone obviously forgot to tell that to the bumble bee. So day by day, it simply proves the scientific definitions wrong and continues to fly anyway with grace and purpose, in spite of the disabling labels of powerlessness tendered by armchair human sceptics, for whom memory of the awe-inspiring sacred laws and power of Nature is simply a matter of convenience.

(continued)

In a similar mode, the Capoeira Roda (i.e. Ring of Liberation) enabled its enslaved African pioneers to find their own ability to dance, communicate and move gracefully behind the disabling labels of oppression and exclusion in the Quilombo dos Palmares of Brazil, over 500 years ago. And today, in spite of such prevailing negative social stratifications, Capoeira at its visceral level acknowledges no class, colour, creed, race or blood, and is genuinely respected by its practitioners – now worldwide – as 'pure love' or 'playing without fear'. In other words, when one enters the Capoeira Roda it's what one learns after one thinks one knows it all that counts. In his book *Capoeira and Candomblé*, Merrell (2005) further contexualises this unique 'music–dance–sport–play' activity when he affirms that there is little or no need for language in the Roda. Rather, there is only a sensing, a consciousness through the *bodymind-kinesomatic* activity.[5] This encapsulates the feeling of what there is to feel deep within the fabric of each player's bones. Moreover, it epitomises an awareness with the inner trust of so-called lower organisms like the ostracised bumble bee, which have not yet been conditioned to surrender to those cognitively constraining 'human virtues of disbelief, skepticism, cynicism, or nihilism' (ibid.: 58).

Still, to induce the Capoeira Spirit in *bodymind-tacit* mindfulness, there must be the *Axé* (pronounced ah-SHEH). This term is the name the Yoruba slaves from Western Africa gave to wo/mankind's 'life force' – a creative principle analogous to the Eastern notion of *qi*.[6] In Capoeira, the phenomenology of that creative force or *élan vital* refers to the good vibes and powerful energy which enables the capoeiristas to know what needs to be done within the sanctum of the Roda, and as a collective of *bodymind-kinesomatic* vibrations, they just do it! In fact, *Axé* and *kinesomatics* represent the fundamental essence of Capoeira, where two *bodyminds* in silent reciprocal discourse negotiate a recursive relationship of *conformity–resistance–change–conformity–resistance–change*, through an intricate vocabulary of personal, stylised, movements. Unified in motion, they complement each other to the extent that, like 'human pylons', both capoeiristas relay a continuum of polyrhythmic and infinite possibilities which instinctively result in a subtle interweaving, yet purposeful performance. To attain this phoenix-like state of transfiguration and to know it can be akin to aspiring towards their highest AML need/ potential, or what the ancient philosophers of the East would call the *Tao* in sport.

Capoeira in the Roda thus becomes a spiritual roadmap to self-discovery, emotional literacy, and to understanding the universal paradoxes of this 'dance of war', wherein the politics is pure, and consequently the savagery simply more refined. As Capoeirista warrior Tesha-Dawn Safiya Brathwaite so eloquently reflected after a recent *Batizado*[7] in 'Capoeira – I Breathe You' (2009):

To know one's self is an unbearable ache.
To contemplate the human condition I cannot bear.
Thoughts live in me, feed off my sweet flesh.
My need to be perfect.
My need to not just be.
I cry,

(*continued*)

[5] That natural intelligence existing within a unified state of body and mind, where one instinctively knows *how* to do things, which then become manifest by imagining (visualisation) and feeling the body going through certain motions, before actually realising those movements. For example, the Jamaican athlete Usain Bolt imagining his winning performance before actually stepping onto the track to *do it*.

[6] Vital energy which flows within all living beings.

[7] Batizado – A baptism into the art of Capoeira.

I yearn and long to be free of the need for you to see that which I need to see in me.

You wrench my soul and I love you because you free me.

But I cannot have you until I learn to free me.

Capoeira – I breathe you.

For you are nothing at all.

As a combative theatre sport, Capoeira is therefore a quintessential experience of processual arrangements, in which it would be futile to exhaust one's mind in an attempt to unify 'defeat and joy', 'struggle and serenity', 'anarchy and peace', 'fear and confidence', since to do so would only connote what the Taoist elders call 'three in the morning'. What is this 'three in the morning'? Consider the story of the man who fed monkeys with chestnuts and said to them: 'Three portions in the morning, four in the afternoon.' The monkeys all became sad. The man then compromised: 'All right then, four in the morning and three in the afternoon.' The monkeys all jumped around with excitement. Note that the food and the quantity had not changed, only the processural arrangement, which initially triggered sadness and then happiness – two sides of the same coin (see Lin, 2007). So, it's what someone learns after they think they know it all that counts in managing the 'three in the morning' processural arrangements of Capoeira – a game which never becomes a finished product. Why? Because there is unrelenting change within the Roda's liberation space and pace, with no fixed rules, tempo or movement repertoire to interrupt the players' motivation to attain their true potentialities.

Of course, what each capoeirista learns during this martial rite of passage is the art of 'pure love' or 'playing without fear' – the *sine qua non* of creative vitality. Such animated fearlessness thus becomes essential to attaining true spiritual awareness, and key to the revivification of those indigenous souls sequestered and beleaguered by the antiseptic staleness of the larger colonial culture. For quite often, oppression comes in the form of convention, and Capoeira has served strategically for centuries as an indigeneous antidote to the oppressive processes of bourgeoisie routinisation in Brazil. But more importantly, it is what each capoeirista manifests in the Roda or Ring of Liberation, when thought (visualisation) becomes tacit and prompts a rise in his/her physical optimum arousal level. At such an instinctive height of consciousness, the players' anxiety, motivation and focus are ideal, and this results in peak performance. From then on, the power and effulgence of their 'improvigraphy'[8] compels and comports all capoeiristas to humbly converge with the spirit of Capoeira (à la the bumblebee in flight) while dancing with great acrobatic athleticism and kinesomatic intelligence, and seeking *moksha*[9] amidst the polyrhythmic rays of Nature's sun.

Finally, it is axiomatic that the messianic spirit of freedom is embodied in the capacity and courage of all capoeiristas to improvise. For whereas indigeneous bodies were once enslaved, indigenous spirits are now emancipated to create and interpret according to 'natural intelligence', and the laws of the moment. It is that basic ability to freely initiate and 'improvigraph' with such *joie de vivre* which denotes one of the central differentiating factors of this African-derived, extralinguistic martial arts from all other martial arts. And as such, Capoeira remains both paramount and indispensable to the salvific struggle for survival and authentic existence in Afro-Brazilian life today. *Axé!*

(*continued*)

---

[8] Improvised movement choreography, created within the spontaneity of the moment.

[9] Sanskrit (*Moksha*) which literally means *release*.

> **Discussion question**
>
> 1 Discuss the cross-cultural prospects and quandaries in applying the motivational psychology of 'pure love' or 'playing without fear' underpinning the 'bodymind-kinesomatic' activity effectively demonstrated in the Brazilian Capoeira Roda, to the empowerment of human capital in a conventional Western sports enterprise you are familiar with.

When a capoeirista enters the Roda, s/he embarks on a *bodymind-kinesomatic* journey of anaesthetising complexity. This enactment demands the biopsychological coordination of a giddying multiplicity of neural and muscular facets in an extremely discriminating yet integrated mode. For instance, picture the African-American basketball legend Michael 'Air' Jordan flying through space, while simultaneously bringing a ball around his body with his right hand and then powering down an acrobatic slam in a National Slam Dunk Exhibition. There is an elaborate interface between his eyes and the hands, as they work in harmony with one another, from action to reaction, and then anticipation of more action through refined movements of attenuation. It is this inner sense of 'e-motion', when thought becomes tacit and the body is in total synchronisation with the mind, that signifies the *bodymind-kinesomatic* activity of Capoeria. In Case 8.1, the message of such a subtle co-dependency between perceptual (visualisation) and motor systems effecting optimum arousal level and rapid-fire peak performance in the game, is quite a poignant one. This is particularly so when one observes that 'traditional' and 'regional' capoeristas who do not essentially play to acquire medals (a tangible reward in sports), are instead quite satisfied to strive for 'personal bests' in their 'improvigraphy' (which can be juxtaposed with aspiring towards their highest AML need or potential).

Of great significance here is the manner in which these capoeristas from all walks of life embody the 'metaphysics of motivation' confirmed by the bumble bee, which aerodynamically should not be able to fly, since its weight-to-lift ratios are all wrong. On the other hand, the saga of the bumble bee itself is no different to that of autistic human beings, who are to all intents and purposes segregated from their psycho-sociocultural milieu in terms of non-verbal communication. Like the bumblebee, they do not know that they are not strong enough, not fast enough, or even not attractive enough, yet they 'keep on flying anyway' with incorruptibility, being driven by their inner voice – a silent, extralinguistic dialogue between the body and the mind: *bodymind*. Such an extraordinary, harmonious co-dependency of *bodymind-kinesomatic* intelligence and spatial awareness oftentimes takes these autistic savants quite effortlessly beyond the boundaries of our traditional comfort zones, and gives the lie to scientific neo-Cartesian claims that wo/mankind's profound wisdom is reductionistic, not integrative, and not related to our underlying dignity: to our *Ubuntu*,[10] flowing, for many, from our resemblance to the universal creative source.

In the turbulent world of American professional sports, the remarkable basketball story in Case 8.2 of Jason McElwain (nicknamed J-Mac) stands as living testimony to this *bodymind-kinesomatic* dynamic of 'pure love' or 'playing without fear', when an autistic player is allowed to fulfil that highest AML need and creates his own slam-dunk scoring bonanza – a feat many sports scientists believe even a professional player would find challenging today.

---

[10] An ancient South African Bantu word meaning humanness.

Case 8.2 J-Mac: autistic person or *bodymind-kinesomatic* spirit in flight?

Born on 1 October 1988 and diagnosed with autism when he was three, J-Mac grew up exhibiting behaviour typical of many autistic children and had trouble interacting with other kids. However, during his teenage years he was enrolled at a number of special schools, where both speech and behavioural therapists helped him to gradually nurture his social and academic skills. J-Mac was always infatuated with basketball, so Jim Johnson, the basketball coach at Greece Athena High School in Rochester, New York, appointed him mascot of the team.

On 15 February 2006, it was Greece Athena v. Spencerport High School, with a major division title at stake. Greece Athena had a substantial lead, so Johnson made the benevolent decision to allow J-Mac to play during the last four minutes, thereby keeping a promise he made to the young lad just before this last game of the season. Although cheered on by a huge ovation from the crowd, J-Mac missed his two initial shots. Disappointed, but not discouraged, Johnson (as he later confirmed) prayed 'Dear God, just get him a basket'. Then the transfiguring power of *bodymind-kinesomatic* intelligence was suddenly released, performed and manifested 'without fear', when J-Mac scored six three-point shots and one two-pointer. By the time he concluded his four-minute fusillade, the crowd dashed onto the court in celebration, and J-Mac had been transformed from an ambitious autistic savant to actual team lead scorer, who declared after the final buzzer rang 'I was on fire. I was hotter than a pistol!' The amateur video[11] of his electrifying exhibition was not only posted on the internet (attracting hundreds of thousands of viewers globally), but it triggered a frenetic scramble for the rights to his life saga by Hollywood agents after being shown on national television.

J-Mac's story evoked such an overwhelming response when it was reported in 2006, that the then American President George W. Bush confessed he wept after seeing the video clip of America's newest improbable hero literally 'flying' in the face of all neo-Cartesian logic and scientific laws of aerodynamics. J-Mac has since appeared on the *Oprah Winfrey Show*, shaken hands with Hillary Clinton, and his performance has been voted the best sports moment of 2006 in an ESPN (cable television network) poll. He also earned a film contract with Colombia pictures, a book contract with a best-selling ghost writer and is now represented by a personal agent at the prominent New York-based William Morris agency. So, is it Jason McElwain: autistic person or *bodymind-kinesomatic* spirit in flight? How about Hollywood slam-dunk hero: hotter than a pistol? I rest my case and await the movie.

Source: Based on Tony Allen-Mills in *The Sunday Times*, 4 March 2010, 24.

Discussion question

2 How do you see the AML principles of benevolent decision making and trust as exemplified by J-Mac's coach, contributing toward managing diversity and increasing the efficacy of HR strategies and practices in the business of sports.

---

[11] See http://www.youtube.com/watch?v=Tui8EOdv_VU&NR=1

'J-Mac's' mother, Debbie McElwin, observed that the whole experience was an immense confidence booster for her son. But it can be further averred that with his transformation from team manager to star of the show, he not only affirmed his leadership 'expectations' as the squad's highest scorer ever, but, approximating the capoeirista warriors in the Roda, he also fortified his self-image of sovereignty in the process. Here we must acknowledge the importance of self-image to motivation and the 'impact of expectancy' when managing people in sports.

Self-image is a person's own view of him/herself. It is:

- learned (acquired through important life experiences);
- moulded by the reactions of others (e.g. parents, peers, coaches);
- susceptible to change;
- extremely important both on and off the sports field.

Self-image also affects:

- motivation (drive to pursue some goal);
- learning (acquisition of new knowledge or new skills);
- athletic performance (as well as performance in other areas);
- personal relationships (liking for others and acceptance by others);
- life satisfaction (realisation of personal goals);
- personal satisfaction (how a person feels about themselves).

It can be argued that Coach Jim Johnson therefore encouraged 'J-Mac' towards cultivating a positive self-image, by:

- showing acceptance;
- offering specific praise;
- giving him personal attention;
- emphasising his self-responsibility as a team mascot.

Coach Johnson also demonstrated a level of interpersonal competence deficient in many non-self-actualised individuals. He showed himself to be an 'emotionally intelligent'[12] sports leader, as opposed to the scientific management style associated with the American engineer F.W. Taylor. As described above, this martial approach to the imposition of 'lean' in workplace organisation and job design is based on the classical principle of giving as much initiative as possible to managerial experts about how tasks are done. These experts

---

[12] In his text *Working With Emotional Intelligence* Daniel Goleman (1998) contends that the world of work has essentially neglected an extremely important array of skills and abilities – those which deal with human relations and emotions. Goleman focused specifically on the need to have appreciation for one's own emotional life, adapting one's own feelings, and understanding the emotions of others, while being able to work with and have empathy for other people. He wrote of various methods to improve our emotional competence (especially where children are concerned), while he averred that the business world in particular would be a more convivial environment if employers and employees nurtured emotional intelligence as conscientiously as they now endorsed cognitive intelligence or the IQ (see also Gardner, 1999). Goleman's stance on the limitations of cognitive intelligence and such related tests is supported quite robustly by Segall et al. (1990: 59) in their earlier publication *Human Behaviour In Global Perspective*.

then define exactly how each meticulous aspect of every job is to be carried out by their acquiescent subordinates, whose psychological contract dictates a simple-minded colonial maxim: 'when the gaffa says jump, we say how high' (see Watson, 1995).

By keeping his promise to J-Mac, Coach Johnson showed he had transcended this dysfunctional (Protestant) work ethic, and skilfully cultivated the healing power of mindfulness, rooted in the ability to give to others, as well as receive from them. This is particularly important in the sphere of human resource management theory, which regards the organisation's human resources as potential 'talent' or investments that can benefit both the firm and the worker if properly managed. We can therefore see the functioning of HRM philosophy in this case study as Coach Johnson signposts J-Mac to his personal growth opportunity. Off the basketball court and into the traditional sports organisation office, where so few managers reach their capacity for 'emotional intelligence' (EQ), implementation of the HRM theory not only establishes personal growth prospects and planned career experiences for employees. Indeed, such activities also result in greater self-actualisation for everyone by capitalising on employees' personnel needs, their capability for career enhancement and overall organisational effectiveness.

By accepting J-Mac for what 'he needs to and must be', Coach Johnson therefore *interacted* with him as a *bodymind-kinesomatic* spirit in flight, rather than merely an autistic person overly excited about basketball. And as a human being, he *influenced* J-Mac's own positive view of himself by his show of respect for his capacity,[13] potentiality[14] and reserve,[15] and *empowered* him towards self-actualisation through a demonstration of concern, while providing a major source of specific but reassuring and informative feedback. This AML approach to HRM contrasts significantly with the Tayloristic scientific management style mentioned above, in which managers perceive their employees mainly as a 'cog in the wheel' of production and planned work to be as uncomplicated and repetitive as possible to realise the highest output. Furthermore, the essential lesson one can extrapolate from both Cases 8.1 and 8.2 is that if sports managers were more competent in 'giving' to their staff through an alliance of *interaction, influence* and *empowerment*, they would also receive more from these employees and thus facilitate their own AML need for self-actualisation. However, this lesson cannot be learnt properly without first acknowledging the underlying competencies or intelligences which correlate the triad of *interaction, influence* and *empowerment* to effective HR leadership in the sports industry.

---

[13] Coach Johnson did not just perceive J-Mac as merely a person disabled by autism. He considered him as possessing a distinctive personality characteristic for the successful performance of the role of team manager. His AML capacity was therefore further revealed in the speed, intensity and soundness of his mastery of the basketball techniques and procedures relevant to scoring seven times, in four minutes, with six shots at long range.

[14] It can be argued that Coach Johnson recognised in J-Mac an objective trend of personality development that was 'real' when everything needed for his AML point of self-realisation was present.

[15] With Coach Johnson's support, J-Mac was able to tap into his reserve or 'standby power supply' in the realm of kinesomatic activity and spatial knowledge. This is an intuitive source from which the fresh forces of all human organisms are drawn, without any irreparable damage to the said organism. By accessing such a 'standby power supply', it can be further argued that J-Mac's energy depletion was made good during his AML process of self-regulation, and he realised his dreams of becoming the team's leading scorer, along with securing a Hollywood contract, a lucrative book deal and becoming an inspirational speaker across the USA – all enviable tangible rewards.

Multiple intelligence and motivation in HRM

In a modern business mileau where managers do not hesitate to tell their staff lies to boost morale (see Goleman, 1997; Winstanley and Woodall, 2000), Coach Johnson's level of interpersonal competence enabled him both to fulfil his need for self-actualisation and to demonstrate a greater cross-capability understanding, caring and concern for J-Mac and his team-mates alike. In his text *Intelligence Reframed: Multiple Intelligences for the 21st Century* (1999) Harvard University Professor Howard Gardner concluded that interpersonal competence is one of seven different kinds of minds or intelligences.

An adaptation of these seven intelligences is as follows:

1 **Linguistic intelligence** – the ability to think in words and to use language to express and appreciate complex meanings. Linguistic intelligence allows us to understand the order and meaning of words, and to apply metalinguistic skills to reflect on our use of language.

2 **Musical intelligence** – the capacity to discern pitch, rhythm, timbre and tone. This intelligence enables one to recognise, create, reproduce and reflect on music, as demonstrated by composers, conductors, musicians, vocalists and sensitive listeners. Interestingly, there is often an affective connection between music and the emotions, and mathematical and musical intelligences may share common thinking processes.

3 **Bodily-kinesthetic intelligence** – the capacity to manipulate objects and use a variety of physical skills. This intelligence also involves a sense of timing, and the perfection of skills through mind–body union.

4 **Logical-mathematical intelligence** – the ability to calculate, quantify and consider propositions and hypotheses, and carry out complex mathematical operations. It enables us to perceive relationships and connections, to use abstract, symbolic thought, sequential reasoning reasoning skills, and inductive and deductive thinking processes.

5 **Spatial intelligence** – the ability to think in three dimensions. Core capacities of this intelligence include mental imagery, spatial reasoning, image manipulation, graphic and artistic skills, and an active imagination.

6 **Interpersonal intelligence** – the ability to understand and interact effectively with others. It involves effective verbal and non-verbal communication, the ability to note distinctions among others, a sensitivity to the moods and temperaments of others, and the ability to entertain multiple perspectives.

7 **Intrapersonal intelligence** – the capacity to understand oneself – one's intelligence and feelings – and to use such knowledge in planning and directing one's life, and the human condition in general.

Like Goleman's 'emotional intelligence' construct, Gardener's theory has been applauded as a meaningful way to account for the knowledge that we are culturally different and do not all have the same psychological conditioning. It infers that managing human capital will be more effective if human cultural differences are taken seriously, and people can learn to bolster their 'weaknesses' through their strengths and share their expertise. This way, they can be appreciated for the gifts they possess and can in turn appreciate others for the gifts they bring to share. Such an assertion not only gives further credence to Maslow's initial model of human needs, but also suggests that as humans we were not born with these hierarchical needs. Instead they are acquired through our cultural experiences or interrelationship with our external environment. For example, we can see both Maslow's and Gardener's theories at their strongest in Case 8.3, where an attempt is being made to account for why individuals perform optimally at some times and below par at other times. Here, we note that a more radical and fundamental AML approach to managing human capital needs to be considered, so that, particularly within the business of sports, neither players nor employees would continue to remain under-valued, under-trained and under-utilised.

Case 8.3 Interplaying anthropomaximology with people strategy

Research in the early 2000s suggested that the psychological superiority of the Australian national rugby league team was responsible for their record of six consecutive World Cup wins, which at the time was unbroken from 1975. This remarkable conclusion from a Teesside-led research team could be put forward because other research studies had shown the physical and tactical preparation of northern and southern hemisphere teams were essentially similar. Those two obvious explanatory factors could therefore be eliminated when looking for the causes of the phenomenal success enjoyed by the Aussies at the time.

The researchers, led by Michael Sheard, served questionnaires on seventy members of the French, Irish, Welsh and English national teams. Controversially, the southern hemisphere sides of Australia and New Zealand refused to participate in his research, but in a neat side-step, Sheard reasoned that Australian nationals currently playing their rugby in Wales could be included. Sheard's finding was that players who had started their playing careers in Australia and were competing in the main in Australia, were top of the rankings for self-confidence or self-belief. Viewed from the perpsective of nationality alone, other measures such as 'mental toughness' – or motivation to succeed – and 'hardiness' – the ability to perceive a potentially dangerous situation as a challenge – were scored highest by Welsh nationals. Sheard felt that this finding was reinforced by the observation that the only side ever to lead against Australia in their successful run (in the 2000 World Cup tournament) was in fact the Welsh side.

Sheard posited that the Australian side's self-confidence on its own could explain their complete domination of the sport at the time. An Australian side would emerge on to the pitch for a physical confrontation with their opponents in which they were not only at least equal in terms of tactical preparation and fitness, but also completely convinced they would win. This would also lead to the benefit of a self-reinforcing positive feedback loop, where victory bolsters confidence, leading to another victory and a further boost to confidence, and so on.

Sheard was of the opinion that self-confidence could be built and improved by any team by means of activities such as role-plays, where players visualise and enact important tactical situations, that in the run of an actual game were important to a match-winning outcome.

Source: New Scientist, 29 March 2001.

Discussion question

3 The Australian Rugby League's psychological superiority can be characterised as one of underlining contrasts: on the one hand there is the pragmatism of the Anglo-Saxon colonial influence, and then, on the other hand, Aboriginal traditions of spirituality and local shared values. Explore the potentials and dilemmas these contradictory cultural values can generate for developing an AML people strategy using role-play in a Northern hemispheric business of sports context.

The results of the research highlighted in the case study confirm that to be successful in any business venture, whether in the northern or southern hemisphere, we must understand how the brain works through visualisation (or the cognitive rehearsal of an event) and how to apply it in our working life. The gist of the study is that our effort to satisfy needs will depend on our belief that through vivid visualisation we can expect such efforts to be followed by a certain result which will bring required rewards. Furthermore, the study suggests that the more appealing an employee considers a particular incentive and the greater the likelihood that the physical and mental exertion of effort will lead to that incentive, then the more positive will be the mental feedback loop and resultant physical energy the individual will put into his/her work. This is clearly demonstrated in the field of professional lawn tennis, as we explore the psychological driving force behind the 6–4, 3–6, 6–2 defeat by the world No. 1 Serena Williams (USA) in her fifth Australian Open final (2010), and twelfth Grand Slam victory, which ruined the hopes of Belgium's Justine Henin achieving what would have been an extraordinary Belgian double of winning a first Grand Slam straight back after retirement, just as her colleague Kim Clijsters accomplished at the US Open in September 2009.

It was reported that Williams, who was a lot more commanding and match-tight throughout that decisive game, left the court with a satisfied grin after again (reminiscent of the 'bumblebee in flight') defying her critics who felt confident that her less than brilliant play in the early rounds would acutely affect her ability to get the job done in the final, devoid of a major struggle. Saving her best shots for last, and with superlative serving, Serena said it was inspiring to have her icon Billie Jean King watch the game from the stands as she decisively matched King's achievements on the international list of all-time Grand Slam champions (a tangible reward). However, it is vital to note that the real motivation behind Serena's unparalleled achievement actually came from elsewhere. As she herself recounted:

> I think everyone was [cheering] for Justine. But you know what really helped me out? This one guy [in the stands] was like, 'You can beat her, Justine; she's not that good.' I looked at that guy and I was like, 'You don't know me' [with a wag of her finger for extra emphasis]. I think I won all the games after that, because that's totally rude.
>
> (Cambers, 2010)

Therefore, in singing the praises of Serena's rewarding anthropomaximological experience, we can confidently acknowledge that within the AML process, an employer/employee's behaviour and psychological superiority is influenced by:

- a lucid visualisation of what s/he wants to take place;
- his/her educated guess of the likelihood of the thing occurring;
- how strongly s/he believes that the experience will satisfy a higher need.

Interestingly, as a home-schooled African-American, nurtured in the poor and sometimes violent suburb of Compton in Los Angeles, USA, Serena's exorcistic conquest against her European rival and the 'Doubting Thomases' in the stands, also speaks volumes when we confront another long overestimated hereditarian folk taxonomy – that human cognitive intelligence depends effectively on ethnicity. Time and again, it has been professed by white academics overwhelmed by their nature v. nurture studies of essentially carefree and upper-middle-class subjects in the North Atlantic, that the resulting differences in wo/mankind's performance were genetically determined. Furthermore, such studies only opportunely involved ethnic minority populations from underprivileged backgrounds, while disregarding the complex genomic diversity which reflected deeply historical, cultural and linguistic impacts on their gene flow, after several generations of ancestral admixture (Bryc et al., 2010).

However, post-modern genetic research has at long last confirmed that a person's ability to make use of his or her genetic potential can be positively influenced, especially if that person is supported and permits others to assist within a socio-economically advantaged, rather than impoverished environment. In other words, seeds that are scattered on infertile soil won't ever grow into large plants ('The Parable of the Sower', Matthew 13: 5–8). We have become conscious of this observable fact earlier in the chapter with the case of J-Mac. But, by studying violinists in Berlin, for instance, education researcher Anders Ericsson and colleagues have also shown that Caucasoid master musicians are not born that way. Instead, this meticulous empirical data – subsequently replicated in the USA – proved that only those who had practised dutifully for more than 10,000 hours by the age of 20 went on to become virtuoso performers (Blech, 2010 [online]; Ericsson et al., 2009). Notably, this analogy does not only hold for Caucasian musicians, but even speaks across nationalities and disciplines to the pretentious metaphors of Asian maths, Russian chess or African sports prodigies – figures of speech that we now know do not have any biological basis whatsoever (Rossi, 2002; Ericsson, 2009). And as for Serena, she has resolutely avowed:

> Luck has nothing to do with [my success] because I have spent many, many hours, countless hours, on the court working for my one moment in time, not knowing when it would come.
> (Williams, 2007)

Thus, for the purpose of this chapter, we can safely postulate that anthropomaximological proficiency is a reflection of our nurturing environment, as well as our nature-bred talent(s). And based on the behavioural approach of the sports employer/employee during this AML process, the following implications should be considered:

- The HR manager should be unambiguous with employees when explaining what exactly is expected from modern working practices.

- Employees should be able to see a direct link between their labour output and the rewards such hard work generates.

- Rewards (psychological and fiscal) should fulfil workers' needs for security, esteem, independence and personal self-development.

- Complex reward or bonus systems are unlikely to increase the effort of workers because employees cannot relate harder work to higher wages.

Such implications forge the relationship between effort, satisfying reward and performance (see Porter and Lawler, in Graham and Bennett, 1995: 17) in a world where research has shown that the aspirations and values of management tiers are varying (Cashmore, 2002). Emerging from the twentieth century is a new breed of sports managers who seek a career that mirrors their own personal/emotional values and frames of mental faculties (human multiple intelligences) rather than those of the sports organisation. Thus, while managers in general are admitting serious dissatisfaction with existing organisational life and the pressures being exerted on them to do 'more with less', the motivational force driving enlightened HR leaders is the opportunity to seek greater self-determination and sovereignty in a corporate milieux where stress costs the sporting and other industries over £370 million a year (ILAM *Leisure News*, 2002: 1). Such open-minded HR managers clearly understand the magnitude of an employee's reserve biopsychological potential (intelligence) to sort out information which can be stimulated in a cultural locale, to resolve a crisis or generate products that are of value within that particular culture (Gardner, 1999). Moreover, it is argued that within the sporting business, the liberal HR managers who, in adopting the AML approach, offer more comprehensive occupational health-support services which address these reserve biopsychological potentials (multiple intelligences) and socio-physical needs of their employees can better boost worker performance and cut health-care risks and costs (Attridge, 1999).

 ## The sports HR Manager as a Yenza strategist

As I live in the multicultural UK where foreigners play a most important role in sports, I can safely admit that I was first made aware of the intrinsic value of HR strategic/'chess-like' decision making by my dear mother and life-mentor, Helena Marjorie Brathwaite.[16] Like an alchemist, transmuting implicit ontologies, existential psychologies and epistemologies into an explicit ethno-philosophy at a high level of sophistication and reflexivity, Mom fondly reminded me many times in the Caribbean rhythmical dialect of an expression that says 'Only a fool see ting in day time and tek firestick to look for it in de nite'. When translated for the benefit of the Euro-American reader, the proverb intertextualises the constructs of the epistemological edifice that gives us the following conjoint meanings:

- 'Only a fool will know something and yet act as if he is ignorant of it.'
- 'What a fool believes he sees, no wise man has the power to reason away.'

These interconnected 'truths' are very discernable and manageable patterns of critical thought and comprehension, which can be equated with the popular 'Acres of Diamonds' story I have heard so many Western management gurus rework as prolegomenons for their public speeches on both sides of the Atlantic. Such speeches tell of a man who left his large estate in Africa unexplored for years and years to seek riches all over the world, until one day he returned home to find diamonds in his own backyard. The intellectual thread of both proverbs is the same. When thinking about a human resource or people strategy, avoid the temptation of living in a 'glass world' (i.e. searching outside for the answers that lie inside). Instead, dig deep for the diamonds (driving force) within your own backyard.

Yenza, a popular Zulu word in Southern Africa which means 'do it', signifies the 'dig deep' principle, which revolves around strategic action (i.e. doing things). According to

---

[16] A retired secondary schoolteacher who also taught the 1976 Montreal Olympic Games 100 metres gold medallist Hasely Crawford at primary school level in the Republic of Trinidad and Tobago, as well as initially introducing her third grand-daughter Miss Rochelle Ballantyne to the intellectually challenging game of chess, and effectively nurturing her talent as a young child. Rochelle, in particular, has since progressed to ably match skills at a 2008 simultaneous chess display in New York with Garry Kasparov, one of the greatest chess grandmasters of all time, who distinguished her game from all the other players. Moreover, she is currently the 18 and Under Champion of the 2010 United States Chess Federation's All Girls Nationals sponsored by the Kasparov Foundation, and winner of the Academic Distinction Scholarship to the University of Texas at Dallas, valued at $68,000 (see Smith, 2010 and Dellamaggiore, 2010).

organisational sociologist Dr Piet Human (1998), the *Yenza* trajectory dictates that until policies and strategies developed on a theoretical level are moved beyond the paralysing comfort zones of debate, planning or further research, they will always remain imperfect. The concepts must be tested or manifested in the real world. Therefore, instead of waiting until everyone is totally happy with each strategic element before implementation, the concepts must be actualised while being tested, cultured and improved during the process. This means that the Sports HR Manager transforms his organisation from a mere bureaucracy to what Human characterises as a 'revocracy', or institution which can fulfil a 'revolutionary role' within the community it serves. In this context, the Sports HR Manager graduates from being a mentally paralysed 'bureaucrat' to become the *Yenza* strategist or 'revocrat' who proactively reshapes and recreates the organisational 'revocracy' via a three-pronged approach:

- **Attention**: initially finding out or determining 'what' needs to be accomplished in a 'real world' context;

- **Intention**: thinking about and framing an appropriate strategy which specifically outlines 'how' the HR problem will be tackled;

- **Commitment**: eventually 'doing it', i.e. taking the necessary action by executing the said strategy.

When developing such a 'cutting edge' Yenza HR strategy towards creating a 'revocracy', a number of critical factors must be addressed in determining the 'driving force' of a sports organisation. As highlighted in Figure 8.2, we see nine elements which range from *natural resources* to *return/profit (cash and kind)* being featured. For the Sports HR Manager or revocrat each of these requisites is important, but the first – *natural resources* – is obviously the 'catalyst' through which the other eight can be realised. The term *natural resources* refers to people skills level, staff capacity, biopsychological potential and reserve, and management capability. The *natural resources* are also postulated to epitomise the energy and consciousness of organisation and change.

Therefore, in utilising the Yenza approach to construct a proactive sports HR strategy based on such sub-requisites, two critical questions must be addressed:

Figure 8.2 Fundamental HR strategic decision making

- What kinds of human capital are needed to manage and run the sports organisation and to meet the strategic business objectives?

- What people-oriented programmes and initiatives must be planned and employed to invite, improve and hold on to skilled staff so that the sports organisation can compete successfully?

In order to properly respond to these questions, we must address the seven key dimensions of organisational consciousness (see also Barrett, 1998). This construct of organisational consciousness is based on the premise that employee fulfilment, social responsibility and environmental stewardship are the recipe for increased productivity and creativity in the future. It also implies that the revocracy ideals which a sport organisation embraces have been more and more of an influence in its ability to recruit the best talent and market its services.

A macro-derivative of Maslow's hierarchy of micro-needs comprises seven dimensions of organisational consciousness (see Figure 8.3), which include:

- **Society**: Input to improvement of public conditions from a long-term perspective.

- **Constituencies**: Considered partnership with consumers, providers and the local population. Also involves ecological awareness and worker fulfilment.

- **Culture**: Concrete affirmative organisational culture established on 'shared vision' and principles, conviction, honesty and corporate cohesion.

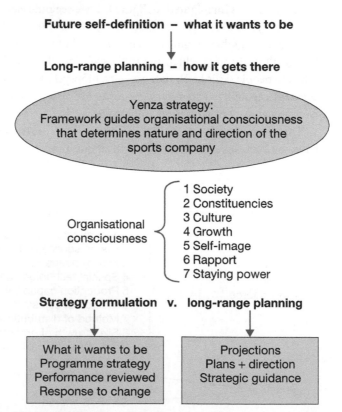

Figure 8.3 Organisational revocracy driving force

- **Growth:** Corporate innovation and development based on co-operative learning, worker involvement and improvement of sports services and natural resources.
- **Self-image:** Corporate change for the better with regard to provision and quality of services, staff competence, systematic designs and procedures.
- **Rapport:** Highlighting exchange of ideas and interaction with employees, consumers and suppliers.
- **Staying power:** Focus on economic security, production output and corporate growth.

When applied to managing the people element in sports, it is fair to assume that senior business executives may well focus on maybe one or two of the above dimensions while neglecting the rest. However, what is needed is an HR stratagem directed at bonding the relationship between all seven dimensions at the organisational level (as illustrated in Figure 8.4). In this context, we see the benefit of proactively consolidating both the sports organisational 'Vision' and 'Driving force'. In reality this Yenza approach means that emphasis must be placed on not only retraining staff, but also on:

- considering the business strategy, accentuating the main driving forces and the implications of these driving forces for the human side of the sports business;
- developing a mission statement relating to the human capital constituent of the business;
- conducting a SWOT (strength, weaknesses, opportunities and threats) analysis of the sports management system, the PESTLE (political, economic, social, technological, legal and environmental) impact of the external and business market milieu and the human resources capability;

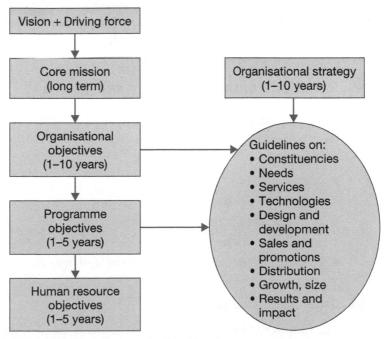

Figure 8.4 HR stratagem at the organisational level

- carrying out a meticulous HR review with emphasis on the sports organisation's culture, organisation and people/HR systems (COPS);
- revisiting the business strategy and juxtaposing it against the SWOT and the COPS analyses, while identifying and prioritising the critical people issues;
- accentuating the decisive options/consequences for managerial action regarding each critical HR issue and translating them into an action plan based on wider objectives linked to the following specialist HR matrix:

   wo/manpower planning;

   recruitment and selection;

   training and development;

   management development;

   organisation development;

   performance appraisal;

   pay and reward;

   communication.

Once the revocracy action plan has been developed around the critical issues and the targets/dates for achieving the essential objectives linked to the HR areas above have been set, execution and appraisal of the said action plans must proceed.

Thus the effectual development of a Yenza HR strategy in sports ensures that the aims and objectives which have been set are reciprocally supportive so that the appropriate reward and payment mechanisms are incorporated with relevant training and career development plans. However, it cannot go without denotation that the management of a sports organisation gains little advantage in training its human capital, only to then put a damper on things by failing to make available any adequate professional and personal improvement prospects. As such, it is important that we now gain some insight into the logistics of the HRM revocracy matrix as it relates to the sports industry.

Functions of the HRM matrix in sports

Having explored the motivational and strategic dimension of HRM, we can now examine the revolutionary mechanics of the modern HRM matrix, which can be broken down into the following departmental functions:

- organisational and job design;
- employee resourcing;
- employee development;
- performance management;
- managing the employment relations and legal dynamics.

Organisational and job design

The adequacy of a sports company's structures, communication networks, authority and responsibility systems, etc., and the implementation of measures for improving them, are critical features of new formulations of HRM. Therefore, the operational sum and substance of a sports organisation's revocracy must be concerned with:

- the immediate manifestation of its technical activities;
- organisational maintenance (i.e. personnel, management accounting and facilities management;
- operational support and the flow of work (e.g. quality control);
- top management (the wider organisational strategic direction and policies);
- middle management (the co-ordination and synchronicity of activities which accommodate a bonding with the support functions).

All these requisites are served through the role of HR, which ensures that the organisation provides competent communications between each activity, whilst remaining resilient.

However, job and organisational design are closely interrelated to all key HRM activities, as well as recruitment and selection, learning and development, pay and rewards and employee relations. Job design or the use of motivational rationale to the structure of work for improving productivity and satisfaction is also essential to the recruitment and selection function. Thus, a sports company that provides a range of high-value-added consultancy services using skilled workers within a team-based organisational grouping will definitely have more rigorous resourcing priorities than a sports firm which specialises in large-scale project-oriented activities operated by unskilled volunteers, who are superintended in the classical pyramid-shaped organisational order of ranking (see Bratton and Gold, 2003 and Dowling et al., 2008).

Approaches to job design are normally classified as:

- **Job simplification** – a job design whose intention is to emend task efficacy by cutting the number of tasks a single employee must carry out.
- **Job rotation** – a job design that methodically transfers employees from one job to another to replenish them with diversity and stimulation.
- **Job enlargement** – a job design which blends a sequence of assignments into a fresh and more comprehensive job to give employees variety and challenge.
- **Job enrichment** – a job design that consolidates accomplishments, recognition and other high-level motivators into the work to help the sports employee achieve a sense of self-commitment, self-planning, self-motivation, self-discipline, self-management and, with such self-development, to enable influencing of his/her own reward through participation.

So, in order to situate the intent and outputs of jobs, along with the mode by which such job outputs will be determined, and the medium or assignments by which these outputs will be attained, it is meaningful that in the job analysis (or formulation) and design function, the sports HR revocrat must pay careful attention to motivation and job satisfaction, as discussed earlier in this chapter.

The result of the job analysis is normally a job specification or calculated statement of the mental and physical activities involved in a job, and other germane factors in the socio-physical milieu. Such a record of the requirements of each task is essentially an assessment

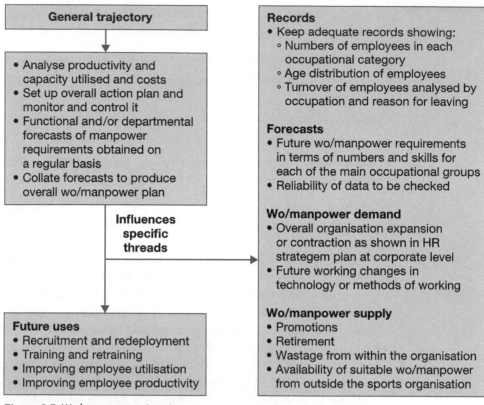

General trajectory

- Analyse productivity and capacity utilised and costs
- Set up overall action plan and monitor and control it
- Functional and/or departmental forecasts of manpower requirements obtained on a regular basis
- Collate forecasts to produce overall wo/manpower plan

Influences specific threads

Future uses
- Recruitment and redeployment
- Training and retraining
- Improving employee utilisation
- Improving employee productivity

Records
- Keep adequate records showing:
  - Numbers of employees in each occupational category
  - Age distribution of employees
  - Turnover of employees analysed by occupation and reason for leaving

Forecasts
- Future wo/manpower requirements in terms of numbers and skills for each of the main occupational groups
- Reliability of data to be checked

Wo/manpower demand
- Overall organisation expansion or contraction as shown in HR strategem plan at corporate level
- Future working changes in technology or methods of working

Wo/manpower supply
- Promotions
- Retirement
- Wastage from within the organisation
- Availability of suitable wo/manpower from outside the sports organisation

Figure 8.5 Wo/manpower planning

of the relative importance of identified duties along with those which take up significant proportions of time and are problematic. The job specification also quantifies data on the scale of activities of each employee or section(s) controlled by employee(s) and sets frequencies of tasks and duties, while listing the management processes to be carried out, along with re-forming the group's main tasks into an ordered structure. Consequently, sports HR revocrats may use both the job analysis and the resulting specifications for wo/man power planning, or for assessing and developing an operational plan that focuses on hiring the right HR for a job and training them to be productive (see Figure 8.5). From this HR planning, further blueprints can be developed for:

- recruitment and selection based on a comprehensive classification of the vacant job;
- appraisal so that an assessment can be made of how well an employees has completed the mandates of the job;
- the creating of training and development programmes which help to appraise the knowledge and skills needed in a job;
- constituting rates of pay connected with job evaluation;
- eliminating risks and identifying hazards in the job;
- re-formulating the organisational framework by reappraising the design, importance and interrelationships of various jobs.

Employee resourcing

Judging from the 'tug-of-war' between the UK soccer club Manchester United and its counterparts in Spain (Barcelona and Real Madrid) and Italy (AC Milan) over the favoured player David Beckham, it is clear that the only major demarcation between the sports organisation and its competitors is the sum total and class of human resources that it can lure and retain. Therefore, with vacancies identified from the wo/manpower plan and person specifications drawn up in tandem with a knowledge of the responsibilities from job descriptions, it is only then that the sports HR revocrat can decide on the trajectory to find the most appropriate candidates. This proactive approach must obviously consider the socio-legislative and politico-cultural framework within which the recruitment and selection is taking place.

A case in point, illustrating the ongoing variations on the theme of racial differences and the related explanations, would be the recent medical declaration by Dr Roger Bannister (who on 6 May 1954 ran the first recorded sub-four-minute mile) that black athletes have tendons that are superior in development due to climatical/environmental determinants (see Gardiner et al., 1998: 135).

When it comes to recruitment and selection within a manpower plan, the question can then be advanced that once the sports HR revocrat chooses the media, sets the recruitment campaign in train, arranges the necessary interviews and assessment centres and categorises each candidate into a shortlist for final selection, would the HR department then decide to favour a black professional or volunteer over candidates of other ethnic origins based on the stereotypes which would inevitably result from this type of corroborated bio-scientific pronouncement? Ever mindful of the attention-grabbing lawn tennis game (Williams v. Henin) discussed earlier, to follow such a unilateral track or the reverse discriminatory approach, where a European athlete is chosen over a non-European in view of corresponding racial ideals, or even within the context of those who have *obvious disabilities* (see also Yaniv, 2009: 29), would certainly be a legally risky decision on the part of the sport HR recruiters/selectors. It is therefore imperative for sports HR staff and the managers responsible for interviewing applicants to be properly trained in structured cross-cultural interviewing techniques, as well as the use of valid, reliable EQ/multiple intelligence v. IQ-based selection tests, which will reflect the company's commitment to diversity and the type of applicant sought.

Many companies, and not least those in the sports industry, experience problems in recruiting the required number and quality of employees required for the posts. The reason may well be that not all possible sources of recruits have been thoroughly explored, including universities, technical colleges, recruitment agencies or even volunteers, which over the years have proved to be a most vital resource within the sports milieu. People volunteer to work in sports for diverse reasons:

- a love of the particular sport activity;
- obtaining job skills or a desire to gain experience in the area of sport with a view to working professionally in the field later on;
- a desire to make a contribution to the community;
- a need to fill leisure time with useful work.

Volunteer supporters in sports can be organised in one of two ways: *integrated* or *autonomous*. If the sports organisation prefers to integrate volunteers into the company, then volunteers become like additional staff members working in individual departments. This system is an uncomplicated one, and is normally used by smaller and medium-sized firms. Because it is integrated, it requires no special liaison, but its success usually depends on the volunteer skills of individual department heads, and these are, naturally, quite variable. A strengthening of this system has been to have a part-time employee recruiting and liaising with volunteers. On the other hand, larger sports companies often have an *autonomous* organisation that has its own officers, meetings and plans, although it exists solely to support the work of that one sports organisation. As with professional graduate workers within the traditional corporate context, working in such an *autonomous* framework with volunteers who may be either multi-skilled technicians or unskilled amateurs enthusiastic about the development of their sporting interest can be particularly rewarding or very frustrating. It all depends on whether the interview (one-to-one or panel type) and subsequent induction programme has provided the new recruits with adequate information about the job they are required to carry out. They should include a job description:

- job title;
- job title of immediate supervisor to whom volunteer/job holder reports;
- job title of each person reporting to the job holder;
- overall responsibility;
- summary for each immediate subordinate volunteer of the overall purpose of the job or the main functions or activities that are carried out or for which his/her responsibility is attached;
- details and full picture of the organisational structure and subordinate organisational structure including the number and type of staff.

With particular reference to consultants who work with volunteers, managers who use volunteer labour, and chairpersons of voluntary groups, the voluntary group may include several informal organisational structures. For example, there are:

- the totally voluntary community group;
- the funded organisation dependent on volunteers to function;
- committees or groups within institutions (especially universities and sports clubs) established for a specific purpose.

During the induction, the sports HR staff should be mindful of and prepare to address the potential problems such organisational structures may share. These issues along with their recommended solutions include:

1 **Too many goals** – Most volunteer groups attempt more than they can actually accomplish. Their goals are so broad and ambiguous that the effort often fails, thus creating dissatisfaction in volunteers, leading to rapid turnover.

   Solution: One method, based on consensus and group decision making, is for volunteer groups to set aside a block of time to devote totally to a planning workshop design session, during which brainstorming, priority-setting, individual programme objective charts and the execution of these objectives may be set in train.

2 **Lack of an adequate contract between the group and its membership** – This is one of the broadest and most fundamental problems facing volunteer groups. Moreover, most groups do not allow the members to indicate their resources, experience and backgrounds during an interview or even during induction. Hence, a specific agreement between members and the organisation regarding what each person can and will do is quite rare. Moreover, discovering members' resources and establishing members' time commitments usually occurs informally and haphazardly, costing the group much maintenance time. Under-utilisation of volunteer skills and experiences is often the result.

Solution: There are a number of methods for developing this contract. The use of group meetings to share individual resources and group expectations is useful, along with the provision of specific, written statements of expectation for each volunteer to help clarify individual responsibilities. Moreover, the creation of a permanent agenda item where questions are asked at each meeting can legitimise explicit discussion about the HR manager's and the volunteers' mutual expectations.

3 **Lack of leadership and accountability** – Unwillingness to confront the problem of leadership liability is common in volunteer groups. Since most sports volunteers are not paid, this issue is especially uncomfortable. Failure to establish adequate leadership structures and to make the leaders (and even volunteers) accountable for their responsibilities can be extremely serious.

Solution: An effort can be made to select project leaders for each major programme attempted – a task which can be assumed by an active sport volunteer. If money is available, a full-time volunteer can also be useful in maximising the contribution of volunteers through regular volunteer staff meetings and orientation sessions, which can help examine progress toward objectives, create group cohesiveness and a climate of support.

4 **Lack of rewards or recognition** – Volunteers are known to quietly assist a sports organisation, but not receive due recognition for their contributions.

Solution: It is important that qualified staff receive first consideration for full-time staff training programmes, which could help make them more employable. Such training sessions can include decision-making methods and other group-process activities, along with workshops on process issues such as structured experiences, role-plays and discussions which may help the group generate process objectives for improved functioning.

5 **Lack of attention to group process** – Within the framework of the Protestant work ethic, volunteer groups are usually left to 'get on with the job' and not much attention is paid to group dynamics, the problems that hinder group effectiveness or the possible preventative actions.

Solution: Examples of preventative actions would be assigning a process observer whose existence would make group dynamics a legitimate discussion item. S/he would also be able to persuade the group to pursue the subject or prevent certain members from dominating. The role of the process observer can then revolve so that all members become accustomed to observing process. A checklist of process objectives can also be an important aid for the observer.

The resourcing of full-time staff and volunteers can therefore be a rewarding experience for a sports HR revocrat, especially when all participants in the relationship have a mutual respect and desire to co-operate in meeting designated needs. However, it can be even more of a positive initiative when the HR revocrat ensures that everyone concerned is provided with a clearer view of his/her role, and the responsibilities and rights of the volunteer within the organisation s/he is associated with and of the people whom the volunteer's effort endeavours to assist are properly identified.

Employee development

With a significant dual function of application and motivation, employee training and developing the ability to improve leadership within a wo/manpower plan also serves to enhance the subordinates' ability to perform the tasks required by the sports organisation. This therefore leads to overall organisational efficiency and maximises the job satisfaction of both employers and employees (including volunteers). But it is not unusual for sports organisations to function without clearly defined training policies which involve:

- the objectives of training;
- the range or scope of the training schemes;
- the limitations of expenditure on training;
- the commitment of management.

The sports organisation's methodology for training its leaders and subordinates can be uneconomical and wasteful if the approach is not a systematic one based on:

- Assessment of the job;
- Performance levels for quality and codes of ethics;
- Performance accomplishments;
- Requirements of the training and development programme;
- Origination of the training as course of action;
- Administering of the training programme;
- Checking of the training results;
- How the training can be improved next time.

(Adapted from Graham and Bennett, 1995: 228)

Moreover, such a systematic approach must also demonstrate the long-term training needs of the sports employer/employee/volunteer, which can be assessed on the basis of the organisation's wo/manpower forecasts, job analyses and performance reviews. These long-term training needs can then be used to prepare training plans which set out:

- problem areas of the sports organisation;
- proposed action by the HR department;
- the personnel responsible for such action;
- costs of the training proposals;
- future benefits (including who are the beneficiaries) of such training.

Once the training needs have been identified and the training plan designed, the sports HR revocrat must then ensure that each of the main groupings of employees are fully taken into account by the plan and the current training proposal, which must be flexible in nature. Accordingly, due regard must be given to the internal training programmes and courses, which also need to be based on a proper appraisal of collective and individual training needs, so as to ensure that the overall objectives of such courses are clearly defined in terms of the standards of performance which must be attained for the good of the organisation. It is therefore expected that the syllabus of the internal training programmes and courses should be logically planned and properly linked to the overall HR and organisation's revocracy objectives, while the individuals responsible for delivering the training must be adequately trained and skilful in conducting the courses with a balanced mix of informal instruction, discussion, projects, case studies and functional practice where necessary. Upon completion of the training courses, an evaluation of and (if necessary) adjustments to the programme must be made in the light of follow-up action after training so as to make sure that what has been taught is in effect being implemented by the recruits.

Performance management

Incorporating the employee development process with results-based performance assessment is the next step in ensuring that individual group accountability is increased and innovation encouraged within the sports organisation. Such integration includes:

- performance appraisal;
- goal-setting for individuals and departments;
- suitable training programmes;
- performance-related pay and rewards.

Whether a written *performance review* from the sports HR revocrat, with separate comments on past success/failures for future improvement, or a *potential review* which assesses the employee's suitability for promotion and/or further training, or even a *rewards review* for determining pay rises, there are various types of performance appraisal schemes. They include variations on the following:

- **Grading** – employees are designated into predetermined merit groupings such as outstanding, fair or poor standards on guideline judgements with regard to specific points (e.g. industry and application, loyalty and integrity, co-operation, accuracy and reliability etc.).
- **Merit rating** – here numerical points are allotted on guideline judgements to give an overall score.
- **Results-oriented** – targets are set and results jointly agreed between the sports HR manager and employee.
- **Target setting and reward** – in this context, bonuses are linked to achievement.

Particularly in the world of sports, the appraisal mechanism does subject managers and administrators to a discipline of performance standards quite unlike those continually experienced by athletes. During the organisation appraisal process, comparisons are made between actual performance and agreed standards and targets, which do not assess undefined personality traits of the person being appraised. The performance review results are normally made available to employees and, where appropriate, counselling meetings after the performance review are held to further discuss the appraisee's strengths and weaknesses. From this point, review reports are analysed, training and development needs are agreed and promotion potential established based on the appraisee's career interests and ambition. Furthermore, and like many traditional organisations, the appraisal process can be linked to pay reviews, although some companies may claim the performance review results are not just salary incremental and that associating appraisal and pay reviews creates chaos and discord during what is supposed to be a holistic process.

An alternative to such an argument is the use of a skills-based system of rewarding staff for their exhibited skills and knowledge and their capability in undertaking a set of tasks at some benchmark level. For instance, a member of staff responsible for the planning and administration of a sports conference or regional track and field games opted to pursue an e-learning programme in computerised database management. S/he eventually used those skills not only to update the company's sponsorship portfolio but also to provide the marketing department with access to a wider network of sponsors which resulted in increased funding. It is appropriate that the productivity growth which resulted should be used to provide a pay rise, since the skills-based system has been linked directly to achievements and a more enhanced sales pitch and through creativity. Sports HR revocrats should also note that such organisational rewards for creativity can be given both *extrinsically* (i.e. via annual performance appraisals or the assignment of bonuses) or assigned on *intrinsic* motivation – in this context we can see the HR manager as custodian of Maslow's 'motivators' and Gardner's 'multiple intelligences' discussed earlier – by recognising the important value of creative efforts as well as the skill and perseverance required to generate creative solutions to organisational issues. Moreover, to amplify the impact of such 'compensation' in promoting personal creativity, it is imperative that sports HR revocrats themselves be creativity role models. As role models, they can therefore consistently focus their and the employees' attention on engendering creative ideas to resolve complex organisational issues.

Managing employment relations and legal dynamics

The quality of employment relations at all organisations determines whether employees will feel they are either valued members of the company or mere 'chattel labourers'. Sports HR revocrats are also aware that during the last half of the twentieth century, conflict management and resolution have emerged as a very important competency of organisational leadership. As a matter of fact, recent studies by the American Society of Human Resource Management (SHRM) have rated conflict management as a topic of equal or slightly higher importance than planning, communication, motivation and decision making (*SHRMagazine*, 2011: 27). Thus HR managers in general are becoming more interested in the sources of conflict management, which emphasise psychological factors such as misunderstanding, communication failure, personality clashes and value differences. As highlighted by Brathwaite (2004), many Western managers look upon conflict as a negative experience rather than the life-blood of business, with those in the UK culturally perceiving 'challenging' as 'confronting', and therefore holding fast to the FEAR (i.e. False Evidence Appearing Real) that challenging decisions will inhibit their long-term career prospects. These managers therefore just want to 'manage'. The obvious retort here would be to 'manage' what? This is the key to their problem, since such managers fail to realise that it is people they are managing and without these people, the corporation or sports organisation will fail to exist. However, the managers, who maintain a dim view of conflict, firmly believe that it:

- diverts energy from the real task;
- destroys morale;
- polarises individuals and groups;
- deepens differences;
- obstructs co-operative action;
- produces irresponsible behaviour;
- creates suspicion and distrust;
- decreases productivity.

On the other hand, there are those corporate organisational leaders who understand the positive and creative values intrinsic to conflict. As one leading UK law firm, Executive Partner, admitted quite appositely:

> It took a while to work out that running a law firm is about managing people's [conflicting] emotions, that much of it is about communicating and listening to them. If I can't get things done, it's usually because I've forgotten this. (Tyler, 2010: 13)

When this testimony is translated within the managerial jurisdiction of sporting organisations, we see that 'conflict' can also serve to:

- open up an issue in a confronting manner;
- develop clarification of an issue;
- improve the quality of organisational problem-solving;
- increase employee involvement;
- provide more spontaneity in communication;
- initiate growth;
- strengthen a relationship when creatively resolved;
- help increase productivity.

Therefore, ensuring a working climate of trust and solidarity is crucial to good people management, and, particularly in the case of sports, the understanding that conflict is also a creative and positive occurrence is helpful in monitoring and developing a non-violent yet 'go-ahead' organisational culture, akin to that initiated by Arsène Wenger amongst his football players at Arsenal, whom he encourages to 'play without fear'. As such, five principal methods of interpersonal conflict resolution are identified for consideration by sports HR revocrats. These include:

- **Withdrawal**: avoiding or retreating from an actual or potential situation.
- **Smoothing**: defusion by emphasising areas of agreement and de-emphasising areas of difference over conflictual areas.

- **Compromising**: searching for solutions through negotiations which bring some degree of satisfaction for conflicting areas.

- **Forcing**: where appropriate, exerting one's viewpoint at the potential expense of another, thus leading to an often open competition and a win–lose situation.

- **Confrontation**: addressing a disagreement directly and in a problem-solving mode, allowing both parties to work through their disagreement.

In managing the employment relationship at work, the 'psychological contract' has also become a 'front burner' issue as more employees consider their quality of working life and their personal beliefs as influenced by the company, with particular reference to agreed terms and conditions exchanged between each employee and the organisation. The postulate of the 'psychological contract' provides a challenge for the organisation where managers fail to communicate with one voice, make promises they cannot keep and render null and void the ethical essence of the written contract, which dictates that all employers are legally bound to a 'duty of care' as far as their employees are concerned. Moreover, employees have recently gained additional rights under the Human Rights Act of 1998, which was enforced from 2 October 2000 and gave 'further effect to rights and freedoms guaranteed under the European Convention on Human Rights' (cited in Ewing, 2000: 5; see also *Council of Civil Service Unions v Minister of State for the Civil Service* [1985] AC 374). Included in the extensive menu of new rights which are now in keeping with the grain of UK law is the unequivocal prohibition of 'torture' and 'inhuman or degrading treatment or punishment' (Article 3) and 'slavery or servitude' and 'forced or compulsory labour' (Article 4). This ensures that even volunteers in the sports mileau are protected to a considerable degree from 'bullish' or 'abusive' supervisors and do have rights to freedom from discrimination (Article 14) in the execution of their responsibilities.

However, while the employee does have the benefit of being galvanised under the EU's macro-legal umbrella, of especial importance within the micro-framework of the employment relationship are the rights inherent in the contract of terms and conditions for service. The contract is a written statement of terms which includes:

- the name of the employer and employee;
- date and details of start of continuous employment;
- information on previous service towards the candidate's length of service;
- pay intervals, rates of pay or pay scales;
- hours of work;
- holiday entitlement and related pay;
- public holidays;
- sickness procedures and sick pay;
- pension and pension schemes;
- notice period from both sides (employer/employee);
- job title;
- disciplinary rules in detail;
- person who administers discipline procedures.

The underlying logic of the Employment Law contract is to ensure that both parties must act reasonably and not undermine each other during the execution of their duties. This is essential for the contract to be binding. The employer further requires that the employee must be fit and competent, ready to work in good faith and to obey 'reasonable' instructions. However, the rights of the employee must also be well understood by the employer in an effort to maintain a 'duty of care' towards all subordinates. The employee must receive:

- payment even if service is not produced to defined limits;
- itemised pay statements;
- access to a trade union and permission to engage in the activities of the trade union, which normally interfaces with HR over matters of employee grievance, discipline, pay bargaining and general negotiations on employment conditions;
- time off with pay for activities such as trade union or public duties, and (if made redundant) the opportunity to seek employment or retraining.

 ## Conclusion

In this chapter an attempt has been made to cover a wider range of complex issues and to offer some meaningful insight into the key elements of the HR function within the sports industry. In essence, the emphasis has been placed on the fundamentals of anthropomaximology, motivation and the neurodevelopmental intelligences within the HRM context. We have established that to maintain the competitive advantage and understand the nature of human capital in the sports milieu, managers must be revocrats and acknowledge the biopsychosocial needs of their subordinates on the micro level, while appreciating the Yenza strategic imperatives of the organisation and its customers on the macrocosmic stage. These two paradigms in effect are influenced by new technology and creative processes which cascade down and impact in diverse ways on the employees and their work, as well as on the overall HRM function and process within the sports organisation.

We therefore end on a philosophical note. And it is to say that in view of the EU's Social Charter and as far as employment and sport law are concerned, the dynamic matrix of HRM will continue to act as a compelling force which drives sports managers to place more emphasis on the problematics of employee rights along with the motivational advantages of maintaining a multicultural workforce that increasingly embraces volunteers of diverse skills and backgrounds. As such, it is to the greater benefit of European Sports HR Managers to understand the importance of creating an environment not only of adequate physical facilities/equipment and finances, but one in which employees can do their best work to serve a supportive public, who loyally invest in the sports industry.

Discussion questions

4 Using an appropriate theoretical model, compare and contrast what you think are the, or might have been the, motivating factors for tennis player Serena Williams, Formula One racing driver Lewis Hamilton, and the paralympian Tanni Grey-Thompson. How might this influence how you would manage each of them?

5 Select a successful sports professional such as Marcello Lippi, the manager of Juventus, Cathy Freeman, the Australian athlete, or Phil Knight, the CEO of Nike. To what extent do you think this person displays the characteristics of multiple intelligence noted earlier in the chapter? How has this enabled that person to become a successful sports professional?

6 If you were the manager or strategist for Fiorentina, the Italian football club, Jan Ulrich, the German cyclist, or Andrzej Golota, the Polish heavyweight boxer, what would you do to improve their performances and why?

Keywords

Anthropomaximology; impact of expectancy; motivation; multiple intelligences; yenza.

Guided reading

For useful general International HRM textbooks the reader is referred to Harzing and Pinnington (2010), Marchington and Wilkinson (2008), Dowling et al. (2008), Henderson (2008) and Bratton and Gold (2007, 2012).

Williams and Adam-Smith (2009), Bamber et al. (2004), and Lewis et al. (2003), provide good coverage of international and comparative employee relations, while Lewis (2003) and Ewing (2000) respectively cover the more specific areas of human rights and employment law in the workplace. The interrelationships of work, stress and health are explored by Bamber (2011) and Attridge (1999). Lucas (2001) offers a practical approach to personal self-development. Managing employee needs is explored by Swindall (2010), and Attridge (1999).

For sports law, James and Cremona (2010) and Gardiner et al. (1998), are recommended, and sports culture is explored by Cashmore (2002).

The concepts of anthropomaximology and Yenza are fully developed by Dellamaggiore (2010) and Kuznetsov (1982). Yenza is addressed by Human (1998).

Recommended websites

Bullying In The Work Place: www.bullyonline.org/
Economic, political and collective bargaining developments in the EU: www.eiro.eurofound.ie/
Legal Resources In Europe: www.jura.uni-sb.de
Multiple Intelligence Test: www.nedprod.com/Niall_stuff/intelligence_test.html
Reward Management: www.rewardstrategies.com
Strategic/'chess-like' decision-making: http://goodfilm.org/film/d/190/Brooklyn+Castle
UK Trade Unions: www.tuc.org.uk/tuc/unions_main.cfm

References

Attridge, M. (1999) 'The business response to biopsychosocial needs of employees: a national survey of benefits managers', Study presented at the American Psychological Association Conference: *Work, Stress and Health: Organisation of Work in a Global Economy* in Washington, www.apa.org/pi/wpo/niosh/thursday2.html

Bamber, G. et al. (eds) (2004) *International and Comparative Employment Relations*, London: Sage Publications.

Bamber, M. (2011) *Overcoming Your Workplace Stress: A CBT-based Self-help Guide*, London: Routledge.

Barrett, R. (1998) *Liberating The Corporate Soul: A Values Driven Approach To Building A Visionary Organisation*, New York: Butterworth Heinemann.

Blech, J. (2010) 'How hereditary can intelligence be?', www.spiegel.de/international/zeitgeist/0,1518,716614,00.html

Bratton, J. and Gold, J. (2007) *Human Resource Management, Theory and Practice*, 4th rev. edn, New York: Palgrave Macmillan.

Bratton, J. and Gold, J. (2012) *Human Resource Management: Theory and Practice*, 5th edn, Basingstoke: Palgrave Macmillan.

Brathwaite, T.W. (2004) 'Human resource management in sport', in J. Beech and S. Chadwick (eds), *The Business of Sport Management*, London: Pearson Education.

Bruno, S.T. and Thompson, M. (2000) *Templar Organization: The Management of Warrior Monasticism*, Author House.

Byrc, K. et al. (2010) 'Genome-wide patterns of population structure and admixture in West Africans and African Americans', *Proceedings of the National Academy of Sciences of the United States of America*, 12 January, 107 (2), 786–91.

Cambers, S. (2010) 'Justine Henin eyes Paris after Serena Williams thwarts her at the last', www.guardian.co.uk/sport/2010/jan/31/justine-henin-australian-open

Capoeira, N. (1992) *Capoeira: os fundamentos da malicia*, Rio de Janeiro: Record.

Cashmore, E. (2002) *Sports Culture*, London: Routledge Publishers.

Cooper, J. et al. (2009) 'Available alternative incentives modulate anticipatory nucleus accumbens activation', http://scan.oxfordjournals.org/content/4/4/409.full.pdf?keytype=ref&ijkey=r2Mcp0D6p7P9mfI

Dellamaggiore, K. (2010) *Brooklyn Castle* (Featuring Rochelle Ballantyne, The United States Chess Federation National 18-under chess champion), http://goodfilm.org/film/d/190/Brooklyn+Castle

Dowling, P. et al. (2008) *International Human Resource Management*, 5th edn, London: Thompson Publishing.

Ericsson, K.A. (2009) 'The scientific study of expert levels of performance can guide training for producing superior achievement in creative domains', in Proceedings from International conference on the cultivation and education of creativity and innovation, Beijing, China: Chinese Academy of Sciences, 5–27.

Ericsson, K.A. et al. (2009) 'An expert-performance approach to the study of giftedness', in L. Shavinina (ed.), *International Handbook of Giftedness*, Berlin: Springer Science + Business Media, 129–53.

Ewing, K.D. (ed.) (2000) *Human Rights At Work*, London: The Institute of Employment Rights.

Gardiner, S. et al. (1998) *Sports Law*, London: Cavendish Publishing Ltd.

Gardner, H. (1999) *Intelligences Reframed: Multiple Intelligences for the 21st Century*, New York: Basic Books.

Goleman, D. (1997) *Vital Lies, Simple Truths: The Psychology of Self-Deception*, London: Bloomsbury Publishing.

Goleman, D. (1998) *Working With Emotional Intelligence*, London: Bloomsbury Publishing.

Graham, H. and Bennett, R. (1995) *Human Resource Management*, London: Pitman Publishing.

Harzing, A. and Pinnington, A. (eds) (2010) *International Human Resource Management*, London: Sage.

Heider, F. (1958) *The Psychology of Interpersonal Relations*, New York: Wiley.

Henderson, I. (2008) *Human Resource Management for MBA Students*, London: CIPD Publishing.

Hull, C.L. (1952) *A Behavior System: An Introduction to Behavior Theory Concerning the Individual Organism*, New Haven, CT: Yale University Press.

Human, P. (1998) *Yenza: A Blueprint For Transformation*, Cape Town: Oxford University Press.

ILAM *Leisure News* (2002) 5–11 September, 1.

James, M. and Cremona, M. (2010) *Sports Law*, London: Palgrave Macmillan.

Knutson, B. et al. (2003) 'A region of mesial prefrontal cortex tracks monetary rewarding outcomes', *Journal of Neuroimage*, 18, 263–72.

Kuznetsov, V.V. (1982) 'The potentialities of man and anthropomaximology', *Journal of International Social Science*, XXXIV (2), 277–89.

Landers, D.M. (1978) 'Motivation and performance: The role of arousal and attentional factors', in W.F. Straub (ed.), *Sport Psychology: An Analysis of Athlete Behaviour*, Movement Publications.

LeVine, R.A. (1970) 'Cross-cultural study in child psychology', in P. Mussen (ed.), *Carmichael's Manual of Child Psychology*, Vol. 2, 3rd edn, New York: John Wiley, 559–612.

Lewis, P. et al. (2003) *Employee Relations: Understanding The Employment. Relationship*, London: FT Prentice Hall.

Lin, D. (2007) *The Tao of Daily Life*, New York: The Penguin Group.

Lucas, B. (2001) *Power Up Your Mind: Learn Faster, Work Harder*, London: Nicholas Brealey Publishers.

Marchington, M. and Wilkinson, A. (2008) *Human Resource Management at Work: People Management and Development*, 4th edn, London: CIPD.

Maslow, A. (1943) 'A theory of human motivation', *Psychological Review*, 50, 370–96.

Merrell, F. (2005) *Capoeira and Candomblé*, Princeton, NJ: Markus Wiener Publishers.

Morgan, G. (1997) *Images of Organization*, London: Sage.

Pert, C. (1997) *Molecules of Emotion*, London: Simon & Schuster.

Rossi, E. (2002) *The Psychobiology of Gene Expression*, London: W.W. Norton & Company.

Segall, M.H. et al. (eds) (1990) *Human Behaviour in Global Perspective: An Introduction to Cross-Cultural Psychology*, New York: Pergamon Press.

Senge, P. (1990) *The Fifth Discipline*, London: Double Day Currency Publishers.

SHRMagazine (2011) June, p. 80.

Smith, S. (2010) 'All-girls nationals: Ballantyne ties with Chen and wins UTD scholarship' (April), United States Chess Federation Official Website, http://main.uschess.org/content/view/10322/585/

Spence, K.W. (1956) *Behavior Theory and Conditioning*, New Haven, CT: Yale University Press.

Swindall, C. (2010) *Living for the Weekday: What Every Employee and Boss Needs to Know About Enjoying Work and Life*, London: John Wiley & Sons.

Tyler, D. (2010) 'Managing Careers', London, *The Lawyer* (July).

Watson, T. (1995) *Sociology, Work and Industry*, London: Routledge & Kegan Paul Ltd.

Williams, S. (2007) 'Creating a successful plan for women', www.tv.com/serena-williams/person/13891/trivia.html

Williams, S. and Adam-Smith, D. (2009) *Contemporary Employment Relations: A Critical Introduction*, Oxford: OUP.

Winstanley, D. and Woodall, J. (eds) (2000) *Ethical Issues In Contemporary Human Resource Management*, London: Macmillan Press.

Yaniv, O. (2009) 'Big man with a big heart', *New York Daily News*.

Branding and marketing in sport

Norm O'Reilly, University of Ottawa
Ted Graham, Operator Consulting
Lindsay Rennie, MacLaren Momentum

Learning outcomes

Upon completion of this chapter the reader will be able to:

- provide background and strategic knowledge on sport marketing;
- acquire the necessary tools and understanding to build a marketing plan for their sport property;
- comprehend the global importance of sport marketing;
- appreciate the importance and place of brand in sport marketing;
- apply the concept of brand equity in sport;
- understand the role of brand management in sport;
- appreciate the consequences of strong brand equity.

Overview

This chapter presents a vast area of material in a short time, with the aim to introduce the key concepts and tools around sport marketing and branding in sport. Both sport marketing and branding are extensive fields themselves, with their respective bodies of literature and practical use both being considerable and well developed. Thus, in response to the challenge of presenting such an extensive array of information, the chapter is organised in such a way as to enhance the information provided and to emphasise applied learning through case studies and practical tools.

In many books on sport marketing, the concept of brand is included as a chapter. In chapters on sport marketing, brand is most commonly included as a sub-component of that chapter. This chapter takes the approach of equally emphasising sport marketing and brand. The rationale, based on the experiences of the authors, is that brand has become vital to all aspects of a business, including marketing. Similarly, driven by the growth of sponsorship and online distribution, sport marketing continues to grow in its importance in overall marketing budgets. Thus, the two important marketing concepts are presented here together.

The chapter is organised in five sections. First, marketing – the field – is presented briefly. Second, sport marketing is introduced, defined and the key aspects of the process presented. This section includes a presentation of the entirety of the steps required to develop a marketing plan for a sport product, including the necessary tools. Second, sport marketing research is introduced. Acquiring the necessary information is paramount to any marketing endeavour and sport is no different. The research tools available to the sport marketer are introduced and explained. Third, building on the information provided to that point, the outline of what makes up a sport marketing plan is presented with links to the tools discussed in the previous sections. Fourth, the concept of brand is introduced followed, fifth, by a section that applies brand to the sport setting. This content includes specific direction on how sport marketing should look at brand and its various aspects. Sixth, a conclusion links the material together. Short case studies are included throughout the chapter, with a longer, more illustrative one presented following the conclusion.

 ## Marketing

Marketing has been established as a key function of business for generations. Along with finance, human resources, accounting, operations, sales and others, marketing is installed as part of organisation culture. The American Marketing Association (2007) defines marketing as follows: 'marketing is the activity, set of institutions, and processes for creating, communicating, delivering, and exchanging offerings that have value for customers, clients, partners, and society at large'. The American Marketing Association (AMA) definition changes from time to time and reflects the evolution of the field. A few noteworthy concepts from the current definition include marketing viewed as a long-term activity that is integral to an organisation (the previous definition had it more as a function, inferring a more short-term and departmental role).

The key differentiator of marketing from the other organisational functions/units is that it is the revenue generator of the organisation. It is marketing that sets the stage for sales, established price points, structures product development, promotes products and services, and establishes distribution. Inherent in our understanding of marketing are the concepts of exchange, value and relationships.

Exchange refers to the core idea that marketing occurs when two parties exchange products, services or cash amongst each other where both feel satisfied with the exchange (i.e. they got value equal to or great than what they gave in return). For example, if Doug expresses interest in purchasing a specific brand of car, once he learns the price, he will make a decision if the car will provide for him value that is worth that price. Similarly, the car manufacturer has set a price at which it achieves its own objectives.

Value is an expression for the overall benefit provided to a consumer by a product or service offering. It captures all the elements of the offering, including its functional (e.g. hunger, transportation, entertainment) and intangible (e.g. association with a high-profile brand, self-actualisation) benefits.

Relationship is a relatively new concept in marketing. It speaks to the need to focus on long-term relationships with customers as opposed to seeking single exchanges. This is inherent in the AMA's new definition and its long-term perspective. Building relationships takes place at personal and organisational levels.

Sport marketing

Sport marketing is the application of marketing to sport. It has two general forms: (i) marketing through sport and (ii) marketing within sport. The first is much larger, where a non-sport organisation uses sport as a platform to market its non-sport products and services (e.g. beer, cars, banks, consulting companies, etc.). The second involves sport organisations marketing through sport. For example, think of Speedo marketing its products to swimmers or Nike or Adidas promoting their sport equipment products.

There is considerable discussion in the marketing literature about how sport marketing differs from other forms or industries within marketing. Many viewpoints exist. We refer to sport marketing as an aspect of marketing that provides organisations and brands, both in sport and outside of sport, with a series of marketing opportunities based on sport and the powerful, dynamic and passion-laden attributes it possesses that result from a single attribute of sport that differs from other attractive marketing properties such as arts, charity, health and education. This distinction lies in the fact that sport has outcomes which are not certain, over which the sport marketer has no control. It is not scripted or planned. There may be a heavy favourite but they/he/she may lose. This reality of an unplanned outcome has negatives (e.g. how can a game day promotion be a success if your team loses badly?) but the upside of excitement, passion, swings, emotion, highs and lows far exceed those negatives. In Canada, where we the authors are from, this reality was on display during the gold medal game of men's ice hockey at the 2010 Olympic Winter Games in Vancouver, when Canada beat the United States in overtime with a goal by Sidney Crosby. With a reported two-thirds of the entire population watching, an outcome that could have been scripted – but was not – led to an outpouring of national pride rarely seen in the country's history.

In addition, others have pointed to the emotional ties that differentiate the associations that consumers have to sport from other products and services. Consider, for example, the diehard fan who gets a tattoo of their favourite team or player. Or the loyal fan who has underwear, bedsheets and towels of their favourite club.

From a marketing perspective, sport is an experience which allows for marketing to take place at a very specialised and very far-reaching level. Think of how yachting allows organisations to target a very specific niche market of influential yachtspeople or how mega sport events like the Olympic Games, FIFA World Cup and the Super Bowl provide reach to billions of engaged people.

Case 9.1 Sport marketing 101 – Red Bull

In a global beverage market where energy drinks have proliferated, Red Bull remains the most popular energy drink in the world on the basis of market share. You may know the tag line 'Red Bull gives you wings', but what has given Red Bull its wings in its leadership of this competitive category? Sports marketing clearly has played a huge role in personifying the brand. When you see the names of events like Air Racing, Crashed Ice and X-Fighters, you may think that this is the roster of an X-Games competition. It is, rather, just a few of the Red Bull-created sports that have become global phenomena.

As the market for energy drinks has seen the entrance of more and more competitors over the last decade, so has there been a glut of brands in this category attempting to secure premium sponsorship positions in events that naturally hold a brand association for the youthful energy drink consumer – extreme sports. Red Bull has not shied away from pursuing such sponsorships and has established its name alongside such existing high octane sports as surfing, auto racing and freeride mountain biking as well as individual athlete sponsorships in skiing, snowboarding and wakeboarding. But it is its created sports that are allowing it to break the clutter and provide the ultimate in branded content.

Looking at two such creations, Crashed Ice and Air Racing, it is easy to see how the Red Bull brand is brought to life in a couple of different literal interpretations of 'giving you wings'. With Crashed Ice, a combination of downhill skiing, boardercross and hockey, competitors skate a downhill course wrought with steep drops and hairpin turns, not to mention three other racers whose moves are all equally unpredictable. Events held in different global locations attract as many as 50,000 spectators, millions of dollars-worth of public relations value and are produced for broadcast to convert even more Red Bull drinkers through television and online exposure.

Although air racing already existed, Red Bull Air Racing was the creation of a new and exciting category that injected high-G, low-level, air-show manoeuvres into conventional, closed-course pylon racing. The result is a thrilling spectacle held in front of thousands of fans in eight countries during the 2010 series. Like Crashed Ice, the brand exposure lives on beyond the live events through broadcasts distributed around the world.

So many brands look for the best possible convergence of values, culture and personality through sports in the existing landscape. Red Bull has shown that in categories that naturally lend themselves to a particular sport culture, you can buy off the rack but nothing beats tailor made!

Discussion questions

1 Why has sport marketing helped Red Bull?

2 Red Bull charges a price much higher than its competitors ('premium pricing'). What allows it to do this?

3 Why do you think Red Bull sponsors both events and athletes?

4 Red Bull purchased the New York franchise in Major League Soccer (MLS) in 2009. Why would it have done this?

Sport marketing is a process whereby the marketer researches many aspects of the market, defines the target consumers, builds a strategy to reach the target, implements that strategy, and evaluates its effectiveness. The process has two general steps (discover consumers needs/wants and satisfy them) which lead to four procedural steps (see Table 9.1) where (i) an extensive array of back research is undertaken, (ii) the target markets are defined, (iii) the strategic elements of the marketing mix are developed and (iv) the success of the strategies are evaluated and altered as/if necessary. Table 9.1 below outlines the sport marketing process.

Situational analysis (Step 1 in Table 9.1) involves a series of analytical reviews to give the marketer a strong understanding of the situation within which they need to develop marketing strategy. First, a review of the organisation for which the marketer works allows for an articulation of the strengths and weaknesses of the organisation, its products and its brands. This review should look at all aspects of the company over which the organisation has 'control' (i.e. the ability to change), with a particular emphasis on areas where it could have competitive advantage over its competition and areas where it may be deficient to its competition. Second, an external analysis of the 'uncontrollable' factors of which the marketer needs to be aware, consider and potentially build contingencies for. These are often organised using the PEST approach (Political, Economic, Social and Technological factors), where each of the four areas is reviewed and opportunities (i.e. possible environmental developments which could be advantageous) and threats (i.e. areas of potential concern) are identified. Third, a competitive analysis is carried out where three forms of competition are identified and analysed, including direct competitors (i.e. those product offerings that fulfil the same need or want to a consumer), future competition (i.e. potential new entrants who may come in the future) and substitutes (i.e. those offerings which can take the place of your product but that are not direct competitors). For example, for the Atlético Madrid football club in the Spanish Premier Division known as La Liga, Real Madrid (another club in Madrid in the Premier Division of La Liga) is a direct competitor, a possible move by another club to the Madrid region is a potential new entrant, and any

Table 9.1 Sport marketing strategic process

Step	Specific tasks
1 Situational analysis	An assessment of the marketing situation, including (i) internal analysis of the organisation, including its strengths and weaknesses, (ii) external analysis: political, economic, social, technological and competitive trends, opportunities and threats, (iii) competitive analysis: key competitors, possible new entrants and substitute products, and (iv) consumer analysis of potential customers.
2 Segmentation, targeting and positioning	STP is the process of defining your target markets and value proposition (i.e. how your products will be positioned in the minds of consumers versus the competition). It involves (i) segmenting the population of consumers into homogeneous groups (i.e. segments), (ii) determining which segments to target and (iii) positioning your product/brand for each target market.
3 Marketing mix	Also known as the '4Ps', the marketing mix is the marketing strategy for the Product, Price, Promotion and Place for each of the target markets selected in Step 2 above.
4 Evaluation	All elements of the marketing mix are evaluated regularly and continuously altered based on those evaluations.

other activity that Madrid residents could partake in (movies, a date, going to the gym, concert, staying at home, etc.) is a possible substitute activity to purchasing a ticket to attend the game or watching the game via television, online streaming or listening on the radio. Fourth, a consumer analysis is undertaken of all potential consumers. Such an analysis needs to take a variety of aspects into consideration. Table 9.2 provides an approach (via the questions to ask and find answers to) that can be adopted.

Segmentation, targeting and positioning (STP) is the key strategic phase in the sport marketing process (Step 2 in Table 9.1). It involves a three-step approach to defining the focus of the marketing plan that allows for efficient and focused marketing strategy to be developed. It takes the array of data and knowledge accumulated in the research stage and streamlines it. Specifically, segmentation divides the market into homogeneous groups that are accessible; targeting decides which of these target(s) we will pursue; and positioning is how we want the selected target(s) to perceive us and our products versus those of the competition. The first stage is segmentation, which is the process of reducing the entire population of potential customers down to those specific, mutually exclusive groups that can be considered for targeting as they are likely to respond to action in a similar manner. Although a few global corporations with high-awareness mass-market products (e.g. Microsoft, Pepsi-Cola, Coca-Cola, etc.) are able to launch far-reaching marketing plans, the vast majority of organisations have limited resources and smaller markets to reach. This is where segmentation comes in, as it allows for efficient custom marketing that is based on specific segments that are more easily reached and are more likely to respond to the offering of interest. For example, consider the lines of running shoes offered by Nike and how the different shoes are designed for specific sections of their customers (based on price, sport, quality, performance, etc.). A tool for completing market segmentation is provided in Table 9.3.

Table 9.2 Consumer analysis framework

Consumer knowledge	Question(s) to ask
Population	Who are the potential consumers of your product/services? What constitutes the market?
Want and/or need	What does the market buy? Why do they buy it? What need(s) and/or want(s) are fulfilled?
Occasions	When are offerings purchased and/or used?
Access	Where are offerings available?
Purchase process	Who is involved in the purchase? Who makes the buy decision? Who influences it? How do they buy it?
Consumer characteristics	What social class, culture, language and race are they from? What reference groups and role models to they follow? What demographics (age, income, lifestyle, etc.) define them? What motivates them to buy in your market? What attitudes/beliefs do they hold about your products?

Table 9.3 Steps to complete market segmentation

Step	Details and directions
1 Market definition	Noting that a sports marketing strategy can target a number of potential general markets, including spectators, participants, sponsors and media partners, set the boundaries for your market of potential customers (i.e. any customer who 'could' potentially purchase your product or service).
2 Justify segmentation	Determine if segmentation is a cost-effective undertaking (i.e. only undertake segmentation when it makes financial sense). For example, deciding to sell team shirts to the supporters of a local gymnastics club to help fundraise would not warrant a segmentation as the potential revenues would be less than the cost of undertaking the segmentation).
3 Scan for high-impact areas of reach	Research to determine what your customers and potential customers are passionate about (e.g. active lifestyles, strong community, youth, etc.) and their key demographic attributes (e.g. ethnicity, culture) to focus segmentation.
4 Identify relevant bases of segmentation	Identify the most important bases of segmentation by which to break the total market down into homogeneous and mutually exclusive segments. Bases include income, ethnicity, activity levels, family composition, education level, gender, age, religion, sexual orientation, marital status, lifestyle, profession, habits, personality traits, home ownership, values and any other relevant base.
5 Segment using most relevant bases	Assess and determine the most relevant bases (2 to 4) of segmentation. Then, based on those most relevant bases, aggregate potential consumers into groups (segments) that will respond similarly to marketing action.
6 Individual segment analyses	For each segment identified, examine in detail the nature of that segment by identifying who is in that segment, what value they want, the process they follow to purchase your product(s) and the distribution channels that reach them.
7 Check for viability of segments	Check the resulting segments against four criteria: 1 Responsiveness – is each identified segment 'different' in how it will respond to marketing action? 2 Measurability – can each segment be measured? 3 Accessibility – is each member of each segment accessible via marketing action? 4 Substantiality – is each segment large enough to justify marketing action and generate profit?

Targeting follows the segmentation process. It is a relatively simple yet vitally important step as it will determine the targets of the marketing strategy(ies) and tactic(s) to be developed. Specifically, targeting is the process of assessing each of the market segments in order to determine which one or ones to pursue based on the following criteria:

- **Size** – is the segment large enough (or will it be large enough) to generate the necessary business?

- **Differentiation** – is the segment different enough from the others? Can we achieve an advantage over the competition in this segment?

- **Profitability** – can the segment generate the requisite sales for the organisation to be successful? Do we have the necessary resources to pursue this segment?

- **Measurability** – are you able to measure sales attributed to that segment?

- **Accessibility** – are you able to access that segment through existing or easily implemented marketing channels?

- **Compatibility** – is the segment compatible with the organisation?

Based on these criteria, the marketer can select the segment(s) with the greatest potential for profit.

Case 9.2 High-profile target markets in sport

Due to a variety of political, social and technological factors, governments and large organisations around the world are interested in reaching a few specific target markets for a variety of objectives. These include:

1 **Aboriginal peoples** represent a group of high interest for governments in many countries of the world, where sport is considered as a potential source of improvement in the lives of aboriginal peoples following years of discrimination. Some specific activities include the North American Indigenous Games and the Arctic Games.

2 **Women** represent an important target for both governments and corporations. From the corporate perspective, women represent an important target market who make the buying decisions in many situations. From a government perspective, in many countries the activity levels of girls are much lower than boys, leading to efforts to increase participation levels of young women. An example of an organisation created for this purpose is the Canadian Association for the Advancement for Women in Sports and Physical Activity (CAAWS), created in the early 1980s, with a mandate to increase the involvement of girls and women in sport at all levels.

3 **Youth** in developed countries are of high levels of interest due to increasing health issues (e.g. obesity) in youth and their increasing buying power and interactive lifestyles.

4 **Athletes with a disability**: through the success of the Paralympic Games and the Special Olympics, athletes with a disability are a focus of governments and organisations alike.

Discussion questions

5 For each of the four groups above, how could sport marketing support the efforts of governments?

6 Select a for-profit corporation of your choice. For each of the four groups above, how could sport marketing be used by that corporation to improve their business success?

7 List three other important target markets.

Positioning is the final stage of STP. It results from the targeting process and focuses only on the target segment(s) identified previously. Essentially, this phase positions the offering in the mind of the consumers in the target market(s) versus the competition. For each target identified, there will be a separate positioning (e.g. for three target markets, three positioning statements). Positioning is the place that an offering (product or service) occupies, relative to other substitute and competitive offerings, in the minds of the consumers of the particular segment. Repositioning is the process of altering your position in consumers' minds (e.g. chocolate milk moving from a children's beverage to an adult beverage/post-exercise recovery drink). In practice, positioning is about finding that 'open' place where your offering is differentiated from the competition. This is often accomplished by focusing on (i) usage environment (track spikes specifically for sprinting), (ii) an attribute (e.g. Nike and athletic high performance), (iii) price (e.g. discounts for students or seniors or alumni on tickets), (iv) association with an endorser (e.g. David Beckham and Gillette), (v) competitive difference (e.g. Gatorade Sport Science Institute), (vi) by specific use (e.g. long-distance golf ball), (vii) by niche advantage (e.g. PowerGel and endurance sport), (viii) by lifestyle (e.g. running stroller for babies), and (ix) specific attribute (e.g. comfortable bike seat). The tool that marketers use for positioning is the perceptual map. A perceptual map is a two-dimensional representation of the minds of the consumers in that target market. The two most important bases of segmentation are used for the axes of the map and then each competitor (or substitute in some cases) is place on the map based on how they are perceived by the target market of interest. An example of a perceptual map is presented in Figure 9.1, depicting the competitors in the sports and energy drinks category for the market of North American men 18–25 years of age.

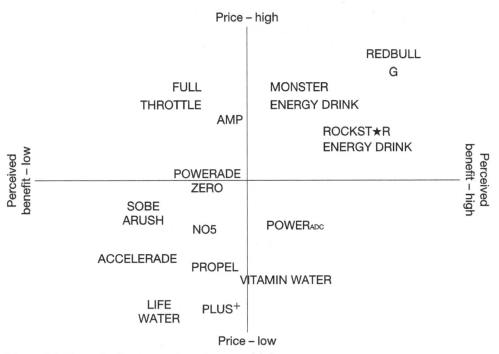

Figure 9.1 Perceptual map: sports and energy drinks

(Note that the perceptual map is based on author opinion and not empirical research. It is meant to be an example for teaching purposes not as a depiction of exact empirical research.)

A perceptual map is built in four steps: (i) draw the axes based on the two most relevant factors for the industry; (ii) assessment of market segment and each competitor; (iii) plot of each on the perceptual map; and (iv) research to validate the draft perceptual map and the positions of each competitor.

The marketing mix – or marketing strategy – is the third step in the sport marketing strategy process (Step 3 in Table 9.1). This step is based on the work done in the previous two steps and is encapsulated under the 4Ps (or the four established strategic elements of marketing strategy). Importantly, a distinct marketing strategy is required for each target market identified in Step 2 (STP). For example, if a marketing strategy for ticket sales for the San Francisco Giants of Major League Baseball (MLB) has identified three targets (e.g. individual season ticket holders, walk-up ticket purchasers and corporate flex-pack purchasers), then a separate marketing strategy is developed for each of the three targets, each with its own set of the 4Ps. Each of the 4Ps is described in the following subsections.

Product

The first strategic element of the marketing mix is product. Product refers to the offering that is provided to the consumer. There are four product forms: tangible good, service, idea and behaviour. A tangible good is something that is a traditional product like a football, a net, a court or a tennis racquet. A service is intangible and is typically experiential (e.g. attending a game, coaching, etc.). An idea is a concept that might be pitched to an investor or a foundation (e.g. a new youth sports camp for young athletes with a disability). A behaviour is the focus of the field known as social marketing and involves the marketing of human behaviour (e.g. doping-free sport). No matter what the product type, the marketer can alter the functionality, features, uses and benefits of the product based on their STP analysis. Sport products include events, game nights, athletes, teams, leagues, brands, merchandise, equipment, and much more.

Price

Price is the strategic element over which the marketer has the most immediate control, being able to alter prices (i.e. reduction or increase) almost immediately. Price takes on many forms (ticket price, price for a merchandise purchase, cost to attend a game including tickets plus food plus parking plus souvenirs, etc.). Pricing strategies can be complex and varied, but generally they can be classified as either skimming ('a profit maximisation' approach) or penetration ('a market share maximisation' approach). The boundaries for pricing are set by what is known as the 'pricing window' within which the marketer can select the price to charge, with the bottom of the window being the minimum price required to keep the organisation in business and the top being the maximum amount that one customer would be prepared to pay.

A key construct in marketing related to price is the idea of perceived value. Perceived value is how a consumer perceives your offering. It is measured as perceived quality/price, where perceived quality is the quality of your offering in the mind of your consumer. When value is compared amongst competitors, it provides direction on increasing or decreasing both/either/none of perceived quality and price in an effort to enhance the value offered to consumers (aka the value proposition).

Promotion

Promotion is best defined by the promotional mix or the strategies and tools available to communicate with your target market(s) and share information about your offering(s) to them. We include eight items within the promotional mix, namely:

- **Sales promotions** – are promotions aimed to encourage sales of products quickly. Examples include two for one sales, buy one get one free, 25 per cent off, coupons, etc.
- **Advertising** – the purchase of time or space (e.g. TV commercial, banner ad online, radio spot, newspaper ad, etc.) for the display of a promotion for your offering.
- **Publicity** – ascertaining coverage in a legitimate news source (e.g. article or quote in the newspaper, online commentary, etc.), which consumers view positively.
- **Sponsorship (cash)** – is the partnership between a sponsor and a sponsee (or property) where the sponsor provides cash in return for association with the sponsee and the marketing value provided. The association between the sponsor and the sponsee is then activated by both parties.
- **Sponsorship (in-kind)** – is the partnership between a sponsor and a sponsee (or property) where the sponsor provides product and/or service in return for association with the sponsee and the marketing value provided. The association between the sponsor and the sponsee is then activated by both parties.
- **Public relations** – involves the sport organisation engaging a professional public relations (PR) firm which seeks to maximise the positive publicity received by the organisation.
- **Personal selling** – the one-to-one selling of a product (by phone or in person) by a salesperson. The most prominent examples are corporate ticket sales in professional sport, where the sales representative for the team makes calls and builds relationships.
- **Online personal selling** – the one-to-one selling of a product (by internet only: website, chatroom, Facebook, etc.) by a salesperson. The most prominent examples are corporate ticket sales in professional sport, where the sales representative for the team makes calls and builds relationships.

A very important note on promotions is the idea of IMC (integrated marketing communications), where none of the members of the promotional mix exist in isolation; an effective marketing campaign employs multiple members of the promotional mix working together. For example, if Red Bull signs a new sponsorship deal with a superstar, it can announce the news with a press release (publicity), build images of that star into its other promotions (advertising) and use the story to sell other sponsorship (sponsorships) – all tactics for an integrated approach to promotions, using the sponsorship in other promotional tactics.

Place

The final of the 4Ps is place, or distribution, which is how the product is produced and delivered to the customer. This involves what is known as the distribution chain where all the steps in product development from raw materials to consumer are noted.

The final element of the sport marketing process is evaluation (Step 4 in Table 9.1), which will not be examined in detail here. However, it is vital to stress the need to clarify the objectives of all partners prior to any marketing campaign, determine how to measure them (metrics), set baseline or benchmark points, and select a value and reliable MBA to manage it.

Sport consumers

The consumption of sport comes in four forms: spectatorship (in person), spectatorship (via the media), participation and indirect. Each is explained in Table 9.4.

Case 9.3 Levels of consumption: NFL football

The National Football League (NFL) is one of the most prominent sporting leagues in the world. Consumption of the NFL by fans happens at a variety of levels, including:

- In-person spectatorship is not just the three hours of the game but the tailgating experience makes it a full-day event. This has led to a whole sub-industry of tailgating gear including team branded coolers, camping chairs and plastic tablecloths.
- TV viewing – NFL draws the highest TV audiences of all North American pro sports and therefore has a multi-billion dollar TV contract. The Super Bowl is the most watched event in the US and 30-second ad rates are $3 million. Fans ritualise their viewing by gathering at a friend's house or meeting at a sports bar. This has been a major force in driving the HD TV revolution.
- Gambling – Linked to the live spectators and TV viewers. Gambling is part of the Sunday ritual. The NFL knows this and, without acknowledging the gambling community, it serves them completely by dictating the level of disclosure with which teams must comply with respect to reporting injuries.

Discussion questions

8 How would a marketer working for the NFL plan for the various levels of consumers?

9 Discuss the effects of the internet on sport consumers.

Table 9.4 Forms of sport consumption

Consumption form	Description
Spectatorship (in person)	The individual attends a sporting event/game in person. Includes purchase of a ticket to a professional sport event and accompanying a family member to watch them practice.
Spectatorship (via the media)	The viewing of a sporting event/game by television, online, radio, print, etc.
Participation	The individual participates directly (e.g. completing a 5km run, playing in a squash ladder, member of an intra-mural basketball team, men's masters hockey, etc.).
Indirect	Consumption of sport through indirect means including playing video games, purchasing merchandise, gambling, participating in fantasy leagues, etc.

Market research in sport

The alignment of demographic and psychographic profiles between a brand and a sports organisation is one of the key drivers to the formation of a partnership so that the brand may effectively market the product or service to the audience that the sport provides. As we also know, brand strategies evolve over time – progression through the product life cycle, changes in the market environment due to competitor activities and so on. As brands continuously explore creative ways to connect with consumers, they engage those consumers for feedback to determine what their attitudes, opinions, needs and wants are. Research is often a significant investment for firms and part of that cost is associated with simply finding the right people to talk to. A sports partnership can help alleviate that cost as the sport itself supplies a pre-existing collection of like-minded individuals that can be surveyed on topics such as product usage habits, brand preference, brand opinion and attitudes.

One of the most valuable aspects of sports marketing is that it is measureable. Sports properties like teams, leagues, associations, etc. measure their efforts in the form of such metrics as ticket sales, sponsorship sales and fan opinions of their product. Corporate brands involved in sports marketing, typically through sponsorship, determine their return on investment through outcomes such as total audience reached, leads generated and engagement of employees and consumers.

If one was to believe the media portrayals that have floated around over the course of the recent global economic downturn, it could easily be concluded that marketing expenditures on sports sponsorships are a corporate extravagance that must be a wasteful use of resources. Fortunately, sponsorship industry professionals have the tools to use measurability as the key rationale to make and/or keep sports sponsorships part of the integrated communications mix. However, the appropriate investment in research to determine sponsorship effectiveness has not been made as consistently as it should: 2010 data from IEG and Performance Research indicates that 36 per cent of brands don't spend anything on custom research to measure sponsorship performance, while another 40 per cent spend less than 1 per cent of rights fees (*Sport Business Journal*, 2010). This often comes down to conceptions from the property that it is up to the sponsor to research their own programme's effectiveness while the sponsor is of the belief that the property should be spending some of those rights fees to produce research.

Staying with the sport sponsorship context, it is simple to make the case for investing in research if it is your job to manage the sponsorships. This is because sponsorship strategy and tactics are often not as well understood by upper management and finance people who, in a time of budget contraction, decide what stays and what goes. Everyone in business understands advertising on a basic level – buy some media, make an ad and people will see it, to put it in an oversimplified way. Sponsorship basics such as property selection, rights negotiations, fulfilment of negotiated entitlements and activation are often not as intuitive as advertising in terms of understanding what they contribute to the marketing objectives of the company.

With research, the strengths of sports marketing can be convincingly portrayed in ways that other marketing mix elements are unable to replicate. The automotive industry is one of the most prolific in regard to investment in sports marketing, so let's look at a couple of examples from this area. An auto manufacturer with a premier-level sponsorship in a national amateur sport organisation wanted to be able to measure key consumer attitudes and opinions about its brand as it related to the sponsorship. With an appropriate investment in field research around its properties, here's what it found out:

- 26 per cent of recreational participants in the sport were able to name the company as a sponsor of the sport unaided;

- 81 per cent indicated that the company's involvement in the sport gave them a positive impression;

- 57 per cent indicated that their next vehicle purchase intent was for a vehicle from that company (almost double the company's actual share of the market at the time).

Reference was made earlier about leads being a valuable measurement of sponsorship effectiveness. Commonly through consumer promotions or incentives, consumers are willing to provide some personal information. It is one thing to have a name and an email address and know that this person is inclined toward a sport that your company sponsors. It is quite another to perform basic research as part of the lead gathering process that allows this top-line knowledge to be leveraged in the context of your brand. A sport that automotive companies are always represented in is alpine skiing, whether it be ski resorts, clubs or national team programmes. One such sponsor was able to utilise research effectively within its lead generation tactics. Alongside the basic personal information any company would gather, it asked three simple questions:

1 What car are you driving now?

2 What car are you planning to buy next?

3 When are you planning to make that purchase?

Think about everything you now know about your prospects on the basis of this information:

- their name and email address;
- that they are a skier;
- they drive in wintry conditions;
- they need room for a lot of gear (i.e. ski equipment);
- whether or not they currently are a customer;
- whether or not they are intend to remain or become a customer;
- their purchase window.

Armed with the prospect's name and email address and their permission to be contacted by the company (always recommended), you can now put a very targeted communication together toward this highly qualified lead. Incentives such as lift tickets in return for a test drive or a free ski box with purchase were especially successful for this company.

Sports marketing contributes differently than all other elements of the marketing communications mix and the value of the results that can be garnered from research are highly influential in determining future strategic direction. More companies need to free up the money to achieve these lofty ends.

The sport marketing plan

Due to time and length restrictions, a full sport marketing plan is not included here, however Table 9.5 includes an example of a typical table of contents in a sport marketing plan.

Table 9.5 Elements of a typical sport marketing plan

Element	Description
Executive summary	A short overall summary of the plan.
Market research	The research undertaken to support the plan, including sections on (i) methodology (i.e. what research was undertaken, how and why), (ii) secondary data acquisition (what data was acquired from secondary sources), and (iii) primary data collection – what activities were undertaken (e.g. interview, focus group, observation) when no secondary sources were available or new.
Situation analysis	Review of the external and internal analyses undertaken.
Consumer analysis	Report on the analysis of consumers and their market.
SWOT analysis/key success factors	Summary of the situation analysis and consumer analysis that captures the key points in a SWOT model (Strengths, Weaknesses, Opportunities and Threats) that is a common business tool to outline the state of the organisation and your position.
Competition analysis	Report of the review of the competition and substitutes, including those who may be new entrants, those who are key existing competition and those substitutes that take the place of our product.
Product offering	An articulation of the product(s) and service(s) offered. This section includes description of the efforts put in place to continue the work.
STP	A very detailed section that provides the segmentation chart and perceptual map(s) for the kids to see.
Sport marketing strategy	Detailed and supported review of the 4Ps.
Financial elements of the strategy	A section including a budget, draft financial plans, draft pricing model and more.
Implementation plan	A succinct plan (steps, who, when) of how the strategy will be implemented.
Control	This outlines the evaluation plan (baseline measures, metrics chosen) to assess the effectiveness of the campaign.
Contingency plan	A plan for what happens if things do not go as planned.

Brand

Throughout academia and practice, there are several definitions of the concept of a brand. The famous ad guru, David Ogilvy (1985), defines a brand as 'The intangible sum of a product's attributes: its name, packaging, and price, its history, its reputation, and the way it's advertised'. US-based brand consultancy Persuasive Brands (2011) offers the following definition: 'A brand is the essence or promise of what will be delivered or experienced.'

The two definitions are similar in the idea that a brand comes down to the creation of an expectation from a consumer and its ability to deliver on that expectation. Although

Ogilvy focuses on the 'intangible' element, the expectation is really based on the physical and perceptual, tangible and intangible.

Brand in practice

Brands are an essential part of how we make decisions and behave in everyday life. It affects the products and services we purchase (and how much we'll pay for them), the companies we work for (and how much effort we put in beyond the bare minimum) and the charities we support. Although a brand is sometimes seen as synonymous with a logo or a name or a design, it is really the culmination of every experience a person has with that brand. This can include the way the receptionist greets you, the time it takes someone to answer the phone or even the accuracy of your invoice.

In recent years many telecommunications companies have desperately tried to create or refresh their brands to win new customers or secure loyalty. In Canada, Bell recently launched a campaign claiming 'everything just got better with Bell'. In other words, all customer service interactions, phone service, television, etc. got better just as soon as the ad campaign launched. Unfortunately this only served to make the public even more sceptical about the brand because it wasn't able to deliver on such an ambitious promise. In other cases brands like Harley Davidson become trusted friends. Harley symbolises the open road, freedom and America. Many Harley riders have gladly tattooed the company logo on their bodies and will wax poetical about even the smallest components of the motorcycles. Each year Harley employees compete with one another for the honour of taking the annual ride with customers. This ride is a chance to step off the assembly line and understand what kind of passion these customers have for the brand. No detail is overlooked, including elements like the distinct sound the muffler makes (a patented element of Harley). This kind of loyalty has allowed the company to make considerable revenue on ancillary products from clothing to restaurants.

Brands can also be used to attract top talent. For years, Google had never used mass advertising channels but did invest in a billboard on the freeway in California that was completely blank with the exception of a mathematical formula with a missing variable. The message? 'If you can solve this then we want to talk to you'. The website listed on the bottom of the billboard was for their recruiting site. If you're part of the rarefied group of top engineering talent then this ad speaks to you but it also speaks to potential users of Google – wouldn't you want to use the search engine that spends its marketing budget to find the very best engineers and not the one with the most expensive golf sponsorship?

Brand in sport

Why do brands choose to associate with sports entities?

As with the definition of a brand, there are a variety of answers to that question. However, the common thread that is found in any rationale behind this practice is that there is value to the organisation in the brand association. Sports leagues, teams, associations and individual athletes can represent many different attributes – excellence, toughness, heritage, flair, etc. The brands that associate with these entities are seeking an effective transference of such positive attributes. It is a way to personify a brand's positioning and its selling proposition.

Value proposition

Depending on the terms of the agreement, a relationship with a sports organisation can also serve as part of the value proposition for a brand. As we saw in our definition of brand, it essentially boils down to consumer expectations. If a consumer pays the top price and receives the highest quality product or service, their expectations are met. Similarly, if a consumer pays the lowest price and receives the lowest quality product or service, their expectations are also met. However, if a consumer pays a price for a product or service and receives quality that meets or exceeds their expectation and they are able to access a sports experience that is relevant to them, the value proposition has shifted positively. This can serve to solidify an ongoing relationship with a brand for a consumer.

Differentiation and competitive advantage

There are many competitive industries where points of differentiation are narrow. Beer, cola and snack foods are just a few of dozens of examples. In such competitive industries, a sports-related association is something else for a brand to be recognised for. Offering benefits through sports partnerships is strategically used to gain a competitive advantage. Whether it's the bank or credit card company that offers access to advanced ticket sales for a big event or the quick-service restaurant that offers collectible action figures, the brand is delivering something that its competitors cannot by virtue of its association with a sports organisation (e.g. BMO – Power of Blue).

Case 9.4 Brand equity/brand value

Brands help companies create value by securing future revenue streams for their owners. Some of the best known brands in the world have a value in the billions of dollars and well branded companies tend to outperform other companies in the stock market and recover from crisis because of the trust that they've built up in customers, employees and shareholders.

Global brand consultancy Interbrand has a widely respected method for calculating brand value which relies on three key inputs:

1 the financial performance of the branded products or services;

2 the role of brand in the purchase decision process (percentage based on the portion of the purchase decision that can be attributed to brand – luxury brands like perfume have a very high role of brand which approaches 90 per cent);

3 the strength of the brand (i.e. a score based on a qualitative and quantitative rating of how well the brand is able to guarantee future return against the competition).

The 2010 ranking of the most valuable brands includes the following top 10:

1	Coca-Cola	70,452 ($m)
2	IBM	64,727 ($m)
3	Microsoft	60,895 ($m)
4	Google	43,557 ($m)
5	GE	42,808 ($m)

(*continued*)

6	McDonald's	33,578 ($m)
7	Intel	32,015 ($m)
8	Nokia	29,495 ($m)
9	Disney	28,731 ($m)
10	Hewlett-Packard	26,867 ($m)

Discussion questions

10 Which do you expect to rise in value in 2010 based on this methodology? Which do you expect to fall?

11 How would you value brands like Facebook which have minimal profit but widespread awareness?

12 Which industries do you think have had changes in the role of brand over the last 10–20 years?

Cost effectiveness

The format most commonly followed to associate a brand with a sports organisation is through sponsorship. In sponsorship, the corporation will pay a fee to the sports organisation in exchange for a set of negotiated rights and benefits. Typically, the corporation will then invest marketing dollars over and above the fee to 'activate' the sponsorship or, in other words, make it more relevant to their consumers and thereby more directly aligned with marketing objectives.

As with any business decision where there is an allocation of limited resources, there is an opportunity cost to investing in sponsorship. This opportunity cost in a marketing context is the cost of not investing those marketing dollars in more traditional media, public relations or some other element of the marketing communications mix. From a strategy standpoint, corporations accept this opportunity cost because sponsorship is unique among all forms of marketing communications in its ability to establish both brand relevance and a deep engagement with customers and prospects. From a budget standpoint, there is also a cost effectiveness consideration. It is an established industry norm in sponsorship assessment that the value criteria sought is such that for every dollar of rights fees paid, more than a dollar's worth of media exposure is delivered by the property. This is contrasted by the fact that, typically, sponsorship represents a higher cost per buyer reached than traditional mass advertising mediums but the vehicle is more targeted (meaning less wastage of the message) and offers the opportunity for two-way communication with customers and prospects.

Reaching a desired audience

One of the fundamentals of business is that there must be a market for your product or service in order to be successful. Therefore, marketers spend a great deal of time and effort defining a profile of their target consumer. The profile is generally constructed on the basis of demographics (age, gender, income, education, etc.) and psychographics (lifestyle, attitudes, opinions, tendencies, etc.). Likewise, sports organisations, particularly leagues and teams, also have a demographic and psychographic profile of the audience they attract.

Where there is an alignment of demographic and psychographic profiles between the sport and the brand, there is a mutually beneficial reason for the two to partner up. For example, North American beer companies are constantly in pursuit of the elusive 18–24-year-old male target demographic. Generally speaking, action sports have been particularly adept at attracting this audience and, as a result, have done very well at attracting beer sponsorships.

Outside of demographics and psychographics of the audience, assessment of a sports partnership opportunity involves weighing the relevance or fit for a brand. This gets further into how the brand image and reputation is defined. The fit must be on the basis of fundamentals like culture and aura. For example, consumers perceive PGA golf and America's Cup Sailing events to have a 'lifestyles of the rich and famous' feeling to them. As high-end events, they are a fit for high perceived quality brands like BMW, which has a strong presence in both of those sports.

The key variable of desirability of an audience may simply be based on the demographic element of where they are located geographically. A brand's marketing objective may be to defend its share in the markets where it is strongest. Or it may be to establish a better presence in markets where it is weak. In any case, the regionality of sports franchises may serve as a strategic approach to meet such objectives. Conversely, the national or multinational reach of larger sports entities (e.g. NFL, Olympics, FIFA) may serve to cover large parts of the world at once for a brand.

Depending on where a brand is in its product life cycle – introduction, growth, maturity or decline – a longer term partnership with a sports entity can be utilised more tactically. Theory dictates that at the early stages of introduction and growth, the focus is to generate awareness and educate consumers about the product. As such, a sports property is a chance to expose a large number of like-minded individuals to a new product offering – i.e. sampling. As brands become more mature, marketers seek to innovate on such elements as finding new usage occasions or ways to generate more usage per occasion. A sports partnership may grow a market by creating more usage occasions. For example, food and beverage companies that obtain exclusive serving rights for a professional team have a captive audience of several thousand per game day.

Brand consistency

In order for a brand concept to become established in a consumer's mind, it is important for that brand to be consistent. The product or service must deliver on its intended use at a quality level that meets or exceeds the consumer's expectation on the basis of the price they paid. The brand must also be consistent in the way that it is presented to consumers for a proper brand image to form. A brand that positions itself as having an appeal dedicated to men one day and to women the next is not being consistent. The product itself has not changed but a consumer would not get a sense of what that brand stands for.

When engaging in a sports partnership, a company must be extremely diligent in determining what sport to associate with and what it is meant to accomplish for the brand. It must be regarded as a long-term strategy since jumping in and out of partnerships is not only a wasteful use of marketing resources but runs counter to the establishment of consistency. A true sports partnership is like a marriage – it must be entered into for all the right reasons and should not be abandoned at the first sign of trouble.

Timing

In media planning, there are different approaches that can be taken to the timing of in-market presence. A strategy that is often employed is to go from periods of non-advertising to advertising or low-volume advertising to high-volume around key selling periods such as Christmas or back-to-school. Sports properties can be used tactically in a similar fashion depending on when their peak audience periods are. For example, in Canada one of the highest television audiences annually is for the World Junior Hockey Championships. This tournament runs through the holidays from Christmas to just after New Year. For a Canadian-based retail brand that is looking to break through the clutter of Boxing Week advertising, an association with Hockey Canada which operates the Junior National Team or with the International Ice Hockey Federation which operates that tournament would make strategic sense.

Case 9.5 *Volleyball Canada* magazine

Volleyball Canada magazine was a speciality sports magazine geared to competitive volleyball players who wanted to improve their game and read about the emerging heroes in Canadian volleyball.

Circulation of the quarterly magazine was over 100,000 and most of the readers were 12–18 years old, had registered for a club programme (i.e. outside of school) and would spend an average of $400 on volleyball-related equipment or apparel. Much of these purchases happened in the back-to-school time frame and some athletes would be both indoor and beach players, which meant that they would be gearing up in June as well.

Typically the Olympic Games would be a huge feature in the magazine and time spent with the magazine would 'spike'. The issue before the games (often in June) would be a preview of the athletes in contention, with in-depth analysis of the competition and what the teams or athletes needed to do to be in contention. The issue after the Games (often late September) would have expansive photo spreads, behind the scenes interviews and long form features on the event.

Discussion questions

Assume you wanted to sell more of your athletic apparel to this market:

13 How would you assess if this media vehicle was the appropriate way to reach the audience?

14 When would you start advertising? What would be some of the risks associated with starting sooner or later?

15 Who or what would you want to appear in the ads? Models? Athletes? Product shots?

Case 9.6 Tiger's brand – Fall 2009

Will the Tiger Woods fiasco mean the end of athlete sponsorships?

Accenture, Tag Heuer, Gillette, AT&T, Gatorade, Upper Deck, EA Sports and Nike all had their names in the news in late 2009 after the fateful night that Tiger Woods ran his SUV into a fire hydrant and released the flood of salacious trysts that he had been hiding from his family and his adoring public.[1] Suddenly, the iconic Tiger, who had always been associated with attributes such as 'heart of a champion', 'confidence', 'strength', 'skill' and 'excellence' was characterised by such terms as 'liar', 'philanderer', 'home wrecker' and 'coward'.

Shortly after the scandal began, a USA Today/Gallup poll showed Woods' 'favorable' rating dropped to 33 per cent from 85 per cent the last time the survey had been conducted in June 2005. His 'unfavorable' rating surged to 57 per cent from 8 per cent.

Meanwhile, a *Washington Post*-ABC News poll found more than four in ten Americans held an unfavourable view of Woods and more than a third – whether golf fans or not – believed companies should not continue to use Woods to endorse their products and services.

The aforementioned companies needed to react to their association with Tiger Woods as the brand that they originally chose to partner with had now altered drastically and decided to drop out of site by taking an indefinite leave from the PGA Tour. Their reactions took the following forms:

Accenture: With Woods present in 83 per cent of the consulting firm's paid media from January to October 2009 through its 'Go on. Be a Tiger' campaign, it ended its sponsorship stating that Woods is 'no longer the right representative'.

Tag Heuer: Days after initially deciding to end the partnership, Tag Heuer recanted and stated that it would continue the partnership. A statement from the President and CEO of the company indicated that Woods' image would be downscaled in certain markets as he was on hiatus from professional golf.

Gillette: Procter & Gamble had 9 per cent of the Gillette brand's paid media invested in campaigns that included Woods from January to October 2009. It did not end the sponsorship but announced that it would not air any ads featuring Woods for the foreseeable future.

AT&T: After only entering into a multi-year contract with Woods in early 2009, AT&T ended the sponsorship agreement.

Gatorade: After releasing a signature product called Tiger Focus in early 2008, the company announced that the product would be discontinued. However, reports stressed that the timing of the announcement was coincidental and that the decision had been made prior to Woods' fall from grace. Gatorade stated that the contract with Woods would continue.

Upper Deck: The company released a statement from the CEO stating that its agreement would continue and that Tiger and his family had the company's full support.

(continued)

---

[1] This does not represent an exhaustive list of Tiger Woods' sponsorship agreements as he also has other contracts including TLC Laser Eye Centers and NetJets. These eight companies have been selected for illustrative purposes.

EA Sports: With its 2010 version of Tiger Woods PGA Tour video game well along in development, the company announced that it would be releasing the game to market as planned. It did, however, emphasise that its relationship with Woods was based on his performance as an athlete, thereby creating separation from his personal life.

Nike: Woods' largest sponsor took no action to distance itself from its association with the golfer or to discontinue the agreement. In fact, Nike founder Phil Knight was quoted as saying 'When his career is over, you'll look back on these indiscretions as a minor blip'.

Final score on these eight sponsors: two drop him, three continue partnership but limit/discontinue image use, three say it's business as usual.

Tiger is certainly not the first athlete with a raft of endorsements to be involved in a scandal. One of the world's other most famous athletes, Michael Jordan, divorced his wife amid rumours of infidelity and gambling problems. Enter Michael Phelps' name in the search bar on Google and you'll find the words 'drugs', 'scandal' and 'bong' among the hits automatically generated.

So the question is: given that high-profile athletes have repeatedly shown that in spite of their sporting achievements they are capable of living imperfect lives, should brands continue risking millions of dollars and their reputational standing on sponsoring them?

The answer really boils down to strategy. If there is a clear and strong relevance for Brand A to have a relationship with Athlete B that the consumer can easily make sense of, then yes, those brands should make these investments in spite of the risk. However, if the relevance is as thin as 'as a company, we're good at what we do and as an athlete, they're good at what they do – it's a match!', then the upside of the relationship is not great but the potential downside of the association amidst a scandal certainly is.

Let's look at two of the opposite extreme reactions from Tiger Woods' sponsors. The Accenture brand's intersection with Tiger Woods is much further removed than that of Nike's. This is really at the core of why Accenture had to end its sponsorship and Nike could continue its sponsorship.

Nike products are a tool of Tiger's trade. His performance on the golf course that separates him from all others who play the game today is achieved by hitting a Nike golf ball with a Nike club while his Nike golf shoes support his feet, his Nike shirt wicks the sweat away from his skin and his Nike cap keeps the sun out of his eyes. It doesn't get more interconnected than that!

Also important to note is that, although Tiger Woods was the beginning of Nike Golf, he is not the extent of it. There is a raft of PGA Tour players who are Nike-sponsored, who consistently perform at a high level and win tournaments. Nike can continue its relationship with Tiger in light of this scandal and expect to profit from it with Tiger returned to playing because its authentic brand positioning in the sport is tied completely to the performance of Nike-sponsored PGA pros, Tiger being the best among them. Who Tiger sends naughty text messages to away from the course has little impact on that brand authenticity.

When it comes to Accenture, neither Tiger Woods nor the average weekend hacker integrates their consulting firm with their golf game – before, during or after. The campaign 'Go on. Be a Tiger' is all a metaphor for excellence. Metaphorically speaking, that excellence on the course does not transcend being a morally corrupt person off the course and, as a result, the brand association no longer serves Accenture.

(continued)

Also noteworthy is that Tiger Woods was the only PGA Tour player with whom Accenture had a relationship. Such a focused spotlight underpinning Accenture's strategy gave the negative PR maximum impact.

This is not to say that only sports companies should sponsor athletes and that direct product usage is the only relevant association. It comes back to the earlier point of brand relevance that the consumer understands and a tangible intersection point for the brand with the athlete. For example, just look at the success that breakfast cereal Wheaties has had over the years using individual athletes on its cereal boxes under the banner of 'Breakfast of Champions'.

This leads to an important distinction between sponsoring a sporting event, league or team and sponsoring an individual athlete. Accenture holds the title sponsorship to the Accenture Match Play tournament within the World Golf Championships series of events. This sponsorship puts it in front of the golf audience locally where the tournament is held and, more importantly, globally where it is carried through media outlets. The golf audience demographic certainly includes business executives who engage in the selection of consulting firms for their organisations, thereby heightening their brand awareness with that segment.

Clearly, there are audiences for a pro sport like PGA golf. Those audiences may be enhanced and intrigued by individual athletes in the sport, like Tiger Woods. However, when the brand association is taken to the level of sponsoring the individual athlete it then becomes an alignment of personalities. As Accenture and many others have learned, personalities can change and throw a pretty big wrench into your plans when they do.

Sources: Developed from: www.msnbc.msn.com/id/34434249/ns/business-sports_biz/; www.msnbc.msn.com/id/34434249/ns/business-sports_biz/; www.marketingmag.ca/english/news/marketer/article.jsp?content=20091216_145128_10184; www.tagheuer.com/the-news/events/index.lbl?uh=7A0340BD-3234-4B37-9DF9-3E223EC799AE; www.marketingmag.ca/english/news/marketer/article.jsp?content=20091216_145128_10184; www.canada.com/sports/golf/latest+sponsor+drop+Tiger+Woods/2395622/story.html; www.msnbc.msn.com/id/34434249/ns/business-sports_biz/; www.msnbc.msn.com/id/34434249/ns/business-sports_biz/; www.easports.com/blogs/itsinthegame/post/slug/ea-sports-moves-forward-with-tiger-woods-pga-tour-online-launch-in-january; www.reuters.com/article/idUSTRE5BD2PV20091214

Discussion questions

16 Discuss the concept generally of athletes as brands. What are the key elements? At what point does an athlete become a brand? Then apply the concept to your favourite athlete and discuss which type, if any, of corporations would be interested in association with that brand.

17 Do you agree with the decisions made by each of the sponsors in the case with regard to maintaining or ending the association between their brand(s) and the Tiger Woods brand?

18 Can Tiger Woods revive his brand? How?

Discussion questions

19 Select a non-sport organisation which could market one of its products or services through sport in your home city. Segment the market for that product.

20 Using your response to the previous question, select your target market(s).

Keywords

Brand; brand consistency; competitive advantage; cost effectiveness; differentiation; evaluation; exchange; market research; marketing mix; marketing; perceptual map; place; price; product; promotion; relationship marketing; segmentation, targeting and positioning; situational analysis; value; value proposition.

Guided reading

The recommended websites and the references listed below provide a good range of appropriate reading. To these can be added David Edelman's article 'Branding in The Digital Age' in the *Harvard Business Review* (December 2010 Issue), especially the Consumer Decision Journey section.

Recommended websites

AdvertisingAge: www.adage.com
America Marketing Association: www.marketingpower.com
Brandkarma: www.brandkarma.com
Brands and Branding – Interbrand Publication: www.interbrand.com
European Marketing & Management Association: www.eummas.org
European Marketing Academy: www.emac-online.org
European Marketing Confederation: http://www.emc.be/
Forbes Sports Money blog: http://blogs.forbes.com/sportsmoney/profile/
Global Brand – Millward Brown Publication: www.millwardbrown.com
Marketing Magazine: www.marketingmag.ca/
McKinsey Quarterly: www.mckinseyquarterly.com
Power Brands – McKinsey: www.mckinsey.com
Wikibrands – Sean Moffitt and Mike Dover: www.wiki-brands.com

References

American Marketing Association (2007) 'AMA definition of marketing memo to academic community', 17 December 2007.

Ogilvy, D. (1985) *Ogilvy on Advertising*, New York: Vintage.

Persuasive Brands (2011) 'Brand definition', www.persuasivebrands.com/Topics_Brand_Definition.aspx

Sport Business Journal (2010) 'Is measurement up to sponsors or properties? Answer: Yes', www.sportsbusinessjournal.com/article/66358

Sports finance

Michael Barker, Coventry University Business School

Learning outcomes

Upon successful completion of this chapter, the reader should be able to:

- identify the sources and uses of finance in professional sports;
- understand the principles of management accounting;
- provide a basic analysis of financial statements;
- conduct a break-even analysis;
- appraise the business planning process.

 Overview

This chapter will provide some insight into the world of sports finance, investigating where and how finance is currently sourced within professional sport and how it is subsequently utilised and consumed by professional sports teams, clubs, organisations and individuals. The chapter will explain the principles of management accounting and how it is relevant for the sports industry, with specific emphasis on decision making, both in the short and long term. This is followed by analysis of the three financial statements that provide the important and essential financial information required by the owners of sports businesses, investors, shareholders and other interested stakeholders such as the media and spectators. The chapter will also explain the concept of break-even analysis, with further analysis of the relationship between costs and revenue following changes in the levels of activity.

Finally the chapter will end with an appraisal of the business planning process and how it is relevant to all organisations, but with specific reference to professional sports. Each learning outcome will be explained with worked examples and illustrated by real information from leading sports clubs and teams.

Introduction

It will become evident as this chapter progresses that the world of sports finance has changed dramatically over the past 50 years with the greatest revolution being in the last 20 years, following the increased availability of higher levels of television revenue within most professional sports. Whether it's within the traditional US sports, or the advent of the English Premier League, professional rugby union or most recently the Indian Premier League in cricket, the amount of money in sport has increased exponentially over this period. This chapter will provide insight into how finance is sourced and consumed within sport and look at the financial and accounting tools available to assist the decision makers within such businesses.

Sources and uses of finance

Businesses have always needed finance, either to start a business, to assist in expansion or purely to meet its financial commitments on a daily basis. Obtaining finance prior to the 'credit crunch' was relatively straightforward. Businesses would seek finance from their bank, in the form of a bank loan or overdraft. Other options could be the issue of new shares, perhaps the sale of assets or maybe the intervention of other third parties such as venture capitalists. Following the 'credit crunch' the acquisition of finance has become a different proposition with banks less prepared to invest in businesses, now deemed to be risky when once classed as safe. Sports businesses have faced the same issues and have appeared risky and less attractive to investors, but these businesses, especially those involved in professional football, operate and survive like no other businesses. How is this possible? The following analysis will demonstrate how sport and finance come together in an unusual business model; we will look at the sources of finance and how it is consumed within sport.

While sports businesses have sought finance from traditional means such as banks and investors, they have been able to benefit from accessing finance from other different areas. This benefit will depend upon the type of sport in which either individuals or teams compete. The levels of finance that can be enjoyed by a successful professional golfer or tennis player will differ from that open to professional teams, which may not be so successful in their field.

The greatest change has been the introduction and availability of television money in professional sport. Case 10.1 (on page 212) compares the example of the English Premier League with that of the NFL in the US, but other sports have also benefited from the injection of television revenue. For example, following the collapse of the Setanta deal with English Premier Rugby, US broadcaster ESPN stepped in with a deal worth £54 million to show league and cup matches over a three year period (*Independent*, 2009). Similarly, the

2008 TV deal signed with broadcasters Sky Sports and Five to show domestic and international cricket in the UK is worth £300 million over four years (BBC, 2008). Such deals are essential for the survival of these sports but offer considerably less than the money available to other sports such as football and US sports.

Along with media deals, sponsorship remains an important source of finance for professional sports. Sponsorship opportunities can manifest in many different ways. For the individual this could be in the form of endorsements where financial payment is made by companies in return for the promotion of the company's products and services. Clubs benefit from shirt sponsorship and naming rights for stadia. Indeed, while more prevalent in the US, this has become more popular in Europe with the Allianz stadium the home of Bayern Munich, Surrey County Cricket Club play at the Kia Oval, formerly the Fosters Oval and the Brit Oval, whilst the Reebok, Emirates and Ricoh are the homes of Bolton Wanderers, Arsenal and Coventry City respectively. Greenberg and Anderson (2004: 127) remarked that 'corporate naming rights has become the norm, the public acceptance has grown and the increasing costs of building these facilities, make it necessary to maximise facility revenues'. Governing bodies will generate revenue for their sport through the sponsorship of tournaments or the sponsorship of leagues and cup competitions. Examples of such diverse sponsorship are shown in Table 10.1.

It is evident from the figures quoted above together with the benefits enjoyed from media deals and other sources such as merchandising that there are considerable sums of money available to professional sport. It could be argued that as successful teams and individuals attract more sponsorship and prize money, the distribution of finance is unevenly weighted in their favour. While this is undeniably the case, such success also results in a greater consumption of finance, in the pursuit of maintaining their position within the sport. This is best illustrated through the largest single expense within a professional team sport, which is players' wages – more of which later. Some sports have employed a salary cap to ensure some form of equality and competitive balance amongst the sides competing within the league. In the National Football League (NFL) in the US, the salary cap in 1994 was $34.6 million for each team but this has risen to $128 million in 2009, the last year of the most recent arrangement. Major League Baseball adopted

Table 10.1 Examples of sports sponsorship deals

Club/individual/event	Sport	Sponsor	Detail	Worth
Andy Murray	Tennis	Adidas	Clothing and equipment	£10m over five years
Singapore Open	Golf	Barclays	Prize money	At least $5m per year
National Football League (NFL)	American Football	PepsiCo	Rights to NFL trademarks	$560m over eight years
Arsenal FC	Football	Emirates	Stadium naming rights and shirt sponsorship	£100m over 15 years
Bayern Munich	Football (German)	Deutsche Telekom	Shirt sponsorship	Undisclosed but 'performance related'
Twenty20 tournament	Cricket	Friends Provident	Prize money	Undisclosed

Source: www.sports-city.org

a different system called the 'luxury tax' where teams would be fined for exceeding a predetermined salary limit. Such taxes would be used to support the game at grass-roots level. While prevalent in North American sports, it is far less common in Europe. A reason for this could be the franchise nature of US sports where teams compete in leagues without the threat of promotion and relegation. The Super League, which is the professional rugby league competition in England, employs a salary cap, which currently stands at £1.65 million for the top 25 players in each club and has remained unchanged for three years (BBC, 2010). The Super League also operates a licensing system for its teams, which is comparable to the franchise arrangement in US sports.

Football in Europe continues without a salary cap, largely due to the clubs' opposition to this but also it would contravene European Union rules on employment law and restraint of trade. With fierce competition in national leagues and in the European tournaments such as the Champions League, market forces remains the determining factor when setting a player's salary.

Case 10.1 A comparison of the National Football League in the US and the English Premier League

What is the impact on sport of the uneven distribution of television revenue?

As mentioned, it is English football and American football that attract the highest amount of TV revenue. This case study will briefly study the development of both and compare how each sport distributes the revenue.

For English football the revolution began in 1992 with the advent of the BSkyB deal. Prior to 1992 televised football was restricted to terrestrial stations with very little live football. With the introduction of satellite technology, BSkyB was keen to promote and develop its channels, and so outbid other terrestrial competitors to secure the rights to the newly created 'Premier League'. The cost was an unprecedented £305 million for a five-year contract. BSkyB, now Sky Sports, has maintained its rights to live football despite challenges from the European Union, in terms of unfair competition and competition from other broadcasters such as Setanta and ESPN. (Although ESPN was successful in obtaining some of the rights lost by Setanta following its demise in the UK.) The current deal which started in 2010 is worth £1.78 billion for four years (*Daily Telegraph*, 2009), an incredible deal in terms of the economic climate but reflects the importance to Sky Sports of football in maintaining its market share and attracting new subscribers. Indeed, BSkyB has recently exceeded the level of 10 million subscribers in the UK for the first time and football remains central to its growth strategy (*Media Week*, 2011). Whilst 50 per cent of this revenue is distributed evenly amongst the clubs in the Premier League, 25 per cent is distributed according to TV appearances and the remaining 25 per cent shared as prize money depending upon the club's finishing position in the League.

This distribution model differs from the National Football League in the US where all TV revenue is distributed evenly amongst all franchises. Franchises are limited in number, owned by wealthy individuals who in the past have moved the franchises to

(*continued*)

different cities in search of a new fan base. Franchises are expensive to purchase but the rewards are high. The current television contracts in place are vast and unlike the UK it is the terrestrial networks that are the main providers. The deal through to 2011 will see CNS, NBC and Fox pay $3.73, $3.6 and $4.27 billion respectively to broadcast live matches. Cable provider ESPN will pay $8.8 billion for a deal to 2013 (SportsBusiness, 2007). With no promotion or relegation the aim is to provide parity and equality within the clubs, and along with the salary cap and the draft system, to some extent this could be said to be successful with 17 different franchise winners of the Super Bowl since 1967 whilst only four different clubs have won the Premier League since its inauguration in 1992.

Discussion questions

1 What would be the impact on English football if the total television money available was distributed evenly amongst all clubs and not partly on appearances and performances?

2 Could you envisage the franchise model ever being successful in English football?

Understanding the principles of management accounting

A simple definition of accounting is the provision of financial information to be used by internal and external stakeholders. Accounting has two distinct streams:

- **Financial** – the regular production of financial statements to satisfy legal and international accounting requirements. Whether a sports business is publicly or privately owned annual reports will be produced, showing the profitability and value of the business for a given period.

- **Management** – the production of management information is far more frequent and not restricted to periods of reporting such as quarterly or annually. The users will tend to be internal. They will be the decision makers who will use the information to steer and direct the business in particular directions. It is this area that is investigated in more detail below.

What exactly is management accounting?

The Chartered Institute of Management Accountants defines management accounting as combining accounting, finance and management with the leading edge techniques needed to drive successful businesses. Chartered management accountants should: inform and formulate strategic decisions; plan and control; determine capital structure and financing; optimise the use of resources; measure and report financial and non-financial performance to managers and other stakeholders. www.cimaglobal.com/About-us/what-is-management-accounting

Inform and formulate strategic decisions

Sports businesses that begin or perhaps have new owners will develop a strategy to deliver the objectives of the business. This initially could be quite modest such as promotion to a higher division within a league structure, by a certain time. To help achieve this a club will probably require a new injection of finance into the business to fund new players or maybe ground improvements. Professional football clubs in the UK have seen how important the ground has become as a source of improving levels of finance. Existing stadia were seen as being inadequate for the maximisation of revenue, in terms of both increasing ground capacity and the opportunities for corporate hospitality and conferencing. This can be best illustrated by Arsenal FC whose move from Highbury to the Emirates Stadium has increased match day income by £50 million per year (Arsenal, 2009). Once professional clubs reach the pinnacle of their domestic game, their strategy could become more ambitious and involve improving their global status through success in international competitions.

Planning and controlling

Any strategy will be required to be underpinned by a business plan, which will set out how the aspirations of the club will be met financially. Whilst the planning process is critical in terms of its accuracy and detail, its successful delivery will be achieved through the effective use of budgets. Lussier and Kimball (2004: 392) identified that 'budgets and financial statements are important tools. The information they contain is key to making decisions of all kinds'. Budgeting is a process that allows a business to monitor its actual performance against its planned income and expenditure so ensuring remedial action can be taken if budgeted income is not being achieved or if budgeted costs are being exceeded.

A difference between budget and actual costs is called a 'variance'. It is often the role of the management accountant within a business to calculate and investigate the causes of variances. Variances can be classed as favourable if they increase profit or adverse if they decrease profit. Variances should only be investigated if the difference is meaningful, e.g. a 5 per cent variance on a budget worth £100 would not be worthy of investigation. However a 5 per cent variance on a budget of £1 million would require further investigation to understand the causes of the variance.

For sports businesses the use of budgets to control and manage expenditure is a very useful tool. We have seen that American football and Rugby League football in the UK both employ a salary cap. This is imposed by the regulators of the sport to ensure financial security and some form of competitive parity within the clubs. This is in stark contrast with the UK football industry where the wages have increased hugely, to the extent that player and staff wages are the largest expense within a club. For example in 2008/09 Chelsea's wage bill was £149 million or 68 per cent of its turnover; however the wage bills of Wigan and Portsmouth were 89 per cent and 78 per cent of their turnover respectively (*Guardian*, 2009). Such high levels are unsustainable for many clubs and in Portsmouth's case resulted in a high level of player transfers out from the club together with numerous changes in ownership and considerable financial insecurity.

Determine capital structure and financing

We have seen earlier in this chapter how the impact of finance within professional sports have increased tremendously over the past few years. The level of money within many sports such as football, cricket, rugby union and the traditional US sports has surpassed levels previously enjoyed. With greater available rewards in terms of TV revenue and sponsorship comes greater financial pressures in the form of higher wage demands, ground improvements, buying new players and meeting expectations of its spectator base. It has become even more critical that businesses have a firm financial structure. We highlight below the change in the type of football ownership where clubs have become laden with the interest payments associated with the transfer of debt into clubs. An example is that of Liverpool FC, which despite the refinancing of its debt in 2009 by the previous owners was unable to fund the construction of a new stadium. Indeed the new owners have indicated that redevelopment of the current stadium is the only viable option for increasing capacity.

Optimise the use of resources

For sports businesses, like all businesses, it is essential they utilise their resources most effectively. In amateur sports this is probably even more essential because the levels of finance are low in comparison to professional sports and may rely on government funding, sponsorship or lottery funding as the main means of support. UK Sport reduced levels of funding to certain sports such as handball, shooting and water polo following their poor medal haul in the Beijing 2008 Olympics. Resources are not unlimited so it looked to optimise its resources by concentrating support in the more successful sports.

Measure and reporting of financial and non-financial information

A key function of management accountancy is the provision of information to internal and external stakeholders. Whilst the production of financial statements may be a legal requirement, their understanding and interpretation will help with the delivery of a business strategy through highlighting strengths and weaknesses and ensuring effective operational and financial control is in place. This will be illustrated through a brief description of the financial statements below.

A basic analysis of financial statements

Businesses exist to make profit. They require timely and accurate financial information to advise and support decision making and it's only when businesses fail to make profit on a consistent basis that they cease trading. This information will provide a picture of their financial state of health, in terms of their current performance and stability.

There are three financial statements that all businesses, including sports, will require. They are:

- the income statement (or profit and loss account);
- the balance sheet (or statement of financial position);
- the cash flow statement.

Each is considered in turn.

The income statement

The income statement provides a summary of the amount of profit or loss that has been generated over a given period. Simply, the income statement records the amount of sales income achieved in the given period, offset by the expenses that the businesses has incurred in the same period. If sales exceed expenses, profit will be generated. If expenses exceed sales, a loss will be incurred. Sales income is generated through economic transactions that increase a business's wealth. For example, a professional sports club will have many sources of income, e.g. ticket sales, merchandising, TV income and sponsorship. These will be reported as sales income on the income statement.

Similarly, it will incur many forms of expenses, e.g. player and other staff wages, match day expenses, ground maintenance and more increasingly considerable levels of interest payments. Typically, a business that incurs continual losses will cease trading; however, professional sports businesses are often unique and football in particular contradicts all rules for business survival. Of the 19 Premiership teams who had declared their financial results for the year to July 2008, a total of 14 made losses totalling £282.9 million before tax (*Guardian*, 2009). Football clubs have a tremendous capacity to survive. Kuper and Szymanski (2009) identified that of the 88 English football clubs operating in 1923, 97 per cent still existed in the 2007/08 season. In any other field, such businesses would have ceased trading but football remains a special case, due partly to the support of its owners but maybe more importantly its position in its community and with its supporters. This is supported by Chadwick (2009: 192), who noted that 'other brand managers can do little more than crave the strength of loyalty, affiliation, and identification displayed by some sports fans towards "their team"'.

An example of a typical income statement is illustrated in Table 10.2.

Notes on the income statement

The sales and expenses descriptions included in Table 10.2 are typical examples and are by no means exhaustive. Income statements will be reported in a format that reflects the income generated and cost base of that business. Internally the income statement may be produced on a monthly basis, but annually to satisfy the legal and statutory requirements for the production of annual accounts. It could be used as an internal tool to monitor performance against a predetermined annual budget. Any significant variances to budget should be investigated with corrective action taken, if required. Sports businesses may measure performance at an operational level and exclude items such as player trading, which fall outside day-to-day activities. The example in Table 10.2 illustrates a professional

Table 10.2 Income statement for a professional sports club for the period ending 31 December 2010

Sales	000's
Match day attendances	14,000
TV Income	5,500
Sponsorship deals	1,250
Merchandising	2,500
Other, e.g. hospitality and conferencing	750
Total sales	**24,000**
Cost of sales	**(10,500)**
Gross profit	**13,500**
Costs	
Salaries and wages including players	(9,000)
Utilities including electricity and gas	(1,500)
Business rates	(1,000)
Legal and professional costs	(1,700)
Ground expenses	(500)
Administration including ticketing, general office costs	(1,000)
Depreciation	(200)
Other costs	(800)
Total costs	**(16,700)**
Net profit or loss before interest and taxation (Operating profit)	**(2,200)**
Interest payments	(1,000)
Net profit or loss after interest before taxation	**(3,200)**

sports club whose expenses have exceeded its sales and therefore it has incurred a loss in the trading period to 31 December 2010. Such levels of persistent losses would not be sustainable in the long run and may force clubs into administration or liquidation, if new investment is not available to support and maintain the club.

The balance sheet

Whilst the income statement records information for *a* given period, the balance sheet (or statement of financial position) provides the financial position of a business *at* a given time. A balance sheet might report the position at 31 December, if the business uses a calendar financial year for its accounting period. The balance sheet will measure the wealth and value of the business by capturing the value of the assets and the liabilities of a company at that given point.

What are assets?

Assets are resources owned by a business which will provide economic benefit in the future. Assets are differentiated between non-current and current assets. A non-current asset can either be tangible, e.g. property or machinery, but can also be intangible, e.g. goodwill. A tangible non-current asset such as a new stadium would be included in the balance sheet. The value of such an asset would be reduced over its estimated life with the corresponding charge reflected on the income statement as depreciation. While non-current assets are long term, i.e. exist for more than one year, current assets are considered short term, in that they are utilised and accessed more quickly in the operation of the business. Examples of current assets commonly found on a balance sheet include cash held in bank accounts, trade receivables, which is the value of money owed to the business by its customers and stock such as club merchandise.

What are liabilities?

While assets provide benefit, businesses will also owe money to other parties in the form of liabilities. Similar to assets, liabilities are classified as short term and long term. Examples of short-term liabilities or current liabilities include trade payables, which is money owed for the goods and supplies it has received and not yet paid for, and perhaps an overdraft held at a bank, which is money owed to the bank. Current liabilities will have to be settled within the year. Liabilities classified as long term exist for more than one year; examples are bank loans and other finance arrangements such as leases or mortgages.

Net assets

A typical balance sheet is configured with the following subtotals.

Non-current assets plus current assets equals total assets

Current liabilities plus non-current liabilities equals total liabilities

Total assets minus total liabilities equals net assets

The net assets figure provides one half of the balance sheet. To complete this financial statement, it is balanced by capital and reserves.

Capital and reserves

The total value of capital and reserves will equal the value of net assets. It represents the value of the company. The component elements will include the following:

- **Called up share capital** – this is the value of the initial investment made by the owners into the business. This could be classified as a long-tem liability and would remain until the owners remove or sell their investment, or the business ceases trading.

- **Share premium account** – surplus generated through the sale of shares at a price greater than their original value, if the business is publicly owned.

- **Profit and loss account or retained earnings** – when companies produce a profit, they are faced with a decision. They may release profit to their shareholders, in the form of a dividend. Dividends will be paid to the shareholders in proportion to the number of shares owned. Any remaining profit would not be distributed and would remain as 'retained earnings' on the balance sheet and would constitute part of the wealth of the business.

A typical balance sheet is illustrated in Table 10.3.

Table 10.3 Balance sheet for a professional sports club at 31 December 2010

	2010	2009
	000's	000's
Fixed assets		
Land and buildings	20,000	18,000
Equipment	2,000	2,000
Total Fixed Assets	22,000	20,000
Current assets		
Cash held in bank	2,000	3,050
Stock	1,250	700
Debtors	1,500	800
Total Current Assets	4,750	4,550
Total assets	26,750	24,550
Current liabilities		
Creditors: amount falling due within one year	(3,000)	(2,000)
Long-term liabilities		
Creditors: amount falling due after more than one year	(12,000)	(7,600)
Total liabilities	(15,000)	(9,600)
Net assets	11,750	14,950
Capital and reserves		
Called up share capital	10,000	10,000
Share premium account	2,000	2,000
Profit and loss account	(250)	2,950
Total shareholders funds or equity	11,750	14,950

Notes on the balance sheet

The balance sheet will demonstrate the value of a business at a point in time. Financial managers will study this carefully, ensuring that the business maximises its value. It is essential that the company has sufficient liquidity to meet its current liabilities. Conversely, if a business has too much cash held on its balance sheet it may wish to utilise this in more productive ways, such as purchasing new fixed assets or perhaps even new businesses to add further value to its overall worth.

The cash flow statement

The final financial statement to consider is that of the cash flow statement (see Table 10.4), which measures a business's liquidity, essential for business survival. The statement is required to demonstrate how, during the accounting period, a business has raised its funds and how they have been used. Cash that has entered the business is called an 'inflow' and will include items such as cash raised from its activities, the sale of any assets, perhaps a transferred player and the injection of new finance into the business. Cash that leaves the business is called an 'outflow', examples of which are payments relating to its activities, interest payments, payments for taxation and capital items such as the purchase of a player into the club.

Table 10.4 Cash flow statement for a professional sports club for the financial year ending 31 December 2010

Reconciliation of net cash inflow	
Operating profit	(2,200)
Add back depreciation	200
Working capital adjustments	2,250
(movements in stock, receivables and payables from previous balance sheet	
Net cash inflow	**250**
Taxation paid	(0)
Interest payments	(1,000)
Scheduled payments to other clubs for players	(2,000)
Net cash position	(2,750)
New financing into club	1,700
Decrease in cash over previous period	**(1,050)**

The cash position is calculated by adjusting operating profit for non-cash items such as depreciation. Depreciation is an accounting adjustment to reflect the value of an asset so no actual cash leaves the business. The final cash position is calculated by comparing movements in working capital such as receivables, payables and stock, with outflow items such as the payment of interest, taxation and for assets. The resulting increase or decrease in cash can be reconciled by comparing this to the movement in cash held on consecutive balance sheets. This is best illustrated with an example of a cash flow statement (using information provided by our earlier income statement and balance sheet).

Notes on the cash flow statement

The importance to a business of its cash position cannot be underestimated. The much-used adage 'Cash is King!' is very true. A company may generate annual profits but could struggle if its assets are tied up in stock and receivable balances and so is unable to meet its liabilities. The cash position represents a more accurate view of the business and so is used when performing an appraisal of new capital projects.

The three financial statements are essential tools for businesses to manage its operations. It provides its internal users such as owners and managers with the information to take remedial action if necessary and also provides external users with a fair and accurate position of how a business is performing. Potential investors will have the information they need to make decisions concerning whether a business is ripe for fresh investment. The financial statements shown in Tables 10.5 and 10.6 are those for Arsenal Holdings plc for the period to 31 May 2009 and provide a perfect illustration of its current performance and worth.

Table 10.5 Consolidated financial statements for Arsenal Holdings plc for year ended 31 May 2009

Consolidated profit and loss account

	Operations excluding player trading £'000	Player trading £'000	Total £'000
Group turnover	309,750	3,589	313,339
Operating expenses	(250,950)	(23,876)	(274,826)
Operating profit/(loss)	58,800	(20,287)	38,513
Other adjustments	455	23,177	23,632
Profit on ordinary activities before finance charges	59,255	2,890	62,145
Net finance charges			(16,633)
Profit on ordinary activities before taxation			45,512
Taxation			(10,282)
Profit after taxation retained for the financial year			35,230

Consolidated balance sheet

	2009 £'000	2008 £'000
Fixed assets		
Tangible fixed assets	440,369	449,517
Intangible fixed assets	68,446	55,665
Investments	730	406
	509,545	**505,588**
Current assets		
Stock	168,758	189,182
Debtors	55,489	46,279
Cash at bank and in hand	99,617	93,264
	323,864	**328,725**
Creditors falling due within one year	(314,096)	(334,252)
Net current assets/(liabilities)	9,768	(5,527)
Total assets less current liabilities	**519,313**	**500,061**
Creditors falling due after more than one year	(292,748)	(310,203)
Provisions and charges	(32,235)	(30,758)
Net assets	**194,330**	**159,100**
Capital and reserves		
Called up share capital	62	62
Share premium	29,997	29,997
Merger reserve	26,699	26,699
Profit and loss account	137,572	102,342
Shareholders funds	**194,330**	**159,100**

Table 10.6 Arsenal Holdings plc: consolidated cash flow statement for the year ended 31 May 2009

	2009 £'000	2008 £'000
Net cash inflow/(outflow) from operating activities	62,305	(21,013)
Player registrations	(12,335)	4,010
Returns in investment and servicing of finance	(17,689)	(19,655)
Taxation	(7,622)	(4,177)
Capital expenditure	(2,950)	(6,944)
Net cash inflow/(outflow) before financing	**21,709**	**(47,779)**
Financing	(15,356)	(67,186)
Increase in cash in the year	**6,353**	**19,407**
Reconciliation of operating profit to net cash inflow/(outflow) from operating activities		
Operating profit	**38,513**	**26,733**
Amortisation of player registrations	23,876	21,757
Profit on disposal of fixed assets	(42)	(19)
Depreciation	11,682	11,555
Decrease/(increase) in stock	25,940	(82,958)
Increase in debtors	(4,680)	(1,172)
Increase in creditors	(32,984)	(3,091)
Net cash inflow/(outflow) from operating activities	62,305	(21,013)

Source: www.arsenal.com

Concept of break-even analysis

Businesses are often faced with making short-term decisions such as, if I introduce a new product, how much will it cost to produce and how many will I need to produce and sell before I will earn profit? A powerful tool to assist with this decision is that of 'cost–volume–profit' analysis (CVP), which measures the relationship between changes in sales and profit following a change in the levels of volumes. We will perform a break-even analysis to determine the point where a business makes neither a loss nor a profit. This is best explained through firstly understanding the classification of costs and how they behave.

There are two approaches to the classification of costs. The first approach is to regard costs as either direct of indirect. Direct costs will be economically linked to a service or product. So when, for example, a manufacturer produces a cricket bat, he will incur costs which can be directly associated with the manufacture of the bat. The materials used, such as willow, cane and rubber, will be classed as direct materials and the workforce necessary to produce and construct the bat will be treated as direct labour. Such costs are deemed direct as they can be economically identified with the manufacture of the cricket bat. The business will also incur costs during the process that are necessary for the production but are not easily identifiable with the manufacture of one particular product. Such costs are classed as indirect costs or 'overheads' and will include the costs running a factory, such as rent and rates, heating and lighting and other labour costs not directly involved with production, such as supervisor and maintenance salaries. This approach relies heavily on the effective capture of overheads and their subsequent absorption into total product costs. Absorption costing incorporates overheads into total production cost by using a method applicable to the production process. For example a labour-intensive process may use labour hours as its basis for absorption, whilst a more capital-intensive process would use machine hours as its basis. As businesses continue to employ sophisticated technological processes in production, the level of overheads will continue to be high and necessitate detailed analysis to accurately determine the true product cost and the subsequent selling price.

A different approach to cost classification is to consider their behaviour. What happens to costs when you increase or decrease production? There are two simple outcomes, costs either change or remain the same when your activity changes. Costs that vary with changes in activity are called 'variable' costs and costs that remain unaltered are 'fixed' costs. (This assumes that fixed costs cannot be eliminated in the short term.) This is a simplistic approach and costs can display both variable and fixed behaviour, called 'semi-variable' costs – more of which later.

Let's look at a possible cost-card for the manufacture of a cricket bat. The main materials to be used are traditionally a wood called 'willow', some form of cane for the handle and rubber for the grip. More of these materials would be required as you produced more bats. If one bat requires 1kg of wood, manufacturing 20 bats would require 20kg, that is 20 bats @ 1kg of wood each, assuming no wastage. This would apply to the quantities of cane and rubber used too. The next variable cost to be incurred would be that of labour. Cricket bats were traditionally handmade but are now more likely to be machine produced so the labour directly identified for each process would be classed as a variable cost.

Finally, there may be other costs that will vary with production but are small and difficult to associate with the manufacture of just one bat. Examples in this case could be the linseed oil used to treat the willow and perhaps the glue used to stick the handle together. These will increase with production, but the quantities used in making one bat are so small they will be treated as a 'variable overhead'. These costs, together with direct materials and labour, are therefore the variable costs of manufacturing a cricket bat.

The cricket bat manufacturer will also incur fixed costs. As mentioned earlier, examples could be the costs associated with the running and operation of the factory, insurance costs and possibly the salaries of staff in the administration and sales departments. These fixed costs will not vary with activity. The rent and rates payable will be the same whether 1 or 1,000 bats are produced. The concept of a 'semi-variable' cost was mentioned earlier, for our manufacturer such a cost could be the electricity required to operate his machinery. Before production begins the business would be liable for a standing charge from its energy provider. This cost will be fixed and would not vary with further activity. However, once production begins, units of energy will be used and a variable cost will be created.

Classifying costs in this manner is a useful tool for businesses in assisting with short-term decision making. Our cricket bat manufacturer can determine whether to produce a new design quickly, if he can measure his variable costs. If the fixed costs are already being met by his existing business, profit will be achieved if the selling price of the new bat exceeds its variable costs. This form of profit is called 'contribution'. It can be viewed as a contribution towards the fixed costs. If the sales revenue exceeds the variable cost, a positive contribution is achieved. If this contribution is then greater than the total fixed costs, net profit will be earned.

Let's look at a possible scenario for the production of a cricket bat. Its variable costs are as follows:

Variable costs (per bat):

Materials	£18
Labour	£6
Variable overheads	£1
Total variable costs	**£25**

If the current selling price is £50, positive contribution of £25 will be generated.

Selling price of £50 less variable costs of £25 equals contribution of £25

Every cricket bat produced and sold will generate contribution of £25 to offset against fixed costs. The manufacturer will not earn net profit until his fixed costs are met.

If the fixed costs are £100,000 for the year, how many cricket bats will be needed to be produced before net profit is generated? This analysis is called break-even analysis. The point where the total contribution equals total fixed costs is called the 'break-even point' or BEP. At this point no profit is made and no loss is incurred.

What is the break-even point or BEP for our cricket bat manufacturer?

$$\text{BEP} = \frac{\text{Total fixed costs}}{\text{Contribution per cricket bat}} \quad \text{or} \quad \frac{£100,000}{£25} = 4,000 \text{ cricket bats.}$$

This can be represented by a traditional break-even chart as in Figure 10.1. The manufacturer has to produce and sell 4,000 bats before any net profit is generated. If the manufacturer is determined to reduce this level, he will either need to look at increasing the sales price or reducing the level of variable costs, assuming the fixed costs cannot be changed in the short term. This process is called 'cost–volume–profit' (CVP) analysis (see page 222). Our manufacturer may decide that the cricket bat is being sold too cheaply so may decide to raise the selling price to £60, which would increase contribution to £35 (£60 selling price less £25 variable cost). This price change would reduce the break-even point to just 2,857

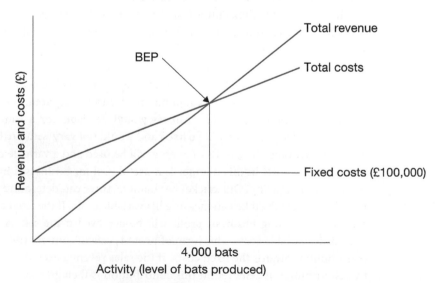

Figure 10.1 Break-even point analysis

cricket bats (£100,000 fixed costs divided by the new contribution of £35). Such a price increase may have a detrimental impact on the number of bats he sells and customers may look to cheaper competitors. He may decide to look at reducing his variable costs but this could have implications for quality if cheaper materials are sourced. In the longer term he may look to revise his fixed costs such as renegotiating the level of rent he incurs on his premises. We can see how useful CVP analysis is for businesses. Implications for other sports businesses could be the pricing policy for match day tickets, the manufacture and selling of club merchandise, such as replica shirts and the financial feasibility of pre-season tours to other parts of the world that are becoming so popular now. (For more detailed analysis refer to Proctor (2009).)

Case 10.2 The Indian Premier League success story

The successful introduction of Twenty20 cricket in England in 2003 was followed by the creation of the Indian Premier League in 2008. The annual tournament is competed by teams owned by businesses predominately from India. Ownership of teams reflects the franchise model used in the US and in January 2008 an auction to purchase a franchise generated $723.59 million for the eight franchises on offer. The largest bid being that of the Mumbai franchise, bought by Mukesh Ambani's Reliance Industries Limited for $111.9 million. Each franchise bid for players with a cap of $5 million, Mahendra Singh Dhoni was the most expensive player at $1.5 million.

Despite the high level of franchise fees and the high salary costs of the players, the franchises were hugely attractive due to the prestige of owning a team and for the potential benefits to be achieved through the high levels of revenue generated by the competition. Team owners would receive 80 per cent of broadcast revenues, 60 per cent of sponsorship revenues, 100 per cent of team sponsorship, 80 per cent of ticket revenue, 87.5 per cent of merchandising and 100 per cent of all hospitality revenues at each ground.

Indeed, by the end of the second tournament in 2009 all eight franchises were reporting a profit. This is despite the fact that the second tournament was played in South Africa following security fears during the general election in India.

Source: www.premierleaguecricket.in

Discussion questions

3 What factors would a new potential franchise owner have to consider when conducting a break-even analysis?

4 What other benefits could a franchise owner expect by owning a team?

Appraising the business planning process

For any business starting out or for any potential new owner of an existing business, the production of a business plan is essential. The function of the business plan is two-fold: it includes all the necessary information required for the entrepreneur to start the business and more importantly provides potential investors with the financial information required to decide whether such a business is viable and a sound investment proposition. For the small, local sports club it may be as simple as the preparation of a business plan with their bank manager to obtain finance or for larger businesses it could be far more complex and involve funding from major banks and other financial institutions.

What does a business plan contain?

A business plan will contain all information pertinent to the starting of a new enterprise. Such information will be non-financial as well as financial. Taking the non-financial aspects first, businesses will seek to demonstrate the purpose of the enterprise: What is the strategy of the sports business? How will this strategy be achieved? This strategy will be underpinned by research into the sector or sport, which will support achievement of the strategy. An example of such would be the recent success of the IPL. Since the introduction of Twenty20 cricket in England in 2003, entrepreneurs in India have realised the potential of this format of the game in their country. The strategy of the IPL was to create the world's best Twenty20 tournament using the best players in the world. Before this could be introduced, it would be necessary to conduct research into whether national or global businesses would support the venture and more importantly whether the cricket-loving public of India would embrace this tournament by attending matches or watching on television. With research indicating that this was feasible, the owners of the IPL constructed the business plan necessary to deliver the tournament. We have seen how successful the IPL has been, so the business plan is being delivered although it's only in the second year of a 10-year plan; there is potentially a big challenge to retain enthusiasm and excitement for spectators and sponsors alike.

Whilst it is critical to have the business idea realised through a coherent strategy, this will only succeed with a robust financial model in place. The financial aspects would include the three financial statements analysed earlier: the income statement, the balance sheet and the cash flow statement. The income statement would forecast the likely income and expenditure that would be incurred over a predetermined period, e.g. five years. Forecasting income and expenditure accurately will be essential to ensure forecast sales growth is not too aggressive and consequently unachievable, whilst being realistic about the future level of costs. Utilising financial ratios is advisable to measure future performance. For example, a declining return on capital employed (ROCE) ratio would suggest problems with the sales and costs forecast in relation to the level of investment being employed in the business. The balance sheet would be prepared using information supplied from the income statement together with assumptions concerning the level of assets and liabilities in the business. For example, what assets were purchased to start the business, how much cash is held, the level of debtor and creditor days, and the level of long-term liability to fund the business. Finally the cash flow statement will illustrate that after initial cash outflows due to start-up and launch costs, the business will be generating sufficient cash inflows to ensure liquidity and the survival of the business. Accurately forecasting cash flows through discounting is essential when deciding upon the feasibility of new projects. If a club is planning to construct a new stadium, can it produce the finance to fund the project and, as important, what are the future cash flows. How much additional revenue will be generated through increased attendances and improved opportunities with catering, merchandising, hospitality and conferencing.

 ## Conclusion

It is evident that the world of sports finance has developed into a complex model over the past three decades. The rewards available due to television revenue and sponsorship opportunities have increased tremendously but, despite this, business survival remains difficult, with controlling player's salaries and levels of debt the main challenges. Despite the economic conditions of the last two years, sport remains a vibrant attraction to global businesses. The continual growth of the IPL, the strength of the Champions League and the success of world events such as the Olympics and World Cup provide professional sport with fantastic finance opportunities. This chapter has not considered the future impact of the internet or mobile technologies; nor has it considered the benefits to be achieved through the large Asian markets, such as branding.

We have seen the importance of financial statements to a business, which is a key tool in its everyday operation and an integral part of its business planning. Businesses can benefit from the use of cost–volume–profit analysis to assist with its short-term decision making. Finally, we saw how the concept of management accounting that incorporates all aspects of strategy, planning and control, financing, information provision and utilisation of resources can be effectively applied to all aspects of professional sports businesses.

Case 10.3 The UK football industry: who owns your club?

Historically, the levels of finance that existed in the game were very low by current standards. Football clubs were often owned by local businessmen, e.g. Sam Longson at Derby County or Bob Lord at Burnley, who not only supported their clubs on the pitch but more importantly off the pitch with funding. Clubs that survived remained relatively unscathed due to this patronage, until the late 1980s and early 1990s, which witnessed a total of 17 clubs, including Manchester United, Leeds United and Tottenham Hotspur, being offered for public ownership on the stock market. As Dobson and Goddard (2003: 189) noted 'the costs of stadium redevelopment, and spiraling player salaries and transfer fees, were both creating significant pressure for football clubs to find new sources of finance'. This change corresponded to the game's greatest development, the advent of the BSkyB television deal that began in 1992. This deal created the Premier League and was worth £305 million over five years. This has radically changed finance within the game. As Conn (1999: 20) commented, 'the £305 million was to make the football club chairmen and owners a fortune, but for Sky it was money well spent'. Seeing the future potential revenues to be earned, it led to the intervention of rich speculative investors who transferred clubs from public ownership back into private hands. As of November 2009, only Arsenal from the Premiership remained a publicly listed company. The most celebrated owner is Roman Abramovich, who has invested over £1 billion since he purchased the club in 2003. This investment could potentially be dwarfed by Sheikh Mansour bin Zayed Al Nayhan who purchased Manchester City and has also invested similar amounts since the purchase in 2008.

(continued)

Whilst these two examples of ownership are for outright purchases of clubs, the foreign ownership of clubs such as Manchester United and Liverpool presented these clubs with different financial challenges, namely the financing of debt through interest payments. Both clubs were purchased by American owners with experience of owning US sports clubs within the franchise model. Malcolm Glazer and family, who bought Manchester United FC, also own the American football club Tampa Bay Buccaneers, whilst the previous owners of Liverpool FC, George Gillett and Tom Hicks, previously respectively owned Canadian ice hockey team Montreal Canadiens and the baseball team Texas Rangers. Indeed, the new owners of Liverpool, fronted by John Henry, are the current owners of US baseball side the Boston Red Sox.

On securing full ownership of the club Malcolm Glazer refinanced the deal in 2006 and secured large parts of the debt against the club's assets. In the first five years of ownership the club paid approximately £260 million in interest, money that could have been used on improving the team or facilities. This takeover led to considerable unrest among many supporters, some of whom formed a new club, FC United of Manchester. The club remains relatively safe financially but failure on the pitch together with any additional refinancing problems may cause uncertainty in the future.

Such levels of debt are not unique to English football, with clubs such as FC Barcelona and Real Madrid managing similar high levels of debt. An additional challenge to all clubs in Europe is the new financial fair play regulations imposed by UEFA which require clubs to break-even in football-related activity by the 2012/13 season.

Discussion questions

5 What would be the implication on English football if the levels of TV money were to fall dramatically at the next renegotiation of the Sky contract?

6 What impact will the new UEFA financial fair play rules have on football in Europe?

Discussion questions

7 How will sport take financial advantage of the internet and mobile technologies without affecting its television contracts?

8 How will international cricket look in 20 years following the success of the IPL?

9 What are the financial implications for the future of individual sports sponsorship arising from the Tiger Woods scandal?

Keywords

Break-even analysis; contribution; cost–volume–profit analysis (CVP); financial statements; franchise; management accounting; salary cap.

Guided reading

Management accounting can be investigated in more detail through journals such as *Management Accounting Research* and the *Journal of Management Accounting Research* published by the American Accounting Association. The Chartered Institute of Management Accounting (website www.cimaglobal.com) provides relevant information on current trends in the subject.

Sports finance, economics and politics are covered excellently by David Conn in the *Guardian*. More detail on sports sponsorship can be discovered in sports journals such as *Journal of Sport Management* and *Sport Management Review*.

Recommended websites

Bleacher Report: www.bleacherreport.com

David Conn at the *Guardian*: www.guardian.co.uk/sport/david-conn

Sports City: www.sports-city.org

Indian Premier League: www.iplt20.com

National Football League: www.nfl.com

Sports Business International: www.sportbusiness.com

Annual football financial report from www.deloitte.com

References

Arsenal F.C. (2009) www.arsenal.com/news/news-archive/arsenal-holdings-plc-results-for-year-end-may-31-2009

BBC (2008) http://news.bbc.co.uk/sport1/hi/cricket/7542774.stm

BBC (2010) http://news.bbc.co.uk/sport1/hi/rugby_league/8744795.stm

Chadwick, S. (2009) 'From outside lane to inside track: sport management research in the twenty-first century', *Management Decision*, 47 (1), 191–203.

Chartered Institute of Management Accounting (2012) www.cimaglobal.com/About-us/what-is-management-accounting/

Conn, D. (1999) *The Football Business*, 1st edn, Edinburgh: Mainstream.

Daily Telegraph (2009) www.telegraph.co.uk/sport/football/leagues/premierleague/4538951/BSkyB-strengthen-grip-on-Premier-League-football-in-1.8bn-TV-deal.html

Dobson, S., and Goddard, J. (2003) *The Economics of Football*, 1st edn, Cambridge: Cambridge University Press.

Greenberg, M. and Anderson, A. (2004) 'The Name is the Game in Facility Naming Rights' in S. Rosner and K. Shropshire (eds), *The Business of Sports*, London: Jones and Bartlett.

Guardian (2009) www.guardian.co.uk/football/2009/jun/03/english-premier-league-debt

Independent (2009) www.independent.co.uk/sport/rugby/rugby-union/news-comment/guinness-premiership-sign-espn-deal-1840568.html

Kuper, S. and Szymanski, S. (2009) *Why England Lose and Other Curious Football Phenomena Explained*, London: HarperCollins.

Lussier, R.N. and Kimball, D. (2004) *Sport Management: Principles, Applications, Skill Development*, Mason, OH: Thomson South-Western.

Media Week (2011) www.mediaweek.co.uk/news/rss/1051723/Sky-passes-10m-subscribers-profits-rise-26/

Proctor, R. (2009) *Managerial Accounting for Business Decisions*, 3rd edn, Harlow: Pearson Education Limited.

SportsBusiness Daily (2007) www.sportsbusinessdaily.com/article/114714

Managing small and not-for-profit sports organisations

Cameron O'Beirne, Curtin University

Learning outcomes

Upon completion of this chapter the reader should be able to:

- identify a range of operational issues that facilitate the effective management of small and medium sports enterprises;
- develop an awareness and appreciation of the components of small and medium sized sports enterprises;
- demonstrate the characteristics of the not-for-profit sports organisation;
- outline the strategic issues facing not-for-profit sports organisations.

 Overview

This chapter provides a general overview on the management of two types of sport business; the small to medium sized enterprise (sometimes called an SME), and the not-for-profit sport organisation. Issues that influence the activities of both types of sport business will be identified and reviewed, including the task of operations, strategic planning, financial activities and the role of customer or participant interactions. Later in this chapter we examine the differences between types of sport businesses and how they differ in management.

Introduction

The small to medium sized sports enterprise

The SME as a sport organisation can be as diverse as a retail sports merchandiser, a sports information service, commercial sports medicine and sports science providers, tourism and recreation providers and event managers. Table 11.1 provides a description of the types of SME sport business that may exist. The sport SME has been identified as a key contributor to the growth of the leisure industry (Berrett et al., 1993), not only in the UK but globally as well. The changing nature of participation in and consumption of sport influences the types of business function that occur and, consequently, the types of sport SMEs that exist. Trends in sport participation away from formal club and association membership to a more unstructured fee for service arrangement is becoming increasingly prevalent. Changes at the social and cultural level are linked to the growth of new commercially operated sport and recreational activities such as indoor cricket, workplace-based sports, touch football, leisure centres and gymnasiums, and swimming centres.

Sport SMEs interact with other sport businesses, particularly those involved in the not-for-profit and participatory type activities which include sport and recreation clubs. There is also considerable overlap as many not-for-profit sporting organisations attempt to develop commercial arms to their operations.

Characteristics of the sport SME

Notwithstanding the large variation in the type of sport business that sport SMEs are engaged in, most sport SMEs have certain characteristics that define them as SMEs. These include:

- providing goods or services to a market;
- focus on making a profit;
- small management structures;
- few employees;
- privately or independently owned.

Table 11.1 Examples of sport SMEs

Sector	Example
Professional services	Fitness centre operations, professional coaches and athletes, sports medicine and sports science, tourism
Venue and events	Planning, construction, management, amusement parks, parks and gardens, tourism
Goods and equipment	Livestock, manufacturing and retailing
Media	Print, TV, cable, satellite and internet

Table 11.2 European Commission definitions of size of enterprises

Criterion	Micro	Small	Medium
Max. number of employees	9	49	249
Max. annual turnover	–	€7m	€40m
Max. annual balance sheet total	–	€5m	€27m
Max. percentage owned by one, or jointly by several, enterprise(s) not satisfying the same criteria	–	25%	25%

Internationally, SMEs may be considered differently. In the UK, section 248 of the Companies Act of 1985 provides the following criteria for evaluating company categories:

Small enterprise
A turnover no greater than £2.8 million
A balance sheet total no greater
　　than £1.4 million
50 employees or fewer

Medium enterprise
A turnover no greater than £11.2 million
A balance sheet total no greater
　　than £5.6 million
250 employees or fewer

SMEs are sometimes categorised based upon the number of employees they have. The Small Business Service (Atkinson and Hurstfield, 2003) describes these categories as:

- micro-businesses are those with 0–9 employees;
- small businesses have 10–49 employees;
- medium-sized businesses have 50–249 employees; and
- large businesses 250+ employees.

Similarly, the European Commission has adopted a single definition of SMEs which uses the figures given in Table 11.2.

 ## Issues for the sport SME

Like other SMEs, the sport SME faces a number of issues that will affect the viability, and ultimately the profitability, of the business. Four key areas need to be addressed:

- developing a customer-focused business strategy;
- building a competitive edge;
- operational planning;
- cash flow management.

Developing a business strategy

The key element to success in any business is that of possessing a clear strategy designed to minimise wasted effort and maximise results. Devising a business strategy is a process of exploring opportunities, identifying and evaluating options and determining a plan of action to achieve realistic results. The business strategy will establish the way in which the business will operate and ultimately succeed.

A business strategy could start with a simple analysis using the SWOT technique that is discussed in detail in Chapter 9. SWOT is an acronym for Strengths, Opportunities, Weaknesses and Threats, where the 'SW' are internal factors affecting the business, and the 'OT' are external influences. Each of these descriptive categories is used to look at the business from an objective perspective.

 ## A customer focus

A key component in developing a business strategy is the need to understand customers. What motivates customers to purchase your products or services? Importantly, remember that customers do not buy goods or services, they buy benefits. For example, when people join a health club, some are buying a lifestyle, some are buying social interaction, and others may be buying fitness. The products and services offered in the marketplace are constantly changing but basic buying motives such as health, beauty, safety, comfort, convenience, enjoyment and economy change very slowly.

Using the health club example, what can be offered people who only have time to work out in the evenings or have children to look after? The business may open at times that are *convenient* for them, and perhaps organise a crèche facility, thereby offering a *benefit* that appeals to their basic buying motives.

As well as understanding customers' buying motives, we can ascertain more information using a simple form of market intelligence. Using certain questions we can uncover vital information to assist in the growth of the business by understanding our customer demographics:

Who uses the product or service?
decides to make the purchase?
actually makes the purchase
buys from me?
buys from the competitor?

Where is the product or service used?
do customers find information?
do customers decide to buy?
do customers actually buy?
are the potential customers located?

What benefits does the customer want?
is the basis of comparison with other products or services?
is the rate of usage?
price are customers willing to pay?
is the potential market for the product or service?

Case 11.1 Paddling a new wave: stand up paddle surfing as the new boom aquatic sport

Stand up paddle surfing and cruising is a relatively new sport which involves standing on an oversize surfboard and using a long shafted canoe paddle to manoeuvre the board through surf, catch waves, or cruise along rivers and other waterways. Stand up paddle surfing is derived from its Polynesian roots. The Hawaiian translation is Ku Hoe He'e Nalu; to stand, to paddle, to surf, a wave.

Purportedly established in the 1950s, its renaissance in the early 2000s saw innovation and new products enter the somewhat stagnant surf market. Established core brands in the windsurfing arena, such as Naish and Starboard, and new players like C4 Waterman and Surftech produce a wide range of boards for all sorts of applications.

So why has stand up paddle surfing (or SUPing as it's sometimes called) exploded onto the surf and lifestyle market with such a bang? Firstly it's accessible; unlike riding a surfboard, you can take out a stand up paddleboard on any body of water. People are using them on lakes, ponds, rivers and in the surf.

Secondly, it's easy to learn; non-surfers can learn to SUP fairly quickly, and many of the SUP brands have made a conscious effort to educate consumers about etiquette and board responsibility by producing education videos and website resources to teach consumers about SUP safety and proper etiquette along with how to do the sport correctly.

Lastly, it has a wide range of potential customers; from seven years to 70, age is no barrier, and there is no constraint on where the activity can take place, be it open water or lakes and rivers, and there are no fees or access costs aside from the board and paddle.

Source: Seabreeze website: www.seabreeze.com.au/news/stand%20up%20paddle/sup-execs-comment-on-growth-of-stand-up-paddle_2882784.aspx

Discussion questions

1 What sports or other recreation pastimes do you think stand up paddle surfing has taken people from?

2 What other opportunities exist for the development of stand up paddling in other areas of business and recreation?

Small business life cycle

The nature of businesses change over time, as societal, environment and consumer demands and pressures change. As a result, the sport SME needs to be agile enough to be able to respond to changes in the environment in which it operates. It is useful to identify different stages of the small business life cycle, each of which places different demands upon the business and management of small businesses. Table 11.3 illustrates the sport SME life cycle, the different phases of growth (or decline) and the goals of each phase. Also, the role of the owner of the business is described. It is important to note that in most sport SMEs the owner plays a number of roles, from marketing, to leadership, through sales and even cleaner!

Table 11.3 Small business life cycle

Phase	Start up	Take off	Harvest	Renewal
Goal	Survival	Sales	Profits	Revival
Role of owner	Initiator	Developer	Administrator	Successor
	Innovator	Implementer	Manager	Reorganiser
		Delegator	Leader	
Typical crises	Confidence	Cash flow	Leadership	Inertia
	Cash flow	Delegation	Complacency	Succession

Research in the area of sport SMEs (Byers and Slack, 2001) has suggested that owners of small leisure businesses typically engage in adaptive decision making based upon a number of factors such as the size of the business, limited human and financial resources, and the person's own involvement in the leisure or sport as their primary hobby. Looking at the typical crises that can occur in the small business life cycle in Table 11.3, how do you think the sport SME owner can overcome these issues?

Start-up phase

This initial phase can best be characterised by enormous uncertainty. Typically, the owner lacks confidence in the business and has all-consuming thoughts of failure: Will it be profitable? What will happen if it doesn't work? The fledgling business will almost certainly face a cash crisis caused by a large amount of initial capital and inertia before sales occur.

> **Discussion question 3**
>
> A large proportion of SMEs fail in this critical time. What do you think are some of the reasons this occurs?

The successful sport SME owner needs to be a good initiator, innovator and organiser during the start-up phase. An idea has to be transformed into a viable and realistic enterprise through generating enthusiasm, sound business strategy, planning and working towards creating a strong competitive advantage.

Take-off phase

The take-off phase is characterised by a sharp increase in sales volume, with the priority being to capitalise on your competitive advantage. At this time the business is growing quickly and more resources in infrastructure, staff and other items may be required to support the increased sales volume. The additional investment, though, can cause more cash flow problems that need to be monitored and allowed for. Planning for cash flow is a key component and is discussed later in this chapter.

During this time the business is growing too quickly for one person to handle and overwork and stress can start to have negative influence if not managed. A delegation crisis will occur unless the owner makes the transition from being just an owner, to an owner-manager. Accompanying this shift, management and operational policies need to be developed and implemented, i.e. 'the what to do and how to do it' so that the owner can focus on more strategic activities of the business. Learning how to delegate responsibilities to others whilst exercising sufficient control to keep the business on track is a key aspect of this phase.

Harvest phase

Following the rapid growth in sales the business begins to stabilise and enters what is termed the harvest phase, which is typified by a prolonged period whereby making profits is the primary goal, you are literally reaping what you have sown. However, accompanying this time of continual profits and 'business as usual', the focus can become more internal, with cost efficiencies, accounting and management policies taking up a lot of the business time. Administration detail and paperwork may become all-consuming, and enthusiasm may decline in the business. Complacency on the part of the business owner may lead to a vacuum in strategy and leadership within the business, and the business may start a gradual decline.

Renewal phase

This phase begins with the recognition and awareness that the business's competitive advantage has eroded. If this phase is not recognised, the business will typically continue to decline, lose staff and sales, and ultimately close. The goal is revive the business's competitive advantage and restore its ability to harvest. In this phase the successful sport SME operator will be a reorganiser and revitaliser. The objective is to breathe new life into the business by reasserting or defining a new competitive edge for the business. A reversal in declining sales, profits and cash flow occurs as the enterprise's assets begin to pay their way once again.

Building a competitive edge

Like any other business, the sport SME needs to explore an edge or advantage over other similar businesses and competitors to be profitable. This competitive edge will differentiate the business from competitors, and assist customers in selecting which products or services to purchase. Australian research into the factors of success in sport SMEs (Department of Industry, Science and Resources, 2001) identified key factors of accomplishment for the sport SME that include:

- strategic alliances for growth and new markets, enhancing efficiency through effective management of supply, production and distribution;
- operation changes to ecommerce systems and procedures including the establishment of a website and raising revenue through the promotion of the internet as an additional sales channel;
- part ownership offers to secure funds for growth;
- decision to change banks because of service dissatisfaction;
- expansion being assisted by an accountant or other professional.

Another key component to building and maintaining a competitive edge, especially in the take-off and harvest phases of the small business life cycle, where staff become paramount to the success of the business, is the ability of management to keep staff motivated and rewarded for their efforts.

This can be achieved through a number of means, including: keeping staff informed and providing them with ownership of aspects of the business; properly remunerating staff; offering profit sharing arrangements, bonuses, commissions and the like; providing an exciting and interesting environment in which to work; providing career development and training; and keeping the management structure flat and encouraging open communications.

Case 11.2 Touch Wine: using industry and sport to support the community

Touch Wine is a unique sporting event that combines touch rugby, a charity focus and an established business industry to drive a number of outcomes. The brainchild of wine marketer Mathew Dukes, Touch Wine was started to provide a networking opportunity for the Australian wine industry, and to give something to charities that need support.

Since the inaugural event in 2005, Touch Wine has raised over $360,000 for Hutt Street Centre, a charity group based in Adelaide, South Australia. The Hutt Street Centre aims to meet the most basic of human needs for people who are homeless – the dignity of a shower and a private toilet, a proper sit-down meal, access to laundry facilities, a safe place to store their belongings and to have people who care about them. Hutt Street Centre provides a sense of hope for people who are struggling with everyday life through mental illness, poverty, family breakdown, addictions and domestic violence. The success of Touch Wine can be attributed to the backing of the wine industry, support of corporate sponsors mainly from the wine industry, and the use of celebrity sportspeople to promote the event, such as former Wallaby Captain Nick Farr-Jones.

Touch Wine 09 offers the public a day of wine tasting in the city parklands, with food, children's entertainment and a sporting competition of touch football. Played between over 60 winery teams in a round robin format to determine the winner, crowds watch the event whilst enjoying the wines from the teams competing. After lunch a celebrity challenge match takes place, adding to the fun of the day.

As well as the competition, the event also offers the wine industry from grape pickers to growers, wine makers to exporters, a unique opportunity to gather together to have fun, to bond as a team and to give something positive back to the community. More than 1,000 individuals from the wine industry directly participate in the event.

Find out more at www.touchwine.com.au/

Discussion questions

4 What does this sort of event provide for the people involved? What benefits – social, economic and promotional – can you list?

5 What other sports and industry could this type of event be adapted to?

Operational planning

The operational plan for the sport SME is concerned with day-to-day processes of the business, procedures, workflow and efficiency. The main purpose of the operational plan is to assist the business owner to work smarter rather than harder.

The process of completing an operational plan enables the owner to determine what commitment is required to make the business a success. Planning significantly increases the chance for survival and prosperity by focusing attention on areas in which Sport SMEs sometimes get lost.

Formalising the plan

The most important aspect with any plan is to formalise it. This means writing it down in a format that is easy to read and can be referred to when necessary, or used by external parties such as financial institutions if support is required in the future and documentation of business goals is requested. The plan provides a way to examine the consequences of different strategies and to determine what resources are required to launch or expand the business. Components of the plan need to include the following items:

Heading	Detail
Introduction	Stating the objectives of the plan as simply as possible, i.e. what is it you want to do?
The industry	Indicate the present status and opportunities for the industry in which the business will operate. Discuss any new products, new markets and customers. Identify any national, regional or economic trends that could have an impact on the business.
The business	Briefly describe what type of business is to be engaged in. Indicate its name, how it is organised and its main activities (retailing, service provision, manufacturing, wholesaling or some combination). Identify the status of the business, such as start-up, expansion or purchase of an existing enterprise. Describe its location and facilities.
The offering	Describe exactly what is going to be sold or offered as a service. Emphasise those factors that make the product or service unique or superior to those already on the market. Discuss any opportunities for the expansion of your product/service or the development of related products/services. If the product processes or services require design or development before it is ready to be placed into the market the nature and extent of work should be included.
The market	Identify your customer profile. Determine the size of the market. Assess the competition. Estimate sales.
Marketing strategy	Based on the assessment of the market, explain pricing policies, and tactics for advertising and promotions.
Management and staffing	Describe the skills and abilities of the management and explain roles within the business. State duties and responsibilities of all staff. What will be the costs of staffing?
Financial forecasts	Provide forecasted profit and loss cash flows and balance sheets that indicate the projected financial status of the enterprise. If the business already exists, show its current financial position before proceeding to a forecast.

Cash flow management

Cash flow management is one of the most important aspects for operations within the sport SME. Financial accounting systems measure profit by matching revenues (what you earn) and expenses (your costs). Unfortunately, commonly used accounting processes do not distinguish between financial transactions and cash transactions. Consequently, cash flowing into the business is not profit as it may be used in areas of the business such as expenses, stock or operating costs. Case 11.3 explains why profits are not cash.

Case 11.3 Dolphin Surfcraft: cash flow and profits

Dolphin Surfcraft manufactures surfboards for surfers worldwide. It has customers in Australia, the UK, Japan and the USA. International customers are given 30 days' credit on their purchases, which enables more sales to be made as international wholesalers can then move stock and sell it on without the capital outlay. This resulted in sales of $10,000 in the first month, which doubled every month after that. However, Dolphin pays for raw materials in cash, which is 50 per cent of the retail price. Operating expenses are 10 per cent of sales revenue and must also be paid for in cash. The result is a net profit margin of 40 per cent and after four months of trading, a profit of $60,000 is seen.

	Month 1	Month 2	Month 3	Month 4	TOTAL
Sales revenue	$10,000	$20,000	$40,000	$80,000	$150,000
Expenses					
Stock	$5,000	$10,000	$20,000	$40,000	$75,000
Operating	$10,000	$20,000	$40,000	$80,000	$150,000
Profit	$4,000	$8,000	$16,000	$32,000	$60,000

However, on closer inspection of these figures, some discrepancies occur in the cash flow. Because the international wholesalers don't have to pay for purchases for 30 days (receipts), and expenses must be paid for immediately (payments) the actual cash flow of the business is in reality in overdraft by $20,000 as $80,000 from month 4 sales revenue is tied up with what are called trade debtors (the international wholesalers). Subsequently without cash flow planning this business could run out of cash and go out of business.

	Month 1	Month 2	Month 3	Month 4	TOTAL
Receipts	$0	$10,000	20,000	$40,000	$70,000
Payments	$6,000	$12,000	$24,000	$48,000	$90,000
Cashflow	($6,000)	($2,000)	($4,000)	($8,000)	(20,000)

Discussion questions

6 What steps could this business take to improve cash flow?

7 How could this business improve efficiencies in the way it manages its cash flow?

Summary

This section has provided an overview of the characteristics of the sport SME, and the types of goods and services that may be provided by such a business. Key issues for the sport SME were identified, and the small business life cycle discussed as relevant to the sport SME. The next section of this chapter focuses on a different type of sport organisation: the not-for-profit sport organisation.

Managing the not-for-profit sport organisation

The not-for-profit sport sector plays a vital role in the overall model of sport business and it has been suggested that the importance of not-for-profit sport in its ability to deliver health, societal and other outcomes for the community should not be underestimated (Australian Sports Commission, 1999). The not-for-profit sport organisation (NPSO) typically involves volunteer management structures and a large participation base.

Not-for-profit sport organisations can range in size from a local darts club with limited resources, to a bigger, financially secure Olympic sport. Since the early 1980s, the not-for-profit sport system in countries such as Australia (Shaping Up, 1999), Canada (Kikulis et al., 1992) and the UK (Sport England, 2003) has undergone radical change, with a shift away from volunteer administration and structures to a more professional way of administering and controlling sport activities. This transition is illustrated in Table 11.4. Moreover, these changing paradigms have assisted in determining the management of the NPSO so as to provide value to members and supporters alike.

What features determine a not-for-profit sport organisation

The not-for-profit sport organisation can be categorised in a number of ways. Kikulis (2000) provides two useful definitions for the not-for-profit sport organisation based upon certain criteria. One is that of the straightforward, simple sport organisation, the 'kitchen table' sport organisation. 'Kitchen table' sport organisations are so named as most decision making in the organisation and administration typically occurs around the kitchen table or something similar. These sport organisations are typically characterised by the following attributes:

Table 11.4 Changing management of volunteer sports systems

Level of involvement	Traditional	Contemporary
Club	Volunteer committees and boards.	Volunteer councils and boards. Some clubs may have a paid administrator.
Regions/state/counties	Volunteer councils and boards.	Volunteer board that oversees function and determines policy. Professional management and paid staff with defined roles and duties.
National	Volunteer councils and boards determine key decisions. May have had a paid administrator.	Volunteer board that oversees function and determines policy. Professional management and paid staff with defined roles and duties.

- an absence of a central office location, paid staff, and strategic plans;
- heavy reliance placed on volunteers that hold a number of different roles within the organisation;
- the structure has few hierarchical levels;
- the sport organisation is governed by few formal rules, little specialisation of volunteer roles or tasks, and;
- decision making is centralised with a few volunteers.

Contrastingly, the more sophisticated so-called 'executive office' sport organisation can be defined by the following characteristics:

- has an organisational design defined by structures and systems;
- has a number of professional staff with specialised roles;
- has specialised roles for volunteers;
- has comprehensive plans, policies and programmes;
- has a decision-making structure that is decentralised to professional staff with reduced volunteer involvement.

Strategic issues for the not-for-profit sport organisation

With increasing demands placed on the not-for-profit sport organisation (NPSO), a range of issues emerge that shape and form the functions, structure and policies of the typical NPSO. Broadly speaking, they include but are not limited to the following:

- stakeholder relationships;
- governance and control;
- strategic direction;
- processes and policies.

Stakeholder relationships

As with any organisation, the NPSO has a range of stakeholders, all with levels of accountability, reporting and influence within the organisation. Not-for-profit sport organisations characteristically have three key groups of stakeholders with varying levels of involvement:

- **Legal:** Legal owners are usually those bodies or persons identified in an organisation's constitution or articles of association who own the NPSO. They may be affiliated clubs or regional associations that form the umbrella body which controls the sport. Legal owners have the right to make changes to the NPSO constitution or articles of association, appoint or elect members to various boards and control finances of the NPSO.
- **Moral:** These stakeholders are usually more difficult to define as they may have no definitive constituted role within the organisation but nevertheless influence the way that the NPSO operates. This group can include players, coaches, officials and fans or spectators of the sport.

- **Business:** Stakeholders in this category include all entities and individuals with which the NPSO has a business or contractual relationship. These can include staff of the NPSO, sponsors and suppliers of goods and services, and in some cases the general public as paying customers.

Governance and control

Chapter 2 introduced governance issues for sport business and provided an appreciation of ethics and the regulatory framework within which sport business needs to operate. The governance structure of the NPSO creates systems that enable stakeholders of the organisation to interact with and contribute to the operations of the NPSO. Most governance structures include:

- formal documentation that defines the rules and regulations of the NPSO, usually through a constitution or articles of association;
- a board or committee of directors whose duty is to govern the NPSO on behalf of the members and stakeholders;
- a board committee structure with defined portfolios of responsibilities within the NPSO that control the operations of the organisation on a day-to-day basis. This may include paid staff who may have the delegated authority to control the NPSO on a day-to-day basis.

With greater responsibility now required of NPSOs, including increased financial accountability and duty of care to participants, a key concern surrounding a conflict of values between volunteer boards and paid professionals can and does occur. Work by Kikulis, Slack and Hinings (1992) and O'Beirne (2001) highlighs that with increasing bureaucratisation of volunteer not for profit sporting organisations, tensions arose and paid professionals conducted duties and made decisions that were once the preserve of volunteer participants.

Why does conflict occur? One suggestion is that due to the nature of the rich traditions and deeply embedded values prevalent in most sport organisation (Kikulis et al., 1995), volunteer board members are reluctant to 'let go' of governance and decision making. Consequently, the involvement of a paid sport executive can be characterised by disagreements, conflict and negotiation to ensure the traditional role of the board and other volunteers in governance, operations and decision making is maintained to some level. A vital step in negating conflict is the need for strategic direction, coupled with policy formulation and implementation within the NPSO discussed next in this chapter.

Strategic direction

The strategic direction of the NPSO, outlined within the organisation's strategic plan, will typically include the board's vision for the NPSO, accompanied by clearly articulated results to be achieved (sometimes called KRAs – key results areas or variation thereof), with each KRA having broadly stated objectives and outcomes with related strategies. Strategic direction is characteristically developed by the NPSO through a consultative process driven by the board and staff, with key stakeholders having representation and input where necessary. Importantly, the strategic direction of the NPSO must be dynamic, so that continual refinement and updating can occur in response to factors in the NPSO's environment that can and will affect the sport growth.

As well as being internally driven, Bryson (1995: 29) suggests that the influence of an organisation's external stakeholders is critical in determining a strategy, although confusion can occur in measuring the performance of the organisation, as the external stakeholder (such as sponsor or the media) 'judge the organisation according to the criteria they choose, which are not necessarily the same criteria the organisation would choose'.

This argument has been supported by Slack (2000: 4) who suggested that corporate sponsors who fund sport organisations expect a 'significant degree of commitment from athletes whose interests in terms of their competition become subordinate to the sponsors desire'. Notwithstanding these comments, the NPSO must be mindful of the need to ensure the organisation has clearly established goals, as well as objectives and strategies for achieving them, and that they have ownership by all stakeholders.

Case 11.4 Beach cricket: formalising an Aussie tradition

Beach cricket is an informal version of the game of cricket, long played in Commonwealth countries around the world. In Australia, the environment of sunshine and beaches allows beach cricket to be played by families enjoying a day at the beach.

Usually consisting of an old bat, a tennis ball and an ice cooler for wickets, beach cricket has specific rules, such as hitting the ball into the water on the full is out, and 'one hand once bounce' when caught after hitting the ground once also being out. Other variations involve 'tip 'n' run', whereby you must run whenever you hit the ball, if the likelihood is you will get out.

In Australia, brewing giant XXXX created an event using a team of Australian cricketing legends to promote and showcase their multi-million dollar beach cricket campaign aimed at beer drinkers. The promotion integrated a competitive six-a-side beach cricket tournament that was televised and included themed packaging for beer and major cricket kit giveaways.

The beach cricket competition featured cricket legends from Australia, England and the West Indies, and was played at customised 'stadiums' on various beaches around the country. The competition proved extremely popular and encouraged a lot of people to the beach to watch the competition, as well as setting up their own beach cricket games using branded cricket gear from XXXX.

Discussion questions

8 What other sports that have formal rules could take this approach to encouraging participation?

9 Why do you think that this event was driven by marketing of beer and not by community participation by the game's stakeholders?

Processes and policies

Policy has previously been described as 'an expression of the values and perspectives that underlie organisational actions' (Carver, 1991: 37). Generally policies describe the course or general plan of action adopted by the NPSO. Policy writing is very particular; words are used carefully in order to ensure precise meaning or intent, as well as aiming to convey the most meaning without verboseness. Importantly, when NPSOs develop and then apply policy, care needs to be taken that users of the policy are able to adequately interpret the policy in order to achieve the outcome intended. Policy is only worthwhile if it is applied, and the NPSO needs to ensure that a process is in place to see to this.

Within the NPSO's environment, the growth of contemporary policies that reflect wider societal values has been at the forefront of sport organisation development in recent years. Specific policies and procedures for dealing with a wide range of issues that affect the NPSO can be developed. These may include policies and processes for risk management within the organisation, child protection, the use of drugs in sport, special populations, as well as event management and the conduct of international events (O'Beirne and Broadbridge, 1999). An example of a specific policy concept is outlined in Case 11.5.

Case 11.5 Engaging the customer: changing the governance of Surf Life Saving, Western Australia

Surf Life Saving is the premier coastal rescue authority in Australia. Consisting of over 250 clubs around the Australian coastline, with over 100,000 members, Surf Life Saving provides volunteer beach patrols during summer, using a variety of rescue methods to save over 2,000 people every summer on local beaches.

In Western Australia, the organisation sought to reposition itself after a strategic review that highlighted the need to appeal more to the community it served. Surf Life Saving Clubs were seen by the community as places that were closed to the public, and surf lifesavers were perceived as authoritarian, aloof and difficult to communicate with.

To ensure relevance to the communities that the organisation serves, a cultural change was highlighted as needed by Surf Life Saving to be able to be more inclusive as a movement and embrace the communities in which it operated. It was recognised that the value and reach of SLSWA operations and the opportunities for SLSWA and its members extend far beyond the current operating structure and practices. To this extent the organisation remodelled its core purpose to reflect this change, and used a tagline to illustrate this:

'SAVING LIVES AND BUILDING GREAT COMMUNITIES'

The CEO of SLSWA, Paul Andrew (2011), commented on the shift as

the move away for from our previous core purpose of 'Save life. Care for life. Building lives', is seen as a must in the changing culture of surf life saving. 'Save life, Care for life, Building lives' is seen to have a focus that is insular within our own organisation and not broad enough to engage the communities that we seek to embrace.

'Saving lives and building great communities', encapsulates and extends our core business beyond our current boundaries while reaching out and embracing the community.'

As an organisation and especially at club level SLSWA saw the need to have processes in place to understand the needs of the wider community and facilitate the necessary change to embrace them, and enhance relevance as an important community partner. In doing so, Surf Life Saving became an initiator and is now identified as a progressive and inclusive organisation – a community leader. New government policies and initiatives such as the focus on battling obesity, the need to better protect

(continued)

children and the continued push to engage more ethnic or minority groups provided opportunities for Surf Life Saving in WA to deliver on this message. Projects that engaged ethnic minorities by teaching them surf awareness skills, and brought disadvantaged youth to the beach, proved very popular.

Community trends of 'fast food' participation in sport and recreation also saw the introduction of events open to the public where a Bronze Medallion and patrol hours (the minimum requirements for surf lifesavers) were no longer required for participation.

Discussion questions

10 Why do you think SLSWA adopted this strategic intent to drive their sport business?

11 What current socio-economic issues could be adopted by similar organisations to change focus to become more reflective of society in general?

Conclusion

This chapter has provided a wide-ranging overview of the management of two types of sport business; the sport SME and the not-for-profit sport organisation. Characteristics of both categories of sport business were identified and discussed in the context of the business they are engaged in. The sport SME is a diverse provider of goods and services across a wide range of business types. We have identified the changing nature of participation in sport and the accompanying growth of commercially operated sport and recreational activities, goods and services. A number of issues related to operating the sport SME were discussed that focused on developing a clear business strategy, building a competitive edge, completing operational planning and proving cash flow management, all with the aim of making the business successful and profitable.

Conversely, the not-for-profit sport organisation provides a contrasting model of sports business. Two different types of NPSO were identified: the kitchen table sport organisation, and the executive office sport organisation, and the changing management of the NPSO in a contemporary environment was explained. A number of strategic issues were identified, including stakeholder relationships, governance and control, strategic direction and policy formulation and processes.

Discussion questions

12 Using the definitions provided for categories of not-for-profit sport organisations, provide a snapshot of two sport organisations for both the executive office type and the kitchen table type. List the features related to the typology definitions for both sports. How do they differ? What are the key resources that the kitchen table sport lacks?

13 Determine where in the small business life cycle a local sport SME is. How would it move to the next level and continue to grow the business? What resources are required to allow the business to be developed further?

14 Using the operational plan guidelines, write an operational plan for a local sport SME.

15 Provide an example of a 'kitchen table' sport you know of. Why have you defined it as a kitchen table sport organisation?

Keywords

NPSO; SME; SWOT analysis.

Guided reading

Further information on the application of organisation theory within sport business is available in Slack and Parent (2006). This book provides a comprehensive overview of the sport organisation within a contemporary framework.

Recommended websites

The following websites may provide useful starting points for further knowledge on the management of SME sport business:

The UK government small business website at www.smallbusiness.co.uk/

Businesslink.org is the website of Business Link, the UK national business advice service at www.businesslink.gov.uk

The Department of Sport and Recreation of the Western Australian Government has a comprehensive list of online resources for not-for-profit sport associations at www.dsr.wa.gov.au/publications. These include templates for conducting club meetings, draft constitutions, strategic planning information and guides, member protection policies, insurance guides and job descriptions for office bearers.

The Sport England website also has a comprehensive research page at www.sportengland.org.uk/research.aspx which outlines a number of publications available free online or by mail order. These include information facilities management, general sport club development, volunteer investment and sport and the environment.

References

Andrew, P. (2011) *Surf Life Saving*, WA President's Forum, Perth, June.

Atkinson, J. and Hurstfield, J. (2003) *Small Business Service Annual Survey of Small Businesses: UK 2003*, Brighton: Institute of Employment Studies.

Australian Sports Commission (1999) *Active Australia – A National Plan 2000–2003*.

Berrett, T., Burton, T.L., and Slack, T. (1993) 'Quality products, quality services: factors leading to entrepreneurial success in the sport and leisure industry', *Leisure Studies*, 12, 93–106.

Bryson, J.M. (1995) *Strategic Planning for Public and Non Profit Organisations: A Guide to Strengthening and Sustaining Organisational Achievement*, San Francisco: Jossey-Bass.

Byers, T. & Slack, T. (2001) 'Strategic decision making in small business within the leisure industry', *Journal of Leisure Research*, 33 (2), 121–36.

Carver, J. (1991) *Boards that make a Difference*, San Francisco. Jossey-Bass.

Department of Industry, Science and Resources (2001) *Game Plan 2006: Sport and Leisure Industry Strategic National Plan*, Commonwealth of Australia, Canberra: ACT.

Kikulis, L. (2000) 'Continuity and change in governance and decision-making in national sport organisations: Institutional explanations', *Journal of Sport Management*, 14 (4), 293–320.

Kikulis, L.M., Slack, T. and Hinings, B. (1992) 'Institutionally specific design archetypes: A framework for understanding change in national sport organizations', *International Review for the Sociology of Sport*, 27 (4), 343–70.

Kikulis, L.M., Slack, T. and Hinings, B. (1995) 'Towards an understanding of the role of agency and choice in the changing structure of Canada's national sport organizations', *Journal of Sport Management*, 9 (2), 135–52.

O'Beirne, C. (2001) 'Exploring the on-line sports organisation: the need for critical analysis, *Cyber Journal of Sports views and Issues*', June 2001, www.sptmgt.tamu.edu/

O'Beirne, C. and Broadbridge, M. (1999) 'Developing sport through hosting international or major events: a resource for sport', Ministry of Sport and Recreation, Perth: State publishers.

Slack, T. (2000) 'Studying the commercialisation of sport: The need for critical analysis', *Sociology of Sport*, 1 (1), www.brunel.ac.uk.depts/sps/sosol/v1i1a6.htm.

Slack, T. and Parent, M.M. (2006) *Understanding Sports Organisations*, 2nd edn, Champaign, IL: Human Kinetics.

Shaping Up (1999) *Shaping Up: A Review of Commonwealth Involvement in Sport*, A report to the Federal Government, Canberra: Ausinfo.

Sport England (2003) 'Delivering best value through sport', *Sport England website*, www.sport england.org/whatwedo/best_value/bestval.htm

Strategy and environmental analysis in sport

Andy Adcroft, University of Surrey

Learning outcomes

Upon the completion of this chapter, the reader should be able to:

- understand the complex nature of strategy and identify the key points of similarity and difference between different definitions;
- explain the importance of strategy in the management of sport;
- analyse the key elements of organisations and environments which determine how strategy is carried out;
- explain how different organisational characteristics and environmental circumstances require different approaches to strategy and different skill sets on the part of strategy makers;
- identify the most appropriate form of analysis according to the circumstances of different sport organisations.

Overview

This chapter focuses on the nature of strategy and how this influences the direction and behaviour of sport organisations. The chapter begins with an explanation of what we mean when we talk about strategy and how this means different things to different people. The chapter also looks at the common elements of strategy across different theories, schools and concepts in order to understand what it means to be a strategist in a sport organisation. The chapter considers three issues crucial to the development of strategy:

- the philosophy of strategy and whether strategy is a science or an art;
- the process of strategy and whether strategy is based around planning and analysis or trial, experimentation and emergence;
- the drivers of strategy and whether the crucial determinants of a strategy are the organisation or the environment.

The chapter concludes with a discussion of the relationship between theory and practice and what this means for a strategist in a sports organisation.

Understanding strategy

In November 1986, Alex Ferguson took over as manager of Manchester United. At the time of his appointment it had been over 20 years since they had last been champions and they were second bottom of the First Division. In May 1999 they won the European Cup. In less than 13 years, Manchester United had gone from being a team on the verge of relegation to being the best team in Europe and, in terms of revenue and support, the biggest football club in the world. It did not happen by accident, easily or quickly. It happened strategically. The manager explained, 'Putting them in a position to challenge consistently would be a long haul . . . would have to build from the bottom up . . . through every layer of the organisation . . . all had to believe' (Ferguson, 1999: 242). The success of one of the biggest sports organisations in the world is a good example of strategy in action: it has elements of vision, analysis, planning and implementation; it contains both creativity and practice; and, perhaps most important of all, it is not just about the individual elements of strategy but how they are linked together.

Seeing a strategy unfold is a lot easier than formulating a strategy or understanding the theoretical foundations of the study of strategy which allows us to make sense of what sports organisations do when they act strategically. Chaharbaghi and Willis (1998) explain why recognising strategy when you see it is easier than understanding strategy by suggesting that it is because there is no single and universally accepted definition of *strategy*. They found over 50 different definitions and explanations of strategy in common and regular use. This reflects the diversity in the practice of strategy not only in sport but in every arena where strategy is important. Some influential writers on strategy have suggested that this is actually of real benefit (see, for example, Mintzberg et al., 1998). Having different explanations of strategy gives us different ways in which we can examine strategy in action. In sport no two games, matches or races will be exactly the same and in the business of sport no two organisations or their circumstances will ever be the same and so having multiple choices of how we analyse them is important.

There is, though, common ground on which strategy stands. Three of the most common assumptions on which the theory of strategy is built are:

- Strategy is about the future. A strategic manager in a sports organisation is less concerned with where the organisation has come from but is very concerned with the next step for the organisation and the step after that and so on. Vision is, therefore, central to strategy.

- Strategy is about how the whole organisation fits together. Strategic decisions can be identified in sport organisations because they have the widest ramifications and implications. Decisions taken by a strategist will have an impact on all the other elements of the organisation.

- Strategy is about the relationship between the organisation and the environment in which it operates. Strategy matters because it influences how the organisation copes with the competition in an industry or market or how the organisation accesses the resources it needs.

Mintzberg (1987: 11) takes these assumptions and develops the '5 Ps for strategy' which can 'help practitioners and researchers alike to manoeuvre through this difficult field'. The first is *Plan*, which raises the notion that something happens before strategic actions take place. Actions are developed consciously; a professional sports team will rarely take the field without a clear idea of how they will play. The second P is *Ploy*. This raises the idea of strategy as having the specific purpose of beating the opposition; plans are frequently built around the weaknesses of the opposition as well as your own strengths. *Pattern* refers to the results of strategic actions and behaviours induced; what happens once play has started is constantly changing as new patterns emerge, some intended and some otherwise. The fourth P, *Position*, tells us that strategy locates an organisation in its environment; the ability of a team to win is the product of the interactions of all the players and competitors, not just one. Finally, strategy is about *Perspective* and how the organisation, for example, sets objectives, decides how those objectives will be met and how it wants to be viewed by the outside world. The success enjoyed by our earlier example, Manchester United, illustrates how the relationships matter more than anything else. The perspective of the club centres on the symbiosis between success on and off the field where both are needed to drive the club forward. Success on the pitch is part plan (what happens in training), part ploy (the scouting of the opposition) and part pattern (being able to improvise when needed). Their position, in footballing and business terms, is the result of how these elements are blended together.

At the most fundamental level, strategy is about two decisions; managers in sport organisations must first decide what they want to achieve and then decide how they are going to achieve it (Whittington, 2002). Michael Porter, elaborates on this and suggests three propositions of how strategy can be viewed (Porter, 1996):

- Strategy is a race to an ideal position. It is a race between competitors and not a journey that just one engages in alone. Whether the ideal position is winning a tournament, making profit or developing a supporter base, sports organisations will face competition from other sport organisations in trying to achieve it.

- Strategy is the creation of a unique and valuable position involving a different set of activities. Strategy is about how you make yourself different compared to the competition. Teams will have their own styles and tactics, businesses will have their own products and services. These differences have a purpose and that is to bring value to the team or organisation.

- Strategy is about making trade-offs and deciding what to do and what not to do. All resources are finite: football teams have only 11 players and rugby union teams just 15; businesses have access to limited human, financial and physical resources. Making yourself strong in one area may mean you become weaker in another. Strategy is about managing strengths and weaknesses.

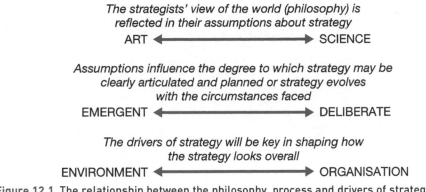

Figure 12.1 The relationship between the philosophy, process and drivers of strategy

Strategy is, therefore, a complicated phenomenon. Adcroft and Teckman (2008) say that it is about how an organisation *performs* combined with how it *competes*. By performance, they mean the organisational elements of strategy such as vision, motivation, integration and change. With competing, they refer to the external elements of strategy and how the organisation interacts with outside elements such as competitors. This reflects the assumptions discussed earlier but there is still much debate about how they translate into the way strategy is done. The chapter will discuss three of these debates about strategy and how they can help us generate a better understanding of the strategic management of sports organisations. Figure 12.1 explains the relationship between these issues.

Case 12.1 England win the Rugby World Cup

In 1997 Clive Woodward took over as the head coach of the English rugby union team. When he started, he had no office, no secretary and very little institutional support for what he wanted to achieve. Six years later, England won the Rugby World Cup. How was the England team transformed from chronic underachievers to world beaters in just six years?

Woodward is one of the more interesting characters in rugby union. As a player during the amateur era of the game, he enjoyed success at club level in England and Australia and was also an international player with England and the British Lions. Following his retirement from playing, he built up a successful career in business, first of all with Xerox in Australia and then with his own leasing company in the UK as well as becoming a well-respected coach with a number of clubs in England. What Woodward brought to the England set-up was a wealth of experience and achievement both on and off the field in rugby and a sharp strategic mind honed during his business and management career.

Despite having access to the highest quantity and quality of resources, before 2003 England had never won the Rugby World Cup. According to Adcroft and Teckman (2008) their problem was not that they weren't competitive, but that they simply didn't perform to the highest standards. Figure 12.2 shows the difference in England's performance and competitiveness in the 1991 World Cup (where they were runners up)

(*continued*)

and the 2003 World Cup (which they won). The most significant difference was in the performance levels of the team.

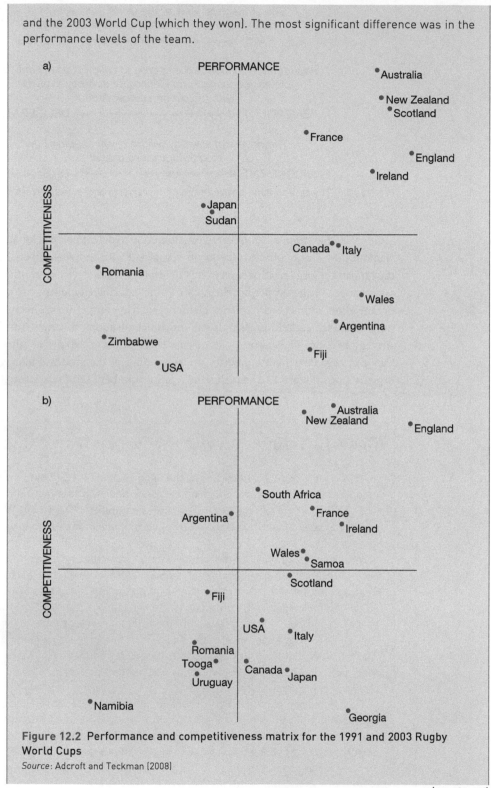

Figure 12.2 Performance and competitiveness matrix for the 1991 and 2003 Rugby World Cups

Source: Adcroft and Teckman (2008)

(*continued*)

The vision that Woodward provided for the England team was clear and unambiguous: they were to become 'the world leader' and 'the best in everything we do' (Woodward, 2004: 168). In delivering this ideal position, Woodward developed seven principles from his experiences in business and sport:

Body and soul: Being involved in the England rugby team required total commitment. Players, for example, may play for their clubs but their primary commitment was to the national team.

The value of employees: The primary resources available to England were the players and these resources had to be nurtured, developed, rewarded and constantly updated if better players became available or existing players retired. The players should expect the same level of commitment to them from England as England expected them to make.

Beyond number one: The culture of the England set-up is based on never resting on your laurels or being complacent but always looking to the next challenge.

Noses pointing in the same direction: Everyone involved in the England rugby team must work towards the same goal, from the coach and captain, through to the players and administrators.

Critical non-essentials: There is a constant drive to find elements which are unique and valuable and so will contribute to a competitive advantage even if they are outside of the core activities of the team.

Re-evaluate structure: Constantly look at how things are organised and managed at all levels, always be prepared to try new things and change if necessary.

No compromise: Having a vision is only useful if decisions are taken and actions carried out that allow that vision to be realised.

Central to the success of the England rugby team was a clear strategy which articulated not only what was to be achieved but also how it was to be achieved. This required changes to the structure and management practices of England but, more importantly, changes to the culture and behaviour of the team and its support staff.

Discussion questions

1 What do you think were the most important changes made which allowed England to be successful under Clive Woodward? Why?

2 Think about a sporting organisation you are familiar with. Do you think the approach taken by Clive Woodward would be successful in that organisation? Give reasons for your answer.

The philosophy of strategy

In this section we are going to consider the implications of strategic decisions for sport organisations. In football, for example, the most important global tournament is the World Cup held every four years. The two most successful nations have been Brazil and Germany. Each has appeared in the final seven times, Brazil have won five and Germany have won three of their appearances. Whilst both of these teams have gone into the finals of the World Cup with the same overall objective, to win the tournament, they have adopted fundamentally different approaches to playing in the tournament. We can broadly characterise Germany as adopting a scientific approach based around, for example, organisation, clear lines of responsibility, planning and preparation, analysis of the opposition, playing to preset patterns and so on. The Brazilian approach is much more artistic, where the emphasis is on individual skill, improvisation and creativity. Different teams will adopt different approaches to achieving their objectives and so we need to think about the different factors that determine how an organisation meets its objectives.

Any organisation's strategy is determined by just two things: the organisation itself and the environment in which it operates. In terms of the organisation, there are many different characteristics which will influence how strategy is made and these characteristics can be tangible and intangible, visible and invisible (Ambrosini et al., 1998). In 1995, for example, rugby union turned professional, which created a series of challenges for rugby clubs. Prior to professionalism, the strategic objectives of rugby clubs were based on Corinthian principles of participation, the spirit of the game, and so on. Post-professionalism these clubs had to change and take on a new set of strategic objectives which combined sporting objectives with business objectives based around developing a customer base, generating revenues from a variety of sources, managing an expanding wage bill and so on. It is not just the stage of an organisation's development which influences strategy from within, as there are many other factors such as size, leadership, structure, ambitions, resources and assets. The other side of the strategic equation is the environment and this also has an influence on how strategy is made; for example, organisations which operate in competitive environments will have different strategic behaviours to those which operate in uncontested circumstances. The degree of regulation in an environment influences strategy and globalisation has had a significant impact on many sports. Madichie (2009), for example, has identified some implications of these changes for the football industry in the UK.

Strategy is, therefore, a complex activity with many different dimensions. This gives rise to the two main *philosophies* of strategy, art and science, discussed in the World Cup example. When we talk about strategy as being art we are talking about a particular view of the world: the world is complex, interrelated and unpredictable and this determines how strategy should be carried out. As an illustration, when strategy is viewed as art a premium is placed on the intuition and creativity of the strategic leaders. Having a feel for what is going on is seen as being more important than rigorous analysis as this is the underpinning of creativity and the development of new strategies which are different to those which may have been employed in the past or by rival organisations. Mintzberg (1987) suggested that strategy is something which could be 'crafted', which raises a set of important implications for the strategist and the sports organisation. Consider Major and Minor League Baseball in the United States. In Major League Baseball, the clubs are often multi-billion dollar organisations with fan bases running into millions, stadiums holding tens of thousands of supporters and players often on contracts worth over $100 million. Minor League Baseball operates on a much smaller scale and there is much less at stake when strategic decisions are taken. For a small team like the Connecticut Defenders with average attendances of less than 6,000, it is possible to see how strategic decisions could be taken on the basis of intuition and without a long analytical process. Could the same be said of the New York Yankees where every game is a sell-out in a stadium which cost over $1.5 billion? Given the environment in which the Yankees operate, where they must compete not only on the pitch but also for supporters, television revenues and players, can they find a unique and valuable position without some elements of creativity? How can the Defenders progress through the Minor Leagues without a well-thought through-strategy? Strategy is indeed a complex activity.

The opposite view, strategy as science, begins with the assumption that the environment is a fundamentally rational place and the different players in that environment (businesses, customers, suppliers and so on) will act in a rational manner: Sport organisations are expected to behave in a way most suited to meet their objectives, supporters make rational decisions about which matches to attend or replica shirts to buy and so on. Rationality means the environment is predictable and so planning long-term strategies is possible. The first proponent of this view was Andrews (1965), who suggested that strategy was about analysing the environment in order to understand the available opportunities and threats faced, identifying the strengths and weaknesses of the organisation and then formulating an appropriate strategy. What is usually central to any scientific approach to strategy is the activity of analysis. From a scientific perspective strategy is frequently a linear process made up of defined steps which are combined together with a clear and coherent logic.

When we analyse the strategies of most sport organisations and the strategic behaviours of people within them, we are likely to find elements of both art and science in strategy making. If strategy was solely about art then it would be an activity driven by *trial and error*, where intuition is wrong as often as it is right, which gives rise to levels of risk unacceptable in sport organisations with global reach like Manchester United and the New York Yankees. On the other hand, if strategy was solely scientific in nature, it would result in all organisations coalescing together when faced with a common set of rational threats and opportunities in their environments. Organisations like Manchester United and the New York Yankees would not be able to generate a distinctive competitive advantage for the long term. This suggests that the underpinning philosophies of strategy are clear-cut in theory but not always in practice, the next section of this chapter will consider the extent to which it is the same for the process of strategy.

The process of strategy

The 'Rumble in the Jungle' between Muhammad Ali and George Foreman in 1974 is probably the most famous bout in boxing history. In this fight, the 34-year-old Ali won the heavyweight title from Foreman, a fighter many experts felt was unbeatable. This fight is a good illustration of how an implemented strategy can become very different to the strategy intended. Mailer (1975) argues that Ali's strategy going into the opening round was to surprise Foreman with unexpected punches and knock him out. The strategy failed. Ali's response was to say to himself 'I'm going to find a way to master this man' (ibid.: 183) and he improvised a new strategy, the *rope a dope*. Seven rounds later Ali knocked Foreman out. There are two important lessons from this example. First, things rarely go exactly to plan: a competitor may respond in an unexpected manner, consumer tastes may shift suddenly or there could be a shock to the economic system. The second lesson is that if a strategy is not working, then it has to be changed. Porter (1996) argues that strategy is about creating positions which are unique and valuable; a strategy that does not work can be unique but never valuable. Ali went into the fight with a deliberate strategy but won with a strategy that emerged from the circumstances.

When we talk about deliberate strategies, we are referring to strategy having a distinct and clear planning dimension (Lynch, 2009). Consider the different levels of decision making and action that take place when a sport organisation behaves strategically. At the highest level, decisions are taken about objectives. These may involve decisions about targets for performance in terms of, say, positions in a final league table, matches to be won and so on. It can also involve business objectives with things like market share, revenues and profits, share prices and so on. Objectives on their own are meaningless as they have to be supported by decisions about how they are going to be reached. This is frequently referred to as the policy level and could involve decisions about how a team is going to play, the type of player that may be recruited, how revenue is going to be generated from television, merchandise, through the turnstiles and so on. The strategy of the organisation is still unrealised; things have been planned but not implemented. The final stage in the process is the shift from decision making to action. This is the stage where the team will implement what has been practised on the training ground, the new replica kit will be launched, the new stadium opened and so on. The key element is that the three dimensions of strategic behaviour are linked together in a coherent and logical manner. Within a deliberate framework, organisations work towards clearly defined goals, have explicit plans about how those goals are to be met and these plans are put into action throughout the organisation (Lynch, 2009).

The most common form of deliberate strategy is built on the analysis–choice–implementation cycle. Strategic analysis of the organisation and its environment is carried out and strategic decisions are taken about where and how the organisation will compete. These decisions are then put into practice until future analysis suggests that the strategy has to change. Thus strategy is linear and has a clear starting and finishing point. What happens if something unexpected occurs? Strategy may have to become an activity which emerges from the circumstances faced by the organisation (Hamel, 2000). An emergent framework for strategy is different to a deliberate framework in a number of key ways. In sporting terms this is the difference between a rugby union team executing a well-practised move from a set piece and the same team creating a move from broken play. Similarly, it could be the Quarterback in an American Football team calling a play compared to what happens when the ball is intercepted.

There can be no set pattern to an emergent approach to strategy. It may be based around improvisation and depend on the ability of the strategist to be creative or it could be based around trial and error and the willingness of the strategist to take risks to secure a competitive advantage. It could also involve the strategist adopting a wait and see posture and developing strategy as a collection of short-term adjustments to changes inside and outside of the organisation. Under an emergent framework of strategy, we move away from the view of strategy as something that is linear and time-bound to something which is much more random, chaotic and lacking in a definite beginning and end. Strategy is an iterative, ongoing process involving constant change and development such that the strategy will frequently end up looking nothing like how it started or was intended.

Different organisations will, therefore, adopt different approaches to strategy making. Some sport managers will work in organisations operating in the type of environment which will support deliberate strategy making whilst others will work in organisations

Table 12.1 Characteristics of deliberate and emergent organisations and the environments in which they operate

	Deliberate approach to strategy	Emergent approach to strategy
Organisational type	Well-established, possibly large organisations which have operated for a number of years.	Small and growing. Likely to be relatively young.
Organisational structure	Hierarchical or bureaucratic. Clear divisions of responsibility. Vertical communication the order of the day.	Flat structures without clear divisions and tiers of management. Horizontal communication dominates.
Organisational culture	Rigid and well established. Significant influence on how things are done and what is done.	Still forming. Open to change. Fluid.
Environmental conditions	Stable markets with limited competition. Unlikely to be significant change.	Dynamic and constantly changing. Possibly many competitors.

which must be more emergent in approach. Table 12.1 offers a number of illustrations of what we could expect to see in organisations and their environments which adopt these two approaches to strategy.

As in the previous section, most organisations, sport based or otherwise, will not be deliberate or emergent in their strategy making but rather may have elements of both and will, over time, shift between deliberate and emergent approaches. For example, as organisations grow and become more successful it may be inevitable that they become more deliberate in their strategy making; it is harder for larger and older firms to be nimble and responsive than it is for smaller and younger firms in the same way that individuals become more set in their ways and risk-averse as they grow older. One of the most interesting conundrums in strategy is how these organisational forces for deliberate strategy making are often in conflict with forces in the environment which demand constant and ever more dramatic change. The challenge in all this for the manager in the sports organisation is finding that balance and the ability to do that often depends on whether strategy is an organisation- or environment-driven activity and that is the issue the next section in this chapter will consider.

Case 12.2 Four teams, four strategies: the top of the English Premier League

Since its inception in 1992, the English Premier League has been dominated by four clubs: Manchester United, Arsenal, Chelsea and Liverpool. On occasion, other teams such as Blackburn Rovers and Leeds United have been able to make an impact but none have been able to sustain a position as a top four club. The ability to sustain a position at the top of the league has been dependent on a combination of two things: first, what happens on the pitch and, second, what happens off the pitch with the business performance of each club. Not only is it possible to identify each team by the way it plays, it is also possible to identify some key differences in the strategic approaches taken by each club.

(continued)

Table 12.2 shows the revenue generated by each of these clubs from match day activities (such as ticket sales), the broadcasting of matches both in the UK and overseas and commercial activities such as sponsorship and merchandising. A number of interesting patterns emerge. The most important of these is that the financial success of a club is determined by the success of the team; the total revenue generated by each club grows when the team does through, for example, increased broadcasting revenue and ticket sales. In 2008 Manchester United generated significantly higher revenue than the other clubs, Chelsea and Arsenal operated at roughly the same level and Liverpool lagged somewhere behind. Revenue generated is important because, over the long term, it determines how much each club can spend in the transfer market buying new players.

Table 12.2 Revenue generated by four Premier League clubs (€, million)

	2005	2006	2007	2008
Manchester United	246.4	242.5	315.2	324.8
Chelsea	220.8	221.0	283.0	268.9
Arsenal	176.3	192.4	263.9	264.4
Liverpool	181.2	176.0	206.5	210.9

Source: Deloitte (2007, 2009)

If this revenue is broken down into its constituent parts, we get further insights into the strategies that each club can and does employ. Table 12.3 provides this data and some interesting patterns can be seen. Manchester United has been successful in generating increasing revenue from all activities and has, for example, increased the size of its ground and made investments in exploiting the brand overseas. Arsenal's main increase in revenue has come from investment in a new ground but it has been much less successful on the commercial front. Chelsea has been unable to generate increasing revenue from the broadcasting of its games and Liverpool has been unable to generate increasing match day revenues.

Table 12.3 Breakdown of revenue generated by four Premier League clubs (€, million)

	Match day		Broadcasting		Commercial	
	2006	2008	2006	2008	2006	2008
Manchester United	103.1	128.2	65.9	115.7	73.6	80.9
Chelsea	83.4	94.1	76.1	77.4	65.1	77.0
Arsenal	63.8	119.5	79.4	88.8	49.2	56.1
Liverpool	47.2	49.5	72.0	96.4	56.8	65.0

Source: Deloitte (2007, 2009)

Table 12.4 summarises some of the key strategic moves made by each of these clubs in recent years and identifies a key challenge faced.

(continued)

Table 12.4 Key strategic moves and challenges

Arsenal	Chelsea	Liverpool	Manchester United
Invest in a new stadium to increase revenues.	Establish Chelsea as an international brand.	Focus on team performance rather than business performance.	Exploit global brand to maximise commercial revenues.
Invest in young players rather than expensive established players.	Invest in established players to bring success quickly.	Invest in a mixture of young and established players.	Expand capacity of stadium.
Key strategic challenge	*Key strategic challenge*	*Key strategic challenge*	Invest in a mixture of young and established players.
Increasing commercial revenues.	Match day revenue limited by stadium capacity.	Increasing match day and commercial revenue.	*Key strategic challenge*
			Meeting international competition from clubs like Real Madrid for revenues and players.

Discussion questions

3 To what extent do you think each of these clubs has adopted a proactive strategy or had a strategy imposed on them by their circumstances? What are the implications of this for how the clubs will compete with each other in the future?

4 Which of these clubs do you think has the most sustainable competitive advantage and which has the least sustainable competitive advantage? What do you think should be the strategic priorities of these clubs?

The drivers of strategy

In the formulation of strategy, which is the most influential, the organisation or the environment? Against Norway in 1993, the manager of the England football team, Graham Taylor, changed his strategy to counteract the opposition and England lost. Having a strategy driven by the strengths of the competition failed. As a counterpoint, in the 2005 Ashes England developed a series of strategies which were aimed at nullifying the strengths of Australia, and England won a close series by 2 to 1. Having strategy determined by the competition works. The strategic response of Australia to losing the Ashes in 2005 was to follow an approach which centred on the team's own strengths and they won the return series 5 to 0. New Zealand went into the 2007 Rugby World Cup with a style of play built around the team's strengths. They were clear favourites to win the tournament as they had been pretty much unbeatable in the preceding two years. In the quarter final against France they continued with this style of play regardless of what the opposition did. They lost. Building a strategy around your own strengths can bring success but it can also bring failure. These examples show that strategy can be driven by the competition faced and also driven by the resources and talents available. When strategy is driven by external forces, we can broadly characterise this as *positioning* and when strategy is internally driven we can characterise this as a *resource-based view*.

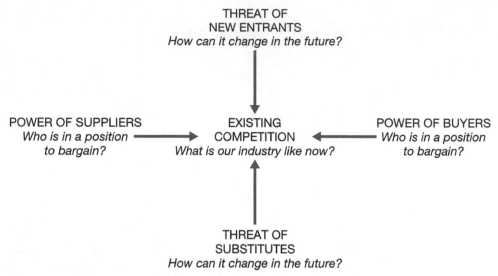

Figure 12.3 Porter's Five Forces model

The most significant exponent of a positioning approach to strategy is Michael Porter and a discussion of his work is useful in establishing some of the principles of this approach (see, for example, Porter, 1979 and 1980). The positioning approach to strategy begins with the assumption that the aim of any firm is to maximise its returns. In the case of traditional businesses this is usually thought of in terms of profit maximisation but this is not always a useful way to think about sport organisations. For example, is Manchester United driven by the objective of winning football matches (and hence titles and trophies) or by the objective of making profit? In practice, the answer is probably both as they are closely linked to each other. The second assumption is that an organisation's ability to meet its objectives depends on the degree of competition faced in the industry or market. The higher the level of competition, the harder it is to make large profits. Using Manchester United again, this translates into the quality of opposition faced on the football pitch and the competition faced in the business arena. The final assumption of this positioning school is that competition is a multi-dimensional phenomenon which happens at a series of different levels and this gives rise to Porter's Five Forces model (Figure 12.3).

This approach focuses on competition at different levels in an industry: the intensity of competitive rivalry, the threat of new entrants, the threat of substitute products, the bargaining power of buyers and the bargaining power of suppliers. In making use of this model it is useful to think about the key strategic questions that need to be answered and we can identify three in the case of Manchester United:

● What is the state of direct competition now?
  We could think about the number and size of competitors, the degree of differentiation between competitors, the exit barriers to the industry and so on.

  How intense is the competition Manchester United faces on and off the pitch?
  Do different teams employ different strategies and tactics?

How do clubs hold on to their existing supporters and attract new supporters?
Which clubs have competitive advantages?

● How likely is it that competition will change in the future?
Competition could change in terms of new products or services entering the market or competition could changes in terms of new firms entering the industry.

Will supporters of football be attracted to other sports?
Will new teams be promoted and will they be a significant threat to Manchester United?
What resources might new clubs have?
What about international competition?

● Where does power lie in the industry?
This refers to the forward relationships a firm engages in with the buyers of its product or service and the backwards relationships with the firms that supply the necessary inputs for the firm. Do buyers have choices about where they make their purchases and does the firm have a choice about where it buys its inputs?

How loyal to Manchester United are its supporters?
Could they move to support another team?
What is the relationship between Manchester United and other clubs when buying and selling players?

At the opposite end of the spectrum to the positioning approach is the resource-based view. This suggests that strategic success is driven by the organisation and not the environment (see, for example, Wernerfelt, 1984 and Rumelt, 1984). This approach is also built on a number of assumptions and the first of these is that, in an increasingly competitive and dynamic world, the survival of any organisation depends on its uniqueness; building strategies around what your competitors do is problematic as you will inevitably try and copy elements that make them successful which will make you similar and not unique. Another assumption of this approach to strategy is that the things which make you unique should be sustainable and not things that, for example, competitors can replicate. The most influential writers from this perspective on strategy are Gary Hamel and C.K. Prahalad, who introduced the notion of 'core competencies' as factors within organisations which provide benefits to customers, cannot be easily copied and can be leveraged into a number of different products and services (Prahalad and Hamel, 1990). In assessing competitive advantages derived from within organisations, they suggest that four factors are crucial: durability (the rate at which they will become obsolete); transparency (the rate at which they can be understood by competitors); transferability (the ease with which they can be copied); and replicability (the extent to which copying will bring similar results).

So is strategy driven by the organisation itself or by the environment in which it operates? Whilst there are theories, concepts and approaches which suggest that strategy is one thing or the other, in practice strategy is probably both. The Adcroft and Teckman (2008) framework of strategy as how an organisation performs combined with how an organisation competes argues that the success of a strategy is determined by the blend of internal and external elements; throughout an organisation's life cycle the emphasis on internal and external drivers will shift and change according to the circumstances faced and, as we have seen elsewhere, it is perhaps the ability of the organisation to change which matters most.

Case 12.3 Matchroom Promotions and the Prizefighter concept

Founded by Barry Hearn in the mid-1970s, Matchroom Promotions is one of the UK's leading sports promotion businesses. It is also one of the most innovative. The business began by promoting a number of little-known snooker players on a small professional circuit and now covers sports ranging through snooker, pool, darts, ten pin bowling and boxing.

Over the past 30 years, the company has developed a clear modus operandi in its strategic approach to developing new markets for sports, and this tends to take one of two forms. The first approach is to promote a sport through the leading people who play the sport. For example, Matchroom's promotion of snooker in the 1980s was centred on six-times world champion Steve Davis and, in darts, the company focused its efforts on 14-times world champion Phil Taylor. The second approach taken by the company is to change the format in which the game is played and presented. The aim of this approach is to take a minority sport and make it appealing to as wide and mainstream an audience as possible. Thus the firm has developed new formats in all of the sports in which it has been involved and the latest example of this is the Prizefighter concept in boxing.

Boxing reached its peak in the UK in the early 1990s with record viewing figures for high-profile bouts on television and the high numbers of boxing shows put on by a variety of promoters across the UK. In this period, Matchroom's efforts focused on the middleweight division and a series of domestic fights involving boxers like Chris Eubank, Nigel Benn, Michael Watson and Steve Collins. Over the past decade and half, however, the sport has been in decline and there are a number of factors which may explain this. For example, as boxing made the shift from free-to-air television to pay-per-view, any increases in revenue have been more than outweighed by falling viewing figures. This means that even the best boxers in the UK no longer have a wide national profile where they are well known outside of boxing circles. Boxing also has to operate in an ever more competitive market for viewers and supporters.

The Prizefighter concept aims to revolutionise how boxing is perceived and consumed. Instead of a boxing show focusing on one big fight and a series of smaller fights on the undercard, Prizefighter offers an elimination tournament in which eight boxers compete in a winner-takes-all format. This format offers a series of short intense bouts where excitement is maximised through the fast pace of each fight. In this approach, every bout matters as it influences the final outcome. The intention is to attract a new audience to boxing to revitalise an industry in long-term decline.

Discussion questions

5 What do you think are the most important core competencies of a sports promotion business like Matchroom? To what extent are these core competencies portable into more popular and mainstream sports?

6 Consider an area of sports with which you are familiar. To what extent do you think that the Matchroom Promotions strategic approach would work in that area? Give reasons for your answer.

Conclusion

This final section of the chapter considers two issues. First, we will consider the relationship between the theory and practice of strategy and, on the basis of this discussion, we will then consider the characteristics of the successful strategist in a sport organisation. The obvious point to make from the theory and examples in this chapter is that frequently there seems to be a disconnection between the theory and practice of strategy, indeed this is often true of many management disciplines not only in sport but in all contexts. The three theoretical issues in strategy that this chapter has considered (philosophy, process and drivers) are all set up as extremes; strategy is seen as being one thing or another. This reflects, for example, Michael Porter's view that the worst strategic position to hold is one where the firm is *stuck in the middle* and trying to be all things to all people. Thus, strategy is usually seen as being about science or art, emergent or deliberate in process or driven by an organisation or its environment. The problem is when this theoretical perspective collides with strategy in practice and we see a much more grey, blurred and messy world than theory could have us believe. Concepts like Porter's Five Forces model suggest that there is a neat and tidy dimension to strategy where the role of the strategist is to place different environmental forces into separate boxes and develop an understanding of the key issues. Perhaps the real world of sport and business is more complex and interrelated than this and there is a real blurring between industries and the forces which influence the nature of those industries.

The relationships between the theory and practice of strategy are summarised in Figure 12.4.

If the real world of strategy is so different to the theory of strategy, the obvious question to ask is *does the theory have any value*? The answer to this question is no and yes. Theory on its own probably doesn't have a lot of value outside of a textbook but how we use that theory has great value. Theory has a value because it provides a framework through which options can be generated and assessed. It has a value because it provides a point of comparison between how strategy happens now and how it can happen in the future. It is

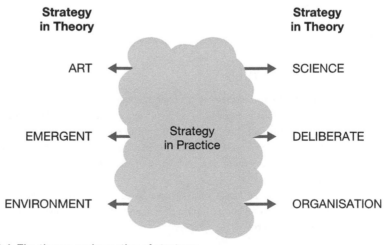

Figure 12.4 The theory and practice of strategy

useful because it identifies the extremes so that the strategist knows the continuum within which they must find a unique and valuable position for their own organisation. In this case, the value of theory is in how it can be used and this raises the issue of the strategist: can we create a picture of what an ideal strategist would look like? Possibly not because strategy is specific to the circumstances in which it is made and implemented. Would Sir Alex Ferguson have been as successful at Chelsea, Arsenal or Liverpool? Can we take his strategic approach and apply it to rugby, cricket, baseball or any other sport? What we can do is draw up a set of characteristics that it is probably important for a strategist to have. A strategist needs vision and the ability to articulate that vision. A strategist needs to be forward looking. A strategist needs to take a helicopter view of an organisation. A strategist needs to be able to plan and analyse but also be creative and intuitive. In short, a strategist needs many things and hopefully this chapter can help you understand what they are and the challenges they will involve.

Discussion questions

7 Consider a sport organisation that you know well. What is most important strategically to this organisation, on- or off-field activities? What challenges does this create for strategists in the organisation?

8 Choose a leader in a sport organisation. How would you characterise their strategy making? As an art or as a science? Or a blend of the two? Why did you reach those conclusions?

9 Use Porter's Five Forces model to strategise about a sport organisation's strategic options. On the basis of your analysis, which option is best? Compare this with the actual strategy of the organisation. What does this teach you about the use of this model specifically and strategy models in general?

10 Consider the strategy of a sport organisation you are familiar with. What have been the main organisational drivers of this strategy? What have been the main environmental drivers of the strategy? Do you think the organisation has a competitive advantage and, if so, is it sustainable? Why do you reach these conclusions?

Keywords

Art; deliberate; emergent; environments; organisation; science; strategy; vision.

Guided reading

For an excellent overview of strategic management in general, the reader edited by Faulkner and Campbell (2006) contains a number of landmark articles. For a more models-based approach to strategy, Johnson, Scholes and Whittington (2008) offer a well-structured approach.

Mike Brearley's book on captaincy in cricket (2001) offers a useful insight into the mind of the strategist and how the messy real world of strategy can be effectively managed using some relevant theory.

Adcroft and Teckman's (2009) special edition of *Management Decision* entitled 'Taking sport seriously' is a useful compendium of articles written from a sports perspective and many of these are strategic in nature.

Recommended websites

The Journal of Sport Management: www.humankinetics.com
The European Association of Sport Management: www.easm.org
Institute for Strategy and Competitiveness: www.isc.hbs.edu

References

Adcroft, A. and Teckman, J. (2008) 'Theories, concepts and the rugby World Cup: using management to understand sport', *Management Decision*, 46 (4), 600–625.

Adcroft, A. and Teckman, J. (2009) 'Taking sport seriously', special edition of *Management Decision*, 47 (1).

Ambrosini, V., Johnson, G. and Scholes, K. (1998) *Exploring Techniques of Analysis and Evaluation in Strategic Management*, Harlow: FT Prentice Hall.

Andrews, K. (1965) *The Concept of Corporate Strategy*, Illinois: Jones-Irwin.

Brearley, M. (2001) *The Art of Captaincy*, London: Channel 4 Books.

Chaharbaghi, K. and Willis, R. (1998) 'Strategy: the missing link between continuous revolution and constant evolution', *International Journal of Operations and Production Management*, 18 (9/10), 1017–27.

Deloitte (2007) *Football Money League: The Reign in Spain*, Manchester: Sport Business Group.

Deloitte (2009) *Football Money League: Lost in Translation*, Manchester: Sport Business Group.

Faulkner, D.O. and Campbell, A. (2006) *The Oxford Handbook of Strategy*, Oxford: Oxford University Press.

Ferguson, A. (1999) *Managing My Life*, London: Hodder and Stoughton.

Hamel, G. (2000) *Leading the Revolution*, Cambridge, MA: Harvard Business School Press.

Johnson, G., Scholes, K. and Whittington, R. (2008) *Exploring Corporate Strategy*, Harlow: FT/ Prentice Hall.

Lynch, R. (2009) *Strategic Management*, Harlow: Pearson Education Ltd.

Madichie, N. (2009) 'Management implications of foreign players in the English Premiership League football', *Management Decision*, 47 (1), 24–50.

Mailer, N. (1975) *The Fight*, London: Penguin Books.

Mintzberg, H. (1987) 'The Strategy Concept I: Five Ps for Strategy', *California Management Review*, Fall, 11–24.

Mintzberg, H., Ahlstrand, B. and Lampel, J. (1998). *Strategy Safari: The Complete Guide Through the Wilds of Strategic Management*, Harlow: FT Prentice Hall.

Porter, M. (1979) 'How competitive forces shape strategy', *Harvard Business Review* (March–April), 137–49.

Porter, M. (1980) *Competitive Strategy: Techniques for Analysing Industries and Competitors*, New York: The Free Press.

Porter, M. (1996) 'What is Strategy?', *Harvard Business Review* (November–December), 61–157.

Prahalad, C.K. and Hamel, G. (1990) 'The core competence of the corporation', *Harvard Business Review* (May–June), 79–91.

Rumelt, R.P. (1984) *Resources, Firms and Strategies: A Reader in the Resource-based Perspective*, Oxford: Oxford University Press.

Wernerfelt, B. (1984) 'A resource based view of the firm', *Strategic Management Journal*, 5 (2), 171–80.

Whittington, R. (2002) *What is Strategy (and does it Matter)?* London: Thomson.

Woodward, C. (2004) *Winning!*, London: Hodder and Stoughton.

Managing sport operations: quality, performance and control

Terri Byers, Coventry University, UK

Learning outcomes

Upon completion of this chapter the reader should be able to:

- explain the nature of operations management in sports businesses and link operations to other research in organisation studies/theory which helps to enrich the traditional perspective of operations;
- discuss a variety of issues facing operations managers in sports businesses;
- examine the nature of quality and customer satisfaction, and their relevance for sports businesses;
- identify a range of performance measures that can be used by managers in sports organisations and discuss the implementation of measures (and associated problems);
- recognise a variety of issues for managers who are responsible for managing performance in sports organisations;
- critically discuss control in managing operations.

Overview

The purpose of this chapter is to introduce students to the concept of operations management in sports businesses. While there is an abundance of research in 'mainstream' operations management, there is considerably less known about the operations function within sports organisations. While it is incorrect to 'assume' sport businesses are different from other businesses, there is some evidence to support the unique elements of certain sport businesses and so the operations function can vary when looking at sport products and services. This chapter examines both mainstream literature and its application to sports businesses and, where appropriate, identifies research that has been conducted specifically in sport organisations.

Also relevant to understanding 'operations' is the literature on organisation theory. There is considerably more theoretically and empirically diverse research in this field and so this chapter will integrate some key concepts from organisation theory (Byers, Slack and Parent, 2012) which help to provide greater detail of how operations work in practice. Concepts such as conflict, change, control and others are integrated throughout the chapter and case studies.

The complexity of the 'operations management' concept, combined with the variety of contexts in which sport businesses are found, is reflected in the numerous examples and case studies presented. Due to the increasing growth of the service sector in the sports industry, this chapter focuses on issues of importance to the 'service operations manager'. However, as a holistic approach to understanding operations, quality and performance in sports businesses is taken, some comparisons to manufacturing are made. Context is considered important when examining operational issues in sports businesses, hence the chapter discusses organisations of various sizes, and from the public, private and voluntary sectors. Key organisations found in the operational environment of sports businesses are also identified.

Consumers of sport-related goods and services are increasingly discerning and knowledgeable. Consequently, the concepts of *quality* and *customer satisfaction* are examined in this chapter. Due to the rapid growth observed (Business in Sport and Leisure, 2002) and the increasingly competitive nature of the sports market, this chapter examines a range of *performance measurements* that can be used to help sport businesses monitor and evaluate their organisations' operations.

The concept of control pervades all that managers do, including those responsible for the operations function. However, control is a complex phenomenon that involves all members of an organisation and so we examine some aspects of control important to understanding operations and organisations generally.

Case 13.1 National sport governing bodies (NSGBs)

NSGBs are not traditionally included in research on 'operations management' yet they are a unique and interesting case when looking at the operations function. In the UK, there are over 150 NSGBs recognised by Sport England. Rather than developing their own strategic goals and aims based on market analysis and competitive rivalries, NSGBs operate in a very constrained environment, historically, financially and with regard to services and products delivered. This is not just true of NSGBs in the UK but can be said of all of these organisations in Canada, the USA, Asia and Australia, for example.

Historically, NSGBs were created to provide services to members of their sport which enabled athletes to train and compete on equal terms and under standardised rules (Henry and Lee, 2004). Many people who work in NSGBs are volunteers and, as Slack and his colleagues (1998) demonstrated, volunteer-run sport delivery has a very strong culture and close personal motivations were the driving force behind much as of the work of NSGBs in the 1980s. During the 1990s, governments began to realise the importance of sport to national culture and pride, and so decided to provide financial support to NSGBs with the condition that the organisations produced formal strategic plans detailing their elite performance strategy for several years into the future. This in turn saw more NSGBs hiring professional paid staff with the appropriate skills in strategic planning and management to complete this task and access central government money. This money fuelled further professionalisation of sport through coaching, athlete medical services and administration of the emerging relationship between sport and the media.

In the UK, Sport England provided approximately £480 million to 46 governing bodies over a four-year period, with the NSGBs agreeing to produce plans in line with Sport England national strategy for sport – grow, sustain and excel. While governing bodies can interpret this to a small degree, their purpose/mission (if they wish to access the considerable funds from government) is largely determined by government. For instance, the British Equestrian Federation's (BEF) motto of 'more people', more horses, more places, more medals' is suitable considering that they must process horses and people through their systems to produce international elite medal performances but still clearly resonates with Sport England's desired strategy for NSGBs producing increased participation, facilities and elite athletes.

The context in which NSGBs operate is important for understanding operations management within these types of organisations. In providing their services to members, NSGBs do not operate 'for profit' but attempt to raise funds in pursuit of their members' needs for expertise, training, facilities and so on. They rely on a vast range of different people, some paid, some in a voluntary capacity, to deliver services in a highly professional manner. The BEF liaises with coaches, physiotherapists, veterinarians, media/broadcasters, policy makers, sponsors, athletes, academic experts, legal services and discipline governing bodies (e.g. British Dressage, British Show Jumping) to deliver services for ten equestrian-related sports. These needs are entirely external to the BEF and so co-ordinating resources can be a very complex task to meet members' needs (which also is complex, coming from ten different sports). They also sit on the new European Equestrian Federation to liaise with the Federation Equestrian Internationale (FEI) on European interests in Equestrian-related sports.

(continued)

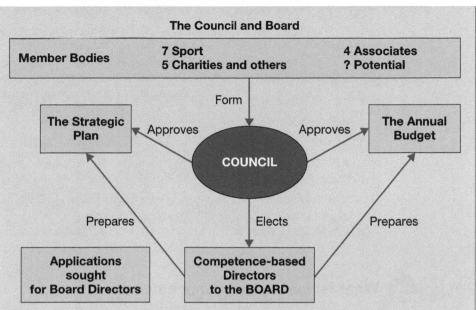

Figure 13.1 Structure of the BEF board

Source: *Structure of the BEF*, British Equestrian Foundation (R.H.G. Suggett, 2010) British Equestrian Federation www.bef.co.uk

NSGBs provide administrative guidance and rules for sport to operate fairly, ethically and sustainably. However, they do not operate outside of the law and their rules are created within the constraints of national law. When 'operations management' is discussed in generic texts, they often refer to private sector organisations and so do not spend significant time discussing the contextual constraints on how operations function. In NSGBs, the constraints have considerable impact on the structure and operation of the organisations which differentiate them from their private (and public) sector counterparts. The mixture of paid and voluntary staff adds to the difficult situation in which NSGBs operate – while paid staff have an economic incentive for work, volunteers have personal motivations for involvement. Volunteers still play an important role in NSGBs, as evidenced in the BEF where the board of directors work in a voluntary capacity and each is responsible for a portfolio, including sport development, international affairs, participation, equine development, commerce/treasurer and public affairs/communications (see Figure 13.1). Although voluntary, there are clear operational guidelines produced by the BEF to specify the conduct of directors. These are called 'Terms of Reference for the Board' and include direction on core values, standards and conflict of interests. Under standards, for example, the role of board members is specified as:

- engage fully in collective consideration of the issues, taking account of the full range of relevant factors, including any guidance available;
- have a strong commitment to the BEF and knowledge and experience of operations and be constructive within the context of a formal strategy/business plan;
- respond appropriately to complaints; and
- ensure the board does not exceed its powers or functions.

(*continued*)

It is noted that members of the voluntary board have collective responsibility for the operations of the BEF – a considerable task for non-paid members of the organisation. As we continue through this chapter, and you get more detailed knowledge of what operations is and how it is conducted, make some notes on how these theories may (or may not) apply in the case of national governing bodies such as the BEF.

Discussion questions

1 Who controls the strategic direction of equestrian sport in Britain? How?

2 How are individuals controlled or influenced to work towards the strategic aims of the BEF?

3 What contextual features of equestrian sport in Britain influence the control and regulation of the development of equestrian sports?

What is operations management?

There are many different ways to define operations management. This section examines the meaning of operations management from three perspectives:

- operations management as a transformation process;
- operations management as a function of the organisation;
- operations management as a management activity.

A transformation process

Operations management is concerned with creating, operating and controlling a transformation system that takes inputs of a variety of resources and produces outputs of goods and services needed by customers. (Naylor, 2002: 5)

Operations management [is] the management of processes, people and resources in order to provide the required goods and services to a specified level of quality, doing so in the most cost-effective way. (Johnston and Clark, 2001: 4)

The definitions above reveal that 'operations management' is concerned with the *process* of ensuring a product/service is delivered or a product is manufactured according to some predefined specifications. Of course, many sports businesses provide both products and services. Brookbank Canoes and Kayaks, England (see www.paddlesport.co.uk) is a specialist supplier of new and second-hand canoe/kayak clothing and equipment products. These products are brought to customers via a retail service and a worldwide mail order service. In addition, Paddle Sport provides canoe and kayak courses to children and adults. As a process, operations management is concerned with the transformation of 'inputs' into 'outputs'. Therefore, at Brookbank 'operations' is the process of transforming the kayaks, the employees, the water into a service/activity desired by customers but the function is overseen by the general manager and not a specific 'operations manager'. This is mainly due to the organisation being relatively small and not requiring the complexity of different types of managers. The transformation process may be a manufacturing process or a

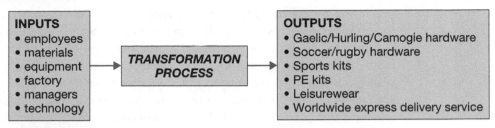

Figure 13.2 Operations as a transformation process – the example of Gaelic Gear

Figure 13.3 Operations as a transformation process – example: global sports management

service process. Figure 13.2 shows an example of operations management as a transformation process in a sports equipment manufacturing business, the Irish-owned company Gaelic Gear, supplier and manufacturer of sports clothing, equipment and other innovative products (see www.gaelic-gear.com).

Figure 13.3 illustrates operations management as a transformation process in a sports consultancy firm, Global Sports Management, an international sports business that offers a comprehensive range of management services for players and coaches, particularly in the sport of Rugby Union. Global Sports Management (see www.gsmworld.co.uk) offers services in contract negotiation, insurance cover, investment planning and tax advice for leading sports professionals.

The transformation perspective is useful in highlighting the important role of managers in producing goods and services. In general, sports businesses can transform either one or a combination of:

● materials (e.g. Spalding Sports UK Ltd, sports equipment manufacturer);

● information (e.g. Optima Sports International, consulting company);

● customers (e.g. Sports Direct, retail shops).

However, operations management is more than a concern with efficiently transforming inputs into outputs (Russell and Taylor, 1998). Next we look at operations as a function of the organisation.

A function

Operations management can be considered as one of the basic functions of an organisation, alongside marketing, finance and human resources. While marketing establishes demand for products and/or services and finance provides the necessary capital, operations is responsible for delivering the product and/or service to the customer, according to the specifications agreed with marketing and within the budget agreed with finance. The human resources function ensures the proper and correct administration of employee rights. The relationship between marketing and operations is particularly important to ensure that customers are satisfied with a product or service. That is, marketing efforts need to be consistent with what the operations function is actually producing so that customer experience is in harmony with or exceeds customer expectations. While the 'operations management as function' perspective provides another useful piece to the puzzle of 'What is operations management?', the final approach allows for a more detailed and specific examination of the concept.

A management activity

In some sports businesses, there is a designated 'operations manager'. In many instances in the sports industry, although the person may not be called the 'operations' manager, they perform many or all of the duties of an operations manager.

As a management activity, Naylor (2002) suggests that operations management concerns the achievement of organisational goals through working with and through people, realising the greatest benefits from limited resources and balancing efficiency, effectiveness and equity. As indicated by this statement, the operations manager has many areas of responsibility. Slack et al. (1998) suggested that these responsibilities include:

1 Understanding the strategic orientation of the organisation

'An organisation without a strategy is like a motorist on a long journey without a map' (Hope and Mühlemann, 1997). Strategy represents the long-term plans or intentions of a business. The development of strategic plans can take place at different levels of an organisation. Corporate strategy (also known as business strategy) is the long-term plan for an entire organisation and is often represented by a mission statement. For example, the mission statement adopted by Nike is 'to bring innovation and inspiration to every athlete in the world' (Nike, 2003).

The intricacies of 'strategy development' are beyond the scope of this chapter. It is sufficient, for the purposes of understanding the operations function, to know that strategy essentially answers basic questions about the nature of a business and about its future direction. The mission statement of Nike conveys to employees and customers the commitment of the company to provide innovative products that inspire athletes (athletes are defined by Nike as any person with a body) to perform. It is this commitment to innovation that should inform the activities of the various departments of Nike, including research and development, marketing and operations, if the strategic aims of the organisation are to be realised.

2 Develop an 'operations strategy'

Functional strategies indicate how each individual department of an organisation (i.e. operations, marketing, finance, etc.) contribute to the corporate strategy. Russell and Taylor (1998) suggested that strategic decisions in operations are concerned with:

- products and services;
- processes and technology;
- capacity;
- human resources;
- quality;
- facilities;
- sourcing;
- operating systems.

They also suggested that each of the above-mentioned elements must fit together to complement one another. The products and/or services offered by a company determine the firms' operations strategy. For example, products and services can be classified as 'make-to-order', such as sports management and marketing consultancy businesses where the service is offered in response to customer needs and according to their requirements. 'Make-to-stock' products and services are produced for a general market in anticipation of some demand. Examples include sports textbooks, equipment and clothing. A key operational issue is the forecasting of demand for these products. 'Assemble-to-order' products and services are produced as standard units with optional components, which are added according to customer requirements.

Processes can also be classified as projects, batch production, mass production and continuous production (see Figure 13.4). The process chosen should complement and enable the product or service being delivered. Therefore 'make-to-order' products, designed to customer specifications, would be impossible to produce using a mass production system. If the 'made-to-order' product is 'recommendations' from a sport management consulting firm such as Global Sports, a project-based process would be more efficient and effective.

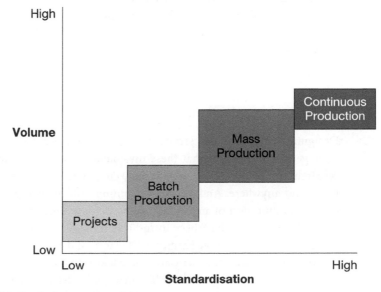

Figure 13.4 Product process matrix
Source: Russell and Taylor (1998: 44)

Operations strategy must consider the capacity and demand issue for the effective production of sports goods and services. Here there are a wide variety of questions to be addressed within the specific context of the sports business. However, some possible questions may be:

- How much capacity is required – to meet average, potential and low demand?
- How will the company handle excess demand?
- What is the best size for a facility? Should demand be met with large facilities or many smaller facilities? Where should facilities be located?
- If international markets are part of the firm's overall strategy, should products be made and sold in other countries? What are the legal, ethical, cultural and organisation structure issues that may arise?

The issues associated with quality saturate every strategic decision. Operations managers must address target levels of quality, measurement systems and the role of systems, processes and people in delivering quality and maintenance of quality standards. Few sport organisations are completely vertically integrated, making all parts and raw materials that are used in the production. Therefore, strategic decisions are needed with regard to what items should be outsourced, how suppliers should be selected, how the quality and dependability of suppliers should be maintained and how many suppliers should be used, for example. Operating systems, such as the information technology system or the planning and control systems, facilitate strategic decisions on a daily basis. It is imperative that these systems are designed to support and enable the organisation's strategic vision.

Aside from developing the operations strategy, consideration must been given to implementing that strategy. It is at this point that concepts from organisation theory are particularly helpful to aspiring managers as it is concerned with the practicalities of managing. Implementation of strategy may require managers to deal with conflict and resistance, particularly if the strategy is radically different from its predecessor. Likewise, managing change becomes important and doing so using the most appropriate tools. These are complex issues which are covered in great detail in Slack and Parent (2007) and in the former version of the text, Slack (1997). The remainder of this chapter also draws more specifically on organisation theory to complement what is known about how operations management is performed.

3 Design organisational products, services and processes

Designing a new product, service or organisational process begins with an 'idea'. Sports managers should realise that these invaluable 'ideas' may come from the organisation's research and development department, customers, competitors, marketing, suppliers – just about anywhere. And it is not uncommon for 'new' products, services and processes to be a modification of an existing phenomenon. Many models and frameworks to assist in the design process have been introduced for services and manufacturing (see Chase and Aquilano, 1995; Haywood-Farmer, 1988; Hope and Mühlemann, 1997; Russell and Taylor, 1998). Some models are generic and some take into consideration the special characteristics of services. Haywood-Farmer (1988) developed a three-dimensional framework to classify services according to the degree of service customisation, the degree of labour intensity and the degree of customer contact and interaction (Figure 13.5).

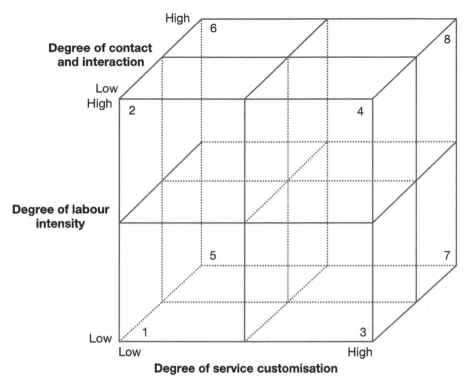

Figure 13.5 Three-dimensional classification scheme
Source: Haywood-Farmer (1988: 25)

Design for manufacturing is primarily concerned with maximum efficiency and minimum costs. Processes are often standardised to produce consistent quality and specifications of a product. However, to remain competitive, sports manufacturers must also consider the role of innovation in their products, services and processes. Relative newcomer to the sports industry, United Colours of Benetton, in its launch of a new line of 'sportswear', applies its innovative delayed-dying process to its sports clothing in order to produce contemporary colours as the market demands.

Manufacturing design processes may be modular (standardised parts to create a finished product) or designed for assembly (procedure for reducing parts in assembly, evaluating methods of assembly and examining assembly sequence). Increasingly, organisations are considering designing for environment (minimising material and energy use) and for quality (can be defined by organisation or by performance measurement standards). Technology is a central component of sports manufacturing businesses. Through CAD (Computer-aided design), CAE (Computer-aided engineering) and CAD/CAE systems, sports manufacturers can design and produce mass or bespoke products in relatively short time periods.

Boussabaine et al. (1999) developed six models to assist professionals involved in feasibility studies at the design stage for sport centres. The models focus on modelling the total energy costs, related to providing safe and comfortable conditions in sport centres. More recent models, such as the 'Effective product/service design' approach proposed by Verma et al. (2001), have recognised the importance of integrating marketing and operations management decisions. The authors' models also highlight the importance of considering operational difficulty levels when designing products and services.

Service design begins with developing the 'service concept' (Desrumaux et al., 1998). The service concept is a clear identification of the service's characteristics. Heskett (1987) suggested that identification of the service concept requires three questions to be answered:

- What are the important elements of the service(s) to be provided? (State in terms of results produced for the customer, employee and the company.)

- How are these elements to be perceived by the target market segment? (Also consider perception of employees, general public, other populations.)

- What efforts does this suggest in terms of designing, delivering and marketing the service(s)?

It is important that the service concept addresses customer needs but not to the detriment of employee needs. In a service setting in particular, it is the employees who are in direct contact with customers. It is therefore essential that the service concept incorporates a common set of values that employees appreciate and support.

In designing new products/services, managers are initiating change within their organisation. It is important here to recognise that change to one aspect of an organisation is likely to require changes to many other aspects and so new product/service development does not happen in isolation and without consequences for how the organisation is structured, how the workforce conduct their duties and the culture of the organisation. Slack and Parent (2006) discuss four areas where change can take place in sport organisations and that these areas are interconnected so that a change in one will cause a change in the others. The four areas are technology, structures and systems, people and products/ services. If the operations manager is encouraging development of new products and services (e.g. new fitness equipment, running shoes, leagues, etc.), new staff are likely to be required to produce and sell the product/service, new technology may be needed to develop and/or produce the product/service and new structures/systems (e.g. job descriptions for new employees, new product feedback system from customers, training for sales staff, etc.) will also be necessary.

4 Control the product (delivery) of goods and/or services

Traditional conceptions of control in organisations are underpinned by assumptions of individuals as rational entities that can be directed towards organisationally legitimate behaviour by management systems. A variety of disciplines, including engineering (Gertosio et al., 2000), accounting (Anthony, 1965; Chua et al., 1989), cybernetics (Ashby, 1956), sociology (Johnson and Gill, 1993) and psychology (Salaman and Thompson, 1985) have examined control as a task to be performed by managers. To some extent this is true in that managers can employ administrative controls such as policies, formal procedures, job descriptions, accounting procedures and employee appraisals in order to monitor organisational and individual performance.

However, as suggested by Hopwood (1974), control in organisations is not limited to these administrative devices. These formal policies and procedures are 'controls' (external mechanisms such as disciplinary procedures) rather than 'control' (directing or influencing behaviour in a desired direction). Furthermore, controls can be implemented in a direct and coercive manner or achieved more subtly through socialisation (Das and Teng, 1998), language (Boden, 1994), capital (Bourdieu, 1985), emotion (Fineman, 2000) and the manipulation of norms, values and culture. For a more in-depth discussion of these subtle forms of control, see Mintzberg and Quinn (1998). For a discussion of control in voluntary sport organisations see Byers (2007, 2009). Byers (2009) highlights the role of power and the relationship between managers and subordinates as important to understanding how control functions in organisations. The concept is strongly rooted in an organisation's history and social context so can vary significantly, even between similar types/structures of organisations.

5 Measure and improve organisational performance

It is important for sports managers to monitor and, where necessary, improve organisation systems, processes and products/services. To do this, organisations must be customer focused and proactive in assessing aspects of the organisation and/or its staff. A wide variety of measures can be used to assess organisation performance, including financial measures such as processing costs, total revenue, operating profit and labour costs. However, there are many more non-financial measures that may give managers a warning that financial performance may be threatened, such as customer satisfaction, employee retention, customer loyalty, facility utilisation and waiting times. For example, if the manager of a sports performance laboratory regularly monitored customer satisfaction through a monthly survey, the results of which over a six-month period indicated a decline in customer satisfaction, the manager could take steps to improve the aspects of the service which people were dissatisfied with and prevent loss of business (and revenue).

The topic of performance measurement is discussed in greater detail later in this chapter. However, as a management activity it is important to emphasise that managers should focus on the 'improvement' of performance. Therefore, *measuring* customer satisfaction, as in the example of the laboratory manager, is insufficient to improve organisational performance. Rather, the manager must then take steps to address issues of failing performance. This may be in the form of a further survey to ascertain exactly the nature of dissatisfaction, or if it is clear why customers are not satisfied then to make changes and to inform customers that changes have been made.

Service operations management

Operations management is primarily concerned with the internal practices of organisations. 'Internal practices' constitutes an overwhelming number of different topics. There is a considerable body of generic literature (concerned with a wide variety of industries) devoted to the study of operations as a function of the organisation, as a process and as a management activity (see for example Hope and Mühlemann, 1997; Fitzsimmons and Fitzsimmons, 2001; Johnston and Clark, 2001). Likewise, research into the internal operations of sports organisations (primarily commercial and public sector) has grown substantially in the last few decades (see Slack, 1997; Slack and Parent, 2006; De Martelaer et al., 2002).

To discuss all of these is beyond the scope of this chapter. However, there are some key issues that are of interest to sports managers. There has been considerable research in sports businesses, focused upon operational issues of service quality (see for example Thwaites, 1999; De Knop et al., 2001; Westerbeek and Shilbury, 2001) and customer satisfaction (see Kelly and Turley, 2001; Van Leeuwen et al., 2001) with less interest being shown in performance measurement. There is, however, considerable practitioner and industry focus upon performance measurement in sports businesses. It is perhaps only a matter of time before academics begin to investigate this relatively uncharted terrain of sports organisations.

The majority of operational research in sport (and in some cases leisure or recreation) businesses has focused on the service sector. This is not surprising considering the growth of services in the world economy and the growing participation rates in sport. Mintel (2009) suggested that the value of the overall sport participation market rose 17 per cent between 2004 and 2008, worth nearly £4.4 billion. With increased participation has come increased consumer spending on sport equipment and clothing. Mintel (2008) reported a growth in sports clothing consumption from 2007 to 2008 and an even faster rate of growth for sport equipment, with technical innovation driving sales.

Services

This section examines the concept of services and the implications for operations managers of the unique attributes of managing a 'service'.

There are four characteristics of 'services' that are not usually associated with manufacturing. As suggested by Hope and Mühlemann (1997), these characteristics are:

- intangibility;
- perishability (i.e. a service cannot be 'stored');
- heterogeneous (nature);
- simultaneity (of production and consumption).

These characteristics have important implications for the operations manager in a sports organisation. Intangibility refers to something that cannot be touched, which results in difficulties in measuring and defining the service. The perishability of a service refers to the urgent nature of service delivery in that there cannot be a surplus 'inventory' as there can be with tangible products. For example, if a Rugby League match only sells half of the available seats, those seats cannot be stored and sold again. Thus capacity management in the light of fluctuating demand for sport services becomes a key concern.

This highlights the fact that production and consumption of a service are simultaneous. Again, there is a sense of urgency about a 'product' that is both produced and consumed at the same time. It is difficult to ensure that the service is provided in a standardised manner, especially if several different people may be involved in service provision at different time periods. While staff training may remedy some of the problems presented by this service characteristic, we cannot train customers in the same way. Therefore clear signposting, layout and appropriate décor are considerations for operations managers.

Finally, the heterogeneous nature of services means that each time a service is performed, it is unique. That is, each customer may have different questions or requirements, the interaction between service staff may be different according to the customer and it is difficult and sometimes undesirable to standardise procedures to the extent that staff do not have the freedom to deal with customers' needs as they arise.

These characteristics are most evident in, for example, sport marketing and management firms such as Fast Track, a leading sports marketing agency in the UK (www.fasttrackagency.com). This company provides services to clients on communications, marketing, sponsorship and event management. The services may include some tangible form (e.g. a report or consultative document); however, many aspects of the service or event are quite intangible until the day of consumption, and may be unique for different customer requirements (heterogeneous). Likewise, the finished product is perishable in that the information is likely to be of some urgency for the client and not particularly useful after a certain deadline. Fast Track works with a wide variety of clients internationally and provides short case studies on its website of the work it has completed (www.fasttrackagency.com/clients.asp).

Customer satisfaction and quality

Garvin (1984) identified five approaches to defining quality:

- the transcendent approach;
- the manufacturing-based approach;
- the user-based approach;
- the product-based approach;
- the value-based approach.

The transcendent approach views quality as 'of the highest standard'. Here, quality is seen as innately excellent in nature, such as a newly built sports stadium with the latest technological and architectural innovations, compared to a local community centre sports ground. According to this view, the stadium would be classed a 'quality' facility and the community centre does not represent a 'quality' facility.

The manufacturing-based approach views quality as conformance to some specification. Therefore a quality product is one which conforms precisely to its design specification. This view suggests that a novice gymnast who performs a simple floor routine with precision demonstrates a quality performance, whereas a senior gymnast performing more difficult skills but making a few mistakes and receiving a lower score than the novice, is classed as a lower quality performance.

The user-based approach deems quality to exist if a service/product meets the requirements of the customer/user. That is, the service or product is 'fit for purpose'. Therefore, an inexpensive tennis racket which allows an individual to enjoy the game on Saturday afternoons with friends can be viewed as a quality product. However, a 'top of the line' carbon fibre racket can also be viewed as a quality product if it is required by its user for accuracy of play, minimal injury and speed/power of play. Arguably, this perspective confuses quality with satisfaction, where satisfaction exists when customer expectations are met (Hope and Mühleman, 1997).

The product-based approach is a quantitatively defined approach where more equals better quality and measurable characteristics are of greatest importance. From this perspective, a golf club which produces a 300m shot is of higher quality than one which produces a 280m shot. Alternatively, less is sometimes deemed of a higher quality, such as the fastest 100m sprint time at the Olympics, or a sports marketing consultant who could produce a marketing plan for your new business in one day would be considered of a higher quality than the consultant who took one month!

Finally, the value-based approach takes 'cost' into consideration by viewing a product of quality as something that provides value for money. This is obviously a subjective judgement performed by a customer; for example, a £10 ticket (in regular seating) to watch the London Knights is seen as of higher quality than a £200 ticket in a corporate box.

Parasuraman et al. (1985) initiated much of the subsequent research into quality as an important construct in organisations, with their Gap Model which identified the 10 determinants of 'service quality'. The determinants were later refined and reduced to five dimensions, namely reliability, responsiveness, empathy, assurance and tangibles (Parasuraman et al., 1988). Perceived service quality was measured as the difference between customer comparisons of their expectations for what should happen and what actually happens in a service encounter, along the five dimensions named above. If a difference existed along one of the dimensions, it was characterised as a gap. To measure the gaps, the authors developed a 22-item questionnaire called SERVQUAL. This instrument is probably the most frequently adopted approach to measuring service quality (Haksever et al., 2000) but has been challenged by researchers on several bases (see Buttle, 1996; Robinson, 1999). Van Dyke et al. (1999) cautioned on the use of SERVQUAL to measure quality of information services, adding to doubts of the effectiveness of the instrument in different contexts.

Not dissimilar to quality, satisfaction can be defined in a number of ways. However, Howat and Murray (2002) point out that satisfaction, as an affective state, occurs when an individual's needs and/or desires are met. In other words, when the needs of a customer are fulfilled, the customers feels satisfied.

Oliver (1997) referred to customer satisfaction as a subjective experience, a 'judgement' that a product and/or service has provided a certain level of fulfilment, or pleasure. According to Patterson and Spreng (1997), satisfied customers are more likely to use a service repeatedly and will relay positive information to potential customers (i.e. their family, friends, etc.). Satisfaction, therefore, may provide managers with a valuable indicator of future support for their organisation and service.

More importantly, Howat and Murray (2002) suggested that meeting customer expectations for key service quality dimensions should create satisfied customers who are loyal to a service and recommend the service to others. In their study of a sports and leisure centre in Australia, these authors argued for an examination of the 'critical incidents' associated with sports services, in order to provide specific diagnostic information about quality and facilitate sport managers' ability to implement required improvements in quality.

Critical incidents were defined as 'specific moments-of-truth' (Wels-Lips et al., 1998: 286) and 'memorable in some way to the people involved' (Bitner et al., 1990: 72). Therefore, critical incidents can occur at any time while a customer is consuming a sports service, including interactions with personnel, physical features, other customers and other visible aspects of the service. A well-accepted premise of critical incidents is that they can evoke either extremely positive or extremely negative experiences for customers.

Measurements of quality in sport service settings

Several scales have been proposed for measuring service quality in sports businesses and services. While this is not an exhaustive account of these studies, the discussion below includes some early and more recent examples of how service quality has been measured in various sport settings.

McKay and Crompton (1990) developed REQUAL after examination of leisure and recreation services. This measure and subsequent versions developed by Wright, Duray and Goodale (1992) and Backman and Veldkamp (1995) were each developed in the context of public recreation services, the findings of which are arguably restricted in generalisability to this context, given that there are often significant differences in perceptions of quality in public versus private businesses (Crompton et al., 1991).

Kim and Kim (1995), examining Korean sports clubs, developed QUESC, a scale including 11 dimensions of service quality. This measure was later translated into Greek by Papadimitriou and Karteliotis (2002) and found to have inconsistent conceptual validity and inconsistent internal consistency reliability. McDonald et al. (1995) developed TEAMQUAL to assess service quality in professional sports. The CERM developed by Howat et al. (1996) focused on Australian leisure clubs. Criticisms of this instrument include its lack of dimensions used to measure the service quality construct, as it only included three dimensions.

Although several models have been developed, the literature on service quality in the sports industry is relatively limited (Alexandris et al., 2001). Issues related to all service quality measurement instruments are concerned with the validity, reliability and contextual appropriateness of the measure. The suggestion has also been made that a more accurate measure of quality may be obtained by measuring perceptions only (Cronin and Taylor, 1992; Teas, 1993). Alexandris et al. (2001) have recently provided a valuable contribution to the service quality literature by focusing on perceptions of service quality (measured by using SERVQUAL) and the resultant behavioural consequences of those perceptions (measured using a model proposed by Zeithaml et al., 1993).

Van Hoecke and deKnop (2006) proposed a framework for the analysis of quality in gymnastic clubs. Their system was subsequently used by the National Gymnastics Federation for a certification programme for club quality. Shonk and Chelladurai (2009) developed and tested a model of service quality in sport tourism. Examining a Major League All-Star sporting event in the USA, they found that the quality of the contest itself was the most important dimension of quality contributing to the sport tourists' level of satisfaction. It was also suggested that the tourists' satisfaction was a major factor in their decision to return to a sporting event or particular destination.

Quality standards

Quality standards are underpinned by the manufacturing-based approach to quality, in that they require businesses to 'conform to specified requirements' in order to achieve the recognised 'quality seal' (Kelemen, 2003). These standards are a mechanism that allows managers to measure and improve quality in their organisation. Some managers also believe that implementing quality standards helps to build a culture of excellence and achievement in their organisation. However, quality standards are also used as a marketing ploy by organisations or are adopted due to institutional pressures from customers, government and/or industry guidelines.

For the operations manager, quality standards help to ensure consistency in the way in which products and/or services are designed, manufactured and/or delivered as a service in their organisation. Historically, the development of standards has grown from manufacturers to be adopted by industry and finally to be developed into international standards such as the ISO9000 series (Conti, 1999). Organisations may choose from a wide variety of quality standards, including Investors in People, Chartermark, ISO 9000 and ISO 14000 (environmental variation). Sports facility managers have adopted quality initiative such as the ISO series since the 1980s (Sport England, 2001); however, McAdam and Canning (2001) report that the service sector generally has been relatively slow in implementing ISOs. Lack of acceptance may be due to the difficulties encountered by many firms, including the resource implications of implementing, achieving and maintaining the standards, the lack of congruence between ISO and industry priorities and the relatively low importance that customers place on this registration (Ogden and Grigg, 2003).

In an attempt to resolve the disparity between international standards such as ISOs and the contextual demands of the sports industry, QUEST was developed in 1996 by Sport England as a sport-specific quality initiative (Sport England, 2001). As of January 2000, 650 QUEST Manager's Guidance packs were sold, with 119 sports facilities having achieved QUEST accreditation and 50 sport organisations actively engaged in the process (Sport England, 2001).

 ## Sports events

Bitner (1992) discussed the importance of the 'servicescape' (the man-made physical attributes as opposed to the social environment) to satisfaction levels given the considerable amount of time a customer spends observing his/her surroundings at a sports event. Wakefield and Blodgett (1994) noted the significant impact of the perception of the sports facility upon satisfaction with the service experience. Research into sports events has shown the level of satisfaction experienced by sports fans is based on their comparison of their predictive expectations of the service encounter and what actually occurs (Zeithaml et al., 1993).

Informed by the sports marketing and services literature, Kelley and Turley (2001) conducted an exploratory study that empirically assessed the importance of service attributes sports fans use when evaluating the quality of service and their levels of satisfaction with the sporting event. With 316 fans from four different basketball games in the southeast of the United States, the study included respondents of a variety of ages, education levels and incomes, and approximately 60 per cent males and 40 per cent females took part in the survey. From a pool of 35 attributes, generated from existing literature and pre-test information, the perceived importance of each was ascertained through a seven-point scale with (1) as least important and (7) as most important. Results suggested that there are nine quality factors concerned with sports events and some of these are unique to the sports event context. For example, the 'game experience and showtime factors' were revealed in data analysis to be unique service quality dimensions for sports events (Kelley and Turley, 2001: 165). Interestingly, the data also highlighted that different categories of customers placed different weights on quality attributes. Therefore, operations managers may need to consider how to ensure that different homogenous groups' needs are catered for and well managed, rather than assuming a crowd to be a single target market. Alternatively, some sports events may attract a more homogeneous crowd (i.e. dressage, polo matches, sheep dog trials), making it easier for marketers and operations managers to address service quality perceptions.

Case 13.2 Sport England: quality focus

Sport England (SE) is the government agency responsible for developing the foundations of successful sport in England. It intends to achieve this through facilitating growth in the community sport system of clubs, coaches, facilities and volunteers. The broad strategy devised by Sport England is focused on 'grow, sustain, excel'. The growth objective includes attracting 1 million people to participate in sport and to have more children/young people taking five hours of physical activity in schools.

Within the 'sustain' element of the strategy, SE believes that to keep people involved in sport, they must enjoy it and it is therefore necessary to measure whether this is happening. Understanding and measuring quality and satisfaction are a significant part of the SE 2008–11 strategy. SE sees the measurement of quality as essential to developing a world leading community sport system. Through a satisfaction survey, it measures the satisfaction of participants in 45 individual sports and full detailed results are available online (www.sportengland.org/research/sport_satisfaction.aspx). The survey measures satisfaction across three target groups: general participants, affiliated club members and the talent pool. Satisfaction is measured across 10 areas: value for money, performance, social/belonging, facilities and playing environment, organisation (people and staff), organisation (ease of participating), diversion and release, exertion and fitness, officiating, coaching. The importance of this survey, published in 2009 (Active People Survey 3) and subsequent surveys (Active People 4, 5, 6) published annually is considerable as they are used by Sport England in investment and planning decisions.

Another area where quality is important for SE is in the performance measurement and accreditation scheme 'Clubmark', introduced in 2002:

- to ensure that accredited partners apply core common criteria to ensure that consistent good practice and *minimum operating standards* are delivered through all club development and accreditation schemes;
- to empower parent(s)/carer(s) when choosing a club for their children;
- to ensure that Clubmark accredited clubs are recognised through a common approach to branding;
- to provide a focus around which all organisations involved in sport can come together to support good practice in sports clubs working with children and young people.

(continued)

The minimum operating standards are in four areas:

- the playing programme;
- duty of care and safeguarding and protecting children and young people;
- sports equity and ethics;
- club management.

The many case studies provided by SE on clubs which successfully achieved Clubmark status (see www.clubmark.org.uk/resources/case-studies) demonstrate the operational issues for clubs when seeking such external verification of the quality of their service provision. The many benefits, including financial, are also evident through the case studies.

To look critically at external measures of quality, we can ask the question: If your club does not have Clubmark, does this mean you are not a good club? The answer is, of course, 'no' but the accreditation of quality by Sport England makes it easier for the public to assess your club quickly and with confidence – this makes the decision of whether to engage with the club or not easier for the consumer. Some clubs may build a reputation for quality and have their own systems for monitoring quality. External verification standards are not an easy option for developing a reputation for quality as they involve hard work and careful administration. However, if a system such as Clubmark is adopted sufficiently throughout clubs, it becomes 'the way to organise and manage quality' and is questioned less and less by the club community.

Discussion questions

4 Examining some of the case studies of clubs who have received Clubmark, what are some advantages and disadvantages of gaining such accreditation of quality?

5 Do you think the advantages of Clubmark outweigh the disadvantages? Why or why not?

6 As a Chairperson leading a club what measures would you take to ensure your club gained Clubmark? How would you manage any resistance from other committee members to the work needed for a successful application for accreditation?

Performance measurements

Johnston and Clark (2001) suggest four main reasons why organisations should measure performance. These are:

- communication;
- motivation;
- control;
- improvement.

Performance measurements indicate to employees those aspects of the organisation's operations that are deemed important by managers. The measures inform employees what the organisation requires of them, within the context of the corporate strategy. For example, if a golf club manager measures how many club memberships are sold by (designated) staff per week, this communicates to staff that the number of members is important to the organisation. However, if the golf club manager measures too many aspects of an employee's performance, there may be confusion over what exactly is important. If performance measures are carefully chosen by managers and linked to a reward system, they can serve to motivate employees. Quite importantly, these measures should support the strategic aims of the organisation and may focus on, for example, speed of service delivery, quality of service, personal attention during service provision or standardisation of service offered.

Performance measures can serve as a formal mechanism of control in sports businesses. By measuring performance, managers are receiving feedback on how well organisational objectives are being met. For this information to be useful, there must also be a means of instituting appropriate action when targets are not being met. Finally, managers should measure performance in order to drive improvements in organisation processes, people and systems. Through performance measures, managers can identify those aspects of the organisation that enable and/or constrain reaching the objectives of the organisation.

Caton et al. (1999) suggested that performance measurements demonstrate, either qualitatively or quantitatively, the extent to which an organisation is achieving its aims and objectives. This definition is useful but limits the concept of performance to an 'organisational' level. A more comprehensive view is offered by Staw (1986), who recognised that performance measures can be taken at the individual, group or organisational level. Therefore, 'performance' of each of these factions can be measured in relation to how well they are progressing towards achieving organisational objectives. Furthermore, the implications of any differences in these levels of performance measures have been referred to by Edgar (1996) as a 'strategic gap', where an organisation cannot meet long-term objectives until individual, group and organisational performances are consistent in working toward organisational goals. There are several measures of performance discussed in the literature, including benchmarks and service blueprints.

Organisations need to evaluate their performance on a variety of dimensions. Traditionally, measures of organisation performance have been through financial figures alone. However, there are many useful non-financial data that may be obtained and explain performance in a more detailed and in-depth manner. The most advantageous use of performance measures for sports managers would be a balance of financial and non-financial measures. Financial measures include, for example, share price, return on capital employed, and ratios. Non-financial measure include customer feedback, staff turnover, staff satisfaction, quantity and type of complaints and facility utilisation.

Benchmarking

Hope and Mühlemann (1997: 244) describe benchmarking as 'the process of continuous improvement'. Benchmarking is the measurement of an aspect of an organisation's performance against an internal or external target. Benchmarks are used widely throughout the sports industry in public, private and voluntary organisations. The process of benchmarking can help managers assess performance, set performance targets, realise new methods of working, stimulate creativity and innovation in performance and make considerable improvements throughout an organisation.

Internal benchmarking is the comparison of operational units within an organisation and often takes place in large firms. For example, JJB sports retail outlets may benchmark across retail outlets, in terms of sales, turnover, customer satisfaction or staff satisfaction. Organisations can benchmark their performance against that of their strongest competitor, in an attempt to establish 'best practice'.

Two organisations that currently provide a benchmarking service for local authorities in UK sport are Sport England, which operates a national benchmarking service for sports halls and swimming pools, and the Association of Public Service Excellence, which provides a service for sport and leisure facilities as part of its Performance Networks.

A wide variety of frameworks are available for sports managers to use as performance measurement systems. These include the Balanced Scorecard, Customer Value Chain, EFQM Award, Investors in People (UK), Charter Mark (UK), the Speyer Award (Germany, Austria, Switzerland), New Public Management, ISO certification and country/industry-specific quality assurance and certification systems. This section examines two of the best known, the Balanced Scorecard and the EFQM Award, as they aim to provide a comprehensive measure of organisation performance, and are not just focused on one aspect of organisations, such as people.

Balanced Scorecard

The Balanced Scorecard was developed by Kaplan and Norton (1992) and encourages a variety of measures of performance with the overall aim of revealing the important links between strategy and operational performance. In fact, this method has been embraced by a rapidly growing number of large corporations as a vehicle to help effectively manage corporate performance and strategy. Anthony and Govindarajan (1998) stated that the Balanced Scorecard is tool that can be used by managers to focus, improve communication, set objectives and provide feedback. There are four key 'cards' within this approach, each requiring managers to ask some fundamental questions about their operations:

- financial perspective (how do we perceive our shareholders?);
- customer perspective (how do we perceive our customers?);
- process perspective (in what processes should we excel to succeed?);
- learning and innovation perspective (how will we sustain our ability to change and improve?).

Each of the above perspectives should be considered in consultation with the organisation's vision and strategy. An entire industry of consulting, computer software and independent organisations has grown out of the work of Kaplan and Norton. This is perhaps due to the fact that each organisation should have its own version of the Balanced Scorecard (Gautreau and Kleiner, 2001). That is, an organisation must develop measures within each of the perspectives, which fits its own strategy and goals.

EFQM

For more than ten years, the European Foundation for Quality Management (EFQM) Excellence Model has continuously helped to improve business results. The performance measurement system aims to give employees a better working environment and provide customers with the best possible value and quality. Introduced at the beginning of 1992, the model was used as a framework for assessing applications for the European Quality Award. It is the most widely used organisational framework in Europe and has become the basis for the majority of national and regional quality awards, including the sports-specific QUEST.

The key principles of the model are as follows:

- results orientation – attempt to delight all organisation stakeholders;
- customer focus – sustaining customer value;
- leadership and constancy of purpose;
- management by processes and facts;
- people development and involvement;
- continuous learning, innovation and improvement;
- partnership development;
- corporate social responsibility.

The EFQM model was designed to suit all sectors – public, private and voluntary. However, a public and voluntary sector version has been produced in order to demonstrate some of the slight differences between the private and other sectors. In the public and voluntary sectors, self-assessment and improvement needs to address the management role and how it interfaces with the political role. Therefore, the EFQM Excellence Model does not seek to assess the quality or excellence of political policies, but rather the management of excellence within organisations. Recognising the importance of contextual variables upon the management of business operations, there is also a version of the EFQM model for small firms.

The sports management literature on performance measurement is rather limited (Caton et al., 1999). However, it is only a matter of time before the academic community focuses on the many recent developments in performance measurement in sports businesses. Public sector sport has been increasingly conscious of the need to compete with private and voluntary sector provision of sport opportunities.

Case 13.3 Performance measurement: Goodform Ltd, UK

Goodform Ltd works alongside two other companies that fall within the Goodform Group: the Membership Management Company (MMC) and Sportswise. MMC provides services to governing bodies and clubs to maximise revenue generation and communication with core supporters and customers through introducing and/or managing their membership schemes formally and systematically. Sportswise, Goodform's market research arm, is an independent market research agency working for national governing bodies, professional clubs, associations, commercial companies and public sector/not-for-profit firms that are involved in sport and leisure.

From the company's website, we can see the purpose/values of the company:

> . . . a clear focus on client aims, targets, needs and markets, providing tailored sales and marketing strategies and delivering the right support and resource to deliver and implement the strategy.

(continued)

The key values listed by the company include: innovative, sports-made, customer focused, vibrant, specialist and quality (see www.goodform.info/page.asp?section=186 &sectionTitle=Our+Values for further explanation and to explore their website).

All sport organisations measure their and their employees' performance in some way. Some companies have elaborate, formal mechanisms to track performance and reward or reprimand employees in comparison to relevant targets (e.g. sales). Other organisations take a less rigid approach and see performance measurement as a developmental tool. Goodform Ltd is one such company. Regardless of the purpose of the performance measurement system, it is vital that it reflects the aims, objectives and values of the company so that there is a logical rationale between what the company is trying to achieve and how employees are encouraged to do this.

Goodform Ltd is a relatively small company. Managing Director Stuart Dalrymple states, 'I think the bottom line is we get measured on how much data or revenue or enquiries we generate for our clients so internally we tend to measure individuals on a similar basis'. Within the company, individuals are measured on a six-month basis using a standardised self-appraisal form. The appraisal is used to assist employees rather than strictly measure and reward/reprimand. Therefore, the objectives stated on the form are: 'to assist you and your Manager to have an open discussion about your role at Goodform, your current level of performance, your aspirations and to consider your future training and development needs'.

Self-appraisal means that the employee takes initial responsibility for completing the form, noting their perceived competencies, job role, constraints, achievements and development needs. This is then reviewed with their line manager and any discussions, action points or requirements agreed before being committed to the final report. The self-appraisal is specifically divided into four sections: work review (looking to the past), review of competencies, training and development needs and the future (next 12 months). An interesting part of the appraisal form is the section on competencies. There are a number of competencies which employees must consider their performance against: communication skills, accuracy/attention to detail, customer focus (understanding needs), initiative, ability to prioritise work, commitment/drive/ energy (motivation), planning/organising, analysis/decision making, leadership, team working and knowledge/understanding broader issues.

Discussion questions

7 Do you think Goodform's appraisal of staff is an effective measure of performance?

8 Does the self-appraisal sufficiently help the company achieve its goals and values?

9 What would you suggest to Goodform to improve the effectiveness of its performance measurement within the company? Is the self-appraisal enough?

In sport business involving elite sport or professional sport, the focus is not only on performance measurement of the organisation itself but on athletic performance as the key indicator of organisational success. These figures and statistics are readily accessible in the media and through governing bodies in the form of league tables, medal counts and other win/loss statistics. In the 2010 Winter Olympics, much was made of the outstanding success of the Canadian team which was top of the table in medal points and achieved the most gold medals of all countries competing. This no doubt will be seen (and promoted) as indicative of the performance of not just the athletes but the whole Canadian sport system, including coaches, administrators, sponsorship, event organisers and volunteers.

Is performance related to operations? If we take the case of Canada above, a relationship can be seen between operations and performance. The Canadian success at Vancouver 2010 was the result of careful planning by the Canadian Olympic Committee and 13 Canadian winter sports federations over a five-year period. From January 2005, £75 million was targeted at these sports with medals in mind. Financial and human resources were managed with the one goal in mind – success on the podium. Operationally, this involved coordinating training, coaching, transport, communications and monitoring progress to ensure that the goal would be reached.

The operational environment: sports industry business

The operational environment for sports business is to some extent unique to the specific sport or industry sector. However, there are a number of organisations that offer important services to businesses operating in the sport industry. While this list is in no way conclusive, some of the key organisations include:

- The Sports Industries Federation (TSIF), which plays a role in coordinating the sports industry in the United Kingdom and provides a strong voice to government and the media.
- Business in Sport and Leisure (BISL), which is an umbrella organisation representing the interests of over 100 private sector sport, hospitality and leisure businesses. BISL acts as a lobbyist to government and the media.
- The National Association for Sports Development, which provides support, advocacy and professional development for companies involved in the development of sport.
- Institute of Sport and Recreation Management, which aims to improve the management and operation of sport and recreation services through standards, training, information and consultancy services.
- European Operations Management Association, the leading professional association for those involved in operations management. This is a European-based network devoted to bridging the gap between research and practice.
- International Association for Sports Information, which provides information forums on the sports industry and advises on planning, operations and development of sports information.

There are a number of challenges facing operations managers in today's competitive industry. This section briefly highlights some of these challenges. They may not be unique to the sports industry but do affect the industry in a specific way, simply because of the different context in which sports businesses exist. This context is characterised by continuous change (markets, trends, customer expectations), technological innovation, increasing regulation and governmental pressures. Consistent with the main focus of this chapter, we will examine operational challenges relevant to service organisations.

Challenges facing operations managers in sport can be grouped into broad and specific categories. Broad operational issues include:

- **Globalisation**: Sport is a global concept, as are many sports products and services. Technological innovations allow sport managers to offer products and services to customers all over the world rather than only to a local market. This expansion of the marketplace presents the manager with logistical difficulties of communication, purchasing and customer care. There are also social and political implications of the globalisation of sports businesses, such as the exploitation and corruption of workers in developing countries.

- **Culture**: A key challenge of globalisation is for the operations manager to offer products and services to different cultures, with different values and norms or basic assumptions. Dimensions of cultural differences include the individual versus collective nature of people, affective versus affective-neutral tendencies and reliance on present/past in life versus reliance on the future to guide behaviours.

- **Social responsibility**: Increasingly, organisations are under pressure to demonstrate social responsibility. This has translated into greater attention by operations managers to issues of customer safety, social impact of products and services, staff safety, pollution and disabled access.

- **Environmental responsibility**: Most pollution and environmental disasters are the result of some operational failure. Environmentally friendly materials, processes and services are increasingly found in such sport sectors as golf (impact of golf courses, environmental management of turf), equestrian sport (European grants for construction of environmental facilities), packaging and distribution of sport equipment and risk and environmental impact assessments by local sports clubs offering competitive and recreational opportunities.

- **Managing complexity**: These broad pressures coupled with specific contextual demands (size, structure, nature of the service) of each business means that sports operation managers are expected to coordinate and control many interrelated components.

Specific operational concerns are nearly endless and should be identified by operations managers for their own organisation. Examples of specific challenges include:

- knowing the customer;
- understanding what the organisation is selling;
- managing customer experiences;
- understanding, implementing and adapting organisational corporate strategy;
- improving the organisation through performance measures;
- capacity demands.

 ## Conclusion

The subject of operations management is a complex and intricate weave of concepts, research findings and organisational contexts. In this chapter, we have looked at the public, private and voluntary sectors of the sports industry. Increasingly, while these sectors have unique characteristics, they are under similar pressures and compete directly with one another for custom and human/financial resources. Operations management is a function of sports businesses, it is an activity engaged in by sports managers (formally or informally) and it is a process integral to competitive and sustainable business practices.

Traditional operational issues have not been fully explored by sport management academics. However, there have been some admirable attempts to begin investigating this important aspect of the sports industry. Most notably have been the studies into customer satisfaction in sports/leisure centres as well as in professional sport. Other progress is being made in examining quality in sport businesses and in service provision in the sports industry. Greater attention needs to be paid to the issue of performance measurement in sport organisations. A number of sector-specific measures of quality and performance, such as the RYA Berth Holders Charter and QUEST for public sport/leisure centres, have been examined in this chapter. However, there is a vast selection of other performance measurement systems available to sports managers such as ESQM, the Balanced Scorecard and Investors in People. The key to the successful adoption and utilisation of these systems is to consider their fit with the particular context of the sport organisation in question and how these new systems will be implemented and managed.

While there are many responsibilities of operations managers (developing operations strategy, designing products and service, measuring performance, etc.), there are also broader issues that have an impact on the role of the manager. These issues, including globalisation and pressures of social and environmental responsibility, mean that the operations function is a complex and intricate part of organisation success.

Case 13.4 Managing operations in a small sport business: Cyprus-based company GPK Sports Management

History and services

GPK Sports Management was founded in 2003 and is based in Limassol, Cyprus. The company is dedicated to meeting customer needs and forging long-term relationships with clients. The company was mainly focused on football player management and pre-season camps for local teams abroad. In 2009, more partners were taken on at the firm and services expanded to include basketball player management, television rights reselling and event management. The company has conducted business in Greece, Israel, Ukraine, Poland, France, Italy, Bulgaria and Dubai and now utilises work placement/interns, temporary contracts, alliances and part-time employees to meet the demands of the growing company.

The directors of GPK are licensed by FIFA and FIBA to provide all their clients with professional services that cover every aspect of the player's career. Negotiating on behalf of a player requires a thorough knowledge of the legislation, exhaustive research, a complete awareness of the marketplace and the ability to present a case in a clear and authoritative manner. GPK, in collaboration with its legal advisers, fulfils all of these requirements to assure clients an excellent contract. GPK is dedicated

(continued)

to enhancing players' images and making their names recognised throughout the professional football/basketball community as well as among the general public. Through a carefully planned marketing campaign a client's income potential during and after their playing career is maximised. GPK offers each client the highest level of financial expertise and integrity, working with experts at top international firms. In addition, GPK assists clients with their personal finances by helping to establish banking relationships, secure home mortgages, and evaluate insurance needs and tax planning services.

The agency provides its clients with services reaching beyond their sports career. These include travel arrangements, relocation assistance and medical referrals, or any other service that makes life a little easier to manage. Through its resources, relationships and innovative thinking GPK helps its clients realise the full potential of their brand name. The sports marketing team provides clubs with assistance in their quest for lucrative merchandising and sponsorship agreements.

GPK collaborates with professional sport centres both locally and abroad to ensure the success of a pre-season training camp. Appropriate accommodation, impeccable facilities and excellent organisation are some of the benchmarks that GPK adopts. International and European games bring together the most successful teams as well as the best players in the world. GPK can offer television channels the right to broadcast these games live.

Operations and control

Crucial to the operations of this business is socialising/networking, media control and public relations (PR). The prominence of social interaction and networking means high uncertainty in operations and constant negotiation. Some uncertainty can be managed with careful use of 'contracts' for temporary employment as demand requires. For example, when seasonal events are being organised, the company hires additional staff. Also, each partner has his/her own portfolio of customers and operational responsibilities. Control mechanisms include some administrative controls such as monthly and quarterly meetings to evaluate performance and strategy, making adjustments as needed. However, much 'control' is accomplished through regular personal communication (social and self-control mechanisms), as is common for small firms.

Large companies which manage athletes and events can and do utilise confidentiality contracts to ensure that when employees leave the business they do not abuse the contacts and knowledge gained through employment. They may also have clauses in employment contracts to prevent employees from taking employment with competitors for a period following their release from their current contract. However, as Athos Antomiou, Director of GPK Sports Management said:

> You can have this policy on big agencies but on small ones like ours it's not possible. You can't force someone to stay and work . . . he will simply do nothing proactive for the company. The only contracts we do have, is with our customers (players).

For small businesses, there is less scope for inefficiency without financial consequences. Hence, their workforce must be encouraged to be active and make a contribution at all times. How this is achieved (social/professional controls, contracts, etc.) depends upon the unique circumstances of the organisation.

(continued)

Quality and performance

Financial and non-financial targets are set at the beginning of each season but the business is unpredictable and sometimes more work does not necessarily equate to an increase in sales or turnover. Non-financial measures of performance include networking targets, since this is a key operational necessity for GPK and other such organisations. New relationships with key people are sought each year. There are also performance indicators which are not easy to measure but are essential to GPK's success, such as the level of trust built with existing stakeholders and the contribution this makes to long-term relationships.

The key operational challenges for GPK are not dissimilar to those of other small businesses. Development of the business client list and reputation can be slow and require significant resources. Usually financial resources are limited while the business grows and so time and commitment are the main resources invested in operations and strategy implementation. Directors, partners or employees are expected to multi-task and be flexible in response to market demands and business needs. For GPK, this personal investment has resulted in a company offering superior services to athletes, forward-thinking and innovative solutions for clubs and a solid basis on which to build its operational and strategic goals for expansion.

Discussion questions

10 What are the main differences in managing the operations of a small business versus a large business?

11 What are the challenges for managing the operations of GPK Sports Management?

12 If hired as the Operations Manager for GPK, describe how you would undertake your new role.

Discussion questions

13 Why is it important to study 'operations management' in sports businesses?

14 What would you argue is the major difference between managing operations in a small sport business in comparison to medium–large organisations?

15 Discuss the challenges for national sport governing bodies in managing their operations as opposed to a private sector sport business.

16 What can organisations do to control the quality and performance of their service offering? Compare the BEF to GPK Sports Management and discuss how or if your response to this question differs.

17 What is the difference between customer satisfaction and service quality?

18 How can organisation theory research help to understand the operations function in organisations?

Keywords

Benchmarks; change; control; customer satisfaction; operations; quality; quality standards; service.

Guided reading

There are a variety of sources which refer to service operations 'generally' and broadly cover the key issues for service operations managers, for example Mahadevan (2010) and Heizer and Render (2010).

For research that can help an understanding of the nature of services and the implications for managers see Bitner (1992).

For sport-specific discussions of the key issues in service operation management, readers may consult Schwarz et al. (2010) and McMahon-Beattie and Yeoman (2004).

For an introduction to concepts from organisational theory which can assist the operations manager to perform their duties (including managing change, conflict and decision making) see Slack and Parent (2006).

For examples of studies focusing on specific aspects of service quality and managing performance see Kelley and Turley (2001).

Recommended websites

The following websites have been mentioned in this chapter and provide further details of organisations in the sport industry and issues of quality and performance management.

Sport England: www.sportengland.org/

GPK Sports management: www.gpksports.com/

goodform: www.goodform.info/

Youth Sports Trust's quality standards: http://gifted.youthsporttrust.org/page/quality-standards-intro/index.html

Quest/NBS: www.questnbs.org/

Sport England's 'Performance measurement for the development of sport' report: www.toolkitsport-development.org/html/resources/3F/3F087249-B1C6-4BFA-BB63-42DF308CAC30/best%20value%20through%20sport%20performance%20measurement.pdf

References

Alexandris, K., Dimitriadis, N. and Kasiara, A. (2001) 'The behavioural consequences of perceived service quality: an exploratory study in the context of private fitness clubs in Greece', *European Sport Management Quarterly*, 1 (4), 280–99.

Anthony, R.N. and Govindarajan, V. (1998) *Management Control Systems*, New York: McGraw Hill.

Anthony, R.N. (1965) *Planning and Control Systems: A Framework for Analysis*, Boston, MA: Harvard University Press.

Ashby, W.R. (1956) *An Introduction to Cybernetics*, London: Chapman and Hall.

Backman, S.J. and Veldkamp, C. (1995) 'Examination of the relationship between service quality and user loyalty', *Journal of Park and Recreation Administration*, 13 (2), 29–41.

Bitner, M.J. (1992) 'Serviscapes; the impact of physical surroundings on customer and employees', *Journal of Marketing*, 56 (21), 57–72.

Bitner, M.J., Booms, B.H. and Tetreault, M.S. (1990) 'The service encounter: diagnosing favourable and unfavourable incidents', *Journal of Marketing*, 54, 71–84.

Boden, C. (1994) *The Business of Talk*, Oxford: Polity Press and Blackwell Publishers.

Bourdieu, P. (1985) 'The social space and the genesis of groups', *Theory and Society*, 14, 723–44.

Bouussabaine, A.H., Kirkham, R.J. and Grew, R.J. (1999) 'Modelling total energy costs of sport centres', *Facilities*, 17 (12/13), 452–61.

Business in Sport and Leisure (2002) *The Active Annual: Business in Sport and Leisure 2002 Handbook*, Cheam: BISL.

Buttle, F. (1996) 'SERVQUAL: Review, critique, research agenda', *European Journal of Marketing*, 30, 8–32.

Byers, T. (2009) 'Voluntary sport organizations: Established themes and emerging opportunities'. *International Journal of Sport Management and Marketing* 6 (2), 215–228.

Byers, T., Henry, I. and Slack, T. (2007) 'Understanding Control in Voluntary Sport Organizations', in M. Parent and T. Slack (eds), *International Perspectives on the Management of Sport*, London: Elsevier, 269–286.

Byers, T., Slack, T. and Parent, M.M. (2012) *Key Concepts in Sport Management*, London: Sage.

Caton, M.A., Webb, P. and Patterson, J. (1999) 'Using performance indicators within Australian national and state sporting organisations', *The Sport Educator*, 11 (2), 30–33.

Chase, R.B. and Aquilano, N.J. (1995) *Production and Operations Management: A Life Cycle Approach*, 4th edn, Homewood, IL: Irwin.

Chua, W.F., Lowe, T. and Puxty, T. (1989) *Critical Perspectives in Management Control*, London: Macmillan.

Conti, T. (1999) 'Quality standards development in a hypercompetitive scenario', *The TQM Magazine*, 11 (6), 402–8.

Crompton, J.L., MacKay, K.J. and Fesenmaier, D.R. (1991) 'Identifying dimensions of service quality in public recreation', *Journal of Park and Recreation Administration*, 9 (3), 15–27.

Cronin, J.J. and Taylor, S.A. (1992) 'Measuring service quality: a reexamination of extension', *Journal of Marketing*, 56, 55–68.

Das, T.K. and Teng, B.S. (1998) 'Between trust and control: developing confidence in partner co-operation in alliances', *Academy of Management Review*, 23 (3), 491–512.

De Knop, P., De Bosscher, V., Van Hoecke, J. and Van Heddegem, L. (2001) 'Quality control in youth sports clubs: a project of the government of Flanders', *Book of Proceedings*, 9th Congress European Association of Sport Management, Victoria-Gasteiz, Spain.

De Martelaer, K., Van Hoecke, J., De Knop, P., Van Heddegem, L. and Theeboom, M. (2002) 'Marketing in organised sport: participation, expectations and experiences of children', *European Sport Management Quarterly*, 2 (2), 113–34.

Desrumaux, P., Gemmel, P. and Van Ossel, G. (1998) 'Defining the service concept', in B. Looy, R. van Dierdonck and P. Gemmel (eds), *Services Management: An Integrated Approach*, London: Financial Times Pitman Publishing.

Edgar, D.A. (1996) 'The strategic gap: a multi-site, short break perspective', in N. Johns (ed.), *Productivity Management in Hospitality and Tourism*, London: Cassell, 38–54.

Fineman, S. (ed.) (2000) *Emotion in Organizations*, London: Sage.

Fitzsimmons, J.A. and Fitzsimmons, M.J. (2001) *Service Management: Operations, Strategy, and Information Technology*, New York: McGraw Hill.

Garvin, D. (1984) 'What does "product quality" really mean?', *Sloan Management Review* (Fall), 22–44.

Gautreau, A. and Kleiner, B.H. (2001) 'Recent trends in performance measurement systems: the Balanced Scorecard Approach', *Management Research News*, 24 (3/4), 153–56.

Gertosio, C., Mebarki, N. and Dussauchoy, A. (2000) 'Modeling and simulation of the control framework on a flexible manufacturing system', *International Journal of Production Economics*, 64 (1–3), 285–93.

Haksever, C., Render, B., Russell, R.S. and Murdick, R.G. (2000) *Service Management and Operations*, New Jersey: Prentice Hall.

Haywood-Farmer, J. (1988) 'A conceptual model of service quality', *International Journal of Operations and Production Management*, 8 (6), 36–44.

Heizer, J.H. and Render, B. (2010) *Operations Management*, London: Prentice Hall.

Henry, I. and Lee, P.C. (2004) 'Governance and ethics in sport', in J. Beech and S. Chadwick (eds), *The Business of Sports Management*, Harlow: Pearson.

Heskett, J.L. (1987) 'Lessons in the service sector', *Harvard Business Review* (March/April), 118–26.

Hope, C. and Mühlemann, A. (1997) *Service Operations Management*, London: Prentice Hall Europe.

Hopwood, A. (1974) *Accounting and human behaviour*, London: Prentice Hall.

Howat, G. and Murray, D. (2002) 'The relationships among service quality, value, satisfaction, and future intentions of customers at an Australian sports and leisure centre', *Sport Management Review*, 5 (1), 25–43.

Howat, G., Crilley, G. Absher, J. and Milne, I. (1996) 'Measuring customer service quality in recreation and parks', *Australian Parks and Recreation* (Summer), 77–89.

Johnson, P. and Gill, J. (1993) *Management Control and Organizational Behaviour*, London: Paul Chapman Publishing.

Johnston, R. and Clark, G. (2001) *Service Operations Management*, Harlow: Financial Times Prentice Hall.

Kaplan, R.S. and Norton, D.P. (1992) 'The balanced scorecard: measures that drive performance', *Harvard Business Review*, 70 (1), 70–79.

Kelemen, M.L. (2003) *Managing Quality*, London: Sage Publications.

Kelley, S.W. and Turley, L.W. (2001) 'Consumer perceptions of service quality attributes at sporting events', *Journal of Business Research*, 54 (2), 161–66.

Kim, D. and Kim, S.Y. (1995) 'QUESC: an instrument for assessing the service quality of sport centres in Korea', *Journal of Sport Management*, 9, 208–20.

Mahadevan, B. (2010) *Operations Management: Theory and Practice*, London: Pearson.

McAdam, R. and Canning, N. (2001) 'ISO in the service sector: perceptions of small professional firms', *Managing Service Quality*, 11 (2), 80–92.

McDonald, M., Sutton, W.A. and Milne, G.R. (1995) 'TEAMQUAL™: measuring service quality in professional team sports', *Sport Marketing Quarterly*, 4 (2), 9–15.

McKay, K.J. and Crompton, J.L. (1990) 'Measuring the quality of recreation services', *Journal of Park and Recreation Administration*, 8, 47–56.

McMahon-Beattie, U. and Yeoman, I. (2004) *Sport and Leisure Operations Management*, London: Thomson Learning.

Mintzberg, H. and Quinn, J.B. (1998) *Readings in the Strategy Process*, London: Prentice Hall.

Naylor, J. (2002) *Introduction to Operations Management*, 2nd edn, Harlow, Financial Times Prentice Hall.

Nike (2003) www.nike.com

Ogden, S.M. and Grigg, N.P. (2003) 'The development of sector based quality assurance standards in the UK: diverging or dovetailing?', *The TQM Magazine*, 15 (1), 7–13.

Oliver, R.L. (1997) *Satisfaction: A Behavioural Perspective on the Consumer*, Boston, MA: McGraw Hill.

Papadimitriou, D. and Karteliotis, K. (2000) 'The service quality expectations in private sport and fitness centres: a re-examination of the factor structure', *Sport Marketing Quarterly*, 9, 157–64.

Parasuraman, A., Zeithaml, V.A. and Berry, L.L. (1985) 'A conceptual model of service quality and its implications for future research', *Journal of Marketing*, 49 (4), 41–50.

Parasuraman, A., Zeithaml, V.A. and Berry, L.L. (1988) 'SERVQUAL: a multiple item scale for measuring consumer perceptions of service quality', *Journal of Retailing*, 64 (1), 14–40.

Patterson, P.G. and Spreng, R.A. (1997) 'Modelling the relationship between perceived value, satisfaction and repurchase intentions in business-to-business, service context: an empirical examination', *International Journal of Service Industry Management*, 8 (5), 414–34.

Robinson, S. (1999) 'Measuring service quality: current thinking and future requirements', *Marketing Intelligence and Planning*, 17 (1), 21–32.

Russell, R.S. and Taylor III, B.W. (1998) *Operations Management: Focusing on Quality and Competitiveness*, Upper Saddle River, NJ: Prentice Hall.

Salaman, G. and Thompson, K. (1985) *Control and Ideology in Organizations*, Milton Keynes: The Open University Press.

Schwarz, E.C., Hall, S.A. and Shibli, S. (2010) *Sport Facility Operations Management: A Global Perspective*, Oxford: Elsevier.

Shonk, D.S. and Chelladurai, P. (2009) 'Model of service quality in event sport tourism: development of a scale', *International Journal of Sport Management and Marketing*, 6 (3), 292–307.

Slack, T. (1997) *Understanding Sport Organisations*, London: Human Kinetics.

Slack, T. and Parent, M. (2006) *Understanding Sport Organisations*. London: Human Kinetics.

Slack, N., Chambers, S., Harland, C., Harrison, A. and Johnston, R. (1998) *Operations Management*, Harlow: FT/Prentice Hall.

Sport England (2001) 'Quality management: putting the facility to work for sport', www.sport england.org/whatwedo/place/quest.htm

Staw, B.M. (1986) 'Organizational psychology and the pursuit of the happy/productive worker', *California Management Review*, 4, 40–53.

Suggett, R.H.G. (2010) *Structure of the BEF*, Stoneleigh: British Equestrian Federation.

Teas, R.K. (1993) 'Expectations, performance evaluation, and consumers' perception of quality', *Journal of Marketing*, 57 (4), 18–34.

Thwaites, D. (1999) 'Closing the gaps: service quality in sport tourism', *Journal of Services Marketing*, 13 (6), 500–16.

Van Dyke, T.P., Prybutok, V.R. and Kappelman, L.A. (1999) 'Cautions on the use of the SERQUAL measure to assess the quality of information systems services', *Decision Sciences*, 30 (3), 877–91.

Van Hoecke, J. and deKnop, P. (2006) 'Development of a relevant quality system for gymnastics clubs: an application of the principles of total quality and service management in traditionally organised sport', *International Journal of Sport Management and Marketing*, 1 (4), 359–77.

Van Leeuwen, L., Quick, S. and Daniel, K. (2001) 'Determinants of customer satisfaction with the season ticket service of professional sports clubs', *Book of Proceedings*, 9th Congress European Association of Sport Management, Victoria-Gasteiz, Spain.

Verma, R., Thompson, G.M., Moore, W.L. and Louviere, J.J. (2001) 'Effective design of products/ services: An approach based on integration of marketing and operations management decisions', *Decision Sciences*, 32 (1), 165–93.

Wakefield, K.L. and Blodgett, J.G. (1994) 'The importance of servicescapes in leisure service settings', *Journal of Services Marketing*, 8 (3), 66–76.

Wels-Lips, I., van der Ven, M. and Pieters, R. (1998) 'Critical services dimension: an empirical investigation across six industries', *International Journal of Service Industry Management*, 9 (3), 286–389.

Westerbeek, H. and Shilbury, D. (2001) 'An empirical holistic framework for service quality research in the sport entertainment industry', 9th Congress European Association for Sport Management Conference Proceedings, 360–61.

Wright, B.A., Duray, N. and Goodale, T. (1992) 'Assessing perceptions of recreation center service quality: an application of recent advancements in service quality research', *Journal of Park and Recreation Administration*, 10 (3), 33–47.

Zeithaml, V.A. and Bitner, M.J. (1996) *Services Marketing*, New York: McGraw Hill.

Zeithaml, V.A., Berry, L.L. and Parasuraman, A. (1993) 'The nature and determinants of customer expectations of service', *Journal of the Academy of Marketing Science*, 21, 1–12.

The internet, online social networks and the fan digital experience

Boris Helleu, University of Caen Basse-Normandie
Maxence Karoutchi, Sports Social Media Consultant, founder of Sportbizinside.com

In this world we live in now, everybody becomes media.

(Shaquille O'Neal, former NBA Player)

Learning outcomes

Upon completion of this chapter the reader should be able to:

- identify digital fans and their practices, and define 'social media' in a new way;
- appreciate the variety of platforms involved, their full technical diversity and their social usages;
- understand the online social networks' capacity for indirect monetisation;
- highlight the marketing potential of socio-digital systems.

 ## Overview

Since it first emerged in the nineteenth century, professional sport has expanded its audience and become a global phenomenon by taking advantage of successive innovations in the information sector: newspapers, radio, television, and now the information and communication technologies. This chapter presents an overview of the use of the internet, and in particular of online social networks, in the field of sport. A review of the literature suggests that a large number of digital systems exist, in some cases predating the popularisation of the term 'social media'. Because they are both social and technological, these systems signal the advent of a new era in sport as entertainment, which we call the 'Online Digital Experience Generation'. The fan is placed at the centre of a digital ecosystem which involves the athletes, the clubs, the leagues and the media – but also the stadiums and arenas. Fans can now interact with, modify and produce content, thereby increasing their role as co-producers of the sporting show.

The purpose of this chapter is to review the methods and practices which, as Clavio (2010) notes, were not part of the lexicon a decade ago. Our description will be regularly illustrated by case studies reflecting recent best practices and data. By their very nature, however, these will no longer be entirely new by the time the reader opens this book.

Introduction: the online digital experience

We begin this chapter with Aaron Sorkin, the famous screenwriter (*The West Wing*). This story relates to an isolated incident, but may convey an important truth: Sorkin began his TV career with *Sports Night*, a television series about a fictional sports news show. He then found international success in the movies with *The Social Network*, a film devoted to the launching of Facebook by Mark Zuckerberg, and *Moneyball*, adapted from the famous book by Michael Lewis (2003). It is all rather as if Aaron Sorkin's career were a reflection of the increasingly obvious linkages between sport and the online social networks. In real life the show *Sports Center*, ESPN's daily sports news broadcast, has more than 2.6 million followers on Twitter and 5 million fans on Facebook.

This is another piece of evidence that the World Wide Web, as a medium of global communication, has changed our social relationships. By way of illustration, the social networking service Facebook reports 845 million active monthly users, including 425 million mobile users. The microblogging platform Twitter has more than 350 million users, sending out more than 300 million tweets per day. But the opportunities for sharing this content and for digital interactions are not limited to these two systems. Foursquare, the location-based social networking website created in 2009, has more than 15 million users. Instagram, the photo-sharing application launched in 2010, reports that 400 million photos were uploaded in 2011. And these tools can be linked to each other so that, for instance, a photo created with the Instagram application can be georeferenced on Foursquare and then shared on a Twitter and/or Facebook account.

These systems are now being adopted by sports fans. Although there are various ways of becoming involved and behaving, the most loyal and passionate fans seek a more active role. They are not merely the spectators for a show that is limited to the field of play, but truly actors in a show that extends into the stands. This is shown, for example, by Richelieu and Pons (2000) when they compare the entertainment experience and rituals at games involving FC Barcelona and the Toronto Maple Leafs. Ultimately, what social networks are making possible is an extension of the space in which the match can be experienced.

Indeed, by using digital space and the social media, we are changing the paradigm. Technologic innovation has taken sport from being an event that must be seen to an event that must be experienced. In *The Elusive Fan*, Rein, Kotler and Shields (2006) distinguish three sports generations:

- The monopoly generation (1900–1950) is identified with the emergence of modern sport. You had to go to a stadium to see a match.

- The second generation is the television generation (1950–1990). It became possible to watch an event outside the stadium and around the world.

- Lastly, the highlight generation (1990–present) is that of the new media technologies. Here, as the authors note, 'satellite radio and television, the internet, cell phones, and video games have all changed the sports experience to make it more global, mobile, and personalized' (ibid.: 44).

That being said, it is no longer just a matter of being able to access sports information anywhere and at any time. We may have just entered a fourth stage: the online digital experience generation. Fans themselves can now create content and share it with a community. What the online social media make possible is to live, share, distribute and comment on their feelings about sport inside or outside the stadium, in front of the TV or at fan fests. And so, because fans can interact among themselves and also with the brand, the product, the teams and the athletes, we are no longer in the realm of transactional marketing but of relational marketing and experiential marketing (see Schmitt, 1999), because the brand, the product and the sports service are no longer merely consumed but experienced, usually as part of a shared-interest community. Adapting Cova and Cova (2004), we might say that in the digital sports experience:

- Fans are not only consumers: they want to be involved.

- Fans both act and react: they want to share their emotions.

- Fans are looking for meaning.

- The experience is not limited to match day: fans can create it whenever they want.

 ## Fans can generate content: it's a whole new ballgame

In an article devoted to British soccer, Gibbons and Dixon (2010) regret that 'the significance of the Internet as a site for fans to interact remains under-investigated'. Although the academic literature devoted to sport and social media is certainly in a youthful, rapidly growing stage, study of the internet as it applies to sport is not a novelty. In 2000 Beech et al. devoted an article to the use of the internet in marketing by British clubs. The web was already perceived as a global communication tool for the delivery of information, the creation of multimedia content, interactions with fans, promoting the product or brand and for selling tickets and merchandise. The authors observe:

> many commentators are now claiming that the technology is leading to a new era in marketing. Sport has not been immune to such rapid developments and is increasingly using the Internet as a medium through which clubs and teams can effectively communicate and establish stronger relationships with supporters.

Since that time the internet has substantially altered the fan experience, thanks to technologic advances. Turner (2008) has examined how web-based technology is enhancing the television viewing experience. But technology has also altered social usage of the internet. This progress is not only technical but also social in nature, as emphasised by Ioakimidis (2010):

> Creating value for fans has become more difficult because they want more benefits from online experiences, including the development of social connections. Teams could take advantage of the fans' attachment by creating interactive web spaces, extending team experiences, and building fan loyalty.

The term 'social media' implies that above and beyond the technical criteria they make it possible to find 'peers', and to interact with them by engaging in a multitude of activities.

Use of the term 'social media' is now widespread. However, Stenger and Coutant (2011) wonder just what a social medium might be. They also point out that the term covers a number of very different systems and uses which, as regards the majority, predate the designation 'social media'.

- Blogs (weblogs): a personal journal published on the World Wide Web, usually produced by a single individual, or sometimes by a small group of contributors. Blogs have become widely popular since the late 1990s. The Twitter platform (founded in 2006) is a spin-off from a blog.

- Online communities: the discussion forum remains the best-known and oldest form of online discussion.

- Websites for sharing video content (YouTube, Dailymotion, etc.), photos (Flickr), links (Delicious) and music.

- Socio-digital systems such as Facebook, Orkut and professional tie-ins like LinkedIn and Viadeo.

- New platforms such as Quora, Foursquare, Instagram and Pinterest.

These systems share the idea of involving the user. Instead of a passive role, prisoners of the information that they dig up for themselves on websites, the public now has the ability to produce content. Kwak et al. (2010) note that such user-generated content requires:

- being publicly posted on a website or a social networking site accessible to a selected group of people;

- demonstrating a quest for creativity;

- having been created outside professional routines.

There have been many developments. They have strengthened the ties between the clubs and their fans. In the early days of the internet a club's official website would offer a content that was devoid of interactivity (score, player bios, the club's history, sports-related information, an exclusive interview, photos and the occasional video). Then the fans began to talk to each other (internet forum) and to speak from time to time with club personalities (chat room). Finally, the emergence of Web 2.0 encouraged the continuing involvement of fans as a way of generating content that was directly linked to their favourite club (the sharing of photos, videos, information and feelings). In a further step, online media strengthened the connection between the fans and their team. In an investigation of fans' use of the media, Phua (2010) shows that 'of the four media types tested (print, broadcast, online, and mobile phones), online media were found to have the greatest impact on fan identification and collective self-esteem'.

To quote the title of the book by Sanderson (2011b), 'It's a whole new ballgame'. Henceforth, the time shared by fans and their clubs will no longer be limited to the match in the stadium or on TV. For example, the growth of connectivity and the proliferation of platforms now enable the fan:

- Three days before the match: fascinated by the club's history, the fan actively participates in the writing of a Wikipedia article on the subject (for more, see Ferriter, 2009).

- Two days before the match, on a specialist discussion forum, the fan reads and comments on the key issues of the coming match.

- The night before the match: the fan completes an online betting slip, and tinkers with the composition of a fantasy league team (for more, see Ruihley and Hardin, 2010; Hutchins et al., 2009).

- Match day: the fan updates his/her Facebook status, geolocates the position of his/her seat in the stadium, takes a few photos, comments on the goals on a Twitter account (congratulates the player who has just scored for the home team), looks at the scores of other matches and watches the slow-motion replay of the goal he/she missed while doing all this. A club app allows him/her to order a beer.

- Back home the fans can discuss the match on a forum, watch the goals again on YouTube (for more, see Zimmerman et al., 2011), share photos and videos on their Facebook pages, and search the images on a gigapixel FanCam.

- The day after the match: they read the online press and the blogs (for more, see Kwak et al., 2010).

- The day after that: looks at the club's Pinterest page, which suggests some online purchases.

Case 14.1 Some sports social media facts

According to GMRmarketing (infographic 'Sports and Social Media', February 2012):

- 81 per cent of people prefer the internet for their sports news (41 per cent Twitter/ Facebook – 40 per cent websites).
- When the game is on TV, 83 per cent of people will check sports social media.
- 63 per cent will even check updates while they're sitting in the stadium.

According to Coyle Media (infographic 'Who is Following NHL Clubs on Twitter', June 2011):

(continued)

- 87 per cent of people following an NHL club are avid fans.
- 65 per cent live within the club's metropolitan area.
- One in three have 'checked in' using a location-based service. Of these, one in three have checked in at a club hockey game.
- 60 per cent of smartphone users have downloaded a club app.
- 88 per cent are multi-screeners (online via computer or cell phone while watching a game on TV).
- 94 per cent have purchased a product or service as a result of following a brand on Twitter.

According to a National Survey commissioned by Motricity (source: 'Sports Fans Love Mobile Stats, Apps', *Marketing Daily*, 6 March 2012):

- 79 per cent of sports fans have used their device for watching or following sports this past year.
- Of these, 87 per cent check on a sport during an 'inappropriate' time, e.g. when they are in a meeting or, say, on a date.
- 50 per cent have gone to the restroom in order to check the score.
- Nearly a third of sports fans who use mobile devices to check on stats will double-task at entertainment events, including movies, concerts and the like, in total disregard of pre-show reminders.
- Remarkably, very nearly 20 per cent of men confess to having checked scores during a date. And even worse for the fate of their souls in the hereafter, about 14 per cent confess (no pun intended) to having checked a score while in church.

According to Kwarter (infographic 'The Social Engine of Sport', October 2011):

- 40 per cent of fans report that they've become bigger fans of their sport since starting to use social media to follow their favourite team.
- 81 per cent of fans agree that sports viewing should be more interactive.

According to Coyle Media (infographic 'Social Sports Poll', December 2011):

- 45 per cent of NHL fans have used a location-based service to 'check in', 32 per cent of NBA fans and 28 per cent of NFL fans.
- Fans checked in first in restaurants, then in a stadium (30 per cent NHL, 13 per cent NBA, 14 per cent NFL).

Discussion questions

1 Do you recognise yourself in these behaviours?
2 Whatever the sport, the league or the team you support, try to identify the digital systems it offers.

The marketing lesson is that the club is no longer the sole guardian of its digital existence. While actively pursuing their relationships with their favourite club, fans extend their areas of experience beyond the stadium by digitalising them. At this point we find ourselves in a new phase: co-production of the sporting brand's digital presence.

The athletes: to be or not to be . . . on Twitter?

High-level athletes take on the attributes of champions, heroes and models. Moreover, when they stand on a podium they are symbolically raised above ordinary men and women. Athletes are distinguished by their excellence and by a kind of inaccessibility. Not that their words are rarely heard, but they are distributed through the filter of traditional media. When they are found on social networks, athletes confer a sort of proximity. By sharing their daily lives, they come down from the pedestal to engage in a special association with their fans. With Twitter, the athlete is able to talk to them without intermediation. As the Manchester footballer Garry Neville explained during the Soccerex European forum in March 2012:

> It's a brilliant source of information. If you are in the media, or you are a football fan, you cannot not be on it. People who are football fans and I have spoken to, I say look forget the stories about the abuse, follow people and you will get so much information fed so quickly, and that is the reason I use it predominantly, because it is just the quickest source of information. All the journalists' articles, all the news from the Premier League and the Championship – and it's not going to go away. For me it is a good thing.
>
> (www.fcbusiness.co.uk/news/article/newsitem=1722/title=footballers+need+
> social+media+warns+neville)

To answer the question 'What are athletes saying on Twitter?', certain academics have analysed the contents of tweets. Pegoraro (2010) examined a week of tweets by 49 athletes. She grouped the 1,193 listed tweets into the following seven categories: relating to personal life; relating to business life; relating to another sport or athlete; relating to their sport; responding to fans; responding to other athletes; and relating to pop culture. The results show that athletes talk about their daily lives, and make every effort to reply to their fans. According to the author 'Twitter is a powerful tool for increasing fan–athlete interaction'.

Hambrick et al. (2010) conducted a study of the contents of tweets to confirm that the use of this microblogging platform was relational rather than promotional. The authors distinguish six categories: interactivity; diversion; information sharing; content; promotional; and fanship. Thirty-four per cent of tweets fall into the 'interactivity' category: the more an athlete interacts, the more followers he/she has. Twenty-eight per cent of tweets fall into the 'diversion' category: here athletes share items that are more personal, or that at least do not only have to do with sport. Only in 15 per cent of their tweets do athletes talk about their sport or their team. And their tweets are clearly promotional in only 5 per cent of cases. In the authors' view 'The results suggest that Twitter may provide fans with unique insight into the personal lives of athletes and address topics not found to the same extent in mainstream-media sources'.

Nevertheless, the Twitter message as promotional tool does exist. Hambrick and Mahoney (2011) have focused their attention on two precursor athletes who were active on Twitter: the cyclist Lance Armstrong and the tennis player Serena Williams. Twelve per cent of their messages were promotional. Sporting organisations encourage the presence of athletes on the microblogging site to ensure their visibility and for promotional purposes. Many WWE Superstars interact with fans and advertise the Federation's activities. Dana White, the UFC President, uses financial incentives to encourage his fighters to have a Twitter presence. White is proactive on the social networks, and even provides training for his athletes.

Some consciousness-raising is indeed necessary, because a foolish remark can affect the brand image of the club or the league. There are many examples of words that have offended fans, or a wider public. To avoid this, the New York Jets established a 'Dos and Don'ts' list as well as examples of best practices. Through such actions the club encourages online activity by its athletes, professionalises their activities and maximises them by establishing a clear framework. When properly utilised, as Sanderson (2010b) shows by analysing the Tiger Woods case, 'social-media sites are valuable public relations tools that athletes can use to quickly generate support that counteracts perceived negative media framing'.

We have focused here on the area of sport, but the use of Twitter also encompasses the larger areas of entertainment, media, politics, and even teaching. Today it is old news that the social media were important in Barack Obama's 2008 presidential campaign. However, although he is indeed in the top 10 of persons having the most followers, the nine other places are monopolised by artists who target a young audience. The first athlete (the Brazilian soccer player Kakà) appears only in 18th place.

Case 14.2 Top athletes on Twitter and Facebook

Rank	Athlete	Sport	Twitter	Facebook	Total
1	Ricardo Kakà	Soccer – Real Madrid	9,166,953	14,619,780	23,786,733
2	Cristiano Ronaldo	Soccer – Real Madrid	7,805,892	41,545,603	49,351,495
3	Shaquille O'Neal	Former NBA player	5,311,376	2,633,113	7,944,489
4	LeBron James	NBA – Miami Heat	4,006,357	9,789,894	13,796,251
5	Neymar	Soccer – Santos FC	3,717,585	3,148,941	6,866,526
6	Wayne Rooney	Soccer – Manchester United	3,585,306		3,585,306
7	Lance Armstrong	Former road cyclist	3,345,884	2,148,053	5,493,937
8	Ronaldinho Gaucho	Soccer – Flamengo	3,336,590	2,394,088	5,730,678
9	Chad Ochocinco	NFL – New England Patriots	3,312,078		3,312,078
10	Dwight Howard	NBA – Orlando Magic	3,085,544	2,199,332	5,284,876
11	Ronaldo	Former soccer player	2,969,954		2,969,954
12	Tony Hawks	Former skateboarder	2,920,699	2,266,549	5,187,248
13	Dwyane Wade	NBA – Miami Heat	2,873,321	4,365,388	7,238,709
14	Lamar Odom	NBA – LA Lakers	2,777,654	676,390	3,454,044
15	Andres Iniesta	Soccer – FC Barcelona	2,761,894	9,220,980	11,982,874
16	Cesc Fabregas	Soccer – FC Barcelona	2,719,289	288,967	3,008,256
17	Floyd Mayweather, Jr.	Boxer	2,578,131		2,578,131
18	Serena Williams	Tennis	2,541,456	952,607	3,494,063
19	Diego Forlan	Soccer – Inter Milan	2,455,135	2,537,078	4,992,213
20	Rio Ferdinand	Soccer – Manchester United	2,416,077	1,119,800	3,535,877

Source: http://fanpagelist.com, 19 March 2012

(continued)

What are the teams and the leagues doing on the social networks?

As a result of their ubiquitous presence, the social networks, and especially Twitter and Facebook, seem to have become indispensable. In this regard we may cite the example of the WWE, which in 2008 launched 'WWE Universe', its own online social network. The platform ceased operations in January 2011, because the WWE preferred to concentrate on the most widely utilised systems (Facebook, Twitter and YouTube). It is clear that for a club, not having a socio-digital presence might be a mistake, but having said that, just being there is not enough. This observation calls for two further ones:

● The social networks are not replacements for older systems: they complement them. The clubs and leagues still have their websites, which continue to generate significant traffic. Waters et al. (2011) even show that NFL teams promote their website on Facebook to cultivate their relationship with the fans. Moreover, the official websites still provide excellent showcases, especially for highlighting their sponsors (Berardone et al., 2011).

● It is not a matter of accumulating as many fans as possible, but of encouraging an inter-activity, with objectives which vary from one club or one league to another. The goal may be to become known, to promote an event, to encourage online/no line transitions, to act globally or locally or to get to know their fans. These examples are intended only to illustrate the range of possibilities.

We see that Twitter can be used to advantage by sports organisations in search of fame. The humble Jaguares de Chiapas football club (Mexican Division 1) offsets a certain lack of media exposure by an innovative digital strategy. The prime objective of the club's marketing department is to position Jaguares de Chiapas locally by continuing to attract more fans, and to develop the club's brand over the medium to long term so as to arouse the interest of potential sponsors and to occupy media space in Mexico. The club's marketing department detected that one of the main expectations of the fans, as regards digital presence, is to be able to see another aspect of the club's life, and especially that of its players. To promote this, the club replaced the names of the players on their jerseys by their Twitter accounts. The move caused a minor stir, encouraging the teams of other minor sports to try it for themselves (among others the Philadelphia Wings of the National Lacrosse League).

The microblogging site can also be used to promote a sports event. After studying two bicycle-race organisers who used Twitter to promote their events, Hambrick (2012) highlights the three key findings obtained:

- First, the race organizers used a combination of informational and promotional messages to attract followers and share information about their upcoming events.

- Second, they gained most of their Twitter followers within the first few days after creating their home pages.

- Third, gaining early followers who had more followers helped spread information about the events.

Lastly, as emphasised by Schoenstedt and Reau (2010), using Twitter, YouTube, blogs and Facebook is a good way to create a buzz. By examining the case of the Cincinnati Flying Pig Marathon, they show that these tools appeal to a niche audience which is bound to grow. Working in tandem with the traditional media centre, it created an interaction between the participants, the public and the sponsors.

Case 14.3 Top teams and professional sport organisations on Facebook and Twitter

Rank	Team	Sport	Twitter	Facebook	Total
1	FC Barcelona	Soccer – Spain	7,347,283	28,307,793	35,655,076
2	Real Madrid	Soccer – Spain	3,873,485	25,843,033	29,716,518
3	Manchester United	Soccer – England		23,483,615	23,483,615
4	NBA	Basketball	4,728,142	12,911,369	17,639,511
5	Los Angeles Lakers	NBA	2,409,665	12,503,812	14,913,477
6	Arsenal	Soccer – England	1,347,332	9,475,537	10,822,869
7	ESPN	TV network	3,316,993	7,150,013	10,467,006
8	Chelsea	Soccer – England	723,236	9,162,334	9,885,570
9	Liverpool	Soccer – England	853,105	8,749,722	9,602,827
10	AC Milan	Soccer – Italy	424,238	9,063,495	9,487,733
11	WWE	Wrestling	96,731	8,551,429	8,648,160
12	UFC	Ultimate fighting	548,877	7,990,795	8,539,672
13	NFL	American Football	3,107,787	5,035,641	8,143,428
14	SportsCenter	TV sports news	2,569,873	5,168,572	7,738,445
15	Galatasaray	Soccer – Turkey	1,057,466	6,633,877	7,691,343
16	Boston Celtics	NBA	414,669	6,296,399	6,711,068
17	Chicago Bulls	NBA	378,519	5,593,115	5,971,634
18	New York Yankees	MLB	543,629	5,278,923	5,822,552
19	Miami Heat	NBA	495,804	5,184,223	5,680,027
20	Fenerbahçe	Soccer – Turkey		5,452,923	5,452,923
21	India Cricket	Cricket	46	4,987,322	4,987,368
22	Dallas Cowboys	NFL	286,758	4,522,583	4,809,341
23	Pittsburgh Steelers	NFL	293,365	4,206,183	4,499,548
24	New England Patriots	NFL	340,169	3,385,810	3,725,979

(continued)

Rank	Team	Sport	Twitter	Facebook	Total
25	Esporte Interativo	TV network	427,077	3,096,625	3,523,702
26	Boston Red Sox	MLB	23,545	3,458,166	3,481,711
27	NASCAR	Auto racing	511,853	2,782,835	3,294,688
28	Beşiktaş	Soccer	14,132	3,137,827	3,151,959
29	NHL	NHL	1,033,692	2,202,862	3,236,554
30	Green Bay Packers	NFL	246,924	2,826,862	3,073,786

Source: www.sportsfangraph.com/, 19 March 2012

Discussion question

5 This classification is dominated by European soccer teams. However, the leagues and institutions of this sport (English Premier League, UEFA, FIFA, etc.) are missing from the top 30, unlike the North American organisations (NBA, WWE, UFC, NFL, NASCAR, NHL). How can we account for this?

When sports organisations already have a significant digital fan base, the key concepts are relationship and activation. As an example, consider the two clubs which dominate the ranking in the table above. Garcia (2011) shows how the social networks are part of a relationship management model established by Real Madrid to build a long-term relationship with its fans. The author explains:

> One of the most valuable uses of social media for Real Madrid's communication management is to test content, gain feedback, and understand things from their fans' perspective. . . . Real Madrid's success in the use of social media has been to think of each fan as one person and not so much as publics or stakeholders. This approach has been particularly successful in promotions that have been adequately contextualized, creating genuine conversations among Real Madrid fans.

To mobilise its more than 28 million fans, FC Barcelona has launched a Facebook app called 'FCB Alert'. It woos its fans with exclusive content, delivers information, offers interactive features (games, surveys, videos, multimedia content), creates exclusive offers and promotions from the team and the players, and includes the possibility of online purchases. Finally, the application enables FCB to include the fans in a marketing database, so as to better target its future offers.

Fans may even be solicited to become co-producers of their club's digital presence. In 2011 the New Jersey Devils of the NHL launched 'Mission Control', a volunteer programme involving 25 fans who were made responsible for the 'monitoring' and leadership of the club's online community. These volunteers work on a rotating 12 hours per day basis every day of the week, under the supervision of an employee. This has enabled the franchise to increase its number of followers by a factor of nine in a single year, acquire five times as many fans on Facebook, and be nominated for *PRWeek*'s Campaign of the Year trophy in the field of Arts, Entertainment and Media.

Social networks can also be employed for business-to-fans (B2F) and business-to-business (B2B) strategies. This requires the simultaneous activation of the fan base and the

Table 14.1 Selected strategies linking Web 2.0 to relationship marketing goals

Potential goals of relationship marketers	Blogs	Social networks	Content communities (e.g. YouTube)	Forums and bulletin boards	Content aggregators (e.g. RSS feeds)
Increase understanding of consumer needs	Opportunities for direct communication with organisational leadership	Highly interactive, numerous opportunities for engagement	Responses to posted content through comments and views	Two-way potential to drive discussion of current topics	Continued sharing of information highlights areas of significance to fans
Develop long-term partnership	Fan connection increase through dynamic feedback channel	Membership in 'clubs' maintained within social network	Participation opportunities such as video or photo contests increase interaction with fans	Status and credibility of frequent or expert posters can be recognised. Ability to contribute to body of knowledge	Simple way to receive up-to-date communications of content. Opt-in capabilities
Enhance loyalty	Importance of fans' voice recognised	Fan connections increase through opportunities to contribute content such video, photos	Active contributions and posting of content used by fans to demonstrate commitment	Frequent posters build connections with each other, as well as organisation. Commitment enhanced by participation in the conversation	Output from feeds can be redistributed through social network or blog – becomes part of poster's contributions
Enhance value and customer satisfaction	Fans can personalise and control their relationship with the sport	Empowers fans and builds community. Real-time connections	Dynamic nature of content provides fans with new perspectives and access to behind-the-scene activities	Real-time conversation with other fans and industry insiders	Increased access to self-selected information resources
Brand building	Re-tweets can be used to spread information on organisational activity	Proprietary social networks such as Planet Orange provide opportunity for expanded brand recognition	Mixed-media approaches can be used to reinforce the brand	Activity builds awareness with brand and brand extensions	Company-designed content used to enhance brand

Source: 'Meeting relationship-marketing goals through social media: A conceptual model for Sport Marketers', *International Journal of Sport Communication*, 10 (3), 442–37 (J. Williams and S.J. Chin 2010). Reprinted with permission.

involvement of partners. In October 2010 the Carolina Panthers of the NFL carried out a novel treasure-hunt based on social networks: 'The Panthers Purrsuit Social Media Contest'. Teams competed in an orienteering race during which they had to answer riddles and cross the town, departing from the club's stadium (Bank of America Stadium) in the morning. After each stage the teams had to complete an action (physical tests, collecting objects, riddles) and confirm it on Foursquare. All the check-in points for the tests were either in the premises of charities associated with the test, or at the club's sponsors. To earn more points the teams could carry out additional actions, e.g. have a photo taken with one of the company's officers at the check-in and send it to Twitter, or convince a client of this partner company to sing a song and then post it on YouTube. This event is a good example of the integration of B2B and B2C.

- The event had 64 attendees (a number deliberately kept small to ensure that the event ran smoothly); on average each participant had 551 friends on Facebook.

- More than 1,000 photos posted on the principal sponsor's Facebook pages.

- More than 1,200 tweets generated during the event, more than 174,000 Twitter users and more than 2.1 million tweets mentioning the event.

- 1,264 viewings of videos posted on YouTube during the event.

- Nine of the event's partners were part of the strongest trends around the town of Charlotte (where the event took place) on Trendsmap.com.

Major sporting events no longer exist only in the stadium or on TV: they also have a digital incarnation. In February 2012, for example, during the All-Star Weekend, the NBA set up a multiplatform option so as to maximise the digital Fan Experience. The NBA.com Social Spotlight collected fans' tweets, photos and videos. The NBA All-Star Pulse, conceived as 'a visualization of the most buzz-worthy topics trending during NBA All-Star Weekend' measured the event's digital activity. The fans were involved, since they had named the winner by using the hashtag #SpriteSlam on Twitter, generating 15 per cent of all the tweets on the system. The NBA estimates that 240 million fans followed the event via Twitter, Facebook and the Chinese social networks.

Case 14.4 Sporting events go global and digital: the 2012 NBA All-Star Game

Melissa Rosenthal Brenner, NBA Vice President of Marketing:

> Our mission for All-Star is the same as our goal every day of the year, which is to enhance our fans' engagement and enjoyment of the game. And that's really what social media is for us. It's a way for fans to interact with each other on a global basis. We look at everything from trending topics to individual post engagement on Facebook, as well the volume and sentiment of mentions across all platforms. We'll put out a pretty robust analysis post All-Star on volume, sentiment, as well as key tweets or Facebook status updates that really tell the story of what fans feel about our game and feel about the event itself.

(continued)

Matthew Brabants, NBA Senior Vice President of International Media Distribution and Business Operations:

We don't have a one-size fits all strategy. We always have to stay ahead of the trends in social media as user patterns in other countries differ. In Brazil, for example, Facebook isn't the first place fans go to connect. We want to make sure that we're reaching out via Orkut and other social networks. We're working in close communication with third-party groups to make sure they're aware of those trends and are doing it properly. We have a fairly young fan base around the world that's tuning into the NBA, a tech-savvy fan base. A fan base that's using their mobile phones, that's on Facebook, Twitter or Tencent in China. So what we've done is made it a real priority to reach out to those fans directly and integrate with our partners in that outreach.

Source: Peter Robert Casey, Community Manager, Five-Star Basketball
('2012 NBA All-Star Weekend a Social Media Success' Posted: 2 March 2012 huffingtonpost.com)

Discussion questions

6 What is the objective of the NBA's digital strategy?

7 How does the NBA hope to intensify its globalisation via the social networks?

Monetisation

Television rights, merchandising and match day revenues are at the core of the clubs' business model. In a situation marked by economic crisis, worldwide inter-sports competition and the inflation of player salaries, the clubs need to develop new sources of income. The official websites of teams and leagues now include online sales departments. Zhang and Won (2010) have analysed the determinants of licensed sports merchandise sales on e-commerce platforms. Among other findings, they show that fan identification (the degree to which the fan's relationship with the team contributes to their social identity) remains an important criterion in online purchasing. Accordingly, if 'fan identification' favours the buying act, why not use the digital relationship already established with enthusiastic, loyal fans to generate income by other means than online commerce?

Let us admit right away that looking for significant income on the web cannot be the clubs' primary objective. At best, by mobilising a large, active digital fanbase, it could be a business booster. As Sean Parker, the Director of Digital Media of the Washington Capitals (NHL), observed: 'we do look at each platform and say how is it going to extend our brand, are we going to be able to engage with fans and ultimately will this make us money?' In fact, the number of fans and their engagement depend on the club's sincerity in seeking to build a relationship on the basis of enthusiasm. A content that is obviously depersonalised and ultra-promotional could put off fans who see themselves as supporters rather than customers. This is not to minimise the potential return on investment (ROI) of a digital strategy. However, as we have said, this is more a relational and experiential matter than a transactional one. Thus, rather than ROI, the consultant Carson McKee, a specialist in monetisation strategies in sport, prefers to speak of digital return optimisation (DRO), which he defines as 'The methodology of maximizing and leveraging digital and social media assets to achieve specific growth, interaction and/or revenue goals'.

Social networks can facilitate business (sales growth, development of new merchandising products, ticketing and traffic on the official website). Here are some examples:

- Encouraging their fan community to participate (crowd-sourcing) in the design of a new jersey or other merchandising product. In 2011 Olympique Marseille and Adidas developed an application that enabled fans to design a jersey which was then worn by the club's players. By means of such initiatives clubs maximise the success of the product, since their community will be more inclined to purchase the product when it has taken part in its development.

- Social networks also ensure announcements of products by word-of-mouth in an instantaneous manner. A simple photo of a new club jersey circulated on a fan's Twitter account can travel around the world in a flash and enable the club to develop both sales and brand awareness at an international level.

- The crowd in the stadium is another source of income that can be developed. The sharing of content and experience from members of the community during matches can encourage a new audience to come and see the team, drawn in by the buzz created around the club and the recommendations of influential parties.

- Socio-digital systems can generate additional traffic on the club's official site; the club can then obtain better terms for its advertising space and optimise its e-commerce options.

- Lastly, the new media can be used to highlight sponsors and partners. For example, the various sponsors of the 2012 NBA All-Star Game had a dedicated hashtag: Sprite (for the Slam Dunk Contest) and Kia (for the main match) were widely mentioned.

Stadium 2.0

On the same subject Dees (2010) claims that with in-venue devices, smartphone applications and social media the stadium is one tool that corporate sponsors can utilise when seeking activational leverage of their brands. Even though they are in a stadium or an arena, fans can employ communication technologies to optimise their match-day experience. The 'Multimedia use setting' represents a promising field for academic investigation. Kruse (2010) has raised the issue of 'technology use in public' as applied to racetracks. In her opinion, although sports betting requires a mastery of information, use of the new technologies has not developed because:

- there are already adequate traditional sources of information (screens and papers);
- the facilities are not always equipped with wi-fi;
- the people who frequent racetracks do not include the early adopters who use these new technologies;
- a lot of people go to the racetrack without betting, which limits the use of information;
- it is not in the interest of the people who operate the equipment that bettors should be able to optimise their access to information.

These impediments are probably specific to racetracks and their public, and cannot be transposed to sports events generally. Especially as the stadium and the arena are competing with television. The widespread availability of flat-screen TVs, home movies and HD, soon to be followed by 3-D screens, may incline the fan to stay at home rather than go to the stadium. So in order to enhance the in-venue experience, Equipment 2.0 must now provide not just comfort, safety and quality hospitality and services, but also enable activation of the digital experience. Providing this connectivity demands major investments and appropriate infrastructure. Manufacturers of networking equipment and the telecommunications companies are becoming major actors in stadium design.

From this viewpoint the Livestrong Sporting Park in Kansas City is exemplary. Designed in part by Cisco, the stadium aims to provide a 'Technologically advanced experience for fans'. Claiming to represent the forefront of technology, it sees itself as 'creating one of the most engaging and memorable fan experiences'. This technology, also installed in Real Madrid's Santiago Bernabeu Stadium, allows:

- **Connectivity**: provides a reliable broadband connection, enabling everyone to access a range of services.
- **Interactivity**: involves the fans with the stadium, the club and the sponsors via specific applications.
- **Personalisation**: following the match in high definition while choosing the viewpoint.
- **Activation**: highlighting of partners, and making it easy to order drinks in the stadium.

The smartphone then becomes a key tool: it enables access to the stadium by means of a paperless ticket, obtaining information related to the match, the ordering of snacks, the viewing of streaming videos and interactions with persons inside and outside the stadium. This poses something of a problem for Mark Cuban, the owner of the Dallas Mavericks and a graduate of the computing and software industries. He is known for having raised the level of dialogue with his fans, particularly via his blog and his Twitter account. In a recent posting he opposes the use of smartphones in sporting venues. He acknowledges the experiential dimension of the sports event (Case 14.4).

Case 14.5 Do you really need to use your smartphone in a stadium or arena?

'We in the sports business don't sell the game, we sell unique, emotional experiences. We are not in the business of selling basketball. We are in the business of selling fun. We are in the business of letting you escape. We are in the business of giving you a chance to create shared experiences. . . . I want it to be very participatory. I want it to be very social. I want it to be very inclusive. I want it to be memorable. I want it to be so much fun people talk about it to their friends and can't wait to go back. I want every parent to get tears in their eyes when they see their kids jumping up and down whether the score is 2 to 0, or 120 to 84. When they are chanting Lets Go Mavs. When they are dancing and trying to get on the jumbotron. Video and music are two simple components of what we do. We are developing games that our fans can participate in at the arena that hopefully engage them with what is happening on the court. We are coming up with ways to reward our fans for being our '6th man' and adding energy to the arena. (I will save those for another post). We are looking for ways to enhance the emotional attachments created at our game.

(continued)

'I can't think of a bigger mistake then trying to integrate smartphones just because you can. The last thing I want is someone looking down at their phone to see a replay. The last thing I want is someone thinking that it's a good idea to disconnect from the unique elements of a game to look at replays or update their fantasy standings or concentrate on trying to predict what will happen next in the game. There is a huge value to everyone collectively holding their breath during a replay, or responding to a great play or a missed call and then spontaneously reacting to what they see. You lose that if people are looking down at their handhelds. The fan experience is about looking up, not looking down. If you let them look down, they might as well stay at home, the screen is always going to be better there.'

Source: Mark Cuban: blogmaverick.com, 'The fan experience at sporting events – We dont need no stinking smartphones!', 24 December 2011.

Discussion questions

8 Do you think that a matchday experience could be – at the same time – online and offline?

9 Try to think of a sports team app which could be used in a stadium or arena.

Trends

Looking ahead, the interested reader might take note of four trends which could affect the digital aspects of sport:

- **The game:** In 2011 Forbes released a Top-40 list of the World's Most Valuable Sports Brands. In this classification, EA Sports appeared in 8th position, valued at $625,000,000, The success of the Madden NFL and FIFA names is a reminder that sporting passions can also take the form of electronic sport. Taking this idea further, Dwyer and Drayer (2010) find that Fantasy sport participation, though not defined as a social media activity, contains a strong social component. Based on this, Dwyer (2011) showed that Fantasy Football exacerbates the emotions and makes its players even keener to follow matches on television. It is interesting to note that this activity already attracts more than 30 million participants in North America. Perhaps because European soccer generates fewer statistics, its fantasy leagues draw less attention. UEFA is attempting to develop these management games for the European Champions League and Euro 2016.

- **Ambush digital marketing:** Not only must professional sports organisations acknowledge the emergence of digital marketing (O'Shea and Duarte Alonso, 2010), they must also pay attention to the inevitable appearance of the digital ambush. Ambush strategies usually manifest themselves physically during the sporting event (see Chapter 17) but digital platforms can offer spaces for attacks by brands which are not the official sponsor of a major event. Twitter advised the London Organising Committee of the Olympic Games to be on guard for attempts at ambush marketing on its system. For example, Twitter will not authorise non-sponsors to buy promoted Twitter ads using hashtags like #London 2012. In the same way, LOCOG is Foursquare's partner in authorising only official sponsors to have check-ins around the Olympic Park site.

- **Policy:** To protect their rights-holders and avoid excesses by athletes which could damage their brand image, professional sports organisations established the Social Media Policies and Social Media Guidelines (Hull, 2011; Sanderson, 2011a). By way of illustration, MLB encourages its teams, players, managers and coaches to interact with the fans: 'MLB recognizes the importance of social media as an important way for players to communicate directly with fans. We encourage you to connect with fans through Twitter, Facebook, and other social media platforms. Along with MLB's extensive social media activities, we hope that your efforts on social media will help bring fans closer to the game and have them engaged with baseball, your club and you in a meaningful way.' But the players cannot distribute official MLB media property such as video and audio content without the authorisation of the league, and are prohibited from distributing racist, homophobic, sexually explicit and other similar content.

- **Second screen:** Watching television doesn't mean passivity anymore. Television viewers don't use their remote control now as much as they use their smartphone or iPad. The live event is a source of emotion, eustress and comments to share. According to Twitter, more than 150 million tweets were sent out about the Olympics. The 200 metre sprint (which was won by Usain Bolt) sparked 80,000 tweets per minute. It is not uncommon now to find television channels utilising a hashtag in order to gather their digital audience. Getting in touch with social media is not the only thing that can be done with an iPad or smartphone. Mobile applications are designed to enhance the experience of watching sports events. For example, Opta is now a provider of statistical content about the sport (datatainment). If you prefer to play then Kawarter claims to be the 'first gaming network for social TV'; with 'FanCake' you can watch a game, compete against other fans and be rewarded for that.

Case 14.6 The London 2012 'Sociolympics' and the digital 'ambush marketing' threat

The International Olympic Committee's decision to move with the times and embrace the new world of social media at the London Olympics could turn the Games into an unseemly commercial battle if this month's GB kit launch is anything to go by.

While the Stella McCartney-designed Adidas attire attracted predictably effusive tweets from Adidas-sponsored British athletes, some of those who march under the Nike 'Swoosh' were rather less complimentary.

Nike-sponsored Andy Turner, the world 110-metre hurdles bronze medallist, tweeted that the kit 'should have a swoosh rather than stripes', before adding: 'Pretty much all my followers who replied aren't a fan of the kit [and] say it looks like a posh Scottish flag and that it needs more red.'

Turner also mocked the Adidas-sponsored athletes who were singing the kit's praises: 'I love how all Adidas athletes are being diplomatic about the kit – "erm yeah I really like it, it's amazing".'

Betraying the innocence of youth, perhaps, world indoor pole-vault bronze medallist Holly Bleasdale forgot her Nike allegiance for a moment when, on seeing some

(continued)

of her GB team-mates modelling the kit, she tweeted: 'I love the kit!!! You guys look awesome!'

Commercial reality quickly intervened, however, when Bleasdale later added: 'The Olympic kit is niceeee! But I agree with @andyturner110h it would much look better with a swoosh! #nikealltheway.'

This may all sound like harmless banter but such overt plugging could get uncomfortable for the IOC and the national Olympic committees when it comes to the Games, where the most high-profile athletes will enjoy huge global exposure.

Companies like Adidas don't pay millions for exclusive sponsorship rights to be publicly undermined by athletes signed to rival firms.

More worrying for the Olympic authorities, the potential for ambush marketing is huge. Already, many athlete tweets are clogged with tiresome plugs for Starbucks, Costa Coffee and Nando's. With Twitter followers hanging on their every word when the Games get underway, how will they be able to resist the temptation to parade their commercial affiliations?

The issue currently exercising the Office of Fair Trading is not that more and more athletes or celebrities are now endorsing products in their tweets but that they are doing so without making it clear that their affiliation is a commercial arrangement.

It has recently brought a case against a public relations company that is alleged to have been paying bloggers to write positively about its clients.

The OFT insists that all endorsements should be declared as such paid-for adverts, otherwise they are deceptive and unfair.

Such an edict is nowhere to be found in the British Olympic Association's social media guidelines for Team GB athletes, which focus on avoiding giving offence. Making political points is a no-no, since that would infringe the Olympic Charter, but there is nothing to stop athletes regaling their followers about the joys of a Starbucks skinny latte.

The BOA defends its hands-off stance on the grounds of free speech, insisting the advantages of allowing athletes to engage with fans through social media far outweighs the disadvantages, even if that means the odd insult about its Adidas kit.

Privately, the BOA believes the Twitter-following public is savvy enough to recognise a product endorsement when they see one and to take it with a big pinch of salt. But it remains to be seen whether the big commercial players in the Olympic family will be quite so tolerant if this summer turns into a tweeting battleground.

The first Games ever to be held in the full glare of social media action could prove every bit as competitive as the action on the field of play.

Source: London 2012 Olympics: Twitter action at Games could be every bit as competitive as the sport, By Simon Hart, 30 March 2012, blogs.telegraph.co.uk

Discussion questions

10 How can an athlete promote an equipment manufacturer on the social networks?

11 How can a non-sponsor brand communicate about the event?

Conclusion

The internet and online social networks can radically alter our way of experiencing sports events, both inside and outside the stadium. The major changes in prospect are of two kinds:

- **Technological:** While we tend to reduce the social networks to Facebook and Twitter, other systems exist. The photographer Nick Laham has used his iPhone and Instagram to produce portraits of New York Yankees players. A number of teams are investing in Pinterest to target a more female audience; others use Foursquare to reward fans or to generate a presence on sales websites. What systems are in our future? What will they allow us to do?

- **Social:** However much certain teams may boast of having millions of fans on Facebook, and however many athletes are followed by hundreds of thousands of enthusiastic fans, so far these are only the early adopters. Are we on the verge of moving into an era in which the sports event in a stadium or on TV will be followed, for a majority of persons, by gazing at their personal screens?

These new digital practices involve new kinds of knowledge. The occupations of Director of Digital Media, Community Manager, Digital Business Manager and Social Media Consultant are sure to develop. Formerly often confined to trainees, this function has acquired ever greater importance in the clubs. Its task is to establish profiles of the clubs, to create and distribute original content involving the club's actors (players, managers, fans and sponsors), and to lead a community of fans. These tools are often mobilised in strategies for the internationalisation of the club. In particular, this involves the creation of content in several languages for a presence on foreign platforms, e.g. Tencent Weibo, the Chinese microblogging system.

These occupations are already the subject of special training. To correctly choose your training, identify the universities which are active on the social media: do they have a Facebook page and a Twitter account? Do they provide livetweets of lectures? Do they offer a smartphone application? Do they have digital teaching platforms? Do the teachers, for example, maintain an interactivity on Twitter? Have they published texts or reference articles?

Discussion questions

12 Discuss, with examples, how the sports event is no longer just a match but a digitalised happening.

13 What problems might the coming of the online digital experience generation pose for the various actors in a sports event?

14 How should a sponsor position itself via the digital media?

Keywords

Engagement; experiential marketing; online social networks; relationship marketing; sports fan.

Guided reading

The internet, the new technologies and social networking are the subject of special issues of academic journals devoted to sport. These include the *Sociology of Sport Journal* (Volume 26, Issue 1, March 2009), the *International Journal of Sport Management and Marketing* (Volume 10, Issue 3/4, 2011) and the *International Journal of Sport Communication* (Volume 3, Issue 4, 2010). In this chapter we have made extensive mention of this research.

The reference compilation work is that by Sanderson: *It's a Whole New Ballgame* (2011b).
Finally, many of the academics cited in this chapter have a Twitter account. Why not follow them?

Boris Helleu: @bhelleu
Brendan Dwyer: @brendandwyer
Frank Pons: @Frankiepons
Galen E. Clavio: @DoctorGC
Holly Kruse: @hollykruse
Jamie Buning: @jdbug2010
Jimmy Sanderson: @Jimmy_Sanderson
John Beech: @JohnBeech
Joris Drayer: @JorisDrayer
Kimberly Burke: @KimB1222
Laci Wallace: @Prof_LWallace1
Marion Hambrick: @marionhambrick
Matt Zimmerman: @Zimmsy
Meghan Ferriter: @MeghaninMotion
Simon Chadwick: @Prof_Chadwick

Recommended websites

Activ8Social: activ8social.com
Digital Football: digital-football.com
Sports Net Worker: sportsnetworker.com
We are Social: wearesocial.com

References

Beech, J., Chadwick, S. and Tapp, A. (2000) 'Surfing in the premier league: key issues for football club marketers using the Internet', *Managing Leisure* (5), 51–64.

Berardone, D., Nguyen, S. and Turner, P. (2011) 'A content analysis of sponsor representation across professional sport websites: extension of attribute typology', *International Journal of Sport Management and Marketing*, 10 (3/4), 286–305.

Clavio, G.E. (2010) 'Introduction' to Special Issue of *IJSC* on New Media and Social Networking, *International Journal of Sport Communication*, 3 (4), 393–94.

Cova, B. and Cova, V. (2004) 'L'expérience de consommation: de la manipulation à la compromission?', *Les troisiémes Journées Normandes de la Consommation: Colloque 'Société et Consommation'*, Rouen, France, 11–12 March.

Dees, W. (2010) 'New media and technology use in corporate sport sponsorship: performing activational leverage from an exchange perspective', *International Journal of Sport Management and Marketing*, 10 (3/4), 272–85.

Dwyer, B. and Drayer, J. (2010) 'Fantasy sport consumer segmentation: an investigation into the differing consumption modes of fantasy football participants', *Sport Marketing Quarterly*, 19 (4), 207–16.

Dwyer, B. (2011) 'The impact of fantasy football involvement on intentions to watch national football league games on television', *International Journal of Sport Communication*, 4 (3), 375–96.

Ferriter, M. (2009) ' "Arguably the greatest": sport fans and communities at work on Wikipedia', *Sociology of Sport Journal*, 26 (1), 127–54.

Garcia, C. (2011) 'Real Madrid Football Club: applying a relationship-management model to a sport organization in Spain', *International Journal of Sport Communication*, 4 (3), 284–99.

Gibbons, T. and Dixon, K. (2010) ' "Surf's up!": A call to take English soccer fan interactions on the Internet more seriously', *Soccer and Society*, 11 (5), 599–613.

Hambrick, M.E. (2012) 'Six degrees of information: using social network analysis to explore the spread of information within sport social networks', *International Journal of Sport Communication*, 5 (1), 16–34.

Hambrick, M.E. and Mahoney, T.Q. (2011) ' "It's incredible – trust me": exploring the role of celebrity athletes as marketers in online social networks', *International Journal of Sport Management and Marketing*, 10 (3/4), 161–79.

Hambrick, M.E., Simmons, J.M., Greenhalgh, G.P. and Greenwell, T.C. (2010) 'Understanding professional athletes' use of twitter: a content analysis of athlete tweets', *International Journal of Sport Communication*, 3 (4), 454–71.

Hull, M.R. (2011) 'Article: sports leagues' new social media policies: enforcement under copyright law and state law', *Columbia Journal of Law and the Arts*, 34 (3), 457–89.

Hutchins, B., Rowe, D. and Ruddock, A. (2009) ' "It's fantasy football made real": networked media sport, the internet, and the hybrid reality of MyFootballClub', *Sociology of Sport Journal*, 26 (1), 89–106.

Ioakimidis, M. (2010) 'Online marketing of professional sports clubs: engaging fans on a new playing field', *International Journal of Sports Marketing and Sponsorship*, 11 (4), 271–82.

Kruse, H. (2010) 'Multimedia use in a sport setting: communication technologies at off-track betting facilities', *Sociology of Sport Journal*, 27 (4), 413–27.

Kwak, D.H., Kim, Y.K. and Zimmerman, M.H. (2010) 'User-versus mainstream-media-generated content: media source, message valence, and team identification and sport consumers' response', *International Journal of Sport Communication*, 10 (3/4), 402–21.

Lewis, M. (2003) *Moneyball: The Art of Winning an Unfair Game*, New York: W.W. Norton & Company Inc.

O'Shea, M. and Duarte Alonso, A. (2010) 'Opportunity or obstacle? A preliminary study of professional sport organisations in the age of social media', *International Journal of Sport Management and Marketing*, 10 (3/4), 196–212.

Pegoraro, A. (2010) 'Look who's talking – athletes on twitter: a case study', *International Journal of Sport Communication*, 3 (4), 501–14.

Phua, J.J. (2010) 'Sports fans and media use: influence on sports fan identification and collective self-esteem', *International Journal of Sport Communication*, 3 (2), 190–206.

Rein, I., Kotler, P. and Shields, B. (2006) *The Elusive Fan: Reinventing Sports in a Crowded Marketplace*, New York: McGraw-Hill.

Richelieu, A. and Pons, F. (2006) 'Toronto Maple Leafs vs Football Club Barcelona: how two legendary sports teams built their brand equity', *International Journal of Sports Marketing and Sponsorship*, 7 (3), 231–46.

Ruihley, B.J. and Hardin, R.L. (2010) 'Beyond touchdowns, homeruns, and three-pointers: an examination of fantasy sport participation motivation', *International Journal of Sport Management and Marketing*, 10 (3/4), 232–56.

Sanderson, J. (2010) 'Framing Tiger's troubles: comparing traditional and social media', *International Journal of Sport Communication*, 3 (4), 438–53.

Sanderson, J. (2011a) 'To tweet or not to tweet: exploring division I athletic departments' social-media policies', *International Journal of Sport Communication*, 4 (4), 492–513.

Sanderson, J. (2011b) *It's a Whole New Ballgame: How Social Media Is Changing Sports*, New York: Hampton Press.

Schmitt, B.H. (1999) *Experience Marketing: How to Get Customers to SENSE, FEEL, THINK, ACT, RELATE to Your Company and Brands*, New York: Simon & Schuster Inc.

Schoenstedt, L.J. and Reau, J. (2010) 'Running a social-media newsroom: a case study of the Cincinnati Flying Pig Marathon', *International Journal of Sport Communication*, 3 (3), 377–86.

Stenger, T. and Coutant, A. (2011) 'Introduction', *Hermès* (59), 9–17.

Turner, P. (2008) 'Developments in web technology: enhancing the viewing spectacle of sport', in S. Chadwick and D. Arthur (eds), *International Cases in the Business of Sport*, Oxford: Butterworth-Heinemann, 178–91.

Waters, R.D., Burke, K.A., Jackson, Z.H. and Buning, J.D. (2011) 'Using stewardship to cultivate fandom online: comparing how national football league teams use their web sites and Facebook to engage their fans', *International Journal of Sport Communication*, 4 (2), 163–77.

Williams, J. and Chinn, S.J. (2010) 'Meeting relationship-marketing goals through social media: a conceptual model for sport marketers', *International Journal of Sport Communication*, 10 (3/4), 422–37.

Zhang, Z. and Won, D. (2010) 'Buyer or browser? An analysis of sports fan behaviour online', *International Journal of Sports Marketing and Sponsorship*, 11 (2), 124–39.

Zimmerman, M.H., Clavio, G.E. and Choong Hoon, L. (2011) 'Set the agenda like Beckham: a professional sports league's use of YouTube to disseminate messages to its users', *International Journal of Sport Management and Marketing*, 10 (3/4), 180–95.

Section C

Sport management issues

This section considers some of the current issues facing sport business managers. Readers should be aware that the content of this section, more than any other, is likely to change rapidly. Changes in technology, developments in the law and general shifts in sport management practice are likely to be such that readers will need to remain vigilant of the impact these may have for the chapters in this section.

The first purpose of the section is to highlight key factors currently facing sport businesses. Secondly, practices common to most organisations, but which have a particular resonance in the sport sector, are then considered. Thirdly, the section considers the future for sport businesses and reflects upon many of the observations made in this book as the basis for making predictions about what might happen over the next five years in sport.

This section contains the following chapters:

Sports and the law

Sport event and facility management

Sport sponsorship and endorsement

Sport broadcasting

Risk management in sport

The sports betting industry

Sports retailing and merchandising

Sports media and PR

The internationalisation of sport

Sports agents and intermediaries

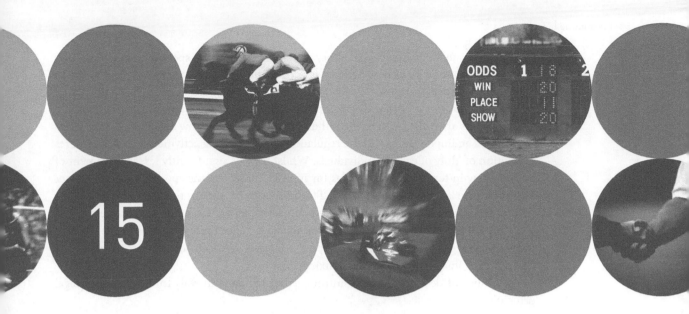

Sports and the law

Karen Bill, University of Wolverhampton
Simon Gardiner, Leeds Metropolitan University

Learning outcomes

Upon completion of this chapter the reader should be able to:

- demonstrate the application of liability and safety in sport;
- understand and apply the concepts that are central to both intentional and unintentional tort law from the perspective of sports participant, referee/governing body and spectator/occupier;
- employ criminal law liability to explain prosecutions for injuries caused on and off the sports field;
- demonstrate the application of legal principles surrounding contract law and their impact on the governance of professional sportspersons' contracts;
- understand the legal principles governing the commercial regulation of sport such as intellectual property rights and match fixing.

 Overview

This chapter provides an insight into how law permeates and regulates many aspects of sporting life from a civil, criminal and commercial perspective. It focuses on those areas which have specifically impacted upon the sports industry and are pertinent to undergraduate students studying sports law from a general perspective and maintains that it is important for anybody involved in either managing or leading a sport to understand their legal responsibilities as well as being aware of the legal context in which their sporting activities take place.

The chapter begins with a discussion around what is sports law, acknowledging the growth in this area of study. The focus then turns to exploring how health and safety legislation plays an important part in the regulation of our sporting activities and then explores the notion of 'duty of care' to individuals. Whilst there is significantly less involvement of criminal law in terms of prosecutions for injuries caused on the sports field, the chapter illustrates case law that has been applied to sport both on and off the sports pitch.

Sport, certainly at the professional and elite level, generates significant business and is therefore subject to regulation in a number of ways, hence the focus turns to the study of commercial regulation in terms of players' contracts, restraint of trade through to the protection of image rights and match fixing.

A number of decided cases are introduced at regular intervals to illustrate key legal principles.

Introduction – what is sports law?

This is an area of academic debate. Although Beloff's book *Sports Law* (2000) refers to the purpose of the Court of Arbitration for Sport (CAS) and how this may facilitate a 'sports law' jurisprudence, Woodhouse (1996) states that 'there is no such thing as sports law. Instead it is the application to sport situations of disciplines such as contract law, administrative law (disciplinary procedures), competition law, intellectual property law, defamation and employment law' (p. 14). Similarly Grayson notes, 'there is no subject that exists which jurisprudentially can be called sports law' (1994: xxxvii).

'Sport is not above, or outside, the national legal system' (Grayson, 2003). According to Thomas 2002, 'the game itself is merely a warm-up for the real contest at some future date in the law courts', and 'foul play and sport are no different from road rage and transport negligence as high risk litigation areas' (Grayson, 2003).

Parallel to this has been the increase in lawyers specialising in sport in areas such as branding, disciplinary and doping and the formation of specialist panels to deal with the increased volume of sporting disputes as more and more money is at stake within sport. This growing professional interest has been matched by academic interest, with proliferation of sports law texts over the last ten years or so, such as those by Gardiner et al. (2006), Hartley (2009), James (2010) and Lewis and Taylor (2008).

Liability and safety in sport

There are a number of generic statutory duties in health and safety that are placed on both employers and employees which equally apply to sport as any other area of employment. Therefore, anyone working in the sports industry needs to be aware of all the duties imposed through various legislation and regulations.

Employers and employees have direct responsibilities under the Health and Safety at Work Act 1974 (HSWA), whilst employers, employees and volunteers have a common law 'duty of care' to other people. The key elements of HSWA (s. 2 and s. 3), require that every employer ensures, as *far as is reasonably practicable*, the health, safety and welfare of any person who may be affected by their activities. By any person, that includes the employers' own acts and the employees and agents such as volunteer sport coaches (vicarious liability). Put simply, it is the balancing of the degree of risk against the time, cost and physical difficulty of taking measures to avoid the risk in a particular activity. Employers are therefore required to identify the risks involved in any sporting activity/event and to take reasonable precautions to prevent injuries.

The Management of Health and Safety at Work Regulations 1999 outlines how employers should achieve the requirements defined under HSWA. Central to these regulations is the conduct of effective risk assessments by employers prior to any activities taking place. A risk involves a hazard which is 'any property, situation or indeed anything which has the potential to cause harm, which can become "realised" under certain conditions' (Royal Society, 1992: 2–3). Depending upon the hazard, to what degree it becomes a risk will depend upon the evaluation of the situation based on the notion of *severity* of outcome, or magnitude of level of threat or impact and the notion of *probability* or *likelihood* of a risk occurring. The hazard then is the source of risk, i.e. a javelin at an athletics meet and the risk would relate to the severity and likelihood of injuries.

$$SEVERITY \times PROBABILITY = RISK\ RATING$$

The Health and Safety Executive (HSE) provides a five step approach to risk assessment. (see www.hse.gov.uk/risk/fivesteps.htm).

Other health and safety regulations further build on HSWA and provide guidance on how specific issues should be addressed in the case of hazards such as chemicals, e.g. chlorine in a swimming pool environment (Control of Substances Hazardous to Health Regulations 2002), situations such as workplace conditions (Workplace (Health, Safety and Welfare) Regulations 1992) and operations such as lifting (Manual Handling Operations Regulations 1992). The reporting of Injuries, Diseases and Dangerous Occurrences (RIDDOR) Regulations 1995 ensures that employers have a duty to report any incidents and accidents that occur in connection with work. For instance, a death or serious injury to an employee or member of public in a sports ground must be recorded in an accident book which is kept to record such incidents as well as 'near misses'. Storage of such records have to be compliant with data protection regulations.

In addition to the more general health and safety there are specific acts and regulations that govern sport, for example:

● The Safety of Sports Grounds Act 1975.

● The Fire Safety and Safety of Places of Sport Act 1987.

Both are concerned with addressing risks to spectators at sports grounds but not with the risks to participants, who are normally covered by the general requirements of the Health and Safety at Work etc. Act 1974.

● Football Spectators Act 1989.

● Adventure Activities Licensing Regulations 1996 require commercial providers of facilities for caving, climbing, trekking and water sports to obtain a licence from the Adventure Activities Licensing Authority in order to operate.

● Activity Centres (Young Person's Safety) Act 1995.

In recent years, many leisure companies and indeed councils have been the subject of prosecutions for breaches of health and safety. A sports centre was fined £15,000 in an incident which resulted in injury to a gym user due to faulty equipment. Leeds City Council was charged with breaching health and safety regulations by failing to prevent people being exposed to health and safety risks on a river walk during a residential course and failure to complete an adequate risk assessment for the river walk activity. It was fined £30,000 after two teenage girls were swept away and drowned during the river walk. A swimming pool complex was fined £15,000 under HSWA for a chemical leak caused by an employee misguidedly placing acid granules into the incorrect tank of a chlorine system, resulting in four people requiring hospital treatment.

The Lyme Regis case in 1993, where four school children were drowned during a canoeing trip in Lyme Bay, Dorset, which resulted in the managing director of the activity centre receiving a four-year jail sentence, helped clarify the principles of *corporate manslaughter*. The Corporate Manslaughter and Corporate Homicide Act 2007 came into force on 6 April 2008. Under the Act a company or organisation can be convicted of manslaughter where a death is caused by the way in which the company manages or organises its affairs and this amounts to a *gross* breach of a duty of care, owed to the deceased by the company. The Act will make it easier for sport organisations to be convicted of manslaughter if their negligence leads to a death. Whilst sports organisations are familiar with owing a duty of care to their customers, they will need to consider more stringent regulations and systems to demonstrate a more explicit and considered health and safety ethos within their day-to-day operations.

Law of tort and sport

The two significant areas of law that have been used to establish liability for injuries caused within sports participation are the criminal law and the law of torts. The criminal law is enforced by the State by bringing a prosecution against individuals who have committed a criminal act. If an individual is found guilty at their trial, they are subject to punishment. It is difficult to formulate a meaningful definition of a tort because the law of torts deals with so many different situations. Essentially a tort is a civil wrong and the person who has suffered loss due to the wrong can sue for compensation. Intentional torts are those wrongs which, when committed, intend to produce harm. They cover a wide range of sporting situations from assault to corruption, defamation and privacy, some of which may become criminal acts.

Defamation imposes a duty on one person not to injure the reputation of another. It can be either libel or slander, as in the case of *McVicar v United Kingdom* (2002) 35 EHRR 22. It is governed by the Defamation Act 1996, which applies to both unintentional defamation and innocent defamation.

There are three elements to defamation:

1 the statement is defamatory and lowers the publics' estimation of the sporting celebrity;

2 the statement actually refers to the sportsperson;

3 the statement was published.

However, the main area of torts, as applied to sport, is negligence to which the courts have considered many analogous situations. Negligence is a tort that imposes a duty on one person to take care not to injure another person. Table 15.1 depicts all the main cases in sport that have involved a duty of care from the position of sports participant, referee/ governing body and spectator/occupier. The cases are presented in chronological order with a brief narrative for each case indicating the decision and what evidential tests were used to establish a duty of care. A number of articles are mentioned at the end of the chapter to broaden the reader's understanding of the legal issues presented in the cases.

Table 15.1 Standards of care applied in sporting situations

Case citation (see section on legal research)	Evidential test for liability
Donoghue v Stevenson (1932) AC 562 Miss Donoghue drank from a bottle of ginger beer to find the decomposed remains of a snail.	'You must take reasonable care to avoid acts or omissions which you can reasonably foresee would be likely to injure your neighbour' (at 580) (Lord Atkin) *Held*: Liable
Hall v Brooklands Auto Racing Club (1933) 1 KB 205 Spectators injured when two racing cars crashed and left the track and tried to claim damages from the organisers.	'there is no obligation to protect against a danger incident to the entertainment which any reasonable spectator foresees and of which he takes the risk' (at 217) (Scrutton LJ) *Held*: No liability
Rootes v Shelton (1968) ALR 33 A water skier sued the driver of his boat who caused him to collide with another boat in the course of a water skiing display.	'the conclusion to be reached must necessarily depend according to the concepts of the common law, upon the reasonableness, in relation to the special circumstances, of the conduct which caused the **plaintiff**'s injury' (at 37) (Kitto J) *Held*: No liability
Wooldridge v Sumner (1963) 2 QB 43 A horse competing in a show bolted from the arena and into two spectators. One of them, a photographer, was injured.	'If the conduct is deliberately intended to injure someone whose presence is known, or is reckless and in disregard of all safety of others so that a departure from the standards which might reasonably be expected in anyone pursuing the competition or game, then the performer might well be held liable for injury his act caused' (at 56) (Sellers LJ) *Held*: No liability
Wilks v Cheltenham Homeguard Motor Cycle and Light Car Club (1971) 1 WLR 668 A motorcycling scrambler lost control of his machine, which left the course and injured two spectators.	'the proper test is whether injury to a spectator has been caused by an error of judgment that a reasonable competitor being a "reasonable man of the sporting world, would not have made"' (at 674) (Edmund Davies LJ) *Held*: No liability
Harrison v Vincent (1982) RTR 8 A competitor in a motorcycle and sidecar race was injured when the brakes on his cycle failed and he crashed into a vehicle, which was obstructing the emergency slip road.	'the injuries sustained by the Plaintiff were not the result of any risk which was inherent in the sport which the Plaintiff should be taken to have accepted' (at 19) (Watkins LJ) *Held*: Motorcycle rider and race organiser liable

(continued)

Table 15.1 (*continued*)

Case citation (see section on legal research)	Evidential test for liability
Condon v Basi (1985) 1 WLR 866 Amateur footballer sued an opponent who broke his leg as a result of a late tackle.	'there will of course be a higher degree of care required of a player in a First Division football match than a player in a local league football match' (at 868) 'reckless disregard of the Plaintiff's safety and which fell far below the standards which might reasonably be expected in anyone pursuing a game' (at 869) (Sir John Donaldson MR) *Held*: Damages for negligence £4,900
Elliott v Saunders & Liverpool FC (1994) QB transcript 10 June 1994 A case against Dean Saunders from Liverpool FC who had tackled Paul Elliott from Chelsea FC resulting in the severance of his cruciate ligaments in the process.	'an intentional foul or mistake, or an error of judgment may be enough to give rise to liability on the part of the **defendant**, but whether or not it does so depends on the facts and circumstances of each individual case' 'did not agree with the **obiter dictum** from *Condon v Basi* in that there might be a higher standard of care required of a player in say, the Premier League . . . The standard of care required in each case was the same' (at (Drake J)) *Held*: No liability
McCord v Swansea City AFC 1996 QBD A case against John Cornforth who challenged Brian McCord for a loose ball and broke his opponent's leg. It was judged to be an intentional foul.	'the error was inconsistent with the defendant's duty of care towards his fellow player' (at 1) (Ian Kennedy, J) *Held*: Player was liable
Smoldon v Whitworth (1997) ELR 249, CA Referee in under 19 colts match held liable for injuries to Smoldon, who broke his neck after a rugby scrum collapsed.	'The level of care required is that which is appropriate in all the circumstances and the circumstances are of crucial importance could not properly be held liable for errors of judgment, oversight or lapses in the context of a fast moving and vigorous contest. The threshold is a high one. It will not easily be crossed' (at 55) (Lord Bingham CJ) *Held*: Referee liable
Watson v Bradford City AFC v Gray & Huddersfield Town AFC (Quantum) QBD 7 May 1999 A claim against a professional footballer as a result of a tackle by an opponent during a First Division league match.	'it must be proved on the balance of probabilities that a reasonable professional player would have known that there was a significant risk that what Kevin Gray did would result in a serious injury to Watson' (at 1) 'a forceful, high challenge, particularly when carried out when there is a good chance that the ball had moved on, was one that a reasonable, professional player would have known carried with it a significant risk of serious injury' (Judge Michael Taylor) *Held*: General damages £25,000. Past lost earnings £152,461. Future loss of earnings £700,500. Lost tax relief pensions benefit £30,000. Loss of bonuses awards £8,265. Medical expenses £12,168

(continued)

Table 15.1 (*continued*)

Case citation (see section on legal research)	Evidential test for liability
Agar v Hyde (2000) 201 CLR the High Court of Australia Claim brought by two rugby union players who, as adult teenagers, had broken their necks in separate incidents and suffered quadriplegia while playing the position of 'hooker' in interclub competition. Both had suffered their injuries when the two sides of the scrum engaged. Their claim was against the international governing body of the sport of rugby union and alleged that it owed them a duty of care in negligence to amend the rules to remove unnecessary risks.	The High Court unanimously rejected the claim. A number of reasons were given, but for present purposes it is sufficient to note that the Court considered that a person's voluntary participation in a sport would defeat any claim where the injury was caused by an inherent risk of participation. To reinforce the point, Justice Callinan described the sport of rugby union as 'notoriously a dangerous game.'
Caldwell v Maguire and Fitzgerald (2001) PIQR 45 Professional jockey was seriously injured whilst riding a two-mile novice hurdle race at Hexham.	Woolf LCJ extracted five propositions as guidance for duty of care: '1 Each contestant in a lawful sporting contest owes a duty of care to each and all other contestants. 2 That duty is to exercise in the course of the contest all care that is objectively reasonable in the prevailing circumstances for the avoidance of infliction of injury to such fellow contestants. 3 The prevailing circumstances are . . . its rules, conventions and customs, and the standards of skills and judgments reasonably to be expected of that of a contestant. 4 The threshold of liability is in practice inevitably high; the breach of a duty will not flow from proof of no more than an error of judgment . . . or momentary lapse in skill . . . when subject to the stresses of a race. Such are no more than incidents inherent in the nature of the sport. 5 In practice it may therefore be difficult to prove any such breach of duty absent proof or conduct that in point of fact amounts to reckless disregard for the fellow contestant's safety.' (at 2) (Woolf LCJ) *Held*: No liability
Pitcher v Huddersfield Town Football Club (2001) QBD 5953 A claim for personal injury suffered as a result of a late tackle in a Division One match resulting in the premature ending of Darren Pitcher's career.	'It was a foul but I am not satisfied it was more. It was an error of judgment in the context of a fast moving game . . . has not in my judgment succeeded in crossing the threshold, the high threshold' (at 19) (Hallett J) *Held*: No liability

(*continued*)

Table 15.1 (*continued*)

Case citation (see section on legal research)	Evidential test for liability
Watson v British Boxing Board of Control Ltd and Another (2001) QB 1134 Negligence case against the British Boxing Board of Control for the inadequacy of medical support when during a middleweight fight Eubank v Watson, Watson was knocked out and suffered serious head injuries.	'The three-stage test in *Caparo Industries PLC v Dickman* (1990) 2 AC 605 is applicable in determining whether in making (or failing to make) rules to regulate professional boxing the board owes a duty of care to individual boxers. The first test, foreseeability of injury. The second test is proximity. Third test, whether it is fair, just and reasonable to impose a duty of care' (at 4) (Lord Phillips of Worth Matravers MR) *Held*: British Boxing Board of Control was liable.
Vowles v Evans and the Welsh Rugby Union and Others (2002) EWHC 2612 The referee in an adult rugby match was held liable for injuries sustained to a player due to repeated set scrums, which left him paralysed.	Morland J was referred to the threefold test enunciated in *Caparo Industries PLC v Dickman* (1990) 2 AC 605 of 'foreseeability, proximity and whether it was just, fair and reasonable that there should be a duty of care' (at 2). The evidential test in *Smoldon* was also applied (at 5) *Held*: Liable. 'Copr. © 2003 West Group. No claim to orig. U.S. govt. works.'
Wattleworth v Goodwood Road Racing Company Ltd, Royal Automobile Club Motor Sports Association Ltd and Federation Internationale De L'Automobile [2004] EWHC 140 Claimant alleged that certain safety barriers in place at the Goodwood motor racing circuit were not adequate, the result of which was that her husband was killed when he crashed into them.	The actions were against the first defendant under the Occupiers' Liability Act 1957 s. 2, for breaching its duty to provide a safe place to race motor vehicles, and against the second and third defendants for their failure to carry out sufficient or adequate inspections of the Goodwood circuit, thereby breaching their duty of care towards users of the race track. Thus, the relative lack of proximity between GRRC and the FIA ensured that no duty of care could be imposed upon the FIA.
Stringer v Minnesota Vikings Football Club, LLC 686 NW2d 545 (Minn. App. 2004) Korey Stringer, an NFL All-Pro offensive lineman, did not receive proper medical care when he collapsed during the 2001 football training camp season. The 335-pound lineman died of heat stroke one day after his collapse. His estate sued a range of defendants including the Minnesota Vikings club doctor.	The doctor and his clinic that were operating as independent contractor to the Vikings, settled the case for an undisclosed sum.
Gravil v Carroll and Redruth Rugby Football Club [2008] EWCA Civ 689 Gravil (Halifax prop forward) was punched in the face by Redruth's second row forward Carroll. Gravil suffered a 'blow out fracture' to his right eye socket and as a consequence he had to undergo reconstructive surgery. All in all, a very nasty personal injury indeed. Gravil brought a personal injury claim against Redruth Rugby Club, claiming they were vicariously viable for the actions of their player.	Overruling view at trials that no vicarious liability could be established in this case, the Court of Appeal held that it was indeed just to hold Redruth liable for the action of one of its players under vicarious liability. The Court felt that the critical question was the nature of the employment and the assault. There was an obvious nexus between the punch and Carroll's employment.

Before any liability in negligence can be established, a duty of care must be proved. The three main elements to tortuous liability are conduct, fault and damage. The modern concept is that defined by Lord Atkin in 'the neighbourhood test' of the famous negligence case of the decomposed snail in the ginger beer (*Donoghue v Stevenson* (1932) AC 562). According to this concept everyone must take reasonable care to avoid acts or omissions which they can reasonably foresee and which would be likely to injure their neighbour.

Hall v Brooklands Auto Racing Club (1933) 1 KB 205 applied the 'reasonable man test' under which, according to Alderson B:

> Negligence is the omission to do something which a reasonable man, guided upon those considerations which ordinarily regulate the conduct of human affairs, would do, or doing something which a prudent and reasonable man would not do.
>
> (*Blythe v Birmingham Waterworks Co* (1856) 11 Exch 781 at 784)

Duty of care by sports personnel

Sport participants owe a duty or standard of care to one another when competing.

> Those who take part in a competitive sport owe a duty of care to other participants and may be liable in negligence for conduct to which another participant may be expected not to have consented.
>
> (*Condon v Basi* (1985) WL 312199)

In *Caldwell v Maguire and Fitzgerald* (2001) PIQR 45, it was held that the standard of care required is reasonable care. In the absence of this standard of care, there may be liability based on negligence in all the circumstances. There is no need to establish reckless disregard on the part of the defendant to establish liability, although if this is found, it will be clear evidence of negligence.

Sport occupiers owe a duty of care to its spectators. Here unlike the above situation, it was established in *Wooldridge v Sumner* (1963) 2 QB 43, that the issue of liability was based on 'reckless disregard'. However, a statutory duty of care is also owed under the Occupiers' Liability Act (OLA) 1957. This applies to lawful visitors, i.e. those with permission, such as seasonal ticket holders. They also owe a duty to unlawful visitors under the Occupiers' Liability Act 1984. Furthermore, a special responsibility applies to minors (s. 2(3)(a) of the OLA Act 1957): 'An occupier must be prepared for children to be less careful than adults'.

Governing bodies owe a duty of care to sports players. *Watson v British Boxing Board of Control Ltd* (2001) QB 1134 was a significant case in that it established negligence against the British Board of Boxing in terms of inadequate medical facilities which left the board bankrupt despite policy considerations with respect to it being a non-profit-making organisation which did not carry any insurance. The evidential test applied was based on that laid down by Lord Bridge in *Caparo Industries v Dickman* (1990) 1 All ER 568.

A referee who oversees a match may also owe a duty of care to the players to ensure no injuries (*Smoldon v Whitworth* (1979) ELR 249). This was a precedent case in that it held that the referee was liable in an amateur context to young players. The more recent case of *Vowles v Evans* illustrates a similar judgment, although this time to an adult amateur team.

Case 15.1 *Vowles v Evans*

Richard Vowles, aged 29, received a dislocated neck with consequential permanent incomplete tetraplegia during a local match between Llanharan and Tondu in 1998 after collapsing after a number of repeated set scrums. During the game the Llanharan loose-head prop went off with a dislocated shoulder leaving Llanharan with a substitute with no experience or any training as a front row forward.

Mr Leighton Williams QC held that as a matter of policy or decision, no such duty exists for a referee to take reasonable care for the safety of adults playing in a rugby match. *Smoldon v Whitworth* [2002] PIQR 137 was distinguishable because there the existence of a duty of care in a colt's game was conceded. Mr Leighton Williams submitted that whether it was fair, just and reasonable to impose a duty upon a referee would depend upon a number of factors, including the interests of rugby as a game and the overall public interest. He stressed that such an imposition would discourage participation in rugby. However, Mr Justice Morland did not consider it logical to draw a distinction between amateur and professional rugby. He asserted that it is open to a player to protect his own interests by insurance cover.

In Mr Justice Morland's judgment the first defendant was in breach of his duty to take reasonable care for the safety of the front row forwards in failing to order non-contested scrums. According to Law 3(5) 'Any team must include suitably trained/experienced players' and Law 3(12) states: 'In the event of a front row forward being ordered off or injured or both, the referee, in the interests of safety, will confer with the captain of his team . . . When there is no other front row forward available . . . then the game will continue with non-contestable scrummages'. Mr Justice Morland in deciding applied the evidential test of liability from that of *Smoldon* in that a full account should be taken of the circumstances of the game and that due to the fast-moving and vigorous contest, the threshold of liability would be high and not easily crossed.

Mr Justice Morland concluded that the lack of technique and experience as a prop was a significant contributory cause. Even if the first defendant may have been entitled to give a trial as loose-head prop as Law 3(12) seems to envisage, he should have kept such a trial under constant review, having regard to the history of repeated and increasingly numerous bad set scrummages.

The claimant succeeded on liability against the first defendant and liability was accepted by the Welsh Rugby Union (WRU). It is a landmark case, which could open the floodgates.

'Copr. © 2003 West Group. No claim to orig. U.S. govt. works'.

For the full case see: *Vowles v Evans and the Welsh Rugby Union and Others* (2002) EWHC 2612.

Discussion questions

1 What evidential test was applied to construct an argument for liability?

2 What is the standard of care expected of a referee?

3 What other cases could one refer to in order to provide guidance?

4 What impact does this case have for sport, in particular contact sports?

5 Discuss the requirements of 'proximity', 'foreseeability' and 'reasonability' and applying the facts of this case, establish why a duty of care is owed to the claimant. Explain the legal basis for your answer.

Damages as a remedy in tort

The aim of damages in tort, as in contract, are to put the plaintiff back in the position s/he would have been if the tort had not been committed.

Defences to negligence

The main ones are as follows:

- *Volenti Non Fit Injuria* (Voluntary assumption of risk): i.e. those participating in sports assume that there are risks involved in participating. The incident of Gary Walsh (Ipswich Town FC and Bradford City AFC) found that such a defence was dismissed as spectators only assume a risk when the ball is in play.

- **Contributory negligence**: i.e. where a sport player has contributed to his or her own injury, perhaps through engaging in horseplay. One could cite the case of *Grinstead v Lywood* (2002) WL 31397573, where an owner of a speedway track sought the defence of contributory negligence from the stewards.

- **Vicarious liability**: i.e. where a third party, often an employer, can be accused of negligence either because the illegal act is authorised by the employer, or because, if unauthorised, it is within the scope of employment. This is not strictly a defence but allows liability also to be shifted to employer. In the case of *Vowles v Evans* the RFU were liable for the lack of duty of care of the referee. Also see *Gravil v Carroll and Redruth Rugby Football Club* [2008] EWCA Civ 689.

Criminal law liability

There is significantly less involvement of the criminal law in terms of prosecutions for injuries caused on the sports field. The type of infliction of injury that has been seen as an assault and therefore potential liability includes fights and brawls that occur adjacent to the sports field, for example the players' tunnel or at the side of the pitch, and have led to convictions for assault offences. In *R v Kamara* [1988] *Times*, 15 April, a professional footballer was convicted of inflicting grievous harm either intentionally or recklessly under s. 20 Offences Against the Persons Act 1861 (OAPA) for punching and breaking the jaw of an opponent after the final whistle for a match had been blown. In *R v Cantona* [1995] *Times*, 25 March, the infamous flying kung-fu kick by Eric Cantona targeted at an opposition fan, inflicted after the defendant had been sent off for an on-field foul, led to conviction for common assault. In these incidents, the claim by both of the defendants was that their actions were in response to racist provocation. Also similar to both incidents, their occurrence was outside of the pitch, beyond the playing rules of the game and the supervision of the referee and arguably not sporting incidents. Consent will not operate here. Both Kamara and Cantona were however 'charged' with wider disciplinary offences under the English Football Association (FA).

Additionally, off-the-ball incidents and away from the play have led to many convictions in team sport for assault and public order offences. There have been a significantly higher number of prosecutions in amateur rugby and football compared to the professional game, which seems to be partly determined by a greater likelihood that offences are reported to the police and that the Crown Prosecution Service will decide to prosecute. In addition, the internal sporting disciplinary procedures at regional level are not enforced so effectively compared to the professional game, which has a national enforcement procedure. More high-profile cases in professional football have occurred than in both the codes of rugby union and league, probably explained by the higher levels of 'violent conduct' in off-the-ball fights that are accepted in rugby. In football, *Ferguson v Normand* [1995] SCCR 770; involved the conviction for s. 18 OAPA 1861, causing grievous bodily harm with intent and imprisonment of Duncan Ferguson for an off-the-ball head butt against John Mistaya during a match between Glasgow Rangers and Raith Rovers. Individuals have also been convicted for public order offences, including *Butcher v Jessop* [1989] SLT 593; when, during the Glasgow derby, a number of Rangers and Celtic players were charged with breach of the peace following a goalmouth 'scrum'. Two players were convicted, one was found not guilty and another had his case 'not proven'. The heavily publicised but relatively minor skirmish between Newcastle players Lee Bowyer and Kieron Dyer is a more recent example, with Bowyer charged under the wide s. 4 Public Order Act offence of fear and provocation of violence. Additionally, police have cautioned professional players for swearing and other anti-social behaviour, by intervening during the actual commission of the game.

More problematic has been when there should be prosecutions in incidents in very close proximity to the point of play, and often termed on-the-ball incidents. The prosecution in *R v Blissett* [1992] *Independent*, 4 December, is an exemplar of the problem of demarcation of the criminal law's involvement. The Brentford footballer Gary Blissett was charged with causing grievous bodily harm under s. 18 of the Offences Against the Person Act 1861 to the former Torquay United player John Uzzell. Up to that time most prosecutions had been for the lesser offence of assault occasioning actual bodily harm under s. 47. Blissett was involved in a flying collision when both he and Uzzell were challenging to get possession of the ball. Uzzell suffered a fractured eye socket and cheekbone, and subsequently retired. The referee saw the incident and Blissett was sent off. Blissett said at his trial that what had occurred was an accident, as the two players had jumped for a 50-50 ball. He had tried to avoid colliding with Uzzell when he realised he was not going to avoid the ball. Acting as an expert witness, Graham Kelly, then FA's chief executive, caused some controversy when he said it was an 'ordinary aerial challenge', which he would see 200 times a week if he attended four matches. He considered that this type of play was one that occurred regularly and of a type that participants implicitly consent to. Blissett was acquitted. No clear guidance was provided as to how the law of consent should be applied to sports participation incidents or how it might be possible to determine where the line of demarcation should be drawn for the criminal law's involvement.

The fundamental issue is therefore determining how consent will operate in these incidents. The recent Court of Appeal case of *R v Barnes* [2005] 1 WLR 910. highlights this issue again. The incident in question occurred during an amateur match in the Thanet local league between Minster FC and the Punch and Judy FC. With 20 minutes to go, Minster was two goals ahead. At the time of the alleged offence, the victim playing for Minster guided the ball towards the corner flag as a means of wasting time. Barnes attempted to tackle him and in doing so committed a foul. Minster was awarded a free kick. The referee, Mr Lawrence, who had over 30 years' experience, interjected in a heated exchange of words between the two and told them both 'to grow up'. Ten minutes later the victim was in a shooting position around seven yards in front of the goal. He scored but just after kicking the ball, Barnes tackled him from behind, making contact with his right ankle. Barnes was reported to have said words to the effect of 'have that'. The victim was seriously injured with damage to his ankle and right fibula. The referee sent Barnes off the field for violent conduct. The foul, resultant injury and sending off are not particularly infrequent occurrences and would usually be dealt within football's disciplinary procedures. However, a prosecution ensued and at the trial the referee considered that in tackling, Barnes 'had gone in with two feet'. Barnes' contention was that he had made a legitimate 'sliding tackle'. In his summing up the judge stressed that although the consequential serious injury was not in dispute, the characterisation of the tackle was however open to doubt. The judge indicated that the prosecution had to prove that what happened was 'not done by way of legitimate sport' and that 'what was done was a deliberate act'. No specific mention was made by the judge on the issue of consent, although the prosecution argued that the phrase 'legitimate sport' used by the judge obviously embraced the issue of consent. Barnes was convicted of a s. 20 OAPA offence which he appealed.

The Court of Appeal found that although the jury had asked for clarification of what was a legitimate sport, they were 'not given any examples of conduct' that might have amounted to it. No attempt was made to determine clearly whether what was happening in the game at the time of the incident was legitimate or not. The Court concluded that 'the summing-up was inadequate' and the conviction therefore unsafe. Lord Woolf attempted to articulate what he believed was the narrow area where there might be criminal liability:

> the starting point is the fact that most organised sports have their own disciplinary procedures for enforcing their particular rules and standards of conduct . . . in addition to a criminal prosecution there is the possibility of an injured player obtaining damages at a civil action from another player . . . a criminal prosecution should be reserved for those situations in where the conduct is sufficiently grave to be properly categorised as criminal [emphasis added].

The Court of Appeal stated that 'the gravity' of the incident would be significantly determined by whether the victim could have consented at law and the test for determining this was an objective one. The criteria 'likely to be relevant in determining whether the defendant's action go beyond the threshold' were: the type of sport; the level at which it is played; the degree of force used; the extent of the risk of injury; the state of mind of the defendant. These criteria were first developed in the Canadian case of *R v Cey* [1989] 48 CCC (3d) 480., concerning criminal liability in ice hockey matches. (Also see Canadian cases of *R v Ciccarelli* [1989] 54 CCC (3d) 121, *R v Leclerc* [1991] 67 CCC (3d) and *R v Jobidon* [1991] 2 SCR 714.)

Regulation of sports business

Sport, certainly at the professional and elite level, generates significant business and is therefore subject to regulation in a number of ways.

Sports employment contracts

Participants in sport fall into three main categories: (a) amateurs; (b) self-employed professionals; (c) employed professionals. It is this last category that is the primary focus.

Professional sportsmen and sportswomen and those who coach and manage them, who are regarded in law as employees, will find themselves subject to and protected by the ordinary law of employment in both its common law and statutory forms.

Status and definition of a sportsperson

In order to ascertain which sports participants are covered by the law of employment it is necessary to understand the legal tests for defining an employee. Under English law it is case law arising out of disputes concerning these practical issues that provide us with the tests to help resolve specific problems. The 'control test' was the traditional common law means for ascertaining whether a person engaged in work was an employee. A person was controlled by an employer if that person was told not only what to do but also how to do it. Arguments that skills possessed by individual sportsmen took them beyond the control of clubs who paid them were quickly discounted, e.g. *Walker v Crystal Palace Football Club* [1910] 1 KB 87 CA. Today a wider multiple test is used where a number of issues will be considered. An interesting development in the context of employee status and sport is provided by the case of *Singh v The Football Association Ltd, The Football League Ltd & Others* (2001) ET Case Number 5203593/99. One of the issues dealt with by the employment tribunal in the case is whether referees can be considered employees of the Football League and/or the Football Association and are thus, for example, eligible to claim unfair dismissal. In line with the authorities, established above, the tribunal placed no emphasis on the fact that referees are normally taxed as self-employed purposes (though S had completed his tax returns as an employee). Similarly, the tribunal emphasised that there is no single test for determining the issue. Rather, a tribunal must 'stand back and consider all aspects of the relationship between the applicant and the particular respondent with no single factor being decisive or determinative but seeking to appropriate weight to all relevant factors'. Thus the tribunal placed little emphasis on facts such as the requirement on referees to wear particular dress or on a referee's lack of entitlement to sick pay or holidays.

Formation and terms of a contract of employment

The ordinary rules of offer and acceptance apply to contracts of employment in the same way as any other type of contract. In accordance with common law principle a contract of employment may, but need not, be in writing. In practice contracts entered into by sportsmen and sportswomen, irrespective of their employment status, will be in writing.

However, in practice it is not that uncommon for an employment contract to be entered into informally through oral agreement, and the full contract is only later put into written form. The following case illustrates the problems this process can cause. In *Stransky v Bristol Rugby Ltd* 11/12/20002 QBD (Eady J) unreported, the club's Director of Rugby was authorised to approach Joel Stransky, a former international player, to discuss his possible employment as a backs coach. Following these negotiations Stransky met the club's chief executive in a restaurant in Bath in April. The terms of the contract were discussed and agreed to over the meal. Stransky returned to his home in Leicester and informed his wife that he had a new job and thus they would be looking for a new home in the Bath/Bristol area. In the months after this meal, to the knowledge of the chief executive, preliminary steps were taken to secure a work permit for Stransky and he was introduced to the players.

The chief executive was also asked to draw up the written contract for Stransky and his response indicated that he was intending to do so. In June, Stransky discovered that the club had decided not to employ him. In court the chief executive stated that he did not recall meeting Stransky for a meal let alone offering him employment. On the basis of the evidence this statement was rejected and the court concluded that a contract had been entered into during the meal in April. Thus the club was in repudiatory (serious) breach in refusing to employ Stransky for the agreed period. Also see *White v Bristol Rugby Club* [2002] IRLR 204.

Obligations of parties under contract

Express terms

The interplay between the standard terms in a sports professional's contract and general employment law is of central importance. This is particularly the case with the rights and duties of the contracting parties. As is generally the case with written employment contracts, many of the respective rights and duties of the parties derive from express contractual terms. For example, on the club's part there are normally express obligations to provide medical treatment and to continue to pay a player's basic wages during periods that he is injured or otherwise incapacitated. Contracts could also contain provisions regulating marketing and sponsorship deals.

Judicially implied duties of the employer:

- The duty to pay wages (but not to provide work). See *Collier v Sunday Referee Publishing Co. Ltd* [1940] 2 KB 647, 650.
- The duty to take reasonable care with respect to the health, safety and welfare of the employee.
- The duty to maintain mutual trust and confidence.

Judicially implied duties of the employee:

- The duty of obedience.
- The duty to take reasonable care.
- The duty of fidelity and not to use or disclose confidential information obtained in the course of employment.

Termination of contract

1 Introduction

Sporting contracts can be lawfully terminated in exactly the same way as any other type of contract – that is by mutual agreement, performance or expiry. However, under UK law there are special rules, primarily as a result of statutory rights of unfair dismissal that apply to all contracts of employment including those entered into by professional sports participants. There is also a common law right not to be wrongfully dismissed by reason of a breach of contract by the employer.

2 Common law

Any employment contract can be terminated without cause if due notice is given. This can be the case with fixed-term contracts, common in the sports world, although the normal expectation is that such contracts will end on the date of their expiry. Non-renewal would not constitute a dismissal. A summary dismissal, where no notice or inadequate notice is given or a fixed-term contract is terminated prior to its date of expiry, is prima facie a breach of contract and thus a wrongful dismissal by the employer unless the employee is guilty of gross misconduct. For this to be the case the employee must be in breach of a term – express or implied – which is at the root of the contract (or have repudiated the contract in its entirety). Disobedience of a lawful and reasonable instruction by the employer *may* constitute gross misconduct.

3 Gross misconduct

It is clear that there is no standard test for ascertaining whether misconduct is gross. The circumstances of the case must be taken into account in determining whether or not the employee has committed a repudiatory (serious) breach of contract. Only if this is the case is the employer justified in treating the contract as at an end.

One group of employees in sport that have a rather precarious employment status are managers of a professional football club. Instant dismissal is certainly par for the course. It is rarely based on allegations of gross misconduct. Indeed, it is often the result of pressure from fans that sometimes rightly and no doubt sometimes wrongly hold the manager to blame if their team's performances are below expectations. The function of contract law here is essentially to provide a legal framework within which an out-of-court settlement can be negotiated; an action for wrongful dismissal is thereby precluded. However, the case of *Macari v Celtic Football and Athletic Co. Ltd* (1998) Court of Session, Case 0/309/6/98, shows how the concept of wrongful dismissal can relate to football managers and discusses the interplay between contractual duties imposed on both employers and employees through the judicially implied terms discussed above. Macari was appointed manager of Celtic in October 1993. In March 1994 the club was taken over by a consortium headed by Fergus McCann. The latter made it clear from the outset that he did not want Macari as manager and excluded him from meetings of the Board (which, under the previous regime, Macari had attended). In June 1994 Macari was summarily dismissed for wilful acts of disobedience. In particular, a failure to comply with a residence requirement to live in or near to Glasgow (Macari had previously been the manager of Stoke FC and his family home remained in Stoke), and his consequent frequent absences from Celtic Park. The Court of Session accepted that the club's treatment of Macari amounted to destruction of mutual trust and confidence. However, the Court rejected his claim for wrongful dismissal as it did not accept that the club's breach of contract justified Macari's wilful failure to obey the reasonable instructions of his employer.

4 Constructive dismissal

This is where the employee can leave his or her employment and claim wrongful dismissal, in that the employer has breached the contract and therefore he or she has been 'constructively dismissed'. Such a situation occurred when the Managers' Arbitration Tribunal of the FA Premier League unanimously upheld Alan Curbishley's claim of wrongful dismissal against West Ham United Football Club. He resigned at the beginning of the 2008/09 season after the Club sold Anton Ferdinand and subsequently George McCartney to Sunderland against his wishes. The Tribunal upheld Curbishley's right to have ultimate sole authority in relation to the sale and purchase of players, which was expressly provided for in the contract, and found that the conduct of the Club amounted to a fundamental breach of contract and that Curbishley was therefore entitled to resign. The findings of the Tribunal demonstrate the critical importance of respecting contracts which need to set out the roles and responsibilities of the parties in clear and unequivocal terms.

In a similar case Kevin Keegan brought an action for wrongful dismissal when he resigned due to players being bought and sold without his permission. However he had no formal term in the contract to that effect.

Case 15.2 Keegan wins damages of £2 million against his former club

Former Newcastle United manager Kevin Keegan was awarded £2 million damages plus interest after winning his case against the club for constructive dismissal.

The panel agreed that in signing Uruguayan midfielder Ignacio Gonzalez, against Keegan's wishes, the club was in breach of a term in his contract. It was also agreed that Keegan would receive no further damages. Keegan parted company with the club, owned by businessman Mike Ashley, in September 2008.

A relieved Keegan said in a statement:

> I am delighted that the Premier League manager's arbitration tribunal has today formally announced that it has upheld my claim for wrongful dismissal against Newcastle United . . . The tribunal has found the conduct of the club in forcing a player on me against my wishes represented a fundamental breach of my contract of employment. I do not believe that there is any manager in football who could have remained at the club in the light of their conduct.
>
> I also want to confirm that a central purpose of my claim has always been to clear my name and restore my reputation. I consider it of vital importance that I was able to let people know about the full circumstances of my resignation and the way in which I had been treated by the club. I hope that this purpose has now been achieved.

Newcastle refused to comment on the case, merely reporting the panel's decision and publishing the official report. The transfer of Gonzalez features heavily in the report . . . The report states that Keegan was offered a deal which was worth an initial £3m per annum for three-and-a-half years, a figure which was the basis behind his initial damages claim in the region of £8.5 million for his agreed spell in charge, and a reported figure in the region of £25 million for the length of his career in football before retirement at the presumed age of 65.

Discussion questions

6 On what grounds was Kevin Keegan successful in his action for wrongful dismissal?

7 How does this case differ from the Curbishley case?

8 Why did Keegan not succeed in his claim for over £30 million in compensation?

Remedies for wrongful dismissal

1 Damages

The normal remedy for a wrongful dismissal, i.e. a dismissal in breach of contract, is damages for actual financial loss suffered. In the case of fixed-term contracts, which are the norm in professional sport, this will, subject to the normal duty of mitigation, be loss of earnings for the period of time that the contract had left to run. The underlying principle in contract law for calculating damages is that the claimant should be awarded a sum of money which would put him in the same financial position that he would have enjoyed had the contract been properly performed.

2 Injunctions

It is a fundamental legal principle that courts will not compel performance of a contract of employment or any contract that involves the provision of personal services. In *Warren v Mendy* [1989] 1 WLR 853. the Court of Appeal refused an injunction to restrain the defendant from inducing boxer Nigel Benn to break his contract with his manager by participating in a match arranged by the defendant. This case was cited and followed by the High Court in *Subaru Tecnica International Inc v Burns & Others* (2001) Ch D (unreported). The court refused an injunction which would have prevented Richard Burns, the 2001 World Rally Champion, from breaking his contract with Subaru by driving for Peugeot.

On the other hand, an injunction was granted for a short period to enforce garden leave provisions in the case of *Crystal Palace FC Ltd v Bruce* (2002) QBD, ISLR SLR-81. At the time of the case Steve Bruce was the manager of Crystal Palace. Bruce wished to leave the club to become the manager of Birmingham FC. Crystal Palace sought an injunction to enforce a 'garden leave' clause to prevent him from doing this. Burton J decided that Crystal Palace might well have legitimate interests to protect as it and Birmingham were both in the First Division and indeed were both rivals for a play-off position at the end of the 2001/02 season. Steve Bruce's departure to manage Birmingham would thus have been duly detrimental to Palace's prospects for the rest of the season. Moreover, the departure of a manager to another club not infrequently results in other members of the coaching and playing staff joining him shortly thereafter. The court granted an interlocutory injunction (pending a full court hearing) for a short period (around two months) to restrain Bruce from leaving Crystal Palace in breach of contract.

3 Transfer of players

Players in professional team sports, notably football, have been subject to being transferred from one club to another in return for a fee from the buying club to the selling club. In England, the system was very restrictive until the case of *Eastham v Newcastle United FC* [1964] Ch 413, where the transfer and retain system as it operated at the time was challenged by the footballer George Eastham as constituting an unlawful restraint of trade. Under the system, on termination of a contract a club could decide to put a player on the retain list. As a consequence the player so retained could not play for any club in any country which was a member of FIFA. If the club refused to place him on the transfer list he had no choice but to accept the offer of a new contract from the club if he wished to work as a professional footballer. These regulations were declared in restraint of trade and created a limited degree of free agency for players at the end of their contract. However, the rules enabling a club to require a transfer fee were upheld.

At the end of 1995 the European Court of Justice (ECJ) delivered its historic ruling in the *Bosman* Case C-415/93, *Union Royale Belge des Societes de Football Association & others v Jean-Marc Bosman* [1995] ECR I-4921. The two limbs of the *Bosman* ruling were based on what is now Article 45 of the Treaty for the Functioning of the European Union (TFEU) nationals to work on a non-discriminatory basis in any Member State. First, the ECJ ruled that out-of-contract players, who were EU nationals, were entitled to negotiate their own contracts with new clubs within the EU without their current clubs being able to demand a transfer fee before a move to a new club could take place, thus creating in essence full free agency. In this context the transfer system constituted an unjustified restriction on rights of freedom of movement. Secondly, the so-called 3+2 rule then in place restricting the numbers of foreign players that could be fielded in one match was declared to be an unlawful constraint on freedom of movement and was contrary to European discrimination law in so far as players from EU Member States were treated as foreigners.

Restraint of trade

The doctrine of restraint of trade is aimed at protecting the right of the individual to work and to promote free and competitive economic conditions. In this respect EU law impacts upon domestic contract law through Articles 101 and 102 of the TFEU and the UK Competition Act 1998.

There have been a number of cases where clubs and players have been successful in suing their sports governing body over issues of restraint of trade and anti-competitive practices (*Eastham v Newcastle United Football Club Ltd* (1964) Ch 413). Here Newcastle United were held in restraint of trade over the FA's transfer rules holding players at the end of their contracts. (See also *Newport Association Football Club Ltd and Others v Football Association of Wales Ltd* (1995) 2 All ER 87.) In cricket *Greig v Insole* (1978) 1 WLR 302 presents a similar conclusion to that of *Eastham*, whilst in horse racing (*Nagle v Feilden* (1966) 2 QB 63) it was held that the Jockey Club was unreasonable in refusing to grant a licence to a woman horse trainer. In rugby (*Williams v Pugh; Russell v Pugh* (1997) unreported), Popplewell J granted injunctive relief to two Welsh Rugby Union clubs against the Rugby Union, restraining the Union from restricting the clubs' activities. Finally, snooker provides a more recent case (*Stephen Gordon Hendry and Others v The World Professional Billiards and Snooker Association Limited (WPBSA)* (2002) ECC 8).

Intellectual property rights

Intellectual property rights (IPRs) are legally enforceable rights which 'give the creator a degree of exclusivity in respect to the use and exploitation of his or her creation' (Lewis and Taylor, 2008). By endorsing products or services, the player can increase their potential earnings. Beckham's earnings on the pitch are dwarfed by multi-million pound deals to endorse brands such as Pepsi, Vodafone and Marks & Spencer, making him 'a footballing superstar who earns over £20,000-a-week for his image rights alone' (*The Scotsman*, 2003).

Nowadays proportionately more time is spent protecting and exploiting IPRs in order to maximise commercial value, such as evident in the recent sale of Manchester United's merchandising business to Nike. This is done through merchandising, sponsorship, broadcasting rights and the use of trademarks, designs and copyright material to reinforce distinctiveness. In *The Rugby Football Union and Nike European Operations Netherlands BV v Cotton Traders Ltd* (2002) All ER (D) 417, the RFU was unsuccessful in defending the distinctiveness of the 'classic rose' under trademark law. Although different countries have their own national law test for eligibility for trademark registration, the law tends to be consistent internationally as to protecting logos, brand names etc. which are distinctive.

In *Torpedoes Sportswear Pty Ltd v Thorpedo Enterprises Pty Ltd* [2003] FCA 901 an Australian sporting company torpedoes sportswear lost its bid to stop Thorpedo Enterprises, a company owned by Australian swimming star Ian Thorpe's parents, from using his nickname 'thorpedo' on a range of products. Torpedoes Sportswear had appealed the decision of the delegate of the register of trade marks rejecting Sportswear's opposition to Enterprise's application to the registration of the trade mark Thorpedo. Bennett J held that Sportswear had not established any of the grounds of opposition. It failed to establish that Enterprises was not the proprietor of the Thorpedo mark or that the Thorpedo mark was substantially identical to the mark 'Torpedoes'. It also failed to establish that Torpedoes Sportswear had acquired a reputation in Australia such that, because of its reputation, the use of the Thorpedo mark would be likely to deceive or confuse consumers.

In the United States' case of *Pro-Football, Inc. v Harjo* (2003) U.S. Dist. Lexis 17180, a group of Native Americans initiated an action to cancel federal trademark registrations owned by the Washington Redskins football team. The Native Americans claimed that the Redskins' trademarks disparaged their people or brought them into contempt or disrepute, in violation of s. 2(a) of the Lanham Act. Conversely, the Redskins argued that their trademarks honoured Native Americans and that the legal 'doctrine of laches' barred the requested trademark cancellation because this claim was delayed for an unreasonable amount of time – the first trademarks being registered in 1967. The court held that the Redskins trademarks neither disparaged Native Americans nor placed them in contempt or disrepute and that the Redskins had made substantial financial investment in their marks over 25 years. The court stressed however that where a more complete factual record can be established, other future trademark cancellation cases may be successful regarding the ongoing Native American sports mascot and logo controversy. In 2009, the US Supreme Court declined the Native American group's appeal.

Image rights

Under English law there is no specific legal protection for individual 'image rights'. The protection is derived from a range of legal provisions. 'Saving face is all a matter of image for the famous' (*The Times*, 2002), as the judgment in favour of racing driver Eddie Irvine demonstrates (*Edmund Irvine & Tidswell Limited v Talksport Ltd* 2002 WL 1876169). Mr Irvine contended that the use a doctored image of him holding what appeared to be a radio to his ear was actionable in 'passing off' as a misrepresentation by Talksport Limited that he was endorsing Talk Radio (now Talksport).

Passing off arises where a trader makes misrepresentations that damage the reputation of someone else (see Lord Oliver's summary in his judgment on *Reckitt & Colman*

Products Ltd v Borden Inc (1990) RPC 341 at 406). Passing-off actions have frequently failed on the basis that there was no common field of activity in which both parties were engaged. In the Irvine case the judge recognised that it is now common practice for famous people to exploit their name and reputation by endorsement of a wide variety of products or services way beyond their own field of activity, in contrast to the narrow approach taken in *McCullock v May* (1947) 65 RPC 58.

The Human Rights Act 1998 and most notably Article 8 – the respect for private and family life – has judicially developed some protection for image rights through a range of cases involving sports and entertainment celebrities. In *Flitcroft v The Sunday People (B & C v A)* (2002) HRLR 25 (in terms of the publishing of Garry Flitcroft's affairs); *Campbell v MGN Ltd* [2004] 2 WLR 1232; *A v B* [2003] QB 195; *Theakston v MGN Ltd* [2002] EMLR 22; *Ashworth Hospital Authority v MGN Ltd* [2002] 1 WLR 2033; *Venables v News Group Newspapers Ltd* [2001] 2 WLR 1038; *Mosley v News Group Newspapers Limited* [2008] WLR (D) 259, something akin to a right of privacy has developed.

Additionally, quasi-legal measures such as illustrated in the *Appeal by The Number regarding Complaint by David Bedford, 27 January 2004* (see decision at www.ofcom.org.uk/bulletins/ adv_comp/content_board/?a=87101) where David Bedford, a former 10,000 metres world record holder, won a ruling against phone directory company, The Number, with its 118118 service over their adverts featuring two runners in 1970s' running gear. Communications regulator Ofcom said the number had caricatured Bedford's image – drooping moustache, shoulder-length hair and running kit – without his permission. Caricature without permission constitutes a breach of Rule 6.5 of the Advertising Standards Code. The Number conceded that it had not sought or obtained Bedford's permission to be caricatured. This process may develop as an attractive remedy in similar cases. However, Ofcom ruled it would be disproportionate to direct that the advertisements not be shown in future, and that the publication of the finding of breach was a sufficient resolution of the matter.

However, other countries have jurisprudence protecting celebrities' images – e.g. 'In Canada and America, there is "the right of publicity". This is an individual's right to control commercial use and exploitation of his persona including image, voice and likeness' (Michalos, 2002). In *ETW Corporation v Jireh Publishing, Inc.* (2003 U.S. App. LEXIS 12488, 20 June 2003), the court established limitations on athlete trademark and publicity rights. ETW Corporation ('ETW'), which is the licensing company owned by golfer Tiger Woods, claimed that Jireh Publishing, Inc. ('Jireh') infringed on its registered trademark 'Tiger Woods' and violated Woods' publicity rights pursuant to Ohio state law.

ETW's legal claims addressed a painting produced by Jireh entitled 'The Masters of Augusta' which commemorated Woods' 1997 victory at the Masters Tournament. This painting including three views of Woods in different poses was produced and sold without ETW's consent. Jireh claimed that this painting's artistic expression was protected by the First Amendment of the United States Constitution, and therefore did not violate American federal trademark law or Ohio publicity rights.

Although ETW had registered Woods' name as a trademark, it had not registered any image or likeness of Woods, and the court ruled that images and likenesses of Woods are not protectable as a trademark because they do not perform the trademark function or designation. When balancing ETW's intellectual property claims with Jireh's artistic expression rights, as guaranteed under the First Amendment, the Court held that Jireh's work had substantial informational and creative content which outweighed any adverse effect on ETW's market.

The Irvine case raised the distinction between endorsement and merchandising. Endorsement involves the exploitation of goods whereas merchandising involves the exploitation of images. More recently the *Arsenal Football Club v Reed* case has been an important registered trademark case for sport businesses.

Case 15.3 *Arsenal Football Club Plc v Reed*

Arsenal Football Club ('AFC') brought an action against Mr Matthew Reed for passing off and trademark infringements after the defendant sold from a stall outside the ground scarves not officially authorised by the club bearing signs referring to the club. AFC's complaint is that the sale of such products bearing its name and logos constitutes passing off and infringes one or more of its four registered trademarks, each of which consists of or includes the prominent use of the word 'Arsenal'. The court held that there had been no passing off committed by the defendant. In relation to trademark infringement the essential function of a trademark was to guarantee origin and hence act as a control for quality. Art. 5(1) of First Directive 89/104 on trademarks provides 'The proprietor (of a registered trade mark) shall be entitled to prevent all third parties not having his consent from using in the course of trade: a) any sign which is identical with the trade mark in relation to goods or services which are identical with those for which the trade mark is registered.' In the circumstance of the case the defendant's use of the signs constituted a link between the proprietor and was likely to jeopardise the guarantee of origin. In Mr Reed's defence he asserted that the name and badges on the replica kits did not function as trademarks as they did not tell people where the goods originated. Rather, the Arsenal marks served merely as 'badges of support, loyalty or affiliation'. The court felt that it was necessary to make a preliminary ruling (Art. 234) to the Court of European Justice concerning the interpretation of the Trade Marks Directive 89/104 in relation to infringement under Art. 5(1) (a). The question referred to the Court was whether or not non-trademark use can represent a violation of registered trademark rights.

The European Court argued that 'in the circumstances' of this case Arsenal should succeed, thus appearing to indicate that Mr Reed was infringing Arsenal's registered trademarks in part due to the material link between his replica goods and Arsenal despite the sign above his stall indicating that the merchandise was unofficial. The Court queried the purchase of the goods away from the stall and the perception of customers then to the origin. The Court of Justice had exceeded its jurisdiction in determining issues of fact and the judge was not, therefore, bound by its final conclusions. Mr Reed appealed over the jurisdiction of the European Court decisions. Mr Justice Laddie stated: 'It was the Court of Appeal which had jurisdiction to overturn or make alternative or supplementary findings of fact'.

'Copr. © 2003 West Group. No claim to orig. U.S. govt. works'.
For the full case see *Arsenal Football Club Plc v Reed* (2003) 1 CMLR 13.

Discussion questions

9 Are there any courses of action left open to Arsenal and if so what are they and how effective do you think they will be?

10 What messages does this send to the replica sports kit industry and to major sponsors like Adidas, Nike etc.?

Match fixing

Match fixing has been identified as a problem in a number of sports for a significant period of time. Those sports such as horse racing that have a close relationship with the gambling industry are particularly prone. Additionally, a range of sports such as snooker, football, cricket and tennis have been subject to match fixing allegations as the opportunities for gambling have increased with technology and more sophisticated gambling procedures such as 'betting exchanges' where the betting company brokers between different customers allowing them to bet against each other. You can back a selection to win or lay it to lose in a great number of sports. International cricket became aware that it had a major problem in 2000 when the South African Team captain Hansje Cronje admitted receiving money in return for providing confidential information concerning team selection to bookies and attempting to get team mates to contribute to purposely lose matches. More recently, in 2011, the playing bans and criminal conviction of three Pakistani international cricketers for proven 'spot fixing' activities during a Test Match against England in August 2010, suggests that cricket still has a problem with this form of corruption (*R* v *Amir & Butt* [2011] EWCA Civ 2914). Spot fixing, as with match fixing, impacts upon the integrity of a sporting encounter, where a particular event in a match is manipulated. In this example, it was the pre-arranged bowling of 'no-balls' at specific points in the cricket match instigated by an illegal bookmaker, where bets could be made predicting this event with little risk for the gambler.

International tennis has similarly realised that some tennis players were vulnerable to corrupt approaches. A report in 2008, the 'Environmental Review of Integrity in Professional Tennis', highlighted five potential threats to the sport: corrupt practices by players and others in respect to gambling; breaches of the rules in relation to not giving best efforts in matches, so-called 'tanking' (i.e. not trying); violation of credentials; misuse of inside information; and illegal or abusive behaviour toward players. Essentially engaging with these problems is about protecting the commercial integrity of that particular sport and sport generally and defending the crucial sporting characteristic of 'unpredictability of outcome'.

Case 15.4 Report urges tennis match fixing investigation

4. We have examined some 73 matches over the past 5 years involving suspected betting patterns. We have further examined 45 of those matches and there are specific concerns about each match from a betting perspective which would warrant further review. Patterns of suspected betting activity have been noted on twenty-seven accounts in two different countries and there are emerging concerns about some players which would warrant further attention. Bearing in mind these matches only relate to Betfair account holders, it is reasonable to assume that other suspect betting is taking place using other international legal and illegal betting markets. So there is no room for complacency. All the indications are that a co-ordinated and

(continued)

focused Anti-Corruption Programme with an adequately resourced Integrity Unit is needed to address the integrity concerns.

7. We judge that cheating at tennis for corrupt betting purposes is the most serious threat and goes to the core of the integrity of the sport. However, although the evidence currently available to prove the precise extent of that threat is limited, as mentioned above, we have examined, more closely, intelligence reports on 45 suspect matches over the past 5 years. The initial assessment of those matches, supported by other intelligence, indicates that a number of account holders are successfully laying higher ranked players to lose/backing lesser ranked players to win. The betting patterns give a strong indication that those account holders are in receipt of 'inside information', which has facilitated successful betting coups both on 'in-play' as well as 'match' betting. Because of the sensitive nature of these issues, the Report does not go into detail on those matches but we have shared further confidential information on them with the Professional Tennis Authorities. In view of the circumstances, we consider there is merit in reviewing those matches in an effort to identify whether the initial suspicions raised did indeed affect the integrity of Professional Tennis, whether there may have been other tennis reasons for the outcome of such matches and, importantly, to identify any intelligence leads for future reference. The scale of the allegedly suspicious matches indicates there is no room for complacency.

15. We judge that the threats to the integrity of professional tennis identified in this Review are real and cannot be taken lightly.

Source: Gunn, B. and Rees-May, J. (2008) Environmental review of integrity in professional tennis, International Tennis Federation, selected extracts.

Discussion questions

11 Discuss the ways that tennis players could manipulate the result of a match.

12 What have the tennis authorities done to engage with allegations of match fixing?

13 What role should gambling firms such as Betfair have in dealing with this issue?

 ## Conclusion

This chapter has introduced a number of relevant legal principles in the study of sports law, drawing upon both the application of existing law to sport but also referring to sport-specific statutory law as sport comes increasingly under the legal spotlight. This chapter has aimed to demonstrate that anyone who is involved in some capacity with sport (be it manager or voluntary coach) must have an understanding of their legal responsibilities and grasp the imperative for legal compliance.

Sports law is an evolving area which is both contentious and dynamic. It is hoped that this chapter has served to whet the reader's appetite for what is a truly captivating area of academic study.

Keywords

Arbitration; defendant; interlocutory injunction; jurisprudence; libel; *obiter dicta*; plaintiff; qualified privilege; slander.

Guided reading

Legal research – case citations

The law which is valid in England is established in either

EU Law   Cases
Statutes   Statutory Instruments

Law Reports – case law

There are various diverse Law Reports and often cases are reported in more than one of these. The cases are referred to by their name, e.g. *Wooldridge v Sumner.*

Some of the main reports for example are:

All England Law Reports   (All ER)
Appeal Cases   (AC)
Kings Bench Division   (KB)
Panstadia International Quarterly Report   (PIQR)
Queens Bench Division   (QB)
Weekly Law Reports   (WLR)

How to cite cases correctly

Cases are referred to by the names of parties to the action. In addition, because there may be several versions of a case reported, the case name is followed by a sequence of numbers and letters which identify where the report is published.

Cases contain five elements:

1 The names of the parties

2 The date – the year in which the case was reported

3 The number of the volume of the law report

4 The abbreviation of the category of law report. Help in expanding fully the abbreviation of the title of the law report is available in publications such as:

Current Law Case Citator (any issue)
Legal Journals Index (any issue)

5 The page number where the case is located.

Here is how a case would be cited:

1	*2*	*3*	*4*	*5*
Condon v Basi	*(1985)*	*1*	*WLR*	*866*

The case is to be found in Volume 1 of the Weekly Law Reports for 1985 at page 866.

There is an increasing array of resources on tort and duty of care in relation to sport. One can refer to the full citation of each particular case but also look at the case commentaries for discussion around the issues within a particular case. Kevan (2001) provides a review of the legal principles involved in sports injuries and the liability of sports personnel, whilst two articles produced by Duff (1999, 2002) discuss the issue of duty of care and reckless disregard. Dovey (2000) focuses on some of the earlier cases in sport around issues of breach of duty and discusses single or variable standards of care. Moore (2002) discusses vicarious liability and level of care of sport officials in sporting events, whilst James (2003) looks more specifically at rugby and discusses the liability of rugby drawing on analysis from the *Smoldon* (1997) and *Caldwell v Maguire and Fitzgerald* (2001) cases and the recent case of *Vowles v Evans and the Welsh Rugby Union and others* (2002) in order to ascertain the evidential test and player's duty of care.

There is a very helpful chapter (6) in *Sport, Physical Recreation and the Law* by Hazel Hartley (2009) entitled 'Safe in our Hands? Risk management and breaches of health and safety: learning from cases and incidents', where Hartley provides a range of statutory health and safety duties in the workplace but also introduces a number of examples of prosecutions for breaches of health and safety brought against individuals and organisations in sport and recreational contexts.

The Health and Safety Executive also provides a helpful guide to the Health and Safety at Work Act, which can be assessed at www.hse.gov.uk/legislation/hswa.htm. RoSPA (The Royal Society for the Prevention of Accidents) provides an advice pack for small businesses and sheet 7, in particular, summarises risk assessment and refers to the five-step approach by the HSE mentioned earlier in the chapter (see www.rospa.com/occupationalsafety/smallfirms/). The British Standards Institution publishes a number of important guidance papers which are particularly pertinent to managers and these can be accessed at www.bsi-global.com/en/BSI-UK/

Other useful sources include Health and Safety Executive (1999a), (1999b) and HELA (2000).

Slapper & Kelly (2001) provide a useful insight and the necessary legal knowledge on the essential institutions, practices and principles of the English Legal System. At (http://www.parliament.uk/index.cfm) a brief guide to the history and procedure of the UK Parliament with links illustrating how legislation is made is available. For a basic text on the Institutions of the European Union and the Community law-making process, read Douglas-Scott, S. (2002). Whilst Craig and de Búrca, G., (2002) is a more challenging book that combines textual commentary with extracts from judgments and other academic literature. There are also a large number of websites devoted to EC Law, i.e. (http://europa.eu.int/), which provides up-to-date coverage of European Union affairs and essential information on European integration.

For those seeking a more detailed commentary on the case of *Arsenal v Reed* and the issues of intellectual property rights then Misquitta (2003) is a useful article. Also see Lewis and Taylor (2008), Chapter G1 and Yap (2007).

Finally, any of the following sports law texts would be a useful resource for all of the different aspects of legal areas discussed within this chapter:

Bill (2009) includes a chapter on sports law by Simon Gardiner which examines the increasing role that the general law has in regulating sport and discusses specific areas of law that have impacted upon the operation of the sports business industry.

Blanpain (2003) reviews the present transfer system imposed by the International Foundation of Football Associations (FIFA). He incorporates the issues of sportsmen and sportswomen as 'workers', the status of players' agents, disciplinary rules and dispute resolution and the disagreements with competition law.

Gardiner et al. (2006) is a leading textbook on sports law, analysing sports law within a socio-economic and cultural context with a focus on sport in Britain.

Hartley (2009) covers a wide range of legal principles and cases and introduces the reader to legal systems, terminology and the use of case law. Key topics, for example, include manslaughter, discrimination and risk management.

James (2010) provides a comprehensive overview of the ways in which the law has impacted on how sport is played, administered and consumed. Of particular interest is a designated chapter on the Olympic Games in the run-up to 2012.

Kevan et al. (2002) is the first book dedicated to the topic of sports injury law. It is a useful guide to organisers and clubs that have a possible liability and for those sports participants who may injure themselves in the sporting environment. The book is aimed at a wide cross-section of people involved in litigation, namely personal injury practitioners to unqualified claim assessors.

Lewis and Taylor (2008) provides widespread coverage on such aspects as the commercialisation of sports events, the legal control of sport and the aspects of self-regulation. It also examines the impact of EC law on sport and the nature of contracts in relation to intellectual property rights.

Parrish (2003) delves into the issues of commercialisation of sport from both a legal and political analysis and raises questions concerning regulation at the EU level.

Bill (2003) and Epstein (2003) are useful resources.

Recommended websites

An online journal for the sports facility industry worldwide: www.panstadia.com

Daily legal update: law@lexisnexis-alerter.co.uk

Europa – the portal site for the EU: http://europa.eu

InfoLaw – Useful links to legal resources: www.infolaw.co.uk

Legal Subject Index, Index to Law School, Academic Law Journals: www.FINDLAW.com

Mondaq article service: www.mondaq.com

The British Association for Sport and Law: www.britishsportslaw.org/

The Institute of Legal Executives' Journal: www.ilex.org.uk/the_legal_executive/journal_home.aspx

The Social Science Gateway – web resources to help with your studies and research: www.intute. ac.uk/socialsciences/

UK Parliament: www.parliament.uk/index.cfm

Villanova Sports and Entertainment Law Journal: http://old.law.villanova.edu/currentstudents/ journalsandmootcourt/sportsandentlj/sportsandentlj.asp

References

Beloff, M. (2000) *Sports Law*, 3rd edn, London: Butterworth.

Bill, K. (2003) 'Sports law on the web', *The Legal Executive Journal*, May.

Bill, K. (2009) *Sport Management*, Essex: Learning Matters.

Blanpain, R. (2003) *The Legal Status of Sportsmen and Sportswomen under International, European and Belgian National and Regional Law*, Alphen aan den Rijn: Kluwer Law.

Craig, P. and de Búrca, G. (2002) *EU Law: Text, Cases and Materials*, 3rd edn, Oxford: OUP.

Douglas-Scott, S. (2002) *Constitutional Law of the European Union*, Harlow: Longman.

Dovey, D. (2000) 'Tort and contact', *The Legal Executive*, 18–19.

Duff, A. (1999) 'Reasonable care v reckless disregard', *Sport and Law Journal*, 7 (1), 44–54.

Duff, A. (2002) 'Reasonable care v reckless disregard revisited', *Sport and Law Journal*, 10 (1), 156–59.

Epstein, R. (2003) 'Law on the web', *The Legal Executive Journal*, February.

Gardiner, S., Felix, A., O'Leary, J., James, M. and Welch, R. (2006) *Sports Law*, London: Cavendish Publishing Limited.

Grayson, E. (1994) *Sport and the Law*, 2nd edn, London: Cavendish Publishers Limited.

Grayson, E. (2003) 'Don't fight the law', Law 4 today – Online legal issues for the UK public and profession, www.law4today.com/sport/sport1.htm

Gunn, B. and Rees, G. (2008) 'Environmental review of integrity in professional tennis', The Tennis Integrity Unit.

Hartley, H. (2009) *Sport, Physical Recreation and the Law*, London: Routledge.

Health and Safety Executive (1999a) *Charity and Voluntary Workers: A Guide to Health and Safety at Work*, HSG192, Sudbury: HSE Books.

Health and Safety Executive (1999b) *Essentials of Health and Safety at Work*, Sudbury: HSE Books.

HELA (2000) *The Relationship between the Safety of Sports Grounds Act 1975* (as amended by the Fire Safety and Safety of Places of Sport Act 1987) and the Health and Safety at Work etc Act 1974, LAC Number 63/2, London: HMSO.

James, M. (2003) 'Referees, scrums and spinal injuries', *New Law Journal*, 7 February, 166–7.

James, M. (2010) *Sports Law*, Basingstoke: Palgrave Macmillan.

Kevan, T. (2001) 'Sport injury cases: footballers, referees and schools', *Journal of Personal Injury Law*, 2, 138–48.

Kevan, T., Adamson, D. and Cottrell, S. (2002) *Sports Personal Injury: Law and Practice*, London: Sweet & Maxwell.

Lewis, A. and Taylor, J. (2008) *Sport: Law and Practice*, 2nd edn, London: LexisNexis Butterworths Tolley.

Michalos, C. (2002) 'Saving face is all a matter of image for the famous', *The Times*, 26 March.

Misquitta, A. (2003) *The Legal Practitioner*, London: Farrer & Co (Mondaq's article service).

Moore, C. (2002) 'Sports related injuries: negligence on the field of play', *Personal Injury Law Journal*, 8 (August), 22–24.

Parrish, R. (2003) *Sports Law and Policy in the European Union*, European Policy Research Unit Series, Manchester: Manchester University Press.

Royal Society (1992) *Risk: Analysis, Perception and Management*, London: Royal Society.

Slapper, G. and Kelly, D. (2001) *The English Legal System*, 5th edn, London: Cavendish Publishing.

The Scotsman (2003) 'Beckham's injury a freak accident, says Alex', 18 February. http://www.scotsman.com/news/uk/beckham-s-injury-a-freak-accident-says-alex-1-546596

The Times (2002) 'Saving face is all a matter of image for the famous', 26 March.

Woodhouse, C. (1996) 'The lawyer in sport: some reflections', *Sport and the Law Journal*, 14 (4), 3.

Yap P.J. (2007) 'Making sense of trade mark use', *European Intellectual Property Review*, 29 (10), 420.

Sport event and facility management

Dave Arthur, Southern Cross University, Australia

Learning outcomes

Upon completion of this chapter the reader should be able to:

- define 'special event' and have a detailed appreciation of the scope of the event management industry;
- demonstrate a broad knowledge of the major processes, plans and skills required of the successful sport event manager;
- demonstrate a broad knowledge of the major processes, plans and skills required of the successful sport facility manager;
- apply aspects of the theoretical knowledge gleaned from both event and facility sections to real life, practical situations.

 ## Overview

In recent years, and in particular since the 1984 Olympic Games were held in Los Angeles, the staging of major special events has become increasingly significant to the sporting organisations concerned and to the cities and countries in which the events take place. Indeed the Sydney 2000 Olympics:

- galvanised a city;
- provided worldwide exposure; and
- established Sydney as a worldwide leader in the provision of elite international events.

In the same manner, the Beijing 2008 Olympic Games showcased China to the world and signified its coming of age in the conduct of international hallmark events. On the commercial side, many sporting organisations, and indeed other stakeholders associated with the sporting industry, are utilising special events as a means of establishing and strengthening relationships with their respective target markets and customers. As a result, management principles embodied in planning, human resource management, financial management, marketing, risk management and evaluation have all been applied to the event industry that has evolved.

Similarly, the growth in sport and recreation facilities since the 1970s has been quite marked as all levels of government have given a higher priority to their provision, along with increased government funding for sporting facility development undertaken by community groups. This increase in facility planning, design and management has seen an increased complexity of skills required by staff involved in the planning and management of those facilities.

The chapter is not designed as a complete 'how to' manual of event and facility management, rather an introduction to each subject.

Event management

What are special events?

Allen et al. (2008: 11) describe the term special events as 'specific rituals, presentations, performances or celebrations that are consciously planned and created to mark special occasions or achieve particular social, cultural or corporate goals'. These can include sporting events, civic functions etc. and may vary in size. They are usually characterised by:

- size (local/community; major; hallmark; mega) and
- form or content (festivals, sports events).

These authors (ibid.) also believe that:

> The term 'special events' has been coined to describe specific rituals, presentations, performances or celebrations that are consciously planned and created to mark special occasions or to achieve particular social, cultural or corporate goals and objectives.

A few examples in the sporting area that may 'fit' this definition would include special events ranging from the Olympic Games, FIFA World Cup, horse racing carnivals such as the Grand National or Preakness, to America's Cup (yachting) and Ryder Cup (golf). However, even the authors note that the 'field of special events is now so vast that it is impossible to provide a definition that includes all varieties and shades of events'. Some special events are therefore characterised according to their size and scale with common categories including 'mega events', 'hallmark events' and 'major events'.

Structure of the event industry

The rapid growth of events at the regional level (for example, Masters Games), at the national level (for example, national titles) and the international level (for example, World Cups) has led to the creation of an identifiable event industry. Allen et al. (2008: 17) believe that 'the industry's formation has also been accompanied by a period of rapid globalisation of markets and communication, which has affected the nature of, and trends within, the industry'.

Perspectives on events

As events take place across all aspects of society, many stakeholders are involved. The perspectives of major stakeholders need to be examined to see whether they have implications for event managers. These perspectives are:

● The government perspective. This includes national, state and local governments. The roles that each play can include ownership or management of the event; being the consenting/regulatory body; service provider; funding body; event organiser and marketer.

● The corporate perspective. Its roles can include the above but can also have more emphasis on a return for their investment.

● The community perspective. Its emphasis is usually upon interaction and forming part of the social landscape that binds the community.

The impact of special events

There are significant impacts on communities which host major sporting and/or entertainment events. It has been widely acknowledged that a combination of the 1982 Commonwealth Games and World Expo 88 was responsible for Brisbane's increased international and national profile, resulting in its rapidly expanding population base, while more recently the Sydney 2000 and Beijing 2008 Olympics showcased these cities to the world. This has led to subsequent increase in tourism opportunities and associated business activities in the respective countries.

Additionally the intense lobbying now involved for the right to host Olympic Games, FIFA World Cups and Rugby World Cups indicates that despite the billions of dollars involved in staging such events, governments around the world see value in event management. For example: Tokyo bid for the 2016 Olympic Games. At the heart of its vision is a momentous concept 'Setting the Stage for Heroes'. The concept paints the city as a world stage with three key elements:

● the city's attractions;

● the city's venues; and

● its vibrant and enthusiastic population.

Tokyo 2016 was committed to combining a world-class Games plan with incredible city infrastructure.

Balancing the impact of events

Much media speculation usually surrounds the financial (economic) impact of special events. However, events do not take place in a vacuum – they can touch almost all aspects of our lives as governments at all levels invest taxpayer funds into the conduct of events. You only need to consider the 'supposed' benefits outlined by cities, governments and sporting organisations that 'bid' for major events. Consequently, there are a full range of impacts that need to be considered by the special event manager. These include:

- social and cultural impacts;
- physical and environmental impacts;
- political impacts;
- tourism and economic impacts.

Many sporting organisations, be they national, state or local, which conduct special events bring many financial benefits to communities ranging from accommodation and merchandising purchases to increased sales for food outlets. The extent of these financial benefits will of course be dependent upon the type, duration, importance and spectator appeal of the event.

When considering economic impact statements it is important that you accurately present anticipated results of the event. It is easy to become cynical about the validity of economic impact statements when two different assessments produce vastly different results. Sometimes an independent association will be seen to have greater credibility than if organisers of the event do the analysis themselves. In the latter instance, the potential exists for a conflict of interest.

Case 16.1 Impact of special events

The proliferation of special events worldwide has encompassed many different sports. Surfing is one such sport that, as a result of the growth of events and other factors such as increased corporate sponsorship and the commercialisation of sport in general, now has an acknowledged and highly professional world championship. Formerly the surfing tour was based around a number of loosely connected events staged on an ad hoc basis. This evolved into a more structured series of events conducted largely at metropolitan beaches, close to crowds and at times more suited to spectators than the prevailing surf conditions. Nowadays the Association of Surfing Professionals (ASP), which has governed the sport of professional surfing since 1976, conducts the World Championship Tour (WCT). The tour, which caters for both male and female professional surfers and an increasing number of niche markets, encompasses venues in places as geographically diverse as Sunset Beach (Hawaii), Bell's Beach (Australia), Figueira da Foz (Portugal), Teahupoo (Tahiti), Nijiima Island (Japan), Santa Catarina (Brazil) and Jeffery's Bay (South Africa). Locations are selected for their status as legendary surfing hotspots and competitions are scheduled at appropriate times with generous waiting periods to ensure optimum conditions. Multinational companies such as Billabong, Rip Curl and Quiksilver compete for naming rights sponsorship of these events and prize money has increased markedly from meagre beginnings. In short, the WCT has become an inextricably linked series of special events that brings with it a number of impacts to the host community.

Discussion questions

1 Discuss the scope of the potential positive and negative impacts associated with the conduct of surfing events in such legendary locations.

2 Do you think the various impacts have changed in line with the change in venue from largely metropolitan to the current locations – if so, how have they changed?

3 Given similar numbers of participants and event management staff, will the economic impact of an ASP event in Tahiti be similar to that for an ASP event in Australia (give reasons for your answer).

The strategic planning function

Strategic planning is a must in the creation and implementation of special events. Catherwood and Van Kirk (1994), stated that:

> planning is a process that must continuously occur . . . until the end of the event. It is crucial to have as a foundation for this ongoing planning a vision, a statement, or concept that can be easily articulated and understood.

The strategic planning process involves determining where an organisation is at present, deciding where it should be positioned in the marketplace, and creating strategies to achieve that position. The conduct of special events can help the organisation reach those goals. Once again, Allen et al. (2008: 91) state that event managers need to be aware that strategic plans should be adaptable and not fail due to:

- overplanning and becoming obsessed with detail as opposed to strategic considerations;
- viewing plans as one-off exercises rather than active documents to be regularly consulted; and
- seeing plans as conclusive rather than directional in nature.

The strategic planning process and event organisations

Many sporting organisations at the national, regional and local level will find themselves with the opportunity to bid for the conduct of a special event. This bidding may range from Tokyo's bid for the 2016 Olympic Games to the local sporting organisation bidding for the right to host a Grand Final or regional tournament. One of the important points in special events management is the need to comprehensively plan and understand the lead time required to successfully complete each aspect for the successful bidding of your event. Lead times vary from anywhere between 10 and 15 years for an Olympic Games to 1–2 years for a smaller local event. For example, the Rugby World Cup in 2007 was awarded to France in early 2003.

The Sydney Olympic 2000 bid was well researched and professionally presented, and required oral, written and visual presentations and negotiations. However, the media speculated intensely on Sydney's bid and Catherwood and Van Kirk (1994: 69) point out that 'behind the scenes lobbying is often more effective than a well written proposal or bid'.

The process of strategic planning and bidding for an event such as this involves progressing through a number of sequential and interrelated steps. Generally this involves the following:

- concept or intent to bid for a special event;
- feasibility analysis;
- decision to proceed or cease;
- formation of a bidding body;
- establishment of organisational structures;
- developing a plan;
- leaving a legacy.

Government special event policy and the bidding process

Many government bodies actively participate in the attraction of major events to their state or city. Therefore these bodies need to implement a strategic planning policy that allows them to undertake major events. On the other hand, sporting organisations also need to be aware of the policies that many government organisations have in place for the conduct of events because they will need to meet the terms and conditions of these policies before their events can be staged or funded.

Each government body will have to develop its own strategy and policies for dealing with special events. Depending on the scope of the event being international, national, state or local, the lobbying and bidding processes will vary in intensity. It is therefore necessary to understand who the key public sector organisations are and whether or not they have specific policies, laws or ordinances pertaining to special events. Support from local, state or federal governments can come in various forms and can greatly assist in the successful operation of your event.

Community involvement in the bidding process

Promoting a favourable community image is extremely important for the sport manager, the sporting organisation and in this case the special event manager or promoter. Think about those special events that have drawn some unfavourable coverage in the press which can affect the community's perception of them. For example, drug-taking at various national and international championships and high speed accidents in motor racing. When these special events draw unfavourable press or attempt to defy community opinion (performance-enhancing drug-taking for instance), support for them can drop alarmingly.

Organisers of special sports events, just like individuals, are expected to be a part of the community scene and act responsibly. Fortunately, sporting organisations and indeed many public sector bodies which conduct events are very much the 'good news' section of the community. Predominantly, sporting organisations and the public sector take pride in themselves and take pride in their community. Strong community relations just do not happen. The development of a favourable image in the community is especially important to many of those public sector bodies.

Conceptualising the event

Event managers must understand their event environment. The context in which the event will take place will play a major role in determining the event concept. This will involve identifying the key stakeholders and their objectives. Once this has been ascertained then the event manager can shape and manage the event.

Once you have determined the need for your event or, in other words, you have your vision in place, then you are able to continue in your planning to understand the market. To gain an overview of these stages in understanding the market, you will need to:

1 assemble key players in your special events team;

2 select those management tools and techniques that will allow the team to work towards its vision by monitoring its progress – project management tools such as Gantt charts, work breakdown structures, critical path charts, policy statements etc. (to be covered later);

3 develop a solid infrastructure;

4 determine the role of private promoters;

5 consider the merchandising and sponsorship opportunities;

6 be aware of the power of the media.

Determining the need for your special event

The following key questions are those that you should answer when researching any event:

1 Can the community support the size of event I am planning?

2 What will be the economic impact of hosting the event?

3 Are there other events on at the same time?

4 What cultural issues might affect interest in the event?

5 Who is my target market? What is it about this market/s that will ensure support for my event?

6 Do I have sufficient resources to professionally promote and operate my event?

7 Has a similar event been conducted before? If so, how did it go?

8 Does the event traditionally attract interest?

9 What is the attitude to the event of the various levels of public sector agencies that I will be dealing with?

10 Are the public sector agencies supportive of hosting events in their communities?

11 Are the participants, teams or entertainers that will constitute the event, available, affordable and willing to do so?

12 What special events are currently available that my city or sporting organisation could bid for? What lead time do these events have?

Matching the event to the market

Matching an event to a particular market is not an easy task. In today's competitive marketplace, you need to develop a yardstick that can help you determine whether the special event will be a success in your community. One of the easiest techniques that can be used by you is to continue your research by talking to a similar city where the special event or preparation for the special event has taken place. The Sydney Olympic Bid Committee undertook discussions with the other Australian cities that had bid for the Games and with Atlanta, USA (the successful bidder for the 1996 Games) in order to ascertain the strategic planning they had undertaken in their efforts to obtain the event and, in Atlanta's case, the right to hold the Games.

Project management for events

The conduct of any special event can be regarded as a project. Consequently the use of project management techniques has many advantages. These include the ability to oversee the initiation, planning and implementation of the event as well as monitoring the event and shutdown. Project management can be defined as a process which covers the management of a non-routine configuration of tasks to accomplish a single set of goals within a limited time span. Some common characteristics of project management and most projects are:

- objectives are clearly defined;
- projects have a limited life;
- they tend to deal with the unfamiliar;
- there is a need to manage risk;
- they are team-based;
- there is a need to manage and balance the often competing elements of time, cost and technical performance;
- resources are drawn from disparate sources;
- management structures tend to be non-hierarchical and tend to cut across well-established existing organisation structures;
- all projects exhibit a project life cycle which can be described by four discernible generic phases:
  - project conception or feasibility;
  - planning or design;
  - implementation or execution;
  - termination or evaluation.

Why is project management useful for event management?

Event managers are often required to harness a wide variety of resources to meet finite goals. These endeavours can be as diverse as:

- managing sporting events;
- managing facilities construction;
- managing promotional campaigns;
- developing fitness programmes;
- setting up sporting competitions.

There are also some problems peculiar to the event management field which the project management discipline is ideally suited to handle. For example, event managers often have to manage projects in an environment where there is only a small formal permanent organisation.

This differs from many other business situations where highly structured organisations are in place with well-defined hierarchies. Management positions in these business organisations are clearly defined and accountabilities, responsibilities and authority are spelled out formally. Formal procedures have been developed and work is allocated according to formalised and defined job descriptions. Staff in those more structured formal organisations can be allocated work to complete as part of their paid full-time employment. Because they are permanent full-time employees they can be held accountable for long-term goals.

Contrast this environment with the one that often confronts the event manager. Some key differences the event manager has to contend with are listed below:

- People undertaking work are often operating in a voluntary capacity.
- There are fewer detailed formalised management positions with well-defined accountabilities, responsibilities and authorities.
- There is less continuity in the employment of human resources.
- Finances are usually not as strong and fundraising is often necessary.
- Well-documented procedures and management benchmarks are less likely to be present.
- Because of the voluntary, temporary and less structured style of much employment, there is unlikely to be an extensive inbuilt system of discipline to ensure things get done.
- The pervading atmosphere often tends to be one of informality, and things can be achieved more through cooperation and team spirit than through a coercive, formal hierarchy.

Event management often involves significant contact with organisations and groups external to the 'home' organisation of the sport manager. These organisations can have an important stake in endeavours being managed by the sport manager. These organisations include:

- community groups;
- government;
- commercial sponsors (an increasingly important area);
- fundraising groups;
- health groups;
- volunteer groups.

The stake and interest that such groups have is often not one which can be categorised as a normal business relationship.

The financial management of events

Financial management can be defined as 'decisions that concern the sourcing, planning, monitoring and evaluation of the money resource' (Allen et al., 2008: 199). If an event is to be run for profit then the generating and allocation of money is extremely important. On the other hand, some events (fairs and festivals etc.) may regard profit as a secondary objective. Whatever the focus, all events must have responsible financial management.

In events such as the Olympics a further major limitation is the 'deadline' or timeframe involved. In the case of the Olympics this is set and cannot be changed so financial practices that anticipate the need to complete targets by certain dates are expected. Therefore, every financial decision in the event environment must take into account the variable, time, and the constant, the deadline.

The management of event finance is a process that starts with forecasting and then sets up budgetary implementation and controls. It is not just about observing the budget but also about decision making that concerns such things as the reallocation of resources, finding new sources of income and reducing unexpected costs.

Not all events have been conducted successfully. In some cases events run at a loss due to over-expenditure, insufficient income or mismanagement. The first two relate to cash flow and the importance of managing this. However, mismanagement has more dire consequences. Mismanagement of finance can lead to unforeseen operational risk (for example, safety issues, crowd control) and even legal problems (for example, fraud). So event managers must have a good knowledge of financial management.

Human resource management

The effective management of human resources is imperative to conducting a successful event. All events must be adequately staffed (be they volunteers or paid), by people appropriately trained and motivated to meet objectives. Some of the initial considerations associated with human resource and special event planning include:

- obtaining paid staff to work on a short-term basis;
- meeting deadlines to hire and train staff;
- anticipating attrition of staff due to the high pressure and tight deadlines;
- preparing for reducing staff numbers quickly once the event is over;
- utilisation of volunteers as well as paid staff.

Human resource strategy and objectives

This process can involve a number of activities including:

- **Strategy**. This should support the event's overall mission and objectives. Areas to be considered include strategies for cost containment involved in employing staff; improved quality by good recruitment and training of staff; improved organisational effectiveness through better job design and organisational structures; and enhanced performance through knowledge of legislation (OHS, EEO etc.).
- **Staffing**. This can be regarded as the main strategic decision as it involves the number of staff needed; skills needed; paid and/or volunteers; training needs.
- **Job analysis**. This involves defining job in terms of specific tasks and responsibilities.
- **Job descriptions**. These are the outcomes of the job analysis and can include job title and commitment; salary and incentives; duties and responsibilities, authority etc.
- **Job specification**. This is derived from the job description and seeks to identify the experience, qualifications, skills, abilities, knowledge and personal characteristics needed to perform a given job.
- **Legal obligations**. Event managers need to be mindful of the laws and statutes that have an impact on the employer and employee relationship.

- **Establishing policies and procedures**. These provide a framework in which recruitment, selection, training, professional development, supervision, termination, outplacement, re-employment and evaluation take place. These policies help managers make quick and consistent decisions, give them confidence to resolve problems, and defend their positions and reassure staff that they will be treated fairly.

Motivating staff and volunteers

Motivation commits people to the event, enthuses and energises them, and enables them to achieve goals. Your ability to motivate your staff is a fundamental component in your repertoire of skills. Without this ability, staff will lack the enthusiasm for achieving your organisation's goals and can even show a lack of concern for the success of the event.

Event marketing – steps in the event marketing process

There are a number of distinct steps involved in creating a successful marketing plan. These steps include:

- segmenting the market which can be chosen by measuring characteristics of the segment (for example socioeconomic, status, gender, age);
- positioning the event in the marketplace;
- developing event marketing objectives;
- choosing generic marketing strategies and tactics for events;
- selecting the event's services and the marketing mix – the marketing mix can involve planning (programming and packaging), pricing and place;
- developing a coherent marketing plan.

Event marketing plans

Events have become a multi-billion dollar industry yet it is still quite surprising how few sporting organisations realise the value of, or have any form of marketing plan (except maybe in some ad hoc manner). The two major groups within event management, that is the for-profit (or professional group) and the non-profit (or amateur group), both need to have sport marketing plans. The most successful events have understood this need to implement an event marketing plan in order to satisfy their objectives.

Just as most sport coaches and managers are familiar with game plans, then so should the event marketer be familiar with an event marketing plan. Effectively it is the corporate game plan. The event marketing plan enables sporting to establish objectives, priorities, schedules, budgets, strategies and checkpoints against which to measure sport marketing performance.

A well-developed marketing plan serves to guide your sporting organisation's performance relative to your marketing objectives. In effect, your organisation needs an event marketing plan because, as the old cliché goes – 'if you fail to plan you plan to fail'. In larger organisations, marketing plans will often be the responsibility of the CEO and other key executives (for example, the president or the marketing and finance managers etc.). In these large sporting organisations the use of key organisational members assures top management involvement.

In smaller organisations, the CEO may have the sole responsibility and, if there are limited resources within the sport, then outside consultants may be employed. Regardless of the situation, there is a need to carefully match the consultant with the level of sophistication of the plan. The ability of the organisation to implement the process must also be considered.

Sustainable developments and event tourism planning

Sustainable development has been described by the World Commission on Environment and Development as 'development that meets the needs of the present without compromising the ability of future generations to meet their own needs' (Allen et al., 2008: 388). Events have increasingly been concerned with the challenges posed by sustainable development. Indeed, some events are based around sustainable development, particularly those involving event tourism. The relationship between events and tourism from the viewpoint of 'destinations' is normally aimed at increasing visitation to that destination (be it a town, region, state or country). This can, ultimately, cause some conflict with the environmental issues and sustainable development.

The 'greening' of events

Most governments throughout the world have agreed to a set of principles for sustainable development (by the signing of Agenda 21 at the conclusion of the Earth Summit in 1992). It is not legally binding; however, the principles do carry a strong moral obligation to ensure their full implementation.

This will mean that event managers need to be cognisant of how the conduct of events in signatory countries would be affected by the efforts of their government. Indeed, even at the local level, event organisers would need to liaise with their local government about the areas covered by Agenda 21. These include such things as:

- solid waste management;
- protection of the atmosphere;
- protection of the quality of supply of freshwater resources;
- environmentally sound management of toxic chemicals.

Interestingly, a number of international organisations have accepted many of the sustainable challenges and engaged directly with it. For example, the IOC and FIFA have become green through a number of sustainable development strategies revolving around tree planting, green energy and building design, and sustainable modes of transport.

Increasing consumer awareness

Undoubtedly there is increasing consumer awareness of environmental issues. Many event managers now respond to the market's concern in environmental issues. Many events have even adopted and stated environmental policies and how their event will impact on the environment.

In recent years a number of events, particularly hallmark and mega events, have attracted the attention of environmental groups. It was mentioned above that the IOC is facing the challenges of sustainable development but there are now 'environmental groups' (Greenpeace, WWF) that are becoming increasingly involved in assessing the impact of any event. These environmental groups have also developed policies that focus attention on event managers and environmental issues.

Event tourism

Just like other aspects of event management the relationship between events and tourism needs a coordinated strategic approach to a destination's overall tourism efforts. The strategic approach can include the:

- conduct of a detailed situational analysis;
- creation of event tourism goals;
- establishment of an organisational structure through which event tourism goals can be progressed;
- development, implementation and evaluation of an event tourism strategy.

The development of destination-based event tourism strategies has been exemplified by government involvement. They have not only created specialist bodies charged with event tourism development but can provide significant funding as well. For example, once the Sydney 2000 bid was won, the state government passed legislation creating organising bodies, ensuring Games security and 'fast-tracking' Olympic-related developments. In smaller cities and towns event tourism strategies may rest with local government, tourism associations or chambers of commerce.

A number of factors have been integral to the increase in event tourism. Government involvement, the establishment of Tourism Councils and the association of major events with tourism have all contributed. The different 'changes' in government 'regimes', particularly those in Eastern Europe, have opened borders.

Staging the event

Staging originated from the development and showing of plays. However, most events can benefit from the techniques used in 'staging'. Staging elements involve:

1. Theming the event and design. This can engender a great experience for the consumer that can be built with the theme of the event and the associated advertising and promotion.
2. Programming. The event manager must create a plan that takes the consumer through a structured progression of various experiences.
3. Choice of venue. Choice is essential to determining many aspects of staging. What resources are available at the venue? The national sporting organisations of many sports have encouraged cities to bid for the national titles and select those bidding cities based upon, inter alia, the venues available.
4. Audience and guests. Consideration must be given to the comfort of the audience and the guests and involves entrances and exits, transport and internal facilities.

5 Stage. This can vary greatly from the smallest park to the largest arena, from the back of a truck to a barge in the harbour, but invariably should be associated with the theme of the event.

6 Power, lights and sound can enhance the experience for the consumer.

7 Audiovisual and special effects. A themed special effect can heighten awareness for the viewer and increase their anticipation (for example, the opening ceremony at the Olympic Games).

8 Decorations and props. This can allow both participants and consumers to feel a part of the event. This is of particular value in the conduct of festivals and cultural activities.

9 Catering is a major element and can also be incorporated into the theme of the event.

10 Performers. The performers are usually the stars of the show and may be sportspeople or entertainers etc.

11 Crew. We looked at human resource management previously; however, many events can be staffed with professional crews. Staging of major events will need skilled engineers, 'roadies', security and even ushers.

12 Hospitality is often offered to sponsors and invited guests. The hospitality experience is important to the corporate success of the event and subsequent business relationships.

13 Production schedule. This schedule may include technical and dress rehearsals and production meetings.

14 Recording the event.

15 Contingencies.

 ## Event logistics

Logistics assists the event manager to identify elements of the event's operations. Movement of materials and people is essential to all special event operations. Consider how any large event is required to 'clear' a stadium of over 100,000 people in the shortest time possible at its conclusion.

Logistics concerns the whole operation, not just during the event, that is, it includes event set-up and shutdown. It can also take place over a comparatively short time and in many instances as a 'one-off' event for the city (for example the Olympic Games). Just as there are logistics companies within the business sector there are now event managers who understand the importance of logistics and adapt its practices to their event.

Also when setting up basic operations consideration needs to be given by event managers to the negotiations that will need to take place with the public and private sector bodies that control venues, security factors, insurance factors, ticket sales, communications and the use of volunteers.

The elements of event logistics can be organised into a 'logistics system' that take into consideration the supply of:

● customers through considering marketing, ticketing queuing and transport;
● product through transport, accommodation, artists, needs;
● facilities through security, power, water, contractors.

These elements lead to the logistical planning during the event of the flow of the audience, artists and equipment around the site; the communication methods to be used; the amenities needed for both participants and audience; provision of consumables; VIP and media arrangements; and emergency procedures. Following the event's conclusion logistics becomes concerned with the event shutdown (removal of equipment etc., cleaning and contract acquittal).

Techniques of logistics management

The tools used in project management can be successfully adapted to event logistics. These tools are dealt with in detail in the project management topic earlier in this chapter; however, they are introduced to you here as well because the dynamic nature of events and the way the functional areas are so closely linked means that a small change in one area can result in crucial changes throughout the event. The most common project management tools helping logistics include:

- scheduling – the use of bar charts, time charts, GANTT charts;
- network analysis – use of critical paths;
- site and venue maps.

Event evaluation and research

This is the process of critically observing, measuring and monitoring the implementation of the event. This is undertaken so you can assess outcomes accurately. Evaluation will help you create an event profile that will outline the basic features and important statistics of the event. It also provides feedback to event stakeholders, and can act as a tool for analysis and improvement of future events.

But when should evaluation take place? Ideally, evaluation should occur throughout the event management cycle. There are three key periods when it is useful to undertake evaluation:

- Pre-event evaluation. Also known as feasibility studies, which take place before the event to see if it is viable to stage the event (for more detail see evaluating the event concept section).
- Monitoring the event. This takes place during the implementation of the event to ensure that it is on track and to take remedial action if required (for more detail here see the project management section).
- Post-event evaluation. This focuses on the measurement of the event outcomes and on ways in which the event can be improved.

Post-event evaluation is often calculated by the event's impact (negative or positive; short term or long term) on the stakeholders and the community. Here many governments show particular interest as they have funded events in the past and view the bigger picture of the impact the event had on the city, state or nation. Much time is spent on evaluating economic impacts; however, event managers must not lose sight of the social and environmental impacts that events have on their communities.

For economic impacts traditional financial indicators are used (for example, net income as a ratio over expenditure). For social impacts indicators such as percentage of locals who attend or volunteer, local business involvement and development of new facilities are utilised. For environment impacts indicators include energy consumed, water consumed and waste management.

Post-event evaluation includes:

- measurement of event outcomes;
- creation of a demographic profile of the event audience;
- identification of how the event can be improved;
- enhancement of event reputation;
- evaluation of event management processes.

The event evaluation process

The event evaluation process has five major stages:

1 Planning and collection of event data required. There is a need to define the purposes of evaluation and therefore what data will be collected. This will include the collection of both qualitative and quantitative data. The purpose of this planning is also to let the host organisation know what the event achieved; to let the sponsor know if their level of awareness was raised; to let funding bodies know of the financial outcomes; to let councils and government departments know of any impact the event may have; and to let tourism bodies know the influx of tourists to the destination.

2 Data collection. Each of the areas listed above will require consideration on how to collect the data. This can be obtained through event documentation, media monitoring, event observation, de-brief meetings, focus groups, surveys and secondary data.

3 Data analysis. Much of the data gathered from the sources above will need to be analysed. Much of it may well be done manually depending upon the size of your event. However, computer analysis can be undertaken with much of the quantitative data.

4 Reporting. Once all data has been collected and analysed comes the task of writing and preparing reports. Consideration needs to be given here on who will receive the reports and the function of the report.

5 Dissemination. This can take place through face-to-face meetings with key stakeholders, general meetings, the media etc.

Legal, risk and Occupational Health and Safety (OHS) management

Liability of organisations, officials, organisers and occupiers

Participants, spectators and even strangers who are injured because of defects of the venue/premise/surface on which the game is played can sue the occupier (and in some instances the organiser) of those venues. When the occupier has received a fee for the use of the venue, the occupier is under a higher duty of care to ensure the safety of the facilities. For those of you who control venues, the question of responsibility revolves around the question of control of the particular property and the capacity of the person who was injured.

Most of the cases concerning injuries result from spectators taking action against the organiser/occupier; a participant who is injured because of the defective condition of the venue can sue the organiser or occupier, as can a stranger, that is someone outside the venue, who is injured by some part of the activity.

The position of the spectator as the potential defendant in legal proceedings cannot be overlooked. Someone who purchases a ticket is expected to behave in a reasonable manner. However, not all fans do behave in a reasonable manner. Therefore, crowd control becomes important to the sport administrator at all levels, particularly at the major sporting events.

Contracts

Event managers will enter into numerous contracts in the conduct of the event. You only need to think of the participants, officials, caterers, consumers and so on. Contracts must abide by contract law.

Duty of care and insurance

A fundamental legal principle is taking all reasonable care to avoid acts or omissions that could injure a 'neighbour'. This is an area of law covered by torts. It is necessary for the event manager to ensure all actions are taken that will prevent any foreseeable risk or injury to the people who are directly affected by, or involved in, the event. This would include staff, volunteers, performers, the audience (spectators) and even the public in surrounding areas. One aspect of the duty of care principle is to ensure that the correct insurance is in place.

Risk management

Risk and safety management is essentially the process of controlling potential risks and minimising potential losses or damage which may occur at your event. Events and the facilities in which they are conducted have a high exposure to potential risk issues and as such it is difficult to operate any event or facility in a risk-free environment. Therefore, risk management and safety issues must always remain a top priority for any event and/or facility manager.

Future trends indicate that people who utilise a facility will become increasingly aware of their legal rights. They will be more likely to instigate legal action against facility owners and managers if those owners and managers fail to provide patrons with a safe environment.

Event organisers and facility managers normally charge patrons for attending functions at their events and facilities. There is an expectation (from the clients and the courts) that when an admission price is charged or a venue is hired, the facilities will be safe for the conduct of the event or activity. It is your responsibility as a facility manager to provide such an environment.

Planning for effective risk management

A facility's legal liability for personal injury claims is usually caused by the facility's failure to meet minimum standards of safety, suitability or sanitation. Consequently management's interest in risk management programmes must ensure that these minimum standards are met. Effective risk management requires an awareness that risk identification is only one process of a comprehensive risk management programme.

The key points to note here are:

- All employees must undertake the role of 'risk manager'. The manager alone cannot undertake all these tasks. Operational employees (those liaising directly with public) are very often the best employees to identify potential risks.

- Communication is crucial. Effective managers must communicate to their staff their commitment to risk management. The staff then communicates this to the patrons. If the commitment is not evident from the manager, then the employees may not communicate to the patrons.

- The specific aspects of the risk identification process are the areas of heavy use, areas of specialised use and areas of expectation.

Facility staff can also become too familiar with the venue and assume activities, services or operating procedures are safe. Risk assessment is an ongoing process and all staff must remain aware of this process. It is recommended that a comprehensive staff training programme be put in place along with arranging regular external audits and peer reviews.

By their very nature, facilities are high-risk areas. The high risks can be due to the wide array of activities that can be conducted (particularly aquatic activities), the difficulty associated with full-time supervision of areas within the facility (changing rooms etc.) and the depreciation of the equipment used in the facility.

If these risks are not managed properly then losses (not only in terms of dollars, but also in time and human suffering) can be expensive. So how does a facility manager do all that is possible to minimise the risk of accidents in the facility?

Risk management checklists

At all events and in all facilities (be they indoor, outdoor or aquatic) there is a constant need to identify risks, deal with them and then evaluate whether the strategies are effectively dealing with the risk.

It should be noted that any system or checklist which is developed is only as effective as its implementation. There is no point in having a comprehensive and complicated system in place if you or your employees do not conscientiously implement it. It is wise to include your employees in the development of a risk management programme. They will have ownership of the programme and therefore will be more likely to see that it is implemented and works.

The principle of duty of care

A duty of care depends upon establishing whether a relationship exists between the facility and the patrons (the two parties involved). The question most asked to determine this relationship is whether the relationship between the parties was such that a facility staff member should have contemplated that his or her act would lead to harming the patron.

The law relating to duty of care was established in a famous negligence case, *Donoghue v Stevenson*. This case involved injury suffered by a woman who drank a bottle of soft drink which contained a decomposed snail. Lord Atkin, who presided over the case, defined the relationship necessary to constitute a duty of care as involving 'persons so directly affected by my act that I ought reasonably to have them in contemplation as being so affected when I am directing my mind to the acts or omissions which are called into question' (*Donoghue v Stevenson* [1932] AC 562).

This test depended upon the reasonable foreseeability of the result. Following this case it has been held in many Australian courts that sportspersons owe each other a duty of care. Similarly, organisers of a sporting event or managers of a sporting facility owe the participants and spectators a duty of care.

It is important to understand duty of care and standard of care. The duty of care is the duty based on the relationship between the occupier (in your case it could well be the facility manager) and the person who enters upon the occupier's land or premises. Therefore one would expect that a duty of care exists between the facility manager (the staff) and the patrons.

The test for the standard of care is how a reasonable person in a particular situation would have acted. In the case of an accident in a facility, the question may be asked: How would similar facility managers have acted given the same situation?

Facility design and management issues

What are the issues and trends in planning a facility?

The number of sporting facilities throughout the world has increased significantly, as has the cost of facilities, so the expected financial viability of facilities is becoming more important. It is therefore essential that those sporting facilities that are planned and designed are done so in a cost-effective manner and are responsive to the changing needs of the community.

In the past many facilities have been single purpose, with little thought being given to multiple usage of the facility, social requirements or even effective management. The community is finding it more and more difficult to support these types of single-purpose facilities. A number of current issues need consideration in the planning stages of sport facility development.

A brief history of sport facilities

Sports facilities, such as the Olympic Stadium in Sydney, the 'new' Wembley or indeed any major stadia around the globe are not new concepts or innovations in the development of sports facilities. In fact, as long as 2,500 years ago, sport facilities had been developed and utilised for the health and well-being of the people. Although the primary purpose at that time may have been to maintain military readiness and entertainment for nobility, these facilities led the way to today's sports complexes.

Modern sports structures

After the downfall of Rome, building monumental sporting structures was halted. In fact, the only structures that were developed were fortress-type buildings, designed to protect the population from harm. There was, however, the construction of bullfighting arenas in Spain and Mexico. With the advent of mass participation and spectator sports in the nineteenth and twentieth centuries, such as football, baseball (USA), cricket etc., more modern facilities were developed. These initial structures could be called temporary as they involved rudimentary seating adjacent to the playing field.

As these sports grew in importance and magnitude, the facilities were correspondingly improved. By the turn of the twentieth century, many major facilities had been constructed, for example Wembley Stadium (UK), Yankee Stadium (USA), Los Angeles Colosseum (USA) and one of the world's largest stadiums in Rio de Janerio (Brazil).

Another reason for the development of major facilities was the reintroduction of the modern Olympic Games in Athens in 1896. Every four years (with the exception of the world war years) modern sports stadia and associated structures were developed to host the major events.

The process of planning and designing facilities

As discussed so far, the need for and the design of facilities is not new. The quality of the management of these facilities can often determine their effectiveness and viability. It has been recognised that facility management plans must be prepared along with the design plans, because once the facility has been erected many management options may be lost. However, the success of any facility is often aligned to its design, not just its management. It is important therefore to have a knowledge of the planning and design process for sporting facilities.

The preparation of planning documents

If any facility is to operate successfully in the medium to long term the design must meet clearly defined needs by developing a planning document. The community or sporting group involved in the development of the facility must ask itself a number of very important and specific questions before commencing this planning document.

Extensive market research is required very early in the planning process to enable all stakeholders to have a clear, concise and consistent understanding of why the facility is being developed and what its role will be. Too often in the past, major facilities have been constructed because the aim was to host a major sporting event, for example the Commonwealth Games or an Olympic Games. Yet events like those games only lasted for two weeks.

In today's economic climate, however, all facilities should now be constructed as multi-purpose and flexible venues. Obviously the facilities must be able to host the major events, but as these events will probably occur only once at the venue, the facilities must also be able to meet the ongoing needs of the community and sporting associations.

Even when designing smaller community facilities the same principles apply. Venues must be multi-purpose and flexible, and extensive market research is vitally important. One valuable research tool is consultation with the community.

The consultation process

The consultation process in designing a community sporting/recreation facility would encompass many community groups (stakeholders). These may include politicians, local businesspeople, sporting/recreation associations, school groups/educational bodies, target markets and the general public.

The consultation process must be structured, planned and orderly, allowing input from all the stakeholders to be considered. To assist in ongoing operations it is important to build up ownership of the facility amongst the stakeholders. Involving these individuals and groups in the original design of the facility is a great start. The stakeholders will be able to help you develop the objectives for the facility.

Community consultation can be a slow process, but is essential for the successful design of a facility. Although the technical tools used to determine the structure and makeup of the facility will vary, the need to consult will not.

It cannot be stressed enough that there is the need to set clear objectives for the facility to allow for its long-term viability, both financially and in its usage by community groups. In your endeavours to establish the facility it is essential that you:

- are clear what the project involves and what you are setting out to achieve – otherwise an inappropriate facility design will be the result;
- select appropriate and reputable companies to work with, both in the planning and construction phases – these companies may not necessarily be the cheapest;
- are aware that money saved in the short term can lead to a false economy or saving in the medium to longer term due to operational constraints and problems that may arise from any shortcuts.

It is important to consult as wide a range of stakeholders as possible because facilities are expensive to construct. This consultation process becomes an essential part of the feasibility study. The feasibility study should determine if, in fact, the construction of the facility is justified; whether the facility will be financially viable (remembering you may wish to run at a loss or subsidise the facility); if the capital cost can be raised and interest payments met; who will use the centre and what type of activities will occur.

Once the decision has been made to continue, the project planning team will need to develop a project brief.

Project briefs

The project brief is an instruction to the design team of what the project planning team expects from the facility. This document can also be used as a checklist of issues and concerns for the design team to discuss with the planning team. Essentially the project brief contains the criteria on which the preliminary design, final design, finished building and operational procedures will be evaluated.

The physical design of the facility

In the physical design of the facility, the various components within the facility need to be considered. These components include the specific spaces that are utilised throughout the facility.

Building the facility

The three control areas of cost, energy and quality are also applicable to the building of any type of facility.

Cost is critical to any facility, as with any project, budgets must be set and followed. The design will be greatly affected by the funds available for the project.

You have undertaken your feasibility study, appointed your planning, design and management teams and developed schematic (and in some instances) detailed drawings. The major question that now needs to be answered in more detail is how much will the facility cost? The answer depends, of course, upon the type of facility that is established. The size and type of the facility, along with the choice of the materials, all influence the capital cost of the facility. Exact costs cannot be determined at this stage; however, relative costs of different components in the facility and the cost of providing different standards for each component can be determined. This analysis of costs can help you decide on the quality of the facility that will be built.

Energy control is an important long-term consideration. Through careful planning and research, ongoing maintenance, heating, lighting, cleaning and material costs can be reduced.

Quality design relates to customer service so understanding the needs and wants of your market will assist you in this area. Safety considerations must also be noted because errors or oversights in this area could lead to expensive litigation or modifications in the long term.

Facility modification

Not all communities can afford or have the need to construct new facilities. Many facilities are suitable for refurbishment. One of the more recent facility design issues being witnessed is that of facility modification, where existing facilities are altered to meet current needs. This is particularly noticeable within aquatic facilities. During the 1950s and 1960s swimming pools worldwide were constructed as oblong boxes designed for competitive swimming; now the pool consumer demands a more leisure/recreational experience.

Joint use of facilities

Constructing new facilities adjacent to existing similar facilities and the joint use of community facilities has also proven successful in recent times. The obvious advantages of this approach include:

- utilising existing facilities, i.e. parking areas, changing rooms etc.;
- not having target markets with different leisure needs in conflict with each other – for example, at an aquatic centre, children would use the water slides, allowing aquarobic classes or older groups to use the 25-metre pool;
- more efficient use of facilities;
- more extensive range of equipment.

Management plans and options

One reason many facilities have difficulty in fulfilling their potential is that they have inadequate or inexperienced management. In relation to new facilities, the development of suitable management plans commences long before the decision is made to construct the facility, while in relation to existing facilities, the implementation of suitable management plans and management options are also vital to their successful operation.

Poor-quality management can lessen the facility's chance of meeting its own objectives or the objectives set by the managing authority. In many instances poor management will lead to the facility being under-utilised by the community. It won't:

- be cost effective as returns from participants will not meet target income;
- meet the needs of the community;
- be adequately staffed.

Just as in the formulation of any business enterprise, it is evident that good management begins with a well-developed and well-written management plan. In the case of new facilities this plan is written in the early stages of development along with the physical planning of the facility.

Management options

During the development of a management plan, the management team will look at the various facility management options available to them. These will include leasing, contract management, a management committee or self-management.

Leasing is a traditional management system that has been used particularly by local government authorities. In most cases leasing only covers the operational aspects of providing the facility.

- Leasing is used extensively by local government for the management of swimming pools.
- Seasonal staff can be employed outside the constraints of local government industrial awards.
- Lessees of facilities may not be up to date with the latest industry trends.
- With leasing, the facility owner is not burdened with day-to-day management issues.

In more recent times, *contract management* has been undertaken by organisations (commercial and community) that specialise in facility management.

- The contractor can introduce management systems and economies of scale through their infrastructure and network of services.
- Contract management has a greater capacity for networking and staff development compared to leasing.
- Questions could be raised in relation to the loyalty of the contractor. Do their main loyalties lie with themselves or the facility owner?
- The information supplied about facility operations may not always meet the needs of council officers responsible for maintaining the contract.
- With contract management the facility owner is not burdened with day-to-day management issues.

A management system that may be adopted by local government and community groups is a *management committee* which oversees the management of the facility and whose members are usually drawn from elected members and appointments.

- The committee can be very efficient or very inefficient, depending on the management skills of the committee.
- If local residents are on the committee, they can generate 'ownership' of the facility in the community.
- A committee of management might have political or personal bias which influences their decision making.

A *self-management* system allows the facility to manage its own affairs once the appropriate staff are recruited.

- The facility must have staff with appropriate management skills and there should be on-going training and development.
- Once staff are managing the facility it is important not to have political and/or bureaucratic interference in the day-to-day operations.

You should be aware that no one management option is necessarily the best. Your aims, objectives and expectations relating to your venue will dictate the most effective management option for you.

Case 16.2 Management rights

You have been appointed the sport, recreation and tourism planner for the Llareggub City Council. The City Council is redeveloping its major sports and aquatic centre. It has asked you to present a brief to members on the proposed development of the facility.

Discussion questions

Explain to the members:

4 some of the recent trends and issues in facility planning and design;

5 the issues that need to be considered in relation to the (i) functional, (ii) technical and (iii) aesthetic components of the facility;

6 the advantages and disadvantages of four management options; and

7 identify the services that you would contract out in the centre. Give your reasons.

Financial and asset management

The financial viability of any facility relates back to design and management issues. If adequate market analysis was undertaken in the design stage of the facility there is every possibility that the facility should meet its financial objectives. If correct analysis was not undertaken then the facility might be struggling financially. Once established, the facility must be managed efficiently and effectively to allow its financial objectives to be met.

Efficient management of a facility implies that management is accomplished with an economy of resources for maximum results. For example, the recreation and sporting programmes are *developed within the facility* with the least possible expense, so that every dollar spent promoting the programmes reaches the largest possible target market and the programmes are offered at a price to maximise participation by the community.

Effective management of a facility implies that the right actions are put in place that will further the objectives of the facility. For example, the sport and recreation programmes offered would be exactly what the community wanted, at a price they could pay, and employees would give the type of service that would make participants want to return.

Facility managers strive for a combination of effective and efficient management. A key area in efficiency and effectiveness relates to the financial management of the facility. Financial management relates to establishing financial objectives, determining pricing strategies and maintaining financial records.

Financial objectives

One of the first steps in financial management is the development of clear objectives, just as it is in the development of a management plan. These objectives will help the facility manager determine if the facility is achieving, or moving towards, financial success. Due to their specific nature, financial objectives should be measurable. Two of the major objectives at the heart of financial management relate to liquidity and profitability.

Liquidity is the ability to generate enough cash to pay the bills. Obviously, the objective here is to have more revenue than expenses, but this may be difficult for a new facility, or a community facility which is reliant upon subsidies from government or other sources.

Short-term liquidity may be the first part of a facility's objective; however, long-term profitability must be achieved in order for the facility to succeed, particularly in the case of commercially owned and operated facilities. Non-profit facilities (usually government owned and managed) may not have profit as an objective, but may strive for a break-even scenario or even a small loss.

Pricing

The financial objectives of the facility will assist when determining the pricing structure under which the facility will operate. Arriving at an appropriate pricing structure is never easy, but is a core responsibility of any facility manager. The purpose of pricing seems to be a key issue. The facility manager must be aware of all the reasons for introducing a price structure into the facility. The pricing strategy must be consistent with the facility's objectives.

Price discounting

Discounting can also play an important part of your facility's pricing policy unless, of course, you have your desired level of usage at all times, which is most unlikely. Discounting provides a means whereby the facility can access unrealised revenue from those target markets that may be incapable or unwilling to pay the full fee for using the facility or attending one of the programmes offered. Three methods of discounting have been experimented with successfully. These methods include yield management, introducing conditions on the service and price bundling or packaging.

Yield management is offering the same service to different target markets at different prices. As a service industry, the facility's service and/or products cannot be 'stored' and used at a later date. For example, once an instructor has completed an aerobic class the product is gone forever. This is the same principle used by airlines where if a plane flies with empty seats the price of that seat can never again be recovered. The aim is to segment consumers and charge different rates dependent on their needs and behaviours.

This price approach must be carefully managed as it can lead to feelings of discrimination if one market is paying more than another for the same service. This in turn can lead to a product or service being devalued in the eyes of the consumer.

Financial records and planning

The keeping of accurate financial records is imperative to allow informed management decisions to be made. Poor recording leads to poor decision making. Facility managers must understand why financial record keeping is important as well as knowing what records to keep and having an understanding of the accounting process.

Some of the specific reasons for keeping records include:

- to meet requirements for government reports, tax returns and licences;
- to determine the current status of the business;
- to measure profitability and performance;
- as data upon which to base forecasts of future performance;
- as evidence in lawsuits;
- as information to present to creditors when seeking a loan;
- to inform potential investors or buyers;
- to inform partners, stockholders, board members or governing bodies;
- to evaluate the results of the responsibilities that have been delegated to others and to monitor employee performance;
- to monitor facilities and equipment for preventive maintenance.

The types of records that should be kept include income, expense, tax record, payroll records, mortgage and debt records, regular financial statements, accounting records, personnel records, facility and equipment records, legal records and administrative records.

The accounting process and financial management mechanisms can assist in determining the financial viability of facilities. Efficient financial management will also determine the asset type of management plan that will be developed by the facility manager.

Asset management

Historically, it would seem many facility owners did not identify asset management as a priority or, in fact, really understand what asset management entailed. Many facility managers believed that asset maintenance was purely preventative maintenance, but it is more than that. Preventative maintenance is but one component of an asset management programme.

Due to the large capital costs required to fund the construction of facilities and the funds needed for ongoing maintenance, effectively managing the assets under your control is imperative. Many facility managers are limited by the funds available for asset management. Therefore the development of an asset management programme will allow facilities to be managed more efficiently and more effectively.

Staffing and customer services

The great majority of facilities will involve more than one employee. Therefore the facility manager will need to devote some time to recruiting, orientating, training and supervising employees. Staff members are a special kind of resource within the facility, because the importance of a professionally committed staff is essential in all service industries. The staff members will be a major component in the success, or otherwise, of all facilities and events.

The success of most sport and recreation facilities is dependent upon the interaction of its personnel with the public and the relationship of employers and employees with each other. In many instances customers of the facility will judge its effectiveness on the friendliness, alertness and performance of the staff. It is therefore imperative that a facility manager fully understands staffing issues.

Staffing culture

Having the 'right' staff for the 'right job' is essential to the successful operation of any event or facility. Your facilities may be immaculate but if your staff do not have the skills or personality to meet and exceed customers' expectations then you will not succeed.

Three specific staffing issues need to be addressed:

1 organisational culture within the facility;
2 the importance of training and developing human resources;
3 job satisfaction for service personnel.

Organisational culture within the facility

According to Robbins and Barnwell (1994) there are ten characteristics that, when mixed and matched, tap the essence of an organisation's culture. These characteristics are closely intertwined with an organisation's design. There is obviously a need for facility managers to be conscious of the ten characteristics that contribute towards an organisation's culture. These characteristics define the culture of the organisation, which can be likened to an organisation's personality.

Individual initiatives The degree of responsibility, freedom and independence that individuals have.

377

Risk tolerance The degree to which employees are encouraged to be aggressive, innovative and risk taking.

Direction The degree to which the organisation creates clear objectives and performance expectations.

Integration The degree to which units within the organisation are encouraged to operate in a co-ordinated manner.

Management contact The degree to which managers provide clear communication, assistance and support to their subordinates.

Control The degree of rules and regulations and the amount of direct supervision that is used to oversee and control employee behaviour.

Identity The degree to which members identify to the organisation as a whole rather than their particular work group or field of professional expertise.

Reward system The degree to which reward allocations (i.e. salary increases, promotions) are based on employee performance criteria.

Conflict tolerance The degree to which employees are encouraged to air conflicts and criticisms openly.

Communication patterns The degree to which organisational communications are restricted to the formal line hierarchy of command.

Quality customer service

Customer service was the buzz phrase of the late 1980s and early 1990s and has continued on into the 2010s. The need to consistently deliver a high level of service to customers is well known. Within event and facility management, the care and service that customers receive will determine the success of the operation.

There are a number of reasons why the need to constantly deliver superior customer service is vital in the day-to-day running of your facility or during your event. These reasons are increased competition, better educated, more demanding customers and word-of-mouth advertising by satisfied customers.

Increased competition not only means that you are competing with a number of other facilities or a number of other events being hosted in your area. It also means that you are competing with many other suppliers for the consumers' leisure/recreation dollar. Your competition may be the local cinema, the tourist and travel agent or any provider of a leisure and recreation experience. Customers may well be looking for substitute products or services other than what you may be providing. This is an important point to remember in order to avoid a marketing myopia approach to customer service. When undertaking a competitor analysis, ensure that you do adopt a broad classification of competition.

Generally, customers of today are far better educated than the customers of 20 years ago. This increased level of education, along with greater competition, has led to higher customer expectations. Consequently, customers are far more demanding than ever before.

Word-of-mouth advertising by satisfied customers is the most effective and cheapest form of advertising. Quality customer service can mean more customers which subsequently leads to increased revenue.

Customer service

For facility managers, emerging developments in customer service have shown that:

- in traditional management texts little reference was historically made to customers, and even less to customer service;
- the cost of acquiring new customers can be five times greater than the cost of retaining existing ones;
- it is important to have the right systems in place to allow your operational staff to meet the needs of the customer;
- inadequate systems, rather than employee mistakes, are often the basis of poor customer service;
- internal customers can be important if operating within a large bureaucracy – offering quality service to these customers can have many benefits in both the short and longer term;
- service still has connections with the words 'servant' and 'servility' – in many instances Australians, for example, still battle with this concept;
- quality is an essential component of all aspects of your event or facility, that is, it is not only restricted to customer service;
- good customer service may be non-personal but it is important to know the level of personal service desired by the customer.

Programming within the facility

There are very few facilities where there are not peaks and troughs in usage patterns. Consequently, to maximise the use of facilities, managers should develop skills in the delivery of recreation programmes within the facility. Because most facilities experience peaks and troughs in their usage patterns, programmes aim to increase usage during those troughs and maximise the financial return during peak times.

Programmes are vital to the success of any community facility. Needs and wants of specific target markets are met, resulting in increased usage of the facility and a positive financial result. Meeting these needs may require a proactive rather than reactive approach. This proactive approach means creating a service or programme that can be offered to the target group to satisfy its needs. Being proactive also means being entrepreneurial. The days are gone when facility managers can sit back and wait to rent their facility.

Scheduling

One of the main reasons for having scheduling skills is that all facilities are built to service the needs of many different clubs, associations, individuals and special interest groups and all these needs must be met. For example, a typical community centre may be servicing the needs of many groups, including sporting groups, students, library users, the general public and staff members – all of whom have different needs and expectations.

Most facilities cater for more than one usage or tenant and as the majority of facilities are government funded or subsidised by the ratepayers, scheduling within multi-functional facilities is necessary. In this regard you should ensure that you have:

- Clear *aims and objectives* for the operations of your facility. For example, one of your facility's aims is to host all State or national indoor sporting titles held within your state. If this is the case then the scheduling of these events takes priority over normal fixture matches.

- *Open communication channels* with your hiring groups and other key stakeholders. Encourage two-way communication to take place.

- *Business and development plans* to guide operations, thus allowing efficient scheduling to take place.

These are the minimum requirements for any facility manager who deals with a variety of different groups and associations. These groups and associations are competing for access to the facility. If you do not have clear aims and objectives as part of your business plan, deciding which groups get priority for bookings will be an inconsistent process and will leave you exposed to claims of favouritism or bias.

Case 16.3 Swimming conundrum

You have been appointed the facility manager of a recently redeveloped aquatic centre. The facility comprises both a 50-metre pool and a 25-metre pool and will operate between 5.00am and 9.00pm, seven days a week. The previous facility manager retired six weeks ago and he related that the old pools were always overcrowded at peak times (especially between 6.00am and 8.00am and 5.00pm and 7.00pm, Monday to Saturday. Due to the overcrowding three swimming organisations (the Old Salts – a Masters swimming organisation of 130 people, the Aquanuts – an aquarobics group of 50 and the local triathlon club of 20 people) became disenchanted and may no longer use the redeveloped facility. You want to attract these important groups back to the proposed facility and have decided to formulate a usage policy and a schedule designed to incorporate programmes for all existing, past and potential user groups. Such groups are as follows:

Learn to swim (including babies, children and adults);	Masters swimming;
Elite squad swimmers;	Aquarobics; and
Triathletes;	General swimming.

Discussion questions

8 Explain when and why you would schedule each activity at certain times during the week.

9 Explain how you would attract the three disenchanted groups back to the facility.

 ## Conclusion

The first part of this chapter discussed some of the basic aspects of event management whilst the latter part discussed similar concepts within the realm of facility management. It is hoped that the chapter provided students with a broad appreciation of both areas and facilitated this through relevant case studies.

Discussion questions

10 Discuss whether the benefits of staging mega events such as the Olympics have been overstated.

11 Discuss whether the large amounts of money invested in high-profile sporting events would better serve the community in other ways.

12 Reflect upon the events that you have recently conducted or attended. Have those events considered all possible revenue generation and cost reduction methods? What could they have done to improve their bottom-line financial profit or reduce their loss?

13 Utilising your own working environment or a facility with which you are familiar, use Robbins and Barnwell's characteristics and evaluate that organisation's or facility's culture.

Keywords

GANTT chart; SMART objectives; special event; SWOT analysis.

Guided reading

Emery (2002) presents the local organising committee perspective on bidding to host a major sports event.

Also recommended is *Perspective. The International Journal of Public Sector Management*, (2002) 15 (4), 316–35.

The Birkbeck Sport Business Centre Research Paper Series provides excellent resources generally, in particular Waters (2008) provides interesting background to the bidding process.

Recommended websites

Association of Surfing Professionals (ASP): www.aspworldtour.com
Fédération Internationale de Football Association (FIFA): www.fifa.com/
International Olympic Committee (IOC): www.olympic.org/
Facility Management Association of Australia (FMA): www.fma.com.au/cms/index.php

References

Allen, J., O'Toole, W., McDonnell, I. and Harris, R. (2008) *Festival and Special Event Management*, 4th edn, Sydney: John Wiley and Sons.

Catherwood, D.W. and van Kirk, R.L. (1994) *The Complete Guide to Special Event Management*, New York: John Wiley.

Emery, P. (2002) 'Bidding to host a major sports event: the local organizing committee perspective', *The International Journal of Public Sector Management*, 15 (4), 316–35.

Robbins, S. and Barnwell, N. (1994) *Organisation Theory in Australia*, Sydney: Prentice Hall.

Waters, G. (2008) 'Bidding for major sporting events; key issues and challenges faced by sports governing bodies in the UK', Birkbeck Sport Business Centre Research Paper, 1 (1), www.sportbusinesscentre.com/images/BFMSE.pdf

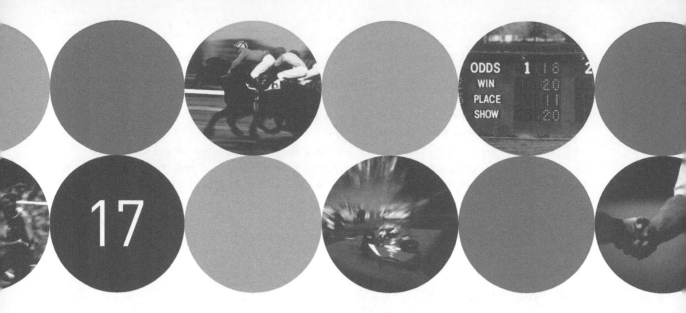

Sport sponsorship and endorsement

Des Thwaites, Leeds University Business School
Yue Meng-Lewis, Bournemouth University

Learning outcomes

Upon completion of this chapter, the reader should be able to:

- define the terms sport sponsorship and endorsement and appreciate the nature of these activities;
- explain the importance of sport sponsorship and endorsement;
- identify the wide range of corporate and brand objectives that can be achieved through sponsorship and endorsement;
- appreciate the major stages in the development of an effective sport sponsorship or endorsement programme;
- identify important management issues in relation to sponsorship and endorsement activities.

Overview

The chapter begins with a definition and explanation of the terms sponsorship and endorsement and relates these to the sporting context. Distinctions between advertising and sponsorship are drawn at this point. The importance of sponsorship is then discussed by reference to growth rates over previous time periods. The focus then turns to the provision of a systematic framework for the development and management of an effective sport sponsorship programme. Major issues include functional location, objective setting, selection, evaluation and control. The discussion then addresses the growth of ambush marketing in the area of sport sponsorship and looks at some of the legal issues that relate to these forms of activity. Finally, the fundamentals of endorsement are introduced, which cover the definition, key theories, as well as advantages and potential risks.

A number of case studies, based on the practical experiences of well-known companies are introduced at regular intervals to illustrate core aspects of sport sponsorship and endorsement. Several leading sporting organisations and athletes also form the basis of case material. Important learning points are reinforced by the use of discussion questions that draw on case material or other issues and topics identified in the chapter.

Introduction

Despite the current interest in sponsorship and endorsement, these activities are not of recent origin. Evidence exists for their use at the time of Caesar's gladiators and in support of artists, musicians and composers in Shakespearean times. The Howell Report (1983) cites Spears and Pond, a firm of Australian caterers as the sponsors of the England cricket tour of Australia in 1861–1862. Over the years, sponsorship has developed into a highly versatile and adaptable medium that has, in part, contributed to the difficulties of creating an enduring definition. Head (1981) described the exercise as 'like trying to harpoon a butterfly in a gale'. There is, however, general agreement that sponsorship represents a business transaction rather than patronage or philanthropy. The commercial dimension is covered in many definitions of sponsorship, for example Meenaghan (1991b) adopts a similar view and identifies sponsorship as 'an investment in cash or kind, in an activity, in return for access to the exploitable commercial potential associated with that activity'. This definition highlights that the primary justification for involvement lies in the material benefit available to the sponsor. In summary, the features of sponsorship are:

- an exchange between two parties: the sponsee receives cash and/or benefits in kind while the sponsor secures a right of association with an activity, event or location;
- the sponsor seeks to achieve a range of marketing objectives through the exploitation of the relationship;
- it is a business relationship rather than corporate philanthropy.

Endorsement is commonly associated with sponsorship and has some similar characteristics. In essence, a company provides an individual with financial or material benefit in return for her/his use, promotion or support of their products. The amounts involved can be considerable. For example, sportbusiness.com reported that in 2009 the world's second-biggest soft-drink producer PepsiCo Inc signed a £1.2 million contract with three-time Grand Slam tennis champion Maria Sharapova over two years. After winning a record eight gold medals at the 2008 Beijing Olympic Games, American swimmer Michael Phelps secured multi-million pound endorsement deals with a number of companies, including Visa, Kellogg, AT&T, Subway and Mazda (China). His four-year deal with Matsunichi, maker of MP3 players, was worth about £2.4 million. National Basketball Association Rookie of the Year, LeBron James, signed a deal with Nike, reported to be worth around £55 million over seven years.

Is sponsorship another form of advertising?

Although a view sometimes expressed is that sponsorship is another form of advertising, sponsorship is now widely believed to be different (O'Reilly et al., 2008). Meenaghan (1991a) distinguishes the two forms of communication in relation to issues of control, message, implementation, motivation and audience reaction. Jones and Dearsley (1989) suggest that sponsorship can deliver additional benefits in the minds of consumers who can see tangible benefits for sport, the arts, community etc. In addition, sponsorship is considered to have more indirect influences on consumer perception in comparison to advertising (McDaniel, 1999; Lardinoit and Quester, 2001). Both McDonald (1991) and Meenaghan (2001) suggested that the existence of goodwill is one of the prime factors that distinguish sponsorship from advertising. Consumers generate an emotional involvement through a sponsorship which has the element of goodwill. In turn, this reduces the suspicion that corporate involvement is purely commercial and subsequently lowers consumers' defence mechanisms.

Marshall (1993) believes that sponsorship can provide a sponsor's communications with valuable elements that would be difficult, if not impossible, to achieve through mainstream advertising. These elements are summarised below:

- *Credibility* – provides validity for product claims.
- *Imitation* – relates good credentials of the event/athlete to prospects/customers.
- *Image transference* – links product with a set of positive image qualities.
- *Bonding* – gains involvement of prospects/customers.
- *Retention* – generates enduring awareness and exposure.

However, Marshall cautions that the attitudes of the public to sponsorship may vary across international borders. Although dated now, his research revealed that German consumers were much more inclined to see sponsorship as another form of advertising, compared to French and UK consumers. The belief that sponsorship could promote a good image for the sponsor and its products was particularly strong in Spain, but much less so in France. These are just an example of the distinctions identified by Marshall, which may have implications for those companies that conduct sponsorship in a variety of international locations. One of the reasons why consumers identify sponsorship as another form of advertising may stem from the fact that companies do not fully understand sponsorship and fail to manage it in a way that exploits its full potential. Some of these issues are developed later in the chapter.

Whilst acknowledging the distinctions between sponsorship and other communication media, the similarities should not be neglected, as they are complementary to each other (Meenaghan, 1991b). For example, marketers use advertising and sponsorship to achieve similar objectives, particularly for improving brand awareness and image (Hoek et al., 1997). Also, in terms of 'information processing, affective response, and behavioural intentions', sponsorship and advertising 'involve comparable consumer behaviours' (McDaniel, 1999: 167). Therefore, Cunningham and Taylor (1995) suggested that the models in previous research based on other marketing communications tools (e.g. advertising) could be applied to the theoretical development of sponsorship response.

Growth and development

Establishing an accurate figure for the amounts spent on sponsorship has proved difficult as many small-scale initiatives go unreported, such as support for village soccer or rugby teams. In addition, the methods for collecting data may vary across countries and institutions. For example, are the reported figures merely rights fees or do they include the costs of exploiting the relationship with other communications media? Are the costs of player endorsements included or excluded? Given these difficulties, it is reasonable to assume that many of the published estimates may be understated.

Several reasons are put forward for the dramatic growth in sponsorship spending, for example:

● escalating costs of media advertising;

● new opportunities generated by increased leisure time;

● greater media coverage of sponsored events;

● inefficiencies of existing media, for example clutter;

● prohibition of advertising by tobacco companies in some countries;

● proven benefits of sponsorship;

● changes of consumers' responses to traditional mass advertising media.

(Eriksson and Hjalmsson, 2000; Seguin and O'Reilly, 2008)

Early entrants into the sponsorship market were drawn from industries such as brewing, tobacco and motor manufacturers. Their success has now encouraged entry by companies from a much broader range of industry sectors such as financial institutions, computer and electronics firms, mobile phone companies, gambling organisations and high street retailers.

The provision of support (in cash or kind) for sports events, teams, performers, stadia etc. has proved the most popular investment vehicle for companies, accounting for approximately two-thirds of worldwide sponsorship expenditure. IEG estimated that in North America, 69 per cent (US$11.6 billion) of all sponsorship investment went to sport events in 2008, followed by entertainment tours and attractions (10 per cent); cause-related marketing (9 per cent); festivals, arts (5 per cent); fairs and annual events (4 per cent), and associations and membership organisations (3 per cent) (IEG, 2008). The particular attraction of sport derives from its high visibility and its capacity to attract a broad cross-section of the community. It can be used to target mass markets or specific niches and offers a means of transcending national boundaries and breaking down cultural barriers. It also generates high levels of television coverage through the provision of all-round family entertainment.

Another significant cause of the dramatic increase in sport sponsorship activity stemmed from the inability of governments to continue to fund sport to the levels necessary to maintain its development. Consequently, sports organisations turned to the corporate sector to make up the shortfall. Indeed, media and sponsorship activities became such an important element in the funding of sport that many sporting bodies and events would find it difficult to continue to operate in their current form without these sources of cash injection. As an example, during 2002, 36 per cent of the turnover of Manchester

United PLC came from media and 18 per cent from commercial activities, of which sponsorship contributed 90 per cent. The club's annual report for 2002 emphasises the importance of numerous relationships with the corporate sector, as shown below. On 1 August a new kit sponsorship and merchandising deal with Nike began, including a 13-year guarantee of £303 million in return for the right to produce all Manchester United branded products worldwide.

- The relationship with sponsors Vodaphone continues to grow as both parties seek to develop revenue-generating services.
- Budweiser has signed up as the official beer of Manchester United, while also agreeing stadium pouring rights.
- Pepsi has renewed as the Club's official supplier of soft drinks.
- Ladbrokes has become the Club's official betting partner in the stadium and its interactive gaming partner worldwide.
- Dimension Data has joined up as the Club's business services provider while also redesigning the website. It has also become a partner in the development in a long-term Customer Relationship Management initiative.
- Terra Lycos has taken responsibility for the development of a Chinese website and acts as sales agent for the English-language site. Lycos UK has become a club sponsor.
- Fuji has agreed to become the Club's official imaging partner and a sponsor – helping pursue new business to business and business to consumer services.
- Century Radio renewed its existing sponsorship.
- Wilkinson Sword became the Club's official male grooming partner.

Case 17.1 The costs of sponsorship

The rights fees that allow companies to associate with particular properties have continued to grow over recent years. While inexpensive properties may still be available, the more prominent teams, competitions or events command significant sums of money. For example, Siemens paid £3.2 million for a six-year sponsorship deal with the GB rowing team to the end of 2012. Samsung has renewed its sponsorship contract with Chelsea FC which lasts three years until 2012/13. Initially in 2005, Samsung signed a £10 million shirt sponsorship contract with Chelsea for a year. However, due to the recession, it is estimated that the current deal is worth £12–14 million. In addition to getting global brand exposure, Samsung also has exclusive rights on all consumer electronics sold through the football club.

Although sports sponsorship expenditure has continued to grow, both in the UK and worldwide, there are some possible concerns. Reports suggested that in 2003 some Formula One motor racing teams had been obliged to cut their asking prices significantly in order to attract sponsors. It was alleged that some middle order teams had been particularly hard hit and that the demise of both Prost and Arrows

(continued)

has been hastened by the withdrawal of commercial support. Reported prices for the 2003 season were significantly down on 2000. Signage on a front/rear wing and sidepod that would have cost £7 million in 2000 was available for £4 million in 2003. Likewise, the cost of wing mirror signage had fallen from £750k to £500k. In addition, the recent global economic recession has put huge financial pressure on car manufacturers. In 2008, one of the major players, the Japanese car manufacturer Honda, withdrew from the F1 owing to the unsustainable cost of competing in the World Championship. Under such a situation, the remaining teams are seeking to cut costs, including smaller, more fuel-efficient engines, which are estimated to save teams up to £38 million in the 2010 season.

Sources include *The Times*, *Evening Standard*, Hollis Sponsorship Bulletin, telegraph. co.uk, sportbusiness.com and cnn.com/worldsport

Discussion questions

1 Do you feel that the situation described above relates purely to Formula One or is the concern a more general one?

2 What are the factors that may contribute to a decline in the value of sport sponsorship properties or limit a company's willingness to be involved in this form of activity?

3 What are the potential impacts of the global financial crisis on a company's sponsorship strategies?

An effective framework for sponsorship management

A feature of the sponsorship literature over recent years has been the reference to greater accountability. Many early sponsorship initiatives were seen as cavalier with limited thought or strategic rationale. This gave rise to the term 'chairman's wife syndrome', suggesting that particular sports were chosen for sponsorship because they appealed to the family members of senior staff within the company. The early literature also suggests that some initiatives that were intended to bestow commercial benefits on the sponsor degenerated into philanthropy because of a failure to manage the process effectively. The recent trend towards greater accountability suggests that both parties to the sponsorship contract should manage the process as effectively as possible to create mutual benefits.

In order that sponsorship can make an effective contribution to a company's communication objectives it is important to develop an effective framework for its management. The adoption of a structured and systematic approach will overcome many of the problems identified in earlier research. Irwin and Asimakopoulus (1992) offer a simple conceptualisation of the main stages in the sponsorship management process.

Step 1   Review of corporate marketing plan and objectives.

Step 2   Identification and prioritisation of specific sponsorship objectives
(corporate and product/brand related).

Step 3   Identification of evaluation criteria and assignment of relative weighting based on the prioritisation from Step 2.

Step 4   Screening and selection of sponsorship proposals.

Step 5   Implementation of selected sponsorship proposals.

Step 6   Evaluation of sponsorship's effectiveness in achieving prescribed objectives.

These issues are discussed briefly in the following section.

The need to consider the corporate marketing plan during the initial step serves to emphasise that sponsorship is one element among a number of promotional activities that need to be coordinated following an evaluation of their strengths and weaknesses. Meenaghan (1991a) uses the analogy of an orchestra where the various instruments combine to create the performance. There is general agreement in the literature that the use of sponsorship or endorsement in a manner that is unhinged from these broader considerations will limit its contribution to the company's overall objectives. It should also be noted that the sponsorship activity should complement other elements of the marketing mix. In this respect, it is important at an early stage to identify the functional responsibility for sponsorship to avoid a situation whereby everyone shows an interest but nobody accepts responsibility.

Following a review of corporate marketing objectives, communication strategy and budget implications, attention turns to the role of sponsorship in the communication mix. Rigorous research into potential sponsorship opportunities will allow the development of clear, concise and focused objectives. This is an important stage in the process as a failure to develop and prioritise sponsorship objectives and to investigate the strengths and weaknesses of particular sponsorship platforms will limit the effectiveness of the programme and militate against subsequent evaluation. One of the positive features of sponsorship is its ability to contribute to a broad range of objectives at both corporate and brand level. Table 17.1 illustrates some of the characteristics and objectives of brand and corporate-level

Table 17.1 Characteristics and objectives of brand and corporate sponsorship

Brand	Corporate
Characteristics	
Short term	Longer term
Market-led	Corporate affairs-led
Decided at brand level	Decided at Board level
Payback tightly quantified	More speculative
Aimed at brand users/potential users	Aimed at opinion formers
Objectives	
Media coverage	Community involvement
Sales leads	Public awareness
Sales/market share	Increase/change public perception/image
Target market awareness	Build goodwill and trade trade relations
Guest hospitality	Staff relations/recruitment

Source: Thwaites (1994)

sponsorships, although it should be noted that some objectives are appropriate to both levels and the list is not exhaustive. Additionally, the nature of the organisation will influence the scope of activity, for example to demonstrate social responsibility is one of the primary objectives for social and environmental sponsors; hospitality is an important objective for art sponsors; 'giving back to the community' is the major motivation for small businesses engaging in sponsorship (Walliser, 2003).

Although sponsorship can be used to fulfil a wide range of objectives, there is some evidence to suggest that specific forms of sponsorship are more appropriate to particular objectives. For example, Witcher et al. (1991) suggest that both sport and the arts are useful platforms for promoting corporate image, but sport offers an advantage in generating brand awareness, media exposure and sales generation.

A feature of sponsorship is its ability to appeal to a broad range of internal and external audiences, for example:

Potential customers	Existing customers	General public
Local community	Business community	Workforce
Distributors	Suppliers	Shareholders
Government	Employees	Media
Intermediaries	Regulatory organisations	

While the attraction and retention of business will be important and give emphasis to potential and existing customers, sponsorship also allows messages to be delivered to other groups that are specifically involved with the company or affected by its conduct or success. The following example drawn from Nationwide Building Society illustrates a major positive aspect of sponsorship, namely the ability to achieve a number of objectives and target a range of constituencies through a single programme.

Case 17.2 Nationwide secures new sponsorship of English FA

Nationwide Building Society and the Football Association (FA) announced on Friday 11 August 2006 a new partnership that will see Nationwide become the exclusive Official England Team Sponsor.

The four-year deal kicked off with England's international against European Champions, Greece, on Wednesday 16 August at Old Trafford and runs until the end of July 2010, after the 2010 World Cup in South Africa.

The deal includes highly valuable inventory including branding on all training kit, media interview backdrop boards, significant advertising signage at all home games and training sessions and also ticket and broadcast sponsorship rights.

Nationwide also has the right to use the official 'Three Lions' crest on its advertising and promotions and will benefit from access to England player images and other personality rights.

The deal also includes the England U21s team, all the England women's teams, the England disabled teams and all the England youth teams.

(continued)

Peter Gandolfi, Head of Brand Marketing at Nationwide, said: 'This is tremendously exciting news for our organisation. As a very large player in financial services, we need to consistently emphasise our brand difference. Sponsorship forms a very important part of our communication process and it's a great way to promote our brand to a huge audience.

'Almost 30 million people in the UK watched England's games at World Cup 2006 and approximately 25 million people in the UK watch football on a regular basis – all potential Nationwide customers.

'We've nearly 600 branches in towns and cities across England and we will be engaging with football supporters, our members and employees through this high-profile football sponsorship. England matches are enjoyed by millions of people and we know that many of our members and employees are massively interested in the fortunes of the national team.'

Football has played a key element in Nationwide's brand strategy since 1999 and the new deal with the FA represents a significant achievement in the renegotiation of the previous sponsorship deal, observes Ardi Kolah, Chief Strategy Officer at sports sponsorship and marketing agency PRISM and author of 'Sponsorship: Strategies for Maximising the Return on Investment', published by SportBusiness (August 2006).

'Sponsors should always keep their sponsorship programmes under review and analyse in detail the return on investment. By applying brand sponsorship valuation (BSV) metrics to its previous sponsorship investment, the Nationwide was able to negotiate from a position of strength and secure a great value deal with the FA – which has also allowed it to aggressively pursue its broadcast advertising strategy at the same time.'

The deal follows in the wake of the new format for sponsorship of the FA Cup and the England Team, announced in February this year.

Carlsberg and Umbro enjoy Official Supporter status of the England Team, alongside their FA partnerships with the England kit (Umbro) and with Wembley (Carlsberg). In addition, McDonald's have a partnership which sees them as sole partner of the Community Shield and leading coaching and community schemes.

Source: www.sportbusiness.com/news/160182/nationwide-secures-new-sponsorship-of-english-fa

The increasing cost of staging sporting competitions has led to a corresponding increase in the number of unsolicited requests for support that companies receive. Against this background it is important to have an effective screening process that can discriminate between the good and bad proposals. Choosing to support an inappropriate proposal is likely to prove expensive given the cost of the initial rights fee and the subsequent expenditure necessary to exploit the relationship. Companies appear to show various levels of sophistication in selecting between proposals. At one extreme are companies that rely largely on intuition and 'gut feeling' while at the opposite end of the spectrum are those who use complex evaluation criteria. A range of factors may be influential in the decision. For example, Irwin et al. (1994) suggest 42 factors, which fall within 11 generic categories:

● Budget considerations.

● Event management issues.

- Positioning/image . . . issues of fit.
- Targeting of market . . . media coverage and immediate audience issues.
- Extended audience profile.
- Public relations.
- Promotional opportunities, e.g. licensing, signage etc.
- Competitive considerations, e.g. ambush etc.
- Sponsorship status, e.g. level, exclusivity etc.
- Alternative sponsorship . . . co-sponsor, in kind supplier.
- Sponsorship type . . . event, competition, team etc.

The factors identified above can be assessed and subsequently weighted depending on their importance to a particular sponsor. Each sponsorship proposal will then gain a total score that forms a basis for decisions about selection or rejection.

Although there are numerous factors that a potential sponsor may wish to consider in coming to a decision on a particular sponsorship opportunity, the issue of fit/congruence has received considerable attention in the literature (see for example Speed and Thompson, 2000). Congruence in the sponsorship literature refers to the direct or indirect relevance (similarity/compatibility) between the sponsor and the sponsored event (Johar and Pham, 1999; McDaniel, 1999; Ruth and Simonin, 2003; Gwinner and Bennett, 2008). Such relevance is positively related to 'memory for sponsorship stimuli and other sponsorship outcomes' (Cornwell et al., 2005: 27). Congruence between sponsor and event could be established logically or strategically (Cornwell, 1995).

There is general support for the view that consumer attitudes towards a particular sponsorship are more positive when they perceive there is a degree of fit between sponsor and sponsee. This fit may take a variety of forms, such as a logical connection between event and sponsor. An energy drinks manufacturer sponsoring an endurance-based sports event would be an example. The fit may also operate at an image level, where both organisations have a similar image or where they have a similar ethos. These issues are explored in the Tetley Bitter case study (Case 17.3).

In addition to sponsor and event fit, companies tend to seek sponsorship opportunities that show a match between brand and audience – in other words, a fit between attendees or participants of an event and the target consumers of the brand (Howard and Crompton, 2004; Cornwell et al., 2005; Ferreira et al., 2008). Socio-demographic variables such as age and gender are often used by both the companies and sport organisations to target specific market segments and promote products (Fennell et al., 2003; Fennell and Allenby, 2004).

Earlier in the chapter, a distinction was drawn between advertising and sponsorship. At this point, it is appropriate to extend the discussion to include the issue of leverage. In essence, this means optimising the value of the association that has been created through the payment of the rights fee. A review of the literature indicates that, in particular, companies who are new to sponsorship may assume that this is the total level of their commitment. In the belief that sponsorship works in a similar manner to advertising, they pay a fee and sit back waiting for a positive response. Sadly, this is unlikely to be effective. The rights fee merely allows the company to be associated with the property. Subsequently, it is necessary to exploit the relationship through other media. The specific nature of the contract, in terms of what is included in the initial cost of association, will clearly influence the amount spent on leveraging. However, figures of up to three times the original sum are suggested in the literature.

One of the sponsorship issues that have raised considerable and ongoing debate is the question of evaluation. On the one hand there are those who argue that the effects of sponsorship cannot be measured or at best are difficult to measure. On the other hand there are those who advocate a range of techniques to measure the effectiveness of sponsorship initiatives. The nature of the company's objectives and the extent to which these objectives are framed in a manner capable of evaluation will influence the choice of method. Several approaches have been adopted, for example,

- measure media coverage/exposure;
- monitor guest feedback;
- measure communication effectiveness (prompted/unprompted awareness or recognition/ recall measure);
- monitor sales leads;
- measure actual sales;
- monitor staff feedback;
- measure awareness by trade contacts;
- measure market share.

The measurement of media coverage appears to be a very popular approach, although its value has been questioned in certain situations. It is important to appreciate that this represents 'an opportunity to see' and as such relates to exposure, not necessarily awareness. Furthermore, there is evidence that companies involved in sport sponsorship have noted the length of time their logo has been displayed during a televised event and translated this into the equivalent cost of rate card advertising. This comparison is flawed, not least because several glimpses of a logo as a backdrop to more compelling action are unlikely to be as effective as a tailor-made advertisement appropriately placed in a suitable media. In addition, recent research indicated that marketers are now also assessing the number of retailers that participate in sponsorship-linked marketing promotions (Crompton, 2004; Cornwell and Coote, 2005), intent to purchase and product trial (O'Reilly et al., 2008).

For long-term large-scale sponsorships, sponsors are more willing to use quantitative evaluations to justify return on investment, increase of sales, the extent to which marketing objectives tied to the investment and improvement of brand loyalty. On the one hand, a brand may benefit from associating with a mega sport event; on the other, the brand may be damaged if the endorser engages in certain disappointing behaviours. Therefore, it is often seen that top-flight endorsement agreements include morality clauses that allow a sponsor to withdraw its sponsorship deal if the endorser failed to perform at a satisfactory level. For example, Nike's 13-year US$500 million sponsorship deal with Manchester United is based on the premise that both Nike and Manchester United are 'true brands and that winning is an inalienable characteristic (i.e., attribute) of the brand and sponsorship' (Mueller and Roberts, 2008: 156; Duguid, 2005).

Case 17.3 Cricket sponsorship

The Joshua Tetley Brewery in Leeds (part of Carlsberg-Tetley) was famous for its leading brand Tetley Bitter. This was one of the most popular bitter brands in the Yorkshire region and exhibited values relating to quality and tradition. The company undertook a number of sponsorship initiatives focused on cricket. This proved successful and the investment included the sponsorship agreements with Yorkshire County Cricket Club and the Scarborough and Harrogate Cricket Festivals and broadcast sponsorship of major international matches shown by BSkyB. An evaluation of these activities suggested that awareness of the brand was strengthening in its northern heartland where the majority of its distribution outlets were located, but also increasing nationally. The market share for Tetley Bitter was growing and 2,300 new distribution outlets were established, following approaches by retailers. These gains were attributed to the complete integration of promotions, perimeter advertising, media coverage, competitions, indirect player product endorsement and sustained press activity.

The company appreciated that in order to build Tetley Bitter into a national brand, it would need to increase awareness, particularly in the Midlands and South of the country. This was achieved through a three-year, £3 million sponsorship of the England cricket teams. The benefits accruing from the agreement included:

- title of Official Sponsor for New Zealand and the World Cup;
- Tetley Bitter name on shirts/track suits of England and England A teams, supplier of beer;
- team photographs twice yearly;
- full-page colour advertisement in all UK international match programmes;
- a maximum of three players for corporate work on six occasions per annum;
- 10 players per year for individual branded photo stories;
- 20 large and 20 small autographed bats;
- 25 signed photos of the team for both home and away series;
- four board perimeter advertising package;
- County Challenge sponsorship.

In addition to the initial cost of association, the company allocated £500,000 for media sponsorship, PR and promotional activity and advertising. This was intended to assist in building awareness of the brand, not only among cricket supporters but also across all bitter drinkers and those who purchase beer on behalf of their families, for home consumption.

Early research carried out before the sponsorship agreement was formalised suggested the link with English cricket would be well received by the target audience. When asked if it was good for the England teams to be sponsored, 44 per cent replied that it was a very good idea, while the same percentage felt it was quite a good idea. When asked how they felt about Tetley Bitter becoming a sponsor, only 7 per cent indicated they were not in favour. Later research highlighted that members of the target audience had been reached through the cricket sponsorship activities. After a

(continued)

half-year period of the sponsorship exposure, 24 per cent of the target audience associated Tetley Bitter with cricket sponsorship, raising the association rate by 20 per cent. Similarly, unprompted awareness of Tetley Bitter as the sponsor of the England teams rose from 2 per cent to 28 per cent during the period, and prompted awareness from 8 per cent to 39 per cent.

Source: Company data.

Discussion questions

4 What were the objectives that Carlsberg-Tetley set out to achieve through sponsorship of the England cricket teams?

5 The notion of fit is discussed earlier in the chapter. Is there a fit between Tetley Bitter and English cricket?

Ambush marketing

Although the amounts spent on commercial sponsorship have continued to grow during the last two decades, this trend will only continue if sponsors are able to see tangible benefits from their involvement with particular properties. For example, Sponsors of the Beijing Olympic Games paid between £12 million and £43 million depending on their level of involvement. These sums can only be justified if the anticipated benefits of the association are realised. As sponsorship activity has grown, so too has the practice of ambush marketing (sometimes known as parasitic marketing). This has been particularly prevalent in the sports area. There are various forms of ambush marketing which limit the scope for developing a comprehensive definition. Initially it was viewed as a practice by which a company, usually a competitor, attempted to secure a benefit by attaching itself to an event without paying a rights fee. In so doing it could generate a positive image for itself while reducing the benefits to the rightful sponsor by creating confusion in the mind of the consumer. For example, at the Atlanta Olympic Games billboards showing the Nike name and 'swoosh' were erected on a building specifically constructed by Nike close to Atlanta's Olympic Park. Reebok was the official sponsor of the sports goods category. The high cost of association with major events and category exclusivity may have encouraged some companies to seek alternative approaches. Legitimate responses to these problems include, for example, the sponsorship of the television broadcasts relating to the event or the sponsorship of national teams that will compete at the event. Although included under a generic definition of ambush marketing these activities are clearly different to the activities described earlier, as no attempt is made to avoid payment.

Some definitions of ambush marketing include reference to the degree of confusion created among the public. As an example, in the 2000 Sydney Olympics, Qantas Airlines allegedly tried to ambush the official sponsor Ansett Air by using the slogan 'The Spirit of Australia', which is very similar to the Games' slogan 'Share the Spirit'. Therefore, to reduce the potential for ambush activity by competitors, it is suggested that sponsors, in association with event owners, fully use all forms of marketing communication to leverage the sponsorship investment and gain strong consumer recognition of their legitimate association.

The growth of ambush marketing poses a potential threat to the viability of corporate sponsorship and, accordingly, both rights owners and potential sponsors have considered ways in which sponsorship rights can be protected. A number of activities are now undertaken to reduce the scope for ambush strategies. For example, event organisers could adopt some of the following approaches:

- Provide category exclusivity, for example only one soft drink company and publicise the name of the official sponsor.
- Control photographic and broadcast images to prevent unauthorised use.
- Control licensed souvenirs and merchandise to limit scope for counterfeiting.
- Offer official sponsors the first option on other promotional activities.
- Seek to purchase poster sites near the major event locations and stadia. These can then be offered to official sponsors.
- Publicise sanctions for unofficial use of copyright material. As an example, SUKOM, the organisers of the Commonwealth Games in Kuala Lumpur, produced the following warning:

> The Games Logo and Games Mascot are actually trademarks of SUKOM and any manner of unauthorised usage is an unlawful act. To protect these intellectual properties, SUKOM has recently issued a press statement in regards to the copyright issue.
>
> SUKOM will commence civil or criminal proceedings against anyone or any company found using the marks without lawful authorisation. An individual will be liable to a minimum fine of RM 100,000,000 or 3 years imprisonment or both and a corporation will be liable to a minimum fine of RM 250,000,000. If one is interested to use the marks or wishes to be involved in the commercial aspects of the games, the best way to go about it is to contact SUKOM's office. There are some marketing sponsorship/licensee programmes readily available.

- Publicise details of companies that are seeking to misrepresent their relationship.
- Establish a group responsible for 'policing' venues etc. and monitoring breaches.
- Package certain rights thereby giving major sponsors the option to gain priority in relation to media opportunities that could be used by competitors as a basis for ambush activities.

The London 2012 Organising Committee (LOCOG) gives its sponsors an exclusive association to the Games in the UK. In order to prevent other companies carrying out unauthorised activities which damage the sponsors' exclusive rights, a number of policies have been introduced. For example, The 'Games' Marks' referring to all of the official names, phrases, trademarks, logos and designs related to the 2012 Games and the Olympic and Paralympic movements are legally protected; some are registered trademarks, and some have copyright protection.

Sponsors cannot rely totally on organisers putting in place all the measures necessary to prevent ambush marketing. They must also take responsibility for maximising their relationship with a particular event and minimising the opportunities for competitors to adopt ambush strategies. This will require a detailed assessment of all aspects of the event where opportunities to ambush may occur and subsequent implementation of a number of counter-ambush strategies. Invariably this will involve additional expenditure. Through early and heavy leverage of their investment, sponsors should seek to develop a position in the mind of their target audience that will be difficult for an ambusher to usurp. McKelvey and Grady (2008) suggested that pre-event education and public relations initiatives could help the public to understand not only the differences between official sponsors and ambush marketers, but also the legal rights of the event organiser.

Case 17.4 Illegal, immoral or legitimate competitive practice?

Federal Express promoted its sponsorship of the United States men's basketball team although UPS was the official Olympic sponsor in the overnight mail category.

PepsiCo developed an advertisement that used famous soccer players wearing shirts with a Pepsi logo and the word PEPSI on the front. The phrase 'Tokyo 2002' was included in the advertisement, together with football images. PepsiCo was not a sponsor of the 2002 World Cup held in Japan and Korea.

At the Commonwealth Games 2002 in Manchester, David Beckham appeared at the opening ceremony in a tracksuit emblazoned with the word Adidas in what was presumed to be a 'clean' stadium.

Visa ran a competition on its Brazilian website that displayed the FIFA World Cup trophy. No authorisation for this activity had been granted by FIFA.

BAE Systems, a defence and aerospace company used advertising that included a number of footballing metaphors and photographs of soccer shirts bearing the number 6. The strap line read 'Who do you think spends this much on defence every season'. The advertising coincided with Manchester United's purchase of the England defender Rio Ferdinand for more than £30 million. Ferdinand plays at number 6.

The Canadian National Hockey League (NHL) has a variety of sponsorship programmes. Coca-Cola signed a contract with the NHL as official soft drink supplier, while PepsiCo obtained advertising rights through Molson Breweries, which had broadcast sponsorship rights to the NHL. In addition to advertising, Pepsi carried out a competition where some statements referred to the cities where the NHL teams were based without specifying the exact team names. The NHL sued Pepsi for confusing consumers as official sponsors as well as associating the brand with the NHL. However, the court believed that it was not illegal, as Pepsi had used disclaimers in the advertising stating that it was not an official NHL sponsor.

Source: Thwaites (1998), sportbusiness.com, Crow and Hoek (2003).

Discussion question

6 Use the examples above as a basis for a discussion of the legality and morality of ambush marketing. Following this discussion, develop your own definition of ambush marketing.

As sponsorship and endorsement activity has grown, so too has the complexity of these relationships. This is illustrated by reference to the Cricket World Cup held in South

Africa during February 2003. Prior to the competition sponsorship agreements were put in place with leading companies such as PepsiCo, LG Electronics, South African Airlines and Hero Honda. To protect these companies from ambush marketing the International Cricket Council (ICC) required players to sign a contract that prevented them promoting rival brands to the main sponsors for a period of 30 days each side of the event. As a number of Indian players had lucrative contracts with rival brands they were unable to sign the contract. The matter was eventually resolved through mediation, although during the competition Samsung ran advertising featuring Indian players, requiring stern action from the International Cricket Council to what they viewed as blatant ambush marketing. This situation is not an isolated example and further conflict between endorsed athletes and rights holders of major events appears inevitable.

Case 17.5 ASA ruling raises risk of ambush marketing

In a development which could cause some concern among London 2012 sponsors, the Advertising Standards Authority has rejected a claim by the Rugby Football Union that an ad campaign for London Pride bitter was ambush marketing.

Fuller's Brewery ran the London Pride campaign during the Six Nations Championships. It used rugby imagery and carried the strap line 'Support English Rugby'. The RFU complained that the ad implied that London Pride was an official sponsor of the England team. Yet this title actually belongs to Greene King's IPA – which is in the midst of a multi-million pound, four-year deal.

The ASA found for Fuller's, however – and made the following statement: 'We considered that readers [of the ad] were unlikely to be misled into thinking Fullers was an official sponsor or partner of the England rugby team. They would expect an advertiser to state if they were an official sponsor and the ad did not claim that Fullers were. We also considered that the text Support English Rugby was not misleading, because Fullers did support English rugby as a sport and had done for several years. We concluded that the ad was not misleading and did not take unfair advantage of the reputation of the England rugby team.'

Source: Hollis Sponsorship Bulletin (2009).

Endorsement

Endorsement has been widely used in advertising in association with consumer products or services. There are many forms of endorsement including using identifiable people such as celebrities or authority figures, unidentifiables (e.g. typical consumers) and even inanimate figures (e.g. cartoon characters) (Strout and Moon, 1990). The celebrity endorser has become very popular in the last decade and is defined as: 'any individual who enjoys public recognition and who uses this recognition on behalf of a consumer good by appearing with it in an advertisement' (McCracken 1989: 311). They are individuals from various fields, such as entertainment, sports, cuisine, business and politics. The primary purpose of celebrity endorsement is to ensure the product or brand gets instant attention. It is an effective way of adding glamour and a new dimension to the product, and therefore generates a higher degree of recall. Several theories have been applied to explain the effectiveness of celebrity endorsers, such as attribution theory (Kelley, 1971), identification process of social influence (Friedman and Friedman, 1979), source effect (McGuire, 1985), meaning transfer (McCracken, 1989) and associative learning (Till, 1998). Previous research indicates that celebrities are particularly effective endorsers and have a significant impact on consumer behaviour, as they are viewed as highly trustworthy, believable, persuasive and likeable. However, other research suggests that the effectiveness of celebrity endorsement may vary depending on other factors, for example the physical attractiveness, expertise, credibility, familiarity and likeability of the endorser, fit or match between the celebrity and the advertised product, product type and market characteristics (Till and Shimp, 1998; Erdogan, 1999; Silvera and Austad, 2004).

Employing a celebrity could have the following advantages:

- gains attention and saliency;
- quick means of brand differentiation;
- building psychographic and demographic connections between the product or brand and the celebrity;
- transferring celebrity characteristics to the product;
- reviving a dull brand;
- obtaining guarantee for the product;
- more favourable advertisement ratings and product evaluations;
- increasing PR coverage;
- creating mass appeal for national/international markets;
- generating sales and profits.

The amounts paid to endorsers are often undisclosed; nevertheless, this does appear to be an increasingly popular form of marketing activity involving substantial financial commitment. For example, in 2004 Gillette signed a three-year sponsorship deal with David Beckham rumoured to be worth between £18 and £30 million and in the same year, Nike's five-year deal with the American tennis star Serena Williams was worth about £25 million.

Notwithstanding its marketing potential, celebrity endorsement may not be effective in some situations. The potential weakness are summarised as follows:

- Celebrity credibility and trustworthiness: the power of celebrity credibility and trustworthiness may become questionable when there is incongruence between a brand and the celebrity.
- Celebrity clutter: consumers may get confused when a celebrity endorses multi-products and multi-brands in one category.
- Celebrity's vampire effect: well-known celebrities can sometimes overshadow the brand and its message.
- Celebrity trap: it becomes difficult to separate the brand/corporate image and the celebrity once companies are automatically linked to the celebrity. Therefore, companies need to

be careful if there is a change in celebrity reputation, or inconsistency of celebrity popularity over time.

- Evidence that the celebrity does not use the brand s/he endorses.

Additionally, misbehaving stars could cause a problem for the endorsed brand. The fundamental premise of celebrity endorsers is about translating the goodwill onto a consumer and linking them to brand traits. Therefore, when a celebrity endorser unexpectedly engages in behaviour which is unacceptable to the targeted consumer, the endorsement effect may be negative. Meanwhile, the celebrity potentially becomes a liability to the sponsor. For example, after Michael Phelps, the American Olympic gold medallist swimmer was caught smoking cannabis mid-way through Kellogg's brand ambassador campaign, the cereal giant dropped the misbehaving celebrity days before the end of the campaign. However, it is suggested that controversy is not necessarily damaging, especially to a youth brand. For example, Rimmel stood by Kate Moss after the exposure of her taking cocaine in 2005. The controversy made the model a bigger star and brands came back to her with even bigger deals. Interestingly, evidence shows that the public are usually very forgiving with sports celebrities, if they are performing well. For example, despite Shane Warne being criticised owing to a series of intemperate actions in both his professional and private life, thanks to his outstanding performance on the field the former Australian cricketer continued to attract marketers and sponsorship deals, including an annual AU$300,000 commentating contract with Australia's Nine Network in 2005, a lucrative deal with Advanced Hair Studio and a two-year agreement with 888 Poker in 2008 (bandt.com.au, 2009).

Although practitioners indicated that a good PR plan and effective management are able to rescue most unexpected situations, considering that celebrity endorsement deals are a significant investment brand managers should research potential relationships carefully. The important factors for choosing the appropriate celebrity endorsers are identified including:

- celebrity attributes: attractiveness, trustworthiness and familiarity;
- celebrity and product fit;
- celebrity and target-audience congruence;
- costs of securing the celebrity;
- celebrity's risk of controversy;
- celebrity's previous endorsement.

(Sejung et al., 2005)

 ## Conclusion

The increasing costs of staging sporting events and the limited support that governmental bodies are able to offer will maintain, if not increase the demand for corporate sponsorship. This will be more likely given the level of debt many countries have built up during the recession. During its early years, sponsorship was often undertaken in a somewhat casual manner with little concern for measurement and accountability. The rigorous evaluation methods used to assess the effectiveness of other promotional tools, such as advertising, were rarely used. Over the years, this situation has changed, perhaps in part due to greater experience with the medium, a tighter economic climate and the increasing costs of association. There is now a general trend in the literature that suggests companies are seeking measurable and tangible benefits from their sponsorship activity. Where this is not apparent there is a willingness to seek alternative ways of achieving their communication objectives.

To contribute to the delivery of tangible benefits there is an onus on the company to develop an effective framework for the management of its sponsorship initiatives. This will ensure that the right properties are selected in the first place and that the opportunities that the relationship offers can be realised. In addition, there is an onus on the owners of the sponsored property to contribute to the development of the relationship. One major criticism of sports organisations has been a tendency to 'take the money and run', which has left sponsors feeling that their rights fee has disappeared into a black hole. To develop a win–win situation rather than a give–take relationship there is a need for greater understanding of the needs of both parties to the agreement. As a former Annual Report of Manchester United stated, 'The purpose behind our partnerships with leading consumer brands is to create mutual commercial advantage'. It is important for the continued growth of sport sponsorship that sporting bodies genuinely adopt this approach and avoid paying lip service to it.

Keywords

Ambush marketing; leverage; rights fee; sponsorship property; sport sponsorship.

Guided reading

Sport sponsorship issues may be investigated through a range of sources. Sport-specific academic journals such as *Journal of Sport Management, International Journal of Sports Marketing and Sponsorship, Sport Marketing Quarterly, Sport Management Review* and the *European Sport Management Quarterly* provide a rich source of information.

Sport sponsorship is also addressed in mainstream management and marketing journals, for example *European Journal of Marketing, International Journal of Advertising, Psychology and Marketing, Journal of Advertising, Journal of Advertising Research* and *Industrial Marketing Management*.

Further sources of valuable information are publications by companies such as Mintel, which provide in-depth reports on a variety of markets. The sponsorship report covers a range of issues including current trends and growth patterns, influences on the market and data relating to different sponsorship options, for example sport, arts, broadcast. The sport section then addresses a number of different sports.

Sport sponsorship is also covered in a variety of sport marketing or sport management textbooks, for example Shank (2009) and Lagae (2005).

Recommended websites

Sport Business International: www.sportbusiness.com
IEG Sponsorship: www.sponsorship.com
Hollis Sponsorship: www.hollis-sponsorship.com

References

bandt.com.au (2009) Caught in the headlines, 6 March.

Cornwell, T.B. (1995) 'Sponsorship-linked marketing development', *Sport Marketing Quarterly*, 4 (4), 13–24.

Cornwell, T.B., Weeks, C.S. and Roy, D.P. (2005) 'Sponsorship-linked marketing: opening the black box', *Journal of Advertising*, 34 (2), 21–42.

Crow, D. and Hoek, J. (2003) 'Ambush marketing: a critical review and some practical advice', *Marketing Bulletin*, 14, 1–14.

Cunningham, M.H. and Taylor, S.F. (1995) 'Event marketing: state of the industry and research agenda', *Festival Management and Event Tourism*, 2, 123–37.

Duguid, S. (2005) 'Brand loyalty: when the shoe is on the other foot', *Media Asia*, 23, 17 June.

Erdogan, B.Z. (1999) 'Celebrity endorsement: a literature review', *Journal of Marketing Management*, 15 (4), 291–314.

Eriksson, J. and Hjalmsson, A. (2000) *Event Marketing as a Promotional Tool*, Lulea: Lulea University of Technology.

Fennell, G. and Allenby, G.M. (2004) 'An integrated approach: market definition, market segmentation, and brand positioning create a powerful combination', *Marketing Research*, 16 (4), 28–34.

Fennell, G., Allenby, G., Yang, S. and Edwards, Y. (2003) 'The effectiveness of demographic and psychographic variables for explaining brand and product category use', *Quantitative Marketing and Economics*, 1, 223–44.

Ferreira, M., Hall, T.K. and Bennett, G. (2008) 'Exploring brand positioning in a sponsorship context: a correspondence analysis of the Dew Action Sports Tour', *Journal of Sport Management*, 22, 734–61.

Friedman, H.H. and Friedman, L. (1979) 'Endorser effectiveness by product type', *Journal of Advertising Research*, 19 (5), 63–71.

Gwinner, K. and Bennett, B. (2008) 'The impact of brand cohesiveness and sport identification on brand fit in a sponsorship context', *Journal of Sport Management*, 22, 410–26.

Hoek, J., Gendall, P., Jeffcoat, M., and Orsman, D. (1997) 'Sponsorship and advertising: a comparison of their effects', *Journal of Marketing Communications*, 3 (1), 21–32.

Hollis Sponsorship Bulletin (2009) http://news.hollis-sponsorship.com/

Howard, D.R. and Crompton, J.L. (2004) *Financing Sport*, Morgantown, WV: Fitness Information Technology, Inc.

Irwin, R.L. and Asimakopoulos, M.K. (1992) 'An approach to the evaluation and selection of sport sponsorship proposals', *Sport Marketing Quarterly*, 1 (2), 43–51.

Irwin, R.L., Asimakopoulos, M.K. and Sutton, W.A. (1994) 'A model for screening sport sponsorship opportunities', *Journal of Promotion Management*, 2 (3/4), 53–69.

Johar, G.V. and Pham, M.T. (1999) 'Relatedness, prominence, and constructive sponsor identification', *Journal of Marketing Research*, 36 (August), 299–312.

Jones, M. and Dearsley, T. (1989) 'Understanding sponsorship', in *How to Increase the Efficiency of Marketing in a Changing Europe*, Esomar Conference, Turin, 11–13 October, 257.

Kelley, H.H. (1971) 'Attribution in social interaction', in E.E. Jones, D.E. Kanouse, H.H. Kelley, R.E. Nisbett, S. Valins and B. Weiner (eds), *Attribution: Perceiving the Cause of Behaviour*, Morriston, NJ: General Learning Press, 1–26.

Lagae, W. (2005) *Sports Sponsorship and Marketing Communications: A European Perspective*, Harlow: Pearson Prentice Hall.

Lardinoit, T., and Quester, P.G. (2001) 'Attitudinal effects of combined sponsorship and sponsor's prominence on basketball in Europe', *Journal of Advertising Research*, 41 (1), 48–58.

Marshall, D. (1993) 'Does sponsorship always talk the same language?', Text of a paper given at the Sponsorship Europe Conference, Monte Carlo.

McCracken, G. (1989) 'Who is the celebrity endorser? Cultural foundation of the endorsement process', *Journal of Consumer Research*, 16 (December), 310–21.

McDaniel, S.R. (1999) 'An investigation of matchup effects in sport sponsorship advertising: the implications of consumer advertising schemas', *Psychology and Marketing*, 16 (2), 163–84.

McDonald, C. (1991) 'Sponsorship and the image of the sponsor', *European Journal of Marketing*, 25, 31–38.

McGuire, W.J. (1985) 'Attitudes and attitudes change', in L. Gardner and A. Elliot (eds), *Handbook of Social Psychology*, Vol. 2, New York: Random House, 233–346.

McKelvey, S. and Grady, J. (2008) 'Sponsorship program protection strategies for special sport events: are event organizers out-maneuvering ambush marketers?', *Journal of Sport Management*, 22, 550–86.

Meenaghan, T. (1991a) 'The role of sponsorship in the marketing communication mix', *International Journal of Advertising*, 10 (1), 35–47.

Meenaghan, T. (1991b) 'Sponsorship – legitimising the medium', *European Journal of Marketing*, 25 (11), 5–10.

Meenaghan, T. (2001) 'Understanding sponsorship effects', *Psychology and Marketing*, 18 (2), 95–122.

Mueller, T. and Roberts, M. (2008) 'The effective communication of attributes in sport-sponsorship branding', *International Journal of Sport Communication*, 1, 155–72.

O'Reilly, N., Lyberger, M., McCarthy, L., Seguin, B. and Nadeau, J. (2008) 'Mega-special-event promotions and intent to purchase: a longitudinal analysis of the super bowl', *Journal of Sport Management*, 22, 392–409.

Ruth, J.A. and Simonin, B.L. (2003) 'Brought to you by Brand A and Brand B', *Journal of Advertising*, 32 (3), 19–30.

Seguin, B. and O'Reilly, N. (2008) 'The Olympic brand, ambush marketing and clutter', *International Journal of Sport Management and Marketing*, 4 (1/2), 62–84.

Sejung, M.C., Lee, W.N. and Kim, H.J. (2005) 'Lessons from the rich and famous', *Journal of Advertising*, 43 (2), 85–98.

Shank, M.D. (2009) *Sports Marketing: A Strategic Perspective*, London: Pearson Prentice Hall.

Silvera, D.H. and Austad, B. (2004) 'Factors predicting the effectiveness of celebrity endorsement advertisements', *European Journal of Marketing*, 38 (11/12), 1509–26.

Speed, R. and Thompson, P. (2000) 'Determinants of sport sponsorship response', *Journal of the Academy of Marketing Science*, 28 (2), 226–38.

Strout, P.A. and Moon, Y.S. (1990) 'Use of endorsers in magazine advertisements', *Journalism Quarterly*, 67 (3), 536–46.

The Howell Report (1983) Committee of Enquiry into Sports Sponsorship, London: Central Council for Physical Recreation.

Thwaites, D. (1994) 'Corporate sponsorship by the financial services industry', *Journal of Marketing Management*, 10, 743–63.

Thwaites, D. (1998) 'Kuala Lumpur 98 The XVI Commonwealth Games', in D. Jobber (ed.), *Principles and Practice of Marketing*, New York: McGraw Hill, 438–40.

Till, B.D. (1998) 'Using celebrity endorsers effectively: lessons from associative learning', *Journal of Product and Brand Management*, 7 (5), 400–409.

Till, B.D. and Shimp, T.A. (1998) 'Endorsers in advertising: the case of negative celebrity information', *Journal of Advertising*, 27 (1), 67–82.

Walliser, B. (2003) 'An international review of sponsorship research: extension and update', *International Journal of Advertising*, 22 (1), 5–40.

Witcher, B., Craigen, J.G., Culligan, D. and Harvey, A. (1991) 'The links between objectives and function in organisational sponsorship', *International Journal of Advertising*, 10, 13–33.

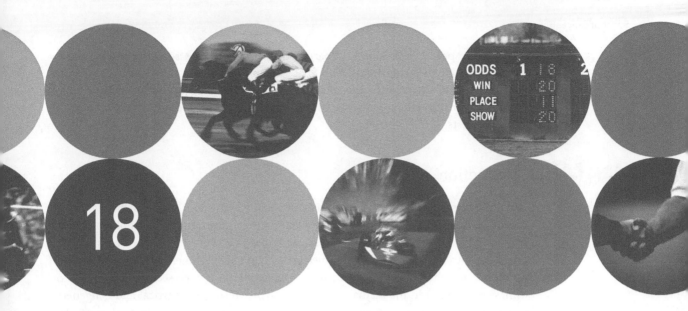

Sport broadcasting

Harry Arne Solberg, Trondheim Business School, Norway

Learning outcomes

Upon completion of this chapter, the reader should be able to:

- identify the characteristics of sport programmes that are of importance when analysing them as commodities;
- analyse the cost structure of sport broadcasting;
- analyse the market behaviour of companies involved in the production and distribution of sports programmes;
- analyse various sale procedures of media rights;
- understand the rationale behind the regulations of sports programmes, such as the Listed Events regulation.

 ## Overview

This chapter focuses on economic aspects related to sport broadcasting. First it describes some characteristics of sports programmes that we need to understand when analysing them as commodities. The same applies to the following section, which discusses the cost structure of sports broadcasting. The next section analyses the market behaviour of broadcasters and transmission companies involved in sport broadcasting. This is followed by analysis of various forms of business integration that have taken place in recent years. The following section concentrates on various sale procedures of media rights. It first discusses alternative forms of auctions. Next, it provides a comparison of individual and collective sale procedures. The third part of this section studies some aspects related to international sale of media rights. The final section concentrates on regulation of sport broadcasting, such as the Listed Events and Anti-siphoning List. It discusses the welfare economic rationale behind these lists, and also provides a brief overview of the content on the existing lists.

Introduction

Sport broadcasting has been characterised by rapid and major changes during recent decades. Galloping inflation on popular media rights is one example. Technology innovations have dismantled the borders between activities that previously were separated. It is now possible to watch sports programmes not only on TV channels, but also on websites and mobile telephones. Parallel with this development, we have seen various forms of business integration in the media industry, involving horizontal, vertical and congeneric integration (integration between firms that produce similar, but not identical products). Sports programmes have also become a popular export product. Matches in team tournaments from Europe and North America are broadcast worldwide. Sport broadcasting has also become subject to regulations. The most common are the Listed Events regulations which prevent events of major importance for society from migrating exclusively to pay TV broadcasters. Additionally, competitive authorities have also challenged the practice of collective sale of broadcasting rights – a procedure regarded as illegal cartel behaviour in other economic activities.

The objective of this chapter is to provide insight to these phenomena. To achieve that, we first have to discuss some characteristics of sports programmes that are important when considering them as commodities being produced and sold in a market.

Sport programmes as commodities

Public goods

The reception of TV signals is an *impure public good*. Pure public goods are non-rivalling and non-excluding in consumption (Samuelson, 1954). The former criterion means that consumption of the good by one individual does not reduce availability of the good for consumption by others. No matter how much a person is watching, he or she does not reduce the quality or the quantity of programmes available for other viewers. The reception of TV signals does not meet the non-exclusive criterion, which is why it is called an impure public good. The broadcaster or the distributor of the signals can easily prevent unwanted viewers from receiving the signals by means of a decoder.

Time sensitive goods

Live sport programmes are extremely time-sensitive goods that cannot be stored without losing most of their commercial value. This particularly applies to sports where the entertainment dimension is highly correlated with the uncertainty of outcome. Very few are interested in watching yesterday's match on TV. The drop in value will be smaller in sports where the aesthetic performance is of importance, for example in figure skating and gymnastics. The high degree of *time sensitivity* represents a major difference from other entertainment products, such as literature, films and music, since these products can be stored without losing most of their commercial value (Gaustad, 2000).

Homogeneous goods

Live sports programmes are homogeneous products. In principle, they have the same consumption value regardless of the type of television service that delivers them. There will hardly be any difference in the quality of the programmes from one channel to another. TV viewers watch identical pictures from live sports events. This also applies to international events, e.g. the Olympic Games and international championships. The core programmes are usually produced by a national broadcaster within the host nation, which in turn distributes these TV pictures to a large number of broadcasters world-wide. This is different from heterogeneous programmes, such as news programmes and documentaries, where different broadcasters can approach issues differently and hence provide viewers with a broader perspective than if they were only covered by one channel.

Low cultural discount

The cultural discount reflects the reduction in value on media products when they are shown beyond the home market. In general, the reduction is lower for sports programmes than for many other media products. Sports in general have the same rules worldwide, which is a characteristic that is favourable for export. Hence, it is not necessary to understand the language to enjoy watching a sporting contest from another country. Nations with close historical and cultural relationships often share similar interests in sports. The same frequently applies to neighbouring countries, a phenomenon which often is a consequence of similar climatic conditions. Multinational squads can further stimulate the interest of specific teams for foreign markets, and hence reduce the cultural discount.

Externalities

Externalities are usually referred to as being the result of an activity that causes incidental benefits or costs to others with no corresponding compensation provided or paid by those who generate the externality. Neither the costs nor the benefits are included in the supply price or the demand price, and are thus not reflected in the market price. Sport broadcasting can generate externalities, for example by encouraging people to exercise. This can improve health conditions and hence benefit the whole society by reducing absenteeism from work. As a consequence of this, more goods and services will be available. Another example is enhanced pride and self-esteem that people enjoy when national competitors have successes in international competitions. Common enjoyment of international success in sporting events might strengthen people's feeling of national identity. The fact that positive externalities are beneficial for the entire society represents a rationale to stimulate the consumption of goods and services which initiate them.

The cost structure of sport broadcasting

Economies of scale and scope advantages

The production and transmission of TV and radio signals has *economies of scale advantages*, which mean that the average costs decline over the entire range of outputs. In general, such advantages apply to processes characterised by *high fixed costs* and relatively *low variable costs*. This characteristic particularly applies to the transmission of TV signals, e.g. by satellite or cable operators which require extremely expensive *start-up costs*. On the other hand, once facilities and other production equipment have been established, the variable costs from using them are very low relative to the investment costs.

Producers involved in sport broadcasting can also achieve *economies of scope advantages*, which refer to advantages from using the same input in more than one production process. Such advantages could result from the joint use of inputs or production facilities, joint marketing programmes, or possibly the cost savings of a common administration. These advantages are particularly beneficial in cases when the common production factor is relatively costly. As an example, a journalist sent on a mission to cover a sports event can contribute in the production of live sport programmes, but also news programmes for the TV broadcaster. In addition, he or she may also work for radio channels and newspapers that are members of the same parental company.

The broadcasters of international competitions have plenty of opportunities to utilise economies of scale and scope advantages. International events, such as the Olympic Games and the most popular international championships, are broadcast to more than 200 nations across the entire world, as seen from Table 18.1. The core programme is usually produced by a domestic broadcaster in the host nation or a local production company. For example, the same applies to European football matches that are broadcast to overseas markets. In principle, they offer the same TV pictures to broadcasters across the world.

Table 18.1 Nations broadcasting the Olympics

Summer Olympics		Winter Olympics	
1960 Rome	21	1960 Squaw Valley	27
1964 Tokyo	40	1964 Innsbruck	30
1968 Mexico City	n.a.	1968 Grenoble	32
1972 Munich	98	1972 Sapporo	41
1976 Montreal	124	1976 Innsbruck	38
1980 Moscow	111	1980 Lake Placid	40
1984 Los Angeles	156	1984 Sarajevo	100
1988 Seoul	160	1988 Calgary	64
1992 Barcelona	193	1992 Albertville	86
1996 Atlanta	214	1994 Lillehammer	120
2000 Sydney	220	1998 Nagano	160
2004 Athens	220	2002 Salt Lake City	160
2008 Beijing	220	2006 Turin	200

Source: multimedia.olympic.org/pdf/en_report_344.pdf

Opportunity costs and sunk costs

Many inputs used in sport programming can alternatively produce other programmes. This means that they will have an *opportunity cost*, which refers to the value the resources could have created in their next best alternative use – in other words, the *value forgone* from not allocating the resources differently. The monetary value of the opportunity costs depends on the income the alternative programme(s) would have generated.

This is completely different for *sunk costs*, which refers to expenditures that have been made, but cannot be recovered. Such costs are totally irretrievable and do not disappear, no matter what action the producer takes. Thus, as a rule of thumb, the sunk costs that are paid for should not influence decisions taken by the firm thereafter.

Let us imagine a TV broadcaster acquiring the rights for a team tournament. We assume that the fee, say €10 million, is independent of the income the programmes generate. Hence, the fee should be regarded as sunk costs and should not influence the number of matches to be broadcast. In general, the rating figures from international tournaments correlate with the participation (and successes) of the competitors from the respective countries. When they are eliminated from the tournament, the national TV audiences are often severely reduced. The Italian channel, RAI, considered suing FIFA since TV pictures revealed that Italy was eliminated from the 2002 World Cup soccer finals due to a mistake by the assistant referee.[1] Similar consequences have been documented on several occasions (Desbordes, 2006; Solberg, 2006a). To reduce such negative effects, the broadcaster may benefit from showing alternative programmes instead of (all) the remaining matches. This illustrates how the opportunity cost can influence the decision-making process. If a sport event becomes less attractive, it takes less to make alternative programmes more profitable.

Media rights

Media rights are here defined as the rights to broadcast from a specific event, normally within a restricted geographical area. Such rights can apply to a TV transmission, but also to other modes such as radio, internet and mobile phones. Media rights have become an expensive part of sport broadcasting in recent years. The most attractive rights have reached levels that were unimaginable some years ago. The values of media rights can be influenced by factors such as:

- the size and the purchasing power of the population in the viewing market;
- the popularity of the sport among the general audience;
- the level of competition on the supply side as well as the demand side;
- whether there is a clear juridical understanding of the ownership issue.

Broadcasters and distributors of TV sport programmes

This section will provide an overview of the producers and distributors of sport broadcasting. It first concentrates on TV broadcasters, which we will categorise as follows:

---

[1] http://media.guardian.co.uk/worldcup/story/0,11974,741487,00.html

- licence fees/public grants (non-commercial public service broadcasters);
- advertising;
- subscription fees (pay TV channels/stations).

Although some channels receive their revenues from a mixture of these three sources, the majority have one major source.

Non-commercial public service broadcasters

The rationale of public service broadcasters is based on elements from welfare economics, i.e. with special attention on providing programmes that have characteristics of *public goods*, *externalities* and *merit goods*. (See Brown, 1996 and Gratton and Solberg, 2007 for more thorough discussion of these matters.) These broadcasters are not allowed to sell advertising or charge the viewers pay-per-view fees. For them, sports broadcasting only represent costs, not any revenues. The inflation on media rights has reduced their involvement in sport programming over the years. Expensive sports rights acquisitions force them to reduce other programme activities. One consequence of this is that commercial broadcasters have taken over sports events that for years were broadcast on public service broadcasters.

Here it is interesting to note the different behaviour between European and Australian broadcasters. While the Australian public service broadcasters gave up the most popular (and expensive) sports programmes such as the Olympics and other international championships in the 1990s, their European colleagues have been unwilling to adopt this strategy. Instead they have continued to bid on these events, often represented by the European Broadcasting Union (EBU). From a welfare economic perspective, the rationale for such a strategy can be questioned. The Listed Events regulation can prevent these events from migrating to pay TV broadcasters (see last section). In recent years, many commercial broadcasters have achieved the same penetration as public service broadcasters. Assuming the programmes are acquired by free-to-air commercial broadcasters, this will allow all of us to watch them without paying any additional fee. (See Solberg, 2007 for a thorough discussion of these matters.)

Advertising broadcasters

The second category of broadcasters earns their income from selling advertising in connection to the programmes. Firms and organisations that purchase advertising on TV want to maximise the promotion of themselves and their products. Thus, advertising revenues correlate with the rating figures during the commercials. Normally the rating figures during the core programme and the commercials will correlate. This category of broadcasters also includes commercial public service broadcasters that are subject to many of the same regulations as the non-commercial public service broadcasters.

Figure 18.1 presents the rating figures of UEFA's Champions League matches shown on Norwegian television for a period February 2000 to May 2003.[2] In total, the core

---

[2] The rating figures were measured by TNS Gallup, Norway on the basis of a sample of 1,000 Norwegian households, comprising 2,400 people (Solberg and Hammervold, 2008). The matches were broadcast on TV3, an advertising broadcaster which at that time transmitted by cable and satellite.

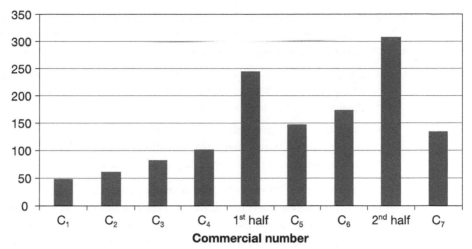

Figure 18.1 TV rating for UEFA's Champions League in Norway ('000 viewers)

programme was interrupted by seven commercial breaks (c_i) – four before the match, two during the break and one after the match was finished. As seen, the commercials attracted significantly lower audiences than the match. Indeed, the two first commercials only attracted in the region of 20 per cent of the viewers that followed the matches. The sections between the first and second halves were the most popular ones and attracted respectively 52 and 61 per cent of the audience that watched the match.

However, maximising the advertising revenues is not only about maximising the rating figures. To advertisers, not all viewers are alike. The greater the spending power of viewers and/or the greater their attractiveness to the advertisers, the more the advertiser will pay to reach them. This creates an incentive to discriminate in favour of households with high income and to offer programmes to which they can relate (Dunnet, 1990).

Subscription-based broadcasters

Subscription-based TV, more commonly known as pay-TV, represents the third category of broadcasters. Their revenues come from the consumer surplus that the viewers would have kept if the programmes were broadcast free-to-air. Unlike advertiser channels, pay-TV channels can take advantage of the intensity of viewers' preferences expressed in financial terms when they construct their price policy. By doing so, it has the potential to make profit from programmes that attract the interest of audiences that are too small to be profitable on advertising channels. Pay-TV broadcasters have strengthened their position in sport broadcasting, particularly in Europe where they have become the leading broadcasters of club soccer tournaments.

The distribution of programmes to the viewers

TV programmes have traditionally been distributed to the viewers by any of the following three alternatives:

- *Terrestrial transmission*, where airwave signals are sent from a broadcasting channel transmitter to receivers owned by viewers, has been the dominant technology for broadcasting programme delivery over the last decades across most continents.
- *Cable transmission*, which uses telephone lines or dedicated separate cable networks where signals are sent along the cables from channels to receivers, represents another alternative.
- *Satellite transmission* became a third alternative for transmission from the early 1990s. With powerful transmitters hovering in orbits above the earth, satellite platforms can distribute signals over a very wide part of the earth's surface.

At the start of the twenty-first century, new technologies such as *broadband* being transmitted by telephone lines have emerged as additional alternatives to those mentioned above. The revenues of these producers come from the same sources as traditional commercial broadcasters, i.e. from advertisers and viewers. Therefore, their market behaviour is similar to the behaviour of traditional broadcasters.

Business integration

The majority of broadcasters and transmission companies do not operate alone, but together with others. In recent years, we have seen various forms of integration, involving both broadcasters and transmission companies.

Horizontal integration is when firms in the same line of business combine with one another. In 2003, Telepiú and Stream, the Italian pay-TV platforms that had broadcast the Italian Serie A, merged into Sky-Italy. A similar merger happened in Spain the same year when former rivals merged into one company, called Socecable.[3]

The broadcasters can achieve a range of advantages by operating within multi-media companies. Competition will be reduced, and it will strengthen the market power of the integrated firms, at the cost of the remaining companies operating at levels along the sport broadcasting value chain. Horizontal integration can involve merger, but also a number of formal and informal alliances, for example collective sale and purchase of broadcasting rights.

Vertical integration is when firms participate in more than one successive stage of the production or distribution of goods or services. *Upward (backward) integration* is when firms are integrating with suppliers of inputs, for example when a TV channel is buying stakes in a team. *Downward (forward) integration* is when firms integrate in activities on a level closer to the final customer, for example a TV channel buying stakes in a satellite or cable operator. Firms that integrate upwards will get more control over the supply of inputs. A company which integrates downwards will obtain more control over the distribution of its own products. A broadcaster which acquires stakes in a club can prevent media rights from being sold to rival broadcasters.

Vertical integration can reduce the risk of *opportunistic behaviour*, which is when the actors are taking advantage of another when allowed by circumstances (Carlton and Perloff, 1999). If a company becomes extremely dependent on specific products or

---

[3] TV-Sports Markets (2003) 7 (7).

inputs, this is a situation their partners can take advantage of. As an example, a TV broadcaster going through a period of declining rating figures may be desperate for attractive content and therefore be willing to pay over the market value – e.g. sports programmes. This is a situation owners of such content can take benefit from. However, if the broadcaster has stakes in clubs, it can prevent them from taking advantage of such situations.

Vertical integration also reduces the risk of being hit by *asymmetric information*. This refers to situations when an actor on the supply side has more or less information than an actor on the demand side, and vice versa. Acquiring sports rights can be risky since rating figures correlate very much with the performance of specific teams and competitors. Revenue-sharing clauses (royalty fees) that tie the fee to income generated by the broadcaster can reduce the risk of being hit by unforeseen shifts in demand. Such agreements, however, create a monitoring problem that is well known from the principal – agent literature (Stiglitz, 1987). The agent (TV broadcaster) will have more precise information about rating figures than the principal (for example a club or a sport governing body). This enables the broadcaster to underreport the rating figures, and hence also revenues. In addition, it can also exaggerate the costs. Such strategies will reduce royalty fees and hence the total rights fees. In the literature, this is known as the *moral hazard* problem and refers to situations where the principal is unable to control the actions of the agent (Douma and Schreuder, 2002).

Such royalty fees have become more common in recent years. When NBC sold more than $615 million in advertising for the 1996 Atlanta Games, a 50–50 revenue-sharing arrangement automatically kicked in, netting the IOC an additional $36 million (Slater, 1998).

Congeneric integration is between firms that produce goods that are related, but not identical. An example can be a media company that includes TV channels and radio channels as well as newspapers. Such forms of integration can generate cost advantages that are initiated by economies of scope advantages (see above). Congeneric integration also enables firms within the same company to promote each other's products. This certainly applies to sports clubs that are integrated in media companies. An article in a newspaper or some minutes of coverage in the news can promote an event much more effectively than ordinary advertising.

Sale procedures of media rights

Auctions

The total profit from broadcasting sports programmes depends on the gap between the revenues and costs. High rating figures, combined with relatively low programming costs, can generate substantial profit. The distribution of this profit, however, can be greatly affected by the sale procedures. Auctions have become the most common procedure for the most popular rights. In principle, an auction does not influence the total profit generated by the programme, only the distribution of it. An effective auction can increase rights fees significantly given the right circumstances. The higher the fee, the larger the proportion of the total profit that falls to the seller.

The most important factor in this matter will be the competition, at the demand side as well as at the supply side. Any seller will benefit from being the sole provider of such products, while there is at the same time fierce competition at the demand side. In contrast, the buyer would prefer to be the sole purchaser while at the same time there are a large number of sellers.

The production and consumption of live sport programmes have to take place simultaneously. This puts pressure on the buyer and seller to agree a deal before the event takes place. Without any deal, neither the seller nor the buyer will make any profit. This, in turn can motivate both parts to behave strategically.

The literature of auctions distinguishes between two categories of auctions, namely *private-value* auctions and *common-value* auctions (McAfee and McMillan, 1987). In private-value auctions each player's valuation is independent of those of the other players. At the time of the bidding, each bidder knows exactly what winning would be worth to him or her, but not what it would be worth to others. This is different in a common-value auction, where the item has approximately the same value to all bidders. However, the bidders do not have precise information about the value of the item, and thus have to estimate it on the basis of the information that is available. The two alternatives represent extreme cases. Real-world auctions will have elements from both categories, which also apply to auctions of sports rights. The values of sports rights will be closely related for commercial channels, but not necessarily 100 per cent identical. Pay-TV channels and advertising channels earn their revenues from different sources. Furthermore, pay-TV channels belonging to different broadcasting platforms may not have the same numbers of subscribers. Nor do all advertising channels have the same penetration. Hence, the broadcasters will not have identical revenue from broadcasting sports programmes. Non-commercial public service broadcasters, e.g. the BBC, do not earn any revenues from sport broadcasting.

We will now take a closer look at *English auction* and *sealed auction*, which have been the most common procedures applied by the sellers of media rights. In an English auction, the process starts with a (low) bid, which is then raised successively until one bid remains. The winner is the one with the highest bid, and who then pays the price he or she has bid. The bidding process ends when the price reaches just above the valuation of the player with the second-highest valuation. The final price in an English auction depends on the gap between the two bidders with the highest reservation prices. The narrower the gap, the higher the price will be.

Revealing information

The income from sport broadcasting is influenced by a number of factors. Many of them will be uncertain at the time the bids are submitted. Firstly, there can be unforeseen shifts in demand due to fluctuations in the business cycle and the popularity of the sport. Secondly, there is also the risk of excess supply if similar sport programmes are broadcast simultaneously. The consequence can be lower rating figures than first predicted. Such uncoordinated actions can create severe financial problems due to the high proportion of sunk costs that characterises this industry.

Since all bidders try to estimate their own valuation of the rights for a specific event, open auction procedures can work to the advantage of the seller, given the right circumstances. Some bidders may have limited experience with sport broadcasting. For them, learning about the rivals' bids may help them to adjust their own assessment. Hence, the unveiling (and sharing) of information that is integrated in an English auction can improve abilities to estimate the income potential correctly. This can motivate risk-averse buyers to bid more aggressively, and hence increase the price.

Sealed – first bid auction

In this procedure each bidder submits one bid and without having any information on the rivals' bids. Since the bids are kept secret, risk-aversive bidders are not provided with the same support to predict the value as in an English auction. This can be a major disadvantage if many sellers are risk averse. On the other hand, the sellers can also benefit from keeping the information about the bids secret. The bidders will face two potential traps. First is the danger of bidding more than necessary, i.e. leaving money on the table. Second is being too greedy and bidding so low that they miss out on a deal that could have been profitable. The bidder(s) will have to balance these two contradictory threats when deciding the strategy. The challenge of the seller is to convince the bidders to emphasise the latter aspect more than the former.

Collaboration

Broadcasters which participate regularly in auctions will learn that bidding wars can be avoided by collaborating. Tacit agreements, where potential buyers desist from bidding on specific rights, can work in their favour by lowering the price. Although such collaboration is illegal cartel behaviour, competition authorities may find it difficult to prove any form of collaboration.

The advantages of horizontal integration were discussed above. Even if the cartel member's income increases, this does not guarantee that the collaboration will last forever. Indeed, the success of a cartel can in itself represent the biggest threat with respect to its duration of secret deals. The benefit from breaking the agreement can come from two sources. Firstly, acquiring the deal solely can increase one's profit, assuming the income from broadcasting exceeds the costs. Secondly, if one of the rivals goes bankrupt, this will reduce the future competition and hence strengthen the market power of those that survive. The cartel members will balance the potential advantages and disadvantages against each other when deciding whether to uphold the collusion or not.

Any seller will wish to prevent collusion among the bidders. The choice of auction procedure can influence whether such collusion is uphold or not. If the seller stages an English auction, all information about the bids will be released immediately. If one cartel member breaks from the agreement, the others will discover it immediately. This will discipline the members. Thus, sellers that fear buyer collusion should not stage English auctions. This is different in sealed auctions where a surprise bid not will be revealed until the auction is finished (Cowie and Williams, 1997). On the other hand, breaking out from the collusion can also have long-term negative consequences. The future competition can grow fiercer if the companies that were cheated on survive, and there is also the risk of retaliation. The consequence can be a permanent state of bidding wars.

Case 18.1 European TV and sports rights 2006

Is Rai-Mediaset cartel ending?

Italy's highest appeal court ruled in November 2001 that Rai and Mediaset had acted as a cartel in the acquisition of sports rights. It said that the broadcasters had agreed to share out virtually all major sports rights from July 1996 to June 1999 in a deliberate attempt to prevent the small commercial channel Telemontecarlo (later to become La7) emerging as a rival. The cartel agreement covered Formula One, cycling's Giro d'Italia and football's Champions League, national team matches and Serie A highlights. Rai was fined L 1.45 billion (€750,000) and Mediaset L 997 million (€515,000).

Two years later, UEFA chief executive Gerhard Aigner complained about the lack of Champions League competition in Italy. The market 'does not correspond to an open market. It's almost as if no one expects their competitors to make a move'. His complaint followed UEFA having to accept a significant cut in television rights fees after Rai decided not to bid. A joint bid was submitted by Mediaset and Sky Italia, but it was dependent on each party being awarded the rights.

There is less evidence of collusion now. In the new bidding for the Champions League, for the three years from 2006/07, Rai won the free-to-air rights with a very high bid (against a low bid by Mediaset), Mediaset took the digital-terrestrial rights and Sky Italia the digital-satellite. Overall, UEFA increased its rights fees in Italy by 80 per cent. Mediaset retaliated by winning the Serie A highlights rights from 2005/06. Rai had shown the highlights since 1970.

Rai also bid aggressively for the 2010 and 2014 World Cup rights. There are said to have been various reasons why it had become more aggressive. First, a new nine-member Rai board was elected in June 2005 for the next three years, and the board was worried that Rai might lose its target audience and market position if did not win major sports rights.

Second, it is said that the new board, led by a left-wing acting president, Sandro Curzi, took advantage of the temporary power vacuum caused by the lack of a president and by the imminent departure of director general Flavio Cattaneo to make bold acquisitions to boost Rai. Third, Rai was under pressure to act positively after being fiercely criticised in the wake of losing some 2006 World Cup rights to pay-television platform Sky Italia.

Discussion questions

1 What is the welfare economic rationale for prohibiting broadcasters from collaborating?

2 Discuss the challenging of monitoring, and unveiling, collaborations between broadcasters.

Individual versus collective sale procedures

The prospect of valuable media rights has made the stakeholders involved in sport broadcasting more concerned about the ownership issue than before. It can be complicated to decide the 'natural' owner of the media rights. In team sports, the *home team* is the sole bearer of the economic risk to a match unless it is played on neutral ground. It has to provide the stadium, security, advertise the game and sell tickets. This represents an argument for regarding the home team as the sole owner. In many cases the visiting team will stage a rematch and hence has a chance to market this game and sell rights of an equal value. On the other hand, *the league* contributes to the product by its organisational and administrative inputs. If a match is a part of a tournament or a league, this usually makes it more valuable than if it was just a friendly match between two clubs. Although many people will find a soccer match between Real Madrid and Manchester United interesting, it will add to the interest if it is also say, a match in the UEFA Champions League.

The practice of collective sale has not been 100 per cent accepted by competitive authorities across the world. One major problem with such procedures is the concentration of rights in the hands of one seller (or a few). A league can be regarded as a cartel, given the special circumstances of the industry (Neale, 1964). Any cartel behaviour is generally regarded as a violation of anti-trust regulations. A similar picture applies to individual sports where international sport governing bodies have tied international competitions together in World Cup series.

The special circumstances in sport related to the importance of upholding the uncertainty of outcome (competitive balance) have given sports clubs and sport governing bodies exemptions from general antitrust regulations. This explains why competition authorities have accepted collective selling of broadcasting rights. In North America, the Sports Broadcasting Act of 1961 provided an antitrust exemption from the anti-trust laws in reaction to broadcasting activity for the NFL, NBA, NHL and MLB, but not for other professional sports. This was perceived to be in the best interests of competitive balance, and hence also for spectators and TV viewers. Collective sale has been the procedure for national broadcasting rights, with the income being equally shared between the clubs. In addition, the teams have also sold their media rights to local TV stations individually. In some leagues, particularly the MLB and NHL, this has generated enormous differences in revenues between teams from large metropolitan areas and teams from smaller cities.

In Europe, the issue of collective selling has been decided differently by the various jurisdictions. In the UK, the Restrictive Practice Courts (RPC) accepted in 1999 the collective agreement between the FA Premier League (FAPL) and BBC/BSkyB. Although the deal was regarded as cartel behaviour, the RPC regarded the benefits from the agreement (redistribution of wealth to smaller clubs) as outweighing any potential detriment through a reduction in competition.

In 1999, the Italian Competition Authority decided that the collective selling of broadcasting rights was in violation of antitrust law. Since then the rights were for several years sold individually, i.e. by the clubs. This was changed from the start of the 2009 season, where the Serie A clubs went back to collective sale (see Case 18.2). The individual procedure was challenged before the start of the Serie A 2002/03 season, which caused a two-week delay. The smallest clubs were disappointed by the low amount they were offered by the broadcasters and threatened to boycott the games. The conflict was solved when the large clubs decided to pay the difference between the amount offered by the broadcasters and the amount the small clubs asked for.

Case 18.2 Central sale paves way for Serie A's cultural revolution

The Italian football league, Lega Calcio, said that the return to the collective selling of Serie A's media rights had laid the basis for a 'cultural revolution' in Italian football.

Rights have been sold individually by the clubs since 1999, leading to a massive disparity in wealth between the big and small clubs and creating fractious relationships between the clubs and broadcasters. The rights from next season are being sold collectively by the league following a change in the law last year.

Speaking exclusively to TV Sports Markets, after launching the tender process for Serie A rights for the seasons 2010–2011 and 2011–2012, the league's director general, Marco Brunelli, said: 'This is the first time since Sky Italia and Mediaset Premium launched that there can be a genuine partnership between the league and its broadcasters, the kind of partnership you find in other European leagues.'

He said that the league and its rights adviser, the Infront agency, were confident that the tender process would be successful. 'We've worked hard to deliver what the broadcasters need and now it's up to the market to respond.'

The league has created one new live time-slot – at 12.30pm on Sunday – which is something that Rupert Murdoch's pay-television platform, Sky Italia, has been demanding for several seasons. There is also the possibility of an additional Serie A live slot – on Monday at 8.45pm – for any broadcaster who acquires the live rights for both Serie A and Serie B.

The league has also increased the opportunities for broadcasters to interview players, with new slots before the match, at half-time – with players leaving the pitch – and after the game. Cameras will also be allowed into the changing rooms to film the coach's pre-match team talk.

'The increased value for broadcasters is not just in the improved rights', Brunelli said. 'There will be higher levels of production, in line with the coverage of the top European leagues, and we as a league will be doing much more to protect the investments made by our broadcasters. We think that the reserve prices we have set are reasonable, given the present state of development of the market.'

Widespread praise

The way in which the league and Infront have handled negotiations with broadcasters prior to the tender was widely praised by industry experts.

A director at one major sports-rights agency said: 'If they pull this off, it will be a true miracle. If the basis for the broadcasting of Serie A for the period 2010–2012 is already laid by the end of July 2009, it will be extraordinary – unprecedented.'

He said that Infront and the league had been forced to operate in an 'unusually unstable' environment. 'There have been so many interests rooting against the collective-selling law – at a political level, within the big clubs and within the broadcasters. The broadcasters don't trust each other and the clubs don't trust each other. If you can create a collaboration which keeps all the broadcasters happy and all the club presidents onside, then you've done something remarkable.'

(continued)

Another agency director described the tender as 'a gesture of peace and collaboration' towards the broadcasters. 'The additional time slots and interviews have some economic value', he said, 'but they have a much greater symbolic value – they say that the league is working hard to give broadcasters what they want, that this is a partnership.'

New interview content

The league and Infront believe that the planned changes to the coverage will improve the experience of the viewer, by, as Brunelli put it, 'creating a narrative that lasts five hours, not just 90 minutes'.

'It's a way of bringing fans closer to the rituals of a match, from the moment the players get off the coach to when they arrive at the final press conference. You get all the little moments that make up a match day for the players and coaches.'

He said that the footage of the coach giving a pre-match talk – which can only be shown once matches are over – should have a 'didactic value' for viewers, giving them a better understanding of what they have just seen on the pitch.

Brunelli said that the league was taking on 'a great responsibility' to deliver what it was promising to the broadcasters but that collective selling made it easier to do so. 'The league is in a position to offer them a single, coherent and complete product', he said.

All 380 games live

The new collective-selling law says that broadcasters should not be obliged to show every game live. In the new deals, winning bidders have to show only 50 per cent of matches live, although it is likely that they will continue to show all games. The league had considered reducing the number of matches for which it sold live rights, along the lines of England's Premier League, which makes only 138 games available, but quickly abandoned the idea.

'The rationale behind the Premier League limiting games is to protect stadium attendances', Brunelli said. 'We don't believe that if you limited the live television games in Serie A more people would go to the stadiums. We need better stadiums to achieve that. Also, if 100 or 180 games were not shown live, they would be, by definition, those least attractive, and therefore those least likely to draw people to the stadiums.'

He said that viewers in Italy had got used to having all games live. 'For nearly 15 years all Serie A games have been shown live. If you suddenly go backwards you are taking something away from the consumer which the consumer has got used to. You are also punishing the broadcasters who have built their business models around showing all games.'

Source: TV Sports Markets, 17 July, 13 (13).

Discussion questions

3 What are the major differences between individual and collective sale of media rights?

4 Discuss whether it is a good idea for the clubs to limit the number of matches being broadcast.

In Germany, the German Competition Act has included an antitrust exemption that has allowed the Bundesliga clubs to continue to market their broadcasting rights collectively. This practice has also been accepted by the European Commission. In January 2005, the German football league and the European Commission agreed to legally binding commitments in the sale of packages of media rights. The European Commission has allowed UEFA to sell the Champions League rights collectively, in an agreement with a pattern similar to the German deal. Hence, UEFA has been asked to split up the rights in several small packages on a market-by-market basis. The reason for this is to avoid the situation that only one channel gets control of all the matches.

In Spain, the most popular clubs have sold their rights individually, while the clubs at the bottom of Primera Liga have sold the rights collectively, together with teams from the second division. A comparison between the English Premier League and the Spanish Primera Liga shows how differently the two models distribute the revenues. Real Madrid and Barcelona, together earned more than the other 18 clubs combined during the 2009/10 season. Of the total revenue of €589 million, the two top clubs earned €307 million (52 per cent). This did not correspond with the pattern in the English Premier League, where the two top clubs, Manchester United and Chelsea, earned 12 per cent of the media

Table 18.2 TV rights Primera Liga 2009/10 season (€ million)

Club	Fee p.a.	Duration
Real Madrid	157	2008/09–2012/13
Barcelona	150	2006/07–2012/13
Atletico Madrid	42	2009/10–2013/14
Valencia	30	2009/10–2013/14
Sevilla	20	2006/07–2010/11
Athletic Bilbao	18	2009/10–2010/11
Villareal	17	2009/10–2013/14
Deportivo	15	2009/10–2013/14
Zaragoza	14	2006/07–2010/11
Espanyol	14	2008/09–2012/13
Getafe	14	2009/10–2013/14
Levante	12	2009/10–2013/14
Racing	11	2006/07–2010/11
Real Bétis	10	2009/10–2013/14
Real Murcia	10	2007/08–2011/12
G-30		
Mallorca	15	2009/10–2013/14
Recreativo	10	2009/10–2013/14
Osasuna	10	2009/10–2013/14
Valladolid	10	2009/10–2013/14
Almeira	10	2009/10–2013/14
Total	589	

Source: TV Sports Markets, 11 (13). The fees in many cases cover a wide range of rights, including Copa del Rey and international rights, rights for home UEFA cup and Champions League qualifying matches, friendlies, perimeter advertising, sponsorship rights

Table 18.3 TV rights English Premier League clubs 2007/08 season (€ million)

	Premier League[4]	UEFA	Total
Manchester United	68	46	114
Chelsea	63	39	102
Liverpool	62	29	91
Arsenal	65	25	90
Everton	58	1	59
Aston Villa	58	–	58
Portsmouth	55	–	55
Blackburn	55	–	55
Manchester City	55	–	55
Newcastle	54	–	54
West Ham	51	–	51
Tottenham	50	1	51
Middlesbrough	47	–	47
Sunderland	46	–	46
Wigan Athletic	46	–	46
Bolton	44	1	45
Fulham	43	–	43
Reading	42	–	42
Birmingham	41	–	41
Derby	40	–	40
Total	1,043	142	1,185

Source: Safety in numbers, Annual review of football finance, Sport Business Group Deloitte June, 2009. Exchange rate: £1 = €1.36 by 01.01.2008

rights generated by the Premier League, and 19 per cent of the total rights including the revenues from European tournaments. Even if the English Premier League almost doubled the total media revenues of the Spanish Primera liga, Real Madrid and Barcelona earned more than twice the earnings of the top two English clubs. The revenues of the bottom club in the English Premier League (Derby) practically equalled the earnings of the Spanish club that came third on the revenue ladder, namely Atletico Madrid. Note that the figures partly refer to different seasons.

International sale of sports programmes

Over recent decades, some sports programmes have become popular export goods. Leagues in Europe and North America earn billions of dollars from overseas markets. One reason for this is the cost structure of sports broadcasting. High first copy costs and low marginal distribution costs create substantial economies of scale advantages that can be utilised by distributing the product to the largest possible audience. Any sale will increase

---

[4] Includes domestic and international rights.

Table 18.4 Percentage of foreign players in European football leagues

Season	England	Italy	Spain	France	Germany	Netherlands
92/93	8.0	n.a	n.a	n.a	n.a	n.a
93/94	10.3	n.a.	n.a.	n.a.	n.a.	n.a.
94/95	12.8	n.a.	n.a.	n.a.	n.a.	n.a.
95/96	17.5	12.4	20.5	n.a.	n.a.	n.a.
96/97	21.3	17.8	29.3	n.a.	n.a.	n.a.
97/98	26.0	21.8	36.4	n.a.	n.a.	n.a.
98/99	27.9	33.8	39.1	24.3	41.2	32.3
99/00	30.6	33.5	40.1	22.9	40.8	35.5
00/01	35.9	35.4	35.3	27.4	44.3	34.5
01/02	38.6	36.4	35.6	32.4	48.3	37.6
02/03	36.7	32.5	29.5	32.9	50.5	37.0
03/04	39.7	33.5	34.5	35.0	49.7	35.7
04/05	39.5	31.0	29.5	38.2	47.6	35.9
05/06	42.9	30.3	34.5	38.9	44.8	40.8
06/07	43.0	29.9	37.6	34.1	49.5	38.3
07/08	n.a.	35.8	38.7	38.3	52.5	36.8

Source: Solberg and Haugen, 2008

profit as long as the distribution costs related to the transaction are covered (Gaustad, 2000). Another reason is the low cultural discount on sports programmes. In recent years, sports clubs have further reduced the culture discount by investing in multinational squads. During the 2008/09 season, 25 per cent of the players in the North American National Hockey League (NHL) came from outside Canada and the US.[5] Likewise, teams in the National Basketball Association (NBA) have imported players from Korea and China. One example is Yao Ming, the Chinese basketball player, who has been very successful in the North American Baseball League (NBA). He has also been an All-Star game starter for several seasons, and his success has substantially increased the interest in NBA in China.

Table 18.4 shows the growth of foreign players in some of the leading European soccer leagues.

Table 18.5 shows the media rights for the English Premier League across seven markets, and also the values of the respective domestic leagues in these nations. The figures show that viewers in the big soccer nations (in this case Italy) are moderately interested in matches from elsewhere in the world. The value of the English Premier League rights were more than four times higher in Scandinavia than in Italy, even though the Italian population is 260 per cent of the Scandinavian population. Also note that the English Premier League rights were about 500 per cent more expensive in China than the Chinese domestic Super League. This illustrates how TV broadcasters and viewers in smaller soccer nations support clubs and players in the big soccer leagues, and in some cases even more than they support soccer in their own nations. In that way, the international sales of media rights widen the income gap between the rich and the 'not so rich' soccer nations.

---

[5] Source: NHL.com

Table 18.5 TV rights for national premier leagues and English Premier League (EPL) – 2006/07 season (US$ million)

	Domestic League (DL)	English Premier League (EPL)	EPL as % of DL
Italy	568	8.9	2%
Netherlands	71.3	4.7	7%
Scandinavia[6]	54.9	39.4	72%
Japan	42.5	12	28%
Australia[7]	7.5	7.3	97%
Korea	5.6	8.3	148%
China	3.8	20	526%

Source: World Football Leagues and TV rights. TV Sports Markets 2006, 10 (21–22)

Market interventions in sport broadcasting

As mentioned above, sport broadcasting can generate externalities, for example by stimulating more people to exercise and making them proud of the national competitors' successes in international competitions. Such externalities, which also have pure public goods elements, represent a rationale for maximising the TV audience.

Throughout the 1990s, the growth of pay-TV channels raised concerns regarding the general public's ability to watch popular sport. European politicians were alarmed in 1996 when News Corporation almost bid the Olympic Rights away from the EBU. Their fears received more fuel when FIFA, the same year, sold the 2002 and 2006 World Cup Soccer finals to the German Kirch corporation and the Swiss ISL marketing agency, instead of to the EBU as it had done in the past. In 2005, the EBU lost the rights for Euro 2008 to Sportfive, a media agency, for a fee of more than €600 million.[8] In 2009, this pattern was copied when the IOC sold the media rights for 2012 and 2014 Olympic Games to Sportfive instead of to EBU.[9]

Pay-TV broadcasters will base their activity on programmes that a sufficient number of viewers are willing to pay to watch. This does not necessarily correspond with mass audiences. If some viewers have very high willingness to pay, it might be profitable to sell the programmes on pay-per-view basis instead of financing them by selling advertising, even if the latter alternative will attract significantly larger audiences.

The development where market forces move such events away from free-to-air channels to pay-TV channels reduces the amount of goods that belong to the public domain. In that way, it represents a cost for society, since welfare is reduced. A consequence of this development is that governments have invented regulations that define sports programmes as a part of the public domain. Late in the 1990s so-called Listed Events regulations were established in several European countries – first in the UK, and later the idea was adopted by the European Commission in the 'Television Without Frontiers' directive 97/36. The principle in the directive is that each member state can draw up a list

---

[6] National rights includes Norway, Sweden and Denmark, while EPL rights also includes Finland.
[7] EPL rights also includes New Zealand.
[8] Source: TV Sports Markets (2005), 9 (3).
[9] Source: http://sochi2014.com/79038 (accessed 13 January 2010).

of events, national or non-national, that it considers as of major importance for the society. The rights to broadcast these events can only be acquired by broadcasters with a minimum penetration decided in the respective nations. By September 2012, nine European nations had implemented Listed Events.

In addition, Australia (Anti-siphoning List), India and South Africa have also implemented similar regulations. The pattern of the South African Listed Events (see Case 18.3) is typical for all nations that have implemented such lists. All of them have the Olympics Games and World Cup football finals, and many also have the final games in UEFA's championship for national teams. As for these two football tournaments, the majority has included the matches of the respective nations, as well as the finals and in some cases also the semi-finals, quarter-finals and opening matches. The UK and Belgium are exceptions to this, and have included the entire tournaments. Additionally, certain international championships and similar events in sports are very popular in particular nations – in South Africa this is rugby and cricket. Some nations have included events that over the years have obtained a special position and resonance, such as the Tour de France and Giro de Italia.

Case 18.3 South African Listed Events regulation
SABC listed-events lobbying 'unlikely' to change much
by Catherine Davies

A review of South Africa's listed-events legislation is generating concern among the country's broadcasters and rights holders, with national sports federations urging the government to reduce the list and state broadcaster SABC lobbying extensively behind the scenes for the list to be expanded. National federations would be the most affected by any additions to the list, which protects free-to-air television coverage of sports events of national importance. Between 50 and 70 per cent of their income derives from television rights fees, the majority from pay-television. Government funding accounts for less than one per cent. Broadcasters, rights-holders and agencies are due to make their presentations to the Independent Communications Authority of South Africa (ICASA), by the end of the month, with the government expected to publish its review early in the new year. 'SABC would like to have everything on the list', said one agency executive. 'They want everything for nothing. And the pay-operators and national federations want nothing on the list. But there's a feeling that the existing list is a fair one, and it's one that the broadcasters have been able to work with.' SABC and Supersport, the pay sports broadcaster owned by Multichoice, have traditionally shared the rights to top sporting events, with one or other usually acting in a gatekeeper role. SABC's arguments for an increased list will not be helped by reports of turmoil within the broadcaster, as evidenced by the collapse earlier this year of a deal for the 2011 cricket World Cup with pan-Asian broadcaster ESPN Star Sports. SABC had agreed a deal worth about $30 million (€24 million) for the rights for International Cricket Council events from 2008 to 2011, but then is understood to have dithered over providing details of its payment plan and bank guarantees. A frustrated ESS then ripped up the draft contract and signed instead

(continued)

with Supersport. Some senior industry executives believe that despite SABC's lobbying there will be little or no changes to the list. The government recently awarded licenses to four new pay-television operators and it would make no sense to over-regulate and squeeze them out by reducing the amount of premium content they could use to drive subscribers. Instead, ICASA is expected to introduce a 'dispute resolution mechanism' to the existing legislation, not because of any outstanding disputes but because the first list, published in 2003, called for such a measure. The list at present includes:

- Olympic, Commonwealth, and All Africa Games
- All South African national team matches, the opening match, two quarter-finals, one semi-final, the final, and opening and closing ceremonies of the football, rugby union and cricket World Cups, as well as football's Africa Cup of Nations Cup
- Finals of the national football, rugby and cricket domestic competitions
- Finals (if South African teams involved) of CAF Champions League, CAF Confederations Cup, Super 14 rugby union
- All South African national team home matches in football, rugby, cricket and netball
- The Comrades and Two Oceans marathons.

Source: TV Sports Markets 21 November 12 (21).

Discussion questions

5 Why are many sports governing bodies negative towards regulations such as the Listed Events?

6 What are the welfare economic rationales that support the implementation of such regulations?

The comprehensiveness of the Australian Anti-Siphoning list leaves the impression that the major concerns have been the entertainment aspect and the inefficiency from charging for public goods. This is underpinned by the following statement of the Minister for Communications, Information Technology and the Arts:[10]

> For many Australians, knowing that they can switch on their free-to-air television and watch a football grand final or a Test match is as important as having free access to Australian-made drama or a daily news bulletin.

Hence, preventing efficiency losses that occur from charging for public goods seems to be a major rationale behind the Australian regulation. This is different in the European Television Without Frontiers directive where the guidelines concentrate more on market failures related to externalities and merit goods, and not the efficiency loss from charging for public goods. The legitimising of the Austrian list uses the phrase: 'event that is an expression of Austria's cultural, artistic or social identity'. Likewise, the Italian list uses the phrase: 'events that have a particular cultural significance and strengthen the Italian cultural identity'.

---

[10] Speech made at the annual conference of the Australian Subscription Television and Radio Association on 8 April 2004.

Neither the Listed Events nor the Anti-Siphoning List indicates concerns for impacts that could improve the health conditions of residents. However, even if such aspects have not been mentioned in the regulations, they nevertheless represent a rationale for implementing them. The more people that are motivated to exercise, the stronger the rationale is.

The objective of such regulations is to move sporting events back into the public domain. Such policies will also affect the rights fees and hence also the owners, ability to make profit from selling them. A high degree of public domain reduces sellers' freedom to exploit the commercial value of the product. As a rule of thumb, the higher the degree of public domain, the lower the commercial value of the ownership will be. Contrary to this, a regime of strict juridical protection improves the owner's ability to make profit from the product, for example in an auction. This also explains the resistance towards the Listed Events regulations from many sport governing bodies.

 ## Conclusion

The production and distribution of sport programmes have characteristics that are both similar to and different from other commercial goods. Sport programmes in general have lower cultural discount than other genres of TV programmes. This refers to the drop in commercial value when the programme is broadcast outside its own domestic market. Investment in multinational squads has promoted teams and leagues worldwide, and further reduced the cultural discount. This explains why professional team tournaments and leagues from Europe and North America earn substantial revenues from selling their media rights overseas, for example to Asia.

The ability to reap economic benefit from international sale of media rights is further enhanced by the cost structure of sport broadcasting. High first-copy costs and low marginal distribution costs create substantial economies of scale advantages that can be utilised by distributing the product to the largest possible audience. Any sale will increase the profit as long as the distribution costs related to the transaction are covered.

The broadcasting industry has gone through a period characterised by various forms of business integration, involving both TV broadcasters and transmission companies. We have seen several examples of horizontal, vertical and congeneric integration. Indications of collaborations have been observed between the sellers and buyers of such rights. This has affected the distribution of market power between the buyers and sellers of media rights, and in turn also the values of media rights.

The special circumstances in sport related to the importance of upholding the uncertainty of outcome have given sports clubs and sport governing bodies exemptions from general antitrust regulations. Therefore, competition authorities across the world have accepted collective selling of broadcasting rights, a procedure that in general is prohibited in other economic activities. Nevertheless, many teams have sold the media rights individually, totally or partly. Experiences from Europe and North America have documented that individual sale procedures distribute the right fees more unevenly compared to collective sales.

Sports programmes can generate positive externalities, for example by stimulating people to exercise. This represents a rationale for maximising the TV audience when special popular events are broadcast. The fact that such programmes and the impacts from them also have public goods elements further strengthens this rationale. The objective of regulations such as the Listed Events and Anti-Siphoning List, which prevent pay-TV broadcasters from exclusively acquiring these events, is to maximise such externalities. However, such regulations will reduce the competition among the buyers of media rights, and hence also the values on the right fees. In that way, they are favourable for the buyers, but to the cost of the owners of the events.

Discussion questions

7 Discuss to what degree the cost structure of sport broadcasting can stimulate international sale of media rights.

8 Discuss the consequences that various forms of business integration can have for sports broadcasting.

9 Imagine that a sport governing body in your country plans to auction the media rights for a popular tournament. They are uncertain whether to stage an open auction or a secret auction, and therefore they ask for your advice on this matter.

Keywords

Congeneric integration; cultural discount; English auction; externalities; horizontal integration; Listed Events; vertical integration.

Guided reading

For further guidance on characteristics of sports programmes as commodities, see Gaustad (2000).

For a thorough discussion of the market behaviour and strategies of various categories of broadcasters, see Gratton and Solberg (2007) and Solberg and Gratton (2000).

For a thorough discussion of the Listed Events regulations, see Boardman and Hargreaves-Heap (1999), Solberg (2002a and 2007) and Gratton and Solberg (2007: Chapter 9).

A thorough discussion of the auctioning of media rights is found in Solberg (2006b).

For more details on the uncertainty of outcome and competitive balance, see Késenne (1996 and 2007) and Szymanksi (2001).

An analytical treatment of principal–agent theory is found in Douma and Scheruder (2002).

For comparisons of sport broadcasting issues in Europe and North America, see Cave and Crandall (2002), Hoehn and Lancefield (2003) and Solberg (2002b).

Recommended websites

The European Listed Events regulation: http://ec.europa.eu/avpolicy/reg/tvwf/implementation/events_list/index_en.htm
The Sports Economists: http://thesportseconomist.com/
TV Sports Markets: www.tvsportsmarkets.com/newsletter

References

Boardman, A.E. and Hargreaves-Heap, S.P. (1999) 'Network externalities and government restrictions on satellite broadcasting of key sporting events', *Journal of Cultural Economics*, 23 (3), 167–81.

Brown, A. (1996) 'Economics: Public service broadcasting and social values', *Journal of Media Economics*, 9 (1), 3–15.

Carlton, D.W. and Perloff, J.M. (1999) *Modern Industrial Organization*, 3rd edn, San Francisco: Addison Wesley Longman.

Cave, M. and Crandall, R.W. (2002) 'Sports rights and the broadcast industry', *The Economic Journal*, 111, F4–F26.

Cowie, C. and Williams, M. (1997) 'The economics of sports rights', *Telecommunication Policy*, 21 (7), 619–34.

Desbordes, M. (2006) 'The relationship between sport and television: the case of TF1 and the 2002 Football World Cup', in C. Jeanrenaud and S. Késenne (eds), *The Economics of Sports and the Media*, Cheltenham: Edward Elgar Publishing House.

Douma, S. and Schreuder, H. (2002) *Economic Approaches to Organizations*, Harlow: Pearson Education Limited.

Dunnet, P. (1990) *The World Television Industry – An Economic Analysis*, London: Routledge.

Gaustad, T. (2000) 'The economics of sports programming', *Nordicom Review*, 21 (2), 101–13.

Gratton, C. and Solberg, H.A. (2007) *The Economics of Sport Broadcasting*, London: Routledge.

Hoehn, T. and Lancefield, D. (2003) 'Broadcasting and sport', *Oxford Review of Economic Policy*, 19 (4), 552–68.

Késenne, S. (1996) 'League management in professional team sport with win maximizing clubs', *European Journal for Sport Management*, 2 (2), 14–22.

Késenne, S. (2007) *The Economic Theory of Professional Team Sports – An Analytical Treatment*, Glensada House, Glos, UK: Edward Elgar.

McAfee, R.P. and McMillan, J. (1987) 'Auctions and bidding', *Journal of Economic Literature*, 25, 708–47.

Neale, W.C. (1964) 'The peculiar economics of professional sports', *Quarterly Journal of Economics*, 78 (1), 1–14.

Samuelson, P.A. (1954) 'The pure theory of public expenditure', *Review of Economics and Statistics*, 36 (4), 387–89.

Slater, J. (1998) 'Changing partners: the relationship between the mass media and the Olympic, Games', Paper presented at the Fourth International Symposium for Olympic Research, 1–3 October.

Solberg, H.A. (2002a) 'Cultural prescription – the European Commission's listed events regulation – over reaction?', *Culture, Sport, Society*, 5 (2), 1–28.

Solberg, H.A. (2002b) 'The economics of television sports rights: Europe and the US – a comparative analysis', *Norsk Medietidskrift*, 10, 59–81.

Solberg, H.A. (2006a) 'International TV sports rights – risky investments', in C. Jeanrenaud and S. Késenne (eds), *The Economics of Sports and the Media*, Cheltenham: Edward Elgar.

Solberg, H.A. (2006b) 'The auctioning of TV sports rights', *International Journal of Sports Finance*, 1, 33–45.

Solberg, H.A. (2007) 'Sport broadcasting – is it a job for public service broadcasters? A welfare economic perspective', *Journal of Media Economics*, 20 (4).

Solberg, H.A. and Gratton, C. (2000) 'The economics of TV-sports rights – the case of European soccer', *European Journal of Sport Management*, 7, 68–98.

Solberg, H.A. and Hammervold, R. (2008) 'TV sports viewers – who are they? A Norwegian case study', *Nordicom Review*, 29 (1).

Solberg, H.A. and Haugen, K. (2008) 'The international trade of players in European club football – the consequences for national teams', *Journal of Sport Marketing and Sponsorship*, 10 (1).

Stiglitz, J.E. (1987) 'Principal and agent', *The New Palgrave: A Dictionary of Economics*, 3, 966–71.

Szymanski, S. (2001) 'Income inequality. Competitive balance and the attractiveness of team sports: some evidence and a natural experiment from English soccer', *The Economic Journal*, 111 (469), 69–84.

Risk management in sport

Dominic Elliott, University of Liverpool Management School

Learning outcomes

Upon completion of this chapter the reader should be able to:

- define the scope of risk for a sports organisation;
- explain the importance of risk and crisis management for sports businesses;
- understand that organisations may incubate the potential for failure themselves;
- identify the range of threats and hazards faced by sports organisations;
- understand the key components of effective crisis incident management.

 Overview

In February 2010 Nodar Kumaritashvili, representing Georgia in the Luge, tragically entered the Olympic record books when he was killed after crashing into exposed steel columns during a training run at the start of the Vancouver 2010 Winter Olympics. A short and quick investigation, lasting less than 12 hours (Donegan, 2010a), reported:

> It appears after a routine run, the athlete came late out of curve 15 and did not compensate properly to make correct entrance into curve 16. This resulted in a late entrance into curve 16 and although the athlete worked to correct the problem he eventually lost control of the sled resulting in the tragic accident. (Vancouver, 2010a)

concluding: 'there was no indication that the accident was caused by deficiencies in the track' (Vancouver, 2010a).

Donegan (2010b), however, reported a number of other incidents on that track including a potential gold-medal winner coming off his sled:

'I think they are pushing it a little too much,' Australia's Hannah Campbell-Pegg said on Thursday after she nearly lost control in training. 'To what extent are we just little lemmings that they just throw down a track and we're crash-test dummies? I mean, this is our lives.'

Following the initial investigation additional safety measures were introduced, although officials asserted: 'We did everything in our power to make it [the track] as safe as we can' (Vancouver, 2010b).

Some 12 years earlier Larry Ellison, CEO of Sun Microsystems and a participant in the 1998 Sydney to Hobart boat race, survived the horrific weather conditions which sank five boats with five deaths commented, in a choking voice:

this is not what racing is supposed to be. Difficult, yes. Dangerous, no. Life-threatening, definitely not . . . the seas were enormous, and the wind made noises we'd never heard before.

(Knecht, 2002: 5)

A casual observer may distinguish between these two examples. Ocean sailors are quite literally at the mercy of the elements and this sport carries many of the potential perils associated with deep-sea fishing, long acknowledged as one of the most hazardous of occupations. However, the Luge takes place on a constructed track, with designed gradients and curves to test the skills of competitors, albeit with, ideally, safety measures designed into the structure. It is man-made. Despite the official statement that everything had been done to ensure safety prior to the Olympics there was still more that might have been done, as evidenced by the further measures introduced following the death of Kumaritashvili. A series of incidents and a reputation as the fastest in the world (Donegan, 2010b) are all suggestive of multiple factors, something more than the official conclusion of 'human error'.

Risk and sport are inseparable and there can be miniscule margins between success and failure, most tellingly in matters of life and death but also in matches and races such as Lewis Hamilton's clinching fifth place in the 2008 Brazilian Grand Prix, to beat Felipe Massa and become Formula One champion by one point. However, our concern is less about attitudes towards risk in the playing of sport and more with risk, crisis and the business of sport. As previous chapters demonstrate, sport is big business, a truly global one and a business which generates large revenues – for example, FIFA estimated that soccer generates a turnover of $250 billion per annum (Tomlinson, 2002). As other sectors must deal with issues of risk and crisis management, so too must sport.

Individuals make judgements about risk every day of their lives, from deciding what to eat and drink to deciding when to cross the road. Following the death on the Luge track the Olympic authorities were faced with a choice between abandoning an event that occurs only once every four years or hoping that the findings from their investigations were accurate and the subsequent stop-gap measures sufficient. This stark choice is reflected in the comments of another Luge competitor, who no doubt realised that he might never get another chance to compete in an Olympic Games, when asked what it would feel like to be the first competitor on the track following the fatal accident: 'Whatever, I could have been the first or the 10th. It's Olympic training. It's a tragedy. I can't personally deal with it until after the Games' (cited in Donegan, 2010a).

Calculated risks are a part of sport, whether it is the decision on the number of pit stops or when to switch tyres in Formula One or whether a player should pass the ball or attempt to score the try in rugby. In most cases the probabilities are uncertain and the range of outcomes unclear, although the best teams and individuals seem able to weigh up this uncertainty intuitively. Perceptions will be shaped by a host of subjective factors, by mood, interactions with those around us, our view of our competitors, familiarity with the situation; all these combine to influence the final decision. Thus, although the risk management process may be aided by the use of scientific tools and frameworks, it is not a science, and it will be shaped by the perceptions of those conducting the analysis and interpreting the results.

The so-called credit crunch of 2007 has had a growing impact upon consumer disposable incomes and may be seen as a potential trigger of financial crisis for sport from lower than expected spectator numbers at the Winter Olympics in Vancouver to the financial difficulties of a number of English soccer clubs. Sport, like any other business, is affected by macro-economic forces and the successful bid by London to be the venue of the 2012 Olympics, which seemed a golden opportunity in 2005, is seen by some as an expense too far in post-credit crunch 2012. The desire for success and the associated glory may encourage some sports organisations to invest rashly and make themselves vulnerable to failure or changing macro-environmental factors.

Although increasingly run as businesses, sport organisations differ from many businesses in terms of their high profile. Sport is often used to achieve political ends, such as China's massive investment in sport in the build-up to the Beijing Olympics, perhaps as a symbol of China's rise in the world order. Boycotts have been widely used as a means of applying pressure, as in the boycotting of Apartheid South Africa. More recently, this high profile has attracted terrorist attacks, as at the Atlanta Olympics, in Lahore on Sri Lankan cricketers and the shootings of Togo footballers in Angola. Attacks on sportspeople or sports events will secure extensive media coverage and publicity.

The fanaticism of some spectators and the associations between competitors and place, be it national, regional or local, distinguish sport from many other industry sectors. The popularity of sports personalities and their place as role models may secure some lucrative sponsorship deals which may end in scandals if they are perceived to have failed to live up to their public image. The examples of former England soccer captain John Terry and golfer Tiger Woods demonstrate this public interest and the concerns of sponsors to protect their own brands should a scandal occur.

Sporting events often involve large, excitable crowds within confined spaces and safety management must be a primary concern of event organisers. These spaces are often used infrequently and pose potential difficulties to manage safely, and stadium disasters remain a feature of sport globally, despite the large investments made in investigating failure, building safe structures and developing management systems.

Another characteristic of sport lies in its often amateur roots and a key question concerns whether or not sports management has kept pace with the tremendous commercial opportunities which have opened up to the industry. Reflecting its amateur origins, a make-do approach to management was evident, one in which a small group or individual was responsible for a wide range of activities, from ticket sales, contract negotiations, match arrangements, health and safety; as one football club secretary commented: 'Ashes to ashes, dust to dust, what the others won't do the secretary must' (Elliott, 1998: 244). Another chief executive reported:

> Unfortunately football being what it is most people do two or three jobs . . . everybody has more roles than they should have, you just do not have the time, it's not an excuse, it's a fact, football clubs can't afford to pay that number of people because the financial structure of clubs is wrong . . . in football it is impossible to do a cash flow for the next month, there are so many unforeseen things that can happen and it is all down to kicking a football on the pitch or drawing a number out of a bag.
> (Elliott, 1998: 160)

Effective risk management, within such a context, is unlikely to receive the attention required – the necessary knowledge and skills set are likely to be missing.

Although none of these crisis types is unique to sport, it may be argued that this industry has a range of risks peculiar to itself. Fortunately from extensive research conducted within the industry and within other contexts a generic framework for considering the risk and crisis through a business continuity management process has been developed. This chapter provides an overview of this and the further reading identified at the end of this chapter provides guidance to more detailed approaches to risk management. The chapter begins by identifying a number of assumptions which underpin this chapter's approach to risk and crisis management, before proceeding to a consideration of the scope of risk and introducing tools for assessing the types of threats and hazards which sports organisations may be faced with.

A crisis management approach

Underpinning this chapter is a crisis management (CM) approach, which is defined here as one that:

- acknowledges the impact, potential or realised, of interruptions upon a wide range of stakeholders;
- recognises that threats often possess social and technical characteristics;
- recognises that if managed properly incidents do not inevitably result in crises;
- assumes that organisations themselves may play a major role in 'incubating the potential for failure';
- assumes that managers may build resilience to business interruptions through processes and changes to operating norms and practices.

The discipline of crisis management recognises a minimum of three distinct phases of crisis, as depicted in Figure 19.1 (see for example, Smith, 1990; Pauchant and Mitroff, 1992). These phases can be conceived of as the before, during and after phases. The pre-crisis stage refers to the period in which the potential for failure is incubated. In the years and months before an incident occurs, decisions will be made that make the organisation more or less vulnerable to crises. Such decisions might include (in)appropriate staffing levels, the discrediting or ignoring of internal and external safety reviews, or a focus upon profit to the detriment of safe working practices. Decisions may be influenced by core assumptions which may later prove to be fallacious. Pauchant and Mitroff (1992) argue that people and

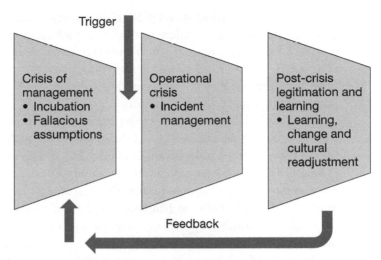

Figure 19.1 Stages of crisis model
Source: Adapted from Smith (1990)

groups within organisations may employ a range of reasons and strategies to resist change, even when events highlight inadequacies in systems, procedures and beliefs. For example, the 1971 Ibrox Stadium disaster was the fourth incident to involve fatalities or hundreds of injuries on Stairway 13 within a ten-year period (see Elliott and Smith, 1993).

The second stage refers to the immediate organisational handling of an incident and includes the immediate period of the crisis, between the crisis taking place and the resumption of operations or activities. Clearly, this period will vary according to the nature of the crisis itself and the ability of the organisation to respond. A distinction must also be drawn between the crisis and the trigger. The cancellation of the ITV digital contract with the Football League in 2002 triggered crises for a number of clubs, especially those recently relegated which retained Premier League cost structures. The impact of this trigger was determined by the existing financial state of the clubs. Those that had taken such events into account within their planning scenarios were better placed to deal with the contract's cancellation than those which had not undertaken any such scenario planning. Similarly, effective crisis management may exacerbate or reduce the impact of a trigger event.

Fitzgerald (1995) describes the period following the advent of a crisis as a 'glide path'; because aircraft will vary in their ability to glide based on environmental conditions, design, load and pilot skills. Similarly, organisations may, following an interruption to their operations, be able to continue their operations, albeit for a short period of time. In general terms, the so-called 'glide path' connotes the manner and speed with which operations are recovered.

The third, and final, stage refers to the period in which an organisation seeks to consolidate and then reposition itself. Of course, stage three feeds back into stage one as organisations may or may not learn from their experiences. This is the area most neglected by managers, not least because of the difficulties it poses as successful learning often requires challenging deep-seated beliefs.

A crisis management approach has evolved from considering how to manage crisis incidents (i.e. phases two and three), to considering how the potential for crisis may be incubated by organisations themselves (see Pauchant and Mitroff, 1992 and Elliott and

Smith, 1993 for a detailed sports industry case study). Thus, although risk management describes the process as undertaken by organisations, a crisis management approach denotes a frame of reference in which crisis is conceptualised as at least a three-stage process, one in which organisations themselves incubate the potential for failure. Here an important emphasis may be seen as seeking to develop resilience before crises and, if they do occur, to learn effectively from them.

For example, Elliott and Smith (2006) argued that the persistent emphasis upon crowd control, reflecting the fallacious belief that soccer hooliganism was the primary issue for the UK soccer industry, is key to understanding how unsafe stadia were designed, built and maintained and how those tasked with managing soccer events repeatedly misinterpreted genuine crowd distress as hooliganism, thus impeding a quick and apt response to disasters. For example, police at Hillsborough physically forced some spectators back into the crush from which they were escaping. Such assumptions help frame how events and management issues are perceived and may have material consequences.

Although risk management is a process undertaken by organisations, crises usually affect a wide group of stakeholders. For example, Brazil's 160 million population mourned, officially, for three days when Ayrton Senna died competing in the San Marino Grand Prix in 1994. Such crisis incidents usually possess social and technical dimensions. For example, the investigations into the causes of Senna's crash indicated a range of socio-technical factors with a number of allegations being made: that the steering column of Senna's vehicle had been cut to satisfy the driver's demand for more space in the cockpit, but that it had been poorly re-welded; that the maintenance of the track was another significant cause. Lovell (2003) suggests that charges against the organisers of the event and the owners of the vehicle were either dropped or 'eased' because of the political connections of key Formula One personnel with senior Italian politicians.

Without wishing to consider the ethical dimensions of this case, it illustrates the range of stakeholders who may become involved, the social and technical dimensions of failure (from the politics to the technicalities of the course and vehicle), that effective management resolved the incident and that the organisations involved probably played a major role in incubating the potential for failure. Although Senna bore the physical risk, Williams the financial risk of a lost vehicle and points in the championship, Formula One faced a threat to its viability and reputation.

In 2008 Formula One faced another serious threat to its reputation when newspapers reported the then FIA President Max Mosley's private sexual activities, including unfounded allegations of Nazi style sado-masochism. Disapproval came quickly from a variety of auto clubs and racing teams such as Toyota, Honda, BMW and Mercedes-Benz (Roopanarine, 2008). The Mosley affair provides one example of the great interest in the private lives of sports personalities. Individual sports personalities, like clubs and events such as the Olympics, are major brands and subject to waxing and waning reputations. Such cases illustrate the scope and some of the faces of risk management.

Managing risk

From a practical perspective there are a number of steps required to manage risk effectively. A process for managing business continuity is shown in Figure 19.2. Step 1 concerns identifying hazards and threats. Step 2 focuses upon developing an understanding of the

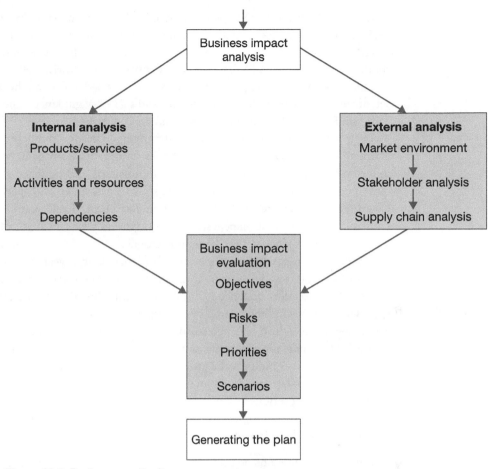

Figure 19.2 Business continuity management process
Source: Elliott et al. (2010)

sports organisations, key activities, temporal issues, supply chain dependencies and micro- and macro-environmental issues and trends. Following on from this, the impact of threats upon business activities will be assessed. Step 3 concerns measuring the risk, assessing its probability and deciding upon priorities. In step 4 alternative options are considered ranging from avoidance (withdrawing from an activity), deferment (wait and see), reduction (improve prevention and control measures, for example, through a continuity plan) or transfer (via insurance).

 ## Step 1: The scope of risk – identifying threats and hazards

Anecdotal evidence collected by the author from many countries across many continents indicates that there remains a strong perception of British soccer spectators as hooligans. There is often a memory of events such as Hillsborough, where 96 people were crushed to death; or of the 56 people who died in the fire at the Bradford Stadium (1985) or 39 killed in the Heysel Stadium in Brussels or the 66 crushed on the Ibrox Stadium's stairway 13. Although hooliganism was only a factor in one of these disasters, its perceived impact lingers in the memory. Our perceptions of risk rarely fit with the true probabilities. Individuals are more likely to die or be injured as they drive to a soccer match than suffer as victims of either hooliganism or of a major disaster. There is a wide range of threats sports clubs may face and a first step is to identify and categorise these.

The scope of risk management can be narrow or broad, reflecting the managerial mind-set of an organisation. Jones and Sutherland's (1999) guidance notes supporting the Turnbull Report (1999) identify fours broad areas of risk.

Their particular concern was with identifying risks for publicly listed companies, although it provides a useful overview of risks for organisations of all types. As the sports industry has shifted towards professionalism, business and financial risks have become more pertinent. For example, the revenue streams associated with playing in the UEFA Champions League are vitally important to Barcelona, Real Madrid and Manchester United. So much so that Manchester United reportedly was insured against the threat of failure to secure a place in the Champions League.

Although the soccer stadium disasters of the past 20 or so years and the well-publicised deaths of spectators and drivers in Formula One have been widely reported, even baseball has seen five spectators die since 1970, all highlighting the potential threats associated with sport which go beyond those faced by participants. These are the most tangible of hazards. But, as the sports industry has become more professional, the threats from other categories of risk have become more obvious, as Manchester United's insurance policy indicates.

Within the soccer industry the growing separation of coaching from business management is one response to this. In an early study of the soccer industry, Fynn and Guest (1994) identified a serious lack of business knowledge. More than 15 years later the problem appears to remain despite structural changes. In 2010 Lord Mawhinney, the outgoing Football League chairman, observed:

> The way football clubs do business fundamentally does not work . . . I think people are taking this issue much more seriously now. What is given to players and agents is not sustainable. There has to be some element of control and restraint.   (see Conn, 2010)

Risk management in business and finance is concerned with strategic management. Organisations such as Ryanair, Procter & Gamble, Mittal and Apple have sustained success through ongoing market research, competitor analysis and a sound understanding of how their competences fit with their environments. Although understanding does not guarantee success, it provides a sound basis for it. The introduction of new formats (for example, Twenty20 cricket) reflects changes in the environment; as spectators' lives change so must the services offered by the sports industry.

Shrivastava and Mitroff (1987) developed a framework for classifying types of resources according to *where* the crisis is generated (internal/external) and *which* systems (technical versus social) are the primary causes. The matrix may be used as the starting point for a brainstorming session for any organisation wishing to identify the range of interruptions it might face. As developing plans for every eventuality may be impractical, the matrix provides the basis for clustering 'families' of crises together and preparing for these clusters rather than for each individual incident. For example, in terms of impact, illegal drug taking amongst key personnel, evidence of bribery and match fixing, and the identification of key staff as racist would all combine both legal and reputational dimensions and might benefit from a similar response. Planners are limited in terms of time and resources and

Table 19.1 Risk matrix

Category of risk	Example	Sports illustration
Business	Wrong business strategy	In early 1970s Adidas dominated the running shoe industry. It underestimated the growth in demand for running shoes and the aggression of new rivals Nike. With relatively low barriers to entry, stronger promotion, sharper pricing and ongoing research and development might have built barriers to entry (Hartley, 1995).
	Industry in decline	Reflecting the decline of County Cricket in the UK, English clubs experimented with the Twenty20 version of the sport, a version that has spread worldwide.
	Too slow to innovate	English Rugby Union resist pressures for professionalism.
Financial	Cyclical risk	FIFA cyclical business leads to negative cash flow in non-World Cup years.
	Credit risk	Since 1992 Football League clubs have fallen into insolvency 53 times, with an estimated £200m unpaid to creditors.
	Misuse of financial resources	Former Yugoslavian footballer Dragan Dzajic faces the confiscation of property over the alleged embezzlement of millions of euros in transfer of players.
	Insolvency	Premiership club Portsmouth AFC insolvent and faces a winding-up order or administration in February 2010 (Fleming, 2010).
Compliance	Tax penalties	
	Abuse of position	Amos Adamu (vice-president of Fifa and Nigerian representative) and Reynald Temarii (from Tahiti) were banned for one year when caught out in a sting by newspaper investigators who pretended to represent a company seeking to buy votes for the USA's World Cup bid.
	Corruption	Former Juventus director Antonio Giraudo sentenced to three years in prison for his role in match-fixing scandal (*Guardian*, 2009).
Operational and other	Succession problems	Inspirational coaches move on with no obvious successor.
	Health and safety	Death of Luge competitor Nodar Kumaritashvili at Vancouver Olympics 2010.
		Stadia management, disasters in Abidjan (2009), Johannesburg (2001), Bastia (1989), Hillsborough (1989).
		Pandemic risks discourage international travel.
	Political	Threat to Formula One Bahrain Grand Prix due to popular uprising, March 2011.
	Reputation risk	Accenture and A&T withdraw sponsorship from Tiger Woods in late 2009 and early 2010. In late 2009 reports of Tiger Woods' marital infidelity were widely circulated (see Donegan, 2010c).

cannot account for all eventualities. Each sport would develop a matrix for its own sector, thus adverse weather might have very different connotations for yachting and cricket. Within each sport there may also be scope for threats and hazards to be identified relating to different levels within the sport, as illustrated by the following cases.

Table 19.2 Crisis typology for sports businesses

	Internal	*External*
Technical/economic	**Box 1** Poor business management Design of Luge in Vancouver Temporary seating collapses Fire Faulty maintenance of key equipment	**Box 2** Credit crunch triggers crisis of liquidity Key sponsor defaults TV rights monies cease suddenly Adverse weather conditions SARS virus threatens travel of sportspeople
Human/social/organisational	**Box 3** Crowd crushing Players strike Drug taking Bribery and corruption Reputation	**Box 4** Political upheaval Threat to reputation and adverse media coverage Legislative change Terrorism Failure of key supplier

Source: Adapted from Shrivastava and Mitroff (1987)

Case 19.1 Poor business management

The world's most popular sport is a mess of a business?

A theme of some crisis research has been with the crisis proneness of some organisations or sectors (see Pauchant and Mitroff, 1992, for example). This proneness reflects core assumptions and beliefs which shape behaviour and manifest themselves in a variety of ways, in the behaviour of many different stakeholders, and in this case at local, national and global levels.

In the week before the 2002 World Cup kicked off in Japan and South Korea Fortune reported an investigation of FIFA. It reported that it was run like a dictatorship, in a way which might constitute criminal offences under the Swiss penal code. With soccer's popularity never higher, the sport has been beset by bankruptcy, financial scandals and power plays. The FIFA president, Joseph 'Sepp' Blatter, was alleged to have awarded $100,000 (1998–2000) to a Mr Kolosokov, for his work on FIFA's executive. Blatter was also accused of paying a Niger referee to discredit the head of the Somalian FA who had reported that Blatter supporters had sought to bribe him. Blatter admitted that the payment to Kolosokov was 'irregular' and admitted to giving the referee $25,000 as an act of personal charity. Estimates of FIFA's accrued losses for the 1998–2002 period ranged between $31.9 million and $115.6 million.

Broadcasting rights to the 2002 World Cup had been sold to the Swiss-based ISSM group which crashed in May 2001. Its collaborator, Kirsch, assumed control of these

(continued)

rights but the non-broadcast commercial rights, also owned by ISSM (from sponsorship through to replicas of the mascot) were brought in-house, under (allegedly) the instruction of Blatter, although with the same personnel involved. Michel Zen-Ruffinen, general secretary of FIFA, expressed surprise that FIFA had chosen not to pursue criminal investigations against the former managers of ISSM.

Reflecting the global popularity of soccer and potential access to consumers in nearly 200 countries, despite these difficulties blue chip sponsors (e.g. Coca-Cola, Gillette, Hyundai, Mastercard) paid millions each for exclusive marketing deals for the 2002 World Cup. Five years later FIFA paid Mastercard a reported $90 million to settle a sponsorship dispute. Mastercard, a sponsor since 1990, believed it had first refusal to extend the deal to the 2010 and 2014 world cups and was unhappy when FIFA had brokered a deal with Visa. Sweeny (2007) reports that FIFA subsequently appointed Jerome Valcke as its new general secretary, eight months after he had lost his job as director of TV and marketing over 'repeated dishonesty' over the Visa sponsorship.

At a national level, despite its successes the football industry seems to provide a regular source of examples of many types of crisis incident. In 2006 Juventus was relegated as a result of a match-fixing scandal, with one of its directors sentenced to three years in prison. The sentence was not served owing to an amnesty for non-violent crimes.

In the English Football League the ongoing dire straits of many clubs' business mismanagement was reflected in 53 cases of insolvency between 1992 and 2010. Creditors such as small businesses, police, charities, hospitals and HM Revenue and Customs had lost an estimated £200 million, pointing to persistent poor corporate governance and the pursuit of inappropriate business strategies. These ongoing failures appear all the more reprehensible given the billions of pounds of new funding earned by the industry during the same period. It seems that high player wages and related expenses, paid in the hope of success on the field, were the most significant costs, coupled with, in some cases, criminal mismanagement. The English industry has been bedevilled with financial problems since at least the early 1960s, which triggered the first of two investigations led by Norman Chester.

As Elliott and Smith (2006) identified, there has been a reluctance for governments to intervene despite the long-standing problems facing the industry, preferring a self-regulatory approach which in reality indulges the football industry. New rules brought in by the Premier League and the Football League represent a bid to deal with difficult questions such as tests for fit and proper persons, financial controls and attempts to rein in reckless spending. On past experience these seemed doomed to failure.

Sources: Conn (2010); Gibson (2010); Oddos (2008); Sweeny (2006, 2007); Tomlinson (2002).

Discussion questions

1 To what extent does the status of FIFA and the global impact the industry possesses allow it to flout or accrue special privileges?

2 What explanations can you identify to account for past failures to regulate the football industry effectively?

The case of the global soccer industry provides evidence of the persistence of a particular approach to business, in which law breaking, dubious ethics and reckless spending might be seen as endemic. It suggests that such behaviours are institutionalised, not only at club level but amongst the higher echelons of the game (see Elliott and Smith, 2006). The ongoing popularity of the sport, around the world, may encourage an anything-goes form of management, not dissimilar to the banking culture which lay behind the collapse of a number of financial organisations in 2007/08. Just as the roots are internal, so too are the remedies in terms of developing a less crisis-prone culture with apt business practices.

Case 19.2 Credit crunches London Olympics

Falling land values hit 2012 Olympics

Figures released by the Olympic Delivery Authority (ODA) indicate that a fall in property prices, triggered by the credit crunch, could see the costs of the London 2012 Olympics rise by up to £150 million. The announcement was made alongside another which indicated that £400 million had been achieved in savings in other parts of the project.

The ODA further reported an overall increase in the cost of the Olympic budget of £21 million, with a further £160 million earmarked to cover maintenance and security at the Olympic park up to 2013. That means the ODA, which has a budget of £8.1 billion, now has anticipated final costs of £7.262 billion, up from £7.241 billion in the three months to December 2009.

Source: Taylor (2010).

Discussion questions

3 To what extent is it possible to prepare for unexpected extreme events such as the credit crunch or major political upheavals?

4 Does the focus upon success on the field, pitch or pool create a managerial mindset not well attuned to managing failure when it arises?

Despite the peculiarities of sports organisations, their fates are potentially influenced by macro-economic factors as much as other sectors. Falling disposable income may see, for example, a switch from watching live sport to watching it at home or in a bar. Merchandise and refreshment sales may also be affected by declining real incomes. Similarly, sponsors may be less willing to back events and teams when revenues and profits shrink. Although it is still too early to see the full impact of the credit squeeze triggered by the 2007 financial crisis, falling ticket sales at major sporting events have been reported, suggesting less revenue for the sports industry.

Case 19.3 Crowd management – a global issue

In 1985, 56 died when a fire swept through the main stand at the Bradford Stadium. Although the Health and Safety Executive (HSE) had expressed concerns about the stand, the stadium was not then covered by the Safety at Sports Grounds Act. There was little pressure on such football clubs to raise standards of safety because of their 'difficult' financial circumstances and an ongoing decline in attendances. In July 1984 the local authority informed the club and the local fire service that:

> The timber construction [of the main stand] is a fire hazard, and in particular, there is a buildup of combustible materials in the voids beneath the seats. A carelessly discarded cigarette could give rise to a fire risk.

On 11 May 1985, with some 11,000 spectators squeezed into this part of the stadium, a fire was ignited when a cigarette end fell amongst some old papers and sweet wrappers. The fire quickly took hold and within less than 2.5 minutes the entire main stand was in flames. Lack of exits and systems to communicate with the crowd prevented a quick evacuation. Spectators fleeing from the fire encountered unattended, locked gates.

In 1989, the deaths of 96 people at Sheffield's Hillsborough Stadium placed crowd safety high on the agenda across Britain and Europe. The tragedy occurred when standing areas became overcrowded. The pens in which the deaths occurred had been created by walls of steel, some of which had been installed for crowd control purposes and others which had been installed for crowd safety, a subtle but vital difference. There was no system for controlling the numbers of people into these enclosures and a strong mindset prevailed amongst football club, police and local authority regulators that the primary problem was of hooligan behaviour. The underlying causes of the disaster combined the technical layout of the stadium and the management of spectators within it.

In March 2009 a reported 22 fatalities occurred in Abidjan, Ivory Coast, triggered by overcrowding and a collapsed wall, with strong echoes of the tragedies at Heysel, Hillsborough and Birmingham respectively. Official reports blamed jostling spectators, a form of scapegoating also reminiscent of earlier stadium disasters. Similar incidents had been reported two years earlier in Zambia and Zimbabwe.

In 2007 in Lille, Northern France, many supporters were crushed due to overcrowding in which fans sought to escape the high fences. Images from this incident resembled images from Hillsborough. The reportedly heavy-handed response of the police at Lille suggests that the crowd's behaviour was misinterpreted as hooliganism, indicating an ongoing failure to learn.

Sources: Elliott and Smith (1993, 1997, 2006); Brown (2007).

Discussion questions

5 How highly does crowd safety figure in sport business priorities?

6 Do you consider stadium disasters manifestations of a deeper crisis of management?

A persistent but often fallacious assumption is that soccer crowds are hooligan. This encourages an approach to stadium design focused upon control, often to the detriment of safety. Further, stewards and police often misinterpret behaviour such as escape as hooliganism and respond accordingly. Elliott and Smith's (1993, 2006) analysis highlights the fatal consequences of such beliefs.

Case 19.4 'What is the difference between a car and a golf ball? Tiger Woods can drive a ball 400 yards'
Social–external reputational risk

The image of Tiger Woods, an athlete with a carefully cultivated family man persona was shaken as a series of news stories linked him to a string of affairs. The story broke in November 2009 when Woods crashed his car into a fire hydrant near his home. News of a number of extramarital liaisons emerged, stories at odds with the popular image of Woods. It was, arguably the sharp contrast between this public image of Tiger Woods, one which had attracted sponsorship, and the revelations around his private behaviour which triggered the damage to his reputation and business interests, not least with Accenture and AT&T cutting sponsorship. Possibly acting on advice, Woods said very little for more than two months.

In mid-February 2010 Tiger Woods finally broke his media silence and spoke to the press. PR specialist Max Clifford (2010) criticised Tiger Woods for this long delay, although observed that in his delivery Tiger Woods appeared genuinely contrite, recognised his own arrogance and hoped that the media would allow him to repair the damage to his family. Clifford also identified a key issue for Tiger Woods had been a failure to build a real relationship with the media in the years before the scandal. Elliott et al. (2010) suggest that such relationships, built up over time, may create a reservoir of goodwill at difficult times and help individuals, or organisations, overcome initial reputational damage. They contrast the destruction of Perrier as an independent entity when tiny traces of benzene were found in its water with Tylenol's rapid recovery as an example of this.

In the days after the press conference Woods' performance was subjected to increasing scrutiny. As Wetherell (2001) demonstrated in an analysis of the late Princess Diana's Panorama interview about her marriage with Prince Charles, such performances can reveal much about how identity is constructed through language and various forms of social interaction. Post-conference scrutiny examined the performance, with some concluding that key elements appeared to have been rehearsed, which raised questions about the authenticity and honesty of the speaker. An invited audience of only close friends, associates and sponsors unable to ask questions demonstrated the management of the event.

It is difficult to estimate the costs of this particular incident, although it appears to have had an impact upon the individual, the sponsors and the sport of golf itself. Ticket sales for golf events are reported to have fallen by 20 per cent and viewing figures by 55 per cent. For Woods, the media event has received a mixed response, and the absence of the Golf Writers Association of America damaged the event's credibility; Woods was criticised for staging it during the week of the Accenture World Matchplay, a former sponsor of Woods.

(continued)

Key learning points include the presence of an extensive literature on reputational crisis management, a process that should commence with the aim of building a reservoir of goodwill before difficulties emerge which are likely to enhance the probability of recovery.

Sources: Wetherell (2001); Clifford (2010); Donegan (2010b, 2010d); Hayward (2010); Elliott et al. (2010).

Discussion questions

7 Tiger Woods is not the first sports celebrity engage in marital infidelity. Identify the reasons why, in your opinion, the reputation of Tiger Woods suffered so dramatically as allegations of his misbehaviours emerged.

8 How do you think sports celebrities could reduce the threat of such media and public fallout, should misdemeanours or misbehaviours suddenly emerge?

9 Should a sport celebrity's personal life have any impact on their professional work?

Another commonly occurring risk is the threat to reputation, possibly growing in importance given the increasing revenues of sports organisations and individuals. Allegations proven or unproven are highly damaging. Allegations of impropriety, whether they have to do with sexual activities such as Tiger Woods and John Terry or financial (Harry Redknapp), drug taking (Ben Johnson, Marion Jones), not turning up for drug tests (Rio Ferdinand) or result fixing (Kieren Fallon) all provide a threat to the people involved and to other organisations with which they are associated, be they sponsors, employers or regulators. It is not whether the allegations are true and proven which counts, rather the threat to reputation is immediate and potentially long lasting, whether fair or not.

As these case studies illustrate, the sports industry may be faced with a wide range of threats, some strategic in nature, others operational failures which have the potential to escalate into a full-blown crisis. The above cases also indicate warning signs in terms of overcrowded stadia, police misperceptions and many football clubs metaphorically sailing close to the wind financially. The threats to FIFA – of business risks, low liquidity, cyclical cash flow, weak corporate governance – may equally apply to other governing bodies as well as to the small and large sports businesses. Similarly, threats to spectator safety inside stadia are as apt to sports such as motor rally, Formula One and Athletics as to Football.

The aim of this section has been to consider the wide range of threats to sports organisations. The frameworks provide a focus for considering the broad scope of risk and for considering which may be the most relevant for any particular sports business. However, as the examples illustrate, threats, when realised, rarely impact on one organisation alone, the nature of risk and crisis is that they encompass multiple stakeholders and sporting organisations are as reliant upon suppliers and distributors as other types of business, as the collapse of Britain's ITV digital ($447 million for broadcasting second tier soccer) illustrates.

Step 2: Identifying and assessing the risk

Two broad approaches to risk assessment have emerged, the heuristic and 'scientific' approaches. The heuristic (rule of thumb approach) is qualitative and based upon judgement. The 'scientific' approach utilises statistical modelling. Toft (1993) has argued that all risk assessment, no matter how sophisticated the modelling, remains inherently value-laden and should therefore be seen as a judgement.

Elliott et al. (2010) offer a qualitative framework for risk assessment, one which emphasises the interdependence of organisations and the importance of a full stakeholder analysis. Key questions to be examined include:

- What is the nature of the hazards with which we are faced?
- What is the potential impact upon our business and other stakeholders?
- What is the probability of a failure occurring?
- What are our key business and operational objectives?
- How do we use our resources to achieve our strategic objectives and add value?
- What linkages and dependencies exist within our supply network?
- What are the potential consequences of the threats identified?
- What seasonal trends or critical timing issues might affect us?
- Is the risk acceptable to our stakeholders and us?
- What should be done to manage risk?

These headings (which lead to related questions) should be adapted to meet the needs of the organisation and would certainly differ, for example, between an industry association and an individual sports club. The purpose of such questions is to stimulate data gatherers and managers to consider risk and how change in any of these broad categories might affect business processes. Elliott et al.'s (2010) framework emphasises the importance of understanding an organisation's internal and external environment. For example, Table 19.3 highlights functional dependencies both within an organisation and its supply chain. Sporting events may be interrupted by failures or difficulties experienced by suppliers or by the failure of backroom activities. An observation of Elliott et al. (2010) was described as the 'soccer star syndrome'. Within the finance sector certain primary activities, such as the dealing rooms, are elevated to a high status with remuneration packages for the 'star dealers' to match. This resembles the football industry because greater management attention is focused upon the playing field than on the unglamorous, but very necessary, backroom and stadium management support activities. Defenders and goal-keepers rarely attract the large transfer fees of top strikers, yet their functions are as vital to achieving the overall objectives of the football team. Identifying the functional dependencies provides an opportunity for examining the linkages between the exciting and the humdrum links that deliver customer value.

The aim of the risk assessment stage is to identify the range of risks and provide some estimation of the degree of threat in terms of severity of impact and probability of occurrence, as depicted in Figure 19.3. Categorisation may occur from a simple ranking exercise, ensuring that high threat events that are likely to occur receive the highest possible attention.

Table 19.3 Functional dependencies

Dependencies	Examples
Operations management and production	Sporting events require crowd management and facilities management
	Supply of uncontaminated food produce
	Crowd monitoring systems
Information and communication technologies (ICT)	Automated crowd control systems
	CCTV
	Communication systems
Marketing (shared brands, marketing and promotion)	Tiger Woods loses sponsorship
Distribution channels (type, number and mix of wholesalers/retailers)	Increasing concentration of power in media companies with TV rights – how to respond?
Purchasing and procurement (raw materials and components from suppliers)	Collective bargaining from professional players unions
	Providers of key sporting venues
Logistics (whether in-house or otherwise)	Direct ticket sales dependent upon postal services for delivery
Organisational support activities (such as legal, finance, etc.)	Lawyers give advice on key contractual issues

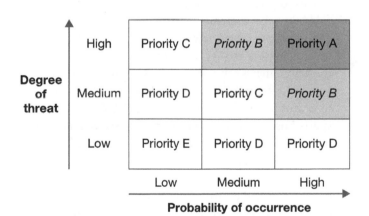

Figure 19.3 Risk assessment matrix

Although risk analysis and assessment may be aided by complex mathematical modelling these can only aid judgement as they are based upon many subjective assumptions. The aim of such tools is to help managers arrive at a considered understanding of the hazards and threats their organisations face together with an understanding of the potential impact upon operational and strategic objectives. The tools are, perhaps, best used to frame the discussion of hazards and risk management and ensure that such issues are not ignored. Resulting from analysis and discussion, a strategy for risk management should be developed.

Step 3: Risk assessment

The hazards of Formula One are obvious, and not surprisingly safety issues receive detailed consideration. In 1982 the Brabham team introduced pit stops; it enabled cars to run with lighter fuel loads and softer tyres and provided an opportunity for sponsors to publicise their logos. There are, however, hazards associated with blasting fuel into tanks via pressure hoses, as illustrated by the spillage of fuel over Keke Rosberg's car during the 1982 Brazilian Grand Prix. Such pit stops were banned until 1994 when Ecclestone, aware of the dramatic impact on television, successfully advocated their reintroduction – the risk was considered worth the television entertainment value (Lovell, 2003). Risk practice results from a trade-off; in this case driver safety versus revenue streams. Despite other accidents pit stops quickly became part of Formula One.

The use of a safety car, in Formula One, to slow competitors following an accident or during dangerous conditions reduces the need for lengthy restarts, an important issue for global television companies. There were concerns that long waits for restarts would encourage bored television viewers to switch channels. Drivers' concerns that the slowness of the safety car could cause the tyre pressure to drop and seriously reduce handling capability were given less consideration.

These two examples illustrate the balance that sports managers strike between conflicting objectives. The purpose of risk assessment and analysis is that such decisions are grounded in a critical evaluation of the evidence; that is, a considered assessment is made. Of course there are dangers that commercial factors will outweigh health and safety, especially where threats to participants are more difficult to quantify.

At the other extreme, sports managers need to assess threats from the macroeconomic environment. Where low interest rates lowered the cost of borrowing and encouraged investment, the credit crunch has had a huge impact upon land and property values. As these are often a key asset and thus collateral for debt, such fluctuations are likely to have an impact upon the amounts lenders are willing to offer, especially in the greater aversion to risk of financial organisations after 2007. Risk management permeates all areas of the sports business, from micro to macro issues. Risk strategies may also be evident in preparations for managing the crisis – the subject of the next section – and in the preparation of business continuity plans.

Simply explained, a business continuity plan (BCP) is the outcome of a thorough process in which the links between an organisation's objectives, resources, environmental context and dependencies are critically examined. The resulting plan identifies how an organisation will re-establish itself in the event of an interruption. It may include a blueprint of key personnel, contact details, equipment, activities, key deadlines etc. in order that any business recovery can be achieved quickly (see Elliott et al., 2010 for a full discussion of business continuity management). The objective of BCP is to ensure that recovery occurs in an orderly manner in a way that supports the strategic objectives of an organisation.

Step 4: Managing the crisis

Even well-run organisations may experience a crisis and proper preparation will result in a greater probability of survival.

Handling events

Major sporting events bring together thousands of people. From boxing to the Olympics to soccer they may be characterised by dynamism, excitement and the unfamiliarity of many spectators with their temporary surroundings. The deaths of spectators watching motor racing or attending soccer matches has encouraged the expectation that sports venues should develop the capability to manage a crisis incident. Time is likely to be of the essence in incidents where there are deaths, injury or serious threats to property, although a longer time frame may be more important where there is a significant threat to an organisation's reputation.

A key component of effective incident management is the crisis management team. In addition to the day-to-day structures required to implement risk management, a command and control structure for managing crisis incidents is needed. A commonly used format is a three-tier structure, as advocated by the Home Office (1997a, 1997b), mimicking the structure used by the British police service which labels the three levels as bronze, silver and gold systems (respectively tactical, operational and strategic). This structure emerged from an attempt to encourage consistency between the emergency services and thereby minimise confusion when dealing with an incident (Flin, 1996).

The purpose of the three levels is to ensure that an organisation's response to an incident is effectively coordinated. Bronze (operational) corresponds to the normal operational response provided by the emergency services where the management is of routine tasks. The immediate response to an incident is likely to be managed at this level. When the emergency services deal with a major incident, the 'bronze commander' is likely to lead a front-line team. Silver (tactical) refers to the command level, which seeks to identify priorities and allocate resources accordingly. During a major incident, it is likely that the silver commander will take charge of managing the incident itself. The role of the gold (strategic) group and commander is to take an overview, to arbitrate between any conflicts at silver level and to assume responsibility for liaising with the media and key stakeholder groups. The 'gold commander' is not expected to participate in the detailed management of an incident (adapted from Home Office 1997a, 1997b). There is no one best way and organisations should plan to use structures that best fit their needs and resources. The three levels identify a minimum of three roles to be undertaken when managing an incident. In smaller organisations one team or individual may perform these distinct roles. Sport abounds with examples of task specialisation, fielders, bowlers and wicket keepers in cricket, forwards and backs in rugby, strikers, midfielders, defenders and goalkeepers in soccer, to name but three. Individuals may switch from defence to attack depending upon need and revert as necessary. This is an apt metaphor for the crisis team. The same individual may fulfil different roles as necessary.

Teams are important because, generally, they outperform individuals, although, as Janis's (1983) groundbreaking work identified, teams may be fallible. Errors may arise from the poor quality of information available, a lack of monitoring key indicators (e.g. accident statistics, budgetary controls), the cognitive abilities of the group and political differences within a group. Sport provokes high emotion, as can be seen from the battle to take Rugby Union from amateurism to professionalism (Jones, 2000), or the media coverage of Bernie Ecclestone (see for example Lovell, 2003). Inevitably, political manoeuvring may reduce team effectiveness. Smart and Vertinsky (1977) identify a range of remedies to the potential difficulties of fallible teams, including the inclusion of independent experts, encouraging alternative viewpoints, protecting minority perspectives and holding crisis simulations. Implicit in Smart and Vertinsky's analysis is the development of the critical team that continually questions decisions and information whilst possessing the mechanisms, personnel and communication channels to support quick and effective action.

Conclusion

The development of risk, crisis and business continuity management processes has developed rapidly during the early twenty-first century in all industry sectors. As the management of sport professionalises and moves away from its often amateur roots it also needs to meet the challenge of dealing with uncertainty and the threat of business interruptions. Indeed, the volatility of many sporting organisations' environments, with close links between performance and revenue streams, in addition to the more tangible health and safety type of operational risks, highlights the relevance of risk and crisis management to this industry. It has been argued that crises impact upon a wide group of stakeholders, not simply the host organisation. A multiple stakeholder perspective is thus the starting point for effective risk management and should flow through subsequent analysis.

A four-stage process has been outlined, briefly, above. It provides a basic blueprint for risk and business continuity management. The process is only constrained by the imagination of the analyst and it is argued that the first stage should consider the widest range of possible failures in all of the areas of risk identified. The second stage is concerned with assessing the impact of a failure upon the sports organisation. A clear understanding of the organisation's objectives is a vital prerequisite to this. The third stage is concerned with calculating the probability of failure. The fourth step involves managers considering alternative options for action ranging from avoidance (withdrawing from an activity), deferment (wait and see), reduction (improve prevention and control measures, for example, through a continuity plan) or transfer (via insurance) and preparing for managing crises.

Discussion questions

10 You are a consultant briefed to prepare a report dealing with risk management across the soccer industry. Prepare a matrix for FIFA and for a professional football club. How might these be clustered?

11 What is a crisis management approach?

Keywords

Business continuity planning; crisis; crisis management; hazard; incident management; risk; risk management.

Guided reading

Although obviously biased, Elliott et al.'s (2010) text dealing with business continuity management provides a practical guide to preparing a business continuity management and crisis incident handling. It includes a range of short case studies from a range of industries. Waring and Glendon's (1998) book provides arguably the best introduction to risk management, including a range of detailed case studies, although none are sports-related. The Financial Times *Mastering Risk*, Volumes 1 and 2, provides a useful overview of current thinking, particularly on business and market risk. Although these volumes are primarily concerned with the finance sector. It is my view that many business and financial risks can be dealt with through effective strategic management and there are many solid textbooks dealing with this. As an introduction to crisis management, Elliott and Smith's (1993) analysis of the football stadia disasters is a readable, applied study that highlights, through case studies, how the potential for crisis is incubated and how organisations respond more or less effectively. This latter is picked up more force-fully in Elliott et al. (2010) and although it deals primarily with the football industry it has a generic relevance. Bernstein (1996) provides the most comprehensive history of risk management to date.

Recommended websites

www.risk-ed.org/pages/risk/sports_risk.htm – A website which deals with a wide range of risk mitigation issues.

www.cabinetoffice.gov.uk/ukresilience.aspx – A comprehensive website of risk and resilience matters pertaining to the UK.

www.hse.gov.uk/ – A clearly signposted website dealing with many health and safety type risks.

www.liv.ac.uk/footballindustry/hooligan.html – Deals specifically with issues of risk and hooliganism, with links to University of Liverpool research.

www.deloitte.com/view/en_GB/uk/article/6a5fb29b3f907210VgnVCM100000ba42f00aRCRD.htm – Deals with research conducted by Deloitte Sports Business Unit.

www.bl.uk/reshelp/findhelpindustry/sports/sports.html – Signposts many reports on sport and business.

References

Bernstein, P. (1996) *Against the Gods: The Remarkable Story of Risk*, New York: John Wiley.

Brown, O. (2007) 'United night of Mayhem', *Daily Telegraph*, www.telegraph.co.uk/sport/football/2308077/Uniteds-night-of-mayhem.html

Clifford, M. (2010) 'He apologises but did he convince', *The Guardian*, Sport, Saturday 20 February.

Conn, D. (2010) 'Inside Sport', *The Guardian*, 10 February, www.guardian.co.uk/football/david-conn-inside-sport-blog/2010/feb/10/portsmouth-cardiff-hmrc-winding-up

Donegan, L. (2010a) 'Luge men back on Vancouver track as IOC lets responsibilities slide', *The Observer*, 14 February, 1.

Donegan, L. (2010b) 'Luge athlete's death in training casts shadow over Vancouver Olympics', *The Guardian*, 13 February, 3.

Donegan, L. (2010c) 'Tiger Woods loses AT&T sponsorship deal', Guardian online, www.guardian.co.uk/sport/2009/dec/31/tiger-woods-dropped-by-sponsor

Donegan, L. (2010d) 'Twelve steps to an American atonement', *The Guardian*, Sport, Saturday 20 February.

Elliott, D. (1998) 'Learning from crisis', unpublished PhD thesis, University of Durham.

Elliott, D. and Smith, D. (1993) 'Learning from tragedy: sports stadia disasters in the UK', *Industrial and Environmental Crisis Quarterly*, 7 (3), 205–30.

Elliott, D. and Smith, D. (1997) 'Waiting for the next one', in S. Frosdick and L. Walley (eds), *Sport and Safety Management*, Oxford: Butterworth Heinemann.

Elliott, D. and Smith, D. (2006) 'Patterns of regulatory behaviour in the UK football industry', *Journal of Management Studies*, 43 (2), 291–318.

Elliott, D., Swartz, E. and Herbane, B. (2010) *Business Continuity Management: A Crisis Management Approach*, 2nd edn, London: Routledge.

Fitzgerald, K.J. (1995) 'Establishing an effective continuity strategy', *Information Management and Computer Security*, 3 (3), 20–24.

Fleming, M. (2010) 'Seven days left to save debt-ridden Portsmouth', *The Independent*, 11 February, http://ft.chadwyck.co.uk.ezproxy.liv.ac.uk/ft/quickSearchDisplayRecord.do?queryString=Portsm outhAFC&articleWordsContaining=all&sortType=reverseChronological&pageSize=25&page Num=1&index=1

Flin, R. (1996) *Sitting in the Hot Seat*, London: John Wiley.

Fynn, A. and Guest, L. (1994) *Out of Time*, London: Simon and Schuster.

Guardian (2009) 'Ex-Juventus director sentenced to three years in jail for match-fixing', www. guardian.co.uk/football/2009/dec/14/juventus-director-guilty-fraud-antonio-giraudo

Hartley, R.F. (1995) *Marketing Mistakes*, 6th edn, New York: John Wiley.

Hayward, P. (2010) 'Imagine if Tiger had given the finger rather than a stream of purification', *The Observer*, Sports, 13 December, 9.

Home Office (1997a) *Business as Usual: Maximising Business Resilience to Terrorist Bombing*, London: Home Office.

Home Office (1997b) *Bombs, Protecting People and Property*, London: Home Office.

Janis, I.L. (1983) *Groupthink: Psychological Studies of Public Decisions and Fiascos*, New York: Free Press.

Jones, M.E. and Sutherland, G. (1999) *Implementing Turnbull: A Boardroom Briefing*, London: Institute of Chartered Accountants of England and Wales.

Jones, S. (2000) *Midnight Rugby*, London: Headline Publishing.

Knecht, G.B. (2002) *The Proving Ground*, London: Fourth Estate.

Lovell, T. (2003) *Bernie's Game*, London: Metro Publishing.

Oddos, S. (2008) 'World Cup 2010 Sponsorship issues', www.docstoc.com/docs/880948/World-Cup-2010-Sponsorship-Issues

Pauchant, T. and Mitroff, I. (1992) *Transforming the Crisis-prone Organisation*, San Francisco: Jossey-Bass.

Roopanarine (2008) 'Ecclestone backs beleaguered Mosley', www.guardian.co.uk/sport/2008/apr/04/ motorsports.formulaone

Shrivastava, P. and Mitroff, I. (1987) 'Strategic management of corporate crises', *Columbia Journal of World Business* (Spring), 5–12.

Smart, C. and Vertinsky, I. (1977) 'Designs for crisis decision units', *Administrative Science Quarterly*, 22, 640–57.

Smith, D. (1990) 'Beyond contingency planning: towards a model of crisis management', *Industrial Crisis Quarterly*, 4 (4), 263–75.

Sweney, M. (2006) 'More fallout from Fifa-Visa deal', *The Guardian* online, www.guardian.co.uk/ media/2006/dec/12/marketingandpr

Sweney, M. (2007) 'Visa scores World Cup coup', *The Guardian* online, www.guardian.co.uk/ media/2007/jun/28/marketingandpr.advertising

Taylor, M. (2010) 'Falling land values hit Olympic Budgets', *The Guardian*, Tuesday 9 February, 3.

Toft, B. (1993) 'Behavioural aspects of risk management', Paper presented at the Association of Risk Managers in Industry and Commerce Annual Conference, London, AIRMIC Conference Proceedings.

Tomlinson, R. (2002) 'The world's most popular sport is a mess of a business', *Fortune*, 29 May, 28–34.

Vancouver (2010a) Official Website Joint VANOC – FIL Statement on Men's Luge Competition, www.vancouver2010.com/olympic-news/n/news/fil-statement-on-mens-luge-competition_ 274462nE.html

Vancouver (2010b) Official Website Luge: Luge start moved as officials defend sliding track, www. vancouver2010.com/olympic-news/n/news/afp-news/luge--luge-start-moved-as-officials-defend-sliding-track_274696Qx.html

Waring, A.E. and Glendon, A.I. (1998) *Managing Risk: Critical Issues for Survival and Success into the 21st Century*, London: ITBP.

Wetherell, M. (2001) 'Themes in discourse research: the case of Diana', in M. Wetherell, S. Taylor and S.J. Yates (eds) *Discourse Theory and Practice: A Reader*, London: Sage.

20

The sports betting industry

David Morris, Coventry Business School

Learning outcomes

Upon completion of this chapter the reader should be able to:

- understand the nature and scope of the sports betting industry;
- identify the major sectors of the industry and analyse the differences and similarities between them;
- understand the major ways in which sports betting is undertaken;
- analyse the major drivers for change in the industry;
- understand the changing relationships between the sports, betting and media industries.

 ## Overview

The overall aim of this chapter is to explore the changing interrelationships between the sports and betting industries through an examination of where they interact, that is in the sports betting sector. The chapter begins with an overview of the main sectors of the gambling industry and the place of sports betting within it. It is also important to understand how sports betting markets work, both at an operational and theoretical level. We then move on to consider whether or not sports betting markets are 'fair' and whether it matters or not. The chapter continues by looking at the motivations of sports betting consumers. The chapter concludes by considering the major drivers of change in the industry – technological change, deregulation, the growth of online media and globalisation.

Two case studies are used to illustrate the major themes of the chapter. The case study questions are designed to reinforce important learning points.

# The sports betting industry

Sports betting is part of the wider gambling industry which, in turn, is part of the leisure industry. Sports betting competes for expenditure with close alternatives such as other forms of gambling and betting on non-sporting events such as the outcomes of elections or even television reality shows. Gambling encompasses games of chance or chance and skill played at casinos, including those played on machines for large prizes in outlets licensed for the purpose (a sector usually known as gaming), bingo halls and the like, lottery games, playing machines for small prizes in pubs and clubs (known as Amusement With Prizes or AWP machines) and sports betting itself. Sports betting can be further divided into betting on animal racing (predominantly racehorses but also greyhounds and in some countries ponies and even camels), football pools and betting on other sports. Sports betting can be undertaken at sports events themselves, at specialist physical retail outlets (often known as betting shops in the UK), by telephone and online either over the internet or via interactive television. The global market for online sports betting was estimated at $4.8 billion in 2007 despite it being illegal in the US and many other countries. The latest developments in the online sports betting sector enable a wide variety of bets to be placed via mobile devices such as smartphones and tablet computers.

In 2008 UK consumers staked just over £62 billion on legal gambling activities, a 61 per cent growth over 2003 levels making it the most rapidly growing part of the leisure industry except for expenditure on video and computer games. This compares with, for example, £35 billion spent on holidays. Within the gambling sector betting accounts for two-thirds of expenditure. Although it is difficult to estimate the share of the gambling market which is accounted for by sports betting it is almost certainly greater than 40 per cent and growing. However, amounts staked (that is the total expenditure on bets without taking account of winnings returned to punters, as the betting industry informally refers to its customers) is, arguably, a misleading measure of market size. Overall, about 75 per cent of stakes are returned to punters in the form of winnings. On this measure net expenditure (stakes minus winnings) on sports betting in the UK is over £6 billion. This compares with just over £5 billion spent on active participation in sports and paying to watch sports events (including Pay TV).

A major trend over time (not confined to the UK) has been the displacement of pool betting on sports by legalised lottery schemes as the favoured means of gambling regular small amounts. For example, the UK football pools market declined by two-thirds in the 1990s. A similar fall in popularity occurred in the Italian football pools market despite the introduction of new products. It is not hard to see why football pools declined in popularity. Essentially they were fairly clumsy to use and sometimes difficult to understand, the average returns poor and the distribution system (often through an army of agents each handling very small volumes) expensive and inconvenient. Lotteries have none of these drawbacks. Even the poor rate of return of stakes as winnings is offset by the feel-good factor of contributing to good causes. The second shift through time has been the gradual decline of horse racing as the major medium for sports betting; in Italy, for example, soccer betting now has a larger share of the bookmaking market than horse racing. Betting on other spots such as golf, boxing and cricket is also growing rapidly, although horse racing is still the most popular betting vehicle.

The reasons why the sports betting market has grown so dramatically in the last few years are not hard to uncover:

- Disposable incomes are increasing and the amount consumers have available for spending on leisure has increased.
- Sports betting has been progressively deregulated in many countries, including the UK. One beneficial element of this is to shift betting activity from the illegal market to the legal one.
- Social attitudes towards gambling have become more liberal.
- Rapid technological change has made it easier to bet, differentiated the betting product, created greater opportunity and choice of how to bet and added excitement.
- The proliferation of sports broadcasting on digital TV has created greater interest in a wide variety of sports.

 ## Who bets on sports?

British data from 2006/07 suggests that 10 per cent of adult males placed a bet with a book-maker on events other than horse and dog racing. Over 7 per cent bet on the 2006 World Cup. The proportion of the UK adult population which used a bookmaker or betting exchange grew from 13.2 per cent in 2004 to 19.7 per cent in 2008, an impressive growth rate of nearly 50 per cent. Of course most of these are occasional, rather than regular, bettors.

The traditional UK regular sports bettor has been male (twice as many men as women bet regularly), works in a manual or semi-manual occupation and probably lives in the north of England or Scotland. The children have left home (empty nesters) or they have had no children. He places fairly straightforward bets on horse racing usually at a betting shop but sometimes on-course. The traditional off-course punter still bets predominantly in betting shops. For such punters there is a betting shop culture into which they have become socialised and which gives them a sense of familiarity and stability. The downsides are clear, at least if you happen to be a bookmaker. However, the pattern is different for newer forms of sports betting such as online betting.

Relatively little is known about online sports bettors, despite the very rapid growth in popularity. One reason for this is that much sports betting is carried out with operators who are based in countries other than where the punter lives. However, a UK survey in 2006 suggested that 4 per cent of the adult population had participated in online sports betting. Estimates also suggest that participation in online gambling (including the National Lottery, online poker etc.) has grown by a factor of three since 2006. Online gamblers tend to be split more equally between men and women and come from higher income groups. However, if we take the intensity of use into account the core group seems to be fairly well-off middle-aged men. The higher socio-economic groups are more comfortable with carrying out financial transactions online and those in full-time employment with less time for leisure activities find online betting a useful option.

Forms of sports betting

There are four major forms of sports betting:

- wagering;
- bookmaking;
- pool betting;
- betting exchanges.

Wagering is perhaps the oldest form of betting. A wager is simply an agreement to pay out an amount of money based on the outcome of an unsettled matter. In sports betting the unsettled matter is the outcome of some sports activity, for example a match or penalty kick or race or whatever. Wagering is probably the oldest form of sports betting. Every wager requires there to be a backer and a layer. The backer bets on particular outcome occurring whilst the layer bets against it. The simplest example is betting on the toss of a coin. A frequent example of a wager is betting on a round of golf among the players. Betting on horse racing in the UK began to be organised as it was realised (in the 1770s) that it was useful to record the results of match races and the wagers made on them. James Weatherby, a lawyer, was recruited to take on this role and that of holding the amounts wagered on each horse (stakes) for future payout to the winners. The role of 'stakeholder' was thus born and the beginnings of the betting industry emerged from private wagering. A wager is a contract between a small number of individuals, often two. Wagers are bets between individuals and it is here that there is an important distinction between wagering, pool betting (betting against anonymous other bettors) and bookmaking (betting against a bookmaker). Parties to a wager set their own odds. Much wagering takes place in the informal economy whereas both pool betting and (legal) bookmaking take place in a highly regulated economic environment. Whilst the terms betting and wagering are often used interchangeably, it is worthwhile making the distinction because it has been revitalised by the emergence of internet betting exchanges.

In *bookmaking* the punter bets against the bookmaker. Bookmakers operate from shops, via telephone, from 'pitches' or shops at sporting venues and, increasingly, via the internet. The bookmaker displays a list of prices (known as 'odds') at which he is willing to take bets. For example, suppose we are interested in backing (i.e. placing a bet on) a particular football team winning the European Champions League. The bookmaker will offer various prices on the different teams, for example, he may offer Manchester United at 3/1 to win. This means that if we bet €1 on Manchester United and they win we will receive €3 winnings plus our €1 stake (less any deductions for taxes). If Manchester United do not win we lose our €1. The 3/1 ('three to one') price says that Manchester United has an expected chance of winning of one in four or 25 per cent. The bookmaker has taken a 'position' on Manchester United by giving punters a price and accepting bets at that price. Of course the bookmaker is taking bets on the different teams in the competition, so if we are lucky enough to win then others will have lost. Whether or not the bookmaker wins or loses overall depends on the distribution of bets he has taken on the event. This collection of bets is known as 'the book' (literally because they were always written down in a book kept for the purpose) and the bookmaker 'makes a book' on the event. This can be a complex and skilled business since there may be many possible outcomes, bookmakers will be competing with each other and other sports betting outlets for business, and the book is made in real time. This latter point means that bookmakers may offer different odds on the same outcome at different points in time depending on how much money is bet on different eventualities and the information available at any point of time. For example, the transfer of a star player may be seen as lessening a team's chances and the bookmaker may need to offer a more attractive price (known as 'longer' odds) to attract further bets on that team.

In an ideal world most bookmakers will attempt to make a book which will give them some profit no matter what the outcome of the event is. Take a very simple example of a football match where the three possibilities are:

- Team A wins;
- Team B wins;
- the match ends in a draw.

Scenario	Team A wins	Team B wins	Draw
A: odds	2/1	2/1	2/1
A: stakes	100	100	100
B: odds	6/4	6/4	2/1
B: stakes	100	100	100
C: odds	6/4	6/4	2/1
C: stakes	100	100	80

Consider Scenario A. In this case each outcome is judged equally likely, having a probability of 33 per cent. If Team A wins the bookmaker pays out 300 to punters who have backed A and nothing to those who have backed Team B or the draw. A similar picture holds if B wins or the draw occurs. Given that the bookmaker has taken in 300 in stakes, no matter what happens the bookmaker will neither win nor lose. In Scenario B he has set the odds so that there is the chance he can win. Notice the odds on the win by either team are not so generous ('shorter') as they are in Scenario A. A winning punter will now only get one and a half times his stake back in winnings plus the original stake itself. Thus, if Team A wins the bookmaker pays out 250 and makes a profit of 50. The same overall distribution occurs if Team B wins. But look what happens if the draw occurs. In this case the book-maker ends up even. Indeed, if he had taken more than 100 in bets on the draw he would have ended up losing money. Scenario C shows an ideal book from the bookmaker's perspective. In this case the bookmaker will end up in profit no matter what the outcome of the match. This occurs for two reasons: the odds on the different outcomes have been set in such a way that the percentage chances add up to more than 100 per cent (40 per cent on Team A winning plus 40 per cent on Team B winning plus 33 per cent on the draw) and ensuring that not too much money is taken on any one outcome.

Note that we have quoted odds here using the traditional British system, often called fractional odds. Many countries use the decimal system. In this case an even money bet (1/1 in fractional odds) would be quoted as 2.0 and odds of 3/1 would be quoted as 4.0.

The decimal odds are the multiple of the original stake which is received in the event of a win. They have the advantage that the odds on multiple bets is simply the product of the (decimal) odds. Odds can also be shown in terms of monetary returns to a standard stake, for example £1 or $100. Such systems are frequently used in pool betting, and in the form of 'moneyline odds' in the US. So a figure of £5 showing on a totalisator bet in the UK would mean that the punter would get £5 for every £1 winning ticket equivalent to fractional odds of 4/1 or decimal odds of 5.0.

Where there are a large number of possibilities, for example in a horse race or who will win a league, bookmakers will attempt to 'lay the favourite'. That is, they will ensure that they do not lose if the most favoured outcome occurs. They will then vary prices on less favoured possibilities ('outsiders') to attract bets on them to cover any payouts on favoured possibilities. So whilst some bookmakers may speculate on particular outcomes of sporting events by making books which leave them exposed to losses if their guesses are wrong, most bookmakers will attempt to make books which have the desirable property (for them) that they cannot lose. Whilst this may seem unfair to punters, we should remember that bookmaking is a retail service and the question is not whether bookmakers make profits but whether or not those profits are reasonable given the service they provide.

Pool betting (usually in the form of totalisator betting), for example the Tote in the UK or the Pari-Mutuel in France, operates like a lottery. Bettors (or punters in common parlance) buy stakes on certain events. All the stakes are pooled. At the close of betting the number of stakes is added up, a deduction made to cover operating expenses, profits, taxes and any other costs, and the total remaining divided up amongst the winning tickets and the pool distributed to the winning ticket holders as a dividend. The important distinction here is that pool bettors bet against each other; the operator of the pool betting system does not take a position on the outcome of any event but simply runs the system and takes a fee for their administrative work. The operator does not bear any risk contingent on the outcomes of the events which are being bet on. In many countries only pool betting is legal. Football pools are a particular form of pool betting. Once the mainstay of the regular weekly 'flutter' (that is betting a small stake on the very small chance of winning a huge return), football pools work by asking punters to forecast the results of football matches. The best known version of this is to select eight games from those played on a Saturday afternoon (in the UK) which the punter expects to end in a draw where goals are actually scored (i.e. other than a 0–0 result). As such they are also an early example of what are now called complex or exotic bets since they rely on forecasting the results of a number of matches.

Betting exchanges, for example Betfair, can be seen as a brokerage for wagers. The problem with wagering, as with barter exchange, is that I have to find someone to wager with. If I really believe that the New England Patriots will win the Super Bowl and the Red Sox the World Series then I would need to find someone else (a New Yorker perhaps) who is willing to bet that they will not at odds we can agree on. It is quite likely that such a person will be a friend or acquaintance and whilst a 'friendly bet' may be fun it can also carry risks beyond the financial ones. Betting exchanges exploit the internet to match bettors with layers; this makes wagering anonymous. Betting exchanges tend to specialise in a relatively narrow set of betting opportunities in order to maximise their ability to match punters. Most of their business is concentrated on sports betting.

 **Types of bet**

The staple bet in the UK is a fairly simple affair. The punter will bet on who they think will be the winner of an event, match or a race. A variant on this is where there are several participants, as in a horse race or golf tournament for example, when the punter may bet 'each way'. This gives a smaller return if the horse, golfer or whatever finishes in the first few places. The exact number of places which will win in this way depends on the number of participants. Much of this betting is at fixed odds, that is the odds are determined at the time of the bet. In horse racing, however, the bet may be struck at the starting price (SP), that is the odds which rule in the market at the time the betting closes just before a race starts ('the off'). Sometimes bookmakers will only accept bets at the SP. This pattern of straightforward win only and each way betting has, in the past, accounted for over 90 per cent of bookmakers' turnover in the UK. The SP is determined by the market at the racecourse even though this usually accounts for less that 10 per cent of total betting turnover on a race.

Complex or multiple or exotic bets, known as 'parlays' in the US, are ones where punters bet on a series of outcomes. The total odds are the multiple of all the odds on each outcome. The simplest example is a 'double' where the punter chooses two events and attempts to predict the winner of both. Suppose that the punter bets $10 on the Patriots to win the Super Bowl at odds of 4/1 and the Red Sox to win the World Series at 5/1. If the Patriots win the punter has $50 'running on' to the Red Sox bet. If the Red Sox win the punter will receive $300 back in total. This is equivalent to odds of 30/1 on the double. Nowadays information technology makes it possible for bookmakers to keep track of very complex bets, for example naming the first five horses home in a race in any order. A common soccer bet is to name the winning team, the final score and the scorer of the first goal. These bets are becoming much more popular especially amongst many younger sports bettors. In many other countries where sports betting is a major industry, for example Hong Kong and Japan, exotic bets are the norm. Exotic bets can also be constructed so that the punter will get some return even if not all the constituent bets are winners. The 'yankee' is perhaps the classic example. For a yankee bet the punter selects four events to bet on. The bet wins if at least two of the events are correctly forecast. There are 11 ways in which this can happen. Six of these are doubles, that is there are six ways in which two of the events can happen. Four are trebles and one is the quad where all four are winners. With 11 betting possibilities the stake needs to be 11 times larger. Multiple bets such as yankees are popular because there are many more ways of winning but they also offer the possibility of a large payout. They also retain interest until at least three of the events have taken place.

Spread betting is perhaps the most sophisticated type of sports betting and enables more interesting bets to be placed on many events. It has not been very exciting, at least in the recent past, to bet on the winner of the Premier League. However, betting on the points won by a particular team may be of more interest. At the time of writing one spread betting company is quoting Chelsea to finish the 2010/11 season with between 84.5 and 86 points (the spread). If I think Chelsea will have a poor season and end up with fewer than 84.5 points then I sell points to the bookmaker. For example, I choose to bet £10 per point that Chelsea will not reach 84.5 points. Suppose they only manage 80 points. In this case I win

£10 per point for every point below the lower end of the spread (84.5), that is I win £45. If Chelsea have a good season I lose. So if they get 90 points I lose 90 minus 84.5 points times £10, that is £55. The opposite of selling is buying and I would choose to do this if I thought Chelsea would have a good season. One consequence of spread betting is that it is quite possible to win (and lose) large amounts of money.

Spot betting has always existed as a form of wagering, but recently it has become available to all for small stakes. Spot betting refers to placing a bet on a specific event rather than the outcome of that event. An example will make this clearer. On 15 September 2010 a leading bookmaker is taking bets on the tennis match between Djokovic and Skugor. Overall it would seem to be a (potentially) very one-sided match; Skugor is being offered at 25 to 1 against to win (that is he is judged to have just under a 4 per cent chance of winning). However, as I look at my iPad, I can also bet on the outcome of the third game in the second set which is just about to start; I can bet live (in-play) on the match. I can now, for example, bet on Djokovic winning this particular game to love (that is, Skugor will not score any points in the game) at odds of 7/1. This is a spot bet. During the day I have multiple opportunities to place live bets on everything from chess to Gaelic football.

Betting markets are a particular form of financial market. In all financial markets, for example those for stocks and shares, there is concern to ensure that they operate fairly, openly and efficiently. Punters will not bet if they believe that markets are 'rigged' in some way so that some group of people 'in the know' have an unfair advantage and will end up winning more than their fair share of the money.

All markets are sustained by information flows. The simple (and simplistic) assumption of elementary economics that everyone in the marketplace has free and perfect information does not really help since it rules out the question of what type of information is needed for an effective market to exist and whether or not this information is easily available to everyone in the market on an equal basis. One important element of information in most markets is price, in betting markets this is represented by odds (however represented) or spreads. The question is whether or not the odds represent a fair estimate of the chance of a particular event occurring. There are a number of areas where concerns have been raised. For example, some people may have access to information that is not freely available to everyone and which would, if widely known, affect the odds. A particular player might be carrying an injury or be feeling unwell. The player and perhaps his friends will know this and may take advantage of this 'inside information' in placing a bet. In extreme cases players might deliberately create particular outcomes. This is much easier to conceal in spot-betting situations. It is also easier when punters lay bets, that is bet on a losing outcome. It is easier to cover up or explain away poor performances.

New forms of betting, for example betting exchanges, and the availability of instantaneous market information, have allowed new forms of activity to grow in betting markets. Arbitrageurs bet on all outcomes to make a profit. Arbitrageurs exploit the small and short-lived opportunities which can occur as markets shift and prices are finding new levels. Some arbitrageurs and traders place up to 1,000 bets per hour on betting exchanges. Typically arbitrage margins are very small and opportunities short-lived, and large amounts have to be bet and decisions made very quickly. Traders exploit market differences between bookmakers or between bookmakers and betting exchanges. Trading has become possible because betting exchanges allow punters to lay a bet, that is bet on an outcome not happening. It may then be possible to lay a low amount on a betting exchange and back at a higher price with a bookmaker and come out with a profit whatever happens.

Hedging occurs when a bet is taken as a form of insurance. Suppose I own shares in my favourite, NFL team. They get to the Super Bowl and, of course, I want them to win. I also expect my shares to go up in value if they win. However, I also need to think about potential financial losses if we lose. I might then be tempted to bet on the opposition on the grounds that if we lose my winnings will offset the fall in value of my shares. Some bookmakers may use betting exchanges as a means of hedging when they are over-exposed to particular horses, usually favourites to win.

And, of course, there is the traditional betting activity of speculating on outcomes. Effective markets probably need all types of participants, although if one set of activities over-dominates there could be problems. Arbitrageurs and traders provide liquidity to the market. Liquidity, the continual flow and turnaround of money, is essential for any market to remain healthy and active. If you are not convinced of this consider the consequences of lack of liquidity in other financial markets following the 'credit crunch' of 2007.

So, can some punters beat the market? If it were widely known that a few professional gamblers or insiders were creaming off the market then it would be very difficult to persuade average punters to bet. In this case the market would only consist of 'professionals' and insiders and the advantages of being one would disappear. Of course, if everyone (or everyone who is interested and cares to find out) has inside knowledge then that information is public and hence no longer 'inside'. At first this sounds odd but inside information really only is inside information if the general public does not believe such information exists or that, if it exists, it is of any use.

Case 20.1 The Davydenko affair

Tennis is interesting from the match-fixing point of view. Most matches are singles game, one-on-one, and there are thus fewer people to deal with and pay off compared with a team sport. There are also a very large number of ways in which matches can be manipulated for betting gain, without throwing the match. A game or set lost here or there, a foot fault or a run of double faults all present betting opportunities.

In 2007 the world number 4, Nikolay Davydenko, lost a match to the world number 87 after retiring in the third set. Just before the match the odds on Davydenko lengthened for no apparent reason. Betfair also noticed that there was an exceptionally high betting turnover (£3.5 million – 10 times as much as usual) for a routine early match in a low-profile tournament. Much of this was bet on his opponent during the second set despite Davydenko winning the first set 6-2.

Of course it might simply be that keen observers of the game had noticed that Davydenko might be carrying an injury and had followed their instincts accordingly. On the other hand, in 2005, a Belgian player had been offered $141,000 to lose a first round match at Wimbledon, the world's premier tournament. Organisers of the French Open were sufficiently worried by the Wimbledon and Davydenko

(continued)

affairs to seek court orders to ban Betfair, Ladbrokes and others from accepting bets on the event.

The Tennis Integrity Unit investigated the Davydenko affair and the player was cleared of any wrongdoing in September 2008. The 14-month investigation was hampered by the fact that many of the phone records which might have been useful in the investigation had been destroyed. Davydenko suggested that some punters may have overheard him talking about his injury to his wife during the match. However, the suspicion that tennis is subject to cheating induced by gambling interests has been reinforced by Betfair's serious and highly unusual decision to void all bets on the Davydenko match and the extreme action of the French tennis authorities in the Paris courts.

Discussion questions

1 Was Betfair justified in taking the extreme step of voiding all bets on the match?

2 Should bets be voided in all cases where a player retires through injury?

3 Should in-game betting be banned?

4 Are unusual betting patterns on a match sufficient evidence to launch an investigation which threatens a player's career? Should players be able to seek compensation if the case against them is not proved?

Why gamble on sports?

Many of the reasons why people gamble on the outcome of sports events are the same as those for participating in many other forms of gambling. The first of these is financial gain, whereby the key feature of placing a bet (or combination of bets) is the hope of future profit. Most gamblers would state that this is their reason for betting. However, this is not an entirely rational position as only around a quarter of bets actually make a positive return. This may mean that gamblers who say that their motive is financial profit are over-optimistic to the extent of suppressing a response which indicates that they are motivated by other factors, for example thrill-seeking.

The second factor is that of intellectual challenge. Here, the idea is that predicting the outcome of a sports event presents a complex problem which requires significant and developed decision-making skills. As a result, a successful or winning bet reinforces the individual's belief in his or her own decision-making ability. Some spread bettors may well fall into this category.

Thirdly, gamblers bet for excitement. Sports offer the build-up to the event, the event itself and the finish. As such, losing can be good value for money, in perhaps the same way that an arcade game, which offers no financial return, can also be good value. Televised coverage of sport, slow-motion replays and so on can obviously add to the excitement. Betting can add a dimension of excitement to either participating in sport, as in wagering amongst friends playing golf, or in being more active spectators. Gamblers who bet for excitement are often attracted by exotic bets where quite large potential winnings can be gained for small initial stakes.

Fourthly, we can identify social interaction as a motivation for betting. Ten per cent of UK gamblers rate winning money as being less important than having a good time. This is clearly not always the case and there are many gamblers who are solitary and private. However, an interest in sports betting can clearly be used to meet others with similar interests. Sports betting may be an adjunct to active or passive participation in sports and reinforce social networks based on a common interest in sports per se. For example nearly half of all male US college athletes (a term taken to mean participants in all sports) gamble on sports.

These four motivations for betting may form a more productive basis for market segmentation than what betting products there are or which demographic groups of people bet since there are clear differences in the promotional approaches and marketing communications which might work for different types of punters.

Some evidence for the idea that some gamblers consume betting, that is treat it as entertainment rather than as a form of financial investment, can be found in the existence of 'favourite-longshot bias' in most sports betting markets (an exception seems to be major league baseball in the US where the opposite tendency has been found). This is the tendency for punters to overbet outsiders and underbet short-odds outcomes and favourites in particular. A number of explanations have been suggested. The best known are that some people enjoy a 'flutter' and that punters 'like a gamble'. Sports bettors enjoying a flutter tend to bet for the fun of it; they restrict their activity to major events such as the Derby or the Grand National horse races and rely mainly on luck to generate wins. Here sports betting is a form of occasional entertainment for which people are willing to pay. In the case of liking to gamble, regular punters are more likely to put on a smallish stake with an outside chance of winning a large sum of money than betting to win small sums of money. This would lead to favourites being underbet. Gamblers who are consuming the activity, that is gambling for reasons other than to make a profit, are often liquidity traders. Such gamblers may have a fixed sum which they are willing to stake and will continue to bet until the stake is exhausted or the time period over which they are active has come to an end or they emerge without having exhausted their stake.

An interesting but under-researched question is whether or not sports bettors are also participants in, or spectators of, sports per se. At one end of the scale there will be those who are gamblers first and foremost but for whom sports betting is the preferred vehicle for gambling. Such punters will only attend sporting events either because the tax regime for on-course (or at-event) gambling is more favourable, as has been the case in the UK and still is in many other countries, or there is useful information to be gained, for example the look of a horse just before a race. At the other end of the scale there will be sports fans for whom a casual bet is part of the entertainment package. In between there will be a range of other possibilities. Overall, however, there does not seem to be any convincing evidence to support the hypothesis that sports betting and paying to watch sports events, whether in person or on pay-TV, are strong complementary goods.

 ## Betting scams and illegal gambling

So far this chapter has been written in a way that would lead the unsuspecting reader to think that all sports betting, apart from occasional private wagers or sweepstakes between friends, took place in the formal economy and was subject to actual and potential regulation.

Of course, this is very far from the truth. For example, in the US it has been estimated that, in the late 1990s, anything between $80 billion and $380 billion was bet illegally on the outcome of sporting events whereas only $2.3 billion was bet legally during a year. In 2010 the illegal Asian gambling market was estimated to be worth $450 billion. Asian bets on the IPL (a cricket league) are thought to be in the region of $150 million per match and the level of betting on a weekend's matches in the English Premier League (soccer) $500 million. In Greece the sizes of the legal and illegal betting markets are believed to roughly equal. Overall, only about 40 per cent of sports betting is thought to take place in legal markets. In China some 70 per cent of national league soccer matches are possibly fixed. Illegal sports betting is thus a global phenomenon, made more so in that gamblers who live in countries where gambling is legal but regulated can bet in other countries and those who live in countries where gambling is illegal have easy access to global markets and the illegal sector.

The relationship between sport and sports betting has always been a difficult one. The laws of both cricket and golf were first codified in 1774 as a response to concern that fair betting was being made very difficult without a clear statement of consistent rules. Even so, cricket has been undermined by betting scandals linked to accusations that players have influenced games ever since. The latest in these is the 'spot-fixing' affair surrounding the 2010 tour to England. Six Pakistani players were accused of deliberately bowling no-balls at a particular point of a Test Match (the 'highest' form of cricket) and influencing the pattern of scoring during a one-day international game. In both cases the allegation is that illegal Asian bookmaking interests are involved. One estimate, by the head of the ICC Corruption Unit, suggests that the amount wagered on an important one-day cricket match can be as much as $1 billion.

Betting scandals have at some time or other affected a wide range of sports including soccer, baseball, boxing, basketball, American football, horse racing, snooker, rugby league, ice hockey and tennis. Illegal gambling and associated match-fixing and spot-fixing allegations are long-lived, ubiquitous and involve very large sums of money. Given the level of illegal sports betting activity it is not difficult to see how some might doubt the integrity of some sports events or even of whole sports. At one end of the scale of wrong-doing we might encounter the minor exploitation of insider information (a star player has mild flu), at the other end we could suspect the systematic manipulation of the outcomes of sporting events. Illegal gambling has a number of adverse effects on sports:

- It brings the integrity of sport into question, which may reduce public interest in the sport.

- It generates widespread negative publicity.

- It reduces the incentive for punters to bet in the legal sector, which will, one way or another, result in reduced revenue for the sports industry.

- It requires sports governing bodies and others to invest heavily in integrity units to attempt to eliminate dubious, and often illegal, practices.

Sports betting has become potentially more susceptible to fixing rather than less so. We would expect that the greater investment in integrity and anti-corruption units and improved detection methods would reduce the opportunities for realising gains from illegal activity. However, we have to set against this the increased opportunities for fixing which the advent of new technology has generated. The development of online betting has enabled gamblers to escape the restrictions of national jurisdictions. Betting exchanges now offer the opportunity to bet on losing (laying) and it is potentially much easier to engineer losing than winning. The massive amounts of money now wagered online make it very difficult to spot dubious large transactions. In-play betting creates innumerable new spot events which can be the subject of bets. 'Proposition' bets are also a potential source of dubious activity. For example, I can bet on the first team to have a throw-in in a soccer match. Such an event would be fairly easy to engineer by a player and would have no effect on the final result of the match. New technologies create new forms of betting, such as in-play and proposition bets, and new business models for the betting industry – betting exchanges and spread-betting – and thus new ways of cheating emerge.

Regulating sports betting

The difficult question is what should be done. Fairly obviously, the sports industry needs to invest in detection and policing, but in some sports this diverts scarce funding from other activities such as grassroots development. A more difficult issue is whether or not sports betting, and particularly online betting, should be legalised. The argument for legalisation is that it reduces the incentive for illegal bookmaking. The proponents of legalisation sometimes point to the harmful effects of (alcohol) prohibition in the US which generated widespread organised crime. Legalisation would also enable betting to be taxed and thus generate funds for policing the market. On the other hand, taxation raises costs and prices and recreates an incentive for illegal activity.

The issue is even more complex when online gambling is under consideration. Online gambling is a global activity, so regulation in one country may have little effect. Internet gambling was made illegal in the US in 2006 but it is still possible to access offshore gambling sites (remote betting) from within the US even though most operators have withdrawn from the market. Punters can easily cross virtual borders. In addition, it is sometimes argued that online gambling, particularly via betting exchanges, is more prone to fraud. However, there is little hard evidence for this. Another concern is that betting exchanges may be used for money-laundering – that is, provide a means of moving illegally gained money around with little chance of detection.

Legalisation may also alienate some sections of the population who regard gambling as an immoral, sinful and socially damaging activity. Again, online gambling may be a particular target. The problem seems to be greater in some countries than in others. If we take the UK as a benchmark, Norway is better, Australia, the US and South Africa worse and Canada, New Zealand, Sweden and Switzerland about the same. Online gambling potentially provides an environment which promotes problem gambling more than traditional betting arenas. For example, online markets provide 24-hour access. In addition, it generates increased event frequency and provides instant reinforcements. On the other hand, losses can be forgotten instantly with the thrill of the next bet. Many online gamblers play in isolation and act on impulse in the absence of the social checks which could be present in a betting shop. Whilst problem gambling seems to be less of a problem than is commonly believed – in the UK only about 1 per cent of gamblers are classified as 'problem gamblers' whereas 29 per cent of the population believe that all types of gambling can lead to problem gambling – the data does suggest that problem gambling is much more prevalent amongst those who use betting exchanges and are involved in spread-betting. The spread of sports betting via mobile computing devices is an additional potential concern.

It is not surprising that different countries have adopted different stances. The UK developed a framework for legalised online gambling in 2005; the US made it illegal in 2006. India and Malaysia are considering legalising some forms of sports betting following recent scandals. In Germany all gambling is illegal; in France, Sweden and Austria it is nationalised. In the US the regulation and legalisation of non-internet gambling is a matter for state jurisdictions. However, sports betting is covered by federal law and is only legal in Nevada, Delaware, Montana and Oregon.

Case 20.2 Sports gambling in the US

The relationship between sports and sports gambling has never been an easy one. Nowhere is this more evident than in the US. The debate is constantly in the eyes of state and federal legislatures and this case study is drawn from US newspaper reports in mid-2009.

In 2009 the US economy was struggling. As is usually the case in hard times, discretionary spending on areas such as attending sports events and buying associated merchandise such as team jerseys slowed down. Both professional (pro) and amateur (university/college) sports teams began to seek new sources of revenue and turned their attention to the possibility of building marketing relationships with gambling companies. Team logos began to appear on state lottery tickets and some basketball games were played at casino hotels.

At the same time state treasurers faced their own problems of rising welfare expenditures and reduced tax revenues. Some states, looking enviously at Nevada – the only state where sports betting was allowed – saw increasing the tax take from gambling as a potentially attractive option, and the best way of achieving that objective was to legalise sports betting. After all, state casinos in Delaware and New Jersey already offered betting on horse racing and the usual casino offerings. Why not add betting on NFL games, baseball, basketball and ice hockey?

However, the major pro leagues (the NFL, MLB, NBA and NHL) and the governing body of college sports (NCAA) were all resistant to any such moves. Sports officials asked a federal court to stop Delaware introducing sports betting, arguing that it would threaten the integrity of their sports by creating incentives for cheating, including game-fixing.

On the other hand some team owners, for example the owner of the NBA team Sacramento Kings (who also happened to be a Las Vegas casino owner), said that a well-designed and implemented regulatory system could remove such problems. To complicate matters further, two state senators from New Jersey supported a lawsuit which sought to have the 1993 federal ban on sports betting declared unconstitutional. Not all agreed; several senators wrote to the federal Attorney General urging him to fight the lawsuit.

Of course the Delaware and New Jersey cases were simply the thin end of the wedge. If Delaware won its lawsuit, then other states would undoubtedly consider sports gambling seriously.

(continued)

A cynical view of the sports leagues opposition to betting on their games would suggest that objections would be fairly rapidly withdrawn if they got a piece of the action, something which was not being offered. After all, they would only need to read this book chapter to realise that there is plenty of betting on their sports already, except that it is illegal and by definition unregulated. It might be better to have it out in the open and negotiate sponsorship deals or some other way of getting a return from it. If safeguards could be put in place to stop sports gambling influencing the outcome of games then what is the harm? We all know what Prohibition did for the US alcohol industry in the 1920s!

Discussion questions

5 Would legalising sports betting have any effect on the incentives for players and others to cheat given the scale of illegal sports gambling?

6 Would punishing sports cheats be an effective way of reducing the incentives for gamblers to try and influence the outcomes of games?

7 Should legalised sports gambling be limited to specific forms of betting, for example multiple (parlay) bets on the outcomes of several matches but not results of individual games?

Conclusion

In this final section we look at the changing relationships between the sports betting and sports industries and, following the emerging themes of this chapter, how these relationships have been mediated by technological change, globalisation and the media industry. These influences are intimately intertwined and need to be considered together.

Recall James Weatherby holding the stake for two rivals wagering on the result of a horseracing match around 1770. In this situation the only available technology probably required that all three parties to the business were present at the location of the match when it took place. Indeed, in the UK only on-course betting was legal before 1961. The invention of the first totalisator machine in Australia in 1913 is a somewhat understated event in the development of sports betting. It made pool betting a reality, and it was also the start of the trend to ever faster calculation of returns to gambling, transactions handling and management of very complex bets. The development of television and, in particular, televised sports events made much more sense of off-course betting since it was no longer essential to attend the event to see for yourself what had happened. Somewhat strangely, however, televisions were not allowed into betting shops until 1986. The next major step forward was probably the use of the telephone for placing bets. Whilst the telephone is a far from new invention it is only relatively recently that credit card transactions could be authorised quickly over the telephone. This opened up telephone betting to the majority of punters who bet small amounts and for whom, on both sides, it was not worthwhile opening a credit account. The emergence of freephone numbers and the rapidly falling costs of making international calls allowed bookmakers to move their telephone betting operations overseas thus avoiding domestic taxes on gambling. At one stage offshore telephone bookmakers were offering to take bets and deduct as little as 3 per cent from winnings to cover costs and profits. Telephone bookmaking rapidly became the preferred option for regular sports bettors for simple economic reasons. The development of smartphones allows punters to access the latest odds and place a bet in a very short space of time. They also allow bookmakers and betting exchanges to provide punters with many more attractive betting opportunities. The internet and iDTV have allowed even greater physical separation of the elements of sports betting yet have combined them in one virtual environment. I can now access the latest odds, place a bet, watch an event and verify the winnings being credited to my account at a keystroke or push of a few buttons on my remote control. With split-screen and information streaming technology I can potentially see all three (the odds, the event and the state of my account) at the same time. I can even place spontaneous bets during an event, for example who will win a tie-break during a tennis match or whether a penalty kick will result in a goal. And, of course, I can bet on any sporting event anywhere in the world. Put succinctly, the development of digital technologies has expanded the available channels of distribution for betting and the range of products on offer. Indeed, betting may be the ideal e-commerce product because there is no physical distribution requirement.

Deregulation has, in part, been pushed along by technological changes. However, ethical and social influences have also played their part. In broad terms, pool betting, including lotteries, has been generally socially acceptable in many countries, though not, of course in the Islamic world. For example, bookmaking is still only allowed on-course in Australia, but their version of pool betting, known as the TAB, has wider distribution than the Tote in the UK with TAB machines placed in bars and clubs. In the UK off-course bookmaking was widespread but illegal before 1961 when the government of the day decided to legalise betting shops and, unsurprisingly perhaps, tax off-course bets.

But the major question and conundrum goes unanswered. The sports betting industry can only exist if there is a sports industry to bet on. Whilst it may be that some sports can survive without capturing any income from the sports betting industry, and may even wish the sports betting industry did not exist, the reality is that the commercial sports industry both faces costs which are a result of sports betting and the non-commercial sector, for example amateur sport, could benefit greatly from additional sources of revenue. How can this dilemma be resolved?

One possibility is for the government to pose a levy on betting which is then used to develop the sport in agreed ways. This has long been the case in some horseracing. In the UK the bookmakers (now including betting exchanges) and the racing industry are required by legislation to agree a levy on bets on horseracing which is designed to provide a 'reasonable return' to horseracing for providing a betting medium. Over the years difficulties have been encountered in reaching agreements given the factors we have already encountered, including offshoring, the globalisation of racing and gambling, the emergence of new forms of betting, the emergence of digital TV and competition from other sports for the punter's pound. All this begs the question why, in the new world of sports betting, horseracing should be treated differently from soccer or cricket.

Why not leave the financial relationships to the market? If sports betting needs sport why not let it 'pay' through sponsorship, joint ventures, promotional activities and other commercially negotiated arrangements? If the level of supply of a particular sport to the market cannot be maintained without an enforced contribution from the betting industry why not simply reduce the level of supply of that sport?

Case 20.3 Is inequality the problem?

Cricket has long been plagued by corruption of one sort or another. Cricket historians claim that match-fixing was one of the major drivers in codifying the laws of the game. The modern game too has been tarnished by a string of accusations of match-fixing and spot-fixing. The most famous of these was the Hansie Cronje scandal of 2000. However, the Pakistan cricket team has featured in many of the recent cases where fixing of one sort or another has been alleged. For example, in 2010, the young Pakistani bowler Mohammed Amir was alleged to have deliberately bowled two no-balls at pre-arranged times during the final Test Match against England. Amir, an 18-year-old from a remote village in Pakistan, was regarded as one of cricket's rising stars. He nevertheless, it was suggested, took a small bribe, said to be £4,000, orchestrated by an illegal Indian bookmaker in collusion with senior members of the Pakistani side, to bowl the no-balls.

Pakistani cricketers are the lowest paid among the major test playing nations. England and Australia players can expect to earn between £250,000 and £450,000 a year for playing for the national side. Players from the other major teams can expect to earn up to £100,000 per year; even the lowest paid Indian test player could expect to equal the top Pakistani players' earnings of a mere £20,000 per year, whilst the lowest paid Pakistani player would only receive about £9,000. These sums compare to the reported £150,000 bribe offered by a British newspaper to Pakistani players for the no-ball spot-fixing.

However, even these salaries are very high when compared with average earnings in Pakistan. At the other end of the scale, the Forbes rich list estimated the annual cricket earnings of the Indian stars M.S. Dhoni and Sachin Tendulkar at over £6 million and £5 million respectively. This includes the very substantial payments major players can attract by playing in the Indian Premier League – an opportunity denied to Pakistani players, ostensibly for political reasons.

Pakistan, according to one international ratings agency, ranks number 143 out of 178 nations on corruption (number 1 is the least corrupt). Bribery and extortion are said to be rife and a number of Pakistani cricketers have suggested that their families have been threatened. The length of a Pakistan player's test career may be subject to influences other than cricketing ability and on-field performances. Some players come from poor areas of the country and may wish to help better the lives of their families and friends back home.

Lord Condon, the first chief of the International Cricket Council's (ICC) Anti-Corruption and Security Unit, argued in 2001 that significant variations between payment and contractual conditions between countries may have been a source of temptation to cheat for some players. He also cited political insecurity, jealousy and potentially short international careers as further factors.

Discussion questions

8 Is corruption in sport an individual issue or are institutional and cultural factors partly to blame?

9 Will punishing individual players be effective in eliminating corruption?

10 Should countries be banned from playing international cricket if institutionalised corruption is thought to be damaging the integrity of sport?

11 How do instances such as this damage the sports betting industry? How do they damage cricket?

Discussion questions

12 Should sports betting companies pay sports event owners for the right to offer odds on the outcomes of events?

13 Who should be responsible for ensuring that the integrity of sport is not undermined through illegal betting activity?

14 What might the effects of increased regulation of betting markets be?

15 Why do sportsmen succumb to inducements to act dishonestly?

16 What issues are raised for sports betting by the globalisation of markets?

Keywords

Backer; betting; bettor; betting exchanges; betting shops; bookmaker; gambling; in-play betting; layer; multiple bets; odds; online betting; pool betting; punter; sports betting; spot betting; spread betting; stake; wagering.

Guided reading

Probably the best way to keep up with market trends in sports betting is to read the regular Mintel Reports on gambling and betting.

Studies of betting consumers and the motivation for betting include Bruce and Johnson (1992) and Jones et al. (2000).

Issues of gambling regulation are covered by Sauer (2001), Miller and Claussen (2001), Paton et al. (2002), and Ward (2009).

A fascinating case study of the financial interrelationships between sport and sports betting is contained in 50th Horserace Betting Levy Scheme: Submission of British Horseracing, March 2010, www.britishhorseracing.com/resources/media/publications_and_reports/50th_Levy_Scheme_Submission.pdf. Betfair's response gives an interesting insight into betting exchanges, and is available at: www.hblb.org.uk/documents/news/Betfair%20response%20to%20Racing's%20submission%20ref%2050th%20Levy%20Scheme.pdf.

The relationship between sport integrity and sports betting is well covered in Forrest et al. (2008).

Recommended websites

Among the many websites which cover sports betting the following are of particular interest:
http://integrityinsport.com covers a wide range of cheating and corruption issues in international sport.
www.gamblingresearchnetwork.org.uk is a group of researchers who collaborate on-line.
The Canadian site www.responsiblegambling.com has useful material on problem gambling.
The Remote Gambling Association www.rga.eu.com publishes excellent research into online gambling including sports betting.
The Association of British Bookmakers www.abb.uk.com promotes the views of bookmakers in the UK, and publishes research in support of its case.

References

Bruce, A.C. and Johnson, J.E.V. (1992) 'Toward an explanation of betting as a leisure pursuit', *Leisure Studies*, 11, 201–18.

Forrest, D., McHale, I. and McAuley, K. (2008) *Risks to the Integrity of Sport from Betting Corruption*, London: Central Council for Physical Recreation.

Jones, P., Clarke-Hill, C.M. and Hillier, D. (2000) 'Viewpoint: back street to high street to e-street: sporting betting on the internet', *International Journal of Retail and Distribution Management*, 28 (6), 222–27.

Miller, L.K. and Claussen, C.L. (2001) 'Online sports gambling – regulation or prohibition?', *Journal of Legal Aspects of Sport*, 11 (99), 99–134.

Paton, D., Siegel, D.S. and Williams, L.V. (2002) 'A policy response to the e-commerce revolution: the case of betting taxation in the UK', *The Economic Journal*, 112 (June), F296–F314.

Sauer, R.D. (2001) 'The political economy of gambling regulation', *Managerial and Decision Economics*, 22 (1), 5–15.

Ward, P. (2009) *Online gambling*, Standard Note: SN/HA/4041, House of Commons Library, www.parliament.uk/briefingpapers/commons/lib/research/briefings/snha-04041.pdf

Sports retailing and merchandising

Leigh Sparks, University of Stirling

Learning outcomes

Upon completion of this chapter, the reader should be able to:

● understand the importance of the sports goods retail sector;

● outline the sports goods retail market structure and discuss how and why it is changing;

● understand the requirements of different forms of sports goods retail outlets, including internet retailing;

● consider a range of management issues in designing, supplying, merchandising and operating sports retail outlets.

 ## Overview

Over the last two decades there has been a transformation in the structure and composition of the sports goods market, in the UK as in many other countries (Mintel, 2008); a narrow market focused on 'games' equipment has been broadened and deepened as sport has taken a more significant place in global culture. The nature of sport has changed with a movement from traditional 'games' such as cricket and tennis to a broad variety of sports ranging from personal health and fitness to extreme and adventure sports. At the same time there has been an increasing internationalisation or globalisation of sport and sports culture. Female sport product requirements and purchasing have taken on greater significance as the nature of sport has changed. The explosion in media awareness and coverage of professional sports and the associated rise of celebrity sports stars have opened up new product and consumer markets. Sports clothing has developed from being a functional requirement into a globally branded fashion statement, i.e. there has been a movement from 'activewear' to 'casualwear'. As a consequence there has been an increased frequency of purchasing of sport clothing, though not always for sports reasons.

This interaction of media, sports and product globalisation and fashion has transformed what is sold and the ways in which it is sold. Sports goods retailing has undergone (and continues to undergo) quite substantial change. The sports retailing sector is now of considerable economic and social significance in many countries. It also offers an insight into changing cultural roles and emphases in sport and sport marketing and business.

This chapter therefore considers the changing characteristics, importance and operations of sports goods retailing. To meet this aim, after a brief introduction to retailing and sports goods retailing, the changing nature of the products that are purchased are considered. Then, as an illustration, the structure of the UK sports retailing industry is assessed. These two areas are then combined into a consideration of particular issues in sports retailing, including targeted consumer marketing, store design and experiential sports retailing, the internet as a strongly emergent retailing channel and merchandising operations. Finally conclusions are drawn.

 ## Introduction

Retailing is concerned with the sale of products (normally individual items or in small quantities) to the final consumer. Sports retailing is therefore the interaction amongst three components (sports, retailing and consumers) all of which have been undergoing considerable change. What we identify as sport, our desires and abilities to participate in sport and our demands to associate with sport have all altered. The meaning we place on sport and association with sport and teams or celebrity 'sports stars' has been transformed. This is evident in many ways and forms, but is clearly reflected in the area of sports goods retailing.

Retailing itself has been a sector undergoing considerable change. The retail sector is no longer the innocent recipient of sports products from manufacturers produced in the hope that someone would need them to 'play the game'. Now, retailers are often amongst the largest businesses in many countries and have a power that exceeds or rivals major manufacturers in many sectors. Whilst it is apparent in many countries and sectors that leading retailers have gained scale and power in distribution channels, it is also true that some manufacturers have also increased their relative position. This is often due to their development and maintenance of powerful brands. In sport, manufacturer brands have expanded enormously and the sector contains some of the leading consumer brands in the world. Companies such as Nike, Adidas, Puma and Reebok are powerful global brands, whilst niche brands like Helly Hansen, Roxy and Ripcurl also have strong consumer attraction. Power is perhaps more evenly distributed between retailers and manufacturers in sports retailing than in some other retail sectors.

Retailers, however, can use their knowledge of changing consumers demands to better serve customers and to reflect tastes, needs and wants. In the sports field it is clear that customer demands have changed in a number of ways. For example:

- the range of sports has expanded;
- equipment has developed through technology and safety enhancements;
- the gender balance of participants and consumers has become less biased towards male and middle-aged categories;
- sports clothing has ceased to be a functional need and in some cases has become leisure-related casual wear;
- style has become as important in some categories (of sport, equipment or clothing) as function;
- demand around major sport events, e.g. FIFA World Cup 2010, Ryder Cup 2010, London's Olympic Games 2012, has become larger and more volatile;
- association and overt identification with sports teams, major brands, major sporting events and sports superstars has risen.

If customer demands and needs have altered in these (and other) ways then it is to be expected that the retail sector generally and specific retailers should have responded to these changes by developing and focusing their retail operations. The sports products we buy and where we buy them has therefore been transformed. The sports retail shop of today looks different and is merchandised differently to sports retail stores of yesteryear. The 'shop' may not even exist other than as a virtual storefront on the internet. It displays, merchandises and sells products, services and experiences in new ways. This change has involved the creation of particular businesses, approaches, brands and methods of operating. For example:

- there has been an increase in sports goods retailing specialists;
- store design ideas and capabilities have developed to meet the market segment targeted;
- club shops and event-based merchandising have expanded at the stadium/event and elsewhere, and there is a strong market in replica and associative merchandise;
- experiential retailing, as at Niketown, ESPN Zone, REI, Dick's Sporting Goods and Tiso Outdoor Experience, has become more prominent;
- internet-based sports goods retailing has expanded dramatically, occasionally as a stand-alone approach but more often as part of a multi-channel (clicks and bricks) operation.

Retailers carry out a number of functions involving bridging production and consumption. Their roles generally involve some or all of the activities in Table 21.1.

Table 21.1 Functions of retailers

Sourcing	Designing product
Buying	Branding
Storing	Distributing
Store location choice	Store layout
Displaying	Pricing
Ranging	Stock management
Merchandising	**Atmospherics**
Customer service	Selling
Discounting	Returning
Reordering	

Retailers put together a set of products in an environment that is attractive to the target market and employ staff to serve these customers. The emphasis in different stores will vary – e.g. price discount, fashion oriented, brand flagship stores – and thus the retailer creates a managed environment in which to sell products and services to consumers. In this regard, sports goods retailing is no different to other retailing. However, the nature of sport and the consumers' relationships with sport does change the balance and outcome of this decision making. For example, whilst product sourcing has moved in many cases to Asia, as with other retail sectors, there may be a heightened concern over the ethics in the supply chain in sports goods (Mamic, 2004).

What do we buy?

The sports retailing market in product terms is normally divided into equipment, clothing and footwear components. Figure 21.1 provides some evidence of how the UK product market has altered in recent decades.

The figure suggests that two main trends have occurred:

- The market as a whole has expanded enormously (though the data in the figure is for current prices so overstates this).

- Whilst this growth has occurred in all three categories, growth in clothing has been by far the most significant. There has been a switch in the market from an equipment focus in the 1970s to a clothing focus in the 2000s.

Before considering these three segments (clothing, footwear and equipment) in turn, the differences amongst the main sports goods markets in Europe are worth developing further. According to Mintel (2004), France is the largest market in Europe on both total and per capita sales bases, probably because of high levels of active participation in sports. This high participation level in, for example, skiing and cycling makes the equipment segment of the market proportionately more important than in other countries. The second largest market in total sales in Europe is Germany, but on a per capita basis they

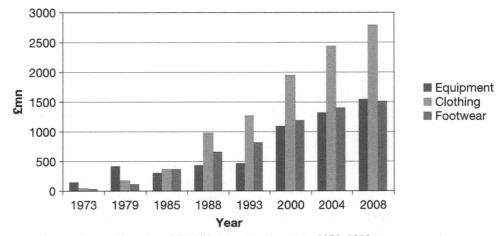

Figure 21.1 The market size of the UK sports goods sector 1973–2008
Source: Selected Retail Business and Mintel Reports on UK Sports Goods Markets 1979–2008

are the lowest of the largest six markets. In contrast, the Netherlands is a small total market but with high per capita sales. The UK market is third on both measures of sales, but it is biased towards casualwear and spectator leisurewear rather than participative (activewear) purchasing. In all markets, however, there has been growth, and increased interest in new retail products and approaches.

Clothing

Sportswear has become fashionable in the UK, and whilst clothing is needed to play sport (activewear or performance wear), many clothing sales are fashion oriented (casualwear or non-performance wear). This growth has been such as to outweigh expansion in the equipment market. British consumers use sportswear as casual, everyday attire, probably based on perceptions of comfort, practicality and durability. Sports brands (Nike, Adidas and Reebok) and replica kit and club branded leisurewear are ubiquitous, found across all ages and genders. For example, less than one-third of football kit sales are for participation purposes, reflecting the casual, fashion and associative dimensions of sports clothing. Sports leisurewear is also seen as fashionable by some because it can be well-cut and flattering to certain (though not all!) body shapes. Fashion sports clothing may also be less durable and more 'disposable' than activewear. In recent years expansion in running and personal fitness markets has increased and in addition club replica merchandise sales have been strong. However, the clothing market has slowed in comparison to footwear and equipment, probably due in part to the recession and in part to changing fashion tastes.

Footwear

The choice of sports footwear for participants in sport has expanded. More fundamentally perhaps, the 'trainer' has become a fashion statement and cultural icon rather than a participatory necessity. The footwear market has expanded considerably on the back of the use of the trainer and its derivatives, for everyday, casual wear. This is now a fashion market where product segmentation techniques – e.g. limited editions, retro styling and customisation such as mi-adidas and nikeid – have been applied strongly.

Equipment

The equipment market has not expanded as rapidly as the other segments and proportionately in the UK has become less important over time. Spending on sport equipment is a reflection of participation levels, the cost of equipment or kit needed and the quantity required to participate. Some sports require little by way of equipment – e.g. swimming (though even this can be very specialised) and aerobics – whereas other sports require some, if not substantial, investment – e.g. golf, fishing, skiing and some home fitness activities. For example, the golf equipment market is proportionately important as it has high participation levels, requires quite a lot of equipment, which can be quite expensive, and there is substantial technological innovation. Specialist golf equipment retailers (e.g. the American Golf and Nevada Bobs) have therefore thrived, whereas in some other sports, specialist equipment retailers are not as prevalent.

In golf and other markets, technological developments such as club, racquet and ball development can be important in encouraging new equipment purchase. Single sector brands like Callaway have a powerful incentive to maintain technological innovation to stimulate demand. Issues of branding and athlete endorsement can also be significant, in both positive and negative ways (e.g. Tiger Woods and Nike). Some similar issues may be found/emerging in alternative and extreme sports where equipment can be technologically demanding, but aspects of branding, design and style overlay this.

This brief review of sports goods products raises a number of implications for sports retailing:

- The switch from equipment to clothing suggests a need for a change in the store design, layout and merchandise mix in retail outlets.

- The fashion orientation (and to an extent concern over style) implies the need for a closer knowledge of the market and rapid adaptation to changes in demand. Volatility in this market has increased. Emphasis has to be placed on the management of the distribution and supply chain functions, with the retail shop being critical to capturing data on, and understanding consumer behaviour.

- Segmentation in the product market for example by gender, sport, equipment and clothing requirements, suggests the potential for segmentation in the retail market at the chain (e.g. female-oriented stores), product (e.g. specialist sports products) and in-store (e.g. separate specialist departments) levels.

- Products with high technological innovation need to be supported at retail level by high-quality environments, information and customer advice and service.

Who do we buy from?

There are many different types of retailers involved in sports goods retailing. The market has undergone considerable change in recent years, as concentration processes have affected retailing generally and sports retailing in particular, leading to consolidation amongst retailers, and as the nature of the sports product market has changed. Figure 21.2 shows that sports products are sold through many different types of retail outlet, but the main market in the UK is to be found in the specialist sector. Over the period from 1988 the nature of the retail store sector has changed. Specialists have become more important, though they have declined a little in recent years as new competitors entered the market – e.g. internet-based retail channels, 'club' shops and mainline retailers such as Tesco and Wal-Mart – and as extreme discount-based competition took its toll.

A number of trends can thus be identified that are affecting the sports retailing sector:

- The size and growth of the UK market has attracted a number of international retailers to the country. The American chain Foot Locker has expanded rapidly in the UK in recent years and the French retailer Decathlon has a number of superstores in the UK.

- Smaller specialist chains focusing on particular markets have a strong position in the UK. For example, outdoor/adventure specialists such as Go Outdoors and Tiso have presence and considerable market reputation. A similar situation exists in board and extreme sports where significant but small players include Snow+Rock and Ellis Brigham. Snow+Rock, for example, attracts male customers looking for expert brands and technical advice.

473

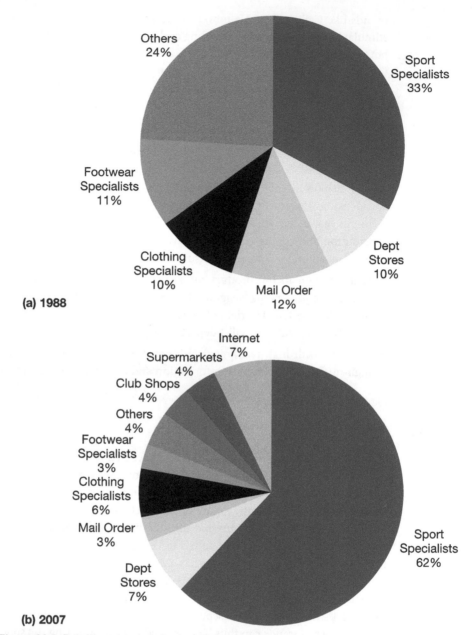

Figure 21.2 Retailing channels in the UK sports goods sector 1988 and 2007

Source: Retail Business and Mintel Reports on UK Sports Retailers and Sports Goods Markets 1988, 2008

- A number of specialist players have begun to explore the potential of multi-channel retailing. Many of the retailers above would, for example, have both physical shops and sell over the internet. Other retailers, such as Cotton Traders, have emerged from a mail order leisure business into a multi-channel physical and virtual retailer. There are also some strong internet 'pureplay' retailers, which have grown considerably in recent years, such as ProDirect (www.prodirectsports.com), Kitbag (www.kitbag.com) and MandM Direct (www.mandmdirect.com).

- Despite the strength of the specialist sports retailers, the power of the manufacturers or sporting brands remains of importance in this market. Leading brands such as Nike, Adidas and Reebok have considerable product presence in sports retailers, but they also have outlets of their own. Similarly, sports clubs brands such as Manchester United have their own retail outlets (megastore, club stores, internet and mail order) as well as selling branded and licensed products through other retailers, e.g. Argos, Tesco, JJB Sports.

- Spectacular consumption sites and/or experiential consumption outlets where products (e.g. clothing and equipment) can be tried in extreme conditions or consumption watched (e.g. ice wall climbing) have attracted considerable attention (e.g. Penaloza 1999). Major players in this market in the USA include Niketown, ESPN Zone, REI and Dick's Sporting Goods.

It also has to be remembered, however, that it is not sports retailers alone that are interested in sport. As Case 21.1 shows, mainline retailers and manufacturer brands use sport as a consumer attractor to their stores and products.

Case 21.1 Tesco, England and the FIFA World Cup 2010

Tesco became an official supplier to the England team for the duration of the FIFA World Cup 2010. Tesco was the only supermarket permitted to use the official England logo in stores, marketing and merchandise. The commercial terms of the deal were not made public, but at a launch in Wembley Stadium Tesco outlined the plan that had been put into place, from World Cup trading cards at every checkout, to additional staff at Tesco Express stores, in anticipation of fans dashing in for pizzas (including football-themed margaritas), beers and snacks ahead of the game, Clubcard promotions and a World Cup web portal.

Promotions on food included partnerships with brands such as Coca-Cola, Walkers and Mars to offer Clubcard holders prizes including tickets to England games in South Africa. Tesco also sold World Cup themed food including St George's flag pizzas and limited edition sandwiches. The bulk of its activity focused on a television and press campaign starring football stars Frank Lampard and Peter Shilton, as well as in-store point-of-sale material and a website to promote a tie-up with Match Attax World Cup trading cards. The partnership saw the supermarket offer exclusive packs including extra cards of international football stars and offer exclusive signed cards, competitions and trading events as the World Cup progressed. The supermarket also used the World Cup partnership to promote its FA Tesco Skills grassroots football school. A TV ad highlighted the free football sessions and starter packs Tesco provided and weekly roadshows with football entertainment throughout the tournament.

The World Cup kicked off on 11 June. Tesco planned to increase its offers on TV, with a deal of the week every week from St George's Day on 23 April, when it launched its World Cup theme in all its English stores. Tesco expected to sell 800,000 flags and 500,000 England footballs as it dedicated its seasonal aisle in all stores to non-food World Cup merchandise. This switched to food when the tournament kicked off.

(continued)

Retail and logistics director David Potts estimated that Tesco's Express stores (they have twice as many now as in 2006) would particularly benefit from shoppers stocking up for games, and expected footfall in its convenience stores to rocket 30 per cent compared with normal levels in the hours immediately before England's games. Tesco is now much stronger in non-food so was able to dress its stores better, sell much more general merchandise and many more televisions (up to 300,000).

Sources: Baker (2010); Danaher (2010: 5); Perry (2010: 32–34); Teather (2010: 29).

Discussion question

1 Why would Tesco wish to make this deal? How could the other leading food retailers such as Asda and Sainsbury's respond?

Given their significance in the structure of the UK sports retailing market, Table 21.2 provides a brief description of the three largest sports specialist retailers.

There are a number of issues that arise from Table 21.2. First, the considerable scale of these businesses is well demonstrated, with substantial sales volumes and number of retail stores.

Secondly, the sector has been concentrating through natural growth and the strategic acquisitions that companies have made. Strategic acquisitions have been combined with significant store expansion programmes, more recently also linked to some store closures and repositionings. In particular, Sportsdirect.com has expanded aggressively in the 2000s at the expense of the previous market leader JJB Sports.

Thirdly, store formats and locations have been undergoing change. Fascias have changed as acquisitions have been made, but much of the expansion has been focused on out-of-town superstores or in-town, larger stores. Scale is thus seen at both the organisational and the operational or store level. Out-of-town superstore or retail park development fits with broad consumer and retail trends. Format development at the smaller scale is also seen, with segmented and focused chains being developed, particularly in expanding specialist markets (e.g. boardwear, outdoor sports).

Fourthly, the sports retailing market is not in particularly good shape. The profits shown in the table are small (often indeed losses) and businesses are not necessarily sustainable at these levels. Price has become much more of a feature in this market recently, exacerbated by the global recession. Market pressures have therefore been seen in the sales and takeovers of major chains e.g. Blacks and store closure plans e.g. JJB Sports. Despite overall growth in the market, it could be that there has been an over-provision of retail space, focusing price competition and/or that the chains are too similar in their positioning.

Finally, the descriptions of the chains point to a recognition that there is need for differentiation in the main market. Different retailers have attempted to focus on fashion rather than value and on high-quality rather than lower mass-market goods. However, this is not an easy task as discounting and price awareness in the market are high. The differences amongst chains therefore may not be that great in the perceptions of consumers. This provides a retail opportunity for smaller niche specialists and those offering something distinctive.

Table 21.2 Leading sports specialists in the UK

Retailer	Description	Financial details
JJB Sports (www.jjbsports.com and www.jjbcorporate.com)	JJB Sports was by the early 2000s, the leading UK retailer of sports clothing, footwear, accessories and equipment, trading from high street outlets and out of town superstores. In 1998 JJB Sports acquired the then market leader Sports Division. Their principal aim is to supply high-quality branded sports and leisure products at competitive or discount prices. They focus on goods for doing sport. Bad business decision making and market changes including strengthening competition have badly affected JJB Sports in recent years. The company has been in real difficulties with financial problems making obtaining stock difficult. They have been forced to reduce their operations and refocus their attention. This has included capital raising, refinancing and closing significant numbers of stores via a CVA. The business is still loss making and is now substantially reduced in scale.	Sales: £930m (2004) £284m (2012) Pre-tax profit: £68m (2004) (−£101m) (2012) Stores: 448 (2004) 192 (2012)
JD Group (www.jdsports.co.uk and www.jdplc.com)	JD Group is a leading specialist retailer of fashionable branded sports and leisure wear. It is based around a sports division, a fashion division and a new outdoors division. There has been a rebranding of many stores (from First Sport – taken over in 2002 – to JD Sports), some store closures and expansion in superstores. It now operates from JD Sports, Scotts, Bank, Blacks and Cecil Gee stores. The company sees its focus as higher-end sports fashion rather than a value-led strategy, and has strong **own-brand** and branded merchandise, supported by an extensive advertising strategy. It has performed well in recent years, attracting a young market. International expansion into France, Spain and Ireland via purchase has taken place. In 2012 JD Sports bought Blacks Leisure and is now embarked on integration, which has seen a large number of Blacks and Millets stores close, with further reorganisation to come.	Sales: £458m (2004) £1,059m (2012) Pre-tax profit: £2m (2004) £67m (2012) Stores: 385 (2004) 919 (2012)
Sports Direct (www.sportsdirect.com and www.sportsdirectplc.com)	Sportsdirect.com (formerly Sports World) is the market leading operator of sports shops and superstores. It is the owner of sports brands including Donnay, Everlast and Dunlop Slazenger. The shops discount aggressively and promise 'unbeatable value and performance' on a range of leading brands, including their own, with a focus on fashion and casual lines. It is more downmarket than its competitors. It expanded aggressively through company takeovers in the 2000s (e.g. Hargreaves, Gilesports, USC) and has also expanded internationally with shops and licensing. It bought Field&Trek, an outdoor specialist, in 2008 and has recently moved more strongly into international retailing and internet sales (c. 8% of UK turnover).	Sales: £398m (2002) £1,599m (2011) Pre-tax profit: £46m (2002) £136m (2011) Stores: 135 (2002) 393 in the UK and 118 international (2011)

Source: Annual Reports

Issues in sports retailing

The description of the sports retailing sector thus far has focused on the structure and composition of the market and the way these have changed. This changing structure is a reflection of the nature of sport, the consumer market, consumers' perceptions of sport and business practicalities. The basic idea of a retailer is a simple one. The business acquires products and makes them available for sale to consumers. Retailers thus have to consider issues of shop location, consumer market segmentation and positioning, store design, buying, ranging and merchandising, logistics and distribution, stock management, staffing and customer service, as well as operational practicalities such as cash flow, security, product availability, heating and lighting etc. Similar issues have to be considered by internet retailers, although often with a different balance amongst the issues.

Covering all of these aspects of sports goods retailing is impossible here. However, it was noted earlier that the market did have a tendency towards similarity and that profit margins were currently low. This section therefore focuses on four particular aspects of sports goods retailing, all of which can be broadly considered as attempts to provide a differentiating proposition in the market:

- approaches to the consumer;
- store design and experiential consumption;
- sports retailing and the internet;
- merchandising operations.

Approaches to the consumer

Retailers attempt to attract customers to visit their stores, make purchases and to keep coming back. There are many ways to do this in sports retailing. It has to be recognised, however, that not all consumers will be attracted to stores by the same stimuli. Indeed, some consumers will actively be turned off by the approach of some retailers – e.g. the in-store environment or the type, range, price and quality of the merchandise. There are trends in consumers' perceptions, desires and life-stages that affect the level and nature of demand. For example, the positive feelings towards sports goods retailers by young teenagers are remarkably strong, but these reduce during later teenage years as participation rates in sport fall and other interests take over (Foresight, 2001). There are also differences between the sexes in terms of perceptions of sports retailers. These are important not only because of the (increasing) scale of the female sports market, but also because of the significant role women play in the purchase of sports products for and by men.

Different reactions to different sports retailers occur. For women, for example, many sports shops are threatening environments that are viewed negatively as being overly male and aggressive:

> Most sporting goods stores smell of stale sweat and old rubber and have techno booming loud enough to vibrate your diaphragm. They display their wares inelegantly, not to say indifferently, stacking them by activity; golf, jogging, swimming. A man's shopping environment if ever there was one.
>
> (www.cada.co.uk/articles/ar_1.htm, downloaded 23 December 2004)

Such stores do not meet the aspirations or requirements of many women in terms of sports goods products, shopping environments and customer service, nor do they fit with how women wish to shop generally.

Some brands have recognised the issues that are raised by these 'standard' environments and by the growing demand from women for sports products. Nike, for example, operates NikeWomen (both stores and online – www.nikewomen.com), which focuses exclusively on the female sports product market. These stores look and feel different to standard Nike stores, having different colours, layout, changing rooms, lighting, product presentation etc. Niketown in London has a significant female component in its overall floorspace mix, based on learning from NikeWomen. The important issue here is not to treat women differently because they are women (gender stereotyping), but to recognise that different consumer segments and markets have different aspirations and needs and as such the retail outlet needs to be designed, merchandised and operated differently.

Case 21.2 takes this approach to a logical conclusion in discussing a retailer run by women for women. This women-only 'activewear boutique' – Sweaty Betty – illustrates many of the differences between the sexes, in terms of both sports goods retailing and retailing generally. It goes beyond that, however, in targeting particular requirements of the female market. Such differences need to be taken into account if retailers are to successfully position themselves for parts of the female (or the male, or both) market. Not all women will react positively to Sweaty Betty. However, it is used here to show how shopping behaviours and aspirations can be taken into account in targeting specific sports and leisure markets. This has to translate into all aspects of the retail store location, design, product mix, merchandising and customer service, in order to create a strongly attractive environment for the target market.

Case 21.2 Sweaty Betty

Sweaty Betty is a young, small, London-focused women-only high street retailer ('activewear boutique') targeting the fashionable end of performance wear. It has been described as a highly targeted contemporary fusion of sportswear, swimwear, outdoorwear and gymwear. The founders believed that they had identified a gap in the market for women-only activewear, arguing that current sports retailers were not meeting women's needs and that women wanted particular things from a sports store. For many women, they felt, the feel-good factor and the overall health and well-being aspects of keeping fit were more important than winning. The retail store needed to reflect these attitudes.

The first store opened in November 1998 and there are now 25 stores and boutiques and a transactional website. Sweaty Betty sells activewear combining fun with fashion and fitness, using superbrands such as Nike and Adidas (including Stella McCartney) and niche brands (including own brands) such as Pure Lime, Venice Beach and CandidaFaria. Celebrity endorsement by, for example, Elle MacPherson and Emma Bunton has helped raise the profile of the brand.

To live up to these beliefs and the purpose of 'increasing the confidence and happiness of women by providing beautiful clothes and subtle inspiration to lead an active lifestyle' the stores do not look like average sports shops. Stores are intensely

(continued)

feminine with soft lighting, spacious environments and fixtures and fittings more synonymous with an upmarket clothing store to create a pleasant boutique shopping experience. The colours are different – high white ceilings and loads of pink. The mood is seductive rather than harsh sell. Changing rooms are prominent and large with flattering mirrors and lighting. This is a deliberately designed environment focusing on the feel-good, health and well-being aspects of keeping fit. Products are high quality and well presented as fashion, music is not overly dominant and the atmosphere is supportive and non-aggressive. Such details derive from the founders' belief that standard sports stores are often too male and threatening, treating women as second-class customers. As the founder of Sweaty Betty, Tamara Hill-Norton, comments: 'why should women have to get advice on, or buy, a sports bra from a spotty male teenager?' Rather than conjuring up images of a typical sports-wear store it aims to position itself as a confidant or friend, someone to provide advice and guide exercisers in the right direction.

A vital aspect of the store offer, which brings together all components of the retail brand, is customer service. Staff are carefully selected to reflect their target customers. As the target customer is likely to recommend stores by word-of-mouth, service is paramount. Sweaty Betty staff are important to the store atmospherics, being enthusiasts themselves, keeping fit and leading active lives. The shop staff know their products and their uses. Their stories feature heavily on the website, which also has useful links to local gyms, running clubs, registered personal trainers and rollerblading evenings. Exercise is seen as fun, and stylish fun at that, but it is recognised that there are more important things in life as well.

Source: Sparks (2008a).

Discussion question

2 In what ways do you feel women shop differently from men for sports products and how could this be reflected in sports shops?

Store design and experiential consumption

Consumers have become more discerning in their shopping behaviour. For some segments of the market the retail experience is as much the driving force for behaviours as the product itself. This implies that much more attention has to be paid to aspects of store design and customer service. Retail outlets are planned and managed consumption environments (this is as true of a discount store as it is for the most exclusive boutique), so design has always been a feature, but recent years have seen considerably more attention paid to design. Good design can be ruined by poor service standards and staff.

It is notable that in a number of instances the idea of the store as a destination has developed – e.g. REI and Niketown. These retailers also have in common a pursuit of what might be called experiential or spectacular consumption. REI (www.rei.com) has become noted for having areas of the stores where consumers can try products. Their highly visual climbing walls have become a distinctive feature of their store design and layout. Store atmospherics are a critical part of the approach of REI and this is allied to a strong sense of social and environmental responsibility, including in-store design and materials use.

Such environmental concerns and store atmospherics are considerable attractions to consumers (Ogle et al., 2004).

The retail store has always been a designed or manipulated space. This has perhaps received its fullest expression in themed retail outlets such as Niketown (Sherry, 1998; Peñaloza, 1999). Niketown, Chicago is described by Peñaloza (1999: 338) as 'a consumption venue, a fastidiously designed five-storey combination of merchandise, celebrity athlete memorabilia and corporate tribute'. The consumption of spectacle at Niketown, where the consumers are part of the 'show', is the key component of the store. Spectacular consumption behaviour is participative in nature, involves knowledge of the production of the spectacle and its consumption and involves consumption of space, cultural meanings and products in what may be termed a hybrid store/museum. Consumers move (or are moved) through spaces and produce meanings of competition, performance, style, recreation and consumption. Through the design they interact with displays of sports celebrities, products and corporate identifiers. Such flagship brand stores (Kozinets et al., 2002) provide additional engagement with the product and the brand (engage by experience) and satisfy the need for shopping (the retail experience) to be more entertaining and/or leisure based. Such extreme combinations of themes, leisure, sport and consumption are at the cutting edge of retail store design. It has to be noted however that such 'shops' do not fit everyone's needs. As with other sports retailing, they may be seen as particularly (male) gendered experiences.

Some of these issues are explored using another retailer in Case 21.3.

Case 21.3 Dick's Sporting Goods

Dick's Sporting Goods is an authentic full line sporting goods retailer offering a broad **assortment** of brand-name sporting goods equipment, apparel and footwear in a speciality store environment. The key elements of the business strategy are:

- authentic sporting goods retailer;
- competitive pricing;
- broad assortment of brand-name merchandise;
- expertise and service;
- interactive store 'within a store';
- exclusive brand offerings.

Dick's offers a full range of sporting goods and active apparel at each price point in order to appeal to the beginner, intermediate and enthusiast sports consumer. The merchandise carried includes one or more of the leading manufacturers in each category. The objective is not only to carry leading brands, but a full range of products within each brand, including the premium items for the sports enthusiast.

Each of the stores typically contains five speciality stores. The 'store within a store' concept creates a unique shopping environment by combining the convenience, broad assortment and competitive prices of large format stores with brand names, deep product selection and customer service of a speciality store. Stores are designed to create an exciting shopping environment with distinct departments that can stand on

(continued)

their own. Signs and banners are located throughout the store allowing customers to locate the various departments quickly. A wide aisle through the middle of the store displays seasonal or special buy merchandise. Video monitors throughout the store provide a sense of entertainment with videos of championship games, instructional sessions or live sports events. Dick's seeks to encourage cross-selling and impulse buying through the layout of the departments. It provides a bright, open shopping environment through the use of glass, lights and lower shelving which enable customers to see the array of merchandise offered throughout the stores.

Dick's sporting goods stores typically contain five standalone speciality stores. These seek to create a distinct look and feel for each speciality department to heighten the customers' interest in the products offered. A typical store has the following in-store speciality shops:

- Golf Pro Shop, a golf shop with a putting green and hitting area and video monitors featuring golf tournaments and instruction on the Golf Channel or other sources.

- The Footwear Centre, featuring hardwood floors, a track for testing athletic shoes and a bank of video monitors playing sporting events.

- The Fitness Centre, providing an extensive selection of equipment for today's most popular fitness activities, including a dedicated cycle shop, designed to sell and service bikes, complete with a mechanic's work area and equipment on the sales floor.

- The Lodge for the hunting and fishing customer, designed to have the look of an authentic bait and tackle shop.

- Team Sports, a seasonal sports area displaying sports equipment and athletic apparel associated with specific seasonal sports, such as football and baseball.

The stores provide interactive opportunities by allowing customers to test golf clubs in an indoor driving range, shoot bows in archery range, or run on the footwear track.

Dick's strives to complement the merchandise selection and innovative store design with superior customer service. The stores actively recruit sports enthusiasts to serve as sales associates because the company believes that they are more knowledgeable about the products they sell. For example, Dick's currently employs PGA and LPGA golf professionals to work in the Golf departments, bike mechanics to sell and service bicycles and certified fitness trainers to provide advice on the best fitness equipment for the individual. The company believes that the associates' enthusiasm and ability to demonstrate and explain the advantages of the products lead to increased sales, and that prompt, knowledgeable and enthusiastic service fosters the confidence and loyalty of customers and differentiates Dick's from other large format sporting goods stores.

As CNN Money.com concluded 'If you like sports, it's hard not to like Dick's'.

Sources: Extracted from the 2010 10-K form for the Securities and Exchange Commission, available for download via Dick's website at www.dickssportinggoods.com; CNN Money.com (2010).

Discussion question

3 What key store design and merchandising features does Dick's exemplify?

Sports retailing and the internet

Reference has been made in this chapter to the presence of sports retailers on the internet or retailers becoming multi-channel operators. This approach has emerged more strongly in recent years. Initially many sports retailers operated informational rather than transactional websites. One argument was that consumers needed to see and touch the products in order to assess their quality. However, as the internet has become more sophisticated and as consumers have adopted the technology and shown a general willingness to purchase electronically, so many websites have become fully transactional and this channel has expanded. As a result, many of the retailers mentioned in this chapter have an online transactional presence.

The sports retail internet presence thus to an extent mirrors the 'real' market. The degree of success is dependent on the standard retail and distribution attributes and effectiveness. There are general sports retailers online such as JD Sports; there are also more casual specialist sports goods retailers such as Sweaty Betty. But the internet also offers some additional features that add to the consumer opportunities to purchase sports products. Consumers online are able to deal directly with some manufacturers and/or brand holders, use a standard retailer, a club shop or an event site (e.g. www.rydercupshop.net), search for the cheapest price and/or the exclusive item or could bid at an auction site. If price is important then comparison sites are a very useful tool, even if it is only to find out the going market price before buying on the high street. If it is an exclusive or hard to obtain item, then a web search may be a good way of tracking it down. This has particular importance in the area of sports memorabilia where specialist sites have emerged. If the item needs customisation – e.g. a replica shirt – this again could be arranged online. Customers may be more in control via internet retailing. It is unlikely that these sites can match the facilities in-store, particularly if store design is properly thought through, but as with 'real' shops, there are good and poor examples of website design. Some sites have extensive visual, aural and interactive features that engage users in the product and the site atmosphere. Others are very functional.

In the UK, the internet has taken 10 per cent of the sports goods market and, according to Mintel (2008), attracts high income and higher social class consumers. It has thus become a major force, raising issues of competition and organisation (Wallace et al., 2009). In addition to the mainstream retailers on the internet, the expansion may be due to the:

- development of specialist pureplay retailers such as Kitbag, ProDirect and MandM Direct with product coherence and expertise and discount prices;
- power of brands in this market, including manufacturer brands, but also club and event brands;
- expansion of click and collect schemes, where the consumer reserves the product on the internet and then collects it (sometimes immediately) from the store (note the technical expertise in real-time stock management needed by the retailer);
- use of the internet as a clearance channel for end-of-line or other products. One example is JD Sports-owned www.getthelabel.com to sell off end-of-line and out-of-style products cheaply.

Merchandising operations

For many outside retailing, selling is often viewed as being the same as retailing but selling is but one component of the retail operation. In some retailers, the skills of the sales staff are critical in the delivery of customer service and the repeat patronage of consumers. The art and science of selling and the quality of the sales staff are of fundamental importance for much business success. In other situations, the lack of quality or knowledge of the staff acts as a negative influence on consumers, as seen in the origins of Sweaty Betty.

Store and selling design varies enormously by situation (Underhill, 1999). The emphasis on design, staff knowledge and staff competency may be vital in some situations, but of no consequence in others. Some stores are dramatic (e.g. Niketown), some are functional (e.g. Sports Direct), others playful (e.g. REI). Some have many staff selling; others simply have takers of money. All, however, are based on retailers' understanding of what works with their customers.

Store-based selling has its own distinctive characteristics. How the product is merchandised and the ways in which design and display interact are important to attracting consumers and obtaining their custom. As a result, much effort is expended in laying out the store and in ensuring that products are presented appropriately. This presentation includes aspects of visual display, as well as essential product information. Depending on the product lines involved and the approach of the retailer, such merchandising may be of lesser or greater importance. Even in supposedly simple retailer situations product display can be sophisticated and help consumers make choices amongst products, and manufacturers are often keen to support retailers with displays etc. Internet retailers have similar selling objectives, but a different set of tasks and expectations to manage, with opportunities for product description, visuals and videos to entice customers, though of course customers cannot touch the product.

Store merchandising and display techniques condition the retail environment in every store. Some of the techniques are rather obvious and relatively easy to identify, whereas others are far more subtle and difficult to discern (Underhill, 1999). Visual merchandising and design direct attention and direction of movement by leading customers around and through the merchandise. 'Hot Spots' in the store are created to encourage consumers through the shop and grab attention. Lighting, music and sports sounds are used in some stores to alter the mood of parts of shops. Colour is used to create an environment or an image – e.g. in a club shop. Touch is encouraged to exploit the tactile senses. Even smells could be used to evoke responses. Some design and display is organised to recreate remembered activities or past triumphs, successes or events. Some, as in Dick's Sporting Goods, allow consumers to play.

Case 21.4 considers two football clubs and their new approaches to retailing in their club shops, via a retail design 'guru' and on the internet.

Case 21.4 Arsenal, Liverpool and George Davies

In late May 2008, one of the largest official football club shops in Europe opened as part of the new Liverpool One mega shopping, leisure and residential complex. With more than 10,000 sq ft of selling space, the new store has a Heritage Wall along one side, a personalisation zone to offer customised Liverpool football club merchandise, a relaxing chill-out area, a dramatic spiral staircase to the first floor and a shirt print

(continued)

area where customers can see their shirts being printed. The store and the wide merchandise range has been designed by Liverpool-born, Reds-supporting fashion and retail guru George Davies (Next, George at Asda, Per Una). His design company S'Porter Limited, established in 1995, specialises in combining fashion with sport.

S'Porter runs three other stores in Liverpool for the club, but until Liverpool One was most known for its development of The Armoury store at the Emirates Stadium. When Arsenal moved to the Emirates in 2006, the club took the opportunity to upgrade and extend the retail merchandise and club shop offer. The Armoury is supported by two other smaller stores (All Arsenal and Arsenal World of Sport at Finsbury Park tube station). S'Porter took on the role of creating a new range of Arsenal merchandise, helping design the new retail spaces and sourcing the products. The Armoury has been exceptionally successful, taking £150,000 each match day, reflecting the event-driven nature of the business.

S'Porter makes money from design and sourcing, with the club making the retail money. With the rising brand power of football clubs and the growing female and young interest, the product and merchandise mix has changed markedly in recent years, becoming more lifestyle and fashion oriented. The retail space dramatically reflects the quality and ambition of the club, whether it be Arsenal or Liverpool.

These club shops are the physical embodiment of the club and attract supporters and visitors alike. Merchandised in modern retail ways and to meet varying customers, they provide new quality for club shops. Similarly, in both clubs the websites are fully transactional for customers who prefer to buy online or who cannot reach the stores. The product is merchandised by activity and segment and the internet features are used to provide a comprehensive and complete club offer.

Sources/further information: Arsenal Football Club (www.arsenal.com); Berwin (2007); Liverpool Football Club (www.liverpoolfc.tv); Weston (2008).

Discussion question

4 In what ways should club 'shops' reflect the changing nature of supporters?

Conclusion

Sports retailing has had to react to considerable changes in sport, the consumer market and retailing itself. There has been a transformation from an equipment product focus to a clothing orientation, which is strongly fashion or leisure based. The breadth of sports and products available has increased, as has the volatility of consumer demand.

Sports retailing in the UK is dominated by a small number of specialist sports retailers, among which Sportsdirect.com is the market leader. The sector has concentrated through takeovers and acquisitions, but at the same time niche markets have opened up, allowing smaller retailers to prosper in some situations. A similar situation exists in other countries.

Keys to success in retailing are understanding the target consumer market and designing and merchandising the shop proposition to meet these consumers' aspirations and needs. Differences amongst retailers in terms of their store positioning are thus emerging more strongly at the edges of the main market, particularly in specialist areas such as outdoor wear, certain markets such as women, and 'new' sports such as extreme or adventure sports. Some of this is organised by the retailers, but in sports retailing manufacturer brands continue to retain significance for consumers. More recently, the internet has broadened the sports retail propositions.

The future of the sports retailing market will be of considerable interest. Profitability in the UK amongst the largest businesses is slight, due to the competition amongst themselves, new mass-market retail entrants and the ability of niche retailers including the internet to erode the core market. There will be a continuing search for formats that closely meet consumers' demands. Closer adaptation to target markets, in both real and virtual stores, is likely to see new and tighter formats emerge as all aspects of the retail operation are aligned with consumer demands. Retail stores will continue to adapt from a purely functional product-based approach to one that involves all aspects of consumers' expectations about sport and sports retailing. Managing the operations of any store will however remain fundamental to success.

Keywords

Assortment; atmospherics; merchandising; own-brands; retailing; shop; specialist retailer.

Guided reading

The sports goods retailing sector is large and significant in retailing terms, with two of the largest sports retailers having over £1 billion in sales. It is remarkable therefore that there is so little coverage of the sector in mainstream retailing texts. None of the leading retail textbooks contain any coverage of sports retailing. This is even more curious given the sports participation and brand recognition rates of teenagers and other student markets. Any standard retail textbook though will provide coverage of retail operations. A good starting point is Sparks (2008b) and you could also consult the more specialist chapters of Sparks (2006a, 2006b).

The best sources of detailed information on the sector/market are market research and consultancy companies that either specialise in the sector (e.g. www.sgieurope.com) or provide regular detailed market updates (e.g. Mintel, 2008 or www.mintel.com), though these come at a price. Many of the retailers mentioned in this chapter have their own websites which provide basic corporate information (to varying degrees of detail and quality) and from which downloadable public reports may be available. Simply visiting retail shops or surfing their websites also provides additional viewpoints or information about their operations. The trade press in the UK is also a reliable source of sports retailing news items, whether from a retail (Retail Week – www.retail-week.com/) or a sports business (Sport Business International – www.sportbusiness.com) perspective.

Specialist academic retail journals include:

- *International Review of Retail, Distribution and Consumer Research*;
- *International Journal of Retail and Distribution Management*;
- *Journal of Retailing*;
- *Journal of Retailing and Consumer Services*.

And in sport:

- *International Journal of Sport Management and Marketing*;
- *Sport, Business and Management*;
- *Sport Marketing Quarterly*.

Recommended websites

Board Retailers Association – www.boardretailers.org
National Sporting Goods Association (USA) – www.nsga.org
Sport Business International – www.sportbusiness.com
Sport Industry Research Centre – www.shu.ac.uk/research/sirc/
Sporting Goods Intelligence – www.sgieurope.com and www.sginews.com
Sporting Goods Manufacturers Association (USA) – www.sgma.com
Sports Goods Business (USA) – www.sportinggoodsbusiness.com
World Federation of the Sporting Goods Industry – www.whsgi.org/

References

Baker, R. (2010) 'Tesco reveals World cup marketing plans', *Marketing Week*, 6 April, www.marketingweek.co.uk

Berwin, L. (2007) 'Kitting out the nation', *Retail Week*, 19 October.

CNN Money.com (2010) 'Retail's rising star', http://money.cnn.com/fdcp?1271899019057

Danaher, T. (2010) 'Tesco expects TV sales to soar with World Cup sponsorship deal', *Retail Week*, 9 April, 5.

Foresight (2001) 'Destination retail: a survey of young people's attitudes towards a career in retailing', Retail E-Commerce Task Force, Foresight, www.foresight.gov.uk/

Kozinets, R.V., Sherry, J.F., DeBerry-Spence, B., Duhachek, A., Nuttavuthisit, K. and Storm, D. (2002) 'Themed flagship brand stores in the new millennium: theory, practice, prospects', *Journal of Retailing*, 78 (1), 17–29.

Mamic, I. (2004) 'Managing global supply chain: the sports footwear, apparel and retail sectors', *Journal of Business Ethics*, 59, 81–100.

Mintel (2004) 'Sports goods retailing UK', *Mintel Retail Intelligence*, March, London: Mintel.

Mintel (2008) 'Sports Goods Retailing', *Mintel Retail Intelligence*, June, London: Mintel.

Ogle, J.P., Hyllegard, K.H. and Dunbar, B.H. (2004) 'Predicting patronage behaviours in a sustainable retail environment', *Environment and Behaviour*, 36 (5), 717–41.

Peñaloza, L. (1999) 'Just doing it: a visual ethnographic study of spectacular consumption at Niketown', *Consumption, Markets and Culture*, 2 (October), 337–400.

Perry, J. (2010) 'A game of two halves', *Retail Week*, 1 April, 32–4.

Sherry, J.F. (1998) 'The soul of the company store: Niketown Chicago and the emplaced bandscape', in J.F. Sherry (ed.), *Servicescapes*, Lincolnwood, IL: NTC Business Books, 109–46.

Sparks, L. (2006a) 'Distribution channels and sports logistics', in J. Beech and S. Chadwick (eds), *The Marketing of Sport*, Harlow: FT/Prentice Hall, 342–64.

Sparks, L. (2006b) 'Sports goods retailing', in J. Beech and S. Chadwick (eds), *The Marketing of Sport*, Harlow: FT/Prentice Hall, 365–95.

Sparks, L. (2008a) 'SweatyBetty: by women, for women', in S. Chadwick and D. Arthur (eds), *International Cases in the Business of Sport*, Oxford: Butterworth-Heinemann, 60–72.

Sparks, L. (2008b) 'Retailing', in M.J. Baker and S.J. Hart (eds), *The Marketing Book*, 6th edn, Oxford: Butterworth-Heinemann, 602–28.

Teather, D. (2010) 'Tesco takes punt on World Cup', *Guardian*, 7 April, 29.

Underhill, P. (1999) *Why We Buy: The Science of Shopping*, London: Orion.

Wallace, D.W., Johnson, J.L. and Umesh, U.N. (2009) 'Multichannels strategy implementation: the role of channel alignment capabilities', *Decision Sciences*, 40, 869–900.

Weston, A. (2008) 'Stairway to Heaven for Liverpool FC shoppers', *Liverpool Daily Post*, 21 May.

22

Sports media and PR

Stephen W. Dittmore, University of Arkansas

Learning outcomes

Upon completion of this chapter, the reader should be able to:

- illustrate the benefits of the two-way symmetrical public relations model for sport organisations;
- understand different approaches to repairing a sport organisation or athlete's image or reputation;
- identify influential groups of individuals which could be considered a sport organisation's publics;
- outline specific social media tools available for a sport public relations professional;
- explain how sport organisations can generate publicity through media relations.

 Overview

The role of public relations in sport organisations appears to have taken on greater importance in the New Media era. This has made the job of a public relations professional both easier and more difficult. More tools, such as social media, are available than previously, and no longer do organisations need to rely on media to carry organisational messages. At the same time, there is a greater need for the development of long-term, meaningful relationships with key publics.

The method for identifying influential publics is also explored in the chapter, as well as what tactics sport organisations can employ to maximize their ability to generate these relationships. It recommends sport organisations focus on developing two-way symmetrical communication approaches which include a direct dialogue with the organisation's publics. It considers the growing importance of social media and examines the benefits of engaging in some of these activities. Suggestions are presented for achieving high levels of publicity through media relations tactics such as news releases and news conferences.

Finally, the chapter explores how sport organisations or individual athletes might manage communication during a crisis, and subsequent efforts to repair a damaged image or reputation.

Introduction

Confusion frequently exists between whether public relations and marketing accomplish the same objective. The two can be considered as distinct yet complementary functions within the sport organisation. Most definitions of sport marketing include objectives such as meeting the needs and wants of sport consumers through an exchange process. This is frequently accomplished through the marketing of sport directly to the consumer, or through sport promotions to the consumer (e.g. Mullin et al., 2007). Much of the literature on sport marketing emphasises the building of mutually beneficial relationships between the organisation and the consumer (e.g. Milne and McDonald, 1999).

Two recent approaches to defining sport public relations emphasise aspects of relationship building as well. Hopwood (2007: 293) noted that public relations is the 'management of corporate image through the proactive and professional management of relationships with the organization's publics'. Similarly, Stoldt et al. (2006: 2) defined sport public relations as a 'managerial communication-based function designed to identify a sport organization's key publics, evaluate its relationships with those publics, and foster desirable relationships between the sport organization and those key publics'.

Let's consider the commonalities of those two definitions. First, both emphasise the role of management, which emphasises the importance of public relations for overall organisation reputation management and not just dealing with media or spin-doctoring. Second, both stress the need to identify specific organisational publics, and the creation of desirable relationships with those publics. As this chapter evolves, attention will be paid to identifying publics and designing communication approaches to reach those publics.

Additional confusion between sport marketing and sport public relations is evident when one considers how public relations fits within the 'marketing mix'. For example, Shilbury et al. (2009) consider a seven-P model which includes the four traditional Ps of marketing (product, price, place and promotion) plus three service-oriented Ps (process, people and physical evidence). Mullin et al. (2007), however, conceptualise a five-P model which includes public relations as a standalone element along with the four traditional Ps. Their rationale for doing so is that some sport businesses (e.g. professional, collegiate sport) experience such high levels of media visibility that PR warrants consideration as a distinct aspect of the marketing mix.

One way to reconcile the proper place of sport public relations is to consider its position within an overall integrated marketing communications strategy (Hopwood, 2007a). She adapted a communications mix from Irwin et al. (2002) for the twenty-first century which includes the elements of relationship building and management, advertising, publicity, personal contact, incentives, atmospherics, licensing and sponsorship.

If advertising is defined as paid media, *publicity* can be thought of as free media, or public attention for an issue or organisation from the media. Hopwood (2007a: 226) rightly concludes: 'Publicity is a great way of generating goodwill and understanding at no financial cost to the organization, so it is not surprising to learn that it is a tool widely used in public relations practice.' Generating publicity for an organisation is frequently considered the most important, and outwardly visible, function of sport public relations professional.

Public relations models

Most public relations literature points to Grunig and Hunt's (1984) conceptualisation of one-way and two-way models of public relations as the definitional approach to viewing public relations communications. This section defines each of these models and considers the utility of each for the public relations practitioner. Grunig's two-way asymmetrical and two-way symmetrical models place much more emphasis on interaction and dialogue. The asymmetrical model incorporates research in an effort to persuade publics to act in desirable ways. The symmetrical model uses both research and dialogue to produce a dynamic relationship between an organisation and its publics resulting in PR actions that are mutually beneficial (Grunig and Hunt, 1984). The element of dialogue is crucial to modern PR practice as it places much more importance on practitioners as receivers of information rather than merely information disseminators.

One-way models

One-way models of public relations focus on the dissemination of information about an organisation to its publics, usually through the media. Specifically, the *press agentry* model involves seeking attention in almost any form. Consider the antics of boxing promoters prior to a big title fight as an attention-seeking form of communication. The public information model focuses on the dissemination of accurate and favourable information about the organisation. According to Grunig and Grunig (1992), this approach was successful at combating muck-raking newspaper stories at the early part of the twentieth century. Specific tactics such as news releases and backgrounders are still essential tools for today's public relations practitioners, though public relations theory has evolved to emphasise the relationship-building activities of two-way models.

Two-way models

Two-way models, on the other hand, place much more emphasis on interaction and dialogue. Grunig and Hunt (1984) proposed both *asymmetrical* and *symmetrical* two-way models. Grunig and Grunig (1992) suggested asymmetrical communication was imbalanced in that it is disseminated from the organisation and attempts to persuade publics to act in a desirable way. The symmetrical model is balanced and uses both research and dialogue to produce a dynamic relationship between an organisation and its publics. Understanding, rather than persuasion, is the principal objective of two-way symmetrical public relations.

To that end, Grunig and Grunig (1992: 291), concluded that 'the two-way symmetrical model should be the normative model for public relations – that it describes how excellent public relations should be practiced'. They stressed that dialogue is one of the most important elements of this model. As Stoldt and his colleagues (2006) noted, the element of dialogue is crucial to modern public relations practice as it places much more importance on practitioners as receivers of information rather than merely information disseminators. Organisational benefits of engaging in public relations dialogue is explored in more detail in the next section.

Two-way model benefits

Organisations employ varied tactics in two-way symmetrical communications in an attempt to develop relationships with key publics, with the ultimate objective being a relationship in which the actions of either entity, the organisation or the public, positively impacts on the economic, social, political, or cultural well-being of the other entity (Ledingham and Bruning, 1998).

Hopwood (2005) examined the use, and non-use, of two-way symmetrical public relations in her case study of English country cricket clubs. She concluded that organisations which overlook the benefits of public relations do so in favour of organisational functions which are perceived as being more lucrative or cost-effective. Sport clubs, she argued, 'which depend upon continual replenishment of supporters for their long-term viability, need to be especially mindful of the implications of ignoring the basic principles of public relations' (Hopwood, 2005: 182).

The use of dialogue has emerged as a successful principle in two-way symmetrical communication. Kent and Taylor (1998: 325) defined dialogic communication as a give-and-take tactic, calling it a 'negotiated exchange of ideas and opinions'. One commonly used tool to exchange those ideas and opinions is an organisational weblog. An organisational weblog is a website with dynamic content and posts by organisational representatives displayed in reverse chronological order. A unique feature of the weblog is the ability for readers, and subsequently the author, to post responses to a particular entry, creating a virtual dialogue.

In one of the early empirical studies to assess the benefits of weblogs in communication, Seltzer and Mitrook (2007) concluded that weblogs 'demonstrate many of the dialogic features and principles that are necessary for achieving the goals and objectives of public relations practitioners'.

Dittmore et al. (2008) tested the benefits of using an organisational weblog in relationship building for a Major League Baseball team. The results of their study are summarised in Case 22.1.

Case 22.1 Benefits of an organisational weblog in relationship building in professional sports

Dittmore et al. (2008) sought to gain a greater understanding of how sport organisations used a social media tool, the weblog, in their day-to-day communications. Their study assessed whether readers of a Major League Baseball team's official weblog perceived the team's weblog as an effective form of two-way communication between the team and its fan base.

The researchers used scales developed by Kelleher and Miller (2006) to measure the presence of conversational human voice (CHV) and communicated relational commitment (CRC) elements within the weblog. Both measures have been shown to be positively related to relational outcomes such as trust of the organisation, satisfaction with the organisation, and commitment to the organisation. CHV was operationalised as a way to 'emphasize human communication attributes capable of being conveyed in a computer-mediated context'. CRC was operationalised as a way to 'emphasise an expressed commitment to building and maintaining a relationship and underscore the nature and quality of the relationship'.

Respondents to the study indicated the team's official weblog scored highly in both CHV (M = 5.37, SD = 0.92 on 7-point scale) and CRC (M = 5.08, SD = 1.29 on a 7-point scale). This emphasises the commitment the organisation has to building and maintaining a relationship with its publics. Sport organisations are challenged by an environment in which publics have much greater access to information and rumours and fan attendance fluctuates greatly based on an organisation's on-field performance. Establishing honest, trustworthy and frequent communication with key publics can help an organisation navigate through variations in the demand for its product. Researchers have consistently noted the organisational advantages of creating a long-term commitment (Milne and McDonald, 1999). Weblogs would appear to be an effective tool in generating that commitment.

In addition to evaluating the two-way relationship benefits of the organisational weblog, the researchers developed a profile of readers of the weblog, effectively creating an online public. Two significant findings regarding the online public were the levels of fan attachment the respondents had and the overall similarities in responses from fans living in the team's home market and those living abroad. First, fans were highly identified with both the team (M = 6.42, SD = 0.77) and the sport (M = 6.11, SD = 0.64), but not as much with individual players (M = 2.82, SD = 1.15). This finding suggests fans of professional sport clubs will continue to consume content from the organisation despite the player makeup of the team.

Second, the ability of a weblog to reach a diverse audience quickly and inexpensively makes this form of communication beneficial for sport organisations seeking to maximise return on their marketing communication efforts. Scoble and Israel (2006: 27) noted that weblogs are the 'lowest-cost communications channel, you can reach thousands, perhaps millions of people for an investment of a few cents and some personal time. Blogs are infinitely more efficient than any other corporate communications medium'. Given the increasing emphasis in the sports industry on globalising brands, the weblog's ability to reach anyone worldwide is attractive.

(continued)

> Overall, this case study would lend support to the notion that an organisational weblog is a highly effective social media tool to develop two-way symmetrical relationships with one of its core publics, its fan base.
>
> *Source*: From 'The use of an organizational weblog in relationship building: The case of a major league baseball team', *International Journal of Sport Communication*, 1 (3), 384–97 (Dittmore, S.W., Stoldt, G.C. and Greenwell T.C. 2008). Adapted with permission.
>
> Discussion questions
>
> 1 Who is the targeted public for a professional team's weblog? Casual fans? Highly identified fans?
>
> 2 What should you do with comments on the weblog which portray the sport club in a negative light?
>
> 3 What barriers exist for organisations considering developing their own weblog?

The benefits of two-way communication are not limited to just fans. In his case study of clubs in the Premiership, Cleland (2009) found a growing interdependence on the part of the media and the clubs for news, information and content. Development of the new media streams has eliminated the reliance on old communications models and created an environment, as he concludes, where the overall importance of local media to organisations has been reduced. It is more likely, therefore, that media organisations may be more critical of sport clubs and ignoring that relationship may prove to create more negative coverage of the club, as Cleland illustrated in his study of Birmingham City and Northampton Town clubs.

Social media as a form of public relations

In the preface of their book, *Putting the Public Back in Public Relations*, Solis and Breakenridge (2009) offered the following definition of social media and its impact on public relations:

> Participation is the new marketing. And to participate, we must become the people we want to reach. The New Media landscape is creating a hybrid of PR, online marketers, market analysts, and customer advocates, to effectively and genuinely engage in the conversations that define Social Media and create relationships with customers.

Their definition suggests that today's social media combines everything mentioned previously in this chapter. It is both public relations and marketing. It is participatory, meaning that it is two-way. It engages conversations, or dialogue. And it creates relationships. Given that, it is no wonder that the importance for organisations of all types to engage in some form of social media became one of the most talked about, and rapidly changing, topics of 2009. This is especially true in sports where the concept of building a community of fans is central to the core business of a club.

The social media tools available to public relations professional are numerous and diverse, but they all share one common underlying attribute: the ability for the user to control the content by sharing it and commenting on it. Popular social media tools include weblogs, social networking sites, microblogging services and file sharing sites.

A typical weblog is 'nothing more than a personal web site with content displayed in reverse-chronological order' (Scoble and Israel, 2006: 26). A unique and important feature of a weblog which distinguishes it from other forms of communication is the ability for readers to post responses to a particular entry. The author of the initial content may read these responses in real time and react to the reader comments, creating a virtual dialogue. Regular readers of weblogs frequently develop relationships with one another through these postings and communities of readers with similar interests may form.

Social networking sites such as Facebook, MySpace and LinkedIn help individual users communicate and stay in touch with friends, families and colleagues. These sites 'are becoming primary mechanisms for connecting with people, ideas, brands, news, and information' (Solis and Breakenridge, 2009: 167).

The most popular microblogging service is Twitter, which permits users to post status updates of 140 characters or less. In addition, users can follow the updates of any number of individuals or organisations and reply or comment on those updates in real time, effectively creating a virtual conversation, similar to a weblog.

File sharing sites allows users to share multiple types of content. YouTube allows users to upload and share video files. Flickr and Picasa allow users to upload and share still photos. Video and photo sharing sites are subject to copyright laws which protect the unauthorised use or dissemination of particular works by persons other than the individual or organisation which created said work. Finally, there are sites such as del.ici.ous, DIGG and StumbleUpon which permit users to share articles or specific pages found on the internet through a bookmarking feature.

During the International Olympic Committee's Congress in Copenhagen, Denmark in October 2009, it was suggested the IOC needed to embrace social media tools such as YouTube, or risk losing younger viewers for life. Sir Martin Sorrell, CEO of London-based WPP Agency, told the IOC: 'The digital revolution has already changed the media landscape and the way in which sport is consumed will never be the same again. Give content to youth in formats they want – short and fast, customizable and easy to share' ('IOC told', 2009).

With all of these tools available, public relations professionals are advised to be cautious about how content is presented on social media because a footprint is left. All content is archived on the internet and searchable through Google and other search engines. As Solis and Breakenridge (2009: 168) state, 'This is your online identity and your online brand. It's yours to create, cultivate, define, and manage'.

 ## Stakeholders/publics

Many different ways exist to conceptualise the audience for public relations. Most definitions will use the term 'stakeholder' or 'public' to classify groups of individuals to which the organisation may wish or need to communicate. However, Stoldt et al. (2006: 50) view the two terms as distinctly different in the world of sport public relations. They argue that 'publics are more specific in nature than stakeholders; a stakeholder group is usually comprised of multiple publics'.

Hopwood (2007b: 296) relied on the public relations theoretical approach known as 'licence to operate'. She concluded business success for sport organisations 'can only be sustained if it exists within a supportive operating environment'.

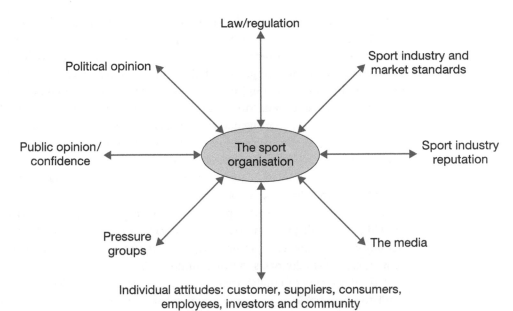

Figure 22.1 Key influences on the sport organisations' licence to operate
Source: Hopwood (2007), adapted from Kitchen (1997)

Common publics which may influence a sport organisation's ability to operate include, but are not limited to: individual attitudes by customers, suppliers, consumers, employees, investors and the community; legal and regulatory bodies; industry associations and standards; industry reputation; media; and more (Hopwood, 2007b). It is important to note that not all of these publics are applicable to all organisations and that each organisation may identify publics which are specific to its organisation and operations.

The key stakeholders which influence sports organisations are shown in Figure 22.1.

Identification and influence of publics

As Stoldt et al. (2006) suggested, multiple public groups make up a larger stakeholder group. For example, a sporting goods business may have multiple retail outlets which sell their products. However, a large chain store may purchase considerably larger amounts of product at wholesale than a smaller sole proprietorship store in a small town. Both would be considered customers of the sporting goods business; however, one (the large chain store) is clearly more important and influential to the profitability of the business since it most likely purchases greater quantities of product.

Publics, therefore, may be thought of as groups of people within a stakeholder group who relate to the sport organisation in similar ways. In fact, Smith (2005) offered five useful characteristics to assist in identifying publics. Publics, he noted should be: (a) distinguishable – that is, they are a recognisable group of individuals; (b) homogeneous – they share common features and traits; (c) important – they have the ability to impact on a business's financial operation either positively or negatively; (d) large enough to matter – they have the ability to warrant attention and potentially use public media; and (e) reachable – they are approachable for interaction and communication.

He also categorised publics in four ways, based on the unique relationship each category has with the organisation. *Customers* of the organisation are individuals who receive the products or services an organisation distributes. This category should include not only current and potential customers, but also secondary customers, or the customers of the organisation's customers (Smith, 2005). Consider the sporting goods business again. Its customer is the large chain store and its secondary customers would be individual consumers. Yet when the sporting goods business faces a recall in its product for performance reasons, it needs to consider not just the impact its communication will have on the retail outlets which purchase the wholesale product, but also the individual consumers who patronise the retail outlets. This is different than a sport organisation which sells tickets directly to an individual consumer.

A second way to categorise publics is through *producers* of the organisation. These individuals provide inputs needed for the organisation to function. Inputs can be human (employees or volunteers), physical (suppliers of raw materials) or financial (stockholders, venture capitalists, donors, sponsors) (Smith, 2005).

A third category of publics are *enablers* to the organisation. These individuals serve as regulators or agencies which establish norms and standards for the organisation as well as groups which can hold influence over potential customers and can assist in making the organisation successful, such as the media and stock analysts (Smith, 2005).

The final category of publics proposed by Smith (2005) is *limiters*, or those publics which can somehow adversely affect the operations of the organisation. These can include activist groups, competitors and individuals opposed to the organisation. Table 22.1 provides a summary of Smith's typology along with sport organisation examples.

Table 22.1 Typology of publics for a sporting goods manufacturer

Public category	Description	Examples
Customers	Receive the products or services an organisation distributes	Retail outlets Individual consumers (current/former/potential)
Producers	Provide inputs needed for the organisation to function	Employees Volunteers Donors Shareholders Investors
Enablers	Serve as regulators or agencies which establish norms and standards for the organisation as well as hold influence over potential customers and assist in making the organisation successful	Industry associations Governmental bodies at various levels Media Stock analysts
Limiters	Publics which can somehow adversely affect the operations of the organisation	Competitors Opponents Activists

Source: based on Smith (2005)

Messaging for publics

Given the potential that so many different publics will be interested in what an organisation communicates, it is natural for a public relations professional to be concerned with how to reach each public in a meaningful way. The current environment of online communication through websites, blogs and social media makes that job both easier and more difficult. It is easier than at any point in history to communicate an organisational message directly to targeted publics without worrying about it being misrepresented, misinterpreted or taken out of context.

On the other hand, it is more difficult than ever to have a message break through all of the forms of content which exist and have the message resonate with the intended public. Steve Rubel (2007), a senior vice president with Edelman, a global public relations firm, called this problem attention crash.

> We are reaching a point where the number of inputs we have as individuals is beginning to exceed what we are capable as humans of managing. The demands for our attention are becoming so great, and the problem so widespread, that it will cause people to crash and curtail these drains.

To that end, Scott (2009) advocates customising messages to specific publics. Rather than focus on publics, he conceives of a 'buyer persona' which is representative of a type of buyer that is identified by having a specific interest in the organisation. He states directly, 'whenever you set out to write something, you should be writing specifically for one or more' buyer personas (Scott, 2009: 143). The language should avoid jargon and be in language the persona uses.

The next section discusses different approaches public relations professionals use to communicate organisational messages directly to specific publics.

Public relations approaches

Given the multitude of possible publics any organisation may have, it is appropriate for public relations professionals to develop unique approaches to reach each of those publics. Traditionally, the most common of these have targeted the publics perceived as most important by the organisation: customer publics such as the community of the club's fans and spectators; producing publics such as investors and employees; and enabling publics such as the media. It is the latter public, the media, to which most of the literature and attention is devoted by sport public relations professionals.

This is largely attributable to the traditional approach to communication in which the organisation functioned as the source for messages which were distributed to the media. The media, in turn, functioned as the channel to deliver those messages to the targeted audience, or public, referred to as the receiver. Thus, conventional wisdom suggested a communication process which flowed like this: source ➔ message ➔ channel ➔ receiver.

The advent of the social media tools discussed earlier has reduced the reliance on the media to deliver an organisational message to receivers. In effect, every company and every person has become a media company. What separates conventional media organisations from non-media organisations is the reach traditional media outlets have. Therefore, it is still necessary for sport public relations professionals to cultivate relationships with the media.

Media relations

As mentioned previously, public relations consists of one-way and two-way models for disseminating information about an organisation. One of the most common one-way models is the press agency model where public relations professionals seek to generate as much publicity, or free media, as possible for their organisation, frequently through the dissemination of newsworthy information to the media (Stoldt et al., 2006). Smith (2005: 159) described the tactics used to accomplish this as 'opportunities for the credible presentation of organizational message to large audiences'. Some of the most commonly employed media relations tactics are news releases and interviews and news conferences.

News releases

The staple of any public relations toolbox is the news release. The goal of a news release is to disclose newsworthy information to the media in as positive a light as possible (Stoldt et al., 2006). The determination of what is and what is not newsworthy is somewhat subjective and frequently made by the media. A good rule for measuring the potential news value of information is remember the acronym TIPCUP, which identifies six values of news: timeliness, impact, prominence, conflict, unusualness and proximity (Thompson, 1996).

Once a decision has been made that some information is newsworthy enough for distribution, the actual means through which the information is disseminated need to be considered. Typically, news releases are emailed to journalists and posted on an organisation's website. However, the advances of alternative or social forms of media create greater opportunities for public relations professionals to disseminate information to wider audiences.

To that end, Scott (2009) encourages public relations professionals not to think of the media as the end user of a news release, but rather write the news release for consumers. The audience for news releases anyone with an Internet connection. He proposed eight 'New rules of news releases' which are represented in Exhibit 22.1.

Exhibit 22.1 Eight new rules of news releases

1 Find good reasons to send news releases all the time, not just when big news happens

2 Create news releases which appeal directly to consumers, not just a handful of journalists

3 Write news releases with keyword-rich copy

4 Include offers which compel consumers to respond in some way

5 Use links in news releases to deliver potential customers to specific pages on an organisation's website

6 Optimise the news release for search engines

7 Include social media tags so consumers can find the news release

8 Drive people into the sales process

Source: based on Scott (2009)

Similarly, Solis and Breakenridge (2009) coined the term social media release (SMRs) to illustrate how public relations professionals should approach disseminating information in today's social media age. They differentiate a SMR from a traditional news release because of its intent, media, socialisation and distribution. They suggest SMRs should be customer-focused, contain links, the ability to interact with customers and be customised to include keywords to improve their pick-up by Google and Yahoo! search engines, a process referred to as search engine-optimised, or SEO.

Regardless of the distribution method, news releases typically contain similar elements which aid the media in recognising that the information contained within is newsworthy. Properly formatted news releases contain a header, lead, body and ending (Stoldt et al., 2006).

The header of a news release contains important information about the organisation distributing the release including the name and contact information of the public relations person, the date and time at which the media can use the information, and a headline to catch the reader's attention. The lead is generally one or two paragraphs in length and summarises the newsworthy information which follows in the release.

A news release body should provide additional details of the lead in an inverted pyramid style with the most relevant information first, followed by the less relevant information. This is helpful for journalists wishing to scan for only the most significant details. Finally, the ending of a news release confirms to the reader the release has ended. Organisations frequently include static corporate language called a boilerplate to position themselves within the sports industry on their own terms (Stoldt et al., 2006).

Interviews and news conferences

A more personal and desirable way for media to obtain information is through interviews or news conferences. Stoldt and his colleagues (2006: 127) described the unique nature of a sport interview as 'an opportunity for organizational representatives to respond to media questions with organizational messages'. Astute public relations professionals should have a strategy in place for responding to media questions with organisational messages. Several ways exist to aid in the process of developing this strategy.

Since the public relations person is usually the first line of communication between the media and the organisation, he or she can exploit this power by gaining as much knowledge as possible of the reporter's topic, story angles and sources. This will aid in developing and shaping a response.

An additional responsibility of a public relations person is to understand the media and the external environment around the organisation. By trying to think like a reporter, the public relations person is better able to anticipate what questions might be directed at the interviewee before the interview begins, and developing a possible response (Smith, 2005).

Public relations professionals are cautioned to recognise that any time they are talking to a member of the media they are essentially being interviewed and things said, or written in emails, can be printed or repeated by the media. It is important to understand the difference between a person speaking 'off the record' and a person speaking 'not for attribution'. Stoldt et al. (2006) described 'off the record' as providing information to the media with the understanding that the media will not repeat the information. They described 'not for attribution' as the disclosure of information the organisation wants known so as to stimulate media interest.

When a public relations professional speaks 'off the record' he or she is placing the journalist in a difficult situation because the journalist now has newsworthy information. Further, the concept of 'not for attribution' can similarly confuse reporters because their stories gain credibility when they identify sources (Lorenz and Vivian, 1996).

Because television is a visual medium and radio is an auditory medium, each needs more than a static news release to effectively and persuasively report a story. News conferences can be an effective way for those two forms of media to generate images and sounds which their audiences expect. This method provides for economies of scale by allowing an organisation to state the same message to multiple members of the media at the same time.

Smith (2005: 197) aptly described a news conference as a 'contrived media happening in which an organizational spokesperson makes a newsworthy statement or reads a prepared news statement'. Once the statement is finished, an opportunity for media members to ask questions generally follows. In sports, it is customary to hold a news conference following the end of a match or an event with the club's manager and perhaps two or three key athletes.

However, knowing when to hold a news conference that does not follow a match can be tricky. Again, it may be useful to consider the news values referred to in the TIPCUP acronym.

Should a sport organisation hold a news conference to announce a new sponsor? That answer would depend on the dollar amount of the sponsorship (impact); whether the sponsor is a local company or international corporation (prominence); and possibly on whether the sponsor is typically involved with the sport (unusualness).

What about a player transfer? Certainly a transfer between rival clubs such as Real Madrid and Barcelona could be considered a conflict, as well as prominent and possibly unusual. However, a transfer from Real Madrid to a club in the US-based MLS may not be particularly newsworthy in Madrid.

Bloggers and new media

Today, sport organisations are repeatedly wrestling with the question of how to manage a new segment of society: bloggers. The ability exists today for anyone in society to author original thoughts and commentary on virtually any subject and have those thoughts published on the internet. No longer do fans of sport organisations need to turn to members of the mainstream media for analysis of how their teams are performing. These fans can simply turn to one another through online communities of bloggers.

This innovation, along with other technologies which deliver news and information instantly to consumers, has placed tremendous pressure on newspapers to maintain profitability. With declining revenues, many newspapers throughout the world are resorting to cutting sports reporters as a means of saving money, driving more consumers to read blogs and other forms of new media to gain insight on their favourite team.

In March 2008, Dallas Mavericks owner Mark Cuban banned a *Dallas Morning News* reporter from the team's locker room midway through the National Basketball Association (NBA) season. The team's new policy denied access to writers whose 'primary purpose is to blog'. The team denied singling out the reporter and cited locker room space and fairness as reasons for the policy's development (Jacobson, 2008). The NBA quickly intervened, ruling that bloggers credentialled from news organisations must be admitted (Arango, 2008).

This instance illustrates the challenges facing sport organisations when dealing with media in the new media age. Traditional definitions of what constitutes a news organisation are evolving. Sport organisations such as the New York Islanders and the Washington Capitals of the National Hockey League (NHL) have issued media credentials to bloggers, many of whom are fans and have no journalistic training.

Gillmor (2006) and Gant (2007) have both written extensively about the evolution of media from a traditional definition to one of 'citizen journalism'. Gant, in particular, distinguished between the function of journalism and the profession of journalism. Among his arguments is the notion that a profession denotes licensure and mainstream journalists would not be likely to advocate a system where the government decides who is, and who is not, a journalist.

Still, most sport organisations cling to a traditional definition of what constitutes a journalist when they make decisions about who should be issued with media credentials. While Stoldt et al. (2006) suggested sport organisations clearly articulate credential policies and make them widely available to all media organisations, research by Dittmore et al. (2009) found that 15 per cent of 78 sport organisations in the United States had no formal policy regarding bloggers.

The International Olympic Committee has addressed this issue head-on by publishing Blogging Guidelines. In its document for the 2010 Olympic Winter Games in Vancouver, the IOC considered blogs 'a legitimate form of personal expression and not as a form of journalism'. Therefore, accredited persons were not restricted from blogging during the Games, however blogs were prohibited from posting interviews with other accredited persons, disseminating moving images or sound from the Games, and posting still photos of sport competition taken from the Games (IOC blogging guidelines, 2009).

Sport organisations are advised to consider the development of a policy as to how they intend to address blogs and blogging as part of an overall media relations approach to communication.

Community relations

One approach to public relations frequently overlooked is the area of community relations (Pedersen et al., 2007; Stoldt et al., 2006). Activities within community relations are designed to enhance the sport organisation's ability to develop those long-term two-way relationships with key publics. The tools utilised to develop those relationships can be dichotomised into direct contact and indirect contact initiatives (Stoldt et al., 2006).

Direct contact initiatives may take various forms but they all involve members of the sport organisation (management, coaches, players, mascots, etc.) making public appearances. This may include speeches, appearances, clinics and open houses. As Stoldt et al. (2006) suggest, this approaches carries three distinct advantages. First, it is face-to-face, allowing for a personal contact between the organisation and a public. Second, individuals who attend these activities are most likely already identified with the organisation and have a favourable attitude toward the organisation. And third, the organisation enjoys a high degree of control over the messages being delivered and how they are presented in these settings.

A more subtle approach to community relations can be seen with the development or support of charitable programmes. Sometimes referred to as philanthropy, these charitable programmes carry several benefits which cannot be achieved through other activities.

A growing line of sport-related literature focuses on the importance of *corporate social responsibility* (CSR) (Bradish and Cronin, 2009). Sport organisations which engage in CSR are frequently considered to be involved in 'cause-related marketing'. This engagement manifests itself in a variety of forms such as event programming, environmental sustainability and corporate citizenry.

The Federation Internationale de Football Association (FIFA) is recognised as one of the first prominent sport organisations to create an internal CSR unit and commit a significant percentage of revenues to CSR programmes (Bradish and Cronin, 2009). The impact of CSR programmes has carried over into professional sports as well. Babiak and Wolfe (2009) noted that the types of CSR programming prominent in professional sports leagues varies considerably from the National Basketball Association's 'Basketball Without Borders' programme where young people attend a basketball-themed camp designed to promote goodwill, education and friendship through sport, to the National Hockey League's 'Hockey Fights Cancer' programme where funds are raised to support cancer research.

Other approaches

While media relations and community relations approaches are useful in communicating with external publics, sport organisations cannot ignore the importance of internal publics such as investors and employees. Each of those publics offer the organisation the ability, or 'licence' as was alluded to earlier in the chapter, to operate by providing a significant resource. In the case of investors, the resource is financial capital, and in the case of employees the resource is human capital. Both warrant some specific attention.

Investor relations

Numerous sport organisations are publicly owned and, as such, must consider investor relations to be one of their critical public relations functions. Often nested within an organisation's corporate communications department, the goals of the investor relations function are to enhance the value of a company's stock and to reduce the cost of obtaining new capital from investors (Cutlip et al., 2000). Investor relations practitioners must not only be accomplished public relations professionals, they must also possess expertise in finance. Specifically, investor relations professionals need knowledge in government regulations relating to financial publicity, policies of national stock exchanges, an understanding of financial statements and the operational strategies embraced by their companies (Miller, 1998).

Specifically, investor relations professionals may be asked to produce annual reports, plan shareholder meetings and coordinate interactive communications with investors and the media. Annual reports function to disclose financial information to shareholders, investment firms and financial media (Treadwell and Treadwell, 2000). Annual shareholder meetings provide shareholders an opportunity to hear directly from a corporation's management team as well as vote on board members and other proposals submitted for shareholder approval. Usually, a public relations person will assist in the execution of annual shareholder meeting in five ways: (a) planning the physical set-up of the meeting; (b) developing handouts and collateral material to be distributed to attendees; (c) coordinating company tours; (d) providing meeting-related information to the media and accommodating media requests for the meeting; and (e) assisting executive in preparing for presentations to shareholders (Cutlip et al., 2000).

Employee relations

Organisations with an employee relations unit commonly house the unit in the human resource department with other important administrative aspects of the organisation are kept such as employee benefits and policies. Therefore, it is easy for a communications or public relations professional to overlook the importance of reaching out to this public. One of the most prominent ways employees can impact on an organisation is in the event of a labour–management dispute, an occurrence far too frequent in sport.

Such was the case during the National Hockey League's year-long work stoppage from 2004 to 2005 when league officials announced that nearly two-thirds of its employees would be laid off due to the labour–management lockout. This instance provides a useful case for considering three benefits to maintaining positive employee relations.

First, satisfied employees are easier to retain than unsatisfied employees. Once the labour agreement was resolved in the NHL, many of the laid off workers had found other employment and needed to be replaced by new employees who would need greater training than the unsatisfied, laid off workers. Second, satisfied employees will be more productive in their jobs. Sport marketer Jon Spoelstra (2001) suggested employees should be valued more than customers because the increase in productivity will satisfy customers whose increased business will benefit the organisation as a whole.

Finally, each employee represents the sport organisation when he or she interacts with people outside of the organisation such as their neighbour, friends and family members. Messages organisations communicate to their employees have the potential to be communicated to external audiences and publics. Therefore, sport organisations are wise to engage their employees in the spreading of organisational messages.

Communicating in crisis

The ability of an organisation to have developed long-term, meaningful relationships with key publics is particularly useful when the organisation is addressing negative publicity or a crisis which has the potential to adversely affect the organisation's reputation. Stoldt et al. (2006: 35) defined a sport organisation's reputation as its ability 'to meet the expectations of its publics and the strength of the relationship various stakeholders have with the organization'.

In the New Media era in which businesses operate today, managing a corporate brand or reputation is more important than ever. It seems commonplace for an organisation to consider itself as constantly communicating in 'crisis mode'. Clearly, incidents such as Ronaldo's alleged solicitation of a transvestite prostitute in 2008, the repeated accusations of illegal doping against Lance Armstrong, and arrests in connection with a match-fixing operation in Germany represent crises for individual athletes and sport organisations. However, not all crises are truly a crisis, some may be conceived of as 'incidents'. For example, a player who is injured during a match and transported to a hospital for examination may not be a full crisis since it is the nature of athletic competition that players may be hurt.

It seems appropriate, therefore, to define what is, and what is not, a crisis. Some definitions emphasise the unanticipated nature of the crisis. Others stress the disruption a crisis can pose to normal operations. And still others focus on the financial implications the unexpected disruption can have. An inclusive definition of a crisis in sport organisations was offered by Stoldt et al. (2000: 253–54): 'a situation or occurrence possessing the potential to significantly damage a sport organisation's financial stability and/or credibility with constituent'. This definition is particularly useful for public relations professionals because it focuses on communication with constituents, or publics.

Building off this definition, it becomes apparent that whenever a sport organisation is confronted with a crisis, its objectives become two-fold. First, it must address the issues in the crisis and communicate with influential publics in order to minimise any potential financial damage the crisis may inflict on the organisation. Second, it must consider how it will manage its organisational reputation going forward. This second objective addresses the 'credibility' of the organisation.

Ulmer (2001: 594) underscores the utility of relationship building with key publics in the time of a crisis by suggesting that the construction of 'reservoirs of goodwill, alliances, and shared understanding' may prevent crises from happening or lessen the effects of a crisis or limit its duration if one does occur.

The following sections address tactics for handling crisis situations when they arise and strategies for repairing organisational image or reputation going forward after a crisis.

Crisis communication tactics

In the event of a crisis, three truths are likely to occur. First, battle for public support is usually won or lost in the first few hours, necessitating a quick response. Second, it is essential to develop a crisis communication plan aimed at frequent and regular communication of organisational messages to the public. And third, the more complex those procedures are, the less likely they are to succeed.

Consider the case of golfer Tiger Woods in autumn 2009. During the week of 23 November, the tabloid, *The National Enquirer*, published a report that Woods was having an affair. Early in the morning on 27 November, Woods was transported to a hospital with facial cuts after crashing his vehicle in Florida. News reports broke the next day that Tiger's wife, Elin, was responsible for his injuries, not the accident. On 29 November, two days after the accident, Woods released a statement refuting the news reports and asked the matter be kept private. He still had not addressed the allegations of an affair.

Over the next few days, additional women came forward with allegations that Woods had had extramarital relationships with them as well. Finally, on 3 December, Woods released a statement apologising for 'transgressions' and again asked for privacy. In the days which followed, additional women alleged similar affairs with Woods, but Woods did not respond.

The case of Tiger Woods is a useful example to illustrate the three truths of crisis communications. First, public support clearly went away from Woods. In order for him to move public opinion, he could have denied the initial allegations of an affair. By not doing so, it implies the affair is true. By not responding immediately following the accident, Woods allowed rumours regarding the nature of the injuries to dominate the media. Again, Woods' lack of denial implied the rumours were true.

Second, Woods only communicated twice through the first 30 days of the incident. Any ability he had to shape the story with his message was negated by the infrequency of his communication. And, finally, much of Woods' communication strategy took place out of the public's view. Certainly he and his agent were communicating with key publics such as sponsors, close friends, etc. His desire to maintain privacy throughout the incident may have alienated him from the general public and such may be the challenge of a high-profile sports celebrity.

Image repair strategies

Once a crisis occurs and an organisation or individual has been found responsible for an offensive action, that organisation's or athlete's image or reputation is damaged. Several approaches can be suggested as ways to repair that image.

Benoit (1997a: 251) defined image as 'the perception of a person (or group, or organisation) held by the audience, shaped by the words and actions of that person, as well as by the discourse and behavior of other relevant actors'. In this sense, it complements the definition of reputation by Stoldt et al. (2006) by reinforcing the notion of two-way relationships between an organisation and its publics. Benoit developed a typology of five image repair strategies: denial, evading responsibility, reducing offensiveness of the action, corrective action and mortification (Benoit, 1997b). Denial simply seeks to shift blame to another or state that an individual did not commit the act. Evading responsibility positions the act as a mishap or suggest the act was meant well. Reducing offensiveness stresses the good traits of the act or minimises the act as not being serious. Corrective action emphasises what the organisation or athlete has done to prevent recurrence of the problem. And mortification is a flat-out apology on behalf of the organisation or athlete.

Considering again the case of Tiger Woods, the only real strategy Woods employed in the first 30 days of the incident was mortification. He issued a five-paragraph apology for 'transgressions' and behaviour on his website. Later, Woods offered some insight into his corrective action by stating, 'I have decided to take an indefinite break from professional golf. I need to focus my attention on being a better husband, father, and person' (Woods, 2009). At no point did he attempt to deny, evade responsibility or reduce the offensiveness of his alleged actions.

In their case study of New Zealand rugby, Bruce and Tini (2008) offered a sixth image restoration typology, diversion. Their study illustrated how management at the Canterbury Bulldogs rugby club attempted to divert attention from a management dishonesty crisis by focusing on players, and later fans, as innocent victims. Bruce and Tini (2008: 112) argued this diversion 'provided an opportunity for the Bulldogs organization to connect with their fans and to limit the overall damage to the sport and team' because fans relate best to players and on-field performance.

Conclusion

The practice of sport public relations is ever-changing. Once it was a profession which relied on a third party, such as the media, to assist in generating publicity. Today, it is an area capable of creating its own communications directly to targeted publics through myriad of tools and outlets. As has been stated, this is both beneficial for the organisation and problematic. Looking into the future, it is possible to identify several areas of uncertainty for sport public relations.

One area of concern is the management of New Media. With so many communication inputs available to an individual, how can sport organisations cut through all of these to deliver messages which resonate with its publics? In other words, how will sport clubs navigate the 'attention crash'?

A second area of concern not completely addressed within this chapter is what appears to be an increase in the amount of crises or image problems confronting athletes and sport clubs. The internet has created a 24-hour news environment where information moves quickly and often without substantiation. Whether the crisis is a star Brazilian footballer being accused of soliciting a transvestite prostitute, or accusations of illegal blood doping in the Tour de France, the need seems greater than ever for organisations and athletes to be skilled at managing a crisis and developing strategies to repair damaged reputations.

Discussion questions

4 Put into your own words the benefits of using two-way symmetrical public relations to communicate with targeted publics.

5 As the public relations person for a club in La Liga, you have been asked to evaluate whether the organisation should include blogs as media when inviting them to attend a news conference. What is your reaction to this?

6 Visit the NBA's Basketball Without Borders website (www.nba.com/bwb/). Evaluate what publics the NBA is trying to reach with this community relations activity. How would you enhance the league's publicity through social media tactics?

7 Which of Benoit's five image repair typologies is most effective in your mind? Identify an organisation or individual which has had a recent crisis and analyse which strategies they have used.

Keywords

Public information model; publicity; publics; social media; two-way symmetrical public relations.

Guided reading

Literature related to sport public relations, media, and communication has dramatically increased in the past six years. The *Journal of Sports Media* is published twice annually by the University of Nebraska Press and is indexed in the JSTOR database. The *International Journal of Sport Communication* is published quarterly by Human Kinetics and is indexed in several databases. Both focus on issues for sport, media and communication. In addition, *Sport Marketing Quarterly*, published by Fitness Information Technology, regularly has research articles related to sport public relations.

In addition, a number of textbooks have emerged in the area. Each seems to cater to a specific aspect of sport, media and communication, beginning with a broad sport communication context (Pedersen et al., 2007), and narrowing to specific texts which consider sport public relations (Stoldt et al., 2006), sport media relations (Hall et al., 2007), and cases and experiences in sport public relations (Favorito, 2007). Nicholson (2007) provides a bridge between the sport industry and the business aspects of the media industry.

Many interesting texts explore the nexus of media, culture, sport and society with an emphasis on European sport, including Boyle and Haynes (2000), Whannel (2002), and Boyle (2006).

Two recent resources which provide thorough, and current, discussions of the role of social media in organisations can be found in Solis and Breakenridge (2009) and Scott (2009).

Recommended websites

Nationals Sports Journalism Center – sportsjournalism.org

Sports Marketing and PR Roundup: Sports Publicity, Marketing, and Brand Building in a New Age – http://joefavorito.com

Sports PR Blog: A look at the sports industry from a PR point of view – http://sportsprblog.com/blog/

References

Arango, T. (2008) 'Tension over sports blogging', *New York Times*, 21 April, www.nytimes.com/2008/04/21/business/media/21bloggers.html

Babiak, K. and Wolfe, R. (2009) 'Determinants of corporate social responsibility in professional sport: internal and external factors', *Journal of Sport Management*, 23, 717–42.

Benoit, W.L. (1997a) 'Hugh Grant's image restoration discourse: an actor apologizes', *Communication Quarterly*, 45, 251–67.

Benoit, W.L. (1997b) 'Image restoration discourse and crisis communication', *Public Relations Review*, 23, 177–86.

Boyle, R. (2006) *Sports Journalism: Context and Issues*, London: Sage.

Boyle, R. and Haynes, R. (2000) *Power Play: Sport, the Media and Popular Culture*, Harlow: Longman.

Bradish, C. and Cronin, J.J. (2009) 'Corporate social responsibility in sport', *Journal of Sport Management*, 23, 691–97.

Bruce, T. and Tini, T. (2008) 'Using crisis response strategies in sports public relations: rugby league and the case for diversion', *Public Relations Review*, 34, 108–15.

Cleland, J.A. (2009) 'The changing organizational structure of football clubs and their relationship with the external media', *International Journal of Sport Communication*, 2 (4), 417–31.

Cutlip, S.M., Center, A.H. and Broom, G.M. (2000) *Effective Public Relations*, 8th edn, Englewood Cliffs, NJ: Prentice Hall.

Dittmore, S.W., Stoldt, G.C., Bass, J.R. and Biery, L. (2009) *Media Policies in the Era of New Media: An Analysis of How Sport Organizations Approach Bloggers and Blogging*, Abstract presented at the 2009 North American Society for Sport Management Conference, 27–30 May, Columbia, SC.

Dittmore, S.W., Stoldt, G.C. and Greenwell, T.C. (2008) 'The use of an organizational weblog in relationship building: the case of a Major League Baseball team', *International Journal of Sport Communication*, 1 (3), 384–97.

Favorito, J. (2007) *Sports Publicity: A Practical Approach*, Oxford: Elsevier Inc.

Gant, S. (2007) *We're All Journalists Now: The Transformation of the Press and Reshaping of the Law in the Internet Age*, New York: Free Press.

Gillmor, D. (2006) *We the Media: Grassroots Journalism by the People, for the People*, Sebastopol, CA: O'Reilly Media, Inc.

Grunig, J.E. and Grunig, L.A. (1992) 'Models of public relations and communications', in J.E. Grunig (ed.), *Excellence in Public Relations and Communication Management*, Hillsdale, NJ: Lawrence Erlbaum and Associates, 285–325.

Grunig, J.E. and Hunt, T. (1984) *Managing Public Relations*, New York: Holt, Rinehart & Winston.

Hall, A., Nichols, W., Moynahan, P. and Taylor, J. (2007) *Media Relations in Sport*, 2nd edn, Morgantown, WV: Fitness Information Technology.

Hopwood, M.K. (2005) 'Applying the public relations function to the business of sport', *International Journal of Sports Marketing and Sponsorship*, 6 (3), 174–88.

Hopwood, M. (2007a) 'The sport integrated marketing communications mix', in J.G. Beech and S. Chadwick (eds), *The Marketing of Sport*, London: Financial Times/Prentice Hall, 213–38.

Hopwood, M. (2007b) 'Sports public relations', in J.G. Beech and S. Chadwick (eds), *The Marketing of Sport*, London: Financial Times/Prentice Hall, 292–317.

IOC blogging guidelines for persons accredited at the XXI Olympic Winter Games, Vancouver 2010 (2009) www.olympic.org/Documents/Reports/EN/en_report_1433.pdf

IOC told to embrace YouTube movement (5 October 2009) www.universalsports.com/news/article/newsid=342643.html

Irwin, R., Sutton, W.A. and McCarthy, L.M. (2002) *Sport Promotion and Sales Management*, Champaign, IL: Human Kinetics.

Jacobson, G. (2008) 'Dallas mavericks bar bloggers from locker room', *Dallas Morning News*, 10 March, www.dallasnews.com/sharedcontent/dws/spt/stories/031108dnspomavsaccess.2cd1e55.html

Kelleher, T. and Miller, B.M. (2006) 'Organziational blogs and the human voice: relational strategies and relational outcomes', *Journal of Computer-Mediated Communication*, 11 (2), http://jcmc.indiana.edu/vol11/issue2/kelleher.html

Kent, M.L. and Taylor, M. (1998) 'Building dialogic relationships through the world wide web', *Public Relations Review*, 24, 321–34.

Ledingham, J.A. and Bruning, S.D. (1998) 'Relationship management in public relations: dimensions of an organization-public relationship', *Public Relations Review*, 24, 55–65.

Lorenz, A.L. and Vivian, J. (1996) *News Reporting and Writing*, Needham Heights, MA: Allyn and Bacon.

Miller, E. (1998) 'Investor relations', in P. Lesley (ed.), *Lesley's Handbook of Public Relations and Communications*, Lincolnwood, IL: NTC Business Books, 161–206.

Milne, G.R. and McDonald, M.A. (1999) *Sport Marketing: Managing the Exchange Process*, Sudbury, MA: Jones and Bartlett Publishers.

Mullin, B.J., Hardy, S. and Sutton, W.A. (2007) *Sport Marketing*, 3rd edn, Champaign, IL: Human Kinetics.

Nicholson, M. (2007) *Sport and the Media: Managing the Nexus*, Oxford: Elsevier.

Pedersen, P.M., Miloch, K.S., and Laucella, P.C. (2007) *Strategic Sport Communication*, Champaign, IL: Human Kinetics.

Rubel, S. (2007) *The Attention Crash*, 1 June, www.micropersuasion.com/2007/06/the_attention_c.html

Scoble, R. and Israel, S. (2006) *Naked Conversations: How Blogs are Changing the Way Businesses Talk with Customers*, Hoboken, NJ: John Wiley & Sons.

Scott, D.M. (2009) *The New Rules of Marketing and PR*, Hoboken, NJ: John Wiley & Sons.

Seltzer, T. and Mitrook, M.A. (2007) 'The dialogic potential of weblogs in relationship building', *Public Relations Review*, 33, 227–29.

Shilbury, D., Westerbeek, H., Quick, S. and Funk, D. (2009) *Strategic Sport Marketing*, 3rd edn, Crows Nest, NSW, Australia: Allen & Unwin.

Smith, R.D. (2005) *Strategic Planning for Public Relations*, 2nd edn, Mahwah, NJ: Lawrence Erlbaum Associates.

Solis, B. and Breakenridge, D. (2009) *Putting the Public Back in Public Relations: How Social Media is Reinventing the Aging Business of PR*, Upper Saddle River, NJ: Pearson Education.

Spoelstra, J. (2001) *Marketing Outrageously*, Marietta, GA: Bard Press.

Stoldt, G.C., Dittmore, S.W. and Branvold, S. (2006) *Sport Public Relations: Managing Organizational Communication*, Champaign, IL: Human Kinetics.

Stoldt, G.C., Miller, L.K., Ayres, T.D. and Comfort, P.G. (2000) 'Crisis management planning: a necessity for sport managers', *International Journal of Sport Management*, 1, 253–66.

Thompson, W. (1996) *Targeting the Message: A Receiver-centered Process for Public Relations Writing*, White Plains, NY: Longman.

Treadwell, D. and Treadwell, J.B. (2000) *Public Relations Writing: Principles in Practice*, Boston: Allyn and Bacon.

Ulmer, R.U. (2001) 'Effective crisis management through established stakeholder relationships', *Management Communication Quarterly*, 14 (4), 590–615.

Whannel, G. (2002) *Media Sports Stars: Masculinities and Moralities*, London: Routledge.

Woods, T. (2009) 'Tiger Woods taking hiatus from golf', 11 December, http://web.tigerwoods.com/news/article/200912117801012/news/

The internationalisation of sport

Simon Chadwick, Coventry University, UK

Learning outcomes

Upon completion of this chapter the reader should be able to:

- summarise how sport is internationalising;
- provide a definition of internationalisation;
- highlight factors that have resulted in the internationalisation of sport;
- present a range of theories that explain internationalisation;
- identify the implications of internationalisation for sport managers.

 Overview

In recent years, there has been a dramatic growth in the internationalisation of sport. This chapter therefore begins by identifying where internationalisation is taking place in sport and provides some initial insights into the reasons why sport has internationalised. Thereafter, definitions of internationalisation will be presented and the characteristics of the phenomenon identified. Respective theoretical contributions to understanding internationalisation will then be addressed, with the implications of each perspective being indicated. Towards the end of the chapter, the implications of internationalisation for sport managers will be discussed, and the chapter concludes with a case study of FC Barcelona.

Introduction

Across the world, many sports have developed as socio-culturally embedded activities, first played as part of local ceremonies, rituals or leisure pursuits. Some sports have remained largely domestic, for instance kabaddi in India; other sports have spread to more countries alongside colonisation and the development of trade routes, for instance cricket; and some sports have developed in a truly international way, such as football and motor racing. In this sense, one can therefore say that even today different sports are at various stages of internationalisation.

At this stage, it is worthwhile considering who and what has been subject to the phenomenon of internationalisation. Given the central premise of sport – a contest between two parties with the intention of their being a winner – there has always been an inevitability that sportspeople will naturally seek out new, different and more challenging opponents against whom to compete. At the same time, there has also been a long-held view that sport is an important way of promoting and facilitating peace, of strengthening bonds between nations, and of encouraging a healthy, active lifestyle. This would explain therefore why events such as the modern-day Olympics and the FIFA Football World Cup were introduced. Clubs and teams have also internationalised for numerous reasons including the support of an expatriate community, the broadcasting of games overseas, and legal or regulatory change leading to the signing of foreign players or the setting up of overseas scouting networks. What has been most stark over the last 5–10 years however, is the way in which the internationalisation of sports personalities and fans has taken place. In notable cases, this has resulted in people such as David Beckham, Anna Kournikova and Yao Ming becoming global icons, and organisations such as the National Basketball Association (NBA) creating an extensive overseas fan base via the creation of an international network of operations.

Motivated more by the quest for commercial gain and market share, internationalisation has sometimes subjugated the sporting dimension of competitive international contests. Alongside these changes, the broadcasting and media coverage of sport as well as the development of markets for sport merchandise has paradoxically motivated, but also emerged as an outcome of, such changes. Indeed, it is now commonplace for the leading organisations, clubs and teams in some sports to produce and sell a variety of merchandise, sell multimedia broadcasting rights and to target product offerings at specific consumer groups across the world. In so doing, this has led to the emergence of a new sporting model to which a number of leading international sports now adhere. Rather than being characterised by sport for sport's sake, off-field performance has become at least as important as on-field performance in some cases. Moreover, instead of focusing on the short-term consideration of winning games, tournaments and events, it is now commonplace in internationalised sport to think in strategic terms, to talk of long-term value generation and to think of returns on investment.

Definitions and the nature of internationalisation in sport

There is no commonly held definition of internationalisation and so one can generally say that internationalisation has taken place when the operations of an organisation have ceased to be exclusively domestic. Dictionary definitions indicate that internationalisation takes place when entities become international in scope or character. They alternatively state that internationalisation involves placing or bringing entities under international control. In the business literature, the following definitions have been postulated:

the process of increasing involvement in international operations;

(Welch and Luostarinen, 1988)

the process of adapting firms' operations (strategy, structure, resources, etc.) to international environments.   (Calof and Beamish, 1995)

In essence, the implications of these definitions for sport have been twofold:

1 Sports organisations have sought to internationally acquire and retain resources – e.g. in the case of labour, football clubs have increasingly bought in playing talent from overseas (for instance, football club Beveren, playing in the Jupiler League in Belgium, once fielded a team of 11 players from the Ivory Coast). Regarding capital, changing ownership patterns and the need for capital project funding has resulted in flows across boundaries (for instance, a large proportion of the funding used to cover the cost of constructing the new Wembley Stadium in London – England's national football stadium – was secured from a German bank, Westdeutsche Landesbank). In addition, land has been purchased by foreign nationals (Mohammed al-Fayed, an Egyptian, now owns Craven Cottage – the home of Fulham Football Club – prime real estate in West London), and even sporting entrepreneurship has become internationalised (for instance, Jefferson Slack, an American, was previously recruited by Internazionale of Milan to head up its marketing operations).

2 Sport organisations have sought to internationally acquire and retain customers – e.g. television, and latterly media corporations. For instance, the English Football Association has historically sold the rights to televised football in more than 70 countries. This continues to be the case, one argument being that media corporations are driving internationalisation in sport. Consider Formula One motor racing: it is thought that an average of up to 100 million people worldwide watch each Formula One race on television. Otherwise, international customers have become increasingly important, with sport organisations becoming more and more reliant on people from overseas buying merchandise, buying tickets to games, subscribing to electronic services and, in a more intangible way, having an affiliation with the organisation.

Factors contributing to the internationalisation of sport

Considering the origins of a sport such as football, numerous activities and games similar to the modern-day version of the game have long been played around the world. Yet it was not until the nineteenth century, when the English codified the game in a way that forms the basis for football today, that football really began to emerge as an international sport. With its vast colonial empire, the English were able to export the game worldwide, although ironically people in the British colonies were actually more receptive to cricket. Instead, the industrial revolution and the development of international trade routes and flows had a much greater impact on the growth of football around the world. Hence, in places such as Spain, Italy, Argentina and South Africa, the sport developed as the result of an influx of overseas workers and industrialists. In this sense, the internationalisation of sport is not a new phenomenon. Indeed, just as other industrial sectors have increasingly operated across international boundaries in recent decades, so too has football and most other sports. Such is the international dimension of sport that we find football clubs such as Manchester United attributed as having more than 1 million fans worldwide, events such as the Olympics being watched by 4 billion people and Formula One motor racing events taking place in countries as diverse as China, Bahrain and Brazil. It seems a long way from foreign railway engineers in Argentina organising football matches against local people to the now oft-used term that football is 'the global game'. At the same time, a sport such as French cycling has gone from being an egalitarian mode of transport to a way of promoting national newspapers (the Tour de France) through to what is now a major international sporting event.

In accounting for the internationalisation of sport, therefore, the following eight factors have had a varying impact on different sports:

1 **Competition and competition formats**. In the pursuit of new competitors, sports people and the bodies representing them have always sought out new rivals. As has already been illustrated, colonial powers and industrially developed nations have long been the source of sports being introduced into countries with little or no history of previously staging them. Alongside the global proliferation of some sports, new creation of new competition formats has helped to perpetuate the international development and popularity of some sports. Tournaments such as golf's Ryder Cup are an example of this, and more recently developed series like the A1 Grand Prix motor racing championship have heightened the sense of international competition.

2 **Socio-cultural shifts**. Throughout many parts of the world, there have been major socio-cultural shifts that have fuelled both the consumption of sport and the way in which it is consumed. Growing disposable incomes and a reduction in working hours in some countries have created opportunities for people to watch, travel to or participate in sport, and such changes have gained momentum due to factors such as the development of low-cost airlines which have made it easier for fans to follow a team or series throughout the year. When Liverpool appeared in the 2007 UEFA Champions League Final, as many as 40,000 people travelled to Athens, even though only 17,000 people were thought to have tickets. At the same time, many countries have also witnessed the development of a celebrity culture in which sporting icons have played a major part. Despite never having won a Grand Slam tennis tournament, Anna Kournikova nevertheless became a major global personality, appearing in advertisements and promotions across the world.

3 **Regulatory change**. Following the Second World War, there has been a major trend towards the liberalisation of free global trade. This has resulted in the removal of barriers to trade flows across the world, although this may not immediately appear to have had a major impact on sport. Yet free trade philosophy has had an immense effect, most notably in relation to the broadcasting of sport. In countries where the state is likely to have once controlled the televising of sporting events, the United Kingdom being a prime example, private corporations are now allowed to bid for, and routinely win, the rights to televise games, leagues, events and tournaments. These corporations are often

non-indigenous, the market being dominated by organisations such as Time-Warner and News International, which operate on a global, boundary-spanning basis. At the same time, such is the commercial orientation of the corporations involved that the maximum financial return can only be achieved through the international sale of the broadcast content they produce. Alongside global trade liberalisation, the emergence of trading blocs such as the European Union has also helped create conditions that have fostered sporting internationalisation. Based upon the principle of 'freedom of movement', the most obvious sporting manifestation of this was the 1995 Bosman Ruling. Having established the right of a player to move unimpeded across international boundaries within the EU, the principles of 'Bosman' were subsequently applied to movements into the EU by players from other European countries (the Kolpak Ruling) and from outside Europe into the EU (the Cotonou Ruling). Free movement as a central tenant of EU philosophy has also been evident in, for instance, the application of competition law. In the case of the English Premier League, the EU Competition Commissioners have long since railed against the domestic, collective sale of broadcasting rights, preferring a more open, liberal and international approach.

4 **Industrial change**. Most sports are likely to have started as a matter of ceremony, thereafter developing according to local custom and practice. With the onset of industrialisation, the role of sport changed somewhat, taking on a more clearly defined role as a form of leisure activity. As teams and clubs organised themselves to compete against one another, an amateur ethos developed whereby formal rules and regulations were encouraged but payments and financial returns were not. In the twentieth century, the sporting model changed again with the onset of professionalism and payments for players. We are arguably now in the fourth age of sport, one where the exploitation of commercial rights and properties has transcended the professionalisation of sport. Increasingly, for commercial partners involved in sport and, indeed, for some sports clubs themselves, the pursuit of profit has become the most important aspect of sport, superseding even the central spectacle of a sporting contest with an uncertain outcome. This fourth age is characterised by its emphasis on revenue generation, cost control and competitive advantage, each of which can be achieved by pursuing international strategies. Hence, whether sports organisations are seeking to enter potentially lucrative new overseas markets in order to sell their products or they have established scouting networks across the world to sport new talent, internationalisation has become an inevitable dimension of a new sporting age.

5 **Resource acquisition**. Given the commercial pressures that many sports organisations now face, the need to access, and possibly control, resources has been a major feature of sport. For teams and clubs seeking to acquire the best playing talent, non-traditional markets have become an important source of players. In the case of Ajax, one of the Netherlands' leading football clubs, this once entailed attempts to set up a franchise network, of which the Ajax Cape Town club became one part. For a football club like Arsenal, an alternative strategy has been to establish an integrated global scouting network which, in this particular case, links the Ivory Coast with Belgium and the UK. In addition, the naturally converging interests of teams and sportswear suppliers, sponsors and other commercial partners have alternatively created opportunities for collaborative, cross-border relationships to develop. Hence, sportswear manufacturers such as Nike

and Adidas have attempted to colonise the world's leading sports even though they are essentially based in only two countries, the United States and Germany respectively. In tandem with this, clubs and teams have been able to benefit from such competition by selecting from the most commercially lucrative kit deals that often extend beyond domestic boundaries. The recent contest between Adidas, the incumbent, and Nike, the predator, to supply the German national football team is a good example of just how competitive internationalised sport has become.

6 **Emergence of new technology.** Sporting contests may have been the basis for social relationships between colonialists and locals or the imposition of alien norms and values on indigenous communities by invading nations. In either case, 200 years ago such contests will have been talked or written about rather than seen or heard. With the advent of first radio and then television, international sport for the first time was transmitted either live or in the form of edited highlights. The growth in satellite technology resulted in the further proliferation of televised sport, introducing different sports to new marketplaces in an array of formats. Digital television is set to result in the even more sophisticated, some might say complex, delivery of sport into international markets – in particular, 'on-demand' facilities, where consumers can decide what and when they want to watch or listen, and in what format. Alongside the new ways of watching sport, there are also new ways of consuming information about it and of buying sport products. The internet, a truly global phenomenon – even if it has developed in equitably across the world – is now a boundary-spanning tool that enables fans and others to consume their sport in a way that was not possible, even as late as the early 1990s. Mobile telephones, especially the third generation of phones, have also enhanced the immediacy of sport's availability, with texting, the internet and downloads now all available to people. A further extension of this is the 'pod' phenomenon, a growing number of 'podcasts' now being available. The more recent emergence of social media sites like Twitter has opened up the world of sport even further to new and diverse groups of people around the world.

7 **Market maturity.** The sports organisations that have deliberately, aggressively and/or successfully internationalised are commonly those from North America and Western Europe. In one sense this is unsurprising given the economic and political power of these regions. However, the nature of domestic markets in countries like the UK and Germany is such that the pressure for sport organisations to internationalise is immense. Proliferating purchase alternatives, particularly in the leisure sector, allied to the maturity of markets, means opportunities for successfully developing new revenue streams are limited. Organisations have therefore sought to sell more products overseas and to enter new international markets. At the same time, markets such as China and India have developed rapidly, the changes spurred on by rapid economic growth and the emergence of a consumer culture.

8 **Mass transportation.** When football in England was formally codified more than 130 years ago, it was simply a domestic pursuit that ultimately came to be played for a while on a regional basis. As the train network grew, so did the number of people travelling to away games. In turn, as car ownership has grown, road travel became the primary means of travelling to away games. Now, fans are frequently using aeroplanes to get to overseas games. Indeed, with the advent of low-cost airlines, many English

fans will routinely travel to the European mainland, not only to watch their team but also simply just to watch a sporting contest. The importance of cheap, widely available transport should not be underestimated. Although the 2007 UEFA Champions League, staged in Athens, was a relatively short trip across the Adriatic for the fans of AC Milan, Liverpool (Milan's opponents) were thought to have five times as many fans as Milan in Athens, with most of the English fans having travelled to Greece on low-cost airlines.

Theories of internationalisation

There is no clear agreement concerning how internationalisation comes about or what drives the phenomenon. What appears below is a brief commentary on the most commonly cited theoretical perspectives. For a more detailed insight into each of these perspectives, it is recommended that readers take a look at one or more of the following: Lam and White (1999), Andersson (2000), Whitelock (2002) and Chetty and Campbell-Hunt (2003).

Industrial network theory

At the heart of network theories is the 'Uppsala Model' which states that organisations are part of a network of other interrelated organisations, although individual firms and groups nevertheless decide which international markets they will enter and why. As such, network theories explain that an organisation's commitment to internationalisation progresses through four stages:

1 no exporting;

2 ad hoc exporting;

3 establishment of subsidiary operations;

4 full commitment to overseas production.

In moving from stage to another, the decision to engage in international operations will be influenced by the culture, language and education of another country. Internationalisation will be more likely to take place where there is a smaller psychic distance between the host country and the overseas country or market.

Implications of this theoretical perspective for sport

A sport organisation such as the football club Ajax Amsterdam is part of a large network of interrelated organisations. This network will include sponsors, sportswear manufacturers, media corporations, players, fans and commercial partners. The recent internationalisation of organisations such as Ajax has seen them move from simply being domestic football clubs, in this case, a Dutch club, to being international business organisations. The most tangible evidence of this in Ajax's case has been the formation of a franchise in South Africa – Ajax Cape Town. One reason the club pursued such a strategy was the relatively small psychic distance between the Netherlands and South Africa, a result of the colonial links between the two countries.

Business strategy theory

Business strategy theory is based on the pragmatic view that internationalisation is only one choice from a range of expansion strategies that are open to an organisation. The decision to pursue such a strategy will ultimately be guided by nature of market opportunity, the nature and extent of an organisation's resources and the philosophy characterising management within an organisation. These in turn will be influenced by market attractiveness, psychic distance between the company and the market, market accessibility and the existence of informal barriers.

Implications of this theoretical perspective for sport

If one is to compare Madrid's two leading football clubs – Real and Atletico – one would find two very different entities. Despite their common characteristics, the former has pursued a strategy characterised more by international development whereas the latter has adopted a stronger domestic focus in its operations. Hence, one can contrast the pragmatism of the two as Real, the economically and politically more powerful organisation, has pursued a more overtly international strategy characterised by overseas growth. In Atletico's case, although its strategy is not exclusively domestic, there has been a much stronger emphasis on targeting domestic and local fans. This has been based on two key factors:

- the established view that Atletico is the underdog's team and therefore represents, for example, the working classes (organisation philosophy);
- an entrepreneurial and innovative approach to marketing communications, that has resulted in series Atletico television advertisements winning creativity awards (organisation resources – management competence).

Innovation-related theory

This perspective holds that innovation is the basis for internationalisation. Organisations are thought to innovate in response to the influence of two factors a) the influence of change agents such as key decision makers; and/or b) the influence of external stimuli such as overseas customers. The response of organisations to either of these two factors will be to move from marketing products domestically to a pre-export phase then through to an experimental and subsequently an active and committed phase of international operation and marketing.

Implications of this theoretical perspective for sport

In 2003, FC Barcelona members elected a progressive young reformer, Joan Laporta, as President of the club. Alongside people such as the Finance Director (Ferran Sorriano) and the Director of Marketing (Marc Ingla), Laporta set about introducing a new business model into the club. These change agents were acting in response to developments in the football industry, including a growth in the importance of sponsorship and the emergence of potentially valuable new marketplaces. In response, the club has been innovative and experimental in the way it has, for instance, embraced sponsorship and targeted new customers. In relation to the former, the club was amongst the last in the world to place a sponsor's logo on team shirts – an international charity: UNICEF. Regarding the latter, one example of the club's innovativeness is the establishment of a series of soccer camps in US states such as New Mexico where large Hispanic communities can be found.

Adapative choice theory

According to adaptive choice theorists, organisations are open, natural, living systems. As such, they are influenced by external events and changes meaning that, in some respects, organisations are in a constant state of flux. They must therefore respond to the world around them and to their changing environments in order to survive.

Implications of this theoretical perspective for sport

If one considers the recent history of English Premier League football clubs, many of them appear to be living organisms that are heavily influenced by external events. A decade ago, numerous clubs were heavily affected by the tendency of clubs to publicly float on the London Stock Exchange. At the same time, the 'dot.com' boom resulted in a large-scale rush to construct elaborate websites. More recently, at the turn of the twenty-first century, clubs began to target markets in the Far East, especially China. Currently, the trend is for new owners to become involved in football, with many American entrepreneurs having bought majority shareholdings in English clubs. The openness and adapativeness of these clubs is just as suitably illustrated when one considers what has happened after each of the developments noted above. Stock Exchange listings have been followed by many de-listings as financial returns have failed to reach expected levels; website developments have become much less elaborate and in many cases are contracted out to specialist companies, largely due to the costs that such developments imposed on clubs; and the rush for market share in places such as China has subsided, due to the competitive nature of the market, the costs associated with targeting it and the unsatisfactory financial returns the market has delivered.

Transaction cost theory

From the transaction cost perspective, all decisions to internationalise are seen as rational economic ones. That is, the costs of taking a particular course of action will be the principal driver for international decision makers. The socio-cultural context and connections of managers and organisations, evident in network theories, are therefore unimportant for transaction cost theorists, unless they have a direct implication on the costliness of a particular decision.

Implications of this theoretical perspective for sport

Over the last decade, transfer fees and salaries have risen dramatically in English football, fuelled by the revenue from large television deals, changes in the transfer regulations and a diminishing domestic pool of skilled labour. In the years since 2000, the English domestic transfer record has consistently been broken with spending on players such as

Wayne Rooney, Rio Ferdinand, Juan Sebastian Veron and Fernando Torres. In addition, annual salary inflation has often run at double figure levels, and it has not been unknown for some clubs to operate at salary levels that have been as much as 150 per cent of club turnover. In attempts to address the financial implications of a challenging labour market, clubs have therefore increasingly sought to acquire players from overseas markets in which cost levels are lower. In the case of a club like Arsenal, a club that has traditionally taken the view that cost control is important, this has meant signing players from countries including Ukraine, Liberia, the Ivory Coast, Denmark, Switzerland, Nigeria and Greece. Indeed, such has been the effectiveness of this cost minimisation strategy that Arsenal has at times fielded a starting 11 in the Premier League consisting solely of overseas players.

Implications for sport managers

Within each of the above theoretical perspectives, it is implicit that there are clear, identifiable and tangible benefits associated with a strategy of internationalisation. In addition to the benefits mentioned above, further benefits might include:

- facilitates access to new markets, e.g. Formula One staging a race in China;
- facilitates access to new sources of labour – e.g. Arsenal and Beveren agreeing to share players;
- facilitates access to new sources of finance – e.g. the English FA securing a German loan in order to fund the construction of Wembley Stadium;
- enables diversification and growth – e.g. Manchester United opening up new retail outlets in Asia;
- promotes market development and growth – e.g. the NBA has been working in Africa both to promote the brand and to help create new market opportunities;
- provides opportunities for collaboration and alliances – e.g. Ajax Amsterdam worked with Cape Town Spurs and Seven Stars to create a new sporting franchise: Ajax Cape Town;
- stimulates learning amongst organisations and managers – e.g. in an attempt to understand and respond to new market opportunities, football clubs including Everton and FC Barcelona have recruited Asian members of staff to build knowledge of overseas markets;
- enables organisations and managers to build competence and capability – e.g. Chelsea has variously recruited staff from Portugal, the Netherlands, Spain, Denmark and Israel in an effort to improve the quality of its management team.

Although internationalisation can bring benefits for sports and sport organisations, it also poses a series of management challenges. Amongst these are:

- **Marketing management.** At the 1998 World Cup Final in Paris, the football world was sent into uproar when it was announced that Ronaldo would not be playing. The player nevertheless appeared on the pitch but seemed to struggle throughout the game. Afterwards, theories abounded that Ronaldo and the Brazilian football authorities had been pressured by Nike to make sure the player took part in the game thereby fulfilling his contractual obligations to the company. More recently, reports have suggested that tennis' Williams sisters have struggled to maintain their form due to contractual demands of some of their corporate partners. Some reports have even suggested that the sisters have been required to play in exhibitions when injured. Whatever the true story in both cases, the two illustrate some of the challenges sport managers can face when trying to market personalities. Using a celebrity to promote a product, a brand or a sport is a rewarding proposition for corporations and the sportsman or woman involved. However, there is also the issue of how to manage the nature and the extent of this activity because too much promotional work may ultimately detract from the very qualities that make the celebrity such a valuable individual in the first place. Indeed, when people such as David Beckham are global icons, this presents particular problems as there may well be extensive travelling involved, which may cause problems for the individual, the team and/or the commercial partner.

- **Organisation management**. Despite spending millions of euros on their respective returns to Formula One motor racing, Toyota and Honda only won one race between them. For strategic marketing purposes, each team's involvement in F1 was very important, as was their intended success in the sport. However, one has to say that the return on their respective investments was poor, resulting in their eventual withdrawal from the sport. It has been suggested that one reason for Toyota and Honda's respective performances was the way in which Japanese companies organise their operations. Such is the geographic distance between the racing team and team headquarters in Japan that problem diagnosis, decision-making and effective communication were major problems. As such, readers should think about how these types of problems might be addressed when sports organisations are involved in international operations.

- **Human resource management**. Take a look at any leading European football team, for example Real Madrid, AC Milan, Bayern Munich, Lyon or Manchester United. What you will invariably find is that each team's squad consists of a rich mix of players from different countries. Immediately the problems of internationalisation should become apparent – how do the players and club officials communicate with each other when they all speak different languages. In the case of, say, Real Madrid, one should recall that during the 2006/07 season, the club's leading centre forward was Dutch, their star midfielder was English, one of their best defenders was Brazilian and the team manager was Italian. It is also worth mentioning that in Spain, Real are nicknamed 'The Vikings' because of the club's history of signing players from Northern Europe. The mix creates challenges other than language; for instance, integrating players and managing multicultural teams is a major issue, especially when one considers the differences in attitudes and behaviour between people from Anglo-Saxon, Northern European cultures and Latin, Mediterranean, Southern European cultures. While such issues may not always be acknowledged or managed effectively, they are paramount if organisational performance is to be optimised.

- **Supply chain management**. Despite the lack of English playing success at the annual Wimbledon tennis championship, the tournament nevertheless remains one of the most important events on both the playing and social calendars. More than half a million spectators from around the world will normally attend the event and part of the overall experience for many of them is eating strawberries and cream – an established Wimbledon tradition. On average, 27,000 kilos of strawberries and 7,000 litres of cream will be consumed at the tournament during Wimbledon fortnight. Given that the strawberries and cream and the tennis are synonymous, this poses some interesting challenges for supply-chain managers. Ensuring that international fans get what they expect is the overall challenge they face; but ensuring the correct quantity and quality of strawberry is sourced is equally important. When one factors in the vagaries of the English weather, the managerial challenge is heightened. Although it might seem almost incidental to sport, strawberries and cream are part of the overall sporting experience and the task for managers therefore is to ensure that the expected experience is delivered to customers.

- **Risk management.** In 2003, there was a major outbreak of the SARS virus in China, which had a major impact on sport in the country. At the time, numerous sporting events were either cancelled or postponed. At the time, China was emerging as an important market for European football teams and many club tours to the country were abandoned. This required some very careful thinking as clubs sought to address the potential risks of touring and of not touring. In the latter case, this meant losing out on an important revenue stream and on the opportunity to establish and build fan affiliation. But the risks of players contracting the virus, allied to the likelihood that stadiums would be cancelled and matches would not take place anyway, ultimately led clubs to cancel their tours.

NB: The points above are not intended to be a definitive list of the challenges facing managers. Rather, it is intended to be illustrative, providing an insight into some of the issues that international sport managers have to contend with.

Case 23.1 FC Barcelona: an international football club in Catalonia

FC Barcelona was founded in 1899 by a group of Swiss, British, Spanish and Catalonian footballers. One could therefore say that from the outset the club was an international one. Whereas football clubs in countries such as England and Italy have traditionally been owned by local businesspeople or industrial families, FC Barcelona was founded as a membership club. This is still the case, with the club achieving a total worldwide membership of 145,000 in 2006. These members are referred to as socios or culés and many of them are members of penés or supporters' clubs, of which there are almost 1,800 worldwide.

Historically, Barca has held something of a stranglehold on Spanish football, along with its closest and bitterest rival Real Madrid. This rivalry became one of the most passionate in world football following the Spanish Civil War, during which Franco's Madrid-based government fought a vicious and bloody campaign against Catalan separatists. FC Barcelona became a symbol of Catalan identity and defiance and, in the minds of many football fans and Catalans alike, has helped to cement the club as 'més que un club' – more than a club. Importantly, many Catalonians, afraid of the Madrid regime, emigrated to places such as Mexico and Argentina, countries that are now important international marketplaces for Barca.

Since 1957, FC Barcelona has played at their iconic home – the Nou Camp Stadium. With a capacity of almost 99,000, it is Europe's biggest football stadium and home games

(continued)

are often complete sell-outs. Many of those who attend games are from overseas but more startling is the fact that the Nou Camp with its museum is one of the most popular tourist attractions in Barcelona, drawing more than 1,160,000 visitors a year.

Arguably the most successful period of Barca's history was that when Johan Cruyff was playing for the club between 1973 and 1978. Cruyff is often thought to have been one of the world's greatest ever players and his impact on FC Barcelona has been profound. Most notably, it appears to have created a Dutch heritage that resulted in Cruyff's return to the club as manager in 1988. More recently, the club has appointed Dutch managers such as Frank Rijkaard, Ronald Koeman and Loius van Gaal, as well as a stream of Dutch players such as Ronald Koeman, Marc Overmars, Winston Bogarde, Giovanni van Bronckhorst, Edgar Davids, Boudewijn Zenden, Philip Cocu, Patrick Kluivert and Michael Reiziger.

In 2003, FC Barcelona members elected a progressive young reformer, Joan Laporta, as President of the club. This signalled major changes at the club, including a newly established focus on targeting international markets. Having commercially fallen behind rivals like Manchester United and Real Madrid, Barca has set up soccer camps in the United States, notably in those areas that have large Hispanic communities, targeted fans in Japan and signed a commercial deal with Tiger Beer in Singapore.

For many years, Barcelona had been one of the last major professional football clubs in the world not to have a shirt sponsor. In 2006 this changed, when the club announced a not-for-profit deal with UNICEF. At one level, this reinforced Barca's international credentials, committing the club to make a series of financial contributions to development projects across the world. At another level, however, it simply added to the activities of Fundacio FC Barcelona, a charitable organisation promoting social/solidarity, institutional/cultural and education/care programmes across the world.

Discussion questions

1 To what extent is it possible for a sports club like FC Barcelona to become major international businesses or brands when they have such important local and historically based identities?

2 In pursuing an international strategy, what might be some of the new market entry challenges facing a sports club like FC Barcelona?

3 How should club managers respond to the challenges you have identified in Question 2 above?

Case 23.2 Li Na serves an ace by flying solo

Before she became the country's most successful tennis player by reaching Saturday's final of the Australian Open, Li Na was almost as well-known in China for her tattoo.

The small rose and heart on her chest might not seem racy on the women's tennis circuit, but it was a strong statement of individuality in a country where tattoos are not popular. She used to cover it up with tape, but no longer bothers.

(continued)

Ms Li's performance in this year's first grand slam event has called attention to another act of rebellion that could have bigger ramifications for the future of sport in China. Two years ago she was one of four female tennis players who were released from the rigid structure of the Chinese sports system and allowed to manage their own careers.

'When I was young, I did what the coaches and leaders told me to do', she says. 'Now I am playing for myself'.

The tussle over the future of the sports system has become emblematic of a wider tension in Chinese society between individualistic younger generations and the paternalistic habits that still pervade.

'Our leaders and media like those who are obedient and lack character, but Li Na is definitely not like that', poet Zhao Lihua said in a blog posting. 'I like her spontaneity. I like her recklessness. I like her being so cool.'

China's Soviet-style sports system achieved its high point at the Beijing Olympics when the host country topped the gold medal table. Promising children are identified at an early age and funnelled into full-time training. Coaches control every aspect of an athlete's career, from when they wake up to which matches they play, and bureaucrats take more than half the winnings.

Yet the system has been coming under pressure since Yao Ming moved to play basketball in the US in 2002. Not only did athletes in big-money sports want to retain more of their income, but the conformity of the Chinese system was found wanting in some sports.

When Mr Yao first played in the US, his coach wanted him to intimidate opponents by slam-dunking the ball. 'He was very reluctant because slam-dunking was frowned upon in China as a sign of individualism', says Brook Larmer, author of a book about the player. He eventually relented after the coach made his teammates run laps of the court each time he refused.

Ms Li has admitted she would not have played tennis when younger without pressure from administrators, but she also left the sport for two years because of her disillusionment with the rigidity of the Chinese system.

When she and three other top players were allowed to leave the system in 2008 and retain more than 90 per cent of their earnings, there was a flurry of criticism from parts of the establishment, especially after early results disappointed.

'The players flying independent have not had an ideal performance', Cai Zhenhua, a senior sports official said at the time. 'At least so far, it is not suitable for more to break out from the system.'

But even before this year's success in Australia, Ms Li and colleague Zheng Jie started to silence critics by both reaching the semi-finals in Melbourne last year. They have also helped galvanise rapidly growing interest in tennis, especially among well-off urbanites.

Source: 'Li Na serves an ace by flying solo,' *The Financial Times*, 28/01/11 (Dyer, G.), © The Financial Times Limited. All rights reserved.

Discussion questions

4 What do you think are some of the major issues in the internationalisation of Chinese sport, particularly for athletes?

5 Looking ahead to the next 5–10 years, what future do you foresee for Chinese sport? Will it be shaped more by domestic or by international pressures?

Conclusion

In some respects, one might argue that sport has always been international. A review of historical literature shows that in many countries games have always been played and that these have often been exported to other countries. As a result, sport has often been a universal phenomenon that has transcended language, culture and geography. However, it is only in recent decades that the international nature of sport has increasingly been recognised as a focus for business managers. There are a number of reasons for this, including regulatory changes and the challenges of acquiring scarce, valuable resources. In this context, various theoretical approaches have been employed in an attempt to explain why internationalisation has become so important in the business world. At this point, however, understanding international sport has received rather less attention. There is therefore still some way to go before we can fully understand why, for instance, there are 100 million Manchester United fans worldwide or why Formula One motor racing holds events in China, Bahrain, Turkey and Malaysia when no drivers or teams from these countries are involved in F1. Some of the reasons why sport has internationalised have been identified in this chapter, although there may be more. The challenge remains for readers to think how the framework of ideas presented in this chapter can be applied to a range of sports, both those that have a strongly specific domestic basis and those that are more clearly 'international'. Above all, as we enter a new age of internationalisation, with new player supply routes opening up, overseas markets forming the basis for increasingly overt commercial strategies and technological developments fuelling media proliferation, managing the process and consequences of internationalisation are key challenges for sport managers. Precedents have already been set in the management of other industrial sectors where internationalisation has taken hold. However, such is the socio-cultural embeddedness of sport, as well as the nature of the product on offer (a contest that has an uncertain outcome), that sport is unique in many respects and therefore requires specific attention in the literature and in practice. It is hoped that this chapter goes some way to addressing this distinctiveness in an international context.

Discussion questions

6 Using existing definitions of internationalisation, how might they be applied to a sport such as football, car rallying, handball or volleyball?

7 For a sport of your choice, identify how it has 'internationalised', indicating the most important factors that have influenced this process.

8 Is the internationalisation of all sports inevitable?

9 Compare and contrast how the US National Basketball Association (NBA) and English Premier League football clubs have internationalised. What lessons can sport managers learn from both cases?

10 If you had to advise a major sport organisation about its internationalisation strategy, what would you tell it?

11 Has/is the internationalisation of sport a good thing or a bad thing?

Keywords

Adaptive choice theory; business strategy theory; industrial network theory; innovation-related theory; internationalisation; transaction cost theory.

Guided reading

Although there are very few studies that provide detailed definitions of internationalisation, the reader is directed to Welch and Luostarinen (1988) and Calof and Beamish (1995) for citations presented in this chapter. Elsewhere, Lam and White (1999), Andersson (2000), Whitelock (2002) and Chetty and Campbell-Hunt (2003) provide an overview of the different theoretical perspectives that have attempted to account for internationalisation. The underpinning forces and benefits of internationalisation are highlighted by Hutchinson et al. (2005). Yakhlef and Maubourguet (2004) and Camuffo et al. (2006) explore the process of internationalisation, indicating how firms move from domestic to international operations. For an overview of internationalisation and sport, it is recommended that the reader take a look at Bridgewater (2006). A more specific analysis of an individual sport and internationalisation can be found in Desbordes' (2006) text on football. Chadwick and Arthur (2007) provide a more detailed insight into the case presented in this chapter – FC Barcelona.

Recommended websites

BBC Business of Sport: www.bbc.co.uk/news/business/business_of_sport/

Business of Sport Management companion site: www.booksites.net/download/chadwickbeech/index.html

ESPN Sports Business: http://espn.go.com/sportsbusiness/index.html

European Association for Sport Management: www.easm.org/

European Sport Management Quarterly: www.meyer-meyer-sports.com/en/produkte/zeitschrift/esmq.htm

Institute of Business Forecasting: www.ibforecast.com/

International Journal of Sport Marketing and Sponsorship: www.imr-info.com/#goIJSM

International Journal of Sport Management and Marketing: https://www.inderscience.com/browse/index.php?journalID=102

Journal of Sport Management: www.humankinetics.com/products/journals/journal.cfm?id=JSM

Long Range Planning: www.lrp.ac/

North American Association of Sport Management: www.nassm.com/

S1M Voice of Leadership: http://voiceofleadership.biz/

Sport Business: www.sportbusiness.com/

Sport Management Association of Australia and New Zealand: www.gu.edu.au/school/lst/services/smaanz/

SportQuest: www.sportquest.com/resources/index.html

Sports Business and Industry Online: www.sportsvueinc.com/

Sports Business Daily: www.sportsbusinessdaily.com/

Sports Business Journal: www.sportsbusinessjournal.com/

Sports Business News: www.sportsbusinessnews.com/

Sport Industry Group: www.sportindustry.biz/

Sport Marketing Quarterly: www.smqonline.com/

Sports Pro: www.sportspromedia.com/

The Sport Journal: www.thesportjournal.org

References

Andersson, S. (2000) 'The internationalisation of the firm from an entrepreneurial perspective', *International Studies of Management and Organisation*, 30 (1), 63–92.

Bridgewater, S. (2006) 'International sport marketing and globalisation', in J. Beech and S. Chadwick (eds), *The Marketing of Sport*, Harlow: Financial Times/Prentice Hall.

Calof, J. and Beamish, P. (1995) 'Adapting to foreign markets: explaining internationalisation', *International Business Review*, 4 (2), 115–31.

Chadwick, S. and Arthur, D. (2007) 'Mes que un club (More than a club), the commercial development of FC Barcelona', in S. Chadwick and D. Arthur (eds), *International Cases in the Business of Sport*, Oxford: Butterworth Heinemann.

Camuffo, A., Furlan, A., Romano, P. and Vinelli, A. (2006) 'The process of supply network internationalisation', *Journal of Purchasing and Supply Management*, 12, 135–47.

Chetty, S. and Campbell-Hunt, C. (2003) 'Paths to internationalisation among small- to medium-sized firms', *European Journal of Marketing*, 37 (5/6), 796–820.

Desbordes, M. (ed.) (2006) *Marketing and Football: An International Perspective*, Oxford: Butterworth Heinemann.

Hutchinson, K., Quinn, B. and Alexander, N. (2005) 'The internationalisation of small to medium-sized retail companies: towards a conceptual framework', *Journal of Marketing Management*, 21, 149–79.

Lam, L.W. and White, L.P. (1999) 'An adaptive choice model of the internationalisation process', *The International Journal of Organisational Analysis*, 7 (2), 105–34.

Welch, L.S. and Luostarinen, R. (1988) 'Internationalisation: evolution of a concept', *Journal of General Management*, 14 (2), 34–55.

Whitelock, J. (2002) 'Theories of internationalisation and their impact on market entry', *International Marketing Review*, 19 (4), 342–47.

Yakhlef, A. and Maubourguet, F. (2004) 'The Lexus and the Olive Tree: a rising mode of internationalisation', *International Journal of Entrepreneurial Behaviour and Research*, 10 (3), 192–205.

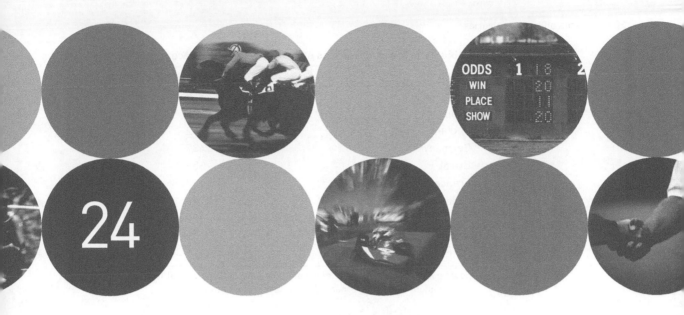

24

Sports agents and intermediaries

Anna Semens, Liverpool University
Adam Pendlebury, Edge Hill University

Learning outcomes

Upon completion of this chapter the reader should be able to:

- understand the structural and economic changes which led to a rise in the number and power of football agents;
- assess the main roles of agents acting for players and clubs;
- differentiate between the main types of agents;
- appreciate the difficulties inherent in the relationship between a player and his agent;
- understand the main regulatory systems currently in place and the difficulties in imposing effective sanctions.

 ## Overview

Over the past two decades the football market has undergone significant change with some players transformed into high earning superstars. The movement towards a competitive labour market has coincided with exponential revenue increases for clubs from broadcasting deals. Yet while clubs tend not to be profitable, players and their agents can make significant sums of money. English Premier League clubs alone spent £70.7 million on agents' fees from October 2008 to September 2009, equating to approximately 11 per cent

Table 24.1 Top ten locations of registered agents (december 2011)

Country	Registered agents
Italy	949
Spain	576
England	502
Germany	437
Brazil	333
France	288
Argentina	216
Bosnia-Herzegovina	124
Nigeria	129
Netherlands	133

Source: Author created from information on www.fifa.com/aboutfifa/organisation/footballgovernance/playersagents/list.html

of transfer spending (Premier League, 2009).[1] Additionally, Football League clubs committed to pay £8.8 million to agents between July 2008 and June 2009, amounting to 22 per cent of football league transfer spending (Football League, 2009). This has led agents to have an increased profile, with the number of registered agents rising by over 500 per cent in the last decade to 5,796, over half of which are located in the traditional football regions of Italy, Spain, England, Germany, Brazil, France and Argentina (FIFA, 2010).

This chapter is primarily concerned with investigating the role and types of agents operating in English football. Based on interview data collected from clubs, players, agents and governing bodies in the UK and Europe and a database of over 900 players and their agents, this chapter explores the historical and contextual issues which help to explain why agents have come to occupy a privileged position in a club or player's transfer decision-making process, before going on to analyse the changes in the football market which have induced agents to perform varied tasks. Once these issues have been addressed, a more complete picture of the current role and types of agents is presented. The remainder of the chapter then explores the interactions between key stakeholders in terms of the principal-agent framework. The final sections explain how problems inherent in this relationship may be allayed, to an extent, through effective regulation, before addressing current issues in the agents industry.

Background and historical context

Agents in English football have been present since the legalisation of professionalism, performing scouting and recruitment tasks for clubs. As clubs developed, they internalised this activity, building their own scouting networks, thus diminishing the role of agents (Roderick, 2001; Taylor, 2006). These changes in the market led agents to seek other roles and

---

[1] Payments made to agents by clubs relate to those made during this period but may relate to transfers completed in previous seasons where the fee is paid across the course of the player's contract. The ratio of agents' fees to transfer spending is therefore slightly lower than 11 per cent.

their position as middlemen between players and clubs, particularly working for players, began to develop. The use of agents in transfers was banned by FIFA in 1936, which believed that they may encourage illegal moves (Berlin Congress, August 1936, displayed in the FIFA collection, National Football Museum). Until the late 1960s the sports agent business was relatively obscure since most athletes were either hesitant to allow someone else to negotiate their contract, or not paid enough to justify their use (Joyce, 1997). With the relaxation of some labour market restrictions there was a resurgence of middlemen becoming involved, despite the FIFA ban still being in place. A combination of developments in technology and labour market liberalisation has enabled players, who have short but potentially lucrative careers, to improve their wealth and bargaining power and agents have become key in aiding players to exploit this.

Broadcasting, first through radio then television, has been the single most important influence on the recent development of football (Dobson and Goddard, 2001; Whannel, 2003). The combination of demographic and technological factors with the rise of television as an entertainment medium, and the TV-friendly nature of team sport making it a favourable medium for advertising, led to aggressive competition from ITV during the 1970s to mount a challenge to the BBC's previous dominance. However, it was not until the introduction of satellite TV and BSkyB's particular ability to outbid rivals for the live rights to major sporting events that there was a serious competitor able to break the ITV/ BBC duopsony as joint purchaser, which had previously kept the rights package fees low (Gannon et al., 2006). BSkyB entered the market in the late 1980s and did not simply want to show football, but wanted the exclusive live rights to it (Lonsdale, 2004).

The top clubs, wishing to gain control of the new TV income, formed a breakaway Premier League for the 1992/93 season and BSkyB outbid all contenders to acquire the live broadcast rights. The final broadcasting deal before the formation of the Premier League generated £44 million for the League clubs across the four years from 1988 to 1992. By 2007 broadcast revenues had increased to over £1.6 billion for the Premier League alone (Deloitte, various years). Additionally, with increased domestic and international television coverage, improved sponsorship and merchandising revenues could be achieved. This exponential increase in income meant that clubs had far more resources available to spend.

At the same time, increasing labour market liberalisation was taking hold. Following professionalism, the system of clubs registering players with the Football League and Football Association was designed to eliminate 'club-hopping', thereby protecting smaller clubs (Russell, 1997). However, in reality it meant that the registration of a player became a tradable commodity, resulting in the transfer market (Morrow, 1999). The retain and transfer system governing this movement of players essentially afforded the club holding the player's registration monopoly power over him. While the player could request a transfer, the club had the final decision on whether or not he was allowed to move based on the level of compensation on offer in the form of a transfer fee (Magee, 2002, 2006).

Contractual terms tended to favour the clubs, with players often being signed on short-term deals, offering them little security (Taylor, 2006). At the same time, the maximum wage exerted downward pressure on a player's earning potential. Disputes and negotiations occurred between the Player's Union, which sought improved terms for players, and the governing bodies, which sought to maintain the status quo, but until the 1960s players still, on average, received salaries far lower than their counterparts involved in more commercialised sports (Taylor, 2006). Restrictive contracts combined with relatively low salaries afforded agents little propensity to act for players. Labour market restrictions slackened over the following decade and legal interventions such as the ruling in Eastham[2] meant players were able to move at the end of their contract and achieve higher wages (Magee, 2002, 2006). Yet the transfer system still favoured clubs, with players having little bargaining power. Though the changing conditions in the football industry led to salary increases for players throughout the 1980s, occupational freedom was still restricted since clubs could demand a transfer fee for out-of-contract players they had offered terms to (Magee, 2002).

The Bosman ruling[3] in 1995 changed the landscape of the football market completely, bringing the contracts of athletes into line with other workers within the European Union (EU) and establishing two main points which impact on the player labour market and by extension on the role that football agents can play. Firstly, out-of-contract international transfer payments are incompatible with Article 39 (now Article 45) of the European Community (EC) Treaty, thus allowing players to move to a new club at the end of their contract without a fee being paid. Secondly, domestic and European leagues are prohibited from imposing quota restrictions on foreign players, thus amplifying the mobility of players across Europe. Previously, clubs in the EU were only authorised to use five foreign players, three of which had to be EU citizens. This was adjudged to be contrary to Article 48 (now Article 39) of the EC Treaty and essentially a pan-European market for players was created (Feess and Muelheusser, 2003). This judgment was extended in 2000 when Kolpak, a Slovakian handball player, successfully argued that as a third country national he should be entitled to the same freedom as EU nationals.[4]

In an effort to quell the impact of the Bosman ruling by reducing the likelihood of players wishing to leave, clubs were willing to renegotiate improved terms as players approached the end of their contract. Longer contracts were also introduced and transfer fees for in-contract players increased as buying clubs tried to prise them away from the club holding their registration. A combination of these factors have enabled the top players and their agents to assume much greater control in the market as clubs attempt to limit the probability of losing a player without recouping a transfer fee.

However, for some players, the ruling in Bosman has led to increased uncertainty. In a more competitive labour market, lower league clubs in particular have been able to regain some of their power over contractual conditions. With higher numbers of players being released at the end of their contract, clubs have been able to offer reduced packages to those who are out of contract elsewhere (Magee, 2006). As the complexity of the market has increased, so too has the need for specialist advice in contract negotiation and in matching players and clubs. The prevalence of agents is a key aspect of the modern game, enabling players to extract more of the revenue that was previously only available to clubs (Roderick, 2001; Holt et al., 2006). However, the role of an agent can vary considerably and some clients expect agents to offer more services than others.

---

[2] *Eastham v Newcastle United FC* [1963] 3 All ER 139.
[3] *Union Royale Belge des Sociétés de Football Association ASBL & others v Jean-Marc Bosman*; Case C-415/93, ECR I-4921.
[4] *Deutscher Handballbund eV v Kolpak* (Case C-438/00) – [2003] All ER (D) 71 (May).

Role

FIFA defines an agent as 'a natural person who, for a fee, introduces players to clubs with a view to negotiating or renegotiating an employment contract or introduces two clubs to one another with a view to concluding a transfer agreement' (FIFA, 2009: 417 FIFA Players Agents Regulations). As this definition reflects, the traditional role of an agent has been in contract negotiation or in providing a link between two clubs in identifying and negotiating the availability of a player for transfer. However, in reality agents can perform a number of tasks throughout the transfer process and in the management of a player's career. Each function is described in turn below.

Brokering transfers

The agent's role as a broker can be the most lucrative aspect of his career. As clubs compete to sign the best talent, agents are able to broker deals between clubs or between players and clubs. Fluidity in the European transfer market has helped to create the opportunity for knowledgeable middlemen to occupy the gap between these stakeholders, with well networked agents able to build up trust between the parties involved. Social networks are pivotal in the distribution of information and control, and as a corollary of that, in the allocation of resources within markets (Burt, 1992). In order to trade efficiently, complete information on all goods and services, sellers, buyers and prices is necessary. However, the diffusion of information occurs over time and individuals that are informed earlier, or more broadly, have an advantage (Burt, 2003). Agents through their clients and contacts are able to bridge connections to other groups and therefore access more complete information quickly, as well as being able to bring together otherwise disconnected individuals, thus giving them a say in whose interests are served when those contacts engage. The broker benefits by separating or arbitraging between two parties (Burt, 1992: 30–34).

According to the EU-commissioned study on sports agents:

> Sports agents act, first and foremost, as intermediaries between sportspersons and sports clubs/organisers of sports events with a view to employing or hiring an athlete or sportsperson . . . Finding a job placement for a sportsperson is the central and specific role of sports agents.
> (KEA, CDES and EOSA, 2009: 2)

This can take the form of introducing the capabilities or legal availability of a player to a club he was not previously known to, or, when interest in a player is known, by ensuring basic terms are agreeable before formal discussions take place. While FIFA transfer regulations state that (Case 24.1) before approaching a player, clubs must obtain permission to speak to him from the club holding his registration, in reality, clubs first approach the player's agent to ascertain whether the player would be interested in a transfer and the level of remuneration that would be expected before opening formal talks. This practice is commonly known as 'tapping up'. A number of clubs have engaged in such practices in recent years, but perhaps the most high-profile case relates to the transfer of Ashley Cole from Arsenal to Chelsea (Case 24.2). By acting as a gatekeeper the middleman can mediate his client's contact with third parties and is therefore able to leverage the value of the information and network he has. Since obtaining a competitive advantage is of paramount importance to clubs, they are willing to offer handsome rewards to agents who can help them achieve this.

Case 24.1 The transfer process

The transfer of players between clubs belonging to the same association is governed by regulations issued by the association concerned (the FA in England), which must be approved by FIFA. The transfer of a player between clubs in two different associations is governed by FIFA.

In accordance with these rules, a club intending to conclude a contract with a professional player must first inform the club holding the player's registration before entering into negotiations with the player or his agent.

The club has the right to reject or accept any bid and this forms the basis of negotiation between the two clubs. The negotiation process continues until the two clubs agree to a fee.

Once there is mutual agreement regarding the early termination of a player's contract, the player and his authorised agent can enter into negotiations with the prospective club. A professional player whose contract with his present club has expired or is due to expire within six months is free to conclude a contract with another club.

In reality, a club may decide they want to sell a player and then either contact other clubs to see if they would be interested, or more likely engage an agent to find a buyer on their behalf. If the agent approaches his player's club and they decide that it is in the best interests of the player to leave, the player can be given permission to speak to other clubs and the selling club informs the agent of the specific fee they wish to achieve to allow the player to leave.

Even though a fee has been agreed between two clubs, it is no guarantee that a transfer will be concluded. It is the agent's job to agree contractual terms on behalf of the player. If more than one club has agreed a fee for the player with the selling club then the player has to choose between them.

Once a transfer is agreed by all parties a number of documents must be lodged with the FA including the transfer forms, financial agreement between the two clubs, player's registration, player's contract and bonus scheme. An agent may only be remunerated by one party. This is usually a fee negotiated with the buying club. Any fee owed to an agent must also be logged in the documents sent to the FA and Premier League or Football League.

The system of transfer windows was enacted in 2002, restricting the new registration of players to two annual periods fixed by the relevant association. As an exception to this rule, a professional whose contract has expired prior to the end of a registration period may be registered outside of that time frame.

Sources: The FA Rules of the Association (2009); FIFA Regulations for Transfers (2007).

Discussion questions

1 Why does the potential buying club have to contact the club holding the player's registration before making contact with the player?

2 What are the benefits and disadvantages of transfer windows?

Case 24.2 The Ashley Cole tapping-up saga

In 2005 record fines were issued to Chelsea, its manager Jose Mourinho and player Ashley Cole after the Premier League found them guilty of being involved in tapping up.

The case centred around the planning of Cole's transfer from Arsenal to Chelsea. Cole and his agent Jonathan Barnett met Mourinho, Chelsea Chief Executive Peter Kenyon and agent Pini Zahavi, who is said to have been there to help broker a transfer deal, while Cole was an Arsenal player, without the prior knowledge of his club. Cole signed a one-year extension to his contract with Arsenal, but just a year later departed from the club for Chelsea.

The independent commission established by the Premier League to investigate the incident found Chelsea to have acted in breach of rule K3, which prohibits a club from making an approach to a contracted player without first obtaining permission from the club to which he is under contract. Chelsea was fined £300,000 and given a suspended three-point deduction.

Mourinho was found to be in breach of rule Q, governing managers' conduct, and was fined £200,000, which was later reduced to £75,000.

Cole was found to be in breach of rule K5, which prevents a contracted player from making any approach to a club with a view to negotiating a contract without obtaining the prior written consent of the club to which he is under contract. The player was fined £100,000, reduced on appeal to £75,000.

While the Premier League had no powers to punish either Barnett or Zahavi, the FA did find Barnett guilty of breaching the Code of Professional Conduct to the FIFA Players' Agents Regulations which requires agents to respect the rights of a third party (Arsenal FC) and Premier League Rule E1(e) by procuring the breach of FAPL Rule K5 (regarding illegal approaches) by Ashley Cole. He was fined £100,000 and had his agents' licence suspended for 18 months, with the second nine months suspended.

Neither the FA nor the Premier League had any jurisdiction over Zahavi, but referred the matter to FIFA, which has jurisdiction as Zahavi is an Israel-registered agent. At the time Cole was an Arsenal player, and the meeting constituted a breach of Article 22 of the FIFA player agents' regulations.

However, as of December 2010, FIFA's investigation was still ongoing.

Sources: 'How the Ashley Cole drama unfolded', 26 September 2006, www.dailymail. co.uk/sport/football/article-336649/How-Ashley-Cole-drama-unfolded.html#ixzz 18yU4a6iW; 'Barnett Decision', FA, 26 September 2006, www.thefa.com/TheFA/ Disciplinary/NewsAndFeatures/2006/BarnettDecision; 'Fifa Closing in on Zahavi', 29 September 2006, www.telegraph.co.uk/sport/football/2346819/Fifa-closing-in-on-Zahavi.html; 'Cole tapping-up evidence revealed', 4 June 2005, news.bbc.co.uk/ sport1/hi/football/eng_prem/4608527.stm

Discussion questions

3 Should restricting a player from speaking to other potential employers be classed as a restraint of trade?

4 Why didn't the FA pursue a case against Pini Zahavi? And how has this situation changed?

The 'middleman' position of an agent is thought to have emerged in the 1970s and 1980s as wealthy football clubs in Italy sought to recruit talent from Eastern Europe, employing intermediaries to overcome the political and legal barriers to facilitate such transfers (Holt et al., 2006: 4). This role was augmented following the Bosman ruling, after which the removal of quota restrictions on the number of foreign players, combined with the expansion of the EU, increased the size of the pool of talent available for clubs to engage – in turn creating a role for agents in providing localised expert information and coordination. Though clubs now have more opportunity to sign top class players, not all have sufficient resources to engage a global scouting network to be able to exploit it. To fill this gap, agents often perform quasi-scouting roles for clubs. The practical implications of this vary according to the level of club the agent works with and the reputation of the agent.

Agents with a good track record of discovering new players are able to develop close relationships with specific clubs that trust their judgement. Some agents have their own network of 'informants' who, on a salaried or commission basis, identify the best young players in a locality on the agent's behalf. Poli (2010) identifies the role of agents in establishing transnational scouting networks in which tournaments are arranged by agents and their associates specifically to this end. Once a player has been identified and introduced to a club, the club will then either offer him a trial or, if suitably impressed with his playing skills, offer him a contract. While clubs will be aware of established players, for those players trying to break into the market it is important to have a well-connected agent to attract the attention of an elite club. This semi-closed network can create a barrier to entry for new agents joining the market.

Agents may also act on behalf of either the buying or selling club in negotiation of a transfer fee. While clubs could negotiate between themselves, they often choose to employ an intermediary to do this on their behalf. This could be to overcome language barriers, or simply because the club's personnel feel that the agent would be better equipped to negotiate the deal. The propensity for agents to represent both clubs and players has led to concern that conflicts of interest could emerge.

Contract negotiation

Once a transfer has been agreed in principle, representing the player in contractual negotiations is central to the agent's role. In concluding a legally binding agreement it is important for a player to take professional advice with respect to employment terms and conditions as well as rights protection. Without specialist representation a general lack of business experience on the part of the player would afford the club an enviable position in the bargaining process. An agent should be able to balance discussions in order to add value to the player's contract by negotiating higher wages as well as bonuses and additional benefits above that which his client would have achieved. Yet it may also be part of the agent's role to make sure that the player is realistic about the level of remuneration he can expect. To achieve optimal outcomes the agent must understand the player's value and his career trajectory, and assess the options of the player in order to make informed decisions. While the player would be expected to have an input in the decision-making process, he may not be directly involved in negotiations until the final stages.

In addition to the need for specialist advice, in many cases the hierarchical structure of sports clubs is such that a player would not necessarily want to negotiate with the manager directly and risk upsetting him. In this case the agent can operate as a buffer providing a useful demarcation between the player on the pitch performing the instructions of the manager and the player off the pitch being able to bargain with the club.

Ancillary/concierge services

The general perception that an agent simply 'does your contract' is clearly no longer the case. With high levels of expenditure on players, there comes an expectation of high-quality play on the pitch which then translates to winning games and by extension enables clubs to generate increased revenues. Part of the agent's role therefore is to ensure that his client is free to concentrate his attention on playing as well as possible. Agents are thus often engaged in carrying out ancillary tasks related to the player's personal life. Players are known to call upon their agents to perform any number of tasks including cooking and cleaning, ensuring their insurance is adequate and up to date, advising them in terms of investment and financial planning, providing advice on close family issues, finding doctors, homes and schools where needed and relevant for the player and his family, as well as coordinating fan mail and press statements. This concierge role has developed as some players have made the transition from being athletes to superstars. While some clubs have developed player liaison departments to address some of these needs, agents still tend to be the first port of call for many players.

Agents of younger players and those at lower levels may pay for equipment on the player's behalf in the hope that an initial investment will be recouped if the player earns a large contract in future. While this level of intervention is acceptable, there have been concerns raised over the issue of agents investing in the early career of a player in exchange for a share in his future transfer rights. A popular practice in South America, following a series of cases FIFA has moved to specifically forbid private investors from 'owning any interest in any transfer compensation or future transfer value of a player' (FIFA, 2008: Art. 29 Player agents Regs).

Commercial advice

Players at all levels can benefit from having a representative negotiate transfers on their behalf, but star players have additional needs concerning commercial contracts. For some, players, their commercial and endorsement deals are more lucrative than their core playing contract. In an increasingly globalised world where the sports, entertainment and media industries have become blurred, the reach of sport has been recognised by, and emerged as a strategic focus for many international corporations. With this, the appeal of associating with elite athletes has developed, enabling companies to market their products to a broad base of potential customers (Mason and Duquette, 2005). These changes in market conditions over the past 15 years have created another role for agents in sourcing ever more lucrative endorsement deals and ensuring that the agreements a player enters into are commensurate with his image and long-term goals. In an increasingly commercialised climate large sums of money are at stake and footballers often do not have the experience or perhaps the time or inclination to satisfactorily assess their best options. Professional advice is therefore imperative.

Player sales

In the aftermath of the Bosman ruling, offering longer contracts to players was seen by clubs as a way to reduce the risk of a player leaving on a free transfer and therefore increase stability. However, in practice this proved too much of a burden for many clubs. Following the Premier League broadcasting contract with BSkyB, the Football League was promised £315 million over three years from rival subscription channel ITV Digital, affording Football League clubs the opportunity to close the revenue gap between themselves and the Premier League. Unfortunately, these rights were overvalued and ITV Digital went into administration in 2002 leaving the clubs with a £178 million shortfall. With limited flexibility in contracts, and having committed huge sums of money to pay players over long periods of time, clubs struggled to maintain their financial obligations. This created another opportunity for agents, who were able to use their network to quickly find buyers for high-earning players. Although clubs could do this themselves, agents with the specialist contacts necessary to operate quickly and efficiently are often given a mandate by clubs to facilitate transfers for players they wish to move on.

Agent typologies

In response to the various roles an agent can play, a number of distinct types have emerged. Magee (2002) identifies four types of agent operating in English football today. The traditional solo agent is identified by Magee as the most popular type. Present since the 1960s, the 'solo agent' tends to be licensed and works alone, dealing mainly with the negotiation of transfers and contracts. A second type of representative, the 'Solicitor/legal adviser', may or may not be licensed and provides a legal service. 'The sports agency' is described as being licensed and able to provide a number of additional services beyond contract negotiation such as brokering commercial deals; and finally the 'promotions agency', which is not normally licensed by FIFA, provides 'career management and promotion opportunities' as opposed to contract negotiation (Magee, 2002: 231).

Whereas Magee distinguishes between different company formations and the services they offer, Poli (2010) describes all agents as performing multiple roles. Full service agencies (FSAs) emerged in the late 1990s and 2000s through a wave of horizontal and vertical integrations where respected solo agents (usually with high-profile clients) were bought out by media conglomerates and other businesses in order for them to gain a foothold in the sports industry. Horizontal integration of smaller agencies also occurred where agents banded together, formally or informally, to capitalise on the network benefits of having a wider reach. FSAs tend to have access to a broader range of services for their clients than a solo agent might. They also gain power by virtue of the players they represent, benefiting from the enhanced awareness which can follow from representing a large number of quality players. The trend of consolidation in the industry has effectively meant that players can get all the services they require in one contact. This makes it very difficult for new individuals or companies to enter the market.

According to Poli (2010) agencies are categorised according to their geographic coverage and the range of professional services they provide, with a distinction made between global or regional companies, and generalists or specialists. The generalists have a wide scope and clientele representing people from across the entertainment industry, whilst the specialists focus purely on the representation of athletes. In addition to scope, location is also important, with companies classified according to where their main client base is located. Regionalists would operate predominantly from offices in one location whereas globalists would have offices internationally. Regional generalists therefore would function within national boundaries or between neighbouring countries but cover a range of services 'from personal management to promotion, public relations, sponsorship, endorsement and fundraising' (Poli, 2010: 211), and represent a range of entertainers, whereas regional specialists perform the same role and have the same geographic coverage but focus their attention on representing athletes, usually footballers.

Empirical data from a sample of 900 players suggests that elements of the typologies identified by Poli (2010) and Magee (2002) apply to representatives active in the English football market. However, at an operational level clubs suggest that there are few differences between alternative types of representative. The main variations relate to the way in which agents are remunerated and the bargaining power they have, which can be determined by the quality of player represented. However, for agents themselves, market structure is very influential in whether or not they succeed as an agent.

The 431 agents currently registered with the English FA do not share the work evenly, with some registered agents not representing any clients, and not all players employing an agent. Approximately 70 per cent of agents represent only one player. Though in terms of numbers there are more solo agents than any other type, FSAs undertake the majority of the business (72 per cent overall), with the top four agencies together representing approximately 64 per cent of the players across the four leagues. An increasing number of former players work with licensed agents to recruit players. Business advisers dealing with all aspects of a player's career apart from his contract negotiation, thus negating the need for a licence, are also popular, with contracts being negotiated by a solicitor or a licensed agent within their network. With ever more complex contracts in place and increasingly negative press surrounding some of the fees agents claim, there has been an upsurge in the number of players employing a solicitor to act on their behalf. This has led to some solicitors' firms developing their own agency arm, which again often involves former players working on client recruitment and providing basic services, with licensed agents and authorised solicitors brokering transfers and negotiating playing and commercial agreements.

 ## Problems

Inherent in the football industry is a close interplay of relations between various stakeholders. Typically in situations of this type problems can emerge, which are often related to the principal–agent dyad. The principal–agent relationship exists 'whenever one party, the principal, hires a second party, the agent, to perform some task on the first party's behalf' (Katz and Rosen, 1998: 220). The principal (player) wishes to induce the agent (agent) to take some form of action which is costly to the agent. Whilst the action taken by the agent may not be visible to the principal, an outcome that is at least partly determined by the actions of the agent is observable (Varian, 1992: 441). Information asymmetries arise since the principal cannot fully observe the actions of the agent, the agent therefore has more information regarding his or her performance and effort levels than the principal. If the agent chooses to act in their own self-interest rather than in the interest of the principal then sub-optimal outcomes can occur, reducing the utility of the principal (Mas-Collel et al., 1995). Common forms of self-interested behaviour are adverse selection, moral hazard (Varian, 1992; Mas-Colell et al., 1995) and ignorance (Lewis and Sappington, 1993). Since agents know more about their own behaviour and effort levels the informational asymmetry favours the agent, who can exploit this asymmetry by acting in self-interest when performing tasks set by the principal (Baker, 1992).

In the case of a footballer and his agent the moral hazard problem could occur due to the player's inability to observe how hard his agent is working. The agent's coming to possess superior knowledge about the player's opportunities, on the other hand, is an example of hidden information. The divergent interests of the player and agent begin with the situation where the player wishes to keep the cost of the job as low as possible, whereas the agent wishes to maximise their own income. The problem is exacerbated since the player has imperfect knowledge of the agent's activities and effort level, and also lacks information about the level of wages and contractual terms offered to players of a comparable standard to himself, whereas the agent will know the contractual terms and conditions of other players he represents. Additionally, the player is likely to be unaware of the effort the agent has made to find suitable alternative clubs or whether the agent has been offered any inducements by clubs to place the player with them (Holt et al., 2006: 16). A number of issues have arisen in which it has been suggested that clubs have paid agents to guarantee that a certain player will sign with them (Bower, 2003).

Holt et al. (2006) suggest the 'Prisoner's Dilemma' as a way of considering the decisions made by teams in deciding whether or not to pay an agent in a transfer deal. The Prisoner's Dilemma is an example of a simple game typically employed by economists to analyse the behaviour of firms in a cartel in which simultaneous decision making between two separate parties occurs. Individual actors in the game will be tempted to pursue their own interests, which may lead to a sub-optimal outcome (Downward and Dawson, 2000). The original game assumes two suspects have been arrested (A and B) on suspicion of committing a major crime and they are not permitted to communicate. In the absence of sufficient evidence, the police are unable to convict either of the suspects for the major crime; however, the police explain to the prisoners that if neither confesses to the major crime they will both be sentenced to one month in jail for a minor offence. If both confess, they will receive 12-month sentences, while if one confesses and implicates the other, who remains silent, the former will be released, while the latter will be sentenced to 12 months for the crime plus an additional three months for obstructing the investigation. The payoff matrix outlining these outcomes is shown in Figure 24.1.

If A confesses, B also prefers to confess and serve 12 months instead of the 15-month sentence he would receive if he did not confess. If A remains silent, then B prefers to confess and be released instead of serving one month. Each understands that the returns based on confession for both themselves and the other suspect outweigh those of silence; therefore the dominant strategy is to confess, irrespective of the actions of the other prisoner. Therefore both confess and are sentenced to 12 months, whereas if both had remained

Prisoner A

Prisoner B		Confess	Don't confess
	Confess	12, 12	15, 0
	Don't confess	0, 15	1, 1

Figure 24.1 The Prisoner's Dilemma

silent then both would have served only one month. Under a one-off game of this sort, rational behaviour suggests the outcome is always sub-optimal (Varian, 1992).

In the context of football agents, Holt et al. (2006) refer to the gatekeeping position of agents and apply the above reasoning to suggest that two football clubs must decide whether to pay an agent to secure the signature of a certain player. Both clubs would be better off refusing to pay the agent, but they also know that if they refuse, but the other team pays, then they will be at a disadvantage and the player will sign for the other club. In accordance with the Prisoner's Dilemma, the dominant solution is sub-optimal for the clubs and 'money is lost to the game' (Holt et al., 2006: 12). The situation in this case is further complicated by asymmetric information as the player may be signed by the club willing to pay the agent, but the player's remuneration or contract terms may be reduced commensurate with the sum expended by the club on the agent's fees.

Conflicts of interest are inherent in the industry, with the dominance of a small number of powerful agents complicating issues further, as one agency may represent a large number of players and the manager at a particular club. Though agents contractually have a duty to act in the best interest of their clients, this becomes problematical when two similar players vying for the same move are represented by the same agent. It is also known that in some cases 'star' players can be used as leverage to secure transfers for less talented players represented by the same agent. Further, the increasingly lucrative potential earnings of players and agents have attracted many individuals to the profession, yet there is concern that some are not qualified to take on such a role, with the absence of stringent qualifications for agents meaning that some players are badly advised (Mason and Slack, 2001, 2003).

Agency theorists suggest that principals can reduce the likelihood of opportunistic behaviour occurring either by introducing some form of monitoring of the actions of the agent or by contracting on the basis of the outcome of the agent's behaviour (Eisenhardt, 1989). A performance-based compensation schedule should act as a deterrent to opportunistic behaviour on the part of the agent by allying the reward of the agent to that of the principal, thus aligning the interests of both parties (Eisenhardt, 1989). However, there is discussion as to the efficacy of this system in the case of sports agents in the US (Mason and Slack, 2001, 2003; Karcher, 2006; Mason and Duquette, 2005).

Under the principal–agent relationship each party is expected to be guided by his or her own self-interest. Contracts should therefore be defined so as to maximise the effort expended by the agent in the light of the inherent uncertainties involved. At the outset of the development of the agents industry there was great uncertainty on the part of players as to their likely career path and also whether hiring an agent would be beneficial to them. Under these circumstances the compensation-based payment scheme was probably an effective method (Mason and Slack, 2001). However, as the industry has developed and it has become more apparent what services the agent will be able to provide, a behaviour-based system would potentially be a better prospect for the principal (Eisenhardt, 1989). This is more closely linked to the way in which solicitors are remunerated. While commission arrangements are employed appropriately in many industries, once an agent represents an established player he is assured substantial rewards and there is no longer any risk of non-recovery of fees (Karcher, 2006: 745). Acknowledging some of these issues, a licensing system was introduced by FIFA in an attempt to regulate the industry.

 ## Regulation

Following concerns about the operation of the transfer market and the potential for large sums of money to leave the game, FIFA introduced a set of regulations relating to the control of football agents in 1994. The aim was to regulate the 'occupation of players' agents who arrange transfers between and within national associations' (Fifa.com). As the global governing body, FIFA set the guideline regulations which the national associations then use to inform their own rules relating to domestic transfers (Holt et al., 2006). Following high-profile cases relating to agents and an investigation by the EC Competition Commissioner, FIFA introduced a new set of more stringent regulations on 1 April 2002. The current set of regulations coming into force on 1 January 2008. FIFA require that National Associations have regulations governing the conduct and use of the services of agents and to become an agent an individual must obtain a licence issued by the national association of the country in which they reside and take out professional insurance. Clubs and players are permitted to work only with licensed agents, though certain parties, including solicitors who are regulated by the Law Society, are granted exemption from sitting the exams; however, in England they must be authorised by the English FA to be able to take part in domestic transfer negotiations. When representing a player, agents must sign a code of professional conduct and use a standard representation contract. A written contract is undertaken between the player and agent which must not exceed two years in duration and which stipulates the remuneration of the agent. The scope of the regulations governs the occupation of agents involved in transfers only and does not cover other contractual agreements between the player and agent to provide ancillary services, such as commercial or financial advice (Dickson et al., 2006).

In 2007 the English FA sought to increase transparency regarding the way agents operate by introducing a new set of rules in which agents were prohibited from acting for more than one party in a transfer (dual representation). Case law adopted following their intro-duction supports this position, with the decision in Imageview[5] outlining that any lack of transparency in a player's transfer in terms of who the agent was receiving commission from enables the courts to render void the player–agent agreement and also order that any

---

[5] *Imageview Management Ltd v Jack* [2009] EWCA Civ 63.

fees from the club–agent agreement should be forfeited. However 'dual representation' represented the reality of conducting business as an agent and there was concern from the industry that the new regulations instead of increasing transparency would simply drive the practice underground. Following protracted negotiations the introduction of the revised FA Football agents' Regulations on 4 July 2009 has allowed the practice of 'dual representation' to exist once more. This is a clear demonstration of the shift from government to governance in which stakeholders are able to lobby and influence decision making according to their own agenda. In exchange for the rule change, Premier League clubs have agreed to publish the sums they spend on agents in transfers.

All stakeholders should comply with regulations set by FIFA and the relevant domestic football association; however, cultural differences and variation in the interpretation and application of the regulations have led to an arena in which agents can easily exploit weaknesses in regulatory systems to assume a powerful position in relation to both clubs and players. In this way the licensing system falls short of its intentions (Magee, 2002: 235; Holt et al., 2006; Fynn and Guest, 1994). Governing bodies have wide-ranging powers to punish any breach of the regulations, from docking points from clubs to suspending an agent's licence, with sanctions imposed according to the severity of the offence (Case 24.2). However, there is concern that the authorities do too little to enforce the regulations and that the potential sanctions which could be imposed following a breach are not stringent enough to act as a deterrent to opportunistic or illegal behaviour (Mason and Slack, 2001; Karcher, 2006). Further, parties involved in the transfer process generally have no incentive to report misconduct (Karcher, 2006).

The 2009 FIFA Congress declared its support for an 'in-depth reform of the player's agents system through a new approach based on the concept of intermediaries' (quoted by the FA, www.thefa.com/TheFA/RulesandRegulations/Agents) Given the failure of the current system to effectively control the market, FIFA is considering withdrawing from its role in regulating agents. While intermediaries are estimated to be involved in over 90 per cent of transfers, only around 30 per cent of international transfers involve a registered agent (Valke, 2009). From October 2011 the focus of regulation is expected to shift from agents to players and clubs, in essence regulating transfer activity more closely instead of trying to regulate access to transfer involvement. Under such a system, players and clubs would have free choice of who they use to represent them, thus annulling the licensing system, but would be forced to comply with certain criteria in transfer dealings. Fifa has also expressed concerns over the level of remuneration agents receive, stating that there is 'no relationship between the transfer fee paid by clubs and the commission paid by an intermediary' and also confusion over whether an intermediary represents a player or club and who is responsible for their fee. As part of the reforms Fifa is expected to set a maximum limit on commissions. With final decisions set to be made it remains to be seen what the impact of these changes will be.

 ## Conclusion

The position of agents has developed in response to structural and economic changes in both the product and labour markets. As labour market restrictions have been removed, players have gradually been able to take control over their own careers. Relatively unskilled in terms of business and negotiation, and unable to recognise and exploit the playing and commercial opportunities arising from the expanded international market, players employed agents to deal with their business affairs and guide their career trajectory. The closed nature of the industry has enabled well-connected agents to establish themselves in a key role transferring knowledge to their clients, affording them more power in negotiations.

The role an agent plays varies greatly according to the player being represented. For elite players who essentially have monopolistic qualities, the Bosman ruling has been a panacea in enabling them to extrapolate greater sums of money in terms of their wages and signing on fees, thus causing their overall package to be more in line with their marginal revenue product. Players seen as irreplaceable have been able to make demands of clubs who have little choice but to meet those demands or lose the player. However, players in lower leagues tend to have much less bargaining power in negotiations as they face a competitive labour market in which clubs can choose between large numbers of equally talented players. Under both circumstances an agent should be able to assist the negotiation process. As well as dealing with the contractual side of their career, for some high-profile players it is likely that an adviser will also be responsible for commercial deals.

Complexities in the market have led to a number of problems with concern that the presence of intermediaries is causing money to be lost to the game. Consequently, governing bodies have attempted to regulate the behaviour of intermediaries in transfers. However, the rules which are in place have done little to address the problems inherent in the market. Successive incidences have meant that a complicated regulatory framework has developed, with reactionary measures taken each time a breach in the rules is identified. This situation has been exacerbated by the lack of uniform enforcement across jurisdictions and between member states, with little incentive for anyone to report wrongdoing. Though governing bodies have acknowledged a number of problems, there has so far been a lack of workable solutions to various issues such as agents taking inducements, and competition for players as well as wider societal issues related to money laundering and child abandonment. These problems are also deserving of more academic attention.

Tradeoffs have been made demonstrating the current negotiated system of governance as opposed to top-down government. This has made any regulatory system difficult to enforce and the suggestions that FIFA seeks to distance itself from regulating agents to focus on controlling the actions of its member clubs and players is not a surprise. The direction of governance will be under close scrutiny over the coming months.

Discussion questions

5 Was the Bosman ruling beneficial for all players? And what impact does this have on agents?

6 Can the agents industry ever be effectively regulated?

7 Why wouldn't clubs simply deal with each other when arranging a transfer?

Keywords

Adverse selection; agent; Bosman; gatekeeper; information asymmetry; marginal revenue product; moral hazard; principal; Prisoner's Dilemma; retain and transfer system; scout.

Guided reading

The European Union Report on Sports Agents provides coverage of the activities of agents in the main European sports. It is available online at http://ec.europa.eu/sport/library/doc/f_studies/study_on_sports_agents_executive%20summary.pdf

Holt et al. (2006) consider the regulatory aspects of football agents in Europe, presenting 23 recommendations to reform the industry.

The Football League produce an annual report on agents fees which details the spending of each club in the previous 12 month period. It is available through the Football League website www.football-league.co.uk/staticFiles/7e/54/0,,10794~152702,00.pdf

Further detail on the operation of the transfer market can be found in *The Economics of Football* by Dobson and Goddard (2001).

The shift from direct control or government of sport, to a negotiated governance of sport approach is discussed in Henry and Lee (2004).

An accessible explanation of the principal–agent model is given in Varian (1992).

Recommended websites

www.thefa.com
www.fifa.com
www.uefa.com
www.eurofootballagents.com

References

Baker, G.P. (1992) 'Incentive contracts and performance measurement', *Journal of Political Economy*, 100, 598–614.

Bower, T. (2003) *Broken Dreams: Vanity, Greed and the Souring of British Football*, London: Simon & Schuster.

Burt, R.S. (1992) *Structural Holes*, Cambridge, MA: Harvard University Press.

Burt, R. (2003) 'The social capital of structural holes', in M.F. Guillen, R. Collins, P. England and M. Meyer (eds), *The New Economic Sociology: Developments in an Emerging Field*, New York: Russell Sage Foundation, 148–89.

Deloitte (various years) *Annual Review of Football Finance*, Manchester: Deloitte.

Dickson, R., Fontannaz, C., Heinrichs, A. and Groeneveld, M. (2006) 'Relationships between Athletes and Agents', in F. Manfredi (ed.), *Football and its Future*, Milan: Egea, 173–214.

Dobson, S. and Goddard, J. (2001) *The Economics of Football*, Cambridge: Cambridge University Press.

Downward, P. and Dawson, A. (2000) *The Economics of Professional Team Sports*, London: Routledge.

Eisenhardt, K. (1989) 'Building theories from case study research', *Academy of Management Review*, 14 (4), 532–50.

Feess, E. and Muehlheusser, G. (2003) 'Transfer fee regulations in European football', *European Economic Review*, 47 (4), 139–54.

FIFA (1936) Berlin Congress, August 1936, records displayed in the Fifa collection, National Football Museum, Preston, England.

FIFA (2008) *Players' Agent Regulations*, www.fifa.com/mm/document/affederation/administration/51/55/18/players_agents_regulations_2008.pdf

Fifa.com, 2010 Player's Agent List, www.fifa.com/aboutfifa/federation/administration/playersagents/list.html

Football League (2009) *Agents' Fees Report*, www.football-league.co.uk/staticFiles/7e/54/0,,10794~ 152702,00.pdf

Fynn, A. and Guest, L. (1994) *Out of Time: Why Football Isn't Working*, London: Simon & Schuster.

Gannon, J., Evans, K. and Goddard, J. (2006) 'The stock market effects of the sale of live broadcasting rights for English premiership football: an event study', *Journal of Sports Economics*, 7 (2), 168–86.

Henry, I. and Lee, P.C. (2004) 'Governance and ethics in sport', in J. Beech, and S. Chadwick (eds), *The Business of Sport Management*, Harlow: Pearson Education.

Holt, M., Michie, J. and Oughton, C. (2006) *The Role and Regulation of Agents In Football*, London: The Sport Nexus.

Joyce, K. (1997) 'The ethics and dynamics of negotiating a professional sports contract', *Texas Entertainment and Sports Law Journal*, 6 (2), 7–11.

Karcher, R. (2006) 'Solving problems in the player representation business: unions should be the "exclusive" representatives of the players', *Willamette Law Review*, 42, 738–74.

Katz, M. and Rosen, H. (1998) *Microeconomics*, 3rd edn, Boston: McGraw Hill.

KEA, CDES and EOSE (2009) Study on sports agents in the European Union: A study Commissioned by the European Commission (Directorate-General for Education and Culture), http://ec.europa.eu/ sport/library/doc/f_studies/study_on_sports_agents_in_the_EU.pdf

Lewis, T. and Sappington, D. (1993) 'Ignorance in agency problems', *Journal of Economic Theory*, 61 (1), 169–83.

Lonsdale, C. (2004) 'Player power: capturing value in the English football supply network', *Supply Chain Management: An International Journal*, 9 (5), 383–91.

Magee, J. (2002) 'Shifting balances of power in the new football economy', in J. Sugden and A. Tomlinson (eds), *Power Games: A Critical Sociology of Sport*, Abingdon: Routledge, 216–39.

Magee, J. (2006) 'When is a contract more than a contract? Professional football contracts and the pendulum of power', *Entertainment and Sports Law Journal*, 1 (October).

Mas-Colell, A., Whinston, M.D. and Green, J.R. (1995) *Microeconomic Theory*, New York: Oxford University Press.

Mason, D.S. and Slack, T. (2001) 'Industry factors and the changing dynamics of the player–agent relationship in professional ice hockey', *Sport Management Review*, 4 (2), 165–91.

Mason, D.S. and Slack, T. (2003) 'Understanding, principal–agent relationships: evidence from professional hockey', *Journal of Sport Management*, 17 (1), 37–61.

Mason, D.S. and Duquette, G.H. (2005) 'Globalisation and the evolving player–agent relationship in professional sport', *International Journal of Sport Management and Marketing*, 1 (1–2), 93–109.

Morrow, S. (1999) *The New Business of Football: Accountability and Finance in Football*, London: Macmillan Press.

Poli, R. (2010) 'Agents and Intermediaries', in S. Hamel and S. Chadwick, *Managing Football: An International Perspective*, Butterworth/Heinemann.

Premier League (2009) Premier League statement on fees paid to agents, www.premierleague.com/ page/Headlines/0,,12306~2234236,00.html

Roderick, M. (2001) 'The role of agents in professional football', *Singer & Friedlander Football Review: 2000–01 Season*.

Russell, D. (1997) *Football and the English*, Preston: Carnegie.

Taylor, M. (2006) *The Leaguers: The Making of Professional Football in England: 1900–1939* Liverpool: Liverpool University Press.

Valke, J. (2009) FIFA Congress Address, Nassau.

Varian, H.R. (1992) *Microeconomic Analysis*, New York: Norton.

Whannel G. (2004) *Sport and the Media*, in J. Coakley and E. Dunning (eds), *Handbook of Sports Studies*, London: Sage.

Section

D

Conclusions

In this final section of the book, the editors consider how to forecast future trends and developments in sport, and provide an assessment of some of the major trends and developments we might expect in the future.

25

The future for sport management

Simon Chadwick and John Beech, Coventry Business School

Prediction is very difficult, especially if it's about the future.
(attributed to Niels Bohr, Danish physicist)

My interest is in the future because I am going to spend the rest of my life there.
(attributed to Charles F. Kettering, American engineer)

Learning outcomes

Upon completion of this chapter the reader should be able to:

- explain the nature of a variety of techniques sports managers can use to predict the future;
- identify sources of information available to sport managers seeking to predict the future;
- identify emerging trends and challenges facing sport managers;
- suggest how sport managers might address these trends and challenges;
- highlight opportunities for the development of managerial practice and academic research as a result of this book.

 ## Overview

The chapter begins by briefly highlighting how sport has developed in recent years. This sets the scene for an examination of the techniques that can be used to predict the future for sport management and the sources of information which enable this process. Drawing from a number of expert views, options for promoting the uncertainty of outcome in a variety of sports are then considered. Beyond this, specific potential developments are considered in each of the five areas covered by this book: the distinctive nature of sport marketing, meeting the needs and wants of sport markets, communicating with the sport market, getting sport products to the market and moving sport marketing forwards.

 ## Introduction

If one reflects upon the history of any sport, in a majority of cases the first game will have been played as a form of leisure pursuit. Inevitably the sport would then have developed and become bound up in the social, political and cultural structures of its country of origin. Consider soccer in England, cycling in France or Australian Rules football and one gets the picture of how these sports have become so intertwined with the historical development of these countries. Throughout the process of codification, professionalisation and commercialisation (see Chapter 1), performers and elite athletes have been at the heart of sport – and rightly so. Without these highly skilled individuals and teams, sport would still be nothing more than a leisure pursuit. But it is now something much more than that. Sport is now variously seen as one of a number of leisure alternatives, a consumer preference, a revenue-generating opportunity – a big business. What happens on the field of play, the pitch or the court is still important, but what happens off it is also becoming increasingly important.

Structuring a league to ensure its attractiveness is now within the domain of the sport manager, yet so too is the sale of replica merchandise, the pricing of tickets and the exploration of new markets. From being highly product focused, sport is now changing by seeking to satisfy the needs and wants of a global, often highly sophisticated, marketplace. The question is: will this trend continue?

 ## Predicting the future

The English economist John Maynard Keynes once said that, in the long run, we are all dead. In this respect, the future is both inevitable and predictable. However, the practice of predicting what might happen in the meantime is rather less precise. The recent dash for a share of the Asian sport market illustrates that what we think might happen and what actually does happen are often two different things. Alternatively, consider the global popularity of soccer; whether in Brazil, England or China, the game is hugely popular. Yet despite several attempts to market the game to an American audience (in the 1970s by buying in stars such as Pele and George Best; in the 1980s by winning the bid to stage the World Cup; in the 1990s by introducing a new league – the MLS; and in the early part of the twenty-first century by signing 'marquee' players like David Beckham), interest remains patchy, largely dictated by ethnic background and class. But there have been notable successes for sport managers. In an attempt to address the decline of a supposedly outdated Anglo-Saxon, colonial sport, strong management led to the introduction of Twenty20 cricket. So successful has been this derivative that some commentators contend that Twenty20 has not only been the saviour of cricket but will also be its future. No one could have predicted this. Equally, no one could have predicted further developments that would emerge: scheduling problems in international cricket; the cricket fatigue being suffered by some fans who, over-exposed to the game, are switching off from it; the threat of terrorism; the staging of Indian Premier League Twenty20 in South Africa; and so forth.

Trying to predict the future would therefore appear to be a difficult task, although choosing not to think about it isn't really an option. Indeed, Glendinning (2001) points out that sport organisations which fail to consider what might happen at a later date are exposed to all kinds of problems. Not least of these are financial difficulty and, potentially, ultimate closure. As such, sport managers need to consider how they can use a range of business forecasting techniques to help them predict the future. Finlay (2000) distinguishes between two types of predictive technique: forecasting and scenarios. The former focuses on the near and middle future, when existing information can be used as the basis for identifying possible trends and developments. The latter is more frequently used when identifying the long-term future, for which there is no information and no precise indication of what might happen.

A forecast can be described as a statement containing projections about the future, and may be undertaken in a number of ways. These include:

1   Time series forecasting, which primarily involves collecting past and current data, and then extrapolating it into the future. For example, if we identify that the match ticket prices at English Premier League football clubs have increased by 2 per cent, 4 per cent and 6 per cent in each of the last three years, we may forecast next year's price rise to be somewhere in the region of 8 per cent. This form of forecasting is often used, primarily because it utilises existing data and is relatively easy to use as a basis for projection. The biggest problem with the approach is the extent to which the past can help to form an accurate picture of the future.

2   Causal forecasting, which takes a similar approach to time series forecasting by using past and current data as the basis for predicting the future. The main difference is that it uses observations about cause and effect relationships between two or more variables to highlight what might happen in the future when a similar relationship is evident. For example, in the past, when advertising expenditure rose by 5 per cent, it may have been observed that the purchase of merchandise rose by 10 per cent. In which case, the sport marketer might conclude that spending more on advertising leads to increased sales of, say, replica team shirts. As with time series forecasting, this approach is useful because it is based upon existing data, but it adds elements of previous experience, particularly in relation to the impact that two variables can have on each other. The two main problems with this are the extent to which a past relationship ever really existed between the variables, and whether a continuing association can be assumed to exist in the future.

3   Judgemental forecasting, which is often used where the data needed for a time series forecast is unavailable, or where there is little experience of a specific set of circumstances. In which case, experts make judgements based upon their knowledge and experiences. For example, the growing interest in American basketball in China is such that we might expect the country to become a major export market for branded NBA merchandise because the Chinese population is both large and fanatical about basketball. This is a good technique for building on the competences and specialised knowledge of many sport managers. Many of them will know 'their' sport well, and

most will have network contacts who keep them informed about important developments. The main concern is that the technique is largely subjective and, as such, predictions may be inaccurate or biased.

Scenarios are pictures of the future developed by those with an understanding of a business or an industry, and are often used to predict the longer term. That is, a time in the future when past or current data may not be applicable. In which case, the precise nature of what might happen to a sport organisation becomes incredibly difficult to pinpoint. Scenarios can therefore be used to develop logical and coherent views of the future, where sport marketers attempt to establish the way things might turn out. In the case of the sponsorship of sport by online gambling companies, whether formally or informally, some sports organisations may be thinking about some of the scenarios should such sponsorships be banned. In countries such as Poland, online gambling sponsorships are already banned; indeed, for clubs like Lech Poznań which had only recently signed a lucrative deal with BetClic, there were significant financial and managerial ramifications. In this respect, scenarios force sport managers to think about the long term. In turn, this enables them to begin thinking about the likely ramifications of their observations. Nevertheless, although scenarios can be methodically and professionally developed, what will happen in five or ten years' time can never really be accurately identified.

There are a number of other techniques that can also be used for generating information about the future, and for making predictions. The former includes brainstorming and Delphi, whilst the latter embraces practices such as model building and impact analysis. Brainstorming is a well-established technique involving groups of creative or insightful people meeting to assess future trends. Extending beyond this rather unstructured practice, Delphi is a more systematic technique where, through an iterative process of discussion, managers reach a consensus about the future. Both techniques are likely to generate qualitative information and may involve observations being made about issues such as the likely future use of the internet by sport managers, or proposals for reforms in sport governance.

This is in contrast to modelling which often uses sophisticated computer software to generate hard quantitative data. Modelling primarily focuses on identifying trends and patterns, and involves making predictions based upon the influence of a number of key variables that are input into the software by managers. For example, when planning a service delivery process, sport managers should be able to generate a computer-based model of the process which can identify the impact of, say, a rise in the cost of producing merchandise, a fall in demand for tickets, maybe even the impact of rain on an event or competition. Impact analysis may also use computer software, but may equally rely on qualitative data analysis.

Sources of information

The techniques noted above are never going to generate a completely accurate picture of the future. Yet the sport manager will still need to ensure that forecasts are as close as possible to what, ultimately, might actually happen. Clearly, the use of a technique such as modelling demands a high level of statistical competence on the part of those using it. Similarly, whilst Delphi is widely used by managers across industry, it nevertheless requires them to have a detailed understanding of their industrial sector. A consideration common to all forecasting techniques, therefore, is the quality of information fed into the forecasting process. Unless the sport manager has accurate information about trends and patterns, they can never convincingly construct a time series analysis. Nor, if they work uninformed, can they expect to make authoritative judgements about the future state of their sport. The way in which information is gathered and analysed is therefore fundamental not only to forecasting, but to a general understanding of how different sports are changing.

One of the most interesting recent developments in predicting the future is known as the Power of Crowds (Surowiecki, 2004). Surowiecki suggests that large groups of ordinary people are actually better than small groups of bright people at identifying what is going to happen in the future, humorously noting that:

> If, years hence, people remember anything about the TV game show 'Who Wants to Be a Millionaire?', they will probably remember the contestants' panicked phone calls to friends and relatives. What people probably won't remember is that every week 'Who Wants to Be a Millionaire?' pitted group intelligence against individual intelligence, and that every week, group intelligence won . . . those random crowds of people with nothing better to do than sit in a TV studio picked the right answer 91 per cent of the time.

Using techniques such as online discussions forums and stock market games, it is thought that crowds are particularly adept at identifying correct answers to questions (for example, whether or not a sport business should open up a new retail outlet in a particular location). What the technique appears to be unable to do is replicate skilled tasks; crowds are therefore much poorer than individuals at, say, implementing and managing a human resource succession plan.

There are two types of information that can be used to assist in the forecasting process: that gathered from primary sources (information collected specifically for the purpose of the forecast) and that from secondary sources (information collected for another reason but which may be used for the purposes of forecasting). Saunders et al. (2003) provide a good overview of the differences between the two sources of information, and discuss some of the advantages associated with each. For a more detailed commentary on the specific sources of information available to sport managers, Scarrott (1999) is an excellent resource. Readers should nevertheless make themselves familiar with the ever growing array of sport business and management information that is available including:

BBC Business of Sport website;

SIM – The Voice of Leadership;

Sport Business;

Sport Business Daily;

Sport Industry Group;

Sports Pro.

The future for sport

More specifically, what of the future for sport? In many ways it is difficult to specifically identify what will happen in the future to individual sports. What is happening to Formula One motor racing at the moment is very different to what is happening to sports such as badminton; and one imagines that the future of these two sports may well be very different. But how different and in what ways is open to debate. This is where the role of formal analysis, prediction and planning comes into play.

It is also worthwhile remembering that, while there may be specific, distinctive forces that will shape and influence sport in the future, there are also what we might call 'mega-trends' or 'macro-forces'. That is, changes so fundamental, so large and so pervasive that they influence everybody and everything in some way. In a 2009 edition of the *Harvard Business Review* (HBR), entitled 'Managing in the New World', a simple question was asked about the future: 'what next'? Here are the changes that HBR identified:

- resources feeling the strain – e.g. competing demands for land and labour;
- globalisation will come under fire;
- trust in business is running out;
- there is a bigger role for government to play;
- management will increasingly be seen as a science;
- shifting consumption patterns will take place;
- the economic rise of Asia will continue;
- existing industries will have to take on new forms and shapes;
- innovation will continue to march on.

In this context, HBR went on to propose that organisations should:

- prepare for slower long-term growth in global consumption: companies that have relied on fundamental market growth, especially for mature products, now need to fight for market share or compete in new categories;
- shift investment to Asia: consumption is clearly growing faster in China and India than in developed markets;
- focus on older consumers: within five years, more than half of all consumer spending in the US will be by consumers over 50, and the proportion of older households is rising in Europe and Japan as well;
- find ways to offer luxuries on a budget: tighter household budgets don't mean lower aspirations – our research shows that stretched consumers in slow-growing economies will still want to feel that they are living the good life.

In 2010, *Forbes* magazine also gave its predictions, this time for the decade to 2020. Amongst the observations the magazine made were:

- 'China hits a great wall': prediction that there will be a market crash in China or that there will be significant state intervention.

- 'Economies go underground': prediction that many people will be working as unregistered, unlicensed and uncounted employees.

- 'Plants will think for us': prediction that plants will think and act like humans.

- 'Consumers will share everything': prediction that people will be using services like eBay to share access to goods and services.

- 'Asia's first water war begins': prediction that China will slowly take control of Asia's water supplies.

- 'India solves its cities': prediction that India will seek to draw billions of pounds worth of foreign investment into the country to create new houses and infrastructure.

- 'Free DNA testing for everyone': predictions that numerous companies will race to provide free DNA testing services.

Alongside these predictions for the future, the views of Robin Mannings, Chief Researcher and Futurologist for BT Innovate, are also worthy of consideration. Mannings has set out his predictions for the long-term challenges that he thinks we are all facing:

- Financial chaos: with current UK debt levels running at 300 per cent of GDP and with other countries also suffering similar debt crises, the economic problems of the last few years are a slow-burner that will continue to cause further, future, possibly even more serious, problems.

- Global pandemics: with bird flu and then swine flu thought to have posed a danger to human health, and with global mobility ever increasing, the threat level of virulent viruses will remain high.

- Extreme weather: weather patterns are changing, the climate is definitely changing, and the climate problems we are therefore likely to face will intensify leading us into a need to radically address both how we consume/produce, and how we respond to the difficulties we will inevitably face.

- Energy demand: a specific issue about the current unsustainable use of sources of energy that one can nevertheless extrapolate from into a more general discussion about future competition for resources and space, allied to the likelihood of major human security worries.

- Demographic shifts: larger populations, ageing populations, more mobile populations, sedentary lifestyles – all will cause major headaches for governments, for the financial system, for health care providers et al.

In the case of the *HBR*, *Forbes* and Mannings, the important question would seem to be: how will each of these mega-issues impact upon sport, how will sport respond and what will sport therefore look like in 50, 25 or even a year's time?

A more dedicated view of the sporting future has been provided by *The Observer* (2010):

- All sport will revolve around the TV viewer.

- China will take gold at rugby.

- Football's old guard will resist technology.

- Test cricket will only be played by four nations.

- Boxing will fight back.
- Twitter will replace the press conference.
- Snooker will die; F1 and skiing on life support.
- NFL takes up a London residency.
- Sportsmen and women will run their own teams.
- Swimming goes slow.

Instead of predicting what will happen to sport in the future, some commentators have actually proposed what should happen in the future (Tables 25.1 and 25.2).

Whether considering the relative merits of *HBR*'s or Mannings' views and their implications for sport, or thinking about the insight provided by those close to sport, we are inevitably left with a simple, yet incredibly complex, question: what next for sport. As the quote from Bohr at the beginning of this chapter states predicting the future is indeed very difficult.

Table 25.1 *The Observer* newspaper's view of the future in sport

Expert	What they said about the future of their sport
Nigel Mansell, former racing driver	'Get rid of driver aids – Technology has taken so much away from the cars and driver aids shouldn't be allowed. I don't even bother to watch races any more'
John McEnroe, former tennis player	'Bring back wooden rackets – The sweet spot is smaller so players need to be more precise. Play let serves: they quicken the pace and add excitement'
Steve Davis, former snooker player	'Make snooker more like bar billiards – I've had enough of watching players clear the table in one visit. Placing a bar billiards-style mushroom between the blue and the pink spots would give snooker that x-factor it lacks'
Barry McGuigan, former boxer	'Same day weigh-ins – Weigh-ins should be put back so fighters can't cheat the scales. At the moment they take place at 2pm the Friday before a fight, which gives boxers more than 24 hours to binge and put weight back on'
Stuart Barnes, former rugby player	'Ban tactical substitutions – When you allow tactical substitutions (and these days it's seven per game) then you are giving too much importance to the coach and not enough to the mental courage required by a player to take him through that pain barrier in the last 20 minutes'
John McCririck, British horse racing commentator	'Ban whips – In 2004, you cannot hit the wife, your kids, or your dog. Yet jockeys hit horses. You cannot justify hurting animals'
David Elleray, former football referee	'Introduce sin bins – I would like to see the sin bin used instead of yellow cards. First, I think it would serve to improve standards of discipline. Second, it makes the system of punishment more just'
Gavin Newsham, golf magazine editor	'Make the hole bigger – Rather than Tiger [Woods]-proof every course in the world, why not throw the game wide open and double the size of the hole, from four and a quarter inches to an almost wok-sized eight and a half?'

Adapted from: *Observer Sport Monthly* (2004)

Table 25.2 The BBC's view of the future in sport

Sport	What analysts said about the future of their sport
Tennis	'Cyclops [the electronic eye] is all very well for helping line judges decide whether a serve is in or not. But it cannot be used once a rally is in progress. And hey – why not get rid of line judges altogether? They don't always get it right [and] they cost money to employ. By underlaying the entire court with sensors and using balls inlaid with a special conductive material, it would be possible to judge with complete accuracy whether a shot was in or out'
Athletics	'The long jump is all very well. But the plasticine marker used to judge fouls on the take-off board has got to go. And why should athletes jump from one small area, anyway? Surely the event should be a test of who can jump the furthest, not who can jump the furthest from one particular point. A chip in the athlete's spikes could be used to give a perfect indication of take-off point from the runway. And replacing the out-moded sand pit would be an impact gel which retains the shape of the jumper for a few moments to allow measurement before morphing back to its original shape for the next jump'
Motor sports	'Cars have air-bags to protect drivers in the event of a crash. Moto GP riders often come off their bikes and injure themselves. Put them together and what do you have? The personal airbag-suit. Okay, so the name's not too catchy, but the concept is good. When a rider is thrown from their bike, their suit instantly inflates and cushions their impact on the tarmac'
Cricket	'The use of the third umpire to adjudicate on run-outs and stumpings is now an accepted part of the game. But why not extend the range of decisions that technology can clarify? Not sure whether a batsman has nicked a delivery to the wicketkeeper? A sensor built into the edge of the bat could send an instant signal to the umpire's ear-piece if it makes contact with the ball'

Adapted from Fordyce (2004)

Case 25.1 Race industry takes the lead

The motor sport industry can point out, with justification, that the 4 million angling population in the UK alone uses vastly more fuel – and hence generates much more globe-warming carbon dioxide – getting to lakes and riverbanks each weekend than is consumed by all forms of motor sport in the same period.

But the problem for an industry that generates billions of dollars in earnings (£5 billion in the UK alone) and employs well over 100,000 directly worldwide is that it is a direct user of CO_2 generating fuels. Unfairly or not, that places it in the line of fire more than almost all other sports.

The potential for the mounting clamour over global warming to result in demands for restrictions on motor sport has not been lost on its participants with a big financial stake in it. These include the sport's world governing body, the Federation Internationale de l'Automobile (FIA); the companies that earn their living from designing, developing and making its cars and other hardware; the racing teams; and the multitudes of other companies – including multinational corporations using motor sport as a global marketing platform.

The industry, says FIA president Max Mosley, appears not to be under imminent threat – 'not yet. But I have no doubt that it will materialise in the next five to 10 years

(continued)

if we don't do anything positive. Although motor sport in reality uses negligible fuel, it is symbolic – remember that in the 1970s fuel crisis there were moves to stop motor sport. We need to avoid that'.

With relatively little fanfare, except for some high-profile initiatives in motor sport's top echelon, Formula One, the industry is already demonstrating the fast responses for which it has become famed. From Indy single-seater car racing in the US to even minor national championships in Europe, it is racing into the use of bio- and other cleaner fuels, and it is gearing engineering programmes to make motor sport much more environmentally efficient. It is not so much jumping before it is pushed as leading the way and challenging others to follow.

For example, the FIA is requiring manufacturers taking part in the World Touring Car Championship (WTCC) to engineer their cars to use only biofuel from the 2009 season onwards. 'With the close relationship between WTCC cars and their roadgoing equivalents we believe that the WTCC is the logical platform to raise public awareness of biofuels', says Jacques Behar, chief executive of KSO, the championship's promoter.

The Indy Racing League, similar in status in North America to F1, this year mandated ethanol, made from renewable resources, as the sole fuel to be used. Its introduction has been in partnership with the US-based Ethanol Promotion and Information Council (EPIC), which is taking interactive display centres to the races designed to educate consumers on the environmental and other implications of using such fuels. NASCAR stock car racing, the biggest crowd puller in the US, has begun a research programme for its own switch to cleaner, alternative fuels. Ford has unveiled a biofuel version of its new Fiesta rally car to run next year in a series forming part of the world rally championship, with some national championships for the cars – notably Sweden's – having already ruled that only biofuel may be used.

Meanwhile an adapted Aston Martin DBSR9 co-driven by Lord Drayson, the UK's defence procurement minister, has become the first bio-fuelled racing car to win a prestigious GT race. 'It goes to prove that running a car on bio-fuel doesn't mean any compromise in performance. I hope that we can get that message across to motorists everywhere', says Lord Drayson.

More radically, a Hydrogen Electric Racing Federation has been launched in North America following a meeting of senior figures including Tony George, chief executive of Indianapolis motor speedway. Devised to promote radical thinking within the motor sport industry, the federation is drawing up a programme to stage races specifically for cars powered by hydrogen electric fuel cells, with the first scheduled before the end of the decade.

'We are at the dawn of a new age of propulsion for the car. From this day forward we will see internal combustion engines in cars inevitably give way to electric power sources', says Peter DeLorenzo, the federation's chief executive. 'The concept of racing hydrogen fuel cell-powered machines is unprecedented and historic, because for the first time in many, many years racing will undertake a key role in the development of radical new technologies for production vehicles that are still on the horizon.'

Such challenges are also being taken up with enthusiasm by motor sport's designers and engineers of the future. In the US, 'Formula Hybrid' has been launched as an inter-collegiate competition under which college and university teams are designing and building race cars with petrol-electric 'hybrid' power trains.

(continued)

Increasingly, such initiatives are becoming coordinated on an industry, rather than individual company or race promotion basis. A few weeks ago well over 100 delegates from around the world attended the most recent conference of the UK's Energy Efficient Motor Sports body, set up by the Motorsport Industry Association with government backing about six years ago to investigate a wide approach to improving the environmental credentials of motor sport. The EEMS has been tackling everything from alternative fuels to radical powertrain technologies.

In the battle for the wider public's hearts and minds, however, it is the progress made in improving its environmental credentials by motor sport's flagship Formula One, watched by hundreds of millions around the world, that will most influence motor sport's future in relation to the environment.

Mr Mosley is putting energy efficiency at the top of F1's research and development agenda and is deeply critical of the past thrust of research and development by competing teams. He describes as 'an inexcusable waste of sponsors' money' the willingness of teams to spend millions of dollars to shave a few tenths of a second or so off lap times through powertrain or aerodynamic tweaks offering no wider benefits to car makers.

We calculated that each four milliseconds saved through engine tweaking was costing US$1m and 20 milliseconds for the same sum through improving aerodynamics. If the wind tunnels were taken off working for F1 and applied extensively to road cars, and if it led to a 1 per cent saving of drag across General Motors' entire range, that's a very significant amount of fuel and it is worth working to that depth of detail – but for F1 cars it's crazy.

From 2011, F1's rules will change in a fundamental fashion. Teams will be restricted to a pre-set maximum of fuel or energy. That, he insists, will result in energy-saving hybrid or other novel powertrain technology to maximise power while minimising emissions. 'It will move the whole research and development effort forward, squarely and fairly into the core research areas of all car makers in dealing with their costliest problem – reducing CO.'

There is now a very active discussion going on, with some manufacturers asking us to just give them a calorific value and make the technology completely free and others saying that would open the field too wide and become too expensive. I think it will end up with a lot of simulations being done so we'll be able to narrow the field down and say the post-2011 technology can be of a certain kind.

It is unlikely, however, to be as radical as that being pursued by students at the UK's Warwick University. They have developed 'Eco One', a largely biodegradable racing car, with a bodyshell made of hemp, tyres from potatoes, brake pads from cashew nut shells and running entirely on biofuel and bio-lubricants.

'Almost everything on the car can be made out of biodegradable or recyclable materials', says project manager Ben Wood.

All the plastic components can be made from plants, and although the chassis has to be from steel for strength, steel is a very recyclable material.

If we can build a high-performance car that can virtually be grown from seed, imagine what's possible for the average family car!

Source: 'Race Industry takes the Lead', *The Financial Times*, 11/09/07 (Griffiths, J.) © The Financial Times Limited. All rights reserved.

(*continued*)

Case 25.2 UEFA warning over Ronaldo £80 million signing

Real Madrid's world record £80 million (US$132 million) deal for Cristiano Ronaldo, Manchester United's Portuguese winger, will destabilise European football, Michel Platini, UEFA's president, has warned.

The Spanish club's offer, accepted by United yesterday, comes days after Real signed Kaka from AC Milan for €68 million (US$92 million) and provides further evidence of the financial muscle that separates Europe's elite teams from the rest.

'It is very puzzling at a time when football faces some of its worst ever financial challenges', Mr Platini, who has repeatedly warned about the amount of debt in European clubs, said in a statement.

'These transfers are a serious challenge to the idea of fair play and the concept of financial balance in our competitions.'

Gerry Sutcliffe, UK sports minister, also questioned the wisdom of the deal, telling the BBC the government was 'concerned about the sustainability of the game'.

But the clubs, which both issued statements saying they expected the transfer to be concluded in the next few days, were keen to emphasise sound business reasons for the deal.

People inside United, which is paying £69m a year in interest to service a £699m debt mountain, denied that the bulk of the money would go towards buying new players, suggesting instead that like other income streams part of the proceeds would go towards interest payments.

'We want to suppress the expectation that we are in the [transfer] market and will be willing to spend big money', said one insider. United has just negotiated a shirt sponsorship deal with Aon, the US insurance group, thought to be worth £100m.

Real Madrid has a EUR300m, four-year bank facility and is likely to spend a large part of it in the first year on high-profile signings such as Ronaldo, according to one club insider.

Real have been hit by the loss of sponsors and corporate hospitality during the recession but the club is still among the richest in the world in terms of assets and cashflow, and has the support of Spain's biggest banks, according to experts.

With 50 per cent of the commercial rights, and the chance that Ronaldo, and future star signings, will boost merchandising revenues, the deal made business sense,

(continued)

said the club insider, as long as the team did well over the next few seasons. 'It is better to buy Ronaldo for EUR92m than pay EUR20m for a player of slightly less calibre and profile', he said.

Real's outlay is being masterminded by Florentino Perez, who was restored to the presidency of Madrid's leading team on June 1, promising to spend heavily to restore the club to the summit of Spanish and European football.

His spending spree on galacticos – great players – in the early part of this decade was underpinned by the proceeds of the redevelopment of the club's old training grounds on Madrid's northern fringe.

Although this week's Real Madrid deals mark a spectacular opening to the summer transfer window, most football finance experts expect clubs to be under pressure from their owners to spend cautiously.

'The market is going to be very iffy', said one football agent. 'So much of the available money is at the top echelon. It is for United to splash the cash.'

Simon Chadwick, director of Coventry University's Centre for the International Business of Sport, said the Kaka and Ronaldo deals signalled both the 'polarisation' of the transfer market and transfer fee inflation.

By moving from England to Spain, Ronaldo will escape the forthcoming 50 per cent top rate tax in the UK next year and will be entering a tax regime where the so-called Beckham Law enables foreign earners working in Spain to pay only 25 per cent in tax.

Ronaldo earned £125,000 a week playing for United and could earn about £180,000 a week at Real Madrid, according to some reports. The strength of the euro against sterling would also add value to Ronaldo's Real Madrid salary.

Source: 'UEFA warning over Ronaldo £80 million signing', *The Financial Times*, 12/06/09 (Blitz, R. and Mulligan, M.) © The Financial Times Limited. All rights reserved.

Discussion questions

4 Is the high-value trading of players such as Cristiano Ronaldo a good thing or a bad thing for the future of football?

5 Find out more about UEFA's Financial Fair Play measures; how important are such measures, and how effective do you think such measures can be?

6 If you had to propose a series of measures designed to safeguard the future of a sport such as football, what would they entail?

 ## Conclusion

Some people insist that the only thing predictable about change is change itself. So at least we know that sport and sport management are not going to remain the same. This does not mean sport managers should be relaxed, unconcerned or casual about change; sport as we traditionally know it will increasingly come under pressure from other forms of leisure expenditure, changing customers' tastes and service expectations and the challenges posed by managerialism, commercialisation, globalisation, new technology and the mega-trends identified by HBR and Mannings. The key over the next 5–10 years will therefore be how sport organisations respond. Whether or not a sport organisation is competing in sport, organising sport or supplying sport, reading the signals and taking appropriate action will be the managerial challenge they all face. This is true whether a sport organisation is a small, medium or large enterprise, or a not-for-profit organisation. The future may seem daunting but, with a carefully crafted strategy, good management and strong leadership, the future provides opportunities for success, not a portent for failure.

Discussion questions

7 Referring to the *HBR*'s, *Forbes*' and Mannings' views of the future, what do you think will be the impact for sport of their predictions?

8 For a sport of your choice, construct a plan to indicate where you should gather information from in order to that the management of this sport remains up to date and relevant.

9 Using the logic of 'The Power of Crowds' (what the people around you are thinking, saying and believe), what future do you predict for a sport with which you are familiar?

10 What do you think is THE single biggest challenge facing sport in the twenty-first century and why? How do you think sport organisations should respond to this challenge?

Keywords

Brainstorming; causal forecast; Delphi technique; image rights; judgemental forecast; modelling; primary data; scenario; secondary data; strategic collaboration; time series forecast.

Guided reading

For students wanting to familiarise themselves with business forecasting techniques, a standard textbook on strategic management Johnson, Scholes and Whittingham's book on strategy (2007) should be sufficient. In cases where students require a more quantitative approach to forecasting, Waters (2001) contains information about the statistical procedures underpinning some of the techniques mentioned in this chapter. The area of business forecasting is also well served by journals such as the *Journal of Business Forecasting Methods and Systems*. This is a good source of information on current forecasting practices and students might find articles by Chase (1998) and Lapide (2002) an interesting overview of recent developments in forecasting. Further resources relating to business forecasting can be found on the Institute of Business Forecasting website which, in turn, provides links to other forecasting resources. Journals in the area of strategy and planning, including *Long Range Planning*, can also prove to be useful reading and are sometimes a good source of information about potential future developments in the business world.

There is also an increasing array of sport business-related information available including journals, websites and current issues publications. A number of relevant websites are listed below, although students will find that *Sport, Business and Management: An International Journal*, *Journal of Sport Management*, *International Journal of Sport Management and Marketing*, *International Journal of Sport Marketing and Sponsorship*, and *Sport Marketing Quarterly* are useful starting points. Market intelligence publications such as Mintel and Keynote are immensely helpful to sport marketers, although the major downside of these is that, unless you have free access through a library, they are very expensive to buy. Students may also find it useful to monitor developments associated with the European Association of Sport Management, the Sport Management Association of Australia and New Zealand and the North American Association of Sport Management. Each of these organisations holds an annual conference at which academics and practitioners present papers of current interest. Their websites are also good sources of information about current and potential future developments in sport marketing.

Amongst the current issues publications, the following are especially recommended: BBC Business of Sport website; *S1M – The Voice of Leadership*; *Sport Business*; *Sport Business Daily*; *Sport Industry Group*; and *Sports Pro*.

Recommended websites

BBC Business of Sport: www.bbc.co.uk/news/business/business_of_sport/

Business of Sport Management Companion site: www.booksites.net/download/chadwickbeech/index.html

ESPN Sports Business: http://espn.go.com/sportsbusiness/index.html

European Association for Sport Management: www.easm.org/

European Sport Management Quarterly: www.meyer-meyer-sports.com/en/produkte/zeitschrift/esmq.htm

Institute of Business Forecasting: www.ibforecast.com/

International Journal of Sport Marketing and Sponsorship: www.imr-info.com/#goIJSM

International Journal of Sport Management and Marketing: www.inderscience.com/browse/index.php?journalID=102

Journal of Sport Management: www.humankinetics.com/products/journals/journal.cfm?id=JSM

Long Range Planning: www.lrp.ac/

North American Association of Sport Management: www.nassm.com/

S1M Voice of Leadership: http://voiceofleadership.biz/

Sport Business: www.sportbusiness.com/

Sport Management Association of Australia and New Zealand: www.gu.edu.au/school/lst/services/smaanz/

SportQuest: www.sportquest.com/resources/index.html

Sports Business and Industry Online: www.sportsvueinc.com/

Sports Business Daily: www.sportsbusinessdaily.com/

Sports Business Journal: www.sportsbusinessjournal.com/

Sports Business News: www.sportsbusinessnews.com/

Sport Industry Group: www.sportindustry.biz/

Sport Marketing Quarterly: www.smqonline.com/

Sports Pro: www.sportspromedia.com/

The Sport Journal: www.thesportjournal.org

References

Beech, J. and Chadwick, S. (2004) *The Business of Sport Management*, Harlow: FT Prentice Hall.

Chase, C.W. (1998) 'The role of life cycles and forecast horizons in a forecasting system: Reebok's perspective', *Journal of Business Forecasting Methods and Systems*, 17 (1), 23–9.

Finlay, P. (2000) *Strategic Management: An Introduction to Business and Corporate Strategy*, Harlow: FT Prentice Hall, 54–80.

Forbes (2010) 'What happens next', *Forbes Magazine*, 186 (5), 50–58.

Fordyce, T. (2004) 'What will the sports we love look like in 2050?', http://212.58.226.40/sport1/hi/front_page/3696988.stm

Glendinning, M. (2001) 'Preparing for trouble in paradise', *Sport Business International*, 1 July, 6.

Harvard Business Review (2009) 'Managing in the new world' (July–August).

Johnson, G., Scholes, K. and Whittingham, R. (2007) *Exploring Corporate Strategy*, Harlow: FT Prentice Hall.

Lapide, L. (2002) 'New developments in business forecasting', *Journal of Business Forecasting*, Spring, 12–14.

Observer Sport Monthly (2004) '10 ways to shake up sport', http://observer.guardian.co.uk/osm/story/0,6903,1315431,00.html

Observer Sport Monthly (2010) 'Sport in 2020: 10 predictions of what we'll be playing and watching', www.guardian.co.uk/sport/blog/2010/jan/10/osm-future-of-sport-2020

Saunders, M., Lewis, P. and Thornhill, A. (2003) *Research Methods for Business Students*, Harlow: FT Prentice Hall.

Scarrott, M. (ed.) (1999) *Sports, Leisure and Tourism Information Sources*, Oxford: Butterworth Heinemann.

Surowiecki, J. (2004) *The Wisdom of Crowds: Why the Many Are Smarter Than the Few and How Collective Wisdom Shapes Business, Economies, Societies and Nations*, New York: Little, Brown.

Waters, D. (2001) *Quantitative Methods for Business*, Harlow: FT/Prentice-Hall, 262–99.

Glossary

Accountability   The requirement of an organisation or person to give an explanation for their actions.

Adaptive choice theory   The view that organisations are open, natural, living systems. As such, they are influenced by external events and changes meaning that, in some respects, organisations are in a constant state of flux. They must therefore respond to the world around them and to their changing environments in order to survive.

Adverse selection   Inability of buyers of a good or service to distinguish between the quality of the product on offer.

Agent   An intermediary operating between two clubs or a player and club in opening and concluding transfer negotiations.

Ambush marketing   A tactic whereby a company attempts to ambush or undermine the sponsorship activities of a rival that owns the legal rights to sponsor an event; often involves creating the sense that they, and not the actual sponsor, are associated with the owners of the event or activity.

Amenity services   Services provided largely to locally determined standards to meet the needs of each local community.

Anthropomaximology   An approach developed in the USSR to study the reserve potential of healthy people and the methods for realising it under conditions of maximum effort.

Arbitration   Settling of a dispute by an outside person or persons, chosen by both sides.

Art   The non-analytical elements of strategy making which frequently include instinct and intuition.

Assortment   The mix of products that a retailer sells in the shop.

Atmospherics   The ambience of the shop, encompassing visual, aural, olfactory, tactile, physical and human (staff) attributes designed to provide an overall sense of the shop.

Backer   Someone who bets on a particular outcome of an event occurring, for example a given team winning a game (see 'layer').

Benchmarks   Targets set by managers to help improve or measure employee or organisational performance.

Betting exchanges   Act as brokerages for bettors by matching backers and layers; betting exchanges usually operate over the internet. Betting exchanges provide a modern version of peer-to-peer betting, however backers and layers are anonymous and are matched by the exchange.

Betting shops   Conventional retail outlets which offer a range of betting activities and related services.

Betting   Staking money on the outcome of a particular event.

Bettor   Someone who makes (places) a bet.

Bookmaker   Someone who takes bets from bettors at agreed odds. Bookmakers make their profit from taking a range of different bets on the same event in the expectation that they will pay out less than they take in.

Bosman ruling   Legal decision by the ECJ which ruled that transfer fees for out of contract players and quota systems limiting the number of foreign EU players were in contravention of the EC Treaty.

Brainstorming   A technique for generating, refining and developing ideas that can be undertaken by individuals, but is more effective when undertaken by a group of people.

Brand consistency   Where the presentation of a brand has consistent messaging, associations and attributes.

Brand   'The intangible sum of a product's attributes: its name, packaging, and price, its history, its reputation, and the way it's advertised' (Ogilvie, 1983).

Break-even analysis   Determination of the point at which the level of sales equals costs, so no profit or loss is generated.

Broadband   Technology that allows a high rate of data transmission.

Bureaucracy   An organisation typified by formal processes, standardisation, hierarchic procedures and written communication.

Business continuity planning   Identifies an organisation's exposure to internal and external threats and synthesises hard and soft assets to provide effective prevention and recovery for the organisation, whilst maintaining competitive advantage and value system integrity.

Business strategy theory   Theories are based on the pragmatic view that internationalisation is only one choice from a range of expansion strategies that are open to an organisation. The decision to pursue such a strategy will ultimately be guided by nature of market opportunity, the nature and extent of an organisations resources and the philosophy characterising management within an organisation.

Business   An organisation which operates in order to make a profit; also the collective word for the activities in which they engage.

Causal forecast   Forecasting technique used to identify the relationship between two or more variables whereby a change in one variable causes a change in one or more of the other variables.

Central Council for Mental Health   Formed in the UK in 1935 to 'improve physical and mental health'.

Change   A process within organisations that can be fast or slow, initiated internally or externally to the organisation and that often results in conflict which requires careful management.

Claimant   Person who starts an action against someone in the civil courts.

Commercialisation   The process increasingly found in sport where a business or businesses from outside the sport have become significant stakeholders in the sport in order to make a direct or indirect profit.

Competitive advantage   A particular attribute by which an organisation can develop a sustainable advantage over its competition.

Competitive balance   The equality in the playing strengths of the teams in any league or cup competition.

Congeneric integration   Integration between firms which produce goods that are similar but not identical.

Congruence   Consumer perceptions of the relatedness and relevance between the sponsor and the sponsored event.

Contribution   Profit generated after variable costs have been deducted from sales revenue. Can be seen as a contribution towards meeting the fixed costs of a business.

Control   Monitoring and if necessary adjusting the performance of the organisation and its members. A complex phenomenon in organisations that involves administrative, social and self control mechanisms that change over time and are employed by managers and employees in an attempt to influence the behaviour of others.

Corruption   The term used to describe actions by an organisation or individual which are unethical.

Cost–benefit analysis   The cost–benefit analysis is an established economic procedure to assess public measurements. Its central purpose is to measure the positive and negative impacts connected with the realisation of events on the social welfare of a defined region or country for a limited period of time.

Cost effectiveness   The evaluation of an expenditure vis-à-vis the value it provides.

Cost–volume–profit analysis   General technique that relates to the relationship between sales, costs and profit, for example with break-even analysis.

Crisis   An incident or event with consequences, which pose a significant threat to the strategic objectives of an organisation.

Crisis management   A term that refers to a three-stage process from the incubation of crisis potential, through incident management to post incident media management and brand repositioning.

Cultural discount   The reduction in value on media products when they are consumed outside their home market.

Culture   A shared psychological framework for ordering and interpreting experiences, and for determining responses to them.

Customer satisfaction   The degree to which a customer has positive opinions of a product or service.

Defendant   Person who is sued in a civil case.

Deliberate   A clear and prescriptive approach to strategy making whereby long-term objectives are clearly articulated and the methods through which they are to be met are planned in significant detail.

Delphi technique   A technique for generating information about the future involving a number of iterative stages through which managers reach a consensual view of what might happen to a business.

Deontology Comes from the Greek 'deon' meaning 'duty'. This ethical approach is based on the notion that a right action morally obliges us to act in a particular way. An action is right or wrong in itself and is not dependent on consequences (consequentialist ethics) nor characteristics or qualities of a good life (virtue ethics). The most common deontological theory is associated with Immanuel Kant.

Differentiation The ability to present your offering as different from competitive offerings.

Digital convergence The technological trend whereby a variety of different digital devices such as televisions, mobile telephones, and now refrigerators are merging into a multi-use communications appliance employing common software to communicate through the Internet.

Disintermediation The process of doing away with middlemen from business transactions.

Doping The presence, use or attempted use of an illegal substance or certain prohibited methods of performance-enhancement in sport. The World Anti-Doping Agency (WADA) define doping as a violation of anti-doping rules set out in Article 2.1 to 2.8 of their code. This can be found here: www.wada-ama.org/rtecontent/document/code_v3.pdf. Doping is most commonly associated with ingested substances, such as anabolic androgenic steroids (AAS), growth hormones, beta-blockers and diuretics or other masking agents, but banned methods also include blood doping and gene doping.

Emergent An approach to strategy making which focuses on short term adjustments to changes either within the organisation or the environment and places a premium on flexibility and improvisation.

Engagement A passionate, emotional and active involvement of the fan with a team, league, sport or event.

English auction An auction where all bidders are informed about each others' bids and where the one who submits the highest bid wins the item and pays the price he or she has bid.

Environments The arena in which strategy is made and executed and includes those elements outside of the firm which will impact on strategy making and the effectiveness of a given strategy such as an industry or market.

Ethos The characteristics, principles or way of life of an individual, group or culture. It differs from the more modern term 'ethics' as it relates to how these characteristics or principles are bound in social practices and values in contrast to a more narrow consideration of right and wrong conduct.

Eustress Good stress, derived from an exciting situation; the opposite of distress, deriving from a threatening situation. Often associated with taking part in, or watching, a close-run competition.

Evaluation The effort to assess the impact of marketing efforts.

Event life cycle To truly assess the economic impact of a sports event for a host city or host destination the complete event life cycle needs to be considered, which starts with the idea, why a bid is launched, and ends with the development of proposals for the athlete and a wider sports community (Kaspar, 2006).

Exchange   The core idea that marketing occurs when two parties exchange products, services or cash amongst each other where both feel satisfied with the exchange (i.e. they got value equal to or greater than what they gave in return).

Experiential marketing   A form of marketing that encourages an emotional relationship between the consumer and the brand/product/service. What is assumed to matter is the immersion of the consumer in a hedonistic and out-of-the-ordinary activity.

Externalities   The results of an activity that cause incidental benefits or costs to others with no corresponding compensation provided or paid by those who generate the externality.

Facility services   Services for people to draw upon if they wish.

Financial accounting   Area of accounting related to the production of financial statements for largely external stakeholders.

Financial statements   The income statement, balance sheet and the cash flow statement report upon the financial performance and well-being of a company.

Formalism/formalist   This takes the position that all legitimate or illegitimate moves in sport can be accounted for by the formal rules of that sport. This view maintains that it is logically impossible for cheaters to win, as by breaking the constitutive rules they have therefore failed to play the game at all (known as the logical incompatibility thesis, as advocated by Bernard Suits). However, one of the problems with the formalist approach is that it doesn't account for situations which are not dealt with by the formal rules, particularly situations of a moral or ethical nature.

Franchising   Type of business model where ownership of a company is contractually agreed with a governing organisation.

Gambling   Sometimes used interchangeably with betting but usually take to be a wider term including betting on games of chance such as cards or roulette.

Gantt chart   A bar chart used to illustrate both the sequence and expected duration of activities within an event.

Gatekeeper   Intermediary who uses his/her position to control access to something or someone.

Governance   The process of governing, and, by implication, of regulating a system based on mutual adjustment rather than on imposition by direct control. Primary stakeholders play a role in governance normally through elected representatives.

Group norms   Informal standards of behaviour and performance that develop from the interaction of the group.

Hallmark events   Hallmark events are major (sporting) events with a limited time of duration and rotate between different host cities and/or host countries (e.g. The Olympic Games, World and Continental Championships).

Hazard   A physical entity, condition, activity, substance or behaviour which is capable of doing harm.

Horizontal integration   When firms operating at the same level along a product's value chain combine with one another.

HTML   Hyper-text markup language is a page description computer language that forms the basis and composition of most web pages on the internet.

Image rights   The legal rights associated with using the image of a sportsperson in marketing and promotional activities.

Impact of expectancy   From a Western perspective, the 'impact of expectancy' can be explained from the angle of seeing another individual's behaviour being affected by (a) what a person wants to happen; (b) his/her estimate of the probability that an event will become manifest; (c) his/her belief that the event will satisfy a particular need.

Incident management   The process of managing a crisis event.

Industrial network theory   Organisations are part of a network of other interrelated organisations; individual firms and groups nevertheless decide which international markets they will enter and why.

Information asymmetry   One party to a transaction has access to more information than the other.

Innovation-related theory   Assertion that innovation is the basis for internationalisation. Organisations are thought to innovate in response to the influence of two factors: (a) the influence of change agents such as key decision makers; and/or (b) the influence of external stimuli such as overseas customers.

In-play betting   Betting on the outcome of a specific aspect of a sporting event whilst it is taking place.

Interlocutory injunction   An injunction which is granted for the period until a case comes to court.

Internationalisation   The process of increasing involvement in international operations; the process of adapting firms' operations (strategy, structure, resources, etc.) to international environments.

Internet   A global system of interconnected networks providing links to millions of computers that allow access to billions of web pages on a huge number of topics. It relies on a system of computer protocols to allow information to be exchanged between networks.

Invariance principle   Policies that restrict the movement of players between teams (i.e. the reserve clause and transfer system) have no impact on the allocation of players amongst the different teams in the league.

Judgemental forecast   Forecasting technique involving the use of opinion, experience and judgement; often used when there is little information about a specific set of circumstances.

Jurisprudence   Study of the law and the legal system.

Layer   Someone who bets against a particular outcome occurring. For a betting transaction to take place there must be a backer and a layer.

Leadership   Influencing and directing the performance of group members towards the achievement of organisational goals.

Leverage   The methods and techniques used to ensure a sponsorship is managed in such a way that it generates the maximum possible value for the sponsor. This often involves other elements in the communications mix.

Libel   Written and published or broadcast statement, which damages someone's character (in a permanent form).

Listed events   A regulation which required that the media rights for sports events of major importance for society can only be sold to broadcasters with a penetration over a minimum level.

Luxury tax   A threshold is set on the amount each team can spend in total on players' salaries. Teams are free to spend more than the threshold but must pay a progressive tax on any expenditure above the threshold level. The money generated by the tax is normally redistributed to the other teams.

Management   The process of planning, leading, organising and controlling people within in a group in order to achieve goals; also used to mean the group of people who do this.

Management accounting   Area of accounting related to the internal management of a business on a day-to-day basis, using techniques such as cost–volume–profit analysis.

Marginal revenue product   The incremental revenue to a firm accruing from employing one additional unit of labour.

Market research   The practice of exploring sources of information to inform marketing planning and action.

Marketing   The American Marketing Association (2007) defines marketing as follows: 'Marketing is the activity, set of institutions, and processes for creating, communicating, delivering, and exchanging offerings that have value for customers, clients, partners, and society at large'.

Marketing mix   The marketing strategy for the product, price, promotion and place (commonly referred to as 'the 4Ps') for each of the target markets.

Maximum wage   Cap on the level of basic remuneration a player was able to earn.

Mega events   Mega events can be defined as 'large-scale cultural (including commercial and sporting) events, which have a dramatic character, mass popular appeal and international significance' (Roche, 2000: 1).

Merchandising   At a retail in-store level, merchandising refers to the variety of products available for sale and the display of those products in such a way that it stimulates interest and entices customers to make a purchase.

MIS   Management Information Systems.

Modelling   Forecasting technique normally involving the use of computer software; the software is used to identify the nature and strength of relationships between variables contained in sets of data.

Moral hazard   Tendency for a party who is insulated from risk to behave behave differently than it would had it been fully exposed to the risk: the party with more information behaves in a manner which could be detrimental to the intentions of the party with less information.

Motivation   A psychological concept with no single universally accepted definition, but which organisational sociologists aver concerns the determinants of *intent, effort* and *tenacity*, factors that push or pull us as individuals to behave in a particular manner.

Multiple bets   Also known 'exotic' or 'parlay' bets are bets on a combination of outcomes in a series of events. For example, betting on the winners of series of races at a meeting or the outcomes of a number of major sporting events.

Multiple intelligences   Howard Gardner argues that his intelligence does not stop at his skin and moves both intrinsically to his bio-psychological make-up and extrinsically to his social and natural environment. Thus, the term encompasses seven intelligences that encompass the biological, psychological, social, naturalist and spiritual dimensions of our life.

Multiplier effects   A multiplier is a factor which indicates to what extent total sales (i.e. income, employment) within the region are changed, in the case of consumer or invest-ment expenditure shifting by one monetary unit.

National recreation centres   Elite residential centres created in the UK after the Second World War.

Need services   Services provided for all, regardless of means.

NPSO Not-for-profit sport organisation   The NPSO is typically a constituted, legal body that is defined under government legislation to undertake activities as defined within its constitution or articles of association. This organisation generally relies upon volunteer management structures and a large participation base. Since the 1980s NPSOs have undergone a radical change shifting from volunteer administration to paid staff to administer increasing levels of competition, administration and development activities of the sport.

Obiter dicta (singular is 'obiter dictum')   Latin phrase meaning 'things which are said in passing': part of a judgment, which is not essential to the decision of the judge and does not create a precedent.

Odds   An expression of the price at which a betting transaction takes place expressed as the chance of a particular outcome occurring. Thus odds of 'evens' (1/1) reflects 50:50 chance of the particular outcome; odds of 9 to 1 against (9/1) reflect a 10 per cent chance (9 chances it will not happen against 1 chance it will). Odds are expressed in different ways in different countries.

On-line betting   Betting over the internet, usually with a bookmaker or via a betting exchange.

Online social networks   Networks that enable a set of activities and of passions related to the creation and to sharing of content within a digital community in a professional or leisure context.

Operations   A process, organisational function and job role which requires 'inputs' to be processed into 'outputs' in the form of a product or service.

Opportunity costs   By choosing to use a scarce good in one way, means losing the oppor-tunity of some other use. Giving up this alternative and thus not being able to generate the related potential benefits is the opportunity costs. This aspect is not often consid-ered, as alternative projects to a major sports event are hard to find.

Organisation   A group of people acting collectively on a formal basis to achieve a common goal.

Own-brands   Products that are produced for and branded by a retailer for their sole use. More accurately termed retailer brands, though private labels is the term used in the USA.

Paternalism   Comes from the Latin 'pater' which means 'to act like a father'. It is the interference by one party (state or individual) over the choices and actions of another *in the interests* of the interfered party. It is the approach by which someone is prevented from acting in a particular way on the grounds of it being for their own good. For instance, laws that force us to wear seatbelts or motorcycle helmets, or not being allowed to buy cigarettes or alcohol below a certain age.

Perceptual map   A graphical representation of how consumers view a product or a brand versus its competitors and substitutes.

Place   Involves the process by which the product is produced and delivered to the customer; also referred to as 'distribution'.

Pool betting   In pool betting bettors buy tickets (stakes) on outcomes which they think will occur. After the event is over all the stakes are aggregated (pooled) and the total (the pool) divided up amongst those who accurately predicted the outcome (winners). Examples include the Tote in the UK and the Pari-Mutuel in France.

Pooled revenue sharing   Teams in a league contribute a share of their revenues to a pool. The contribution is usually calculated as a percentage of their revenues. In a straight pool scheme the contributions are then distributed equally to each team. In a split pool scheme the contributions are not distributed equally to each team.

Price   The value attached to the offering.

Primary data   Data collected specifically for a purpose; sources may include questionnaires, interviews and focus groups.

Principal–agent relationship   Relationship which occurs when one party, the principal, hires a second party, the agent, to perform some task on the principal's behalf.

Prisoner's Dilemma   Simple game typically employed by economists to analyse the behaviour of firms in a cartel in which simultaneous decision making between two separate parties occurs.

Product   The offering that is provided to the consumer.

Professional   Being paid to do an activity as the significant portion of one's income.

Promotion   The set of tactics available to inform consumers of the product(s) and/or service(s) offered.

Protective services   Services provided for the security of the people, to national guidelines.

Public information model   Focuses on the dissemination of accurate and favourable information about an organisation.

Publicity   Public attention to an athlete or organisation, usually gained through the media. Also referred to as 'free media'.

Publics   Groups of people within a stakeholder group who relate to the sport organisation in similar ways.

Punter   A popular term for 'bettor' (*q.v.*).

Qualified privilege   Protection from being sued for defamation given to someone only if it can be proved that the statements were made without malice.

Quality   Usually considered to be the 'highest standard' but definitions can vary depending on the perspective adopted.

Quality standards   Statements which indicate a required level of competence or element of a service.

Relationship marketing   A form of marketing that includes tools and techniques which aim to build and sustain a personal dialogue and a collaboration between a brand/product and a customer in the long term.

Reserve clause   A clause in a player's contract that gives the team he/she plays for the unilateral right to renew his/her contract for another year.

Retailing   The sale of products, normally individually or in small quantities, to a final consumer.

Retain and transfer system   Restrictive system under which clubs had the discretion to renew all players' contracts on an annual basis and even if the contract was not renewed clubs had the right to retain the registration of that player, enabling the club to prevent an out of contract player from playing anywhere.

Reverse order-of-finish draft   A method for regulating the entry of new young players into the league. The team with the worst playing record in the previous season gets the first pick of new young players. The player must play for the team that picks him or not play in the league at all.

Rights fee   The payment made in cash or in kind by the sponsor to the sponsee in order to secure the legal rights of association with an activity or an event.

Risk management   The overall process of ensuring that risks are managed in the most cost efficient and cost effective way.

Risk   The probability that a specified hazard will result in an undesired event.

Rules – constitutive   These are the rules that enable the game to exist. They direct the permitted (and prohibited) means to achieve the end (i.e. winning, scoring a goal, preventing the opposition scoring). If these rules are violated then the game ends. The constitutive rules are also called the 'lusory means'.

Rules – regulative   These are the rules that come into effect when the constitutive rules are broken. They provide restoration to the game through penalty or compensation. For example, a 'corner kick' in football is a way of restarting the game when the constitutive rule referring to the playing area has been broken. This regulative rule is also designed to penalise the team that broke the constitutive rule relating to putting the ball out of play behind the goal line by giving an advantage to the opposition.

Salary cap   A restriction on the amount that teams can spend on players' salaries. Limits can be placed on both the maximum pay of a single player and the total amount the team can spend on all players' salaries.

Scenario   Pictures of the future developed by those with an understanding of a business or an industry, and are often used to predict the longer term. That is, a time in the future when past or current data may not be applicable.

Scenario planning   A method of predicting likely future events.

Science   The analytical elements of strategy making where decision making is guided by evidence and the use of analytical models.

Scout   A person who collects information relating to players or, at times, other clubs by attending matches on behalf of his club.

Secondary data   Data collected for a purpose other than the one a forecaster may use it for; sources may include newspapers, press releases, market research reports.

Segmentation, targeting and positioning   The process of defining your target markets and value proposition (i.e., how your products will be positioned in the minds of consumers versus the competition).

Service   Intangible, heterogenous, perishable, simultaneous by nature, equalling an economic good.

Shop (or store or outlet)   The business location at which retailing takes place.

Situational analysis   An assessment of the marketing situation, including internal analysis, external analysis and competitive analysis.

Slander   Untrue spoken statement which damages someone's character.

SMART objectives   SMART acronym (Specific, Measurable, Achievable, Relevant and Time Bound) – if objectives are not SMART it is hard to ascertain if they have been achieved or not.

SME   Small to medium size enterprise; definitions vary, but the most widely accepted is that such enterprises employ fewer than 250 people.

Social media   Form of communication which allows users to facilitate conversations through the internet.

Special events   The specific rituals, presentations, performances or celebrations that are planned and created to mark special occasions or to achieve particular social, cultural or corporate goals and objectives.

Specialist retailer   A retailer that sells products drawn from only one retail product sector.

Specificity   A term used by the European Union, as in 'the specificity of sport', to identify the unique role that sport plays in society. Often applied to a perceived need for sport as business to require regulation in a way that is unique to sports businesses, and hence different from the regulation of other businesses.

Sponsorship property   The component, feature or name of an event or an activity which attracts the sponsor to make a payment in cash or in kind, and which the sponsor will subsequently acquire and be associated with following payment.

Sport sponsorship   An exchange between two parties whereby the sponsee receives cash and/or benefits in kind while the sponsor secures a right of association with a sport based activity or event.

Sports betting   Betting on the outcome of a sports event or some element of one.

Sports fan   Sport consumer involved in/committed to a team or an athlete. To a greater or lesser extent, a sport fan can be loyal through identification with a team.

Spot betting   Betting on a specific occurrence rather than the outcome of an event, for example, the next scorer in a game, the number of penalties in a game of soccer, or the winner of the third set in a grand slam tennis match.

Spread betting   Betting on an outcome within a range of possibilities, for example, the margin of victory in a game.

Stake   The amount bet on a particular outcome.

Strategic collaboration   Strategy through which one organisation works or combines with another organisation in order to achieve goals that would otherwise be unattainable; includes joint ventures, strategic alliances and partnerships.

Strategy   The set of management decisions and actions through which an organisation pursues its goals and objectives.

SWOT analysis   An analysis for strategic purposes which identifies strengths and weakness within an organisation, together with opportunities and threats posed by the business environment in which the organisation is operating.

Treaty for the Functioning of the European Union   TFEU.

The Sports Council   A UK body created in 1971 to help develop elite performers and increase overall participation.

Time series forecast   Forecasting technique which utilises past and current data as a basis for extrapolating about the future.

Transaction cost theory   States that all decisions to internationalise are seen as rational economic ones. That is, the costs of taking a particular course of action will be the principal driver for international decision makers.

Transfer system   A system where a player's registration can be transferred between teams. If the player is still under contract then a fee can be demanded by the team selling the player.

Transparency   The requirement that the activities of an organisation are open to public scrutiny.

Two-way symmetrical public relations   Called the 'normative' model of public relations, uses both research and dialogue to produce a dynamic relationship between an organisation and its publics.

Uncertainty of outcome   The idea that fans prefer to watch games with less certain outcomes to ones with more predictable outcomes.

Utilitarianism   This is a consequentialist ethical theory which states that an action is right or wrong depending on the consequences that result from that action. The consequences that matter for a utilitarian are those to do with pleasure or happiness. So the morally right action is the one that results in more pleasure or happiness than any other possible actions. It is often associated with Jeremy Bentham's phrase, 'the greatest happiness for the greatest number'. There are problems inherent in utilitarian theory, such as: how is happiness measured (what counts as one unit)? whose happiness do we count (do we include future human beings and/or animals)? and how are we to judge the consequences of actions before they have been carried out?

Value   An expression for the overall benefit provided to a consumer by a product or service offering.

Value proposition   The value provided to the consumer by a given offering.

Vertical integration   When firms participate in more than one successive stage of the production or distribution of goods or services.

Virtual communities   Groups of people with similar interests who communicate and interact in an online environment.

Virtue theory   This is an ethical theory that focuses on the character of a moral agent (person). In contrast to deontological and consequentialist ethical theories, which focus upon rules or consequences to determine right and wrong actions, virtue theory considers the character of the person involved. A good person will therefore necessarily act in a good way. It is primarily associated with Aristotle's concept of 'eudemonia' which can be translated as 'flourishing'. So in the same way that we can recognise a flourishing plant (in contrast to a sick plant) we can recognise a flourishing person as someone that has ideal (intellectual, moral and physical) characteristics.

Vision   A simple statement or a tacit understanding of the way in which the organisation will develop in the future.

Wagering   An agreement, usually between two people, to exchange an amount of money on the outcome of an unsettled matter, for example the toss of a coin or the result of a race. Now often used interchangeably with 'betting' (*q.v.*).

Win elasticity of demand   The responsiveness of match attendances to the winning record of the teams.

Wolfenden Committee   Established in the UK in 1957 to suggest how statutory bodies could assist in promoting the general welfare of the community in sport and leisure.

Yenza   A South African Xhosa and Zulu word for 'do' or 'make'.

Index